Criminal Responsibility for the Crime of Aggression

Original title: Odpowiedzialność karna za zbrodnię agresji

Translation: Anna Konieczna-Purchała

Since the Nuremberg trial, the crime of aggression has been considered one of the gravest international crimes. However, since the 1940s no defendants have been charged with this crime, with some states actively opposing the notion of punishing aggression. The option of trying an individual for aggression is expressly included in the statute of the International Criminal Court. In 2010 the Assembly of States Parties adopted a definition of the crime of aggression and conditions for the exercise of jurisdiction over this crime by the court. The Assembly also agreed that the decision on including the crime of aggression within the court's jurisdiction would be made in 2017 at the earliest. It is still internationally debatable whether the criminalisation of aggression is an outcome to strive for, or whether its abandonment is more preferable.

In *Criminal Responsibility for the Crime of Aggression*, Patrycja Grzebyk explores the scope of criminal responsibility of individuals for crimes of aggression and asks why those responsible for aggression are not brought to justice. The book first works to identify the legal norms that define and delegalise aggression, before moving to determine the basis and scope for the criminalisation of aggression. The book then goes on to identify the key risks and difficulties inherent in trials for aggression.

Following a string of awards in Poland, including the Manfred Lachs Prize for the best first book on public international law, this cutting investigation of aggression is now deservedly made available to the wider world. In its extensive analysis of international trials on aggression, and its synthesis of legal, political and historical rhetoric, this book offers broad and striking insight into the criminal responsibility of individuals on a world stage.

Patrycja Grzebyk is Assistant Professor at the University of Warsaw, Poland.

Routledge Research in International Law

Available:

International Law and the Third World
Reshaping Justice
Richard Falk, Balakrishnan Rajagopal and Jacqueline Stevens (eds)

International Legal Theory
Essays and Engagements, 1966–2006
Nicholas Onuf

The Problem of Enforcement in International Law
Countermeasures, the Non-Injured State and the Idea of International Community
Elena Katselli Proukaki

International Economic Actors and Human Rights
Adam McBeth

The Law of Consular Access
A Documentary Guide
John Quigley, William J. Aceves and Adele Shank

State Accountability Under International Law
Holding States Accountable for a Breach of Jus Cogens Norms
Lisa Yarwood

International Organisations and the Idea of Autonomy
Institutional Independence in the International Legal Order
Richard Collins and Nigel D. White (eds)

Self-determination in the Post-9/11 Era
Elizabeth Chadwick

Participants in the International Legal System
Multiple Perspectives on Non-State Actors in International Law
Jean d'Aspremont

Sovereignty and Jurisdiction in the Airspace and Outer Space
Legal Criteria for Spatial Delimitation
Gbenga Oduntan

International Law in a Multipolar World
Matthew Happold (ed.)

The Law on the Use of Force
A Feminist Analysis
Gina Heathcote

The ICJ and the Development of International Law
The Lasting Impact of the Corfu Channel Case
Karine Bannelier, Théodore Christakis and Sarah Heathcote (eds)

UNHCR and International Refugee Law
From Treaties to Innovation
Corinne Lewis

Asian Approaches to International Law and the Legacy of Colonialism
The Law of the Sea, Territorial Disputes and International Dispute Settlement
Jin-Hyun Paik, Seok-Woo Lee, Kevin Y L Tan (eds)

The Right to Self-determination Under International Law
'Selfistans', Secession, and the Rule of the Great Powers
Milena Sterio

Reforming the UN Security Council Membership
The Illusion of Representativeness
Sabine Hassler

Threats of Force
International Law and Strategy
Francis Grimal

The Changing Role of Nationality in International Law
Alessandra Annoni and Serena Forlati

Criminal Responsibility for the Crime of Aggression
Patrycja Grzebyk

Forthcoming titles in this series include:

International Law, Regulation and Resistance
Critical Spaces
Zoe Pearson

The Cuban Embargo Under International Law
El Bloqueo
Nigel D. White

International Law-making
Essays in Honour of Jan Klabbers
Rain Liivoja and Jarna Petman

Regional Maintenance of Peace and Security
The Distorted Mirrors
Dace Winther

The Changing Nature of Customary International Law
Methods of Interpreting the Concept of Custom in International Criminal Tribunals
Noora Arajärvi

Technology and the Law on the Use of Force
New Security Challenges in the Twenty-first Century
Jackson Maogoto

Criminal Diversity in International Law
The Effectiveness of the UNESCO Convention on the Protection and Promotion of the Diversity of Cultural Expressions
Lilian Hanania

The United Nations and Collective Security
Gary Wilson

Criminal Responsibility for the Crime of Aggression

Patrycja Grzebyk

Routledge
Taylor & Francis Group
LONDON AND NEW YORK

Simultaneously published in the USA and Canada
by Routledge
711 Third Avenue, New York, NY 10017

Routledge is an imprint of the Taylor & Francis Group, an informa business

British Library Cataloguing in Publication

British Library Cataloguing in Publication Data
A catalogue record for this book is available from the British Library

Library of Congress Cataloging-in-Publication Data
Grzebyk, Patrycja.
[Odpowiedzialnosc karna zbroznie agresji. English.]
Criminal responsibility for the crime of aggression / Patrycja Grzebyk.
pages cm. – (Routledge research in international law)
Includes bibliographical references and index.
ISBN 978-0-415-85678-2 (hbk) – ISBN 978-0-203-79745-7 (ebk)
1. Criminal liability (International law) 2. Aggression (International law) 3. International criminal law. 4. International crimes. I. Title.
KZ7075.G79 2013
341.6'2–dc23 2013005486

ISBN: 978-0-415-85678-2 (hbk)
ISBN: 978-0-203-80535-0 (ebk)

Typeset in Baskerville by
Cenveo Publisher Services

Contents

Tables and charts

Tables

Charts

List of abbreviations

ASP	Assembly of States Parties to Rome Statute of International Criminal Court
CCPSH	Code of crimes (offences) against the peace and security of humankind
ECtHR	European Court of Human Rights
ECOWAS	Economic Community of West African States
GA	General Assembly of United Nations Organisation
GAOR	General Assembly Official Records
GC	Geneva Convention of 1949
ICC	International Criminal Court
ICCPR	International Covenant on Civil and Political Rights
ICISS	International Commission on Intervention and State Security
ICJ	International Court of Justice
ICTY	International Criminal Tribunal for the former Yugoslavia
ILA	International Law Association
ILC	International Law Commission
IMT	International Military Tribunal
IMTFE	International Military Tribunal for the Far East
IST	Iraqi Special Tribunal
LN	League of Nations
LNOJ	League of Nations Official Journal
LNTS	League of Nations Treaty Series
NSDAP	*Nationalsozialistische Deutsche Arbeiterpartei* (German National Socialist Workers' Party)
PCIJ	Permanent Court of International Justice
SA	*Sturmabteilung* (Assault Division)
SC	Security Council of United Nations Organisation
SCSL	Special Court for Sierra Leone
SNT	Supreme National Tribunal (Najwyższy Trybunał Narodowy)
SS	*Schutzstaffel* (Protection Squadron)
SWGCA	Special Working Group on the Crime of Aggression established by Preparatory Commission of Assembly of States Parties to Rome Statute of the International Criminal Court

UN	United Nations Organisation
UNTS	United Nations Treaty Series
USSR	Union of Soviet Socialist Republics

Acknowledgements

This book would have not been written without the support and helpful comments I have been very lucky to receive.

I would like to thank first and foremost the supervisor of my doctoral work and my great inspiration, Professor Roman Kuźniar. Without his determination and support the English version of this book would have been impossible. His comments always stimulate the spirit of academic curiosity and encourage inquiry.

I would also like to give my thanks to Professor Roman Wieruszewski and Professor Leonard Łukaszuk, the reviewers of the Polish version of this book whose comments I found immensely helpful. I received the necessary financial support, for which I am very grateful, from the Dean of the Faculty of Journalism and Political Science of the University of Warsaw, Professor Janusz Adamowski, and from the Director of the Institute of International Relations of the University of Warsaw, Professor Marian Haliżak. I am also most indebted to the Foundation for Polish Science, the Polish Ministry of Science and Higher Education and the University of Warsaw for including me in their grant programmes for young academics.

My thanks go to Anna Konieczna-Purchała, the translator of this book, who went above and beyond to ensure the highest quality of the translation. Her efforts made the English version of this book better than its Polish original. I would also like to thank the Routledge team: Catherine Carpenter, Laura Bailey, Nicola Prior and Mark Sapwell.

I am a mother to two wonderful daughters, Zofia and Łucja, and I would not have been able to pursue my academic passions if it had not been for the continued support of my family. My special gratitude goes to my parents Dorota and Bohdan Grenich, my sister, Maja Zawada, and my mother in law, Józefa Grzebyk, who were always there for me, freely offering their assistance. Finally, my sincerest thanks go to my husband, Piotr Grzebyk, who has been an endless source of support, and who has always encouraged me to grow both as a person and as an academic.

Introduction

> War is essentially an evil thing. Its consequences are not confined to the belligerent States alone, but affect the whole world. To initiate a war of aggression, therefore, is not only an international crime; it is the supreme international crime differing only from other war crimes in that it contains within itself the accumulated evil of the whole.
>
> (From the judgment of the International Military Tribunal)

> Indeed no more grave crimes can be conceived of than a conspiracy to wage a war of aggression or the waging of a war of aggression, for the conspiracy threatens the security of the peoples of the world, and the waging disrupts it.
>
> (From the judgment of the International Military Tribunal for the Far East)

Ever since the Nuremberg trial, the crime of aggression has been considered one of the gravest international crimes, on a par with war crimes, crimes against humanity and genocide. It is therefore rather astonishing that since the 1940s no defendants have been charged with this crime, although there has clearly been no shortage of conflicts wherein, theoretically at least, one party should be considered the aggressor. The questions thus arise. Is there indeed a ban on aggression? What is the scope of criminal responsibility of individuals for this type of international crime? Why are those responsible for aggression not brought to justice, even though aggressive war was declared by the International Military Tribunal to be the supreme international crime?

The importance of these questions is not only historical and academic, but practical too. The option of trying an individual for aggression is expressly included in the statute of the International Criminal Court (ICC). The Assembly of States Parties at a review conference adopted, on 11 June 2010, a definition of the crime of aggression as well as a specification of the conditions of the exercise of jurisdiction over this crime by the ICC. At the same time, the assembly agreed that the decision on actual inclusion of the crime of aggression within the ICC's jurisdiction would be made in 2017 at the earliest. It is therefore possible that the ICC will, at a certain point in the future, hear cases unprecedented since Nuremberg: cases against individuals charged with the crime of aggression. Even if no such case comes to trial, the outcome of negotiations within the ICC should be taken into consideration by all bodies and authorities contemplating the option of a trial for aggression.

It is debatable whether actual criminalisation of aggression is an outcome to strive for, or whether it would be preferable to abandon the notion altogether. The relative difficulties and risks that arise out of criminal trials where the charge of aggression is made must be carefully considered. Insight into these problems may prove helpful in understanding why no criminal trials for aggression occur, and why there are states that actively oppose the notion of punishability of aggression.

The purposes of this book are threefold: first, to identify the legal norms that define and delegalise aggression; secondly, to determine the basis for criminalisation of aggression and the scope of this criminalisation (and thus necessarily to establish the elements of the crime of aggression); and, thirdly, to identify the key risks and difficulties inherent in trials for aggression. Consequently, the book consists of three main parts.

The first part of the book discusses delegalisation of aggression. It presents the evolution of approaches to war and to the use of force in the legal perspective. The analysis is rooted in a thorough review of pertinent documentation, from the earliest conventions on peaceful means of dispute resolution, the Covenant of the League of Nations and the Briand-Kellogg Pact to the Charter of the United Nations. Imperfections of these international agreements are pointed out with a view to ensure full appreciation of the precision of solutions that set the perimeter of allowable use of armed force in international relations.

The first part closes with comments on the notion of state aggression; this notion is employed in the Charter of the United Nations. The comments are structured by way of chronologically following the efforts towards a definition of the term, relying on a review of documents again (from the Treaty of Mutual Assistance of 1923 to the African Union Non-Aggression and Common Defence Pact of 2005), along with an analysis of the debates surrounding the adoption of these documents. Particular attention has been paid to the 1974 Resolution No 3314 of the General Assembly of the United Nations, a result of more than two decades of efforts to define aggression within the United Nations system. On the basis of these documents, an analysis is also provided of the elements of the general definition of aggression and of examples of specific acts of aggression.

The second part of the book pertains to the criminalisation of aggression. It begins with a discussion of the main tenets of the debate on responsibility for the waging of the First World War, and the inter-war debates on the various drafts of the statute of an international criminal court and international criminal code, in order properly to present how the legal basis for criminalisation of aggression was forged.

This part includes an in-depth analysis of the statute of the International Military Tribunal and its judgment, the special importance of which stems from the fact that the London Agreement of 1945 was the first-ever international agreement that actually provided for punishablity of the crime against peace. Also discussed in detail are the statute and judgment of the International Military Tribunal for the Far East, as well as laws from the occupation era, internal laws of a number of relevant countries, and the work of the International Law Commission. The analysis of the evolution of sources of legal responsibility for aggression closes with a review of the negotiations on the specification of this crime in the statute of the ICC.

Furthermore, this part of the book discusses all cases of individuals tried for aggression that are mentioned in the literature on the subject, including cases sometimes believed to be precedents for the Nuremberg trial. In reference to each of these cases, an attempt has been made to note and discuss all the elements of the judgment that pertain to the responsibility of each defendant for the crime against peace or a conspiracy to commit it.

The part devoted to criminalisation of aggression ends with a note on the scope of responsibility of individuals for the crime of aggression, following from considerations as to the basis of general responsibility for aggression and analyses of court cases against individuals charged with crimes against peace. The comments on the issue of individuals as subjects of international law, and the principle of individual responsibility, are very brief, since these issues are thoroughly discussed in the literature on international criminal law. Instead, the focus is on the specific elements of the crime of aggression. For the sake of clarity, separate sub-chapters discuss who can commit the crime of aggression and the forms of participation in the crime of aggression. For similar reasons, the grounds for excluding criminal responsibility owing to lack of guilt are also discussed separately.

In the third part of the book, the focus is on the procedural difficulties that in certain cases may render it difficult or even impossible to hear and try cases of aggression, and the potential negative outcomes of proceeding with such cases. It is of course impossible to outline all challenges that a court may face if a decision is made to examine a case of aggression. Nonetheless, an attempt has been made to list and review the issues of primary significance, such as: lack of jurisdiction; refusal to surrender the defendant; protected status of the defendant owing to privileges and immunities; necessity to name a state as an aggressor; inability to ensure fair trial; invocation by the defendant of an amnesty or a statute of limitations. Also discussed is the problem of possible violation of the *nullum crimen sine lege* principle in light of the perceived imprecision of legal norms pertaining to aggression.

In terms of risks connected with trials for aggression, three key areas of concern are pointed out. First of all, there are consequences to consider with regard to ensuring peace and security, especially in the context of a potential conflict of interest between the Security Council and the ICC. Moreover, criminal examination of the crime of aggression may have consequences in terms of bringing perpetrators of crimes to justice in the area of international humanitarian law (given how these crimes are the main reason why aggression has been criminalised). Finally, criminalising aggression may potentially have adverse results for the functioning of the international justice system, such as disruption of cohesion of international criminal law, and damage to the trustworthiness of international courts.

In the course of the research underlying this book, it proved necessary to review the jurisdiction of national and international courts, the resolutions of the various institutions of the League of Nations and the United Nations Organisation, international conventions, documents drafted by and for the International Law Commission and the ICC, as well as reports of a variety of other bodies and organisations. Two selections of documents were exceedingly useful in the process: *Defining International Aggression. The Search for World Peace: A Documentary History and Analysis*, as well as *An International Criminal Court. A Step Toward World Peace: A Documentary History and Analysis*, both edited by Benjamin B. Ferencz. Two other sets of documents were particularly helpful in the analysis of jurisprudence with regard to the crime against peace, namely the 11-volume *Nazi Conspiracy and Aggression* (published under the auspices of the US Government) and the 15-volume *Trials of War Criminals before the Nuernberg Military Tribunals under Control Council Law No 10, Nuernberg October 1946–April 1949*. Also of great use were the two volumes of *The Tokyo Judgment, The International Military Tribunal for the Far East (IMTFE) 29 April 1946–12 November 1948*, edited by Bernard V. Röling and Christian F. Rüter.

As for other resources, Oscar Solera's *Defining the Crime of Aggression* has been invaluable. It contains a chronological review of the efforts to define aggression in a manner that would be satisfactory with regard to the responsibility of both states and individuals. An older publication, *Aggressive War. An International Crime* by Cornelis A. Pompe, also presents a broader perspective on the criminalisation of aggression. Larry May's *Aggression and Crimes against Peace* was also used, although the main thesis of the book (that is, that the crime of aggression should only be tried in court when in its commission, crimes against humanity were also committed) impacts both the structure and the content of the publication rather too strongly. Furthermore, Ian Brownlie's *International Law and the Use of Force by States* and Yoram Dinstein's *War, Aggression and Self-Defence* are noteworthy; both only discuss the issue of criminal liability among a number of other issues, but they do so comprehensively and in great detail.

As for the chapter on legal limitations on the use of force, there is of course a great abundance of relevant resources. It is impossible to draw on every single publication on this topic. Similarly, with regard to the analysis of the efforts towards defining aggression as committed by a state, a number of highly insightful monographs have been published, such as those authored and/or edited by Julius Stone, Eugene Aroneanu, Bengt Broms, Jean Diamandesco, Ahmed M. Rifaat, Ann Van Wynen Thomas, A. J. Thomas Jr and Nicolas Nyiri.

Research on court trials focused on the crime against peace demonstrated that there were many publications on the Nuremberg trials, but quite a shortage of academic studies of other relevant cases. What stands out is the 15-volume publication *Law Reports of Trials of War Criminals*, prepared under the auspices of the United Nations War Crimes Commission, and *Seven Judgments by the Supreme National Tribunal* by Tadeusz Cyprian and Jerzy Sawicki.

Naturally, journals and periodicals in the area of legal studies were also consulted in the drafting of this book. The following were the most helpful: *American Journal of International Law*, *Journal of International Criminal Justice*, and *International Criminal Law Review*.

The original Polish version of this book went on sale in 2010 and, since that date, a number of new contributions on the crime of aggression have been published. They include: *Aggression, Crime and International Security. Moral, political and legal dimension of international relations* by Page Wilson and *The Travaux Préparatoires of the Crime of Aggression* edited by Stefan Barriga and Claus Kress, collecting the documentation of the 15 years of negotiations on the definition of aggression to be adopted in the statute of the ICC. This edition of the book has been updated to reflect the data available thanks to these new sources.

A methodological comment is also necessary in this introductory part of the book. The book uses the terms 'crime of aggression' and 'crime against peace' interchangeably on most occasions. An analysis of the definition of the crime against peace, as adopted for example in the statute of the International Military Tribunal, demonstrates that the term has a broader meaning than the crime of aggression, since it includes not only the planning, preparation, initiation or waging of a war of aggression, but also a war in violation of international treaties, agreements or assurances. However, it is generally accepted in the jurisprudence on the crime against peace that any war of aggression is at the same time a war in violation of international treaties, and therefore the category of crime against peace is usually not subdivided, a trend that has been reflected in this book.

The book's sole focus is criminal responsibility of individuals. Consequently, issues such as responsibility of states or legal persons, much as they deserve thorough study, were only given a passing glance herein. However, determination of aggression on the part of a state is a prerequisite for an individual's responsibility for aggression, and therefore the notion of aggression committed by a state has been given proper consideration.

The biographical notes on individuals charged with the crime of aggression or conspiracy to commit this crime were drafted on the basis of sources indicated later in the book.

This book is a translation and update of *Odpowiedzialność karna za zbrodnię agresji* (*Criminal responsibility for the crime of aggression*), published in 2010 by the publishing house of the University of Warsaw. In 2012, the Polish original was awarded the prestigious Manfred Lachs Prize for the best first book on public international law.

Part I
Outlawing aggression

1 War as an institution of law

War has always been a part of the history of humankind. Over the ages, reasons for wars and how wars were fought changed, but the essence remained the same. Primitive wars were little more than large-scale robberies,[1] and the wars fought by the civilised people aimed higher: at territorial[2] or cultural[3] expansion.

Whether wars result from the innate human nature or whether they are a product of civilisation gives rise to endless debates.[4] The history of international relations demonstrates that both Jean Jacques Rousseau's notion of primitive people being of naturally peaceful disposition, and Thomas Hobbes's theory of the state of nature with its 'war of all against all', fail to find their full reflections in the real world.[5] Researchers have studied primitive tribes that lived in peace, with no knowledge of war, as well as equally primitive tribes for whom war was the way of life.[6]

As a result of the frequency with which it occurred, war came to be treated as a regular and unavoidable part of life,[7] just as it is impossible to eliminate or avoid natural disasters such as earthquakes, fires or floods.[8] Nonetheless, war was never completely accepted. Literature going as far back as ancient times, be it Jewish,[9] Indian,[10] Chinese,[11] Greek or Roman,[12] abounded in anti-war sentiments.

As civilisations developed, theories arose as to the legitimacy of wars. Initially, wars were classified as just or unjust. Later, with the Covenant of the League of Nations, came the idea of legal and illegal wars. The Charter of the United Nations discusses 'self-defence', 'armed attack' and 'acts of aggression' – notions rooted in post-First World War discourse. How these notions are defined became of crucial importance, since the legality of the use of armed force rests on these definitions. It is particularly important to define aggression: outlawing aggression is the basis for its criminalisation and, consequently, the basis for criminal liability of individuals found guilty of waging aggressive war.[13]

1.1 Before the First World War

Until the end of the First World War, the problem of waging wars tended to be considered in moral categories (in particular in light of morality of international relations) rather than in legal ones. Therefore, research both by lawyers and by philosophers discussed war in terms of its being just or not, rather than legal or not.[14] It was generally believed that the outbreak of war does have legal consequences, much as a flood wreaks havoc that later results in a title to compensation. The mere occurrence of war, however, was believed to be beyond the realm of law.[15] Thus, while law might govern the relations between the parties at war (*ius in bello*) and the responsibilities of third parties (the principle of neutrality), no laws apply to the very outbreak of war.[16] The outbreak of war is a fact of life, not a fact of law.[17] The legality of war is a moot point, and so international law must accept war for what it is, whether it is fought for just reasons or not.[18]

Not only did the states hold the right to wage war at will and decide whether these wars were just and legal: they also wielded the power to decide whether a war they were fighting was formally a war. The interesting (if absurd) doctrine of the state of war stipulated that it was up to the warring parties to decide whether a *de iure* war was in effect. Whether a war occurred was thus not judged on the basis of objective criteria, such as active hostilities etc. War in the legal sense only occurred if it had formally been declared or if, in the absence of a formal declaration, one of the states was guilty of aggression towards another and demanded neutrality from other states, or if the state that fell victim to aggression deemed the circumstances to constitute war.[19]

As long as the parties avoided describing the situation as 'war', it was possible to engage in large-scale military operations without admitting that a war was going on. For example, the intervention in China of a coalition of American, Austrian, British, French, German, Japanese, Italian and Russian armies, in order to quash the so-called Boxer uprising (1900–1901), resulted in heavy fighting in Taku, Tientsin and Beijing. Neither China nor the coalition labelled the situation as 'war'. In his letter to the president of the United States and to the German emperor, the Chinese emperor mentioned only 'friendly relations'.[20]

The reverse situations occurred too, where despite the absence of fighting parties claimed to be at war. A good example is the Polish-Lithuanian conflict. Lithuania claimed that since October 1920, when Poland commenced allegedly occupying Vilnius, the states were at war. Consequently, diplomatic relations were suspended and borders were closed.[21] It took the decision of the Council of the League of Nations of 10 December 1927 to end this war.

It is relatively easy to understand why countries may claim to be at war, even if no actual military action occurs. One or both of the countries may seek a propaganda effect, may want to play up the hostility and make a strong statement that the current solution to a territorial dispute is not acceptable. This was the reasoning behind the Polish-Lithuanian conflict. It is somewhat more difficult to explain why parties deny the occurrence of war, even if military operations are in fact underway. The explanation rests on the following factors. A war usually results in a breach in diplomatic and economic relations, a breakdown in transport and travel (owing to the sealing of borders), a suspension of bilateral agreements and the necessity to observe the applicable national procedures for launching a war.[22] Once war occurs, third parties are also bound by the duty to remain neutral. The consequences of war are felt by both of the parties involved, but the weaker party is hit harder, especially in terms of the massive economic losses. Third parties may invoke neutrality to cut off the supply of arms, and the opponent may thus be encouraged to intensify military efforts.[23] Finally, the term 'war' is heavily loaded with psychological and moral baggage that the parties may prefer not to shoulder.[24] Therefore, the parties often prefer to label their actions as reprisals, demonstration of force, peaceful blockade, armed intervention (so-called measures short of war).[25] Certain limitations apply to these solutions, visible particularly well in the case of reprisals.

Reprisals are usually defined as 'such injurious and otherwise internationally illegal acts of one State against another as are exceptionally permitted for the purpose of compelling the latter to consent to a satisfactory settlement of a difference created by its own international delinquency'.[26] In the case of armed reprisals, they may consist of bombings, occupations or blockades. The legality of reprisals was discussed in the ruling of the arbitration court in the case of *Naulilaa* (1928).[27] The ruling stipulated that reprisals: (1) may be used only if international law was breached by the offending state; (2) must be preceded by a request for compensation of losses suffered; and (3) must be in proportion to the action to which they constitute the reaction.[28] States therefore have the option of labelling their actions not as 'war' but, for example, as 'reprisals'. This, however, imposes on them the duty to act in proportion to the offending actions and observe certain restrictions (annexation is for example ruled out).[29]

At the turn of the 19th century, public opinion gained in importance. The ruler's exclusive prerogative to launch war was challenged, in a large part owing to the fact that the burden of actual military action rested on the people, rather than on the sovereign. Consequently, a new viewpoint gained popularity, namely one that proposed that war was the ultimate step, to be used only if all peaceful measures of conflict resolution had failed, and only for self-defence or self-preservation. A number of conflicts at the time found their solutions in the courts of arbitration: the Alabama Claims (1872), the Bering Sea controversy (1892), the British Guyana–Venezuela border dispute (1897), the 'deserters of Casablanca' issue (1909), encouraging the use of amicable measures of conflict resolution. Unilateral and multilateral agreements came into force in which the contracting states pledged themselves to international arbitration and/or other peaceful solutions.

The First Hague Conference in 1899 and the Second Hague Conference in 1907[30] aimed at 'ensuring the most effectual means of insuring to all peoples the benefits of a real and durable peace'.[31] At the first conference, the Convention for the Pacific Settlement of International Disputes (Hague I) was adopted, in which the parties to the convention undertook to accept in principle the employment of good offices and of mediation in cases lending themselves thereto.[32] Pursuant to the convention, the Permanent Court of Arbitration was established, with its seat in The Hague. Unfortunately, both the First Hague Convention of 1899 and First Hague Convention of 1907 failed to impose mandatory arbitration in conflict situations, even though the principle of reliance on arbitration was included in the Declaration to the 1907 Hague I. At the 1907 Conference, the Convention on the Limitation of Employment of Force for Recovery of Contract Debts was adopted (also known as the Drago-Porter Convention, Hague II).[33] Its scope was somewhat limited, since it allowed for the possibility of war if the debtor state was unwilling to submit to arbitration (refused arbitration, neglected to reply to an offer of arbitration) or, after accepting the offer of arbitration, prevented any compromise from being agreed on, or, after the arbitration, failed to submit to the award. Moreover, the convention was not applicable to intergovernmental loans; it pertained solely to loans granted to individuals who had the official support of their governments. The states that ratified the convention – and they were few and far between – made additional reservations, further limiting its impact.[34] Nonetheless, it was the first international treaty to indicate an unlawful reason for launching a war.[35]

Among the regulations on the legal status of war arising out of the Hague Conferences, the Convention Relative to the Opening of Hostilities of 1907 was also adopted (Hague III).[36] It stipulated that hostilities must not commence without previous and explicit warning, in the form either of a reasoned declaration of war or of an ultimatum with a conditional declaration of war. The convention aimed at minimising the potential for war by means of implementing formal requirements on its commencement, thus making it more difficult (albeit minimally so) to launch a war.[37] The covenants of Hague III were almost universally disregarded. None of the Hague Conventions went as far as to outlaw war.

The beginning of the 20th century saw a number of bilateral agreements obliging the parties to solve conflicts by peaceful means. For example, beginning in 1913, US Secretary of State, William Jennings Bryan, negotiated a number of bilateral treaties for the 'advancement of peace'. The basic aim of these treaties was to prevent war by interjecting a conciliation process into a dispute between the parties to the treaty.[38] Each signatory nominated two representatives, one a national and one a foreign citizen, to a permanent commission. These four would then choose a fifth member who could not be a national of either state. The commission would review the underlying facts to the dispute and issue a report on the controversy within one year. The report was not binding on the parties; however, until the report had been issued, the parties agreed to refrain from resorting to hostilities. The Bryan Treaties did not introduce a ban on war, but they provided a period in which to find a peaceful solution to a conflict and to lessen the tension between the parties (a cooling-off period).[39]

As these legal instruments of peaceful conflict resolution were developed, vital conflicts tended nonetheless not to be submitted for arbitration. The regulations, much as they encouraged and required the use of peaceful procedures, left open the option that certain types of conflicts, such as those pertaining to 'honour', 'vital interests' or political issues, remained outside of the scope of the regulation.[40] Hague I included the tell-tale phrasing: the parties agree to have recourse to the procedures outlined therein 'as far as circumstances allow'.

States continued to believe that war is their sovereign right. They sought legitimacy in the need for self-preservation and for security, but held tight to the notion that it was up to the states to decide whether a war meets the criteria set out by ethics and law.[41] The idea of a total ban on war, and consequently of its criminalisation, never entered the discourse.[42] The single exception was the resolution of the Paris World Peace Conference of 1878, which declared: '*la guerre offensive est un brigandage international*'. Resolutions of the Inter-Parliamentary Union, world peace congresses and statutes of pacifist organisations tended to stop at claims of necessity of peaceful conflict resolution, for example by means of arbitration or disarmament.[43]

When the First World War broke out, international law had no universal provision banning war. First, war was accepted as a legal measure of seeking satisfaction of certain claims[44] (which is hardly surprising, given that no international justice and enforcement systems existed[45]). Secondly, legality of wars whose sole purpose was to win new territories was unchallenged (eg the German annexation of Alsace-Lorraine, British and French expansion in Asia and Africa, and the American expansion in Northern America).[46] A war was always legal, whether it was just or not.

Nonetheless, the practice of entering into bilateral and multilateral agreements on peaceful conflict resolution helped eliminate the unshaken notion that war is an extra-legal event, and its outbreak cannot be regulated by the law. The perception of war as extra-legal was doomed, considering that wars are caused by people and not by forces of nature, which by definition are uncontrollable.[47] The above-mentioned legal instruments pertained to the commencement of hostilities (the obligation to follow a conciliatory procedure, to engage in arbitration, to declare formal war). Consequently, war began to be perceived as an issue subject to legal regulation. That in turn meant that certain limitations might be gradually introduced as to the reasons why a war might be launched.

1.2 The League of Nations

The First World War was a tremendous shock for nations that took part in it. Seventy million soldiers were drafted, 10 million people died, 20 million were injured and a further 10 million died of starvation or from epidemics.[48] Consequently, there was an immense determination to prevent a similar disaster from even happening again. It became clear that the right to war is a straight path to self-destruction.[49] A seemingly radical solution was reached: a fundamental shift in the entire world system.[50]

The first ever collective security system was created in the form of the League of Nations. Its creation had been announced by the United States President Woodrow Wilson in his Congressional address of 8 January 1918.[51] The Covenant of the League of Nations, a part of the peace treaties with the states which had taken part in the war on the side of the Triple Entente or joined it during the conflict, was signed by 32 warring states and 13 neutral ones.[52] It appeared that, for the first time in history, there was universal consensus that the threat of war must be eliminated from international relations. However, a look at the provisions of the covenant leaves no such illusions.

The covenant's preamble is very promising. In order to promote international cooperation and to achieve international peace and security, the parties accept the obligation not to resort to war. Similarly promising is Article 10 of the covenant, which stipulates that the members of the League of Nations undertake to respect and preserve as against external aggression the territorial integrity and existing political independence of all members of the League of Nations. In case of any such aggression or in case of any threat or danger of such aggression the council should advise upon the means by which this obligation is to be fulfilled.

In Wilson's plans, Article 10 was of key importance, since it aimed at protecting smaller states from the bigger ones.[53] At first glance, the wording of Article 10 does point to a legal ban on war, with the exception of self-defence,[54] which was one of the reasons why the United States never ratified the covenant (it was feared that owing to the guarantees of Article 10, the world would be pushed towards another war).[55] Canada went so far as to wish for Article 10 to be removed from the covenant.[56]

The problem, however, consisted in the fact that the provisions of the preamble and of Article 10 were not integrated with Articles 11–15 of the covenant. These articles allowed for the possibility of war once applicable procedures had run their course. Furthermore, the system of sanctions envisioned in Article 16 was to take effect only if the state had failed to observe Articles 12, 13 and 15. Article 10 was not mentioned. Also, the Assembly of the League of Nations decided that the members of the league held the sole prerogative to undertake measures to implement Article 10.[57] It was therefore accepted that Article 15 took precedence over Article 10, which weakened Article 10 but at the same time removed the inconsistence within the covenant.[58] There were even suggestions that Article 10 expressed an obligation of the members of the league that was purely moral in nature.[59]

The council of the League of Nations decidedly preferred to base its decisions on articles other than Article 10, in order to avoid an interpretation of its meaning. Article 10 was directly invoked by the council only on two occasions: the Chinese-Japanese conflict[60] and the Spanish civil war.[61] On the other hand, particular members of the league cited Article 10 relatively often.

The Covenant of the League of Nations was, in its essence, a very complex multilateral 'Bryan treaty'.[62] Instead of banning war, it outlined a procedure that had to be followed in order for the war to be legal. In the cases of disputes between league members that might lead to a rupture, the parties were to submit the matter to arbitration, to judicial settlement or to enquiry by the League Council.[63] Another option was to submit the matter to the Assembly of the League. The right to choose this option lay either with the council or, within 14 days of submitting the conflict to the council, each of the parties involved. If the matter was referred to the assembly, its powers were the same as the council's.[64] The award of the arbitrators or the judicial decision was to be made 'within a reasonable time', and the report of the council, establishing the facts of the case and proposing relevant recommendation, was to be made within six months after the submission of the dispute.[65]

Only after the lapse of three months after the award by the arbitrators or the judicial decision, if the other party failed to respect that award or decision, or after the publication of the report, if the council had failed to reach a report unanimously agreed to by its members, a party was free to resort to such action as it considered necessary for the maintenance of right and justice, including a war.[66] A party could not resort to war against a member of the league who complied with the report or the judicial decision.[67] Also, if a report by the council was unanimously agreed to (regardless of the votes of the representatives of one or more of the parties to the dispute), the parties were not allowed to go to war with any party to the dispute who had complied with the recommendations of the report.[68]

The Covenant of the League of Nations considered war legal in the following circumstances (beyond defence against an attack in breach of the covenant). First, when a party failed to observe the award or the judicial decision or a unanimous report of the council, the other party was allowed to commence hostilities after a lapse of three months after the date of the award, decision or report.[69] Secondly, if the council had failed to reach a report unanimously agreed to by its members thereof, other than the representatives of one or more of the parties to the dispute, the parties had the right to take actions they considered necessary, including war.[70] Thirdly, if the dispute between the parties was claimed by one of them, and was found by the council to arise out of a matter by international law solely within the domestic jurisdiction of that party, the council could not make a recommendation as to its settlement, and consequently the parties were also allowed to act as they saw fit.[71] That meant that the Council of the League of Nations had no authority in matters not considered international in nature, but which had in fact the potential to lead to international conflict.[72] Fourthly, if the report of the council was not made within six months, or the award or decision was not reached within a reasonable time, the parties were also free to act as they considered necessary.[73] Fifthly and finally, the provisions of the covenant were only binding on the member states of the league. States were still free to engage in war with other states that were not members of the league.[74]

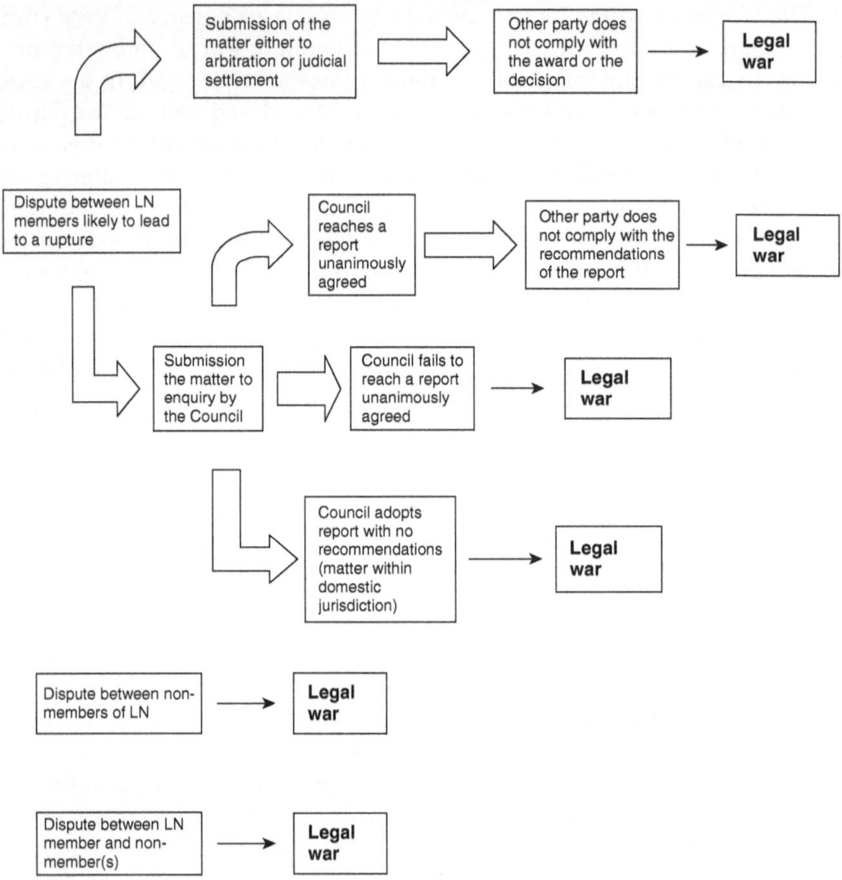

Chart 1.1: Legal war (League of Nations) Source: Author.

Consider the paradox of the situation: the key architects of the League of Nations, that is, the states that had prevailed in the First World War, placed restrictions on their own ability to wage war, but forced no similar limitations on the states that had lost that war.[75] The Covenant of the League of Nations thus left a door wide open for wars.[76]

The shortcomings of the covenant were plenty. What appears to be the main one among them is that the possibility of war, including aggressive war, was only limited and restricted, rather than banned outright.[77] Consequently, war as a method of solving conflicts was still legitimate.

Moreover, the use of the phrase 'resort to war' in a number of provisions proved to be rather unfortunate as well. The states could avoid the scrutiny of the procedures provided for by the covenant as long as they claimed not to be formally at war. Moreover, the doctrine of the state of war was fully accepted by the League of Nations. Was it enough to label the hostilities 'intervention' or 'reprisals' in order to be allowed to engage in armed action against another state? The legality of armed force used in circumstances other than war, in the light of Articles 12–15 of the covenant, came under the consideration of the special committee, which was established as conflict occurred between Italy and Greece (in 1923).[78] The committee gave an answer styled after the Oracle of Delphi. The use of armed force by one member state against another, without observing the procedure set out in Articles 12–15, might or might not be in compliance with these articles.[79] However, if the states wanted in good faith to observe their obligations under the covenant, then it must be noted that Article 12 should be applied to 'any dispute likely to lead to a rupture', and therefore League of Nations members should in any situation likely to result in the use of armed force attempt a peaceful solution first.[80] Over the two-year life span of the League of Nations, the formalistic approach to war held less and less ground.[81] Nonetheless, an interpretation loophole continued to exist.

When considering the shortcomings of the League of Nations, its inefficient system of sanctions appears most prominent. Theoretically, economic sanctions were to be applied by default in cases of breach of Articles 12, 13 and 15 of the covenant.[82] However, it was left for states to decide whether the covenant had been breached and, consequently, whether and against which party the sanctions should be applied. The Council of the League of Nations could issue a recommendation in each case, and it could propose military sanctions, but the recommendations were not binding – they were purely moral in nature.[83] The council itself was hardly a proponent of sanctions, since it tended to believe that use of sanctions may further jeopardise peace, and a mediation attempt is a better solution.[84] The French proposal that an international armed force be established and placed at the League's disposal was dismissed.[85] A permanent Disarmament Commission was established in order to lead in matters of disarmament,[86] but it failed to make progress in this direction. Only once did the League of Nations actually employ sanctions. After the Italian invasion of Abyssinia, on 19 October 1935, the Council of the League of Nations applied economic and financial sanctions against Italy.[87] However, Great Britain and France were unprepared for the massive costs related to the operation, so no sanctions were introduced with regard to strategic commodities such as oil, coal and steel.[88] Germany, Austria, Switzerland and Hungry failed to observe even this restricted version of sanctions.[89] Thus, the theoretical weakness of the League of Nations was fully exposed in practice.

Another shortcoming of the first collective security system was its limited membership. The United States, one of the driving forces behind the covenant and its signatory, never ratified the covenant.[90] Germany remained outside the League of Nations for some time, joining in 1926. However, as early as 1933, both Germany and Japan (following the Manchuria invasion) also left the League of Nations. Earlier, in 1928, Brazil had left and the Union of Soviet Socialist Republics (USSR), a member since 1934, was expelled from the league by a resolution of 14 December 1939 for invading Finland.[91] The efficiency of the League of Nations depended on the power of its key members, France and Great Britain, measured by their attitude towards a breaching state and their readiness to observe the obligations arising out of the covenant.

For all its weaknesses, the League of Nations constituted a major step forward. The Covenant of the League was the first legal act to divide wars into legal and illegal ones, where the defining criterion was whether or not the procedure set out in the covenant had been observed. Thus, the subjective division into just and unjust wars was abandoned. Moreover, pursuant to Article 11 of the covenant (as well as Article 16, with the notion of sanctions), any war or threat of war, whether immediately affecting any of the members of the League or not, was declared 'a matter of concern to the whole League'. War therefore ceased to be a private matter of the parties at conflict and became a matter of interest to all the members of the league which, theoretically, was supposed to extend to the entire international community. The Council of the League of Nations was authorised to use any measures to prevent an escalation of conflict (policing the peace).[92] If the council had been effective, there would have been a chance for elimination of war in the practice of international relations. All that was needed in order to eradicate war completely was a gradual tightening of the system.

1.3 The inter-war period

Throughout the entire inter-war period, efforts continued to eliminate war. The League of Nations provided one forum, but a number of bilateral, multilateral and even universal agreements were executed with the same intention in mind. States from across the Americas were particularly involved.

Immediately after the publication of the first draft of the Covenant of the League of Nations, on 14 February 1919, voices were raised to the effect that war should be banned completely. Such opinions came from the Inter-Allied Associations for the League of Nations in London, the International Conference for the League of Nations in Berne and the International Socialist Congress in Amsterdam. However, at the time, Lord Cecil, speaking on behalf of the Paris Conference, claimed that it was impossible to implement these proposals.[93] The impetus therefore went towards further development of peaceful means of conflict resolution.

The first Assembly of the League of Nations established the Permanent Court of International Justice, which began to operate in 1921. For the first time in history, a permanent international court was in place, available for all states to use at any time when conflicts arose. Unfortunately, the Argentinian proposal to make the court's jurisdiction mandatory in all cases which were not political in nature was never adopted.[94] However, a great number of treaties were signed in which the parties undertook to take their conflicts to arbitration, or attempt to solve them by other peaceful means.[95]

Distrust towards the League of Nation's system stemmed mostly from ineffective enforcement of its sanctions. Since it was up to the states to decide whether to apply sanctions in the case of a breach of the covenant, no default actions in support of the victim of the attack were possible. In order to ensure mutual assistance in case of aggression, the Assembly of the League of Nations asked the Temporary Mixed Commission for the Reduction of Armaments, established by the Council of the League of Nations on 25 February 1921, to draft a 'treaty of mutual guarantee'.[96] The outcome of the commission's work was the Draft Treaty of Mutual Assistance, debated in sessions of the fourth Assembly.[97] The draft treaty stated that aggressive war was an international crime, and that the parties would undertake that no one of them would be guilty of its commission.[98] The parties to the draft treaty were to undertake to furnish assistance to a state that fell victim to a war of aggression if that state had complied with relevant disarmament provisions.[99] The League Council was empowered to designate which party is an object of aggression and whether it is entitled to claim assistance.[100] The parties were obliged to act on the council's recommendation.[101] Unfortunately, the Legal Committee immediately minimised the impact of the ban on aggressive war: its report, drafted at the request of the assembly, claimed that wars could be deemed international crimes only if they had been commenced in breach of the provisions of the Covenant of the League of Nations.[102] Great Britain, Russia, Germany and the United States were all strongly opposed to the draft treaty, mostly owing to the absence of guarantees to ensure actual disarmament.[103] The treaty never came into force.

Parts of the Draft Treaty of Mutual Assistance found their way into the American Draft Treaty of Disarmament and Security, presented to the League of Nations Assembly in 1924.[104] This treaty also denounced aggressive war as an international crime that states should undertake not to commit.[105] In the American proposal, it was up to the individual states to decide whether to apply sanctions against the aggressor.[106] The determination of the aggressor was in the hands of the Permanent Court of International Justice.[107] The United States was not a member of the League of Nations and so was unwilling to let the council make the decision in this matter. This draft was innovative in that it declared not only that war could be aggressive, but so were other forms of armed force engagement ('acts of aggression, even when not amounting to a state of war') and, therefore, they were all banned.[108] According to the draft, states were allowed to use armed force solely for the purpose of defence against aggression and for protection of human life.[109] Unfortunately, the draft was never even seriously debated within the League of Nations.

Yet another attempt to salvage the Treaty of Mutual Assistance occurred in the form of the Protocol to the Pacific Settlement of International Disputes of 2 October 1924, the so-called Geneva Protocol.[110] As the name itself – 'Protocol' – suggested, it was intended to implement the provisions of the Covenant of the League of Nations rather than replace the covenant.[111]

Under the Geneva Protocol, states undertook to recognise as compulsory, ipso facto and without special agreement, the jurisdiction of the Permanent Court of International Justice in cases of legal disputes.[112] Moreover, in cases of other disputes, the option of legal war remained closed if, under Article 15 of the covenant, the council had failed to reach a unanimous report. Given such circumstances, the Geneva Protocol outlined a tiered procedure ending in the dispute's resolution either by judicial means or by arbitration.[113] Owing to the scope of the state's obligation to undergo judicial or arbitration proceedings, Robert Kolb claims that the Geneva Protocol's solution is an example of *totalitarisme juridique*.[114]

The crucial significance of the Geneva Protocol lay in the fact that it attempted fully to outlaw all aggressive war.[115] It asserted that a war of aggression constituted a violation of international solidarity and an international crime.[116] It also forbade any acts that might constitute a threat of aggression against another state.[117] War was allowed only in case of resistance to acts of aggression, or when acting in agreement with the Council or the Assembly of the League of Nations in accordance with the provisions of the covenant and of the Geneva Protocol.[118] With regard to the aggressor, economic, financial and military sanctions were to be employed, and the aggressor was to be charged with costs and reparations.[119] Following the ideas of the Treaty of Mutual Assistance, if the League Council recommended sanctions, the states were obliged to follow this recommendation.[120] The Geneva Protocol even included a definition of the aggressor, as the state which resorts to war in violation of the undertakings contained in the covenant or in the protocol, with violation of the rules laid down for a demilitarised zone held equivalent to resorting to war.[121] However, states were not ready to move beyond the obligations listed in the covenant and the Geneva Protocol never entered into force.[122]

Owing to the failure of the efforts to establish a universal multilateral peace agreement, individual states attempted to ensure their security by means of a variety of bilateral agreements. The Persia-Turkey Treaty of Friendship and Security of 1926[123] is a good example, as is the Persia-Afghanistan Treaty of 27 November 1927.[124] The Soviet Union was very active in this area. On 17 December 1925 it signed a Treaty of Friendship and Neutrality with Turkey, which included a ban on aggression.[125] Subsequent treaties, usually called treaties of non-aggression, gradually introduced new elements. The treaty with Lithuania of 28 September 1926 forbade aggression and also proposed a conciliatory procedure to employ in case of conflict,[126] and the treaty with Persia of 1 October 1927 included also a ban on subversive activity.[127]

Of major importance among these agreements was the Locarno system of treaties of 16 October 1925 and, in particular, the Rhineland Pact between Germany, Belgium, France, Great Britain and Italy.[128] Germany and Belgium, as well as Germany and France, made mutual guarantees not to attack, invade, commence war or occupy, with the exception of legitimate defence, actions stipulated by Article 16 of the Covenant of the League of

Nations, actions resulting from a decision made by the League's Assembly or council under Article 15 paragraph 7 of the covenant, if aimed at the state that attacked first.[129] Importantly, a violation of the Rhineland Pact was to be brought before the League Council first and, until the council decided that a violation had indeed occurred, war was prohibited.[130] However, war was considered acceptable in the case of a flagrant violation of Article 2 of the Rhineland Pact or a flagrant violation of the demilitarisation provisions of Articles 42 and 43 of the Treaty of Versailles, if the above constituted an unprovoked act of aggression and when an immediate reaction was necessary owing to the crossing of the frontier, the outbreak of hostilities or the assembly of armed forces in the demilitarised zone.[131] The parties undertook to settle disputes in a peaceful manner, either by judicial decision (legal issues) or conciliation (other issues).[132] It was stipulated that in cases where the proposals of the conciliation committee were unacceptable, the matter should be presented to the League Council, in accordance with the procedure of Article 15 of the Covenant of the League of Nations. The main objective of the Locarno system of treaties was to ensure the status quo along Germany's western border.[133] Thus Locarno, while it eliminated one potential reason for aggressive war, at the same time created vulnerability in another direction – in the east. No mutual assurances between France and Poland as well as France and Czechoslovakia could change that, and neither could the arbitration treaties between Germany and Poland as well as between Germany and Czechoslovakia.

Despite the controversies that Locarno created, they introduced further restrictions on the use of armed force. The treaties placed restrictions not only on commencing war, but also on other uses of force, such as attack or invasion. Moreover, they developed a system of peaceful conflict resolution. On the other hand, it is debatable whether they did in fact ensure security and fostered the feeling that the right to war was limited. They certainly undermined the position of the League of Nations. Since Germany was expected to join the league at any moment, why at this time enter into additional agreements that forbid war of aggression?[134] Moreover, the terms used in the treaties, such as 'flagrant violation' or 'unprovoked act of aggression', lacked precision and allowed for very broad interpretation.

Meanwhile, the League of Nations continued to propose solutions for elimination of aggressive war from international relations. The assembly, in a resolution dated 25 September 1925, adopting the wording that 'offensive warfare' constitutes 'an international crime'.[135] However, the First Commission of the Assembly drafted a report stating that the resolution was not a reflection of positive law.[136] On 24 September 1927, at the initiative of Poland, the assembly unanimously adopted a resolution banning war of aggression, considering it an international crime and an inadmissible solution to international conflicts.[137] This resolution, like the previous one, was not legally binding, although it was accepted by some as placing a legal obligation on the members of the League of Nations.[138] It was of moral and educational significance, in the opinion of its sponsor, Franciszek Sokal, a Polish representative in the League of Nations.[139] Neither of the resolutions was intended to apply beyond the covenant, and so neither introduced further restrictions in terms of the use of armed force.[140]

Among the documents of the inter-war period, apart from the Covenant of the League of Nations, the other most important undertaking was the General Treaty for the Renunciation of War, also known as the World Peace Act, that is, the Briand-Kellogg Pact of 27 August 1928, which entered into force on 24 July 1929. The French foreign minister, Aristid Briand, approached the United States on 6 April 1927, on the 10th anniversary of the Americans entering into the First World War, with a proposal for a mutual agreement that would serve to 'outlaw war'.[141] The American secretary of state, Frank Billings Kellogg, countered with a proposal to draft a treaty to be signed with all the major states in the world, which might go further towards ensuring world peace than just simply a bilateral agreement. France was more interested in bilateral guarantees, but it acted on the American proposal. Other states were invited to the negotiations of the treaty, including Great Britain, Germany, Italy and Japan.

In the treaty, the parties condemned recourse to war for the resolution of international controversies, and renounced war as an instrument of national policy in their relations with one another.[142] It might appear, therefore, that the Briand-Kellogg Pact went far beyond the scope of the Covenant of the League of Nations. It was, however, not free from shortcomings of its own.

First, the Briand-Kellogg Pact uses ethical notions such as 'condemn' or 'renounce', which might point towards its moral rather than its legal nature.[143] However, no state ever attempted to undermine the legal status of the obligations set out by the pact.

Secondly, following opposition on the American part, the term 'war of aggression' was not used, since it could not be clearly defined.[144] It was replaced by the phrase 'war as an instrument of national policy', which hardly made interpretation of the Briand-Kellogg Pact any easier.[145] It gave rise to a number of questions: since war was unacceptable 'as an instrument of national policy', could it be used 'as an instrument of international policy', or war aimed at furthering a religion or a philosophy?[146] Does the Briand-Kellogg Pact forbid the use of force in the absence of a formal war, and does it forbid reprisals, believed at the time to be a measure of peaceful conflict resolution?[147] Once again, the principle of sovereignty, with its reluctance to accept any restrictions on what a state can do, clashes with the principle of interpreting the treaty in a manner that ensures its efficiency.[148] If the latter were to prevail, any use of force in contradiction of the Briand-Kellogg Pact would be forbidden, particularly in light of the preamble, which expresses the desire for 'peaceful and friendly relations'.[149] The prevailing interpretation of the Briand-Kellogg Pact was that measures short of war were not directly forbidden by it, but were in violation of its spirit.[150]

Thirdly, while the wording of the Briand-Kellogg Pact appears decisive in terms of banning war, the ban did not extend to defensive war, as evidenced by the provision that the party who resorts to war will be denied the benefits furnished by the treaty.[151] It was up to the individual states to decide whether self-defence was required.[152] It was also accepted that war was allowed as long as it was conducted within the framework of sanctions under the Covenant of the League of Nations or under the Monroe doctrine.[153] These exceptions to the general ban on war were not listed in the main body of the Briand-Kellogg Pact, owing to the propaganda needs of the signatory states or, in other words, to their need to mislead public opinion,[154] which strongly favoured a full and complete ban on war.[155]

Fourthly, the pact was something of a missed opportunity in terms of peaceful conflict resolution. The stipulation of the pact is that the parties should seek to resolve their conflicts by peaceful means, rather than obliging the parties to resolve them by such means only.

Fifthly, the Briand-Kellogg Pact carried no sanctions. States were free to decide how they were going to react to a violation of it, as Kellogg himself stressed on 7 December 1928 in his speech to the Senate's international relations committee.[156] The only sanction included in the treaty was the stipulation that a signatory that seeks to promote its national interests by resorting to war will be denied the benefits furnished by the treaty. However, no institution was authorised to decide whether a state acted in self-defence or whether its actions constituted a violation of the pact. In his speech on the occasion of the signing of the Briand-Kellogg Pact, Briand stressed the moral significance of public opinion.[157] The International Law Association addressed the issue of sanctions under the pact in September 1934 in Budapest. According to the association, in case of violation of the pact, its signatories could attack the violating state using measures short of war. The violating state would bear full compensatory liability and neutral states were free to modify their position so as to favour the victim of aggression.[158]

Sixthly, and somewhat obviously, the effectiveness of the Briand-Kellogg Pact was limited to its signatories, that is, war was still allowed with states that had not signed the pact. It was therefore liable to the same problem as the Covenant of the League of Nations, namely that it would be purely regional. However, these fears did not materialise. Immediately prior to the beginning of the First World War, 63 states were signatories to the pact, a massive feat for the times.[159] Before the war's outbreak, only four states remained outside the pact: Bolivia, Salvador, Uruguay and Argentina.[160]

Despite the above-listed reservations, the Briand-Kellogg Pact tends to be perceived as a breakthrough in terms of restricting the use of armed force and outlawing aggression.[161] Representatives of many governments spoke of how the pact changed *ius ad bellum*.[162] In conflict situations occurring after 1928, the pact's provisions were often invoked. The Briand-Kellogg Pact contributed also to the Hoover-Stimson doctrine of non-recognition of international territorial changes that were executed by force.[163] In line with the recommendations of the 27th Universal Peace Congress, held in Athens in October 1929, provisions implementing the Briand-Kellogg Pact were introduced into constitutions and laws of a number of states, renouncing war and an instrument of politics.[164]

Since the ratification procedure of the pact appeared to drag on, the Moscow Protocol was signed on 9 February 1929. An initiative of Maksim Litvinov, a representative of the USSR, the Soviet Union, Estonia, Latvia, Poland and Romania signed the document, thus ensuring earlier entry into force of the Briand-Kellogg Pact in eastern Europe. Attempts – driven mostly by Great Britain and Lithuania – were also made by the Assembly of the League to reconcile the pact with the Covenant of the League of Nations.[165] An 11-member committee established by the League Council presented relevant amendments to the covenant on 8 March 1930. Unfortunately, none of these amendments was ever implemented.

The only successful efforts of the League of Nations were those aimed at adopting successive documents promoting peaceful means of conflict resolution. These included the General Act of Arbitration (Pacific Settlement of International Disputes) of 26 September 1928, which encouraged the use of arbitration, conciliation and judicial measures.[166] It proposed that bilateral and multilateral treaties be signed by states, to oblige them to abstain from attacks, wars and invasions, unless in self-defence, in cases falling under Article 15 paragraph 7 and Article 16 of the covenant or in cases where a decision of the council or the assembly recommended such actions. Thus, all the avenues that were open for war in the covenant remained open. However, when specific solutions were proposed to support victims of aggression, for example by financial means (as proposed in the Finnish draft of a treaty on financial assistance to states victims of aggression[167]), they failed to garner endorsement from the league's members. Work of the disarmament commission in the period 1932–1934 was also fruitless, despite the attention paid at times to the Belgian draft procedure for determining that aggression had occurred, the French proposal for a European Security Pact, the British concept of good services in preventing use of armed force, and the Soviet initiative toward defining aggression. The efforts to adopt a convention introducing guarantees of mutual protection in case of aggression and to continue the disarmament failed, and the definition of aggressor passed at a conference in London in 1933 had a very limited scope.

As the League of Nations appeared ineffective at the task of constructing a security system, the states continued to put their trust in bilateral agreements. The 1930s was a decade of so-called non-aggression pacts. Such treaties were concluded, for example, between the Soviet Union and Poland on 25 July 1932,[168] and between Germany and Poland on 26 January 1934.[169] These pacts were concluded for a limited duration, clearly illustrating the attitude that wars of aggression were not being outlawed permanently.

When Germany left the League of Nations, attention shifted towards regional agreements. France planned to enter into an agreement with its eastern and Mediterranean neighbours, but never managed to complete these plans. On the other hand, the Pact of Organisation of the Little Entente was signed in Geneva on 16 February 1933 between Romania, Czechoslovakia and Yugoslavia,[170] the Balkan Pact on 9 February 1934 between Greece, Romania, Turkey and Yugoslavia[171] and the Saadabad Pact on 8 July 1937 between Afghanistan, Iraq, Iran and Turkey.[172]

The states of the Americas, as well as associations active in their territories, were also actively working to minimise the potential for war in the inter-war period.[173] The Pan-American Conference in Santiago de Chile on 3 May 1923 resulted in the Treaty to Avoid or Prevent Conflicts Between the American States (Gondra Treaty), which condemned the situation of 'armed peace which increases military and naval forces beyond the necessities of domestic security and the sovereignty and independence of States'.[174] The Gondra Treaty proposed that all conflicts and disputes impossible to settle through diplomatic channels be submitted for investigation and report to a permanent commission seated in Washington or in Montevideo. A resolution adopted on 18 February 1928 by the Pan-American Conference in Havana declared that war of aggression constituted an international crime against the human species.[175] It stressed that any and every aggression was illegal and therefore the states of the Americas were to use all accessible peaceful means to settle any disputes among themselves. The Washington Conference (1928–1929) adopted measures implementing new instruments of arbitration and conciliation.[176] The Anti-War Treaty of Non-Aggression and Conciliation (also known as the Saavedra Lamas Treaty) signed in Rio de Janeiro on 10 October 1933 condemned wars of aggression, and imposed the duty to resolve conflicts peacefully not only with other signatories but also with regard to third parties.[177] The original signatories of this treaty were Argentina, Brazil, Chile, Mexico, Paraguay and Uruguay. At the Pan-American Conference in Montevideo, other states were invited to join this treaty, often referred to as a 'twin of the Pact of Paris', that is, the Briand-Kellogg Pact.[178] The invitation was accepted not only by American states, including the United States, but also by Italy, Great Britain, Bulgaria, Norway, Romania, Spain, Czechoslovakia, Finland, Greece, Portugal, Turkey and Yugoslavia. As specified in the declarations supplementing the treaty, all states preserved their inalienable right to self-defence. Subsequent documents adopted at the Pan-American conferences stressed the obligation to settle disputes by peaceful means and the prohibition of intervention into internal and external affairs of any state.[179] In fact, so many of these documents were adopted that on 23 December 1936 the Convention to Coordinate, Extend, and Assure the Fulfillment of the Existing Treaties between the American States was passed in order to codify the treaties renouncing war and establishing measures of peaceful conflict resolution.[180]

Did the legal instruments of the inter-war period, with the Covenant of the League of Nations and the Briand-Kellogg Pact in particular, change the prevailing attitude to war? The answer is: yes and no. They were clearly ineffective, as evidenced by the multitude of conflicts that did occur at the time: the two Manchuria conflicts between the USSR and China in 1929, and then between Japan and China in 1931–1932,[181] the Leticia conflict between Columbia and Peru in 1932,[182] the Italian invasion of Ethiopia in 1935, the Chaco conflict between Paraguay and Bolivia in 1928 (Bolivia, however, was not a party to the Briand-Kellogg Pact), the Japanese-Chinese conflict of 1937, as well as the conflict between the puppet state Manchukuo and Mongolia of 1939 (essentially, a conflict between Japan and the USSR).[183] This list clearly demonstrates that the national leaders of the times held the Briand-Kellogg Pact as well as the other international instruments in very low esteem, an observation put more bluntly by the Polish leader Józef Piłsudski.[184] The German aggression against Poland of 1 September 1939 met with no forceful reaction of the League of Nations, to which Poland itself had contributed to some extent.[185] The resolution of 14 December 1939, which expelled the USSR from the League of Nations for invading Finland, received only 7 votes in favour, from among 14 states.[186]

The League of Nations was only successful in the cases of smaller disputes, such as the conflict between Albania and Yugoslavia (1921) or between Greece and Bulgaria (1925).[187] When conflicts escalated, the league's recommendations fell on deaf ears.

On the other hand, when the Nuremberg tribunal held that war of aggression was a crime even under international law before the Second World War, this ruling was based on the provisions of the Briand-Kellogg Pact and other documents discussed above. The legislative efforts of the international community in the inter-war period resulted in erasing the presumption that all war was legal.[188]

1.4 The United Nations system

The Second World War demonstrated with excruciating clarity that further restrictions on the use of armed force were absolutely necessary. Even before it was over, numerous documents were issued that hinted at systemic change. In the Atlantic Charter of 14 August 1941, Franklin D. Roosevelt, the president of the United States, and Winston Churchill, the British Prime Minister, declared the necessity of renouncing the use of force and announced the establishment of a wide permanent system of general security.[189] The Moscow Declaration of 30 October–1 November 1943 between the United States, Great Britain, the Soviet Union and China confirmed that, in order to maintain peace and security, it is necessary to found 'a general international organization, based on the principle of the sovereign equality of all peace-loving states'.[190] At the Dumbarton Oaks Conference (20 August–7 October 1944), representatives of these four states discussed the new world order. Their proposals and ideas were presented at the conference in San Francisco where, on 26 June 1945, the Charter of the United Nations was signed and the foundation of the contemporary system of universal security was established.

As stated in the preamble of the charter, its aim was to save succeeding generations from the scourge of war. It is therefore not surprising that the charter lists maintaining international peace and security as its first purpose,[191] and all the principles listed in Article 2 of the charter pertain directly or indirectly to limitations of the use of force. The members were obliged to settle their international disputes by peaceful means, in such a manner that international peace and security, and justice, were not endangered.[192] They were also obliged to give the United Nations every assistance in any action the organisation took, and to refrain from giving assistance to any state against which the United Nations was taking preventive or enforcement action.[193] The United Nations Organisation, on the other hand, was obliged to ensure that states that were not its members acted in accordance with the charter's principles as far as necessary for the maintenance of international peace and security.[194] Matters within the domestic jurisdiction of a state were excluded from intervention,[195] in conjunction with the principle of sovereign equality of all the members of the United Nations.[196] However, the norm of greatest importance was the principle forbidding the threat or use of force against the territorial integrity or political independence of any state, or in any other manner inconsistent with the purposes of the United Nations.[197]

The charter employs terms such as 'force', 'aggression', 'self-defence', 'armed attack' and 'intervention'. These terms have been left undefined, on purpose. It was assumed (incorrectly, as it turned out) that a well functioning Security Council, consisting of the former allies, would be able to make quick and objective decisions on a case-by-case basis, and that it would have no major problems with qualifying the circumstances as they arose.[198] In contrast to this assumption, an ultimate decision has not been reached until today whether the notion of 'force', as employed by Article 2(4) of the charter, is to be understood as military force only, since the preamble as well as Articles 41 and 46 refer to it explicitly, or whether it is intended to include pressure exercised by non-military means, such as economic or political pressure.[199]

The term 'war' was barely mentioned, having been replaced by 'use of armed force',[200] and so deliberations on whether a formal war occurred might seem unimportant in light of the charter. However, doubts as to the legality of the use of measures short of war remained. For example, the International Law Commission, having regard to previous practice, never clearly declared that armed reprisals were forbidden.[201] The International Court of Justice (ICJ), in the *Corfu Channel* case ruling issued on 9 April 1949, condemned in principle interventions of any kind, but allowed the possibility of a demonstration of force on another state's territorial waters, if the purpose of this demonstration was to confirm a right that had been violated and thus ensure the opponent's appropriate action in the future.[202] The United

Nations General Assembly resolved that states have a duty to refrain from acts of reprisals involving the use of force.[203]

In principle, the charter allowed the possibility of the use of armed force on two accounts only:[204] in actions authorised by the Security Council[205] and for individual or collective self-defence.[206] Both of these options have been subject to interpretation that tends to broaden their scope.

Primary responsibility for the maintenance of international peace and security was conferred on the Security Council,[207] which should 'determine the existence of any threat to the peace, breach of the peace or act of aggression'.[208] In theory, such a determination is necessary for any action to be taken pursuant to Chapter VII of the charter.[209] In practice, the Security Council so far has tended toward making a general reference to Chapter VII, without qualifying the circumstances under Article 39,[210] which might involve unnecessary debate and controversy. This is understandable, since the determination that a situation fits into any one of the three categories specified in Article 39 has no impact on the measures available to the council under the circumstances. What is crucial from the council's perspective is the determination of what may constitute a threat to the peace, since both a breach of the peace and an act of aggression would both fall into this broader category.

As evidenced by the Security Council's resolutions, the following types of situations were qualified by the council as a threat to the peace: mass scale violations of human rights and a humanitarian crisis,[211] terrorist attacks,[212] failure to implement the council's resolution,[213] failure to release or punish terrorists,[214] maintaining a racially segregated regime,[215] failure to respect the outcome of a free election,[216] government support for rebel forces in another state[217] and dissemination of weapons of mass destruction and means of their transportation.[218] Usually a situation of a threat to the peace involves a combination of the above-listed elements.[219]

Once the council has determined that a situation falling under Article 39 has occurred, in order to prevent an aggravation of the situation, it may 'call upon the parties concerned to comply with such provisional measures as it deems necessary or desirable'.[220] This may include calling the parties to cease fire and withdraw troops, to agree on a truce or armistice, to establish demilitarised zones, to stop the supply of weapons and armed personnel, or to cease violations of sovereignty, independence and territorial integrity.[221] Such measures are without prejudice to rights, claims and positions of the parties concerned. However, if the measures are not implemented, the council should take this fact into consideration.

On top of these provisional measures, the council is authorised to use other measures not involving the use of armed force. These may include complete or partial interruption of economic relations and of rail, sea, air, postal, telegraphic, radio and other means of communication, and the severance of diplomatic relations.[222] The list is not closed or comprehensive, meaning that the Security Council is free to use other measures it considers necessary. If the council decides that provisional measures may or have proven inadequate, it

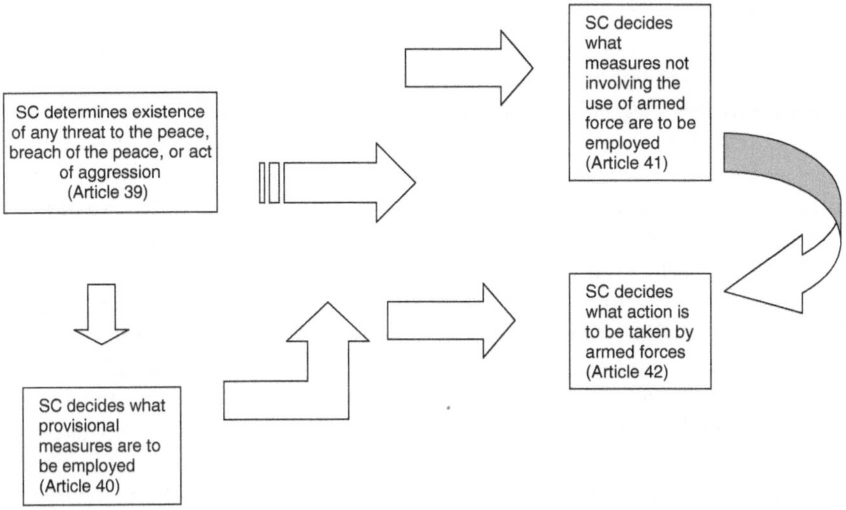

Chart 1.2: Security Council action (Chapter VII of the Charter of the United Nations)
Source: Author.

may take such action by air, sea or land forces as may be necessary to maintain or restore international peace and security (armed action).[223] In contrast to the League of Nations system, members of the United Nations are *ex iure* obliged to employ such measures not on their own initiative. They must act once the Security Council has formulated its position, and this position is binding on the member states of the United Nations.[224]

In order for the council to be able to make effective use of its authority, an armed force must be at the disposal of the council. Such an armed force was to be established under special agreements that the council was to conclude with one or more member states of the United Nations.[225] The agreements were to determine the types and number of troops, the levels of their readiness, location and the nature of the facilities and assistance to be provided. Moreover, a military staff committee was to be established, consisting of heads of military staff of the permanent members of the Security Council. The committee was to be in charge of planning and managing military operations. However, the relevant agreements were never signed and the committee became a 'dormant' structure within the United Nations system. Nonetheless, the Security Council is not without a military force at its disposal.[226] While not explicitly provided for in the charter, a system of peacekeeping and peace-enforcement forces is in place.[227] The armed forces that participate in these operations may be considered a substitute of the United Nations' own troops. It is, however, a deeply imperfect substitute, since the options available to such forces are very limited.[228]

Pursuant to the charter, pending the entry into force of the abovementioned special agreements (which have, so far, not yet been implemented), the five permanent members of the Security Council are authorised to engage in armed action on behalf of the United Nations.[229] Agreements of an ad hoc nature between the council and specific member states are also acceptable,[230] as is authorising specific member states or regional organisations to carry out specific actions.[231] Unfortunately, the wording of the council's resolutions tends to be somewhat vague, and member states disagree as to whether the authorisation to use armed force has or has not been issued in the situation in question.[232] Given the near-permanent tension and disagreements between the members of the council, a binding interpretation delivered by the council itself appears to be impossible to obtain. The issues of the so-called reverse veto (that is, whether the council has the power to end an operation it had previously authorised) raises further doubts.[233] This power should, without question, be vested in the council. Again, however, the possibility that a permanent council member will veto a decision to end an operation arises here, and a situation once declared by the council to be a threat to the peace remains treated as such until the council issues a decision to the contrary.[234]

It appears clear that the council should authorise a military operation prior to this operation's commencement. Yet, on a number of occasions the council authorised operations that, at the moment of authorisation, were already underway[235] and accepted the results of interventions the legality of which was highly doubtful.[236] The practice of using armed force without proper authorisation, and seeking this authorisation only later, is clearly demoralising.

According to the charter, the Security Council was to have a monopoly on the use of armed force. Even the right of self-defence was to be exercised by member states only until the council engages in relevant actions. In practice, however, the council is unable to use its own powers, since any decision of the council may be vetoed by any of its permanent members. The principle of *nemo iudex in causa sua* was not implemented in the charter. Consequently, a permanent council member is free to veto all decisions, including those that pertain to conflicts in which this state is a party.[237] Conflict involving none of the council's permanent members are few and far between, and so it is hardly surprising that resolutions pertaining to threats to the peace have been vetoed a great number of times. Historically, until the 1970s it was the USSR that tended to exercise the veto power the most, while more recently the United States has issued the greatest number of vetoes.[238] The decision to use force in Korea in 1950 was special in this respect, controversial as it was, given that it was included in a resolution adopted in the absence of the Soviet representative in the council.[239]

It could reasonably be expected that the fall of the Iron Curtain would put an end to the rivalry between the East and West, and that real cooperation with view to ensuring peace would be possible within the council. Seemingly, in confirmation of such expectations, the council was in fact able to adopt resolutions with regard to Iraq in the period 1990–1991, Congo in 2003, Sudan in 2006 and Libya in 2011. Attempts are being made to strengthen the collective security system.[240] However, members of the Security Council tend not to plan in terms of the common good. They have no shared vision of the international order. As superpowers tend to do,[241] they are guided each by their own interests, and these interests tend to pull them in opposing directions.[242]

Owing to the Security Council's inability to act decisively, resulting from the tensions between its permanent members, the General Assembly of the United Nations attempted to overcome the impasse by means of the resolution *Uniting for Peace*, adopted in 1950.[243] Under this resolution, if the Security Council, because of a lack of unaninimity between permanent members, fails to exercise its primary responsibility for the maintenance of international peace and security, and there appears to be a threat to the peace, breach of the peace or an act of aggression, the General Assembly is free to act in the matter. If a threat to the peace, breach of the peace or an act of aggression occurs and the Security Council is unable to reach a decision within 24 hours, the General Assembly at an extraordinary session requested by nine members of the Security Council or a majority of United Nations member states, may take – with a two-thirds majority of votes – a decision as to measures recommended under the circumstances. The assembly's recommendation is not binding on the member states, but it may encourage the states to act in a crisis situation. If armed force is used pursuant to a decision taken by the assembly, in most cases it can be interpreted as an exercise of the collective right of self-defence.[244] The legality of *Uniting for Peace* was challenged, mostly by the Soviet Union, on the grounds that it directed the General Assembly to overstep its authority and exercise the powers reserved for the Security Council. However, the ICJ ruled that the charter in its Article 24 confers on the Security Council 'primary' responsibility for the maintenance of peace, and not sole or exclusive responsibility in this respect.[245] Therefore, other bodies of the United Nations are also authorised to investigate threats to the peace.[246] Yet, the procedure outlined in *Uniting for Peace* has been used on only a handful of cases[247] and, as such, cannot be considered to constitute a valid solution to the system's faulty architecture.

Unable to rely on institutionalised guidance, given the inertia of the Security Council and the absence of effective measures for other bodies of the United Nations, states have tended to rely on the right of self-defence to legitimise most of the cases of armed force use.[248] To a large extent, self-defence has replaced a collective security system.[249]

In line with the charter, the right of self-defence may be exercised only in the case of an armed attack, and the measures taken in the exercise of this right should be immediately reported to the Security Council,[250] which will take measures necessary to maintain international peace and security.[251] Thus, under the charter there is a clear distinction between the party who carries out an armed attack and the party who acts in self-defence.

The definition of 'armed attack' is crucial here. The French version of the charter uses, as an equivalent of this phrase, the wording *agression armée*, corresponding rather to 'armed aggression'.[252] Its precise understanding is of the utmost importance for the state exercising the right of self-defence, since the burden of proving that armed attack had in fact occurred rests on the state invoking self-defence.[253]

Cases where one state attacks another by opening fire on its forces are clear-cut and give rise to no doubts, regardless of the types of weapons used.[254] Even if no weapons are used, a situation may qualify as an armed attack: consider a scenario analysed by Yoram Dinstein, where the attacker (state A) enters the territory of the enemy (state B) without the need to use weapons, takes strategic position, and then holds the offensive and awaits the reaction of state B. State B, upon the invasion, will probably be the first to use weapons, and yet clearly it was state A who was the attacker and state B is acting in self-defence.[255]

What mostly inspires debate is the legal (or illegal) status of anticipatory, preventive self-defence, that is, the use of armed force when an attack has not yet occurred, but is expected to occur, as well as pre-emptive, interceptive self-defence, namely the use of armed force in the face of an imminent and unavoidable attack.[256] The difference between these two lies chiefly in the timing: preventive self-defence is aimed at preventing at attack expected in a longer-term perspective, while pre-emptive self-defence is timed immediately before the expected attack. Despite the difference in their meaning, the terms are often used interchangeably, which further blurs the distinction.[257]

The Charter of the United Nations appears to be clear on this issue: self-defence cannot be invoked if an attack did not take place.[258] However, the charter also states that the right of self-defence is inalienable, inherent (or 'natural', in the French version – *naturel*), which suggests that the ramifications of this right are found not only in the regulations of the charter but also in customary law.[259] The provisions of the charter confirm the existence of an old right, rather than establish a new one.[260] In the ruling of 27 June 1986 concerning military and paramilitary activities in and against Nicaragua, the ICJ held that customary international law continues to exist alongside treaty law and that the areas governed by the two sources of law do not overlap exactly, and that the rules do not have precisely the same content[261]. Thus, even if certain actions find no grounds in the regulations of the charter, they may be acceptable under customary law. Considering that, for a very long time, the right of self-defence consisted in essence in the right to undertake any actions aimed at self-preservation,[262] allowing states to invoke 'customary self-defence' may have very dangerous consequences.

Attempts at delimiting the customary right of self-defence tend to rely on the position of the American secretary of state, Daniel Webster, formulated in 1837 in the 'Caroline' affair.[263] Webster claimed that the right might be invoked when the necessity of that self-defence is instant, overwhelming and leaves no choice of means, and no moment for deliberation.[264] Acts justified by the necessity of self-defence must be limited by that necessity and kept clearly within it. Thus, within this formulation, a prior armed attack is not a requirement for invoking self-defence;[265] it suffices if the attack is close and imminent, as is the case with pre-emptive self-defence.

Webster's formulations stop short of providing a clear answer as to whether preventive self-defence, as defined above, is actually legitimate. The danger is not imminent, and the attack is likely, but not certain. Proponents of legality of preventive self-defence claim that, in today's world, with military technologies that allow states to carry out an unstoppable attack within minutes, it is necessary to retain the option of preventive action, provided certain conditions are met (for example, the action is in proportion to the threat).[266] The need for preventive self-defence is supposedly particularly clear in respect of nuclear threats.[267] Another often used argument compares a state that knows that the enemy has often violated the ban on using force, and that also knows the technological means the enemy has at its disposal with a woman who, after years of suffering harassment and violence, attacks the perpetrator before he – for it is usually a man – strikes again.[268]

In the time that the United Nations Organisation has been operational, a number of instances of preventive actions have occurred, such as the American operation in the Bay of Pigs in 1962, the Israeli intervention in the neighbouring Arab countries in 1967, Pakistan's armed operations in the Kashmir region in 1948, 1967 and 1981, and the mainly American strike against Iraq in 2003.[269] The Security Council has condemned only a handful of such incidents (including, for example, the attack on Iraqi nuclear facilities in 1981[270] or on the headquarters of the Palestine Liberation Organization in Tunisia in 1985[271]). It is therefore hardly surprising that sometimes voices are heard in favour of allowing preventive self-defence in certain types of situations[272] or even claiming that customary law is shifting towards the legalisation of the preventive strike.[273] The latter view seems to be rather unfounded. Often, it appears that the appeals to legitimise preventive self-defence in actual fact call for the legitimisation of pre-emptive and not preventive self-defence.

Legitimising preventive self-defence carries with it enormous risks. A state that invokes it relies solely on its own subjective assessment of the likelihood of the danger actually materialising. Consequently, it is extremely difficult to judge whether the actions were justified.[274] Politicians tend to consider the interest of their own state before the interest of the overall system, even if the system is geared towards ensuring their state's security. Therefore, they typically expect worst-case scenarios, and work to prevent them.[275] It is very difficult to draw the line between preventive self-defence and aggression. It would be most practical to assume that preventive war equals aggressive war,[276] in the sense that the restrictions on the use of armed force that are in place today would be safeguarded best in this way. Many states, including the major players will, however, certainly disagree with this position.

Article 51 of the charter mentions not only individual, but also collective self-defence, which considerably expands the scope of acceptable use of armed force. Grounds for collective self-defence include, first and foremost, a coordinated attack against a number of states, and attack against a state that is a member of an alliance.[277] Other situations may also qualify. For example, if state A attacks state B, state A must take into account the possibility that state C may consider the attack to be a threat against its own security, and therefore that it is entitled to act in self-defence.[278] Armed attack may be perceived as a contagious disease that every state has the right to try to combat.[279]

Another type of self-defence consists in the efforts a state undertakes in order to protect its citizens who are located in another state's territory.[280] For a state, its population is equal in importance to its territory, and protecting the citizens is each state's *raison d'être*.[281] If armed action to protect citizens is carried out on the territory of a state whose legitimate government allows this intervention, the scope of the operation is limited strictly to its declared purpose and all relevant legal norms are observed, such action is fully legal.[282] Examples of such operations include the American operation in Lebanon in 1958, the American-Belgian operation in Congo in 1964, the German operation in Mogadishu in 1977, the French-Belgian operation in Zaire's Shaba province in 1978, the Indonesian operation in Bangkok in 1981 and the French operation in Comoros in 1989.[283] The situation is less clear when the state on whose territory the action takes place has not agreed to such action.[284] If a state's citizens or property are attacked outside its territory, can this state consider the attack to constitute legitimate grounds for self-defence?[285] The ruling of the ICJ regarding American diplomatic and consular personnel in Teheran upholds this interpretation.[286] It appears, therefore, that the use of armed force may be legitimate if the following conditions are met: citizens are in danger; the state in whose territory the citizens are cannot or does not wish to protect them; peaceful means of resolving the problem have been exhausted; and that armed action is aimed solely at the protection of those citizens.[287] In theory, under such circumstances the action will be considered customary self-defence.[288] In practice, even the Israeli intervention in Uganda in 1976, believed to be a classic example of this scenario, was highly controversial,[289] not to mention the American interventions in the Dominican Republic in 1965,[290] Grenada in 1983[291] and Panama in 1989.[292] As it turns out, protecting the citizens may be used as an excellent excuse for executing other plans, since there is almost always a citizen in danger somewhere.[293] The same doubts as in the case of preventive self-defence appear here as well. Is it acceptable to intervene in order to ensure the safety of citizens in the future, for example against a terrorist attack? This type of reasoning was used to legitimise the American interventions in Libya in 1986, in Iraq in 1993 and in Afghanistan and Sudan in 1998.[294] In line with the conclusion regarding preventive self-defence, the answer here also appears to be in the negative.

The two above-mentioned exceptions that allow the use of force, namely self-defence and action authorised by the Security Council, provide ample room for abuse. However, states continually endeavour to find other loopholes in the restrictions of the Charter of the United Nations. Since the charter forbids the use of force 'against the territorial integrity or political independence of any state, or in any other manner inconsistent with the purposes of the United Nations', arguments are used to the effect that armed action not aimed at another state's territory or independence is completely legal. Such reasoning omits the essential fact that the wording 'in any other manner inconsistent with the purposes of the United Nations' is intended to include any other instances of the use of armed force;[295] the charter's preamble clearly states that force is only to be used in the common interest, if at all.[296] Moreover, as clearly demonstrated by the charter's *travaux préparatoires*, the 'territory and independence' wording of the charter was intended not as a limitation of the restrictions of the charter, but rather as an expression of how valuable these two elements are for the signatory states.[297]

Use of armed force is, for example, strictly forbidden in the enforcement of a judgment of the ICJ,[298] since under the charter[299] it is the Security Council that decides upon the measures to be taken to give effect to the judgment.[300] The right to recover territories that once belonged to a given state has been refuted, as demonstrated by the reaction to the Iraqi invasion of Kuwait, undertaken under the guise of territorial claims rooted in history.[301] The question is less clear in the case of wars of national liberation, given the abundance of documents that support peoples' right to self-determination.[302] The majority opinion seems to be that a third party may endorse a nation fighting for its independence by means of moral, political and humanitarian support, but may not intervene by military means.[303] However, the minority position, that is, the claim that nations executing their right of self-determination may receive military support or support consisting in making territory available, is also well represented.[304]

Intervention is considered legal if it is undertaken at the invitation of the relevant government,[305] but the use of force under these circumstances has often been controversial, largely owing to questions concerning the legality of the government issuing the invitation.[306] For example, the American intervention in Panama (1989) and the Soviet interventions in Hungary (1956), Czechoslovakia (1968) and Afghanistan (1979) were all justified by having been requested by these countries' governments.[307]

Heated debate has continued since the 1990s as to the legality of humanitarian intervention,[308] that is, a situation where a state or a group of states use force against another state without the latter state's consent, in order to stop large-scale and severe abuse of human rights in that state.[309] Examples of such interventions include the Indian intervention in Bangladesh in 1971, Vietnam's intervention in Cambodia in 1979, France's intervention in Central Africa in 1979 and the more recent intervention by NATO forces in Kosovo in 1999.[310] In each of these instances, the intervening forces were accused of aggression.

Problems with humanitarian intervention arise in the absence of an authorisation from the Security Council, if the situation requires armed intervention. It is generally accepted that the ban on genocide is just as strong as the ban on the use of armed force. Therefore, an intervention not authorised by the Security Council might not be legal (*légale*), but it would be legitimate (*légitime*),[311] although naturally only if certain conditions are met.[312] However, this line of reasoning indirectly challenges the entire notion of legal restrictions of the use of force since it prioritises moral norms over legal ones. The International Commission on Intervention and State Security produced a report devoted to this issue, entitled *Responsibility to Protect.*[313] According to the report's conclusions, if a state is unable or unwilling to prevent a situation where the state's population suffers significantly owing to internal conflict, uprising, repression or the downfall of the state, the international responsibility to protect, including – if necessary – by military means, prevails over the principle of non-intervention.[314] Legitimate reasons for intervention include large-scale loss of life, large-scale 'ethnic cleansing' and, when the intervening parties have the right authority, just cause and right intention, the intervention is the last resort, proportional means are used, and there are reasonable prospects of success of the operation.[315] In order to avoid the accusation that force is used in the intervening party's own interest, the commission recommended that efforts be made to obtain authorisation to intervene either from the Security Council, from the General Assembly or from a regional organisation.[316] The notion of responsibility to protect was also discussed in the 2004 Report of the Secretary-General's High Panel on Threats, Challenges and Change, *A more secure world: Our shared responsibility*,[317] in the 2005 Report of the Secretary-General, *In Larger Freedom: Towards Development, Security and Human Rights for All*[318] and in the documents generated by the United Nations World Summit in 2005.[319] The consensus appears to be that in the face of genocide, war crimes and crimes against humanity states are obliged to intervene but, in doing so, they must observe the procedures outlined in the Charter of the United Nations. The restrictions on the use of force specified in the charter have thus been upheld, including the ban on unauthorised use of force by a state.[320] However, the above-mentioned documents were only a step towards a final resolution of the debate on humanitarian intervention.

The principles of the Charter of the United Nations have been confirmed by a number of other documents adopted by the UN, such as the Declaration on Rights and Duties of States,[321] the Declaration on the Inadmissibility of Intervention in the Domestic Affairs of States and the Protection of their Independence and Sovereignty,[322] the Declaration on the Strengthening of International Security,[323] the Declaration on Principles of International Law concerning Friendly Relations and Cooperation among States in accordance with the Charter of the United Nations[324] and the Declaration on the Enhancement of the Effectiveness of the Principle of Refraining from the Threat or Use of Force in International Relations.[325] Regional organisations have also adopted documents confirming the restriction on the use of force, such as the Chapultepec Declaration of 3 March 1945, the Inter-American

Treaty of Reciprocal Assistance (Rio Treaty) of 2 September 1947,[326] the Charter of the Organization of the American States of 30 April 1948 (Bogota Charter),[327] the Charter of the Arab League of 22 March 1945,[328] the Final Act of the Conference on Security and Cooperation in Europe of 1 August 1975 and the Charter of Paris for a New Europe of 21 November 1990. The ban on the use of force, with limited exceptions, is also included in the Five Principles of Peaceful Coexistence adopted on 29 April 1954 between India and the People's Republic of China.[329] On the other hand, the Constitutive Act of the African Union of 11 July 2000 gives the Union the right to intervene in a member state pursuant to a decision of the Assembly in respect of grave circumstances, namely war crimes, genocide and crimes against humanity, and in order to restore peace and security in case of serious threats to the legal order in a member state.[330] The decision to use armed force is authorised by the Peace and Security Council of the Union. The Act does not address the need to obtain authorisation from the Security Council.

It is hard to miss the radical dissonance between the declarations to abstain from the use of force, and the actual use of force. Research completed by Arthur Mark Weisburd demonstrates that, between 1945 and 1991, states have used force on more than 110 occasions.[331] According to Weisburd, some of these occasions can be termed classic invasions, for example the attack of Great Britain, France and Israel on Egypt in 1956, the Indonesian attack on Dutch New Guinea in 1960, India's attack on the Portuguese-held Goa in 1961, Somalia's attack on Ethiopia in 1977, Tanzania's attack on Uganda in 1978, Vietnam's attack on Cambodia in 1978, the Soviet attack on Afghanistan in 1979, Iraq's attack on Iran in 1980, Argentina's attack on Great Britain in 1982 (the Falklands War) and the Iraqi aggression against Kuwait in 1990.[332] In three of these instances (Iran, Uganda and Goa), the international community offered no negative reaction. After the Second World War, no large-scale conflicts occurred. This, however, is attributable not so much to the efficiency of the United Nations system but rather to the strength of military alliances and effective political discouragement.

1.5 Conclusions

In the first half of the 20th century, the legal status of war changed dramatically. The theory that war was an extra-legal event, perceptible purely in moral categories, lost ground completely. This was largely due to the Covenant of the League of Nations, a document of major importance that divided wars into legal and illegal ones. The covenant, however, was hardly perfect, since it generally allowed war, including aggressive war, as long as the parties waited for a sufficiently long period of time before starting it.[333] The doctrine of the state of war, acceptable under the League of Nations system, left many opportunities for actual war fighting, as long as war was not officially declared.

Attempts to improve the League of Nations system were derailed, as evidenced by the unsuccessful efforts around the Treaty of Mutual Assistance and the Geneva Protocol. The Briand-Kellogg Pact, while definitely a milestone in terms of restricting the use of force, used wording so imprecise that it was open to interpretation that completely undermined its significance.

The Charter of the United Nations, with its absolute ban on aggression, was intended as a radical step forward.[334] Unfortunately, the charter too uses terms such as 'aggression' and 'self-defence' without providing their definitions. Their interpretation relies on customary law, and customary law itself raises a wide range of problems.[335] The lack of precision may be as a result of the fact that the charter arises out of a compromise between states that have paid more attention to ensuring their own positions of power than to creating foundations of durable peace.[336]

In light of the number of interventions that violate the charter's provisions, it is tempting to agree with Thomas Franck's observation that the ban on the use of armed force is dead.[337] The temptation is particularly strong considering that the United States, a permanent member of the United Nations Organisation, uses its hegemonic power to treat the law as an unnecessary burden.[338] On the other hand, states that do resort to violence in breach of the charter tend to claim self-defence. The difference between self-defence, no matter how broadly interpreted, and the use of force as a method of conflict resolution, is fundamental.[339] No state has argued that violations of Article 2(4) of the charter, as they occur, pave the way for unrestricted use of armed force.[340] On the contrary, the ban on the use of force that is expressed in this provision is now considered a *ius cogens* norm,[341] and the ICJ has ruled that these provisions of the charter are equal to customary law.[342] The restrictions introduced by the charter may therefore be viewed with scepticism, although they should by no means be discounted.

2 The notion of aggression

2.1 Towards a definition of aggression

The term 'aggression' first appeared in the language of diplomacy quite some time before The First World War. Its use is often attributed to William Pitt, speaking with reference to the war with France and the time of the French revolution.[1] It was also quite typically used as *casus foederis* in treaties drafted in the 19th and early 20th centuries.[2]

Initially, 'aggression' had no negative connotations.[3] Understood as a military attack on the territory or sea vessels of another country, it was a term derived from the study of military tactics.[4] With time, it began to be combined with an adjective expressing judgment, as in 'unjust aggression', 'defensive aggression' or 'unprovoked aggression'.[5] By the time 'aggression' was used in the legal instruments establishing collective security systems, that is, the Covenant of the League of Nations[6] and the Charter of the United Nations,[7] it had evolved to the point of carrying clearly negative connotations.

Over the years, numerous attempts had been made to define aggression. Whenever the issue was raised, opponents countered that it was enormously difficult, if not possible to do so[8] and, moreover, it was unnecessary and dangerous to try to define it.[9] Arguments were cited against a legal definition of aggression, along the following lines: if aggression occurs, it is necessary to implement sanctions. However, in certain types of cases using coercive measures is not required, and may even result in an escalation of the use of armed force.[10] A definition of aggression may delay the Security Council's operation by placing the council in a position where it has to engage in a debate as to the qualification of the situation,[11] where the council's task is to ensure peace and not to point to the offender.[12] The institutions in charge of maintaining peace and security should be free to use their own judgment in any given situation, in order to be able to react appropriately, and therefore they cannot be bound by a strict legal definition.[13] For the United Nations procedures to be implemented, no definition of aggression is necessary.[14] A situation might arise where a state that in fact bears no responsibility for the hostilities might be determined to be the aggressor.[15] A definition of aggression would thus become a trap for states forced to act in self-defence, while at the same time providing clear signposts for the aggressor.[16] If a list of acts of aggression is insufficiently comprehensive, the aggressor may feel encouraged to commit the acts not specifically listed in therein.[17] New forms of aggression continue to be developed, so a definition developed today may be out of date as soon as tomorrow.[18] Aggression is a natural notion, and thus needs no definition, because everyone knows intuitively what it is.[19] A definition of aggression might be a propaganda tool used in order falsely to accuse states of aggression.[20]

The proponents of defining aggression pointed to a number of useful functions that such a definition might serve. It would be an instruction for the relevant institutions as to what situations qualify as aggression.[21] It would be a deterrent to states contemplating the actions referred to therein, and thus would have a preventive effect.[22] The lack of legal clarity is only favourable to potential aggressors[23] since, in the absence of a definition, it is up to the states to decide whether aggression occurred, and thus to decide whether they are authorised to act in self-defence.[24] If a definition were in place, this kind of blurring of the boundary between aggression and self-defence would be more difficult to accomplish.[25] States must know exactly what actions are punishable, in accordance with the principle of *nulla poena sine previa lege*.[26] Precise understanding of what constitutes aggression would help to mobilise public opinion.[27] It would facilitate the process of offering assistance to the victims of aggression and would protect the rights and interests of states.[28] Moreover, it would make it possible to place liability not only on states, but also on individuals.[29] The Security Council would be forced to act in support of the victim in clear-cut cases,[30] which would eliminate the arbitrary aspect of the council's decision-making and would work to the advantage of smaller states.[31] Adopting a definition would consolidate the international collective security system[32] and would result in a strengthening and advancing international law.[33] It would contribute the process of disarmament.[34] The intuitive understanding of aggression cannot be relied on, considering that, had all the states shared an intuition as to what was good and what was bad, the world would have been paradise.[35]

The issue of aggression was first debated during the process of drafting, within the League of Nations system, of the treaty of mutual guarantee, and its successor, the Treaty of Mutual Assistance. The League's Permanent Advisory Commission on Military, Naval and Air Questions in its opinion on the Treaty warned that repeating the well known phrase 'unprovoked aggression' was not a solution, since – given the nature of contemporary armed action – 'it would seem impossible to decide, even in theory, what constitutes a case of aggression'.[36] For that reason, the commission believed that aggression should be defined in the treaty. The commission also claimed that it was necessary to determine which 'universally recognised' signs signify that aggression has occurred, and thus are a reason that the treaty should be applicable, in order to ensure a reaction of the parties. It was emphasised that the understanding of aggression as mobilisation or the violation of a frontier was no longer adequate, since the process of mobilisation had become highly complex, and it is difficult to determine when it begins and how it develops. As for the frontiers, owing to the creation of neutral zones, political and military boundaries fail to overlap and, moreover, both are often disrespected by air forces. The commission listed certain signals that point to the intent of aggression (essentially, the stages of mobilisation), but it also noted that, in the absence of a fixed test for aggression, governments should rely on their own evaluation of the situation, taking into account 'the political attitude of the possible aggressor: his propaganda; or the attitude of his press and population; his policy on the international market etc'.[37]

The issue of aggression was also discussed by the Special Committee of the Temporary Mixed Commission for the Reduction of Armaments, headed by Lord Robert Cecil and operated by the Council of the League of Nations. The Special Committee endorsed the report of the Permanent Advisory Commission and also attempted to specify which actions constitute undisputable evidence of aggression. However, the conclusion reached by the Special Committee states that no simple test for aggression is available, even though it is possible to point to certain factors that determine that aggression has occurred.[38] Therefore, the League Council should have unlimited discretion in determining aggression. Eventually the decision was made not to include a definition of aggression in the Treaty of Mutual Assistance. However, the treaty was never adopted, regardless of this fact.

The problem of defining aggression returned during the debate on the Protocol for the Pacific Settlement of International Disputes of 1924. The report drafted by the First and Third Committees of the Assembly of the League of Nations stipulated that a presumption of aggression arises in three cases: 'when a resort to war is accompanied: (i) by a refusal to accept the procedure of pacific settlement or to submit to the decision resulting therefrom; (ii) by violation of provisional measures enjoined by the Council ...; or (iii) by disregard of a decision recognizing that the dispute arises out of a matter which lies exclusively within the domestic jurisdiction of the other party and by failure or by refusal to submit the question first to the Council or the Assembly'.[39] The Protocol was never adopted either.

References to aggression were included in the non-aggression pacts that the Soviet Union concluded with other states.[40] For instance, in the non-aggression pact concluded with Poland on 25 July 1932, the following were indirectly considered to constitute acts of aggression: 'any act of violence that breaches the integrity and inviolability of the territory or the political independence of the other Contracting Party, even if such acts were undertaken without a prior declaration of war, and with absence of any of its symptoms'.[41] However, from among the contributions that the Soviet Union made to the definition of aggression in the inter-war period, this formula was not the crucial one.

The issue of aggression reappeared in the report of the Committee on Arbitration and Security of the Preparatory Commission for the Disarmament Conference, that is, in the Memorandum on Security Questions by Politis[42] and the Memorandum on Articles 10, 11 and 16 of the Covenant of the League of Nations by Rutgers.[43] The latter, once again facing the impossibility of arriving at a precise definition of aggression, eventually listed only selected acts that constituted aggression.[44] The breakthrough came with the Soviet proposal of 6 February 1933,[45] presented during the deliberations of the General Committee in response to the French proposals of sanctions against the aggressor.[46] The Soviet proposal stipulated that a state should be considered the aggressor in an international conflict if this state was the first to commit any of the following actions: declaration of war against another state; the invasion by its armed forces of the territory of another state without declaration of war; bombarding the territory of another state by its land, naval or air forces or knowingly attacking the naval or air forces of another state; the landing in, or introduction within the frontiers of, another state of land, naval or air forces, without the permission of the government of such a state or the infringement of the conditions of such permission, particularly as regards the duration of sojourn or extension of area and the establishment of a naval blockade of the coast or ports of another state.

The Soviet initiative was endorsed by China, Czechoslovakia, Estonia, France, Norway, Poland and Sweden, while Great Britain and the United States opposed a discussion on the definition of aggression. Germany, Japan, Italy and Ireland also expressed reservations in this regard.[47] The issue of the definition was to be handled by the Committee on Security Questions, established on 10 March 1933 by the Political Commission and headed by Politis.[48] The Committee in its report of 24 May 1933 presented a draft definition of the aggressor, based to a large extent on the Soviet proposal.[49] The reception of the draft was largely critical, with most states claiming that it was too strict. However, a slightly modified Politis definition was used in the draft convention for limitation and reduction of armaments of 22 September 1933. This convention, however, was not adopted, mostly as a result of reservations as to the disarmament procedure it outlined. The opportunity for adopting a universal definition was thus missed.

Litvinow decided to make use of the experience he had gained when arranging for an earlier entry into force of the Briand-Kellogg Pact among the states of Eastern Europe. Without waiting for the decision whether or not the disarmament convention would be adopted, as soon as April 1933 he approached Poland with a proposal to sign a convention defining aggression with the states of Eastern Europe with which the Soviet Union had previously signed a non-aggression pact, that is, with Finland, Latvia, Estonia and Poland.[50] Poland's response was favourable, on one condition: that Romania also be a signatory of the convention. Consequently, on 3 July 1933, a Convention for the Definition of Aggression was signed between Romania, Estonia, Latvia, Poland, Turkey, the Soviet Union, Persia and Afghanistan.[51]

On 22 July 1933, Finland joined the convention and, on 4 July 1933, also in London, a second convention defining aggression was signed, this one between Czechoslovakia, Romania, Turkey, the Soviet Union and Yugoslavia.[52] The second convention was open and available for other states to join. Poland decided against joining, for two reasons. First, the convention was intended as a universal rather than a regional convention, and Poland believed that a treaty of this kind should be adopted at a disarmament conference. Secondly, Czechoslovakia was a party to the convention, and Poland did not wish to have its hands tied as far as Czechoslovakia was concerned with regard to the possibility of using armed force in order to effect territorial changes. On 5 July 1933, a convention defining aggression was also signed between the Soviet Union and Lithuania.[53]

The convention's definition of aggression (known as the London definition) met with almost unanimous approval from lawyers.[54] However, it had a key weakness: the London conventions are binding solely on those states that have signed them, and therefore the definition's significance was purely regional.[55] Furthermore, from among the 11 states with which the Soviet Union had signed the conventions defining aggression, only one single state had not suffered, at the hand of the Soviet Union, an attack that qualified as aggression under the conventions.[56]

After the London conventions, further attempts were made to redefine aggression on a regional scale. For example, the Saadabad Pact made in Teheran on 8 July 1937 between Afghanistan, Iraq, Iran and Turkey included an enumerative definition, where the list of acts that constitute aggression differed from the list included in the London conventions.[57]

The states of the Americas too endeavoured to define aggression. Initially, there was little support for the need of the definition. Columbia presented its own definition of aggressor in a reservation to the Convention for the Maintenance, Preservation and Re-establishment of Peace between the United States of America and other American Republics signed in Buenos Aires on 23 December 1936.[58] The pan-American Conference in Lima in 1938 rejected the proposal of the Committee of Experts on the Codification of International Law to define aggression.[59] Only the Act of Chapultepec of 1945 succeeded in adopting a regional definition of aggression, stating that 'any attempt on the part of a non-American State against the integrity or inviolability of the territory, the sovereignty or the political independence of an American State shall be considered as an act of aggression against all the American States'.[60] The Act stipulated also that an invasion by armed forces of one state into the territory of another, trespassing boundaries established by treaty and demarcated in accordance with it, constituted an act of aggression. The Inter-American Treaty of Reciprocal Assistance signed in Rio de Janeiro on 2 September 1947 declared that the following may be considered aggression: unprovoked armed attack by a state against the territory, the people, or the land, sea or air forces of another state; invasion, by the armed forces of a state, of the territory of an American state, through the trespassing of boundaries demarcated in accordance with a treaty, judicial decision, or arbitral award, or, in the absence of frontiers thus demarcated, invasion affecting a region which is under the effective jurisdiction of another state.[61]

Yet another definition was adopted in the Iraqi-Transjordanian Treaty of Brotherhood and Alliance, signed in Baghdad on 14 April 1947,[62] where the following acts were considered acts of aggression: the declaration of war, the seizure by an armed force of a third state, of territory belonging to either High Contracting Party even without a declaration of war, an attack on the territory, land, naval or air forces of either High Contracting Party by the land, naval or air forces of a third state, even without a declaration of war, direct or indirect support or assistance to aggressor.[63] It was also noted that the exercise of legitimate defence or actions taken to implement provisions of the Charter of the United Nations would not be deemed acts of aggression.

The most recent attempt to define aggression on a regional scale is the African Union Non-Aggression and Common Defence Pact of 31 January 2005. Under this law, aggression means the use, intentionally and knowingly, of armed force or any other hostile act by a state, a group of states, an organisation of states or non-state actor(s) or by any foreign or external entity, against the sovereignty, political independence, territorial integrity and human security of the population of a state party to the pact, which are incompatible with the Charter of the United Nations or the Constitutive Act of the African Union. The definition is supplemented by an extensive, 11-point long list of acts of aggression, where each of the points further enumerates acts of aggression.[64]

In terms of a universal definition of aggression, another crucial attempt is connected with the Dumbarton Oaks Conference. It was there that the Soviet representatives decided that the peace and security organisation to be established should have, in the definition of its peace and security related powers, not only the expression 'breach of the peace', but also 'acts of aggression'.[65] The United States opposed the notion, claiming that 'acts of aggression' constitute a 'breach of the peace'.[66] The Soviet Union, however, exerted strong pressure, and – together with China – demanded that a definition of aggression be included in the draft of the document establishing the new world order. Both the United States and Great Britain resisted the pressure. Eventually it was agreed that aggression would be mentioned in the section detailing the objectives and principles of the United Nations.[67]

The issue of aggression reappeared at the San Francisco Conference, hardly surprisingly, since 'aggression' had eventually made it into the draft Charter of the United Nations. Smaller states joined in the debate. For them, work on a definition of aggression was an opportunity to limit the arbitrariness of the superpowers in the Security Council. Some of the smaller states understood, however, that the Security Council needed to have a certain degree of freedom in its decision-making.[68]

Bolivia[69], Czechoslovakia[70] and The Philippines[71] proposed their own definitions of aggression. All three proposals copied the model prevalent in the 1930s, that is, were enumerative rather than general in nature. Iran and Egypt made strong pleas for including a clear and precise definition of aggression in the Charter of the United Nations, but offered no proposals of their own. The United States, Great Britain, the Soviet Union and China were strongly opposed to including a definition of aggression in the charter.[72] The dispute was ended by the Third Commission of the Third Committee, which decided (in line with the suggestions of Paul Boncour's report) that there was no room for a definition of aggression in the charter.[73] Boncour's report stressed that a definition of aggression was beyond the capacity of the conference, as well as beyond the objectives of the charter. Moreover, owing to the constant development of methods of conducting hostilities, it is difficult to produce a comprehensive definition of aggression. The report pointed out that the Security Council should have full discretion in determining whether a given act constitutes an act of aggression. Furthermore, defining aggression might lead to a situation where the Security Council would disregard dangerous situations, if they fell beyond the scope of the definition of aggression.

Boncour's report, however, did not put and end to the debate on the definition of aggression. The issue reappeared yet again in the debate over the Yugoslav proposal on the duties of states in the event of the outbreak of hostilities.[74] The draft of this document stipulated that in case of outbreak of hostilities, each state should, within 24 hours, state its readiness to cease fire, and it should be able to withdraw to previously held positions within 48 hours. If a state failed to meet these requirements, it could be considered an aggressor and would be responsible for a breach of the peace. The Soviet Union responded to the proposal by claiming that a definition of aggression was necessary, and proposed a definition that was in essence identical with the one proposed in 1933.[75] In the early 1950s, the cold war began. The Soviet Union realised that a definition of aggression might be useful in limiting the expansion of American influence.[76] The Soviet proposal met with opposition from the United States, Great Britain, Canada, and France, all of whom believed that the determination of whether or not aggression occurred should belong fully to the Security Council. However, in a resolution of 17 November 1950, the General Assembly decided that the issue of definition of aggression should be referred to the International Law Commission, as a part of its work on the draft Code of Offences against the Peace and Security of Mankind.[77] On the same day, the General Assembly also adopted a resolution which read: '... whatever the weapons used, any aggression, whether committed openly, or by fomenting civil strife in the interest of a foreign Power, or otherwise, is the gravest of all crimes against peace and security throughout the world'.[78]

The International Law Commission, debating in 1951, was equipped with the report by Jean Spiropoulos, special rapporteur working on the draft Code of Offences against the Peace and Security of Mankind. The report stated that aggression is 'a concept *per se*', which is not susceptible of definition.[79]

The debate thus began from the question of whether a definition of aggression was possible to construct, and whether it was necessary. Further complicating the commission's work was the ongoing dispute of what exactly was the commission's objective: was it supposed to offer its own definition of aggression, or was it, rather, to focus purely on discussing the Soviet proposal.[80] Once the dispute was settled (in favour of the former option), the next issue arose, namely as to the form of the definition.[81] A general, universal definition would apply to all acts of aggression, regardless of future developments in the technicalities of war, and so the definition would be inclusive in nature. However, a definition of this kind would have to rely on general notions such as self-defence, and that in turn would result in the need to design further definitions.[82] On the one hand, the pitfall of excessive strictness might be avoided.[83] On the other hand, a general definition would have to be inherently imprecise and thus dangerous, since it might delay the reaction of relevant authorities.[84] Moreover, given the wording of the Charter of the United Nations, a general definition would hardly move international law forward.[85]

An alternative to the general definition might be an enumerative definition, consisting in a list of acts that constitute aggression. Such a definition would have the advantage of being easy to apply. At the same time, it would have the disadvantage of possibly suggesting that other acts not included in the list may never be considered aggression.[86] Consequently, the aggressors would just change their manner of operation.[87] An enumerative definition is therefore exclusive in nature.[88] A definition like this might be open-ended, for example by means of granting the Security Council the power to deem other acts, not specifically listed in the definition, to constitute aggression. This, however, would essentially bring the international community back to square one, since the Charter of the United Nations gives the Security Council the right to decide what constitutes aggression, and it does so without the need for a definition.[89] This problem might be remedied by adopting an approach in which the definition would be gradually amended and expanded.

Proposals were also put forward for a mixed definition, that is, a definition that would combine a general notion of aggression with a list of specific acts of aggression.[90] Opponents of this solution pointed out that a mixed definition combines the faults of both types of definitions,[91] while its proponents emphasised that it combines the advantages of both.[92]

The International Law Commission devoted a considerable deal of time and energy to the debate on the definition of aggression. This is somewhat surprising, given that only Jesús Yepes[93] and Shuhsi Hsu[94] endorsed the enumerative approach. Eventually, the commission decided to focus its efforts on seeking a general and abstract definition. In the ensuing years, during work in committees, the debates and arguments returned periodically. Ultimately, after a lapse of a few decades, the mixed definition approach won the day.

The commission also debated the relationship between self-defence and aggression, the notion of indirect aggression, the question of whether, in addition to the employment of force, the threat to use force should also constitute aggression, the extent of the use of force necessary to establish that aggression occurred, as well as the importance of the subjective factor (intent of a given state) and the objective factor (the first shot fired).[95]

The commission did in the end decide to endeavour to construct a definition. Ricardo Alfaro's draft was selected as the basis for further work.[96] The final definition of aggression adopted by the commission[97] was rejected in the final vote by the commission's members with seven votes against, three in favour and one abstaining.[98] Consequently, the commission was unable to propose a definition to the General Assembly; it was only able to present the report of the debates. The result may seem paltry. However, it was the early 1950s, the time of the Korean war and the 'salami-slice' strategy, one of the coldest periods of the cold war. The intensity of East-West tension was so immense that any debate, including a debate within the International Law Commission, was interpreted through the lens of politics. Consequently, there was no willingness on either side to compromise.[99]

The report of the commission was referred to the Sixth Committee of the General Assembly in January 1952.[100] Predictably, it was heavily criticised by the USSR and the entire Eastern bloc. The countries of Latin America expressed their regret at the lack of significant progress, but they understood the difficulties encountered by the commission.[101] The debate demonstrated clearly that there was no consensus with regard to any of the elements of the definition. The subjective factor as well as indirect aggression were matters of discord, as was the function of the definition, not to mention its overall form.[102]

In light of the problems surrounding the issue of definition of aggression, Greece, with the support of the United States and Great Britain, suggested that attempts to arrive at a definition should be abandoned.[103] The USSR, on the other hand stood decidedly by its proposal, amending it only so far as to include the act of aggression consisting in support for armed groups.[104] Bolivia also presented its own draft definition.[105] Eventually, on the basis of an amended draft resolution prepared by France, Iran and Venezuela,[106] the General Assembly, in its resolution dated 31 January 1952, decided that defining aggression should be placed on the agenda of its seventh session, since 'it is possible and desirable, with a view to ensuring international peace and security and to developing international criminal law, to define aggression by reference to the elements which constitute it'.[107] In the same resolution, the General Assembly requested that the Secretary-General prepare a report on the definition of aggression and that he appeal to states to make their opinions known on the definition of aggression when they submitted their opinions on the draft Code of Offences against the Peace and Security of Mankind.

For the 1952 session of the General Assembly, it was necessary to analyse the comments submitted by 14 governments,[108] a report drafted on behalf of the Secretariat by Chafic Malek and Emile Giraud,[109] a number of draft resolutions and a report of the Sixth Committee.[110] It is therefore hardly surprising that the Assembly decided, by means of a resolution of 20 December 1952, to establish a Special Committee of 15 members to address the question of defining aggression.[111]

The Special Committee worked from 24 August until 21 September 1953. It encountered the same problems that had plagued the work of the International Law Commission, including the dispute on the committee's mandate and remit. However, the committee also devoted time to the following issues: how the definition is to be adopted (an amendment to the Charter of the United Nations, a separate convention, a resolution of the Security Council or a resolution of the General Assembly); specific acts of aggression; the relationship between aggression and the maintenance of peace; including a definition of aggression in the Code of Offences against the Peace and Security of Mankind; and the significance of the definition to the individual authorities.[112] In its report, the committee failed to propose a single definition of aggression. None of the draft definitions (proposed by Bolivia,[113] China,[114] the USSR[115] and Mexico, the latter being a variation of the Soviet proposal[116]) gained majority approval. Interestingly, in order to garner support for its definition, the Soviet Union added to its proposal the definition of indirect aggression, economic and ideological aggression, and also agreed that the list of acts of aggression included in the definition is not exhaustive. According to the amended proposal, the Security Council was at liberty to deem other actions acts of aggression too.

The report of the Special Committee was forwarded to the states, ten of whom responded with their comments.[117] In 1954, these comments were debated in the Sixth Committee. The debate demonstrated once again the great diversity of opinions regarding the need for a definition of aggression and the possibility of arriving at such a definition.[118] A relatively attractive proposal submitted by Iran, suggesting that a working group be established with the purpose of designing one text of the definition, acceptable to the majority of members, was rejected.[119] The General Assembly, following a recommendation of the Sixth Committee, adopted a resolution based on a draft prepared by Lebanon, Syria and Yemen, and on 4 December 1954 expanded the Special Committee to 19 members.[120]

The Special Committee, now 19-member strong, met in 1956 to discuss the proposals of definition that had been submitted (by the Soviet Union,[121] Paraguay,[122] Iran, Panama,[123] China,[124] Iraq[125] and Mexico,[126] as well as a draft proposed together by the Dominican Republic, Paraguay, Peru and Mexico[127]) and the Dutch proposal to define not aggression but armed attack.[128] However, once again the committee was unable to present one definition to the General Assembly, and it only submitted a report of its work.[129] It appeared that, in light of the increasingly tense international situation, there was no possibility of consensus. The year 1956 brought the Soviet intervention in Hungary, the Israel-Egypt conflict in the Middle East (followed by the French-British intervention) and the increased American presence in Vietnam. It was therefore pointless for the Sixth Committee to study and discuss the subsequent reports on the progress of the work in the Special committee. consequently, following the suggestion of the Sixth Committee, in a resolution of 29 November 1957 the General Assembly decided that it was necessary to ask the states admitted into the United Nations Organisation after 14 December 1955 to present their opinions on the definition of aggression.[130] The comments submitted in response to this request were to be handled by a committee of 21 members, consisting of the states from among the membership of the General Committee of the General Assembly. This committee was to present a report to the General Assembly once it felt that the right time had come.

The 21-member Special Committee met in 1959, only to conclude that the time was not yet right to engage in a serious debate on the definition of aggression.[131] The debate was rescheduled first to 1962,[132] then to 1965[133] and then – under the pretext of having to study the opinions of the newly admitted members – to 1967.[134] For the decade from 1957 onwards, no real effort was made to move forward towards a definition of aggression. The only issue actually debated in the meetings was the date of the subsequent meeting of the Special Committee. Aggression was a buzzword, but consensus as to the meaning of the terms seemed to be beyond reach.[135]

In the late 1960s, the political climate became somewhat friendlier. A number of new states joined the United Nations Organisation and were determined to pursue a definition of aggression, regardless of the animosity between the two blocs. It was also clear that the absence of the definition of aggression was preventing any progress on the draft Code of Offences against the Peace and Security of Mankind and on international criminal jurisdiction.[136]

In November 1967, the Soviet Union took the initiative once again. It suggested placing the issue of the definition of aggression on the agenda of the General Assembly.[137] The Sixth Committee debated, and afterwards the General Assembly, in a resolution of 18 December 1967, established yet another Special Committee, this one with 35 members. The committee commenced working in 1968.[138] Traditionally, mutual accusations of aggression abounded.[139] This time, however, the committee was very clear on its task and role: it was intended to propose a definition of aggression, and not to present yet another report from a debate on it.[140]

In its first session, lasting from 4 June until 6 July 1968, the Special Committee discussed three proposals for a definition of aggression, submitted respectively by 12 states (Algeria, the Democratic Republic of Congo, Cyprus, Ghana, Guiana, Indonesia, Madagascar, Sudan, Syria, Uganda, the United Arab Republic, Yugoslavia),[141] four states (Columbia, Ecuador, Mexico, Uruguay)[142] and 13 states (Columbia, the Democratic Republic of Congo, Cyprus, Ecuador, Ghana, Guiana, Indonesia, Iran, Mexico, Uganda, Spain, Uruguay and Yugoslavia).[143] All three definitions followed the mixed definition approach.

Importantly, the states that had proposed them were willing to leave aside the issue of indirect aggression and focus on the use of armed force.[144]

The General Assembly viewed with due appreciation the change in the attitude of the states and their willingness to compromise. It therefore prolonged the mandate of the committee, first until 1969[145] and then until other dates gradually in the following years.[146]

In the subsequent sessions, the committee's work focused on three drafts of the definition. The first one was the well known Soviet proposal.[147] The second one was endorsed by 13 states (Columbia, Cyprus, Ecuador, Ghana, Guiana, Haiti, Iran, Madagascar, Mexico, Spain, Uganda, Uruguay and Yugoslavia).[148] The third one was proposed by six Western states (Australia, Canada, Italy, Japan, Great Britain and the United States).[149] Great Britain and the United States had submitted their own proposals for the first time; previously, they had only criticised the other drafts. They were, however, no less sceptical as to the necessity and possibility of arriving at a definition.[150] Working groups were established, which proved to be really efficient. The groups focused on their specific tasks. Later, work was continued in contact groups. Ultimately, a consolidated proposal of the definition was achieved. Counterproposals kept cropping up for a while, but they contributed very little.

Consensus had been established that the definition should pertain to armed aggression only, and only to cases that would trigger Article 51 of the Charter of the United Nations. What still needed to be solved was the reconciliation between the proponents of the 'first shot fired' principle with those who claimed the definition needed a subjective component. That the definition should be mixed in nature remained beyond dispute; on the other hand, heated debates took place with regard to the list of specific acts of aggression. Each state paid particular attention to the acts it felt most at risk of, as well as those that it had in the past experienced.[151]

After a 24-year long struggle to define aggression, in March 1974 the (fourth) Special Committee, after seven sessions, was finally able to recommend a draft definition of aggression on which the committee's members had reached consensus. Still ahead was the task of convincing 100 states that the draft constituted the best available option, and that it gave due consideration to the interests and opinions of all members of the United Nations. It was quite a feat, but the efforts were successful. The General Assembly accepted the committee's recommendation. On 14 December 1974, resolution 3314 was adopted. It included a definition of aggression. According to this resolution, aggression was defined as follows: 'Aggression is the use of armed force by a State against the sovereignty, territorial integrity or political independence of another State, or in any other manner inconsistent with the Charter of the United Nations, as set out in this Definition'.[152] The first use of armed force by a state in contravention of the charter constitutes prima facie evidence of an act of aggression, although the Security Council may decide otherwise, considering the circumstances.[153] This general definition was accompanied by a relatively comprehensive list of specific acts of aggression,[154] although it was emphasised that the list was not exhaustive and the Security Council was free to determine that other acts constituted aggression under the provisions of the charter.[155]

Was this the end of the struggle to define aggression? Not necessarily. It has been argued that Resolution 3314 does not contain a definition, but only a declaration that ignores the minority opinion.[156] It is, certainly, a resolution of the General Assembly, and as such it is only binding on and for the General Assembly. Arguments have been made that the Assembly's resolution is binding on the Security Council too, since it was accepted by all states,[157] but scholars tend to disagree with such claims.[158] Resolution 3314 itself makes a reference to its non-binding character, stipulating that it is intended solely as guidance, helpful in determining aggression.[159] It would be also difficult to argue that the definition contained in Resolution 3314 is a reflection of customary law.[160] However, it is a fact that one of the acts listed in the definition – the sending of armed bands – has been upheld by the International Court of Justice as reflecting a norm of customary law,[161] which in the opinion of many experts was only a confirmation of the fact that a ban on this act also has the status of customary law, as do the other acts of aggression listed in the definition.[162] Given the massive scale of the controversy generated by the process of arriving at the definition, and the doubts and problems surrounding each of the acts of aggression it lists, it is really impossible to claim that there is any generally accepted *opinio iuris* in this regard.

Most of the provisions of Resolution 3314 were implemented, by means of the San Jose Protocol of 1975 to the Inter-American Treaty of Reciprocal Assistance (Rio Treaty).[163] On the one hand, it may be understood as endorsement of the definition of aggression the resolution proposes. On the other hand, it may just be a reflection of the short-lived enthusiasm of those states whose vision prevailed in the work on the resolution (the fact that the Protocol itself has not come into force until now might support this interpretation). The newest regional definition of aggression, included in the African Union Non-Aggression and Common Defence Pact of 2005, largely ignores the solutions adopted in the General Assembly resolution. It is therefore difficult to claim that the wording of the resolution is satisfactory, even if only for developing countries. Moreover, until present times, the Security Council in its resolutions has not even once invoked the resolution of the General Assembly, and the Assembly itself invoked it only twice, on the occasion of Namibia's occupation by South Africa and Israel's occupation of the Golan Heights.[164]

After 70 years of attempts to create a universal, legally binding definition of aggression, still no such definition exists, despite the fact that the term is used by politicians almost every time armed force is in use.

2.2 A definition of aggression

There is no universal, legally binding document which would contain a definition of aggression. However, a variety of legal instruments may be analysed, yielding certain similarities and recurring patterns, which may help reveal the meaning of the notion of 'aggression'.

2.2.1 Chapeau *of the definition*

It may appear that aggression is most simply defined as the unauthorised use of force by one state against another. However, even this general statement gives rise to substantial doubts.

'Force', which is the central element of any definition of aggression, is a term that needs to be outlined with precision. Does it include armed force only, or does it also refer to economic, political and cultural pressures? The Charter of the United Nations is of no assistance here, since its provisions are invoked both by the proponents and by the opponents of a broad understanding of 'force', and therefore of 'aggression'.

It has been argued that economic measures of coercion may destabilise a state just as much as an armed attack.[165] In the case of states that are economically weak, a threat of withdrawing financial assistance may have an immense impact on the ability of this state to make independent decisions. Economic aggression may lead a state not only to the brink of civil war, but also to extreme poverty and starvation.[166] Economic paralysis is a threat to the economic stability of a state, and therefore jeopardises the political independence of underdeveloped countries. Therefore, any action that deprives a state of economic resources, disrupts the balance in international trade, or infringes the fundamental principles of economic security, should be considered economic aggression. Many states agreed that the following acts should be deemed aggression: freezing of credit lines, boycott of imports, embargo, hindering the use of natural resources, nationalisation of local businesses with foreign capital, economic assistance on terms that have the potential to undermine political independence, and entering into disadvantageous treaties.[167] It was emphasised as early as 1931 that the Soviet Union had suggested a protocol on economic non-aggression,[168] placing the issue of economic security at the same level as military security and giving states the right of self-defence in order to protect their economic interests.[169]

Furthermore, there is the question of ideological aggression, consisting in intentional dissemination of controversial behaviours and attitudes with the purpose of manipulation.[170] For example, claims have been made that, had it not been for Nazi propaganda, Austria and Czechoslovakia would not have been weakened to the extent that made it possible to subdue them without the use of military force on a large scale.[171] Since a variety of acts of aggression may be listed, the same should be possible with regard to forms of aggression, including for example economic and ideological aggression.[172]

Including economic, cultural and political pressures into the definition of aggression may open a Pandora's box of problems.[173] It would give states an option to interpret any instrument of economic policy that at present is acceptable, such as for example the introduction of customs duties, as economic aggression. Such actions, however, are fully within range of a state's discretionary power.[174] As for ideological aggression, the notion is difficult to reconcile with the freedom of speech and the freedom of expression.[175] Moreover, the international community cannot guarantee the permanence of governments, an issue connected with a ban on criticism and on encouraging change.[176] It has also been pointed out that broadening the definition of aggression to include economic and ideological aggression might result in states being granted the right of self-defence in the case of, for example, economic pressures;[177] this solution would be hardly conducive to the maintenance of world peace.[178] It is possible to favour an interpretation under which Article 39 and Article 51 of the Charter of the United Nations refer to different types of aggression.[179] Even so, why should economic pressures and propaganda be considered aggression, if before 1919 aggression was understood strictly as actions that resulted in self-defence on the scale of a war?[180] In Nuremberg too the judgments were issued not on charges of aggression, but of aggressive war. Apparently, only actions that resulted in war or war-like activities were considered aggression.[181] Economic and ideological aggression does not have this dimension: since self-defence must be in proportion to the attack, logically a response to economic or ideological pressures should not be military in nature.[182]

With time, it appeared that consensus had been reached, with states conceding that hostile economic and ideological actions may constitute a threat to the peace, but that they are not acts of aggression.[183] Any aggression is illegal, but not all illegal actions constitute aggression.[184]

The least controversial solution therefore consists in considering only situations that involve the use of armed force as aggression. However, agreeing that aggression is connected with the use of armed force is not enough to determine whether any degree of force used constitutes aggression. In the case of smaller incidents, for example tension in regions around frontiers or unintentional crossing of frontiers by small sections of troops, are claims of aggression justified, and therefore self-defence legitimate? On the one hand, the conflict between Greece and Bulgaria of 1925 comes to mind. In its result, Greece was obliged to pay compensation for invading Bulgaria's territory, even though it had been Bulgarian soldiers who had carried out the first attacks on the Greek-Bulgarian border.[185] On the other hand, during the Tokyo trial, the hostilities along the border of Russia and Manchuria in the period 1938–1939 were considered aggression.[186] It seems that in order to invoke aggression, the use of force must be rather grave, in order not to expand too far the right of self-defence. It is necessary to take into consideration both the quality and quantity of force used.[187] Importantly, many definitions only classify the use of force as aggression when the force is a threat to independence. A random round of shots or small-scale hostilities along a border tend not to meet this requirement.[188]

Resolution 3314 gives certain consideration to the *de minimis* clause that had been requested by a number of states. The resolution does not explicitly rule out the possibility of classifying the smallest incident of use of force as aggression. However, it does stipulate that the Security Council may determine that, despite the use of force, an act of aggression has not occurred, if the instant actions are not sufficiently significant.[189] This makes it possible to ignore the smaller incidents but at the same time creates an additional interpretation problem, that is, the necessity to decide whether certain actions are sufficiently significant. The mechanisms adopted in the resolution suggest also that a state that has overreacted to a minor incident may itself be considered an aggressor.[190]

Further doubts pertain also to the question of whether the definition of aggression covers not only the actual use of force, or also the threat of use of force, which is banned by the Charter of the United Nations.[191] Some of the proposals of the definition did consider a threat of force to constitute aggression.[192] However, it is typically difficult to establish whether a threat of force actually occurred and, if it did, whether it was sufficiently serious. The subjective experience of a given state must be given due consideration.[193] For these reasons, in most cases the Security Council determined a threat to the peace only after armed action took place.[194] The Soviet Union was strongly opposed to including the threat of force in the definition of aggression, since it would go against the 'first shot principle' that is strongly endorsed.[195] Consequently, the 1974 definition made no mention of the threat of the use of force.

It seems clear that the notion of aggression is only applicable to international relations. Aggression therefore is always something that one state undertakes against another state[196] (or a group of states in relevant circumstances).[197] As for a definition of what a 'state' is, the Montevideo Convention on the Rights and Duties of States of 26 December 1933 stipulates that the state as a person of international law should possess the following qualifications: (a) a permanent population; (b) a defined territory; (c) a government; and (d) capacity to enter into relations with the other states.[198] The qualification of territory does not necessarily pertain to territory over which the state has full powers – it is difficult to determine the aggressor in cases of conflict in disputed territories, in neutral zones and within temporary demarcation lines.[199] Whether a state or government has been recognised is irrelevant.[200] Otherwise it would be impossible to discuss, for instance, the aggression of North Korea against South Korea, given that the former was not recognised by the majority of Western countries.[201]

In the debates held within the International Law Commission, it was emphasised that aggression could be perpetrated not only by states, but also by nations, as well as peoples not organised into states.[202] The draft prepared by the six Western countries (the six-powers draft) made a reference to non-state units determined by international frontiers and internationally recognised demarcation lines. The African Union Non-Aggression and Common Defence Pact of 2005 includes in its definition of aggression a reference to 'non-State actor(s)' and a 'foreign or external entity' that may commit acts of aggression. However, Resolution 3314 represents the traditional view that only states can commit aggression. Consequently, no aggression occurs in the case of civil wars (including wars of national liberation and anti-colonial wars) where no third party which is another state participates by means of armed force.[203] This brings about the difficulty in reconciling the unlimited use of force within one state with the numerous resolutions in support of the right of self-determination.[204] The view that using force in order to quash a rebellion whose purpose is the exercise of the right of self-determination might be considered aggression was reasonably well represented.[205] Moreover, the practice of the Security Council suggests that an internal situation, including internal conflict, may constitute a threat to the peace. Following this logic, in certain cases the use of force within one state might conceivably constitute aggression. The Soviet proposal of 1933 makes a reference to international aggression, which may either suggest that aggression is only possible in international relations or, conversely, that aggression may also be internal. Many attempts were made to study the possibility of intervention of the colonial power in cases of colonial wars as aggression.[206] Considering that at present, a great majority of conflicts occur internally, it might seem natural that the restrictions on the use of force in international relations should be accompanied by similar restrictions in internal relations.[207]

One of the amendments that Politis introduced into the Soviet draft of the definition of 1933 was a reference to agreements between states.[208] This modification seemed necessary, since not each and every instance of use of armed force is illegal. Even the Charter of the United Nations provides for certain exceptions to the ban on the threat and use of force. A simple definition of aggression might be a negative one: any use of force that is neither self-defence nor authorised by the Security Council constitutes aggression. Even more simply, any use of armed force in contravention of the Charter of the United Nations constitutes aggression.[209] Attempts of this kind were well represented in the debates within the International Law Commission, to mention only the proposals by Alfaro, Gilberto Amado,[210] Roberto Cordova, Georges Scelle[211] and (partially) Hsu. However, during the discussions of the Geneva Protocol as long ago as 1924, Politis had realised the paradox: defining aggression is very simple, in that it suffices to say that the state that uses armed force in contravention of the Covenant of the League of Nations or the Geneva Protocol is an aggressor. And yet statements of this kind fail to provide an answer to the question of whether in fact aggression occurred. If armed force is involved on both sides of the conflict (that is, if the non-aggressor is defending itself), it is difficult to determine who in fact was the party that started the armed action.[212] Determining that certain obligations have been breached is not sufficient for determining the nature of these obligations.[213] This issue is still absolutely valid in the current legal situation. Since we rely on the obligations resulting from the charter, we must face the challenge of defining legitimate self-defence, since aggression and self-defence are the two sides of the same coin.[214]

The notion of self-defence is frequently used (and abused), and attempts to differentiate between aggression and self-defence resemble a walk in a minefield with no good protection at hand. Almost every act of aggression is presented as self-defence,[215] since the notion of self-defence can easily be stretched beyond the strict necessity.[216] In the words of Georges Clemenceau: 'a nation that desires war is in a permanent state of legitimate self-defence'.[217] Relatively often, states claim to have acted in self-defence, but the claim proves false upon examination.[218] Sometimes also states clearly act in self-defence, but other states disagree with this classification of their actions.[219] Accepting war in self-defence opens the notion to dangerously far-reaching interpretations. Gaston Moch, a famous pre-First World War pacific movement activist, claimed that in order to prevent wars, it was necessary to specify with great precision the ramifications of permitted self-defence.[220] There can be no definition of aggression without a definition of self-defence. However, crafting a precise definition of self-defence is equally difficult to defining aggression.[221] In order to define self-defence, it is necessary first to define armed attack, which raises exactly the same dilemmas that arise with every attempt to define aggression,[222] since armed attack constitutes a specific case of aggression.[223]

One of the elements typically invoked in the definition of aggression is the principle of the first shot fired, according to which the state that first uses armed force is to be considered the aggressor.[224] This principle was reflected in the Soviet proposal of 1933 (and every subsequent Soviet proposal). In his 1933 report, Politis confirmed that in his opinion, chronology should be crucial in determining the aggressor.[225] The principle is also what stands behind Article 51 of the Charter of the United Nations, which stipulates that armed attack must occur in order for states to have the right of self-defence.[226] The advantages of this principle include the simplicity of its application and its objectivity, required in a definition.[227] Its consistent application means that even a mobilisation or gathering of enemy forces along the frontier, or incidents at the frontier, give no grounds for an attack. If facing this type of situation, a state may use diplomatic measures, or alternatively it may engage in the same actions as the enemy, but it may not use armed force without becoming the aggressor. The principle of the first shot fired is perfectly functional in simple cases, where a mass attack against another state is taking place. However, usually the use of force escalates. Under the condition of constant tension along the frontier, it is much more difficult to determine who resorted to force first.[228] Inflexible application of this principle may lead to considerable injustice,[229] especially – as has been claimed – if a state is forced to engage in preventive or pre-emptive self-defence, which – particularly for smaller states – may be the only option available to them for responding to aggression.[230] Requiring that a state should hold the attack gives the aggressor a massive technical and technological advantage.[231] Moreover, if a state wishes to use armed force against another state, it may mislead the victim into attacking first:[232] a provocation or forgery of documents testifying to the use of armed force is easily accomplished.[233] Therefore, the determination of aggression should be contingent on specific circumstances, and the fact that a party used force first should not automatically classify it as the aggressor.[234]

To sum up: on the one hand, there is a superbly simple method of determining aggression; on the other hand, there is a whole range of arguments in support of the fact that the party who attacks first not always is the aggressor. The dilemma is difficult to solve. Resolution 3314 adopted a compromise. The principle of the first shot fired was omitted from the general part of the definition, but it was included as prima facie evidence of aggression.[235] Consequently, the principle is not an inherent part of the definition, but it places the burden of proof on the state that was the first to use armed force: this state has to prove that its actions did not constitute aggression.[236]

Many states supported the inclusion in the definition of subjective elements, such as intent or motivation of the aggressor.[237] This would give the definition more flexibility and facilitate making the decision on the basis of all relevant circumstances and, moreover, it would draw a sharper line between aggression and self-defence. The reasons for aggression must be considered an inherent part thereof – otherwise any use of armed force would amount to aggression.[238] Arguments have also been raised suggesting that, in order to invoke aggression, the intent of the given state must be studied, as well as the state's political approach and attitude. This in turn requires a study of the state's propaganda, press and public opinion, as well as the state's actions in the international context.[239] Such a study of the motives eliminates a determination of aggression in the case of mistaken use of armed force, or an accidental outbreak of hostilities.[240]

Furthermore, experts pointed out that the subjective element must not necessarily consist in giving consideration to the intent of aggression. Rather, the ultimate goal of the aggression should be considered.[241] In favour of this approach, the Covenant of the League of Nations had already tied aggression to a specific goal, that is, breach of territorial integrity and political independence.[242] In addition, the draft Treaty of Mutual Assistance of 1923 had made an indirect reference to the goal of the aggressor by stipulating that:

> ... a war shall not be considered as a war of aggression if waged by a State which is party to a dispute and has accepted the unanimous recommendation of the Council, the verdict of the Permanent Court of International Justice, or an arbitral award against a High Contracting Party which has not accepted it, provided, however, that the first State does not intend to violate the political independence or the territorial integrity of the High Contracting Party.[243]

Scelle, who had criticised the inclusion of the subjective element in the definition of aggression, did make a reference to the goal of aggression (expressed as a *modifier état du droit international positif en vigueur*), as well as the potential results of aggression (*troubler l'ordre public*). The goal as one of the elements of aggression was also mentioned in the proposal of the six Western states (the six-power draft), where it was stipulated that aggression consists in: actions in order to diminish the territory or alter the boundaries of another state; alter internationally agreed lines of demarcation; disrupt or interfere with the conduct of the affairs of another state; secure changes in the government of another state; or inflict harm or obtain concessions of any sort. Interestingly, Nicolas Nyiri suggested that in order to determine aggression and not to confuse it with self-defence, it is necessary not only to examine the results of the aggression (attack against the sovereignty of a state, destruction of key opponents), the measures employed therein (threat, diversion, propaganda, declaration of war) and the methods thereof (attack), but also to give consideration to the reasons for aggression (expansion), its goals (intended domination) and the aggressor's intentions (determination towards achieving domination by means of use of force).[244]

The Soviet Union, backed by the entire Eastern bloc, protested against a reference to aggressive intent, as did the Arab states, which argued that reliance on *animus aggressionis* is dangerous in that it is difficult to prove.[245] Whenever the need arises to analyse the circumstances and motivations, it is often difficult to distinguish between the aggressor and the victim.[246] Consequently, incorporating a reference to the aggressor's intent in the definition creates a dangerous loophole of which an aggressor might take advantage.[247] Each aggressor will claim that his actions consist only in exercising his rights, and that there is no aggressive intent.[248] Moreover, applying 'intent' to state authorities is somewhat misdirected.[249] It was also pointed out that Article 2(4) of the Charter of the United Nations makes no reference to intent. On the other hand, the use of force resulting from an error in judgment, and justified by an honest belief that the use of force is legitimate, would likely not be in contravention of the charter.[250] As far as the goals of aggression are concerned, the Soviet proposal of 1933 had already stipulated as follows:

> No consideration whatsoever of a political, strategical or economic nature, including the desire to exploit natural riches or to obtain any sort of advantages or privileges on the territory of another State, no references to considerable capital investments or other special interests in a given State, or to the alleged absence of certain attributes of State organization in the case of a given country, shall be accepted as justification of aggression (…).

Further explanations were added, in the following wording:

> In particular, justification for attack cannot be based upon:
>
> A. The internal situation in a given State, as, for instance: (a) Political, economic or cultural backwardness of a given country; (b) Alleged maladministration;

(c) Possible danger to life or property of foreign residents; (d) Revolutionary or counter-revolutionary movement, civil war, disorders or strikes; (e) The establishment or maintenance in any State of any political, economic or social order.

B. Any acts, laws or regulations of a given State, as for instance: (a) The infringement of international agreements; (b) The infringement of the commercial, concessional or other economic rights or interests of a given State or its citizens; (c) The rupture of diplomatic or economic relations; (d) Economic or financial boycott; (e) Repudiation of debts; (f) Non-admission or limitation of immigration, or restriction of rights or privileges of foreign residents; (g) The infringement of the privileges of official representatives of other States; (h) The refusal to allow armed forces transit to territory of a third State; (i) Religious or anti-religious measures; (k) Frontier incidents.

Politis's definition, as well as the London definitions of 1933, all contained similar lists.

The outcome of the work of the special committees on the definition of aggression appeared to suggest that a consensus had been reached insofar as stating that no goal justifies aggression.[251] Hence, if a state's intention is a breach of political independence, and the motive is for example the desire to free the population from an oppressive government, only the intent should matter, and the ultimate goal should be disregarded.[252] That is why Resolution 3314 stipulates that no consideration of whatever nature, whether political, economic, military or otherwise, may serve as a justification for aggression.[253] Instrumental in this choice of phrasing was the argument that citing goals of aggression in the definition will certainly lead to deeming aggression motivated by other goals acceptable.[254]

The definition of 1974 invoked sovereignty, territorial integrity and political independence of a state,[255] although it lists these factors not as goals of aggression but rather as methods of committing aggression. However, by granting the Security Council the right to interpret the circumstances in contradiction of 'first shot fired', the council was authorised to examine both the intent and the goal of aggression.[256] Consequently, an opportunity for a clear-cut test for aggression was lost, and qualification of each situation as aggression requires a case-by-case evaluation.[257]

As demonstrated by the above comments, all elements of the definition of aggression are controversial, albeit in varying degrees. At the very heart of a definition, aggression should be defined as unlawful use of armed force by one state against another. Problems arise in the attempt to define unlawfulness (owing to the absence of a definition of self-defence), and in determining the level of force necessary to call it aggression. Moreover, the dispute is still open as to what should prevail: who used force first, or who had an aggressive intent and/or desired to achieve a forbidden goal. Further controversies surround the cases of use of force other than armed force, and the use of force internally within one state (internal aggression). Given the scope of doubts and lack of clarity, the solution adopted in Resolution 3314, authorising the

Security Council to give due consideration to relevant circumstances in determining aggression seems reasonable. It does, however, mean that the decades of work towards a definition of aggression were rather futile, since the original construction contained in the Charter of the United Nations had already proposed this very approach.

2.2.2 Acts of aggression

Initially, definitions of aggression consisted solely of lists of specific acts of aggression. The Permanent Advisory Committee of the General Assembly of the United Nations declared that aggression consisted in a mobilisation occurring together with a crossing of frontiers.[258] This two-element test was soon criticised in the course of the debates on the treaty of mutual assistance, when it was decided that a mobilisation is a long process with many stages, and it is rather difficult to determine when it has started, not to mention to track its progress.[259] As for the frontiers, after the First World War, owing to the zones of neutrality established in the period 1919–1920, difficulties arise in specifying the frontiers, since military and political borders are not identical, air forces are not bound by them anyway and sea vessels may engage in hostilities at open sea.[260]

Nonetheless, attempts continued to generate lists of specific acts of aggression. Both enumerative and mixed definitions were popular. Table 2.1 presents a compilation of acts of aggression typically included in these lists.

As presented in Table 2.1, typical acts of aggression include: a declaration of war; invasion of another state's territory; armed attack on the territory, vessels and aircrafts of a state; maintaining armed forces in another state's territory without this state's permission; naval blockade; and support given to armed bands active in another state's territory.[261]

Many documents list a declaration of war first among the acts of aggression.[262] The argument was that a declaration of war is usually accompanied by hostilities, and it may therefore be considered an act of aggression necessitating immediate reaction.[263] Moreover, a declaration of war is an expression of the will and intention of a state to use armed force.[264] However, the significance of this act of aggression faded as wars were more and more often no longer formally declared[265] and states were opposed to determining that the state that declared war first was the aggressor. Following this reasoning, in the Second World War scenario, Great Britain would have to be classified as the aggressor in relation to Germany,[266] and the Netherlands – in relation to Japan.[267] There are also cases where a state, having declared war, has no intention of actually engaging in hostilities.[268] It was on the strength of these arguments that a declaration of war was not included in the 1974 list of acts of aggression. However, the abstract part of the definition makes a reference to the declaration of war by emphasising that the absence of such declaration is irrelevant for the determination of aggression.

Almost every list includes invasion as a separate item. The very term 'invasion' suggests more than a short raid or crossing of frontiers. An invasion occurs when a state sends its troops into the territory of another state and maintains them there for an extended period.[269] A crossing of frontiers is therefore required, accompanied by the troops physically entering at least a part of the territory.[270] Most definitions refer to an invasion by armed forces, which gives rise to reservations.[271] During the inter-war period questions had already been raised as to this wording: if a state sends its police force, or irregular troops, does this constitute an invasion?[272] The answer should of course be in the affirmative, but – in order to dispel all doubts – this wording should be removed, particularly given that the abstract part of the definition of aggression makes it clear that aggression only occurs if armed force is used.

Attack by land, naval or air forces on the territory, vessels or aircraft of another state is typically considered an act of aggression.[273] This phrasing pertains to any attack, regardless of the type of weapons used. However, the expression 'territory, vessels or aircraft of another state' is unclear. Does it cover only an attack on military vessels and aircraft? Does it pertain to an attack on any vessel sailing under the flag of the state, regardless of who owns it, be it a private person or the state? Does it matter whether the vessel carries a few or a few hundred persons?[274] There are no definitive answers to these questions. A possible line of argumentation is as follows: since it is the state that may fall victim to an attack, then the attack must be directed against the state's territory or fleet. That is the reasoning adopted in the 1974 definition, which specifies that it pertains to an attack on the marine and air fleets of a state, rather than on any vessel or aircraft. In light of this definition, an attack directed against a passenger airplane would not be considered aggression.[275] There are, however, other definitions which would classify such an attack as aggression. For example, one of the amendments that Politis introduced to the Soviet proposal of 1933 was replacing the phrase 'naval forces' with 'vessels or aircraft', so as to cover both civilian and military vessels.[276] This is logical insofar as actions taken to protect property or citizens are classified as a sub-category of self-defence. Some states have also stressed that an attack on their air or marine fleets would in fact amount to a coastal blockade.[277] On the other hand, holding or fining foreign vessels and aircraft that illegally enter territorial waters or air space of a state is a right granted to each and every state, a point made especially strongly by Ecuador.[278]

Bombardment is another act typically classified as an act of aggression,[279] probably because it assumes the use of artillery and other heavy weaponry[280] and because it tends to have grave consequences. Arguments have also been made to the effect that, by listing bombardment next to, or instead of, armed attack, the intention was to demonstrate that actions that do not include penetrating another state's territory may nonetheless be considered aggression.[281]

In some proposals acts of aggression include, in addition to invasion and attack, occupation and annexation of the state's territory or part of

Table 2.1 Acts of aggression according to selected documents

USSR Proposal (1933)	*London Convention (1933)*	*Treaty of Saadabad (1937)*	*Bolivia Proposal (1945)*	*Philippine Proposal (1945)*	*USSR Draft Definition (1969)*
'The aggressor in an international conflict shall be considered that State which is the first to take any of the following actions:'	'Accordingly, the aggressor in an international conflict shall, subject to the agreements in force between the parties to the dispute, be considered to be that State which is the first to commit any of the following actions:'	'Each of the High Contracting Parties undertakes in no event to resort, whether singly or jointly with one or more third Powers, to any act of aggression directed against any other of the Contracting Parties:'	'A state shall be designated an aggressor if it has committed any of the following acts to detriment of another state'	'Any nation should be considered as threatening the peace or as an aggressor, if it should be the first party to commit any of the following acts:'	'1. Armed aggression (direct or indirect) is the use by a State, first, of armed force against another State contrary to the purposes, principles and provisions of the Charter of the United Nations. 2. In accordance with and without prejudice to the functions and powers of the Security Council. (…) B. Any of the following acts, if committed by a State first, even without declaration of war, shall be considered an act of armed aggression:'
'Declaration of war against another State' (a)	'Declaration of war upon another State' (1)	'Declaration of war' (1)	'Declaration of war' (b)	'To declare war against another nation' (1)	'Declaration of war by one State, first, against another State' Article 2(A)

Six-Powers Draft Definition (1969)	*Thirteen-Powers Draft Definition (1969)*	*GA Res no 3314 (1974)*	*African Union Pact (2005)*
'II. The term "aggression" is applicable, without prejudice to a finding of threat to the peace or breach of the peace, to the use of force in international relations overt or covert, direct or indirect, by a State against the territorial integrity or political independence of any other State, or in any other manner inconsistent with the Purposes of the United Nations. Any act which would constitute aggression by or against a State or other political entity delimited by international boundaries or internationally agreed lines of demarcation against any State or other political entity so delimited and not subject to its authority. IV. The uses of force which may constitute aggression include, but are not necessarily limited to, a use of force by a State as described in paragraph II. A. In order to: 1. diminish the territory or alter the boundaries of another state; 2. alter internationally agreed lines of demarcation; 3. disrupt or interfere with the conduct of the affairs of another State; 4. secure changes in the Government of another State; or 4. inflict harm or obtain concessions of any sort; By such means as:'	'For the purpose of this definition, aggression is the use of armed force by a State against another State, including its territorial waters or air space, or in any way affecting territorial integrity, sovereignty or political independence of such State (...). In accordance with the foregoing and without prejudice to the powers and duties of the Security Council, as provided in the Charter, any of the following acts when committed by a State first against another State in violation of the Charter shall constitute acts of aggression:'	'Aggression is the use of armed force by a State against the sovereignty, territorial integrity or political independence of another State, or in any other manner inconsistent with the Charter of the United Nations (...)' 'Any of the following acts, regardless of a declaration of war, shall subject to and in accordance with the provision of article 2, qualify as an act of aggression:'	'"Aggression" means the use, intentionally and knowingly, of armed force or any other hostile act by a State, a group of States, an organisation of States or non-State actor(s) or by any foreign or external entity, against the sovereignty, political independence, territorial integrity and human security of the population of a State Party to this Pact, which are incompatible with the Charter of the United Nations or the Constitutive Act of the African Union. The following shall constitute acts of aggression, regardless of a declaration of war by a State, group of States, organisation of States, or non-State actor(s) or by any foreign entity'
	'Declaration of war by one State against another State' (a)		

(*Continued*)

Table 2.1 Acts of aggression according to selected documents (*Continued*)

USSR Proposal (1933)	*London Convention (1933)*	*Treaty of Saadabad (1937)*	*Bolivia Proposal (1945)*	*Philippine Proposal (1945)*	*USSR Draft Definition (1969)*
'The invasion by its armed forces of the territory of another State without declaration of war' (b)	'Invasion by its armed forces, with or without a declaration of war, of the territory of another state' (2)	'Invasion by the armed forces of one State, with or without a declaration of war, of the territory of another State' (2)	'Invasion of another state's territory by armed forces' (a)	'To invade (…) with or without declaration of war, the territory, public vessels, or public aircraft of another nation' (2)	'Invasion (…) by the armed forces of a State against the territory of another State (…)' Article 2(B)(c)
'Bombarding the territory of another State by its land, naval or air forces or knowingly attacking the naval or air forces of another State' (c)					'Bombardment of or firing at its territory and population of another State (…)' Article 2(B)(b)
'The landing in, or introduction within the frontiers of, another State of land, naval or air forces, without the permission of the Government of such a State or the infringement of the conditions of such permission, particularly as regards the duration of sojourn or extension of area' (d)					
'The establishment of a naval blockade of the coast or ports of another State' (e)	'Naval blockade of the coasts or ports of another State' (4)			'To subject another nation to a naval, land or air blockade' (3)	'blockade of coasts and ports' Article 2(B)(c)
	'Attack by its land, naval or air forces, with or without a declaration of war, on the territory, vessels or aircraft of another State' (3)	'An attack by the land, naval or air forces of one State, with or without a declaration of war, on the territory, vessels or aircraft of another State' (3)	'Attack by land, sea, or air forces, with or without declaration of war, on another state's territory, shipping, or aircraft' (c)	'(…) attack, with or without declaration of war, the territory, public vessels, or public aircraft of another nation' (2)	'(…) an attack on its *(of another State)* land, sea or air forces' Article 2(B)(b) '(…) attack by the armed forces of a State against the territory of another State (…)' Article 2(B)(c)

Six-Powers Draft Definition (1969)	*Thirteen-Powers Draft Definition (1969)*	*GA Res no 3314 (1974)*	*African Union Pact (2005)*
'invasion by its armed forces of territory under the jurisdiction of another state' (1)	'The invasion (…) by the armed forces of a State, against the territories of another State (…)' (b)	'Invasion (...) by the armed forces of a State of the territory of another State (…)' Article 3(a)	'the invasion (…) by armed forces against the territory of a Member State' Article 1(c)(ii)
'bombardment by its armed forces of territory under the jurisdiction of another State' (3)	'Bombardment by the armed forces of a State against the territory of another State (…)' (c)	'Bombardment by the armed forced of a State against the territory of another State (…)' Article 3(b)	'the bombardment of the territory of a Member State' Article 1(c)(iii)
'use of its armed forces in another State in violation of the fundamental conditions of permission for their presence, or maintaining them there beyond the termination of permission' (2)		'The use of armed forces of one State which are within the territory of another State with the agreement of the receiving State, in contravention of the condition provided for in the agreement or any extension of their presence in such territory beyond the termination of agreement' Article 3(e)	'the use of the armed forces of a Member State which are within the territory of another Member State with the agreement of the latter, in contravention of the conditions provided for in this Pact' Article 1(c)(vi)
	'The blockade of the coasts or ports of a State by the armed forces of another State' (d)	'The blockade of the ports or coasts of a State by the armed forces of another State' Article 3(c)	'the blockade of the ports, coasts or airspace of a Member State' Article 1(c)(iv)
'carrying out deliberate attacks on the armed forces, ships, or aircraft of another State' (5)	'(…) attack by the armed forces of a State, against the territories of another State (…)' (b)	'(…) attack by the armed forces of a State of the territory of another State (…)' Article 3(a) 'An attack by the armed forces of a State on the land, sea or air forces, or marine and air fleets of another State' Article 3(d)	'(…) attack by armed forces against the territory of a Member State' Article 1(c)(ii) 'the attack on the land, sea or air forces, or marine and fleets of a Member State' Article 1(c)(v)

(*Continued*)

Table 2.1 Acts of aggression according to selected documents (*Continued*)

USSR Proposal (1933)	*London Convention (1933)*	*Treaty of Saadabad (1937)*	*Bolivia Proposal (1945)*	*Philippine Proposal (1945)*	*USSR Draft Definition (1969)*
	'Provision of support to armed bands formed in its territory which have invaded the territory of another State, or refusal, notwithstanding the request of the invaded State, to take, in its own territory, all the measures in its power to deprive those bands of all assistance or protection' (5)		'Support given to armed bands for the purpose of invasion' (d)	'To interfere with the internal affairs of another nation by supplying arms, ammunition, money or other forms of aid to any armed band, faction or group (...)' (4)	'The use by a State of armed force by sending armed bands, mercenaries, terrorists, saboteurs to the territory of another State and engagement in other forms of subversive activity involving the use of armed force with the aim of promoting an internal upheaval in another State or a reversal of policy in favour of the aggressor shall be considered an act of indirect aggression' Article 2(C)
		'Directly or indirectly aiding or assisting an aggressor' (4)			
			'Intervention in another state's internal or foreign affairs' (e)	'To interfere with the internal affairs of another nation (...) by establishing agencies in that nation to conduct propaganda subversive of the institutions of that nation' (4)	

Six-Powers Draft Definition (1969)	*Thirteen-Powers Draft Definition (1969)*	*GA Res no 3314 (1974)*	*African Union Pact (2005)*
'organizing, supporting or directing armed bands or irregular or volunteer forces that make or infiltrate into another State' (6) 'organizing, supporting or directing violent civil strife of acts of terrorism in another State' (7)		'The sending by or on behalf of a State of armed bands, groups, irregulars or mercenaries, which carry out acts of armed force against another State of such gravity as to amount to the acts listed above, or its substantial involvement therein' Article 3(g)	'the sending by, or on behalf of a Member State or the provision of any support to armed groups, mercenaries, and other organised transnational criminal groups which may carry out hostile acts against a Member State, of such gravity as to amount to the acts listed above, or its substantial involvement therein' Article 1(c)(viii) 'the encouragement, support, harbouring or provision of any assistance for the commission of terrorist acts and other violent trans-national organised crimes against a Member State' Article 1(c)(xi)
		'The action of a State in allowing its territory, which it has placed at the disposal of another State, to be used by that other State for perpetrating an act of aggression against a third State' Article 3(f)	'the action of a Member State in allowing its territory, to be used by another Member State for perpetrating an act of aggression against a third State' Article 1(c)(vii) 'technological assistance of any kind, intelligence and training to another State for use in committing acts of aggression against another Member State' Article 1(c)(x)

(*Continued*)

Table 2.1 Acts of aggression according to selected documents (*Continued*)

USSR Proposal (1933)	*London Convention (1933)*	*Treaty of Saadabad (1937)*	*Bolivia Proposal (1945)*	*Philippine Proposal (1945)*	*USSR Draft Definition (1969)*
			'Refusal to submit the matter which has caused a dispute to the peaceful means provided for its settlement' (f)		
			'Refusal to comply with a judicial decision lawfully pronounced by an International Court' (g)		
					'The use of nuclear, bacteriological or chemical weapons or any other weapons of mass destruction' 2(B)(a)
					'(…) military occupation (…) of the territory of another state or part thereof' (B. c)
					'(…) annexation of the territory of another state or part thereof (…)' (B. c)

Six-Powers Draft Definition (1969)	*Thirteen-Powers Draft Definition (1969)*	*GA Res no 3314 (1974)*	*African Union Pact (2005)*
	'(…) the use of any weapons, particularly weapons of mass destruction, by a State against the territory of another State' (c)	'(…) the use of any weapons by a State against the territory of another State' Article 3(b)	'(…) the use of any weapon against the territory of a Member State' Article 1(c)(iii)
	'(…) Any military occupation, however, temporary (…)' (b)	'(…) any military occupation, however temporary, resulting from such [*described above – author*] invasion or attack' Article 3(a)	'(…) military occupation, however temporary, resulting from such an invasion or attack' Article 1(c)(ii)
	'(…) Any forcible annexation of the territory of another state or part thereof' (b)	'(…) any annexation by the use of force of the territory of another state or part thereof' Article 3(a)	'(…) any annexation by the use of force of the territory of a Member State or part thereof' Article 1(c)(ii)
			'the use of armed forces against the sovereignty, territorial integrity and political independence of a Member State, or any other act inconsistent with the provisions of the Constitutive Act of the African Union and the Charter of the United Nations' Article 1(c)(i)
			'the acts of espionage which could be used for military aggression against a Member State' Article 1(c)(ix)
'inflicting physical destruction on another State through the use of other forms of armed force' (4)			

its territory.[282] These acts of aggression are somewhat controversial, since annexation may occur on the basis of an agreement,[283] and military occupation may arise as a consequence of self-defence, especially under the conditions of the so-called 'therapeutic occupation' aimed not at an annexation but at effecting a shift in the enemy's policy and economic, legal and social institutions.[284] If occupation is strictly considered an act of aggression, a state acting in self-defence might be considered the aggressor if it engaged in occupation, however temporary, of the territory of the state that had attacked it first.[285] In this situation, there would be no simple divide between the aggressor and the defender, but rather there would be two aggressors. This is why Great Britain argued that occupation should be considered an act of aggression if it results from another act of aggression.[286]

There is some truth to the claim that if occupation and annexation are considered acts of aggression, acts of aggression are confused with the results thereof, since no unlawful annexation can occur without an invasion. Consequently, if invasion constitutes aggression, then the occupation that follows it is just a subsequent act of aggression (twofold aggression)[287] and it is a case of continuous aggression, and then – if annexation follows – it is a case of permanent aggression.[288] However, smaller states were afraid of the scenario that was realised in Austria and Czechoslovakia in 1938–1939, that is, a situation with no invasion or attack to speak of, but where annexation occurs nonetheless. Resolution 3314 addressed some of the fears of these states, while trying at the same time to give consideration to the sceptical comments regarding the inclusion of occupation and annexation in the definition of aggression. Under the resolution, military occupation resulting from an invasion or attack, or annexation by the use of force, are considered acts of aggression.

The Soviet proposal of 1933 lists among the acts of aggression the landing in, or introduction within the frontiers of, another state of land, naval or air forces, without the permission of the government of such a state or the infringement of the conditions of such permission, particularly as regards the duration of sojourn or extension of area. Such actions generally fit within the understanding of the term 'invasion'.[289] However, violations of the permission to maintain troops within a territory would result in an invasion from within, and therefore without the violation of frontiers, which in turn in the inter-war period seemed to be a *sine qua non* condition of aggression. In order to eliminate doubts in this regard, and to ensure that this act is also considered an act of aggression, some definitions list it as a separate act of aggression, in addition to a typical invasion. Importantly, during the period of work on the definition of aggression within the United Nations system, both the United States and the Soviet Union had their military bases situated in the territories of various states, and these states did consider the possibility of this type of invasion.

The inclusion in the Soviet proposal of 1933 of a naval blockade signalled a radical shift in the perception of this measure, traditionally viewed as a fully acceptable peaceful measure of exerting pressure.[290] Politis stressed in his report that a naval blockade, although not necessarily leading to war, is nonetheless an act implying material force, in a limited but real manner, and only the weakness of the state on the receiving end of the blockade prevents the blockade from being an initial act in the final rupture of peace and resort to hostilities.[291] Thus the blockade, even if initially peaceful, may lead to war if the state against which it is being used decides to respond and react.[292] Despite these arguments, states decided not to include a naval blockade in the list of the acts of aggression included in the Disarmament Convention, arguing that not every naval blockade should lead to sanctions.

When the question of blockades came up for debate within the United Nations, states had already had the experience of the blockade of Berlin. It was therefore argued that a land or air blockade is as serious as a naval one.[293] Landlocked states added that cutting them off from the sea by means of disabling road transport was as serious as a naval blockade was for non-landlocked states.[294] A land blockade therefore should also be considered an act of aggression, in order to safeguard the interests and preserve the principle of equality of all states.[295] In today's perspective, no-fly zones might also be considered a type of blockade that threaten the interests of a given state.[296] However, only the proposal put forward by the Philippines included all three types of blockades: naval, air and land. Opponents of the broad notion of a blockade as an act of aggression claimed that land and air blockades are effected in a state's own territory, that is, territory that is under the state's sovereign power, and therefore may be treated at most as examples of economic aggression.[297] Resolution 3314 defaulted to the traditional notion, and stipulated that only a blockade of the ports or coasts of a state by the armed forces of another state constituted an act of aggression.[298] The Sixth Committee, in its report of 21 November 1974, made a brief mention that the wording of the definition should not be taken as an excuse to justify blocking sea access to landlocked states.[299]

One of the key modifications that Politis introduced to the Soviet proposal of 1933 was listing, among the acts of aggression, the provision of support to armed bands formed in the territory of one state which have invaded the territory of another state, or refusal, notwithstanding the request of the invaded state, to take, in its own territory, all the measures in the state's power to deprive those bands of all assistance or protection. Subsequent proposals sought also to include a situation in which one state provides support to armed bands operating in the territory of another state.[300] States that had experiences of diversion during the Second World War pushed for the inclusion of diversion in the list of acts of aggression.[301] Unquestionably, by using measures such as the deployment of secret agents or supporting certain groups in critical moments a state may be able to undermine the sovereignty of another state as efficiently as with the use of typical military aggression.[302] In the cold war period, open international conflicts were in fact rarer than so-called indirect aggression:[303] for example the issue of Chinese volunteers during the conflict in Korea (Chinese People's Volunteer Army)[304] or fighting in Greece after the Second World War.[305]

Precisely what kind of support might be considered aggression is problematic. The Philippines' proposal included supplying arms, ammunition, money or other forms of aid to any armed band, faction or group, and establishing agencies to conduct propaganda subversive of the institutions of a given state. Such a broad approach proved unacceptable to many states. Democracies in particular pointed out that their hands were tied in terms of controlling what is published in privately held newspapers, owing to the protection of freedom of expression.[306] The International Court of Justice (ICJ), in Military and Paramilitary Activities in and against Nicaragua (*Nicaragua v United States of America*), provided certain guidelines in the matter. It ruled that a state is responsible for the operation of armed groups, if they are the states de facto agents and, in order to consider them as such, it is necessary to establish that the state has effective control of their operations, consisting in organising and directing the groups' operations.[307] On the other hand, supplying arms and offering support, in logistics or otherwise, may qualify as a threat or use of force, or amount to intervention in the internal or external affairs of other states.[308] The ICJ upheld this line of reasoning in its ruling of 19 December 2005 in the case concerning armed activities on the territory of the Congo (*Democratic Republic of The Congo v Uganda*).[309] It is of course immensely difficult to prove that a certain state had full control over the operations of armed groups. Usually, the situation tends to involve tolerance towards the groups' operations, possibly with logistical support.[310] In the light of the above, the definition of indirect aggression in the 1974 definition is particularly disappointing. The definition includes only the sending by or on behalf of a state of armed bands, groups, irregulars or mercenaries, which carry out acts of armed force. Considering that the International Tribunal for the Prosecution of Persons Responsible for Serious Violations of International Humanitarian Law Committed in the Territory of the Former Yugoslavia dismissed the 'effective control' test (applied previously by the ICJ) in favour of a condition of 'general control'[311] and that the Security Council has declared states to be responsible for armed action solely on the grounds of harbouring a terrorist,[312] it appears that presently, any assistance offered to armed groups, with the exception of humanitarian aid, can be considered an act of aggression. A similar approach has been adopted in the African Union Non-Aggression and Common Defence Pact of 2005, which considers the following to be an act of aggression:

> ... the sending by, or on behalf of a Member State or the provision of any support to armed groups, mercenaries, and other organized transnational criminal groups which may carry out hostile acts against a Member State, of such gravity as to amount to the acts listed above, or its substantial involvement therein,[313] ...

as well as:

> ... the encouragement, support, harbouring or provision of any assistance for the commission of terrorist acts and other violent trans-national organized crimes.[314]

Assistance in aggression has occasionally been considered an act of aggression, as in giving a state access to a territory in order to engage in aggression against a third state.[315] This is a consequence of treating support to armed bands as an act of aggression: since a state may be held responsible for the use of armed force against another state by armed groups, it should certainly also be held responsible for supporting another state in the commission of such an act.

Some of the proposals that refrained from limiting aggression to the use of armed force also listed other acts of aggression, such as intervention in another state's internal or foreign affairs.[316] Iraq proposed that aggression should include a refusal to accept a decision of the Security Council or the General Assembly aimed at protecting the peace and preventing international tension.[317] Classifying the refusal to submit to a peaceful procedure of conflict resolution as an act of aggression was also supported.[318] The idea itself was hardly new: the Rutgers memorandum[319] had already included a similar idea, as well as the American Draft Treaty of Disarmament and Security of 1924.[320] After the Second World War, Bolivia included this type of aggression in its definition. However, the idea met with rather a cold reception. Counterarguments claimed that under both the Covenant of the League of Nations and the Charter of the United Nations states had agreed to seek peaceful means of conflict resolution, but they did not accept mandatory jurisdiction of the Permanent Court of International Justice or the ICJ.

Another idea that continued to appear periodically in the debate was to consider a state an aggressor if the state refused a ceasefire[321] or refused to withdraw its troops to their original positions or positions indicated by an international authority.[322] However, states raised the argument that making such an arbitrary decision might be unfair towards a state that fell victim to aggression, since it might suit the aggressor to invade a territory and then proceed to an armistice, engaging in lengthy disputes over who holds the rights to the invaded territory.[323]

The acts discussed above are not intended to constitute a comprehensive list. The very definition of 1974 stipulates that the Security Council may decide that other actions constitute acts of aggression too. On the one hand, this of course diminishes the certainty of law. On the other hand, it is a safety valve which guarantees that in the future acts that have so far not been attempted may be classified as aggression, and also to classify acts whose position was debatable, as aggression.

2.3 Conclusions

To date, no universal legally binding definition of aggression has been achieved. All the definitions in force are regional definitions, such as the London definition or the definition included in the African Union Non-Aggression and Common Defence Pact of 2005. The resolution of the General Assembly of 1974 is not a satisfactory solution. In the words of Benjamin B. Ferencz, everyone realised that the process of adopting Resolution 3314 was somewhat like the birth of a not very pretty baby: the lack of good looks was noted by everyone, but no one was really ready to tell the parents to try again.[324] Moreover, the definition is legally binding only on the General Assembly and – as practice has demonstrated – the General Assembly itself rarely makes reference to the resolution.

It is frustrating that a term as important as 'aggression' has not been defined in a universally binding manner. There is no simple answer to the question why the decades of work proved fruitless. An optimistic approach stipulates that the failures so far are only symptomatic of the difficulties inherent in defining aggression.[325] A more truthful approach would entail accepting the fact that states were not particularly interested in a legally binding definition, since such an outcome would limit their options in the event that armed force was in fact used.[326] The inflexible position of the Soviet Union, which interpreted each suggestion to amend its draft as an attempt to defeat the Soviet Union itself, definitely hindered the work on the definition of aggression within the United Nations system.[327] The definition became entangled in the game of politics, a game from which the states of the developing world emerged victorious, as it was their vision of the definition that eventually made it into Resolution 3314.[328] The United States and its allies approached the issue of the definition not as a legal problem in need of a solution, but as an extension of the cold war front. Characteristically, Americans opposed the Soviet definition with passion, while just a short time earlier Robert Jackson, chief United States prosecutor at the Nuremberg trial, had used it as an authoritative source of law.[329]

Why then was Resolution 3314 adopted at all? Its significance was intended as minimal, and therefore there was little point in continuing to argue over its scope.[330] If the resolution had been intended as legally binding, it would probably never have been adopted. Many states perceived (and continue to perceive) war as an important element of political strategy.[331]

Often, arguments are made to the effect that 'aggression' is a not a strictly legal notion, but rather a mixture of politics, economy, sociology and psychology, with a just a little bit of law thrown in[332] or, conversely, that 'the matter is to a great extent political'.[333] Such claims, however, seem to hold little merit. Since aggression is mentioned in legal acts, then it must be a legal problem and it must be definable. Many concepts used in the law are derived from economics or politics, but this does not mean that they cannot be defined within the system of law. The only obstacle hindering the establishment of a universal legally binding definition of aggression is the absence of the political will to do so.

There is a valid claim that the absence of a definition of aggression has a damaging effect on international relations.[334] With no clear rules to determine what constitutes acts of aggression, states are left to their own devices in trying to make this decision, and may feel justified when they try to prevent such acts independently.[335] The lack of a definition does not seem to be a good solution. A legal order with no clarity as to the obligations it requires is not really a legal order, not even a primitive one.[336] And while obviously aggression cannot be stopped by means of a definition alone, a definition can nonetheless be useful.[337]

In the absence of a universal legally binding definition, it might be worthwhile to reconstruct a definition from the customary law. This, however, is a difficult task. Each of the potential building blocks of the definition has given rise to doubts and lengthy debates with no clear outcomes. Moreover, almost every attempt at a definition excludes from its scope actions undertaken in self-defence. Unfortunately, there is no definition of self-defence either, and thus a vicious circle or, in the words of Otto von Bismarck, 'Zirkelquadratur' is created.[338] A definition of aggression relies on a definition of self-defence, and a definition of self-defence relies on a definition of armed attack, which in the opinion of many constitutes aggression, which brings us back to square one.

Nonetheless, with a proviso to take all circumstances into account, it is possible to point to the very core of the definition of aggression. Resolution 3314 was an attempt to capture this core. Problems arise when the precise scope of the notion is sought, especially when a decision has to be made in favour of either a broad or a narrow approach. However, this is an issue that has haunted every interpreter of almost any legal term since time immemorial.

Part II

Criminalisation of aggression

3 The legal basis for criminalising aggression

It is certainly possible for customary law to grow towards the delegalisation of certain actions. However, it is impossible in this way for a mechanism to develop that would allow for bringing individuals to justice for engagement in such actions.[1] Just because certain actions are unlawful, they are not necessarily criminal: international law provides for a wide array of acts and omissions that are unlawful but for which no criminal sanctions are provided.[2]

If an individual is to be tried for the crime of aggression, and if the procedure is to be carried out *lege artis*, it is necessary to invoke solid legal grounds for the individual's legal responsibility for the crime.

A document that criminalises aggression must, first and foremost, specify all the elements of the definition of the crime of aggression. It must indicate precisely what acts the law forbids (*actus reus*), what the relationship must be between the act and the individual who engages in it (*mens rea*) and which individuals may be considered responsible for the act in question.

In order to determine the framework for criminalisation of aggression, it is useful to begin with a review of the historical cases where individuals have indeed been convicted of this crime. As the review will demonstrate, the legal grounds for the criminalisation of aggression have not been laid out with great precision.

3.1 The Treaty of Versailles

The First World War, with its unprecedented scale, timeline, methods and measures, was a shock for those nations that found themselves participating in it. Public opinion demanded not only that the perpetrators of war crimes should be punished, but also that the same fate should befall those who had started the war.[3] Traditionally, once a war was over, the sins were forgiven, with just a handful of war crime perpetrators punished by national courts. This time, however, it was not going to be an option. The public expected a more radical approach. It became clear that the agenda of the international conference, designed to create a new political framework for Europe, if not for the entire world, had to cover the issues of responsibility of those who had violated international obligations.

The Preliminary Peace Conference, on 25 January 1919, appointed the Commission on the Responsibility of the Authors of the War and on Enforcement of Penalties.[4] The commission was given the task of investigating:

1. The responsibility of the authors of the war.
2. The facts as to the breaches of the laws and customs of war committed by the forces of the German Empire and their allies on land, sea and in the air; the degree of responsibility for these offences attaching to particular members of the enemy forces, including members of the general staffs, and other individuals, however highly placed.
3. The constitution and procedure of a tribunal appropriate for the trial of these offences.
4. Any other matters cognate or ancillary to the above, which the Commission should find useful and relevant to take into consideration.[5]

The commission was therefore appointed to analyse the options for holding individuals responsible not only for war crimes but also for the initiation of aggressive war.

In its report of 29 March 1919, the commission examined documents that were declared to determine that the responsibility for the war lay wholly upon the powers that had declared war in pursuance of a policy of aggression, with the responsibility resting first on Germany and Austria, and secondly on Turkey and Bulgaria. The war was referred to as 'a dark conspiracy against the peace of Europe'.[6] The commission concluded that the war had been premeditated by the aggressors and their allies, who refused to participate in any peaceful efforts, consciously and purposefully leading to a situation where war had become inevitable.[7]

The commission expressed its belief that these actions would certainly be condemned in the future. However, given that states were free to decide whether they wanted to employ the services of institutions such as the International Commission of Inquiry, Mediation and Arbitration, the commission was forced to acknowledge that engaging in aggressive war was not violation of a positive law, and therefore could not constitute a basis for issuing charges and bringing perpetrators to trial before a tribunal, in line with the tasks assigned to the commission.[8] It continued to explain that an answer to the questions of responsibility required extensive research into events of many decades in many countries, and was therefore difficult and complex[9] and was a task fit for historians and politicians, and not for a war crime tribunal.[10] The commission was of the opinion that no criminal charges could be made against the individuals and authorities responsible, but the gravity of the outrages upon the law of nations and international good faith were such that they should be subject to formal condemnation by the Conference.[11] Particularly in light of the violations of neutrality of Luxembourg and Belgium, and the acts that brought about the war, the commission recommended that it would be right for the Peace Conference to adopt special measures, or even to create a special body to investigate the matters. However, it was not stipulated that this body should be a criminal tribunal. The commission noted that, for the future, penal sanctions should be provided for such grave outrages against the elementary principles of international law.

The American members of the Commission on the Responsibility of the Authors of the War and on Enforcement of Penalties, James Brown Scott and Robert Lansing, prepared a significant memorandum. The Americans condemned the violations of neutrality of Luxembourg and Belgium, and declared that their perpetrators should be 'held up to the execration of mankind',[12] but they also stressed that the issues of initiation of war are of moral and not legal nature.[13] They also stated that responsibility for war should not be subject to proceedings before a tribunal,[14] stating that: 'It is up to the statesmen and not to judges to decide whether the violators of the treaties guaranteeing the neutrality of Belgium and of Luxemburg should be subjected to a political sanction'.[15] The Americans proposed that a commission of inquiry, rather than a judicial body, should investigate whether aggression occurred and, if so, whose responsibility it was.[16] The Americans 'found themselves in substantial accord' that, for the future, criminal sanctions should be provided for offences such as initiating a war.[17] At the same time, they pointed out the difficulty in determining whether in reality an act is one of aggression or one of defence.

Eventually, the stipulation was included in the Treaty of Versailles of 28 June 1919 to the effect that the allied powers affirm, and Germany accepts, the responsibility of Germany and her allies for causing loss and damage as a consequence of the war imposed by the aggression of Germany and her allies.[18] The Treaty explicitly stated that aggression had occurred, but it stopped short of banning aggression and of imposing penal sanctions for aggression.[19]

Under the Treaty, Wilhelm II of Hohenzollern, formerly German emperor, was publicly arraigned 'for a supreme offence against international morality and the sanctity of treaties'.[20] The language used in the treaty was purposefully vague and general,[21] since the issue of the emperor's responsibility was considered in political and moral, rather than penal, terms.[22] While it was decided that a special tribunal was to be constituted, it was at the same time provided that 'the tribunal will be guided by the highest motives of international policy, with a view to vindicating the solemn obligations of international undertakings and the validity of international morality'.[23] Moreover, in their response to Germany of 15 January 1920, the allied powers claimed that the regulation that formed the basis of the emperor's charges before the tribunal was not penal in its content, regardless of its form, and that it was an expression of international politics, which is a minimum in a case concerning gravest crimes against international morality, treaties and fundamental principles of justice.[24]

In light of these arguments, it is hardly surprising that claims were made to the effect that the crimes with which the emperor was charged were political or moral in nature, and immorality of certain behaviours does not make them subject to penal proceedings.[25] The assumption that any treaty violation is a crime was exposed as faulty.[26] On the other hand, it was argued that the crimes listed against Wilhelm II were of such a kind that they could be tried without a breach of fundamental principles of law, given that they pertained to premeditated aggression and violations of laws and customs of war, that is, crimes covered by customary law and also, to an extent, by the Hague Conventions.[27] If the Conventions never discuss aggression explicitly, that is only because there was no need to state what the conscience of honest people clearly states itself.[28]

The other peace treaties (made with Austria in Saint-Germain-en-Laye on 10 September 1919,[29] with Bulgaria in Neuilly on 27 November 1919,[30] with Hungary in Trianon on 4 June 1920[31] and with Turkey in Sèvres on 10 August 1920[32]) contained provisions pertaining to responsibility for war crimes, and in the case of Turkey also for crimes against humanity, but did not refer to responsibility for the crime of aggression.[33]

3.2 Inter-war ideas of an international tribunal and penal code

The stipulations of the Treaty of Versailles were hardly satisfactory, and their enforcement was faulty at best. Nonetheless, they contributed significantly to opening a debate on international criminal responsibility of individuals for violations of international law, and thus on the possible establishment of an international criminal tribunal and an international criminal code.

In 1920 Baron Descamps, president of the Advisory Committee of Jurists appointed by the Council of the League of Nations, proposed the establishment (beside the Permanent Court of International Justice (PCIJ)) of a High Court of International Justice, tasked with bringing to justice crimes that violate international public order or the universal law of nations.[34] The proposal met with a critical reception in the committee, in part owing to the fact that it was beyond the scope of work assigned thereto.[35] It was transmitted to the council regardless,[36] and then referred by the council to the Assembly. However, the latter's reaction was also unfavourable. The Third Committee decided that there was no international criminal law that would be recognised by all nations and, moreover, even if the option was accepted that certain crimes fall under any authority's jurisdiction, then the correct course of action would be to establish a dedicated criminal chamber within the PCIJ, rather than to appoint an entire new court.[37] The reservations that the League of Nations so clearly demonstrated towards the notion of criminal responsibility of individuals for crimes against international law was largely due to the fact that the league felt that such efforts were a direct continuation of the efforts to punish those responsible for the horrors of the First World War.[38]

The idea of an international criminal court, and the underlying notion of criminal responsibility of individuals was, however, not entirely dismissed with the decision of the Assembly. It continued to resurface in organisations of lawyers, in particular the International Law Association (ILA), the Inter-parliamentary Union and the International Criminal Law Society (ICLS).

In 1922, at the ILA conference in Buenos Aires, Hugh Hale Bellot spoke of the need to establish a permanent international criminal court. His appeals were well received, and the ILA assigned him the duty of drafting the statute of such a court. The draft was ready in time for the Stockholm 1924 conference, where it was decided that a special committee should be appointed to deal with the issue.[39] The committee polished the draft of the statute of a permanent international criminal court, and the document was adopted at the Vienna conference of ILA in 1926.[40] Under its provisions, the criminal court was to become a part of the PCIJ.[41] The jurisdiction of the court was to extend to all charges of violations of international obligations of penal character, committed by the subjects or citizens of one state or by a *heimatlos* against another state or its citizens.[42] The court should also have power to deal with cases of a penal character referred to it by the council or assembly of the League of Nations for trial, or for inquiry and report.[43] Theoretically, therefore, the crime of aggression might fall under the court's jurisdiction if it was accepted that the ban on aggression constitutes a notion of criminal law; this is clearly not an obvious claim. While documents of the inter-war period typically discuss the criminal nature of aggressive war (eg the draft Treaty of Mutual Assistance of 1923, the draft Geneva Protocol of 1924, the resolution of the Assembly of the League of Nations of 24 September 1927 and the resolution of American states of 18 February 1928), none of these documents was legally binding. Moreover, the term 'crime' was used in them purely in order to emphasise the significance of the ban on war and of the principle that the state rather than an individual is responsible for engaging in war.[44]

The ICLS also debated the need to establish a permanent international criminal court. At a meeting in Brussels in 1926, the International Congress of Penal Law, on the basis of a recommendation prepared by Vespasian Pella and Henri Donnedieu de Vabres, decided that it was the PCIJ that should investigate criminal cases and judge both states and individuals.[45] The crimes to fall under the jurisdiction of the court were to include crimes of aggression and other similar crimes and offences, or any violation of international law committed in times of peace or war, as well as common law crimes which, by reason of nationality of the victim or the presumptive offender, may be considered as international offences that constitute a threat to world peace.[46] However, all violations committed by states or by individuals should be provided for and sanctioned in advance by precise texts, with international conventions defining the crimes and offences within the jurisdiction of the court and prescribing penal sanctions and security measures.[47] The congress instituted a commission that was given the task of drafting the documents for the establishment of the criminal chamber of the PCIJ. On 8 January

1927 the commission appointed Pella to carry out this task, and Pella's draft was accepted by the ICLS on 16 January 1928 and subsequently communicated to the states represented at the Congress as well as the member states of the League of Nations.[48] Under the draft, the criminal chamber should be established within the PCIJ. The draft contained specific instructions on how to proceed towards the chamber's establishment. In terms of *ratione materiae* jurisdiction of the court, the draft relied on the international penal code (which was expected to be drafted at a later stage), as well as treaties to which states may adhere.[49] In addition to offences committed by states and to international offences committed by individuals (which by their nature are incapable of being declared crimes or of being made punishable by national criminal codes), the criminal chamber was to have jurisdiction over such offences committed by individuals, in respect of which jurisdiction may be renounced by individual states by international convention, including in particular crimes and offences omitted in times of peace and likely to endanger the peaceful relations of states, or which ought, by reason of circumstances in which they are committed, to be made subject to international criminal jurisdiction for their effective repression.[50]

The Inter-parliamentary Union too debated the issue of responsibility for aggression in the context of possible establishment of an international criminal court. At the 1925 Conference in Washington and Ottawa, Pella (on behalf of the Permanent Committee for the Study of Juridical Questions of the Union) presented a report entitled *La criminalité de la guerre d'agression et la constitution d'un droit répressif des nations.*[51] In the report, Pella's emphasis was on the notion than an individual should bear responsibility for violations of the international legal order and the law of nations, regardless of whether a state also bore such responsibility.[52] Pella believed that a penal court should be established as a part of PCIJ.[53] In outlining the jurisdiction of this penal court, Pella's strongest focus was on the crime of aggression. The list of punishable acts included not only a declaration of aggressive war by a sovereign, but also abuse of diplomatic privileges with a view of committing acts that are in gross violation of fundamental principles of the international public order, or that constitute preparation for aggressive war, as well as dissemination of information that may be a threat to the peace.[54] Sanctions against individuals were to encompass: a warning, a fine, a reprimand, limitation of freedom, a ban on residence, a ban on serving a diplomatic function abroad, deprivation of freedom and exile.[55] Having heard the report, the conference adopted a resolution by which it declared its belief that aggressive war was a crime, and decided to set up a permanent sub-committee, which (under Pella's direction) was to study the causes of wars and draw up a preliminary draft of an international legal code for the repression of international crimes.[56] The union thus raised both the issue of an international penal court and of the international penal code.[57]

As the ILA and the ICLS both also began to consider the issue of the international criminal code, the two associations decided to open collaboration with the Inter-parliamentary Union, coordinate their efforts and establish (in March 1935) the position of one joint reporter. Pella was appointed to the position. Immediately, in 1935, he drafted a preliminary version of a worldwide code of repression, *Plan d'un Code répressif mondial*.[58] In the draft he proposed that war should be considered a crime committed by a state; war was defined as committing by a state, as the initiating party, one of the acts listed by the Committee on Security Questions of LN Conference for the Reduction and Limitation of Armaments in 1933.[59] He also stipulated criminal responsibility of heads of state, or other persons who took the initiative to commit the acts stipulated in the convention, who prepared to commit such acts or who committed them, or directly incited others to commit them (in particular by means of war propaganda), or participated in armed bands formed in the territory of one state and invading the territory of another state, or gave assistance to such bands, or disseminated forged documents or information that had the potential to be a threat to international relations, or who committed other offences that were a threat to international relations and that were specified in the code.[60]

However, much as the notion of penal responsibility of individuals for aggression became widespread among scholars, states continued to ignore it. It was only after a series of assassination attempts against representatives of European states in positions of power (king of Yugoslavia Alexander I and prime minister of France Louis Barthou) that the states decided to pursue a Convention on Prevention and Punishment of Terrorism and Convention for the Establishment of an International Criminal Court in The Hague.[61] Both conventions were signed on 16 November 1937. The court established by the latter convention was to have jurisdiction only over crimes and offences specified in the former.[62] The crime of aggression therefore fell only very narrowly within this jurisdiction. There was, however, hope that it would be gradually expanded.[63] Unfortunately, this first attempt to establish an international penal court failed. Neither of these conventions ever entered into force.[64]

It appears, therefore, that the notion of criminal responsibility of individuals for the crime of aggression took form after the First World War, but was given serious consideration only by scholars, whose efforts led to the production of draft regulations on international criminal law and an international criminal court.[65] Protocols were not ratified and resolutions of international conferences were not binding, demonstrating that there was little general acceptance of such responsibility.[66] All evidence therefore suggests that in the times before the Second World War, there was no principle in force to the effect that individuals should bear criminal responsibility for aggression.[67] States demonstrated no willingness to adopt binding legal acts that would directly impose such responsibility, which is hardly surprising, given how much resistance there was towards the idea of implementing a total ban on aggressive war.

3.3 The statute and judgment of the International Military Tribunal

Germany initiated the Second World War. During the war, German citizens (admittedly along with citizens of other states) committed numerous war crimes and crimes against humanity. Initially, the allied powers proceeded with a single objective: winning the war. There was little point in discussing how to punish those guilty of international law crimes before the perpetrators of the crimes were defeated and captured.[68] However, starting in late 1941, the allies issued, with increasing frequency, both separate and joint declarations stating their intention to punish Nazi criminals.[69] The declarations contained no specifics as to which crimes were to be punished, and how.

The first suggestion that the Nazi actions should be punished as international law crimes, within a legal procedure involving a court, came from the states under occupation.[70] In a declaration adopted at a conference in London, organised at the Polish and Czechoslovak initiative on 13 January 1942, nine occupied states (Czechoslovakia, Belgium, France, Greece, Luxemburg, the Netherlands, Norway, Poland and Yugoslavia) proposed that, in order to avoid revenge and to satisfy the need for justice of the civilised world, one of the key objectives of the war should be to bring the perpetrators of crimes before an organised judicial authority.[71] In response to the London Declaration, representatives of the United States, Great Britain and the Soviet Union confirmed that Nazi criminals should be brought to court.[72] The significance of these declarations should not be underestimated: initially, it was the proponents of executing the criminal without any trials who had garnered strong support from the governments of the superpowers.[73] Robert Jackson provided a good synthesis of arguments in favour of a court trial when he wrote:

> We could, of course, set them at large without a hearing. But it has cost unmeasured thousands of American lives to beat and bind these men. To free them without a trial would mock the dead and make cynics of the living. On the other hand, we could execute or otherwise punish them without a hearing. But undiscriminating executions or punishments without definite findings of guilt, fairly arrived at, would violate pledges repeatedly given, and would not set easily on the American conscience or be remembered by our children with pride.[74]

The decision to organise trials for Nazi criminals contained no specification as to what crimes they would be tried for. For example, the Moscow Declaration of 30 October/1 November 1943 only announced that the German officers and members of the Nazi party who had been responsible for or had taken a consenting part in the atrocities, massacres and executions would be sent back to the countries in which these deeds were done in order to be judged and punished according to the laws of those countries. As for the masterminds of the crimes, whose actions were not geographically limited, they were to be punished jointly by the allied states. If the wording of the declaration is any indication ('atrocities', 'massacres', 'cold-blooded mass executions', 'brutalities of the Nazi domination', 'terror', 'monstrous crimes', 'hands imbued with innocent blood'), the allies may have intended only to punish the Nazi criminals for war crimes and crimes against humanity. The declaration makes no clear reference to the crime of aggression. Furthermore, no such reference appears in the warning issued to those states maintaining their neutrality not to offer asylum to Axis state citizens,[75] or in the conditions of the armistice with Finland, Romania, Bulgaria and Hungary.[76] It is pointed out in the literature on the subject that it was not until Stalin's speech of 6 November 1943 that the allies started threatening responsibility for the war itself.[77]

The determination of the scope of criminal responsibility of Nazi perpetrators was investigated by the London International Assembly.[78] Eventually, the Assembly recommended that an international criminal tribunal should be instituted, with jurisdiction over war crimes, defined as:

> ... any grave outrages violating the general principles of criminal law as recognised by civilised nations and committed in wartime or connected with the preparation, the waging on the prosecution of war, or perpetrated with a view to preventing the restoration of peace.[79]

The United Nations Commission for the Investigation of War Crimes[80] also pondered the question of whether 'war crimes' included the crime of initiating a war, and whether starting an aggressive war was a crime at all. The topic was discussed at the session of the Commission's Legal Committee (Third Committee). The Czechoslovak representative Boguslav Ecer presented, in March 1944, a report entitled *Scope of the Retributive Action of the United Nations according to their official declarations*, in which he proposed that the commencement and continuation of the Second World War was indeed a crime for which individuals should be criminally responsible and punishable.[81] According to Ecer, the criminal character of the Second World War resulted from its objectives and methods employed in their pursuit.[82] In response to the report, the committee adopted, on 6 June 1944, a draft resolution entitled *Scope of the Retributive Action of the United Nations*, suggesting that aggressive wars should be considered war crimes and therefore within the commission's remit.[83] In the committee's opinion, consequently, crimes committed in order to prepare for or initiate a war, regardless of where they were committed, were to be considered war crimes (and that included crimes that might be committed in order to prevent the restoration of peace).

However, in June 1944 the Plenary Commission decided that these suggestions were too far-reaching, and that the issue of punishability of war itself should be once again investigated by the Legal Committee.[84] The committee established a sub-committee, which in turn produced two reports. The majority report claimed that deeds committed by an individual with the exclusive purpose of preparing for aggressive war or launching such war were not, *de lege lata*, war crimes.[85] However, owing to the fact that such deeds, and in particular the violations of the principles of the law of nations and of international good faith committed by the heads of the Axis states and their satellite states, in order to prepare for a war and to launch a war, were of such magnitude that they should be formally condemned in peace treaties and, in the future, criminal sanctions should be stipulated for such grave violations of principles of international law. These conclusions bear a strong resemblance to the solutions adopted in the Treaty of Versailles. On the other hand, the minority report (drafted by Ecer) claimed that aggressive war was a crime for which individuals should be criminally responsible.[86] However, Ecer stated clearly that his declaration pertained only to one specific war, that is, the Second World War initiated by Germany, and that he was making no general claims as to the criminality of each and every aggressive war.

Both reports were submitted to the Plenary Commission. Many of the commission's members approved of the conclusions of the minority report (Australia, China, New Zealand, Poland and Yugoslavia), but France and Greece opted to support the majority report.[87] Votes fell 6:5 in favour of the minority report. Nonetheless, the commission decided that governments' opinions should be sought, and the delegates should follow their governments' instructions in the final vote.[88] Unfortunately, many delegates received no governmental instructions, and voting on the resolution failed to take place.[89]

In terms of determining whether aggressive war would be considered a crime, the position of the United States was decisive. This position was heavily influenced by the memorandum of 22 January 1945, drafted for President Franklin D. Roosevelt by the Secretary of War, Henry L. Stimson, Secretary of State, Edward R. Stettinius Jr and Attorney General, Francis Biddle. The memorandum suggested that Nazi criminals should be charged with participation in a criminal enterprise as well as 'the waging of an illegal war of aggression with ruthless disregard for international law and the rules of war'.[90] From that moment onwards, the crime of aggression made regular appearances in American proposals.

President Roosevelt assigned to Judge Samuel Rosenman the task of working out, together with other allies' representatives, a consensus as to how to proceed in the matter of the Nazi criminals. At the conference in San Francisco in April 1945, Rosenman presented a proposal. Owing to a variety of constraints, no thorough analysis of the proposal occurred at that time.[91] However, informal consultations did take place, with the following conclusions: the perpetrators were to be judged in a trial; individuals with clear geographical ties were to be handed over to the states where they committed their crimes; as for the Nazi leaders, an international military tribunal was to be instituted, with representatives of the United States, Great Britain, France and the Soviet Union.[92] Rosenman's draft proposed that the tribunal should have jurisdiction over:

> ... b. Invasion by force or threat of force of other countries in violation of international law or treaties.
> c. Initiation of war in violation of international law or treaties.
> d. Launching a war of aggression.
> e. Recourse to war as an instrument of national policy or for the solution of international controversies.[93]

In Rosenman's view, clearly the tribunal was to adjudicate mostly with reference to the crime of aggression.

Jackson's position was similar: he emphasised that Germany had committed international aggression with a view to implementing its own order in other states, which is the gravest offence against international law.[94] Jackson proposed that Nazi criminals should be charged, inter alia, with 'invasions of other countries and initiation of wars of aggression in violation of international law or treaties'.[95] Jackson was perfectly aware that attempts would be made to undermine the legal basis of such charges. He argued that Hugo Grotius had already distinguished between just and unjust war, that is, defensive and aggressive war.[96] Moreover, Jackson pointed to the specific character of international law, which tends to be based on custom, while customs themselves usually arise out of one significant event.[97] Jackson proceeded to argue that the present time also had 'its right to institute customs and to conclude agreements that will themselves become sources of a newer and strengthened international law'.[98] He wrote: 'It is high time that we act on the juridical principle that aggressive war-making is illegal and criminal'.[99] As grounds for his position, Jackson cited the Briand-Kellogg Pact, the Stimson doctrine, the Geneva Protocol of 1924, the resolution of the Assembly of the League of Nations of 1927 and the resolution of the Sixth Pan-American Conference.[100] Interestingly, Jackson believed not only that preparations for military aggression should be punishable, but that the preparation must cover military, naval, diplomatic, political and commercial aggressions.[101]

In June 1945, the United States, France, Great Britain and the Soviet Union decided to convene a conference in London, with the objective of working out an agreement instituting an international military tribunal. The conference took place at Church House in the period between 26 June and 8 August 1945.

The American draft of the proposed agreement referred to the participating states on 14 June 1945, along with the amendments submitted for it, served as a basis of discussions.[102] Originally, the American proposal contained the following wording as to the jurisdiction of the tribunal:

> … c. Invasion of another country by force or threat of force, or the initiation of war, in violation of international law.
> d. Launching a war of aggression.[103]

However, after considering the responses of the other participating states, on 30 June a revised version was proposed, worded as follows:

> … b. Launching a war of aggression.
> c. Invasion of threat of invasion of, or initiation of war against, other countries in breach of treaties, agreements or assurances between nations, or otherwise in violation of International Law.
> d. Entering into a common plan or enterprise aimed at domination over other nations, which plan or enterprise included or intended, or was reasonably calculated to involve, or in its execution did involve, the use of unlawful means for its accomplishment, including any or all of the acts set out … above or the use of a combination of such unlawful means with other means.[104]

On 2 July, the Soviet delegation proposed yet another wording as to the tribunal's jurisdiction:

> a. Initiation of war in violation of principles of International Law and in breach of treaties.
> b. Launching a war of aggression. …
> d. The use of war as an instrument of Nazi policy intended for the extermination and plunder of other peoples …[105]

In order to reconcile the two drafts, the drafting sub-committee proposed another version on 11 July. In this proposal, the tribunal's jurisdiction was limited to violations of international law that were criminal in nature. Such violations were to include, inter alia:

> … b. Launching a war of aggression.
> c. [Invasion or threat of invasion of] initiation of war against other countries in breach of treaties, agreements of assurances between nations or otherwise in violation of International Law.
> d. [Entering into a common plan or enterprise aimed at domination over other nations, which plan or enterprise included or intended, or was reasonably calculated to involve, or in its execution did involve, the use of unlawful means for its accomplishment, including any or all of the acts set out … above or the use of a combination of such unlawful means with other means] …[106]

In line with Rosenman's proposal, a distinction was made between a war of aggression and a war in violation of treaties, and further acts aimed at domination were listed separately. The list includes both actions that are objective (invasion, war in violation of laws) and an action specified by reference to its subjective purpose – domination over other nations.[107]

In response, the American delegation proposed that war of aggression should be defined as 'an invasion of another country in the absence of an attack upon, invasion of, or declaration of war against such country'.[108] Jackson stressed that Germans would want to justify some of their actions by invoking self-defence, and thus it was necessary to adopt a relevant definition of aggression. In his opinion, it should be the definition stipulated by the London Conventions of 1933.[109] The danger observed by Jackson was also noted by Sir David Maxwell Fyfe, who pointed to the example of the invasion of Norway.[110] The London definitions, as Jackson emphasised, provided clearly that no political, military, economic or other reasons could be considered as justification for aggression.[111] This would therefore nip in the bud any attempts to legitimise the German aggression. As a result, the Americans became stalwart supporters of the principle of the first shot fired.[112] For practical reasons, the Americans also wanted the definition of the crime of aggression to include the notion of conspiracy, which in itself was foreign to French law, a fact pointed out by André Gros.[113]

The remaining allies did not share the enthusiasm towards defining aggression along the lines of the 1933 approach. They feared that some of the operations of the allied forces might actually fall under this definition.[114] For this reason, the French delegation, in its proposal of 19 July 1945, suggested that the tribunal should only try the individuals who directed the preparation or conduct of:

> (i) The policy of aggression against, and of domination over, other nations, carried out by the European Axis Powers in breach of treaties and in violation of international law; …
> (iii) The war, launched and waged contrary to the laws and customs of international law.[115]

The French delegation was therefore the first to propose narrowing down the jurisdiction of the tribunal to citizens of the Axis states and their satellite states, a suggestion probably intended to diminish the fears of potential responsibility of citizens of the allied states. With the jurisdiction thus limited, the French were no longer afraid of introducing the subjective component (domination) into the definition; the aggressive nature of German policies was beyond any doubt.[116]

The charge of aggression, which the American delegation insisted on, was troublesome and difficult for the French to accept. The French negotiator Gros stated repeatedly that the statute of the tribunal was to remain a strong reference point for many years to come, and it was therefore desirable to avoid issues that might attract criticism in the future.[117] In Gros's opinion, including the crime of aggression within the tribunal's jurisdiction was precisely such a point of contention. Gros made it clear that France did not believe the waging of an aggressive war to constitute a crime under penal law; in deciding that an individual may bear criminal responsibility for war, the conference would be taking a step beyond the laws in force at the moment. Furthermore, Gros argued that in the future, any state that launches an aggressive war would bear criminal responsibility in moral and political terms. However, under the international laws in force at the moment of the conference, such an approach would not be appropriate. It was possible – he claimed – to try the criminal for conducting an aggressive war in violation of principles of international law, but it was not possible to make anyone responsible just for the fact of waging an aggressive war. Aggressive war was not a crime under the applicable laws, and if the issue of criminality of war was raised at all, it was always in the context of the responsibility of a state, and not an individual.[118] Moreover, no penal sanctions were associated with it. The consequences were limited to compensatory damages.[119] Overall, a state that launches an aggressive war commits a crime, but the state's citizens do not become criminals as a result of it.[120] Gros believed that adopting the French paradigm would result in the criminals being punished, without the need to invent new crimes and sanctions for them.[121] What the Americans wanted, that is, having the Nazi criminal on trial, could be accomplished under the treaties and laws already in existence.[122] He argued further that proving that Germans had violated the treaties and, as a consequence of those violations, they had annexed territories and built concentration camps, would provide sufficient grounds for charging the relevant individuals and assigning responsibility to them.[123] Finally, Gros noted that the scope of the statute of the tribunal did not necessarily have to be identical with the charges brought before it.[124]

The British delegate, Sir David Maxwell Fyfe, consistently represented a constructive approach. In his attempts to steer the debate towards consensus, he suggested that all the delegations shared the belief that aggressive war should be considered a crime, but what was missing was the sanctions.[125] He went on to explain that, in his opinion, it was unacceptable to create a situation where 15–20 individuals could be identified who were clearly responsible for launching the war, but it was not possible to put them on trial. He believed that the charge of aggression was crucial, because it conceptualised the crux of what the Germans were accused of.[126] The British proposal of 20 July therefore listed under the jurisdiction of the tribunal the crime defined as:

> 1. Domination over other nations or aggression against them in the manner condemned or foresworn in (inter alia) the following Pacts of Declarations … .[127]

On the other hand, the Soviet delegation insisted that the purpose of the conference was not to draft a definition of the crime of aggression that would be applicable in the future[128] and that would anyway not be binding in the case of those presently charged.[129] If even the conference establishing the United Nations Organisation decided not to engage in discussion on the definition of aggression, the London conference was even less appropriate a forum in which to engage in this discussion. Following the French delegation, the Soviets insisted that the jurisdiction of the tribunal be clearly limited to citizens of the European Axis states.[130] As for the absence of a definition, Ion T. Nikitchenko explained that the German operations should not be viewed separately, but rather in their totality, thus revealing the full nature of the Nazi policy.[131] Referencing the French and British proposals submitted earlier, the Soviet delegation proposed on 23 July that the tribunal should have jurisdiction pertaining to:

> a. Aggression against or domination over other nations carried out by the European Axis in violation of the principles of international law and the treaties.[132]

This approach, however, would rely on the notion of 'the principles of international law', the scope of which was controversial among the delegates.[133]

It was again Great Britain that attempted to forge a compromise. Drawing on the American, French and Soviet drafts, on 23 July the British delegation proposed the following wording of the tribunal's jurisdiction:

> a. Aggression against or domination over other nations carried out by the European Axis Powers in violation of treaties, agreements and assurances.[134]

The proposal did not meet with universal approval. The Americans continued to insist on the London formula of 1933 and to claim that, in their opinion, aggressive war and war in violation of treaties were not the same.[135] The next British proposal (of 28 July) was therefore modified to read:

> c. Initiation of war of aggression against other nations, or initiation of war in violation of treaties, agreements or assurances or otherwise in violation of international law.
> d. Entering into a common plan or conspiracy aimed at domination over other nations, which plan or conspiracy involved or was reasonably likely to involve in its execution all or any of the above crimes.[136]

The Soviet delegation immediately lodged its objection to placing aggression only in third place on the list, which – in their opinion – failed to denote its fundamental significance. The Soviets also protested against distinguishing between domination and aggression.[137] The British delegation reacted swiftly, proposing on the same day to move aggression to first on the list, and reformulating it to read:

> a. Initiation of a war of aggression or participating in the waging of war of preparing for war in violation of treaties, agreements or aimed at the domination of one nation over other nations and carried out by the European Axis Powers.[138]

The Americans responded with a draft in which the introduction to the catalogue of crimes falling under the jurisdiction of the tribunal stated also that it would have the power and jurisdiction to hear, try and determine charges of crimes against only those who acted in aid of the European Axis powers. As for the crimes themselves, the list opened with:

> a. Initiation of a war of aggression; or initiation of a war in violation of treaties, agreements and assurances, or otherwise in violation of International Law; or participating in a common plan or conspiracy aimed at the domination of one nation over other nations to be carried out by means of any such war ...[139]

In the comments to this draft, the Americans clarified that the tribunal's jurisdiction was limited only to perpetrators from the European Axis powers, but that the definition of the crime itself may not point to the perpetrator.[140]

Eventually, after a debate, the American delegation proposed that the tribunal should have jurisdiction over the crime of war, understood as follows:

> ... planning, preparation, initiation or waging of a war of aggression, or a war in violation of any international treaty, agreement or assurances, or in particular, of the General Treaty for the Renunciation of War, or participation in a common plan or conspiracy for the accomplishment of any of the foregoing [that is, war crimes, crimes against humanity – author].[141]

At Nikitchenko's motion, the name of the crime was changed to 'crime against peace'.[142] Once that was agreed on, consensus had finally been reached.

Eventually, the London Agreement of 8 August 1945 (Agreement by the Government of the United States of America, the Provisional Government of the French Republic, the Government of the United Kingdom of Great Britain and Northern Ireland and the Government of the Union of Soviet Socialist Republics for the Prosecution and Punishment of the Major War Criminals of the European Axis), to which the Charter of the International Military Tribunal was annexed, listed – beside war crimes and crimes against humanity – at the top position 'crimes against peace', defined as follows:

> ... planning, preparation, initiation or waging of a war of aggression, or a war in violation of international treaties, agreements or assurances, or participation in a common plan or conspiracy for the accomplishment of any of the foregoing.[143]

Under the charter, the tribunal was to have the power to try to punish the major war criminals of the European Axis countries who, acting in the interests of the European Axis countries, whether as individuals or as members of organisations, committed crimes against peace, war crimes or crimes against humanity.

Nineteen allied states signed the London Agreement.[144] These signatory states had no impact on the content of the agreement, and practically no impact on the proceedings of the Nuremberg Trial. However, their accession to the agreement was interpreted as general consent to the ideas expressed therein,[145] making the agreement – as Jackson said in his opening statement, 'an organic act which represents the wisdom, the sense of justice, and the will of nineteen governments, representing an overwhelming majority of all civilized people'.[146]

In terms of material jurisdiction, the French delegation was satisfied with the wording of the tribunal's statute, as it made reference to existing agreements, thus undermining any criticism that it was retroactive.[147] The American delegation, on the other hand, had been successful at persuading the other allies to make an attempt to judge the crime of aggression.[148] In his statement opening the Nuremberg Trial, Jackson stated, however, that a weakness of the charter consisted in not defining aggressive war.[149] He noted that one of the most authoritative sources of international law on this subject was the Convention for the Definition of Aggression signed at London in 1933, and he invoked the definition, with the exception of the act of aggression consisting in a harbour blockade.[150] Jackson, however, was fully aware that in the case of Hitler and his supporters, he had hard evidence in his hands, in the form of written records of the conference of the German High Command which clearly spelled out the aggressive intentions of the Nazis.[151] Nikitchenko's words were proven true: since it was evident that Germany had committed aggression, there was no need to define it. Given the evidence held by the prosecution, each and every test would lead to the Nazi actions being classified as aggression.[152]

As for aggression itself, the statute of the tribunal contains no definition of it. Instead, it relies on a norm of non-criminal character, as a normative element under international law.[153] However, it is quite obvious that the conference in London was by no means an appropriate venue for extensive analyses of aggression in the perspective of logic, psychology or theory. The participants of the conference had a clear political objective to achieve, and their task consisted in finding a way of by-passing the restriction of international law.[154] They were expected to work out a legal framework for defeating 'world gangsterism'[155] and not to codify international law, and therefore they constructed the definition of crimes against peace with a particular set of defendants in mind.[156] Consequently, the outcome of the conference, in strictly legal terms, was unsatisfactory to say the least. Instead of a single crime of aggression (a focal point of so many prior debates), the statute specified the crimes against peace, of which one form was the war of aggression and another – a war in violation of international agreements. Moreover, the charter did not consider every act of aggression to be a crime; only aggressive war fell into that category. Yet the analysis of the charges filed at the Nuremberg Trial, and the final judgment made there, demonstrate that the prosecutors and the judges did not follow the London Agreement very closely.

In his opening statement, given on 21 November 1945 on behalf of the United States, Jackson said that international law had to be utilised 'to meet the greatest menace of our times – aggressive war',[157] and that an 'attack upon the peace of the world is the crime against international society'.[158] Jackson claimed that the nations of the world had renounced aggressive wars and wars in violation of treaties. However, it would be incorrect to assume that Jackson consistently made a distinction between these two types of wars. Later in the speech, he spoke of 'aggressive warfare in violation of treaty obligation'.[159] The other prosecutors, even when they attempted to distinguish between aggressive war and war in violation of treaties, did so only in order to focus, depending on the evidence they held, on proving either aggressive intent or treaty violation, to allow the court to conclude that the charge of aggressive war had been proven.[160] The indictment itself constitutes the ultimate proof of amalgamation of the two notions (of aggressive war and war in violation of treaties), since it specifies that the common plan or conspiracy embraced the commission of crimes against peace, in that the defendants 'planned, prepared, initiated, and waged wars of aggression, which were also wars in violation of international treaties, agreements, or assurances'.[161] Furthermore, in the analysis of the specific actions prosecuted under the charge of crimes against peace, the indictment lists the specific acts deemed to constitute aggressive war, and immediately thereafter makes a reference to the appendix, in which each of these wars is considered in the context of violations of specific treaties, agreements and assurances.[162]

The tribunal ignored the distinction between these two forms of crimes against peace. It decided that, since the defendants were charged with aggressive wars, it made no sense to consider each specific war in light of whether and how it violated specific agreements. However, for the sake of order and clarity, the tribunal pointed out the major treaties that Germany had violated.[163] It is therefore legitimate to conclude that the Nuremberg judgment makes no distinction between the crimes of 'aggressive war' and 'war in violation of international treaties'.[164] Notably, however, the tribunal made no attempt to define aggression: it merely reduced it to the specific acts of aggression.[165]

The tribunal, along with the prosecution, gave the crimes against peace a priority, considering them to be the supreme international crimes.[166] It emphasised that its charter reflected the international law as of the moment of the tribunal's establishment.[167] It made references to the Briand-Kellogg Pact, the draft of the Treaty of Mutual Assistance, the draft Protocol on Peaceful Conflict Resolution, the resolution of the Assembly of the League of Nations of 24 September 1927 (noting at the same time that Germany, Japan and Italy had all participated in the adoption of that resolution), the unanimous resolution of American states adopted in Havana on 18 February 1928 and to Article 227 of the Treaty of Versailles, invoking them in support of the view that aggressive war was not only illegal but also criminal in character.[168] Furthermore, the tribunal noted that since in the Briand-Kellogg Pact the states had renounced war as an instrument of national politics, war had become illegal under international law, and those who prepared for it and conducted it committed a crime.[169] Finally, the tribunal pointed out the following reasoning: the Hague Convention IV of 1907[170] forbade the use of certain methods of fighting, but provided for no sanctions; nonetheless, it was accepted that war crimes were punishable. In this light, it is even more clearly acceptable that the violation of norms of much greater importance than the Hague norms should be punishable too.[171] The tribunal relied both on legal and on moral arguments, as – in its own words – 'the prohibition of aggressive war [was] demanded by the conscience of the world'.[172]

Despite the tribunal's claim to the contrary, the charter was not a reflection of the customary law. It was in fact quite an important innovation.[173] It was therefore retroactive.[174] There were no grounds for invoking the Briand-Kellogg Pact, given that neither its makers nor the ILA, in its debates on the Pact at the meeting in Budapest in 1934, suggested any possibility of criminal responsibility for violating the pact.[175] Invoking the Hague Convention IV as evidence of there being a ban on aggressive war only goes to show regrettable misconception as to the difference between *ius in bello* and *ius ad bellum.* Moreover, the entirety of the debates on the criminality of aggressive war, undertaken during the Second World War, as well as the difficult London negotiations, are further indicators that it was absolutely impossible to ascertain, before the war, that customary law provided for criminal responsibility in case of violation of the ban on aggression. Customs are made by means of repeated practice, rather than a declaration of intentions. In this case, there was no such practice.[176]

Making aggression a crime was an American idea through and through. It was the representatives of President Roosevelt first, and President Truman later, who fought to have it included in the statute of the International Military Tribunal. In this context, it is important to remember the words Roosevelt spoke on 21 September 1939, after the aggression against Poland, in his Congressional address:

> You will all remember the long debates on the subject of what constitutes aggression, on the methods of determining who the aggressor might be, and, on who the aggressor in past wars had been. Academically this may have been instructive … But in the light of problems of today and tomorrow responsibility for acts of aggression is not concealed, and the writing of the record can safely be left to future historians.[177]

3.4 Statute and judgment of the International Military Tribunal for the Far East

During the London conference in January 1942, the Chinese delegate, Wunz King, had already argued in favour of considering the problem of court trials of war criminals not only in the context of Nazi perpetrators, but also with regard to perpetrators from Japan.[178] At China's request, on 10 May 1944 the United Nations War Crimes Commission established a Far Eastern Sub-Commission, operating out of Chunking, China.[179]

Just like in the case of Nazi Germany, the allied states issued declarations condemning the Japanese crimes[180] but, until 1945, the declarations invoked only the traditional war crimes.[181] Similarly, the Cairo Declaration of 1 December 1943, issued by China, Great Britain and the United States and announcing that Japanese aggression would be restrained and punished, had minor importance in this respect.[182] Its wording should be interpreted as a reiteration of the principle of a state's responsibility, and not individual responsibility.[183]

On 26 July 1945 China, Great Britain and the United States issued the Declaration of Potsdam, to which the Soviet Union acceded. The declaration defined the terms on which Japan was to surrender.[184] Under these terms, Japanese criminals would be heard and tried for the same crimes as the Nazis. However, the Declaration of Potsdam was adopted two weeks before the London Agreement was signed. It is therefore difficult to establish whether the declaration had unconditionally anticipated the responsibility of Japanese criminals for crimes against peace.[185] Japan accepted the terms of surrender on 2 September 1945, after which Americans began the arrests.[186]

On 19 January 1946, General Douglas MacArthur, as the Supreme Commander of the Allied Powers, proclaimed the Charter of the International Military Tribunal for the Far East, modelled after the statute of the International Military Tribunal.[187] Consultations on the scope of the charter only opened after its proclamation. Nonetheless, the option was offered to states to introduce amendments, and some states did indeed make suggestions, and the charter was amended accordingly.[188]

The Charter of the International Military Tribunal for the Far East stated that Japanese criminals would be charged with offences that included crimes against peace, that is:

> ... the planning, preparation, initiation or waging of a declared or undeclared war of aggression, or a war in violation of international law, treaties, agreements or assurances, or participation in a common plan or conspiracy for the accomplishment of any of the foregoing [that is, war crimes and crimes against humanity – author].[189]

In contrast to the London Agreement, it was stated clearly that aggressive war or war in violation of international agreements, regardless of whether or not it had been declared, is a crime against peace. Aggressive war, regardless of its name, was to be considered an international crime. This modification of the statute of the International Military Tribunal was intended to eliminate the option of the defendants claiming that they could not be responsible for an illegal war, given that they had never declared any war.[190]

Another important difference between the two tribunals' statutes was the stipulation that the Tokyo Tribunal only had the power to try to punish Far Eastern war criminals who were charged with offences which included crimes against peace.[191] Other crimes (war crimes and crimes against humanity) could only be tried if a given individual had also committed crimes against peace.

Just as Jackson had done, the chief prosecutor at the Tokyo trial, Joseph B. Keenan, attempted to define aggression. To this end, he relied on *Webster's New International Dictionary* (sic), where he found two definitions of the term:

> [a] first and unprovoked attack, or act of hostility; the first act of injury or first act leading to a war or a controversy; an assault; also the practice of attack or encroachment; as a war of aggression

and

> [a] nation that refuses to arbitrate or to accept an arbitration award, or any other peaceful method, in the settlement of a dispute but threatens to use force or to resort to war.[192]

Keenan also cited a passage from a book by James T. Shotwell, which read: '[t]he aggressor being that state which goes to war in violation of its pledge to submit the matter to peaceful settlement, having already agreed to do so'.[193]

The Tokyo Tribunal made no attempt to provide a universal definition of aggression. It only noted that, most certainly, unprovoked attacks prompted by the desire to seize the possessions of other nations qualified as aggression.[194] In terms of invoking the basis for charges of crimes against peace, the Tokyo judgment reiterated the relevant passages of the Nuremberg judgment. It was additionally emphasised that the Japanese should not claim to be surprised by such charges, since the emperor himself, on 10 August 1945, three weeks before Japan's surrender, had said: 'It is unbearable for me to see the brave and loyal fighting men of Japan disarmed. It is equally unbearable that others who have rendered me devoted service should now be punished as instigators of the war. Nevertheless, the time has come to bear the unbearable'.[195]

The judges, Radhabinod Pal, Henri Bernard and Bernard V. A. Röling, produced separate statements, devoting more thought to the criminalisation of aggression.[196] Pal's dissenting opinion was the most extensive of these. Pal claimed that wars could indeed be divided into just and unjust ones, but the division had no legal bearing.[197] He criticised the concept of international crimes, believing that no such category could exist in the absence of an international society.[198] He questioned the validity of the Briand-Kellogg Pact as the basis for criminalisation.[199] Röling, on the other hand, argued that aggressive war had not been considered a crime before the Second World War, but he also noted that the victorious states had the right, in order to ensure peace, to take certain precautionary measures, including a court procedure to punish those responsible for launching the war.[200] Bernard too questioned the legal basis for responsibility for crimes against peace invoked by the tribunal; he claimed that the punishability of aggression resulted out of natural law.[201] Bernard was opposed to the Tokyo Tribunal hearing charges related to the war Japan had conducted against China, the Soviet Union and Thailand, since, according to him, the Declaration of Potsdam only pertained to punishing those responsible for the crimes in the Pacific.[202]

The International Military Tribunal for the Far East, even though it focused just as much as the International Military Tribunal, or possibly even more, on the issue of crimes against peace, decided not to define aggression and not to pursue a deeper legal reasoning as to the basis of its criminalisation. The dissenting opinions to the Tokyo judgment, however, revealed the problems pertaining to the absence of a legal basis to charge defendants with the crime of aggression.

3.5 Peace treaties, occupation zone law and national law

Representatives of the states that occupied Germany, operating through the Allied Control Council for Germany, decided on 20 December 1945 to adopt the Control Council Law No 10, intended as a uniform basis for bringing to justice Nazi criminals in all occupation zones, and consequently to follow up on the provisions of the Moscow Declaration of 1943 and the London Agreement of 1945.[203] Control Council Law No 10 provided for the punishability of crimes against peace along with war crimes and crimes against humanity. Crimes against peace were defined as:

> Initiation of invasions of other countries and wars of aggression in violation of international laws and treaties, including but not limited to planning, preparation, initiation or waging a war of aggression, or a war of violation of international treaties, agreements or assurances, or participation in a common plan or conspiracy for the accomplishment of any of the foregoing.[204]

The key differences between the definition of Control Council Law No 10 and the definition contained in the Charter of the International Military Tribunal consisted in listing the invasion of other countries as an example of a crime against peace, and the explicit statement that actions other than those listed could also be considered a crime against peace.[205] Using the term 'invasion' was intended as a method of classifying the German operations towards Austria and Czechoslovakia as crimes against peace,[206] which was fully in line with previously issued orders of the military commanders of the three allied powers regarding the capture of war criminals.[207] Essentially, this amounted to extending the definition of the crime against peace to include the implementation of the national policy of the invading state by force, even if no actual combat took place.[208]

These modifications of the definition of crimes against peace bred further controversy. It was argued that the Control Council Law No 10 makes direct references to the London Agreement and the Moscow Declaration, and makes these documents an integral part thereof. Therefore, the tribunals that proceed on the basis of the Control Council Law No 10 may not interpret crimes against peace in a broader manner than it is provided for in the Charter of the International Military Tribunal.[209] However, it was also pointed out that the judgment of the International Military Tribunal was binding with regard to further trials of Nazi criminals, but only with respect to the facts.[210] It would be difficult to accept that between August and December 1945, customary law had changed much; it was, however, not impossible to reach different conclusions as to this law.[211]

The provisions of Control Council Law No 10 were implemented in the legal regulations in the American,[212] French[213] and eventually also British occupation zones.[214]

Of the bulk of the rulings resulting out of Control Council Law No 10, one judgment is of particular importance, namely the American military tribunal judgment in the so-called 'Ministries' trials, which stated that:

> ... the initiation of wars and invasions with their attendant horror and suffering has for centuries been universally recognized by all civilized nations as wrong, to be resorted to only as a last resort to remedy wrongs already or imminently to be inflicted. We hold that aggressive wars and invasions have, since time immemorial, been a violation of international law, even though specific sanctions were not provided.[215]. ... But even if history furnished no examples, we would have no hesitation in holding that those who prepare, plan, or initiate aggressive invasions, and wage aggressive wars; and those who knowingly participate therein are subject to trial, and if convicted, to punishment.[216]

Provisions concerning the capture and trial of persons guilty of crimes against peace were included in the peace treaties with Italy, Hungary, Bulgaria, Romania and Finland, signed on 10 February 1947 in Paris.[217] No peace treaty was signed with Germany, although the Treaty on the Final Settlement with Respect to Germany, signed on 12 September 1990, is generally believed to be its equivalent.[218] The treaty stipulates that acts tending to and undertaken with the intent to disturb the peaceful relations between nations, especially to prepare for aggressive war, are unconstitutional and a punishable offence.[219] The governments of the Federal Republic of Germany and the German Democratic Republic undertook that the united Germany would not use any of its weapons in violation of the Constitution or the Charter of the United Nations.

Few states attempted to implement the provisions of the London Agreement on crimes against peace into their legislation, possibly owing to the fact that few states had in their territories persons of such high calibre as the defendants in the Nuremberg Trial.[220] The Act on Punishing War Criminals, adopted by the Danish parliament on 12 July 1946, stipulated that the jurisdiction of military courts extends to all crimes specified in Article 6 of the Charter of the International Military Tribunal.[221] A similar approach was adopted in the Greek Constitutional Act of 1945.[222] Also Australian legislation on war crimes, by means of references to other documents, indirectly incorporated crimes against peace as a type of war crimes.[223] American military commissions in the Pacific area were authorised to conduct trials with respect to crimes against peace.[224] Legislation in Poland[225] and China[226] also included provisions on bringing Second World War criminals to trial for crimes against peace, but the judgments rendered on the basis of these provisions contribute little in the way of analysis of the legal grounds for the charge. It was generally believed that under the Nuremberg judgment, aggression was a crime and no further arguments were necessary on the issue.[227]

However, putting aside the legislation strictly connected with Second World War crimes, very few criminal codes provided for punishability of aggression.[228] Polish law is a clear exception in this regard. The Penal Code of 1932 already makes incitement to aggressive war (*wojna zaczepna*) punishable, under the condition that the legislation of the state towards which the incitement was directed considers this act punishable.[229] The Penal Code of the Polish Army of 1944 made it punishable publicly to incite aggressive war (*wojna zaborcza*).[230] The Penal Code of 1969 included no provisions pertaining to international war, although its draft version included a chapter on 'Crimes against peace, humanity and international relations', and Article 135 in this chapter pertained to crimes against peace.[231] However, the whole chapter was deleted from the draft, with the intention that a separate legal act should be devoted to international crimes. Such a legal act was, however, not adopted. Nonetheless, the act on the protection of peace of 29 December 1950 remained in force. Under this act, conducting war propaganda by means of the spoken or written word, the press, radio, film or otherwise, was considered a crime against peace.[232] In particular, a person committed a crime against peace if he or she induced or incited war, facilitated the dissemination of propaganda undertaken by those inciting war and actively opposed or made libellous or slanderous comments against the Peace Protectors Movement (*Ruch Obrońców Pokoju*).[233]

The Polish Penal Code of 1997, currently in force, penalises the crime of initiating or conducting a war of aggression.[234] It has, however, been noted that isolated acts of aggression undertaken by small forces, limited in space and time, will not be punishable, even if they are undertaken at the order of supreme state authorities.[235] Also, preparations for the initiation or conduct of aggressive war, as well as public incitement to initiate aggressive war, are all punishable under criminal law. In contrast, the law provides for no punishment for public incitement to further conduct of a war that has already been launched (*durante bello*).[236]

It may be interesting to consider how the issues relating to the crime of aggression have been regulated in Japan and Germany, that is, two states whose citizens were actually held responsible under such charges.

The Japanese Constitution of 3 November 1946 renounces war.[237] However, no criminal code provisions follow up on this general notion. The Japanese Penal Code of 1907, amended on numerous occasions, penalises the incitement to aggression, as well as attempts to commit this crime, and the preparation and conspiracy toward its commission, but only if this aggression is aimed against Japan.[238] It is punishable to prepare and conspire with the aim of initiating a war, but only if these actions are undertaken privately against another state.[239] It is also punishable to violate an order to maintain neutrality in a war between foreign states.[240] Together, these provisions may be read as precluding punishability in the scenario where the government decides to engage in aggression against other states, since such actions would not be aimed against Japan and would not be undertaken privately.

As for German law, the German Constitution of 1949 contains a ban on preparing for a war of aggression, and specifically on 'acts tending to and undertaken with intent to disturb the peaceful relations between nations, especially to prepare for a war of aggression'.[241] The constitution stipulates also that such acts should be punishable under the law.[242] The German Penal Code of 1998 includes, in its part on specific crimes, provisions on punishability of preparation for a war of aggression[243] and incitement towards a war of aggression.[244] Interestingly, there are no specific provisions banning the initiation of a war of aggression and its conduct. The term 'war of aggression' itself is not defined, and the practice of the German prosecuting authorities demonstrates that the notion tends to be interpreted politically by means of moral rather than legal arguments.[245] Also significant is the fact that the Act implementing a code of offences against international law of 26 June 2002 does not list the crime of aggression.[246]

3.6 Nuremberg principles and the Code of Crimes Against the Peace and Security of Mankind

With the United Nations conference in San Francisco approaching, the problem of responsibility for the crime of aggression was once again brought to the debate in the United Nations War Crimes Commission. Ecer proposed that the conference's attention should be focused on the issue of punishing war criminals. The commission indeed decided to draft a report and prepare recommendations for the states participating in the conference. The conference referred these documents to the executive committee, which was to investigate whether criminal sanctions should be stipulated for a threat of use of force, or actual use of force, by one state against another. In May 1945, the committee put forward the suggestion that any person remaining at the service of any state, if this person violated the principles of international law pertaining to the threat of use of force, or any other principles pertaining to the manner of conducting war, and in particular the duty to respect the commonly accepted principles of humanity, is individually responsible for his or her actions and may be brought to court and punished for these actions in front of civil and military courts of any state in whose hands this person remains.[247] The committee proposed a formula whereby the states would affirm that originally, the Briand-Kellogg Pact was intended to mean that a person who acts on behalf of a state, if this person violates the provisions of the pact, should be punished by a court, and the aggressions of the Axis states constituted a violation of the pact, and therefore the persons responsible for the aggression could be tried and punished for it.[248] These suggestions of the executive committee were received rather coldly by the conference. Only a general formula banning the use of force was included in the Charter of the United Nations. However, together with the establishment of the United Nations Organisation, the problems of criminal responsibility of individuals for a variety of acts, including the crime of aggression, came up for debate again.

The first Secretary-General of the United Nations, Trygve Lie, in his report to the General Assembly presented on 24 October 1946, said:

> In the interest of peace, and in order to protect mankind against future wars, it will be of decisive significance to have the principles which were employed in the Nurnberg trials, and according to which the German war criminals were sentenced, made a permanent part of the body of international law as quickly as possible.[249]

President Truman of the United States was of a similar opinion. In a letter to Justice Biddle he referred to the judge's suggestion that it would be useful to have a restatement and confirmation of the principles expressed in the Charter of the International Military Tribunal in the context of general codification of crimes against peace and security of humankind. Truman wrote that 'code of international criminal law to deal with all who wage aggressive war … deserves to be studied and weighed by the best legal minds the world over'.[250] He also stated he hoped that the United Nations would accept Justice Biddle's proposal. Americans moved beyond the letters too; they drafted a resolution[251] and the draft was accepted almost in its entirety by the General Assembly on 11 December 1946.[252] In the resolution, the General Assembly affirmed the principles of international law recognised by the

Charter of the Nuremberg Tribunal and the judgment of the tribunal, and directed the Committee on the Codification of International Law to treat as a matter of primary importance plans for the formulation, in the context of a general codification of offences against the peace and security of mankind, or of an international criminal code, of the principles recognised by the statute of the Nuremberg Tribunal and the judgment of the tribunal.

The Committee on the Codification of International Law decided that the General Assembly's request and recommendation only pertained to proposing a manner of formulating the principles, and thus the committee was not expected to investigate the content and scope of the Nuremberg principles, that being a task for the International Law Commission, the establishment of which the committee recommended to the General Assembly.[253] The committee suggested that the International Law Commission should be assigned the task of drafting a convention setting forth the principles of international law recognised by the Charter of the International Military Tribunal and sanctioned by the tribunal's judgment, as well as a detailed proposal for a general codification of the crimes against peace and security of mankind. This proposal should specify the position of the Nuremberg principles within such a system.[254] The committee noted that the work of the proposed commission should in no way interfere with the work on the draft international criminal code. The committee thus pointed to three areas of codification: the Nuremberg principles, a code of offences against peace and security of mankind and a statute of an international criminal court. Each of these areas necessarily had to include in its scope the issue of responsibility for the crime of aggression.

On 21 November 1947, the General Assembly decided to entrust to the International Law Commission the formulation of international law principles recognised in the charter and the judgment of the International Military Tribunal, and directed the commission to prepare a draft code of offences against peace and security of mankind, indicating clearly the place to be accorded therein to the Nuremberg principles.[255]

In the commission's debates on the formulation of the Nuremberg principles, a suggestion was made to define aggressive war and to list certain elements of the subjective and objective delineation of the crime of aggression.[256] However, the commission decided that, in light of the fact that neither the charter nor the judgment of the International Military Tribunal defined aggression, the commission was not supposed to tackle the task.[257] Eventually, the Nuremberg principles as adopted by the commission consisted in a literal repetition of selected provisions of the Charter of the International Military Tribunal. This solution may be perceived as disappointing. Certain progress was nonetheless achieved in comparison to the London Agreement. The crimes listed by the statute of the Nuremberg Tribunal was assigned a universal character, and thus the ban on committing crimes again peace was extended to apply to all states, rather than only to Nazi Germany and its Second World War allies.[258]

In its resolution of 12 December 1950, the General Assembly invited the governments of member states to furnish their observations with regard to the Nuremberg principles, and requested that the International Law Commission take account of the observation made both by the governments and by the delegations in the fifth session of the General Assembly.[259] Few states responded to the invitation, and fewer still offered actual insights as to the content of the principles.[260] Lebanon pointed out that listing wars in violation of treaties alongside aggressive wars was redundant, since any war in violation of the treaties qualified as aggressive war. France proposed that aggression should be defined as the use of force by one state against another, where the use of force is not in exercise of the right to legitimate self-defence of this state or another state, or collective action by a community of states. Norway requested emphasis on the notion that a crime against peace does not pertain to military personnel subordinated in their actions, and suggested a complete omission of the notion of participation in a conspiracy. Lebanon, on the other hand, argued that 'planning' should be eliminated, since it falls under the scope of conspiracy. The Assembly's Sixth Committee raised the issue of defining the conspiracy and possibly defining aggression, as well as criminalising war propaganda.

Work on the formulation of the Nuremberg principles proceeded alongside the work on the draft code of offences against peace and security of humankind, which was to include these principles. The commission decided to begin by approaching the states and inviting them to list the crimes they believed should be included in the code. The majority of the states responded by stating that they preferred to see the commission's proposal first.[261] France stressed that the code should most certainly include the crime against peace (war of aggression). The Netherlands presented a broad catalogue of crimes against peace, including the war of aggression and war in violation of international treaties, agreements and assurances, as well as actions committed in the territory of a state that violate the principles of international law or the national law of that state, and are directed against the sovereignty or territorial integrity of another state. Pakistan suggested that the term 'war' should be defined.

The commission appointed Jean Spiropoulos as its special *rapporteur*. In his first report, Spiropoulos proposed to include, as a crime against peace and security of mankind, the use of armed force in violation of international law and in particular, conducting aggressive war.[262] He noted that this approach extended beyond the Charter of the International Military Tribunal, since it criminalised any use of force in violation of international law, and not only a war of aggression or a war in violation of international agreements. Spiropoulos, however, listed war of aggression specifically, to put emphasis on the criminal nature of this gravest of crimes. This was Spiropoulos's attempt to contain the debate within the framework outlined by Article 2(4) of the Charter of the United Nations.[263] He believed that any attempt to define aggression would be a waste of time. Besides the use of armed force in violation of international law and in particular the waging of aggressive war, he proposed listing other crimes that fell within a broad definition of aggression, such as: invasion by armed gangs of the territory of another state; the fomenting, by whatever means, of civil strife in another state; organised terroristic activities carried out in another state; the violation of military clauses of international treaties defining the war potential of a state; and the annexation of territories in violation of international law.[264]

In line with Spiropoulos's vision, initially the members of the International Law Commission focused on the formulation of the ban on the use of force and selecting the terminology for the specification of other crimes. However, the persistence of Scelle, who claimed that a code of offences against peace and security of mankind was impossible without the crime of aggression, the final version of the catalogue of crimes included 'any act of aggression' in first place.[265] The version of the catalogue of offences against peace and security adopted by the commission in 1954 listed:

> (1) Any act of aggression, including the employment by the authorities of a State of armed force against another State for any purpose other than national or collective self-defence or in pursuance of a decision or recommendation of a competent organ of the United Nations.
> (2) Any threat by the authorities of a State to resort to an act of aggression against another State.
> (3) The preparation by the authorities of a State of the employment of armed force against another State for any purpose other than national or collective self-defence or in pursuance of a decision or recommendation of a competent organ of the United Nations.
> (4) The organization, or the encouragement of the organization, by the authorities of a State, of armed bands within its territory or any other territory for incursions into the territory of another State, or the toleration of the organization of such bands in its own territory, or the toleration of the use by such armed bands of its territory as a base of operations or as a point of departure for incursions into the territory of another State, as well as direct participation in or support of such incursions.
> (5) The undertaking or encouragement by the authorities of a State of activities calculated to foment civil strife in another State, or the toleration by the authorities of a State of organized activities calculated to foment civil strife in another State.
> (6) The undertaking or encouragement by the authorities of a State of terrorist activities in another State, or the toleration by the authorities of a State of organized activities calculated to carry out terrorist acts in another State.
> (7) Acts by the authorities of a State in violation of its obligations under a treaty which is designed to ensure international peace and security by means of restrictions or limitations on armaments, or on military training, or on fortifications, or of other restrictions of the same character.

(8) The annexation by the authorities of a State of territory belonging to another State, by means of acts contrary to international law.
(9) The intervention by the authorities of a State in the internal or external affairs of another State, by means of coercive measures of an economic or political character in order to force its will and thereby obtain advantages of any kind … .[266]

The catalogue appeared to be a mixture of general references to aggression (act of aggression, threat to resort to an act of aggression and preparation to do so) with listing of specific acts of aggression.[267] There was no general clause that would pull together all the acts that are listed, since neither aggression itself nor acts of aggression had been defined. The proposal lacked logic and coherence.[268] Despite its shortcomings, it was forwarded to the General Assembly who, in turn, decided that work on the code should be suspended until the Special Committee worked out a definition of aggression.[269]

Such definition of aggression was adopted by the General Assembly in 1974, but work on the code was not recommenced immediately thereafter. It was only in 1978 that the General Assembly invited the member states and international organisations to comment on the 1954 draft of the code,[270] and only in 1981 that the General Assembly asked the International Law Commission to proceed with work on the code, taking into account the progress in international law that had occurred since the previous attempts.[271]

In 1982, the International Law Commission appointed as its special reporter Doudou Thiam. His task was not easy: in the time since the first draft of the code, crimes other than aggression (such as apartheid and drug trafficking, for example) had increasingly become threats to peace and security of humankind. Further debate on the code could no longer focus solely on the crime of aggression. Aggression itself, however, could not be ignored either, and Resolution 3314 hardly made the commission's work easier in this respect. Members of the commission were divided into three camps. The first camp argued that the definition of aggression set out in the resolution must be strictly adhered to. The second camp believed that no definition of aggression was at all necessary. The third camp, with Thiam's support, attempted to generate a new definition specifically for the purposes of the code.[272] None of the solutions was satisfactory. Resolution 3314 could not be disregarded, but its definition had only served a political purpose and had only been adopted owing to its non-binding character. The only provision on responsibility in the 1974 resolution stipulated that a war of aggression was a crime against international peace and gave rise to international responsibility.[273] It was a literal restatement of the formulation used in the General Assembly's Resolution 2625 of 24 October 1970. Resolution 3314, however, failed to specify whether it referred to a state's responsibility only, or whether it extended to individual responsibility too. Moreover, the resolution defined aggression, and not aggressive war.[274]

In the debates on the code, it was always emphasised that for the purposes of criminal responsibility, a definition of aggression should be precise and complete. On the other hand, such a definition might not find acceptance among the member states.[275] Moreover, the commission paid a great deal of attention to the controversial issue of separating the ranges of competence, on the one hand, of the judges who were to rule on the guilt of those responsible for aggression and, on the other hand, of the Security Council, which ruled on the occurrence of aggression and which was free, under Resolution 3314, to consider acts other than those specified in the resolution as aggression. In the light of these limitations, the members of the commission had no illusions as to the possibility of arriving at a satisfactory definition of this crime in the code.

On 12 July 1991, the International Law Commission adopted a catalogue of crimes against peace and security of mankind, with a scope significantly exceeding the 1954 draft.[276] The catalogue included the crime of aggression as well as other crimes, eg the threat of aggression, intervention,[277] colonial domination and other forms of alien domination.[278] As for aggression, it was stated that individuals were responsible for acts of aggression, and the statement was followed by a restatement of the relevant provisions of Resolution 3314.[279] The threat of aggression was defined as declarations, communications, demonstrations of force or any other measures that would give good reasons to the government of a state to believe that aggression was being seriously contemplated against that state.[280]

The draft was generally criticised by the states. The negative reaction was hardly surprising, given the imprecise formulations it contained – owing to the lack of precision the draft failed to meet the fundamental criteria for criminal law regulations.[281] The principal criticism was directed at the penalisation of all types of aggression, including measures short of war, and at the relationship between the Security Council and the bodies that were to judge the crimes of aggression. It was argued that the literal incorporation of Resolution 3314 was inappropriate, since the resolution had been worded for political purposes and, consequently, its catalogue of acts of aggression was open-ended, violating the principle of *nullum crimen sine lege*. Further, the inclusion of the threat of aggression among the offences against peace and security of mankind was criticised, first owing to its overly general character, secondly, owing to the fact that it pertains to states rather than individuals and, thirdly, owing to the problem of penalising threats that did not materialise. Moreover, it was argued that punishability of a threat means that the punishment applies to a stage preceding an attempt at a crime, which is not advisable.

The final draft of the code, adopted by the commission in 1996,[282] still contains the crime of aggression, but omits the wording of Resolution 3314. It stipulates that an individual is responsible for the crime of aggression,[283] defined as active participation in or ordering the planning, preparation, initiation or waging of aggression committed by a state.[284] The threat of aggression was removed from the code.

The General Assembly, in its resolution of 16 December 1996, expressed its appreciation to the International Law Commission for the work it had accomplished, in particular for the completion of the final draft articles on the draft Code of Crimes against the Peace and Security of Mankind. It drew the attention of the states participating in the Preparatory Committee on the Establishment of an International Criminal Court to the relevance of the draft code to the work of the International Law Commission and invited the member states to comment on how they wished to proceed with regard to the code.[285]

In recapitulating the accomplishments of the International Law Commission in terms of codification of violations of international law, it must be stressed that the commission affirmed that aggression gives rise to individual criminal responsibility. The commission's failure lies in the fact that it decided to withhold a specification of what constitutes aggression, despite the option of literally citing Resolution 3314 or making a reference to it. What is penalised in the code is aggression, rather than specific acts of aggression or aggressive war. However, the comments to the code provided by the commission make it clear that the crime of aggression is based on the Charter of the International Military Tribunal, within such scope as it was interpreted and applied by the Nuremberg Tribunal,[286] which may be taken to suggest a narrow interpretation of the wording used by the commission. It is also clearly stated that aggression can only be committed by a state, and also that sufficiently grave violations of Article 2(4) of the Charter of the United Nations qualify as aggression. This comment is clearly a reference to the original idea of Spiropoulos of how aggression should be approached in the code. The code is not binding. However, as the International Criminal Tribunal for the former Yugoslavia ruled, it offers evidence of customary law; it may assist in explaining customary rules the content of which is uncertain or in the process of formulation; and it may point to the majority opinion of the lawyers who represent the biggest legal systems in the world.[287] The General Assembly resolution also suggests that the code drafted by the International Law Commission was intended as inspiration for the law-makers in charge of the statute of a permanent international criminal court.

3.7 The Statute of the International Criminal Court (ICC)

In May 1947, in the course of the work of the Committee on the Progressive Development of International Law and its Codification, Henri Donnedieu de Vabres pointed out that one of the problematic issues with the Nuremberg Tribunal was the fact that the panel only included judges representing the states that had prevailed in the war, and proposed to remedy this problem by establishing a permanent international criminal court.[288] However, the committee decided that, as it was not assigned the task of investigating the scope of the Nuremberg principles, it was clearly not supposed to contemplate the manner of the principles' implementation. However, in its final report, the committee suggested that for the implementation of the Nuremberg principles, as well as for the punishment of other international crimes, it might be advisable to establish an international criminal court.[289] The General Assembly made no references to this point when debating the committee's report.

The idea of establishing an international criminal court reappeared when the General Assembly adopted, on 9 December 1948, the Convention on the Prevention and Punishment of the Crime of Genocide, stipulating that the persons charged with genocide or any of the other acts enumerated in the convention should be tried by such international penal tribunal as may have jurisdiction with respect to those contracting parties which have accepted its jurisdiction.[290] Consequently, the General Assembly approached the International Law Commission with the request to assess the need to establish an international judicial authority to try not only the crime of genocide but also other cases placed under its jurisdiction by international treaties.[291] The General Assembly suggested, as a solution, the establishment of a criminal chamber by the International Court of Justice.

In June 1949, the commission appointed two *rapporteurs.* The first *rapporteur*, Alfaro, argued in favour of the need and possibility of establishing a permanent international court.[292] He claimed that such a court was necessary primarily with regard to the crime of aggression, but he was clear in saying that all crimes to be tried by the court must be defined.[293] The second *rapporteur*, Emil Sandström, admitted that establishing an international criminal court was possible, but considered the pros and cons of this solution and concluded that doing so was not advisable.[294] Many states, he explained, were opposed to the idea of a permanent criminal court, so a consensus as to its establishment would be difficult to achieve within a short timeframe. Furthermore, there was no mechanism to force states to surrender its citizens to the court, particularly in the case of an aggressor who prevailed in the war, and a judgment *in contumaciam* without enforcement would not serve its purpose at all.[295]

The commission accepted that establishing an international judicial authority was advisable and possible, but withheld a recommendation to establish a criminal chamber by the International Court of Justice. On 12 December 1950, the General Assembly appointed a committee with representatives of 17 states, and assigned to it the task of drafting a specific statute of an international criminal court.[296] The committee drafted the statute in 1951,[297] and presented a revised draft[298] after receiving comments from governments[299] in 1953. However, working separately on the draft code of offences against peace and security of mankind and the draft statute of the international criminal court made little sense,[300] since both projects were strictly interrelated. It is therefore not surprising that, once work on the code was suspended in 1954 until a definition of aggression was created, the General Assembly decided on 4 December 1954 to suspend work on the statute of the international criminal court too.[301] Also importantly, in the 1950s France was the only permanent member of the Security Council that was willing to adopt a statute of an international criminal court.

In the 1980s, when the efforts to draft a code of offences against peace and security of mankind were recommenced, the idea of establishing a court that could try individuals charged with these offences also made a comeback.[302] Work intensified when on 4 December 1989 the General Assembly (on the initiative of Trinidad and Tobago), after ignoring for a number of years the appeals of the International Law Commission, as it was discussing the issues of illegal drug trafficking and other transnational offences, approached the commission with the request to investigate, within the framework of drafting the code, the options for establishing a criminal court that would have jurisdiction over such offences.[303] The commission presented subsequent reports in 1992,[304] 1993[305] and 1994,[306] proposing the establishment of a permanent international criminal court with jurisdiction over offences specified in international conventions. However, the problem remained of crimes under general international law, not defined in international conventions, such as for example the crime of aggression. Initially the commission believed that the problems of aggression would be solved when the code of offences against peace and security of mankind came into force. For this reason, the final version of the statute adopted by the commission lists the crime of aggression among the violations of international law to fall under the jurisdiction of the tribunal. The last report of 1994 recommends to the General Assembly that a conference of plenipotentiaries should be convened in order to discuss the draft statute and prepare a convention establishing an international criminal court.[307]

On 9 December 1994, the General Assembly established an Ad Hoc Committee on the Establishment of an International Criminal Court. All United Nations member states, as well as member states of the specialised United Nations agendas, were invited to participate in the work of the committee.[308] The purpose of the committee was to examine the commission's draft of the statute, and taking the steps towards convening a diplomatic conference.

The Ad Hoc Committee, while debating the scope of the material jurisdiction of the court-to-be, also encountered the eternal problem of whether aggression should fall within this scope and whether it was at all possible to draft a definition of aggression appropriate in the context of criminal law. Another problem consisted in shaping the relations between the court and the Security Council, given the necessity to determine that aggression had in fact occurred before an individual could be charged with this crime.[309]

The General Assembly gave consideration to the recommendations of the Ad Hoc Committee and, on 11 December 1995, created the Preparatory Committee on the Establishment of an International Criminal Court to prepare a consolidated draft text for submission to a diplomatic conference.[310] Once again, the three traditional positions were represented within the

Preparatory Committee with regard to the crime of aggression.[311] The first one stipulated that the crime of aggression should be listed in the statute, and its definition should be drawn from the international documents already in existence. According to the second one, the crime of aggression should indeed be listed in the statute, but should be defined anew. In the third one, the crime of aggression should fall beyond the scope of the court's jurisdiction. The delegations undermined the significance of the Nuremberg precedent (it was 'lacking precision, restricted' and had an 'outdated approach') and of Resolution 3314 (it was 'inadequate for the needs of criminal law, imprecise and unclear'). There was also no consensus with regard to the formulation of the crime, that is, whether an abstract definition or a mixed one would be better, the latter one possibly modelled on the proposal of the International Law Commission of 1991. The disputes as to the various definitions of aggression followed exactly the same course as the disputes during the drafting of the definition of aggression in terms of states, or the debates on the code of offences against peace and security of mankind. Furthermore, there was no agreement as to whether aggression consists in the use of armed force only or whether the threat of use of armed force also qualifies; whether aggression only covers armed force or whether political force counts too; whether aggression must be directed against territorial integrity and political independence of a state or whether it could be directed against its sovereignty; and, finally, whether the use of armed force, in order to be qualified as aggression, must be in violation of the Charter of the United Nations, or whether it must also violate the customary international law. There were also proposals modelled on the Nuremberg solutions, that is, relying on undefined notions of aggressive war and war in violation of international agreements.[312]

The Working Group of the Preparatory Committee put forward two proposed versions of a general definition, accompanied by a catalogue of specific acts and also specifying the individuals that may be charged with aggression.[313] The first proposal was formulated in such a way that all disputed terms were placed in square brackets, thus revealing that there was no consensus with regard to any of the elements of the abstract definition of aggression, down to its very name ('crime of aggression' versus 'crime against peace'). The proposal is worth citing in its entirety, given how strikingly it illustrates the scale of the difficulties:

> [For the purpose of the present Statute, the crime [of aggression] [against peace] means any of the following acts committed by an individual [who is in a position of exercising control or capable of directing political/military action in a State]: (a) planning, (b) preparing, (c) ordering, (d) initiating, or (e) carrying out [an armed attack] [the use of armed force] [a war of aggression,] [a war of aggression, or a war in violation of international treaties, agreements or assurances, or participation in a common plan or conspiracy for the accomplishment of any of the foregoing] by a

> State against the [sovereignty,] territorial integrity [or political independence] of another State [when this] [armed attack] [use of force] [is] [in contravention of the Charter of the United Nations] [[in contravention of the Charter of the United Nations as determined by the Security Council].]

This proposal provided yet further evidence of the logical shortcomings of attempting to define aggression by way of *ignotum per ignotum*. The definition relied on further undefined terms, such as 'armed attack' and 'war of aggression'. In terms of positives, the role of the Security Council in determining aggression was specified in the proposal.

The second proposal was somewhat clearer, and it defined aggression as follows:

> [For the purposes of this Statute, the crime of aggression is committed by a person who is in a position of exercising control or capable of directing political/military actions in his State, against another State, in contravention to the Charter of the United Nations, by resorting to armed force, to threaten or violate the sovereignty, territorial integrity or political independence of that State.] [2. [Acts constituting [aggression] [armed attack] include the following:] [Provided that the acts concerned or their consequences are of sufficient gravity, acts constituting aggression [are] [include] the following:] (a) the invasion or attack by the armed forces of a State of the territory of another State, or any military occupation, however temporary, resulting from such invasion or attack, or any annexation by the use of force of the territory of another State or part thereof; (b) bombardment by the armed forces of a State against the territory of another State [, or the use of any weapons by a State against the territory of another State]; (c) the blockade of the ports or coasts of a State by the armed forces of another State; (d) an attack by the armed forces of a State on the land, sea or air forces, or marine and air fleets of another State; (e) the use of armed forces of one State which are within the territory of another State with the agreement of the receiving State in contravention of the conditions provided for in the agreement, or any extension of their presence in such territory beyond their termination of the agreement; (f) the action of a State in allowing its territory, which it has placed at the disposal of another State, to be used by that other State for perpetrating an act of aggression against a third State; (g) the sending by or on behalf of a State of armed bands, groups, irregulars or mercenaries, which carry out acts of armed force against another State of such gravity as to amount to the acts listed above, or its substantial involvement therein.]]

The comments provided for the second proposal do not specify whether the list of acts of aggression is open-ended or whether it constitutes a full catalogue thereof; it is only specified that these acts of aggression should be punishable by appropriately grave sanctions. However, no recommendation has been included whether this refers to the scale of destruction, scale of force used, gravity of the violation, or the impression the act made on the international community.[314]

At the request of Germany in particular, the Preparatory Committee drafted a third proposal of the definition, worded as follows:

> [1. For the purpose of the present Statute [and subject to a determination by the Security Council referred to in article 10, paragraph 2, regarding the act of a State], the crime of aggression means either of the following acts committed by an individual who is in a position of exercising control or capable of directing the political or military action of a State: (a) initiating, or (b) carrying out an armed attack directed by a State against the territorial integrity or political independence of another State when this armed attack was undertaken in [manifest] contravention of the Charter of the United Nations [with the object or result of establishing a [military] occupation of, or annexing, the territory of such other State or part thereof by armed forces of the attacking State.] 2. Where an attack under paragraph 1 has been committed, the (a) planning, (b) preparing, or (c) ordering thereof by an individual who is in a position of exercising control or capable of directing the political or military action of a State shall also constitute a crime of aggression.][315]

The scope of powers of the Security Council was the major problem in this approach. It was also emphasised that the court would only investigate manifest contraventions of the Charter of the United Nations. It was slowly becoming clear that the problem of aggression consisted not only in identifying the material components of the definition of aggression, but also in determining the conditions under which jurisdiction with regard to this crime could be exercised. Moreover, the third proposal of the Preparatory Committee made references to the object and result of the actions of the aggressor.

The Preparatory Committee decided to include all three versions of the definition in the consolidated draft of the statute.[316] It was clear that the definition of aggression would be the most difficult aspect of the conference convened in order to establish the ICC.[317]

On 17 December 1996, the General Assembly summoned for the year 1998 a diplomatic conference with view to adopting a convention establishing the ICC.[318] During the conference, many states voted in favour of including the crime of aggression within the jurisdiction of the court.[319] Consequently, the conference was forced to deal with the issue of its definition. Only the United States, Israel, Morocco and Turkey were completely opposed to the court having jurisdiction over the crime of aggression. These states insisted that aggression was a crime committed by states rather than individuals, and only the Security Council was authorised to decide in regard to it.[320]

Despite the suggestions of many states that the court should have jurisdiction over the crime of aggression, the negotiators had great difficulties in reaching consensus with regard to its definition. The states that supported the inclusion of aggression in the court's jurisdiction stipulated two conditions that were very difficult to satisfy, namely: that an acceptable definition of aggression be achieved, and that the powers of the Security Council be preserved intact.[321]

As a consequence of the impossibility of reaching consensus, a number of the states were willing to give up on including aggression among the crimes under the court's jurisdiction.[322] On 6 July 1998, the Conference Bureau proposed to choose one of two options: either to adopt the third proposal of the Preparatory Committee (of course without the brackets), since it was most popular among the states, even if somewhat unsatisfactory, or to give up on including the crime of aggression in the statute.[323] Then a sudden turn of events occurred: the debate opened again as to whether the crime of aggression should at all be included in the statute, even though after the second round of negotiations, only New Zealand, Liechtenstein, Brazil, Mali, Togo, the United States and the Netherlands were in favour of eliminating aggression.[324] All attempts had been abandoned to define the crime of aggression. The negotiations focused on leaving the crime of aggression in the statute, considering that the conference was drawing to a close.[325] On 10 July 1998, the Conference Bureau announced that the crime of aggression would be included in the statute on the condition that by 13 July all relevant provisions could be agreed on. Should this prove impossible, the bureau proposed to leave aggression out of the statute and explained that the court's jurisdiction could be extended in the future to cover aggression, by means of an additional protocol or an amendment adopted at a review conference.[326] However, many states found this solution unsatisfactory and provided the impetus necessary to adopt, on the last day of the conference, a resolution stipulating that the Preparatory Commission was to draft a proposal of the definition and elements of the crime of aggression, as well as the conditions of exercising jurisdiction over this crime by the ICC. This proposal was then to be presented to the Assembly of states parties at a review conference.[327]

Eventually, the statute of the ICC lists aggression, in its Article 5(1), as one of the four most serious crimes of concern to the international community with respect to which the Court has jurisdiction.[328] Article 5(2) adds that the ICC is to exercise jurisdiction over the crime of aggression once a provision is adopted defining the crime and setting out the conditions under which the ICC is to exercise jurisdiction with respect to it. The only other instruction is that such a provision must be consistent with the relevant provisions of the Charter of the United Nations; this points to an intention to preserve for the future a strong position for the Security Council.[329]

The statute's provision is thus an example of a codified *impasse*.[330] The terms that have been used are general enough to leave room for agreement.[331]

In effect, until the relevant amending provision comes into force, the crime of aggression is de facto not included in the statute.[332]

3.8 The Kampala Conference

The Preparatory Commission began its work in February 1999. In addition to the problem of the formulation of the crime of aggression, its tasks included drafting a proposal of procedural rules and rules of evidence, specifying the elements of the particular crimes, drafting an agreement on the relations between the ICC and the United Nations, laying the foundations for the agreement on the seat of the ICC (to be negotiated between the host country and the ICC), as well as drafting the financial regulations, agreements on privileges and immunities of the ICC, the budget for the first financial year, and the rules of proceedings at the Assembly of states parties. The commission first focused on drafting the documents that were not related to the definition of aggression, since they were essential to the ICC's functioning.[333]

However, at the initiative of Bahrain, Iraq, Lebanon, Libya, Oman, Sudan, Syria and Yemen, the problem of the definition of aggression was again entered onto the agenda, and states began to file their proposals for a definition of aggression.[334] The Coordinator of the Working Group on the Crime of Aggression prepared a consolidated text in which he collected all the proposals that had been put forward.[335] The document served as a recapitulation of the negotiations thus far, and included all the controversial terms.

The states adopted the constructive approach of affirming the necessity to find a methodology in working on the provisions concerning aggression.[336] Italy suggested a topic-based approach: identifying the fundamental controversies and analysing them one by one, so as to avoid the same well known statements.[337] Consequently, the coordinator presented a preliminary list of issues to consider, including the following problems: should the definition be abstract in nature; should it include a list of the acts of aggression; to what extent is Resolution 3314 useful in this regard; what role should the Security Council play in determining aggression; to what extent should the principle of complementarity apply, as well as the principle of *ne bis in idem* and other principles of international criminal law; what should be the investigation procedure in cases of aggression; what regulations should apply to the issue of access to documents that have relevance for a state's security; what rules should apply to international cooperation and judicial assistance?[338]

As the states began to file their comments and proposals, it became clear that the topical organisation of the debate indeed allowed it to become better organised.[339] It also allowed the Coordinator to draft a discussion paper on the specific issues equivalent to the specific elements of the definition of aggression.[340] The document entitled *Historical Review of Developments Relating to Aggression*, prepared by the Secretariat, summarising the rulings so far, proved exceedingly useful.[341] At the same time, debates continued with regard to the elements of the crime.[342]

In September 2002, the Assembly of States Parties appointed a Special Working Group on the Crime of Aggression. Participation in the Group was open to any member states of the United Nations and any member states of the UN agencies, as well as member states of the International Atomic Energy Agency. Subsequently, progress on the formulation of aggression in the statute of the ICC gained momentum.[343] Importantly, in February 2003, the Assembly of States Parties decided that the special working group was to meet at the annual meeting of the Assembly of States Parties, starting with the second session in 2003, and that two to three meetings of the Assembly of States Parties during its annual sessions should be devoted to the issue of aggression.[344] The Assembly of States Parties noted that the special working group was permitted to meet between sessions, but would have to obtain financing for this purpose from one of the governments. Such meetings have became a regular occurrence (so-called Princeton Process), sponsored *inter alia* by Canada, Denmark, Finland, Germany, Lichtenstein, Mexico, the Netherlands, Norway, Sweden and Switzerland.

The first meetings of the working group, held parallel to the sessions of the Assembly, hardly encouraged optimism. For example, Cuba's proposal for the definition of aggression reopened once again the debate on whether aggression only applied to armed force or whether political and economic actions could be considered aggression.[345] However, at subsequent informal meetings, states decided to focus first on the issues directly related to aggression, without working on the definition itself. Once the atmosphere of trust was created, the states were to resume their efforts on preparing the definition.[346] Eventually, the following tradition was worked out: actual negotiations proceeded during the informal sessions,[347] while the formal sessions were devoted to discussing the results of the informal ones, as well as to debating the subsequent discussion papers drafted by the coordinator to summarise the results of the negotiations up to that point.[348] In the course of the group's work, it also appeared that the so-called non-papers on selected issues (such as the conditions for exercising jurisdiction, or acts of aggression of states) were very useful.[349]

The topical focus of the meetings was on the following issues: jurisdiction *ratione temporis* of the court with regard to the crime of aggression; placement of the provisions on aggression in the statute of the ICC; adjustment of the wording of specific provisions in the case of actual extension of the court's jurisdiction to cover the crime of aggression; the application of the principle of complementarity, as well as the principle of *ne bis in idem* and other principles of international criminal law with regard to the crime of aggression (including the problem of responsibility of supervisors and acting under orders); the procedure for adopting amendments regarding the crime of aggression; forms of participation in the crime of aggression; and application of provisions on state secrets. A great deal of time was devoted to considerations of whether it was necessary to determine aggression before the court investigated a given crime, and what body would be authorised to determine aggression. Another heavily debated issue was how to ensure the rights of the accused before an external authority. The form of the definition was also discussed, that is, whether it should be abstract or mixed, with a listing of specific acts of aggression, and whether (and how) Resolution 3314 should be referenced. Moreover, the wording of the acts of aggression committed by the state was debated (whether the terms ' use of force', 'armed attack', 'act of aggression', or 'use of armed force' should be used) as well as the qualification of a state's actions as, for example, a grave violation of the Charter of the United Nations, or the option to limit the court's jurisdiction only to aggressive war. Consideration was given to the issue of objects and results of acts of aggression, and to broadening the definition to include the crimes of attempted aggression and threats of aggression. Elements of the crime were also listed, since it was agreed to codify them as soon as possible, preferably together with the definition of aggression. There were also proposals to grant the Security Council a 'red light' privilege, which would allow it permanently to preclude the investigation of a given case of aggression by the court. Finally, the principle of territoriality in the context of the crime of aggression was also debated.

After years of work, at the last formal session of the group, in February 2009, the final version of the provisions on the crime of aggression was adopted, under the reservation that 'nothing was agreed until everything was agreed'.[350] The group agreed that Article 8 *bis* should be worded as follows:

1. For the purpose of this Statute, 'crime of aggression' means the planning, preparation, initiation or execution, by a person in a position effectively to exercise control over or to direct the political or military action of a State, of an act of aggression which, by its character, gravity and scale, constitutes a manifest violation of the Charter of the United Nations.
2. For the purpose of paragraph 1, 'act of aggression' means the use of armed force by a State against the sovereignty, territorial integrity or political independence of another State, or in any other manner inconsistent with the Charter of the United Nations. Any of the following acts, regardless of a declaration of war, shall, in accordance with United Nations General Assembly resolution 3314 (XXIX) of 14 December 1974, qualify as an act of aggression: ... [followed by a list of acts of aggression as it appears in Resolution 3314 – author].[351]

As evidenced by this wording, the final decision was made to define the crime of aggression by stating who was able to commit this crime, and by referencing the acts of aggression listed in Resolution 3314, while also introducing a threshold clause determining the manifest violation of the Charter of the United Nations.

On the other hand, the Special Working Group found itself unable to present to the review conference a final proposal with regard to the conditions of exercising jurisdiction by the court, and thus the informal meetings that followed were devoted to the elements of the crime and to the conditions for the exercise of jurisdiction.[352]

The revision conference took place from 31 May to 11 June 2010 in Kampala, Uganda. According to the opening remarks of president of the assembly, Christian Wenaweser, the crime of aggression was to be the 'central topic' of the entire conference.[353]

In the initial days of the conference, only the Special Working Group, headed by HRH Prince Zeid Ra'ad Zeid Al-Hussein of Jordan, focused on the amendments pertaining to the crime of aggression.[354] The report of the Special Working Group clearly demonstrates that, in principle, the definition of aggression was not particularly controversial.[355] Consequently, the Special Working Group passed the definition (in the wording cited above, finally drafted in February 2009) to the conference. Along with the definition, the groups forwarded a proposal of relevant amendments to Articles 9, 20 and 25 of the statute of the ICC, mostly technical in nature.[356] The group noted in its report that certain states suggested a necessity to specify with greater precision that actions intended to prevent war crimes, crimes against humanity or genocide do not constitute 'manifest violations of the UN Charter'. Other reservations included the argument that 'threshold of a manifest violation shall be deleted since any act of aggression manifestly violated the Charter' and that the definition 'would not reflect customary law'.[357] As a result, much as the definition drafted by the Special Working Group was lauded as a consensus, there was still the possibility that the debate on the specific elements of the definition would be reopened.

The report of the Special Working Group demonstrates also that there were no doubts as to the applicability of all three options of exercising jurisdiction by the ICC stipulated by Article 13 of the statute (state referral, Security Council referral, *proprio motu*) to the crime of aggression.[358] What was problematic was the determination as to how the ICC should proceed when the Security Council did not make a determination of an act of aggression. The draft Article 15 *bis* on the exercise of jurisdiction in case of state referral or *proprio motu* investigation proposed two solutions.[359] Alternative 1 read as follows:

> In the absence of such a determination, the Prosecutor may not proceed with the investigation in respect of a crime of aggression, [with the option of adding] unless the Security Council has, in a resolution adopted under Chapter VII of the Charter of the United Nations, requested the Prosecutor to proceed with the investigation in respect of a crime of aggression.

Alternative 2, on the other hand, read as follows:

> Where no such determination is made within [6] months after the date of notification, the Prosecutor may proceed with the investigation in respect

> of a crime of aggression provided that the Pre-Trial Chamber has authorized the commencement of the investigation in respect of a crime of aggression in accordance with the procedure contained in article 15.[360]

On top of these options, the Special Working Group noted that suggestions had been made to enhance the internal filter, eg by involving all judges of the Pre-Trial Division or by subjecting the decision of the Pre-Trial Chamber to an automatic appeals process. The issue that seemed to generate the greatest problems was the procedure under which the amendments were to be adopted, and thus whether there should be a requirement that the alleged aggressor state has accepted the ICC's active jurisdiction over this crime. In this regard, the Special Working Group presented to the review conference a wide range of possible solutions.[361] One option was to use the procedure stipulated in Article 121(4) or 121(5). Another option was to agree that all amendments could enter into force for the ICC immediately upon adoption by the review conference, in accordance with Article 5(2) of the statute, while entering into force for states parties one year after their respective ratification in accordance with Article 121(5) of the statute (consequently, the ICC could receive Security Council referrals in principle immediately after adoption, while *proprio motu* investigations and state referrals would depend on the necessary ratifications). A possible 'negative understanding' of the second sentence of the Article 121(5) was suggested; it would require acceptance of the amendments on aggression by the alleged aggressor state in order to be able to initiate proceedings on following a state referral or a *proprio motu* investigation. On the other hand, a 'positive understanding' of Article 121(5) of the statute was suggested too; as a consequence of this understanding, the acceptance by the alleged aggressor state would not be required. Furthermore, it was indicated that the procedures under Articles 121(4) and 121(5) could be combined. As a result, Article 121(5) of the statute would be applicable to the definition as well as to the provisions dealing with Security Council referrals. The exercise of jurisdiction based on Security Council referrals would thus begin one year after the deposit of the first instrument of ratification or acceptance. Once seven-eighths of states parties ratified the amendments on aggression, the remaining two jurisdictional 'triggers' (state party referral and *proprio motu* investigation) would enter into force for all states parties based on Article 121(4) of the statute. Suggestions were even made to the effect that the ICC should be able to proceed with investigations based on a state party referral or *proprio motu* investigations even before the entry into force for all states parties, namely with respect to states that had already ratified the amendments and thus consented to the ICC's exercise of jurisdiction.

Some states (the United States in particular)[362] tried to convince the conference participants that there was no consensus with regard to the definition of the crime, the jurisdictional filter, and when amendments enter into force.[363] Nonetheless, most states were ready for a compromise, and prepared to address the doubts regarding the amendments. No amendments were introduced to the draft Article 8 *bis*, that is, the definition of the crime of aggression, or the elements of the crime. However, to the annoyance of some states (eg Spain) caused by the last-minute nature of the attempts to polish the definition, the decision was made to adopt certain explanations regarding the definition, by means of so-called 'understandings'.[364]

The American negotiators proposed the following wording:

> It is understood that, consistent with the principles set forth in General Assembly, resolution 3314
>
> - only the most serious and dangerous forms of illegal use of force are considered to constitute aggression;
> - a determination whether an act of aggression has been committed requires consideration of all the circumstances of each particular case, including the purposes for which force was used and the gravity of the acts concerned and their consequences;
> - it is only a war of aggression that is a crime against international peace;
> - nothing in this resolution or the amendments set forth in Annex [1] should be interpreted or applied in any manner inconsistent with General Assembly resolution 3314, nor should they be construed, as in any way enlarging or diminishing the scope of the Charter of the United Nations, including its provisions concerning cases in which the use of force is unlawful.[365]

Furthermore, the Americans proposed to add emphasis to the effect that the amendments in regard to the crime of aggression do not constitute a statement under customary international law and that they define the crime of aggression solely for the purposes of the statute of the ICC. They also suggested the adoption of the following wording:

> ... an act cannot be considered to be a manifest violation of the United Nations Charter unless it would be objectively evident to any State conducing itself in the matter in accordance with normal practice and in good faith, and thus an act undertaken in connection with an effort to prevent the commission of any of the crimes contained in Articles 6, 7 or 8 of the Statute would not constitute an act of aggression ...

as well as:

> ... in determining whether an act of aggression is manifest all three components of character, gravity and scale must be sufficient to justify a 'manifest' determination.

Furthermore, the American delegation requested the addition of the passage:

> an act cannot be considered a manifest violation of the UN Charter absent showing that it was undertaken without the consent of the relevant state, was not taken in self-defence, and was not within an authorization provided by the UN Security Council.

Predictably enough, this wording proved to be unacceptable, if only because it reiterated issues that had long been closed, such as the use of the term 'war of aggression' or the requirement to consider the purposes of certain actions. It also relied on imprecise phrases ('normal practice') and repeated other phrases already included either in the statute of the ICC (eg Articles 10 and 17, as well as the preamble) or in the newly drafted Articles.[366] The American delegation openly explained that the purpose behind their proposals was to limit as far as possible the jurisdiction of the ICC and definitely to exclude humanitarian intervention from the scope of the definition.

The efforts of the German delegation were decisive in the success of the negotiations. The final wording of the Understandings was as follows:

> Domestic jurisdiction over the crime of aggression
> 4. It is understood that the amendments that address the definition of the act of aggression and the crime of aggression do so for the purpose of this Statute only. The amendments shall, in accordance with article 10 of the Rome Statute, not be interpreted as limiting or prejudicing in any way existing or developing rules of international law for purposes other than this Statute.
> 5. It is understood that the amendments shall not be interpreted as creating the right or obligation to exercise domestic jurisdiction with respect to an act of aggression committed by another State.
> Other understandings
> 6. It is understood that aggression is the most serious and dangerous form of the illegal use of force; and that a determination whether an act of aggression has been committed requires consideration of all the circumstances of each particular case, including the gravity of the acts concerned and their consequences, in accordance with the Charter of the United Nations.
> 7. It is understood that in establishing whether an act of aggression constitutes a manifest violation of the Charter of the United Nations, the three components of character, gravity and scale must be sufficient to justify a 'manifest' determination. No one component can be significant enough to satisfy the manifest standard by itself.[367]

The wording includes no references to purposes, but – in the opinion of Iran – the reference to 'consequences' of certain acts is equivalent to taking into consideration 'the purpose of the operation' in the definition.[368] In fact, at least in this respect, the understandings may be deemed superfluous: the necessity to pay due attention to the consequences of certain acts results from the general introduction to the elements of crimes, which under Article 9 of the Rome Statute once adopted by a two-thirds majority of the members of the Assembly of states parties assist the ICC in the interpretation and application of Articles 6, 7 and 8. The true problem with the understandings is that their status and legal significance are unclear, and therefore it is unclear whether the ICC is obliged to take them into account.[369]

As for the most heatedly debated issues, that is, the consequences of lack of determination, on the part of the Security Council, of a given situation as an act of aggression, as well as the manner of bringing the amendments into force, three documents were most helpful in that they demonstrated a far-reaching willingness to search for a compromise: the Argentine, Brazilian and Swiss Proposal (ABS) of 6 June 2010, the Canadian Proposal of 8 June 2010 and Slovenian Proposal of 8 June 2010.

Under the ABS proposal, in case of a Security Council referral, the prosecutor first ascertains whether the Security Council has made a determination of an act of aggression committed by a state concerned. If the Security Council has made such determination, the prosecutor may proceed with the investigation. If there is no determination, the prosecutor may not proceed, unless the Security Council asks the prosecutor to proceed pursuant to Chapter VII of the Charter of the United Nations. In case of a state referral or *proprio motu* investigation, the prosecutor 'shall first ascertain whether the Security Council has made a determination of an act of aggression committed by a State concerned'. Where the Security Council has made such a determination, the prosecutor may proceed, and where no such determination is made within six months after the date of notification by the prosecutor, the prosecutor must obtain an authorisation from the Pre-Trial Chamber.

The Canadian proposal was a variation of this mechanism (menu approach).[370] If there is no determination of an act of aggression by the Security Council, this proposal suggested that in order for the prosecutor to be able to initiate the investigation, in addition to the authorisation of the Pre-trial Chamber, it should also be necessary to obtain the consent from the state on whose territory the alleged offence occurred and the state(s) of nationality of the persons accused of the crime (alternative wording mentioned all state(s) concerned with the alleged crime of aggression). The focus in the Canadian version was thus more on securing the consent to the ICC's jurisdiction on the part of the state that might have been involved in the act of aggression, be it as victims or as perpetrators.

Slovenia, on the other hand, suggested the preservation of the Pre-Trial Chamber filter if the Security Council failed within six months to determine of an act of aggression. The commencement of proceedings would hinge on whether 'all state parties concerned with the alleged crime of aggression have deposited instruments of ratification or acceptance of the amendment on the crime of aggression'. If the states have not ratified and/or accepted the amendments, the prosecutor should readdress the possibility of the Security Council referral pursuant to Article 13(b) of the statute.

Following the ABS proposal, the states eventually decided to draft two separate articles, with Article 15 *bis* focusing solely on the exercise of jurisdiction by the ICC via state referral or *proprio motu* investigation by prosecutor, and Article 15 *ter* via Security Council referral. However, compromise as to the protocol for the failure on the part of the Security Council to determine whether or not an act of aggression had been committed was only reached on the last day of the conference. It was only on 11 June 2010 that the option to grant the Security Council the sole power to determine an act of aggression was finally rejected.

The final version of Article 15 *bis* 8 reads:

> Where no such determination is made within six months after the date of notification, the Prosecutor may proceed with the investigation in respect of a crime of aggression, provided that the Pre-Trial Division has authorized the commencement of the investigation in respect of a crime of aggression in accordance with the procedure contained in article 15, and the Security Council has not decided otherwise in accordance with article 16.

The filter was thus made even more restrictive, by means of requiring a decision not by the Pre-Trial Chamber but by the Pre-Trial Division.[371] It was further emphasised that the Security Council may, despite the authorisation by the Pre-Trial Division, suspend or stop proceedings under Article 16 of the statute. This, of course, is superfluous, but the purpose of the provision was to state very clearly the powers vested by the statute of the ICC in the Security Council in order to mollify the proponents of the notion that the Security Council should have very broad impact on the commencement and continuation of proceedings.

As for the exercise of jurisdiction over the crime of aggression in case of Security Council referral, the requirement to ascertain by the prosecutor whether the Security Council made a determination of an act of aggression committed by the state concerned, as well as the provisions on consequences of the determination of situation by Security Council, were removed from the earlier proposals. This was due for example to the fact that in case of Security Council referral, there is no risk that the Security Council (as opposed to the prosecutor) might have no interest in investigating a given situation, considering that it is the Security Council itself that forwards the case to the ICC, and such determination might negatively affect the ability of the Security Council to exercise its competences.[372] Therefore, in case of Security Council referral, the Security Council does not have to determine an act of aggression. It is sufficient for the Security Council to give the prosecutor the green light for the investigation.

However, the agreement on the choice of filter was largely dependent on finding the 'right formula for activation'.[373] That is what made the negotiations on the procedure of adoption and ratification of the amendments on the crime of aggression so difficult. It was this procedure that determined the scope of ICC's future jurisdiction over the crime of aggression, and whether the aggressor state must accept the relevant amendments. As noted by William Schabas, in this regard the states split into the global north (with a few exceptions such as Switzerland and Greece) that argued that the aggressor state had to accept the amendment, and the global south, for which the requirement of consent by the aggressor state was unacceptable.[374]

The ABS proposal suggested for the amendments on state referral and *proprio motu* investigation an adoption procedure in line with Article 121(4), and for the amendments on Security Council referral in line with Article 121(5). As a result, the amendments on state referral and *proprio motu* investigation would come into force relatively late. On the other hand, once they are binding, the ICC would have jurisdiction over the crime of aggression regardless of the consent of the alleged aggressor. Unsurprisingly, this proposal met with 'mixed reactions' from the global north.[375] Slovenia's suggestion was as follows: after ratification by seven-eighths of the United Nations, the Secretary-General should convene a review conference to consider the applicability of the amendment on crime of aggression. Clearly the approach to the adoption procedure (as well as the revisions) was very creative: it was an attempt to produce a new *sui generis* procedure for adopting the amendments, which would in the process undermine the Rome conference consensus and the coherence of the solution agreed upon there. Finally, Canada, in its proposal in response to the expectations of the global north, emphasised the principle of state consent, supplemented with elements of reciprocity.[376]

As it turned out, the crucial element in overcoming the scepticism towards the amendments on aggression was the suggestion of delay in their effective date (already included in the joint ABS/Canada proposal), their revision after the lapse of a specific period and maximum limitation of the ICC's jurisdiction with regard to states that do not ratify the amendments and/or are not parties to the statute, as stated for example in the president's non-papers of 10 June and 11 June 2010.[377] Consequently, the final draft of the resolution lists many restrictions of the ICC's jurisdiction, some of which are essentially repeated (that is, the combination of the opt-out procedure in Article 121(5) with the option to submit an opt-out declaration).

The final version of the resolution states that the adoption of the amendments occurs in accordance with Article 5(2) of the Rome Statute, and their entry into force – in accordance with Article 121(5). Furthermore, Articles 15 *bis* and *ter* 2 stipulate that the ICC 'may exercise jurisdiction only with respect to crimes of aggression committed one year after the ratification or acceptance of the amendments by thirty States Parties'. In paragraph 3 of the above-mentioned Articles, it is pointed out that the ICC will exercise jurisdiction over the crime of aggression subject to a decision to be taken after 1 January 2017 by the same majority of states parties as is required for the adoption of an amendment to the statute.[378] Finally, preamble (4) declares that a review of the amendments on the crime of aggression will take place seven years after the beginning of the ICC's exercise of jurisdiction.

In the opinion of Christian Wenaweser, the Kampala consensus on activation of amendments was achieved not so much owing to the to delay but rather as a consequence of the option available under Article 15 *bis* 4 to lodge (prior to ratification or acceptance) a declaration that a state party does not accept jurisdiction of the ICC over a crime of aggression, as well as the clear mention in Article 15 *bis* 5 that 'in respect of a State that is not a party to this Statute, the Court shall not exercise its jurisdiction over the crime of aggression when committed by that State's nationals or on its territory'.[379] A case of an aggressor state which did not accept the amendments will only be able to proceed on a Security Council referral. Even with regard to such a Security Council referral, the ICC may exercise jurisdiction only with respect to crimes of aggression committed after a decision in accordance with Article 15 *ter* 3 is taken, that is, after a relevant decision is made by the Assembly in 2017 or later, as well as one year after the ratification or acceptance of the amendments by 30 states parties, should it take place later than the Assembly's decision. This principle also applies in case of state party referral and *proprio motu* investigation by the prosecutor.

Despite incorporating these restrictions into the proposed resolution, its success was not a safe bet.[380] There was a risk that the United Kingdom and France might demand a vote, which would make the future of the resolution highly uncertain (many delegations had left before the end of the conference, and under Article 121(3) the adoption of an amendment on which consensus cannot be reached requires a two-thirds majority of states parties). On the other hand, these two states were rather unwilling to stand alone blocking this 'historic agreement'. Surprisingly, it was Japan that lodged a statement just before the adoption of the resolution. In the statement, it expressed its 'serious doubt as to the legal integrity of the amendment procedure', leading to 'undermining of the credibility of the Rome Statute and the whole system it represents'.[381] Japan could not accept a situation where a state party surrounded by non-states parties is to adopt an amendment which 'unjustifiably solidifies blanket and automatic impunity of nationals of non-State Parties'. Despite its reservations, Japan decided not to 'stand in the way of a consensus'. The resolution was adopted formally on 11 June 2010 (in practice, on 12 June 2010; on 11 June at midnight the clocks were stopped) by a popular consensus. It consists of a preamble, Annex I listing the amendments to the statute (Article 8 *bis*, Articles 15 *bis* and *ter*, Article 25(3) *bis*, the new version of Article 9(1) the new *chapeau* of Article 20(3), Annex II listing the amendments to elements of crimes and Annex III with understandings regarding the amendments).

It is difficult to assess whether the solution that was eventually adopted (especially as regards the procedure for the amendments' entry into force) still qualifies as a compromise, or whether it comes dangerously close to a farce.[382] The ICC's jurisdiction over the crime of aggression has not been decided in a final manner. The debate was simply postponed by another seven years. It is not clear whether upon the lapse of this period a 'regular' vote at the Assembly will be sufficient, or whether another review conference will have to be convened.[383] The United Kingdom noted, probably with satisfaction, that it 'looks forward to continuing the discussion of these issues, whether in 2017 or thereafter'. The discussion is certainly not going to be easy, as evidenced by some of the statements in explanation of the position after the adoption of resolutions that have already been lodged.[384] In its statement, France noted that it decided 'not to oppose the consensus, despite the fact that it cannot associate itself with this draft text as it disregards the relevant provisions of the Charter of the United Nations enshrined in article 5 of the Rome Statute'. France went on to explain that it could not accept the solution of Article 15 *bis* 8, which allows the proceedings to go on in spite of the absence of the Security Council's determination of an act of aggression. In the opinion of France, this is a violation of the Charter of the United Nations, since only the Security Council has the power to determine an act of aggression. The United Kingdom and the observer states (China, Russia and the United States) have expressed similar opinions. In effect, all permanent members of the Security Council oppose the solution adopted at the conference – yet cooperation with exactly these five states is a *sine qua non* condition of the ICC's effectiveness.

Japan noted once again that it found the procedure for adoption of the amendments unacceptable, because 'Article 5, paragraph 2, is invoked as the basis with respect to "amendment", whereas article 121, paragraph 5, is invoked as the basis with respect to "entry into force"'. Japan went on to criticise strongly this approach as 'cherry picking', leading to the 'suicide of legal integrity'.

Cuba, Iran and Israel in their statements attempted to undermine the consensus surrounding the definition of aggression. They argued that the definition should be generic and refer not only to the use of armed force by a state, but also other 'forms of aggression that may also violate the sovereignty, territorial integrity or political independence of another State' (Cuba). Iran questioned the decision to use Assembly Resolution 3314 of 1974 as the basis of the definition, and pointed out its 'ambiguity and lack of sufficient legal clarity'.

Clearly, the states gathered at the review conference theoretically accomplished what the conference establishing the ICC required them to do, that is, to adopt a definition of the crime of aggression and agree the conditions of the exercise of jurisdiction over the crime. However, immediately thereafter, the states made a decision that precluded any judgment on the charge of aggression for the next eight years. The first states to ratify the amendment on the crime of aggression were Lichtenstein (8 May 2012), Samoa (25 September 2012), Trinidad and Tobago (13 November 2012), Luxembourg (15 January 2013), Estonia (27 March 2013), Germany (3 June 2013) and Botswana (4 June 2013).

3.9 Conclusions

Aggression was penalised for the first time under the London Agreement of 1945, and under the Charter of the International Military Tribunal that was attached thereto. It was an absolute novelty. At the beginning of the Second World War, none of the four states that later negotiated the London Agreement claimed that aggression was criminally punishable (perhaps with the exception of the Soviet Union, which used the issue for propaganda purposes). Moreover, even during the negotiations of the Charter of the International Military Tribunal, only the United States argued that aggressive war was a crime. Even legal theorists rarely argued during the Second World War that those guilty of aggression should be tried and punished.

The Charter of the International Military Tribunal, much as it constituted a major break-through, had two significant flaws. First, it contained no definition of aggression. Secondly, the crimes it listed were applicable only to citizens of Nazi Germany and its allies.[385] The statutes of the International Military Tribunal and of the International Military Tribunal for the Far East were drafted with a highly political and very specific goal in mind. Therefore, the definitions of crimes against peace included in them were, from a criminal law perspective, drastically imprecise.[386] They were a clear expression of the attitude of 'we may not know what aggression is, but we do know that Germany and Japan committed it'.[387]

It was not until the work began in the International Law Commission on the Nuremberg principles and the code of offences against peace and security of mankind that it was affirmed that the ban on the crime against peace (crime of aggression) applied to citizens of all states, and not only of Germany, Japan and their allies. However, even the cooperation between the most outstanding lawyers specialising in international law failed to produce a result in the form of a precise definition of the crime of aggression. It was as if there was a presumption that aggression was the type of crime that would simply be recognised once it occurred.[388] However, the resolutions of the International Law Commission as well as the resolutions of the General Assembly of the United Nations were not legally binding. Even the binding status of the often-cited Nuremberg principles as universal international law is not certain.[389]

Few states decided to adopt legislation that would penalise the crime against peace committed by the Second World War aggressors. It is therefore not surprising that even fewer states implemented criminal codes that provided for the punishability of aggression directed against another state.

It is interesting that in the 1990s, when the Security Council established *ad hoc* courts, such as the International Criminal Tribunal for the former Yugoslavia[390] and the International Criminal Tribunal for Rwanda,[391] it never extended the jurisdiction of these courts to the crime of aggression. This was hardly a random decision.[392] Including the crime of aggression within the statute of the International Criminal Tribunal for the former Yugoslavia might have been well founded.[393] It was, however, decided that the crime of aggression was political in nature[394] and, since in both cases the problem of aggression was not of primary importance, it was easier to ignore.[395]

The crime of aggression was included in the statute of the ICC, because it appeared after Nuremberg that it would be politically incorrect to place it outside the scope of the ICC's jurisdiction.[396] Furthermore, it would have been surprising if the list of crimes in the statute of the ICC differed from the list in the international criminal code, and the function of the Code of Offences against Peace and Security of Mankind was designed as such.[397] The review conference in June 2010 adopted a definition of the crime of aggression and the conditions of exercise of jurisdiction over it, thus fulfilling the original condition of extending the ICC's jurisdiction over this crime. However, the decision was made at the same time only actually to authorise the ICC to try cases of aggression after 1 January 2017 at the earliest.

Beyond the statute of the ICC, which is yet to enter into force, no universally binding document to date affirms the principle of punishability of aggression. For this reason, it is claimed that the formal extension of the ICC's jurisdiction to cover the crime of aggression proves that the ICC's statute is a result not of codification, but rather of legislation.[398]

Jackson said that new times had the right to create new customs.[399] He was well aware of the fact that there was no precedent pointing to the punishability of aggression.[400] What he was unwilling to accept was that customs arise out of many years of state practice. The Nuremberg and Tokyo trials were incidents rather than precedents,[401] exceptions rather than the rule,[402] and therefore no far-reaching conclusions should be reached on their basis.[403]

The International Law Commission argued that it would be a step backwards to preclude punishability of individual responsibility for aggression, in particular with regard to acts connected with aggressive war, decades after Nuremberg.[404] However, given the absence of documents that would not be directly related to Second World War crimes, that would provide for the punishability of aggression and that would be binding, it is difficult to disagree with the claim that punishability of the crime against peace is a dead norm.[405] While aggression is illegal, it also remains non-justiciable in practice.[406]

4 Trials of individuals charged with the crime of aggression

4.1 The search for precedents

It is easy to find examples, reaching even as far back as the ancient times, of individuals criminally charged with war crimes.[1] However, it is very difficult to point to examples of individuals charged with and tried for the crime of aggression before the Second World War.

The example of Hannibal is sometimes cited; the Romans demanded his transfer into their hands from every ruler of every province where Hannibal stayed, on charges of attempting to persuade other rulers and peoples to establish a military coalition against Rome and of conspiring to breach the pact between Cartagena and Rome.[2] Hannibal committed suicide and thus escaped the Romans, but even if they had managed to catch him, they were far more likely to execute him immediately (as a precautionary measure of sorts) than to put him on trial.[3]

Typically, the execution of Prince Conradin von Hohenstaufen, carried out on 26 October 1269 in Naples, is cited as the first known example of an individual's responsibility for the crime of aggression. The execution was ordered by the new ruler of the Kingdom of Naples and Sicily, Charles of Anjou, brother of Saint Louis (king of France).[4]

Conradin fell victim to the power struggle between the Papacy and the Holy Roman Empire, and specifically to the conflict between the dynasties of the Guelphs and the Ghibellines.[5] Pope Clement IV gave Naples and Sicily to Charles of Anjou, who – having received the investiture of Rome – defeated Manfred, the Sicilian incumbent, in 1268. The Guelphs of Sicily remained faithful to Manfred's dynasty. They persuaded the young Conradin, Manfred's cousin and successor, to try to win his kingdom back. Despite his initial successes, Conradin was defeated in the battle of Triaglacozzo. Charles held him hostage, and subsequently convened in Naples the Great Council, with membership including representatives of the French aristocracy and of Italian cities, as well as the French nobles who sat in his new court. The aristocracy was in favour of either entering into an agreement with Conradin or holding him and his supporters captive. However, Charles took the side of the judges, who suggested that Conradin should be executed. The judgment read out to Conradin on Naples' main square stated that he was guilty of an illegal war (*arma non licita induit*). For this reason, Conradin's execution is cited as the first instance of criminal responsibility for the crime of aggression. However, in Conradin's case, there was a judgment, but it was not preceded by a trial. Therefore, the case is an example not so much of criminal charges for the crime of aggression, but rather of security measures in the form of eliminating a political opponent.

The next case contemplated in the literature of the subject as an example of criminal responsibility for aggression is the case of Napoleon Bonaparte.[6] In the treaty of Fontainebleau of 11 April 1814, Napoleon was forced to renounce power and to retreat to the island of Elba, having been declared to be 'the sole obstacle to the re-establishment of a general peace in Europe'.[7] Napoleon, however, failed to remain on Elba. On 1 March 1815 he landed at Golfe Juan in France and, together with his proponents, began moving towards Paris. The allies, who at the time were conferring in Vienna, upon learning of Napoleon's march towards the French capital, issued a declaration on 13 March 1815, claiming that 'Napoleon Bonaparte is excluded from civil and social relations, and, as an Enemy and Disturber of the tranquillity of the World, that he has incurred public vengeance'.[8]

Eventually, Napoleon ended up in British hands. For Great Britain, the preferred solution would have been his trial and execution by the French. However, the French feared that the public opinion was too favourable towards the former emperor to make this a feasible solution. A different option was therefore selected. Pursuant to the agreement of 2 August 1815, Napoleon was placed under the care of British authorities, with Prussia, Austria and Russia retaining the right to send their observers to the island of Saint Helena where he was to be exiled.[9] The emperor died on the island on 5 May 1821.

It is sometimes suggested that Napoleon's exile and imprisonment on Saint Helena was an individual punishment[10] and therefore it should be treated as a precedent of the Nuremberg Trial in terms of individual responsibility for aggression.[11] Yet it appears to be more accurate to view Napoleon's isolation as a security measure, implemented by the powers and preventive in nature.[12] There was neither a trial nor a judgment issued by any court. Napoleon was exiled under a purely political decision. Importantly, he was not tried for aggression before retiring to Elba, and the exile to Saint Helena was a consequence of his violating the promise to remain on Elba, which can hardly be described as aggression.[13]

Another case presented as a potential precedent is the attempted trial of Wilhelm II of Hohenzollern.[14] During the First World War, the slogan *Hang Kaiser* became popular. There was widespread belief that the war was one man's doing, and the public opinion was convinced of his guilt.[15] Great Britain was in favour of charging and trying Wilhelm, and persuaded France and Italy to support this solution.[16] Despite the resistance from the Americans, the Treaty of Versailles stipulated that Wilhelm should be arraigned 'for a supreme offence against international morality and the sanctity of treaties'.[17] However, the trial never materialised.

On 10 November 1918, Wilhelm crossed the border into the Netherlands, where he was received very coldly.[18] The Netherlands claimed that the former emperor's visit was an unpleasant surprise, but decided to offer him shelter nonetheless.[19] This occurred despite the fact that Switzerland, Sweden and Spain had all refused him asylum, and the German government threatened him with arrest, should he ever decide to return to the country.[20] The allies in Vienna were perfectly well aware that they had no legal measures to force the Netherlands to expel the emperor.[21] However, they did make certain attempts to bring Wilhelm to court. On 28 June 1919, that is, on the day when the Treaty of Versailles was signed, the French *chargé d'affaires* in The Hague issued a note to the Dutch government (on behalf of the allied and associated powers). In the note, he requested that the Netherlands expel Wilhelm, on the grounds that it would prevent him from escaping or hiding.[22] In the response of 10 July 1919, the Netherlands refused to expel Wilhelm, citing Dutch sovereign rights.[23] Once the Treaty of Versailles entered into force on 10 January 1920, the allies issued a number of further notes, demanding the former emperor's extradition.[24] The Netherlands, however, continued to refuse, emphasising in the responses that the country was not a signatory of the Treaty of Versailles and therefore was not bound by its Article 227, while the tradition and honour of the Dutch do not allow them to expel a political refugee.[25] At the same time, the Netherlands asserted that it would employ all security measures necessary to prevent incidents that might be a threat to the peace in Europe.[26]

The Dutch attitude was very convenient for the allies.[27] Great Britain and Italy were no longer invested in the notion of charging and trying the former emperor,[28] and the United States had been opposed to the notion from the start (and once the war was over, it was focused on withdrawing from European affairs completely).[29] France was most interested in bringing the former emperor to court, to the point of contemplating an option of a *par contumace* trial. The idea was, however, abandoned, given that the procedure *in absentia* was not allowed under the Anglo-Saxon legal system and therefore international support would be difficult to gather.[30] The former emperor died in the Netherlands in June 1941, when the occupation of the country by Nazi Germany was taking place.

Wilhelm's case is sometimes treated as an instance of assigning individual responsibility for aggression, but far-reaching scepticism is necessary if this approach is adopted. First, no trial actually took place. Secondly, it is difficult to claim with certainty that the allies intended to try the former emperor specifically for aggression. It was most probably a step designed to calm public opinion rather than a security measure in this case.

Attempts to assign responsibility for the lost war focused not only on Wilhelm II of Hohenzollern. In Bulgaria, on 4 November 1919, Alexander Stambolijski's regime had approximately 200 individuals arrested from among those associated with the government of Vasil Radoslavov, who stayed in Berlin together with the emperor Ferdinand.[31] The indictment was filed on 11 October 1921. It included charges against the former prime minister Radoslavov (who was to be tried *in absentia*) and against Nikola Todorov Zhekov, the commander of the army, who returned from abroad to participate in the trial. The charges were as follows: secret diplomatic preparations for war, unconstitutional declaration of war, and illegal conduct of war.[32] The judgment was entered on 31 March 1923. Radoslavov was sentenced to life imprisonment, and Zhekov to 10 years in prison.[33] The trial proved to be a political success, and so Stamboliyski ordered further arrests on 22 September 1922. He also called a referendum in which he asked whether the government of Ivan Geshov and Stojan Daner was to be tried for starting the second Balkan war in 1913, and whether Aleksander Malinov was to be tried for not ending the war in 1918.[34] Public opinion was in favour of the trial, planned for March 1923. However, before the date came, Stamboliyski's regime was overthrown, and the defendants in previous trails were freed under an amnesty.

Can the trial of Radoslavov et al be considered a precedent for the Nuremberg Trial? Hardly. The defendants were in fact tried for their defeat and the loss of territorial gains, rather than for aggression. The proceedings were motivated by internal politics, and a shift in government was enough to resolve with a negative outcome the question of their responsibility.

Before the Second World War, it is difficult to find a precedent in terms of individual criminal responsibility for aggression. The Nuremberg Tribunal invoked the case of Wilhelm II of Hohenzollern – the *casus* is doubtful, given how the charges against him were formulated and given the fact that the trial did not take place. In one of the judgments in the so-called Subsequent Nuremberg Trial (the Ministries trial, discussed in more detail below) the American Military Tribunal cited the fact that Frederick the Great was summoned by the Imperial Council to appear at Regensburg and to answer, under threat of banishment, for his Saxon invasion and thus a breach of public peace.[35] Admittedly, Frederick the Great paid little attention to the threats. The trial of the Radoslavov government is less well known and, moreover, this trial too was less about the charges of aggression and more about political payback for a defeat. The fact that no precedent exists for the Nuremberg trial should not be surprising: it was only the London Agreement that first formulated and expressed the principle of criminal responsibility for aggression.

4.2 The Nuremberg trial

The International Military Tribunal No 1 was established under the London Agreement of 8 August 1945 and assigned the task of hearing and trying the major German criminals. The scale of the undertaking is best demonstrated by the data cited by the tribunal. The International Military Tribunal held 403 open sessions, heard 33 witnesses called by the prosecutors and 61 witnesses (besides the defendants) called by the defence, and read – on the request of the defence – the affidavits of 143 witnesses. As far as the guilt of specific organisations is concerned, it heard 22 witnesses and read the affidavits of a few hundred thousand individuals.[36]

The adjudicating panel was comprised of representatives of the four powers. The main judges were: Geoffrey Lawrence, President of the Tribunal (Great Britain); Francis Biddle (United States), Henri Donnedieu de Vabres (France), and Iona Nikitchenko (USSR). The alternates were: William Norman Birkett (Great Britain), John J. Parker (United States), Robert Falco (France) and Alexander Volchkov (USSR).[37] Chief prosecutors were Hartley Shawcross (Great Britain), Robert H. Jackson (United States), Roman Andreyevich Rudenko (USSR) and François de Menthon (France).

The indictment was filed on 18 November 1945 at the tribunal's session in Berlin. The Nuremberg trial itself began in Nuremberg on 20 November 1945, and ended on 1 October 1946.[38]

The chief prosecutor in the Nuremberg trial, Jackson, had previously made known his intention to accuse a large number of individuals and officials who were in authority in the government, in the military establishment and in the financial, industrial and economic life of Germany who by civilised standards were provable to be common criminals.[39] Eventually, charges were filed against 24 individuals: Hermann Wilhelm Göring, Rudolf Hess, Joachim von Ribbentrop, Robert Ley, Wilhelm Keitel, Ernst Kaltenbrunner, Alfred Rosenberg, Hans Frank, Wilhelm Frick, Julius Streicher, Walter Funk, Hjalmar Schacht, Gustav Krupp von Bohlen und Halbach, Karl Dönitz, Erich Raeder, Baldur von Schirach, Fritz Sauckel, Alfred Jodl, Martin Bormann, Franz von Papen, Artur Seyss-Inquart, Albert Speer, Constantin von Neurath and Hans Fritzsche.[40] Not all of the accused heard their judgments.[41] Robert Ley committed suicide on 25 October 1945. The case of Gustav Krupp von Bohlen und Halbach was eliminated from the tribunal's proceedings on 15 November 1945 owing to the failing health of the defendant. In the case of Martin Bormann, whom the allies failed to capture, the tribunal decided on 17 November 1945 to proceed *in absentia*.

The prosecutors charged the defendants of four counts. Under count 1, the defendants were accused of participating in the formulation or execution of a common plan or conspiracy to commit, or which involved the commission of, crimes against peace, war crimes and crimes against humanity.[42] The prosecutors intended to demonstrate that there was a conspiracy, established many years before the commencement of the war and aimed at the commission of crimes, including crimes against peace.[43] Consequently, the indictment presented an outline of the stages of the conspiracy.[44]

The prosecution claimed that at the root of the conspiracy was the founding of NSDAP (*Nationalsozialistische Deutsche Arbeiterpartei*), the objectives of which were to be accomplished by means of threat of force, force and aggressive war. These objectives were reportedly as follows: to abrogate and overthrow the Treaty of Versailles and its restrictions upon the military armament and activity of Germany, and to acquire the territories lost by Germany and other territories to be occupied by the 'racial Germans' as *Lebensraum*, or living space. An ideology was thus advertised, according to which Germans were a 'master race', and war was a noble and necessary activity for Germans. At the same time, unconditional obedience to Nazi party leaders was encouraged and demanded. In the following stages of the conspiracy, Nazis seized totalitarian political power in Germany in order to gain full control over the country's economy and begin a mobilisation for aggressive war. Once full domestic control was obtained, foreign aggression commenced. The aggression was comprised of: aggressive action against Austria and Czechoslovakia (1937–1939); aggressive war with Poland (September 1939); general aggressive war, that is, attacks on Denmark, Norway, Belgium, the Netherlands, Luxembourg, Yugoslavia, Greece (1939–April 1941); invasion (on 22 June 1941) of the USSR territory in violation of Non-Aggression Pact of 23 August 1939; and collaboration with Italy and Japan and aggressive war against the United States (November 1936–December 1941).[45]

Count 2 pertained to the 'planning, preparation, initiation and waging of wars of aggression, which were also wars in violation of international treaties, agreements and assurances'.[46] The indictment listed the dates and other particulars of the wars planned, prepared, initiated and waged: against Poland (1 September 1939); against the United Kingdom and France (3 September 1939); against Denmark and Norway (9 April 1940); against Belgium, the Netherlands and Luxembourg (10 May 1940); against Yugoslavia and Greece (6 April 1941); against the USSR (22 June 1941); and against the United States (11 December 1941). Reference was made to count 1 for the allegations charging that these wars were wars of aggression on the part of the defendants, which was probably intended to explain the focus on count 1. Count 3 pertained to war crimes, and count 4 to crimes against humanity.[47] All defendants, with the exception of the absent Bormann, pleaded innocent.[48]

Before the tribunal issued a ruling on the individual guilt of the defendants, it analysed the events that preceded aggressive war and that later ran parallel to it. The tribunal began its considerations with the founding of the German Workers' Party (*Deutsche Arbeiterpartei*) on 5 January 1919; the party was transformed into NSDAP on 29 July 1921. Adolf Hitler publicly proclaimed the party's programme in Munich on 24 February 1920. In the programme, he demanded the unification of all Germans in the Greater Germany, the abrogation of the peace treaties of Versailles and St Germain, and land and territory for the sustenance of the German people.[49] Further, the tribunal analysed how the NSDAP proceeded to win and consolidate power, giving attention to the role that some of the defendants played in the process.[50] Then, the process of rearmament of Germany was discussed, in particular how on 16 March 1935 a law was passed bearing the signatures, among others, of Göring, Hess, Frank, Frick, Schacht and von Neurath, instituting compulsory military service and fixing the establishment of the German Army at a peace time strength of 500,000 men.[51] The tribunal emphasised the development of the German navy.[52] It invoked certain facts predating the acts of aggression in order to demonstrate that both aggressive war and the seizure of Austria and Czechoslovakia were parts of a premeditated and carefully prepared plan.[53]

It referenced the relevant sections of *Mein Kampf* with a view to proving Hitler's aggressive attitude, as well as documents from meetings where aggression was planned.[54]

The prosecution focused on the charge of conspiracy, which was contemplated as a fourth type of crime, in contravention of the wording of the Charter of the International Military Tribunal. The charge of conspiracy was brought against all the defendants, whereas the charge of the crime against peace was only brought against 18 of them. However, the tribunal noted that its charter only stipulates aggression in the context of crimes against peace, and not war crimes or crimes against humanity, and therefore it had decided to contemplate the charges of conspiracy and crimes against peace jointly, since they were identical as to their essence.[55] The tribunal pointed out that there was not one single conspiracy to wage a general war of aggression, but rather specific plans for specific wars of aggression.[56] If anybody was to be sentenced for the conspiracy or a crime against peace, it was necessary to prove that this person had participated in planning a specific war of aggression.[57] In light thereof, it may be considered (at least to an extent) a mistake on the part of the prosecutors that six individuals were charged only with conspiracy, without the charges of planning, preparing and waging a war of aggression. All six of these individuals were acquitted of the charge of conspiracy.

The eight defendants who were sentenced both for conspiracy and for crimes against peace included Hitler's closest confidantes (Göring, Hess, von Ribbentrop and Rosenberg) and the top military and diplomatic officials who had been privy to secret plans and participated in the key conferences where Hitler revealed his aggressive intentions (Göring, von Ribbentrop, Keitel, Raeder, Jodl and von Neurath).[58] From among this group, *Göring* was undoubtedly the most prominent in the Nazi regime.[59] The tribunal noted Göring's actual position as the economic dictator of the Reich and the creator of Luftwaffe's immense power, and the fact that he had tremendous influence over Hitler, at least until 1943 when their relationship deteriorated. Göring himself testified that Hitler kept him informed of all important military and political problems. The tribunal decided that Göring was largely instrumental in bringing the National Socialists to power in 1933, and was responsible for consolidating this power and for expanding German armed strength. It was thanks to Göring that as early as 8 July 1938 the German air forces won an advantage over the other European powers. The tribunal noted that he was one of the five most important participants of the conference of 5 November 1937, where Hitler fully revealed his plans of aggression. He was, by his own admission, 100 per cent responsible for Austria's *Anschluss*, 'overruled objections by the Führer and brought everything to its final development'. In the seizure of the Sudetenland he played a role too, by planning an air offensive. The night before the invasion of Czechoslovakia he threatened to bomb Prague if Hácha did not submit to German demands. Göring attended the Reich Chancellery meeting of 23 May 1939, when Hitler decided to attack Poland.

Table 4.1 Accused and convicted in the trial before the IMT

Name	*Accused of:*				*Convicted of:*				*Penalty*
	1. (conspiracy)	*2. (crimes against peace)*	*3. (war crimes)*	*4. (crimes against humanity)*	*1. (conspiracy)*	*2. (crimes against peace)*	*3. (war crimes)*	*4. (crimes against humanity)*	
Göring	+	+	+	+	+	+	+	+	Death
Hess	+	+	+	+	+	+	**No**	**No**	Life imprisonment
Ribbentrop	+	+	+	+	+	+	+	+	Death
Keitel	+	+	+	+	+	+	+	+	Death
Kaltenbrunner	+	**No**	+	+	**No**	–	+	+	Death
Rosenberg	+	+	+	+	+	+	+	+	Death
Frank	+	**No**	+	+	**No**	–	+	+	Death
Frick	+	+	+	+	**No**	+	+	+	Death
Streicher	+	**No**	**No**	+	**No**	–	–	+	Death
Funk	+	+	+	+	**No**	+	+	+	Life imprisonment
Schacht	+	+	**No**	**No**	**No**	**No**	–	–	Acquitted
Dönitz	+	+	+	**No**	**No**	+	+	–	10 years of imprisonment
Raeder	+	+	+	**No**	+	+	+	–	Life imprisonment
Schirach	+	**No**	**No**	+	**No**	–	–	+	20 years of imprisonment
Sauckel	+	+	+	+	**No**	**No**	+	+	Death

Jodl	+	+	+	+	+	+	+	+	Death
Papen	+	+	**No**	**No**	**No**	**No**	–	–	Acquitted
Seyss-Inquart	+	+	+	+	**No**	+	+	+	Death
Speer	+	+	+	+	**No**	**No**	+	+	20 years of imprisonment
Neurath	+	+	+	+	+	+	+	+	15 years of imprisonment
Fritzsche	+	**No**	+	+	**No**	–	**No**	**No**	Acquitted
Bormann	+	**No**	+	+	**No**	–	+	+	Death

Source: Author.

He was active in the diplomatic manoeuvres to try to prevent the British government from keeping its guarantee to the Poles. He commanded the Luftwaffe in the attack on Poland and throughout the aggressive wars which followed. The tribunal stressed that even if he had opposed Hitler's plans against Norway and the Soviet Union, as he alleged, it is clear that he did so only for strategic reasons. He was enraged about the invasion of Norway, but only because he had not received sufficient warning to prepare the Luftwaffe offensive; his only objection to the war of aggression against the USSR was its timing; he wished for strategic reasons to delay it until Britain was conquered. He was active in preparing and executing the Yugoslavian and Greek campaigns. From the positions which he held, the conferences he attended and the public words he uttered, there could remain no doubt that he was the moving force for aggressive war second only to Hitler. He was the planner and prime mover in the military and diplomatic preparation for war which Germany pursued. The tribunal sentenced Göring to death by hanging.[60] He was, however, not executed. The day before the planned date of the execution, Göring committed suicide.

The next defendant, Hess, was Hitler's closest personal confidant from the unsuccessful Munich Putsch on 9 November 1923 and the imprisonment in the Landsberg fortress until his flight to Great Britain on 10 May 1941.[61] As deputy to the Führer he was at the very top of the Nazi regime. His position made him responsible for all party matters and gave him the authority to issue all decisions in this regard on Hitler's behalf. As minister without portfolio he had the authority to approve all legislation suggested by the different ministers before it could be enacted as law. In these positions, Hess was an active supporter of preparations for war. He supported Hitler's policy of vigorous rearmament in many speeches. He told the people that they must sacrifice for armaments, repeating the phrase: 'Guns instead of butter'. The tribunal emphasised the fact that Hess knew Hitler and his plans very well. He participated in the German aggression against Austria (he signed the law incorporating Austria into the German Reich), Czechoslovakia (at the time of the Munich crisis, together with Keitel he was involved in the secret mobilisation and set up the Nazi government on the seized territories) and Poland (he signed the decrees incorporating Danzig and certain Polish territories into the Reich, and setting up the General Government, that is, the Nazi administration of Poland). Hess, as Hitler's closest confidant (at least until his flight to Great Britain) must have been informed of Hitler's aggressive plans when they came into existence, and he fully supported these plans, as evidenced by the fact that even after his arrival into Great Britain he attempted to justify Germany's action in connection with Austria, Czechoslovakia, Poland, Norway, Denmark, Belgium and the Netherlands, and he blamed England and France for the war. Hess was eventually sentenced to life in prison.[62] The Soviet judge found this ruling unacceptable, and he stressed that, since Hess was declared guilty of the crime against peace, which – in the opinion of the tribunal itself – is the gravest crime of all, he should be sentenced to death.[63] Hess died in 1987 in the Spandau prison in West Berlin.

The defendant von Ribbentrop did not participate in the Hossbach conference of 5 November 1937 but, on 2 January 1938, while still German ambassador to England, he sent a memorandum to Hitler indicating his opinion that a change in the status quo in the East, in the German sense, could only be carried out by force, and suggesting methods to prevent England and France from intervening in a European war fought to bring about such a change; the memorandum was an important piece of evidence against him.[64] The tribunal noted that von Ribbentrop suggested to Hitler the possibility of a military settlement with regard to Austria, Sudetenland, Danzig and Memel, and that he also went beyond the suggestions: he was an active participant of the aggressive actions against Austria (on 12 February 1938, von Ribbentrop attended the conference between Hitler and Schuschnigg at which Hitler, by threats of invasion, forced Schuschnigg to grant a series of concessions designed to strengthen the Nazis in Austria; he signed the law incorporating Austria into the German Reich), Czechoslovakia (in August 1938, he participated in a conference for the purpose of obtaining Hungarian support in the event of a war with Czechoslovakia; he was present at the conference of 14–15 March 1939, at which Hitler, by threats of invasion, compelled President Hácha to consent to the German occupation of Czechoslovakia) and Poland (he participated in a conference held on 12 August 1939, for the purpose of obtaining Italian support if the attack should lead to a general European war; Ribbentrop discussed the German demands with respect to Danzig and the Polish Corridor with the British ambassador). Ribbentrop was advised in advance of the attack on Norway and Denmark and of the attack on the Low Countries. He attended the conferences at which the proposed attacks on Greece and Yugoslavia were discussed. He also consulted with Rosenberg in the preliminary planning for the political exploitation of Soviet territories and, in July 1941, after the outbreak of war, urged Japan to attack the Soviet Union. The tribunal sentenced von Ribbentrop to death.[65] The sentence was carried out.[66]

The next defendant, Rosenberg, participated in the Munich Putsch of 9 November 1923, and worked to keep the NSDAP together while Hitler was in jail.[67] Recognised as the Party's ideologist, he developed and spread Nazi doctrines, and his book, *Myth of the Twentieth Century*, had a circulation of over a million copies. He set up the *Hohe Schule*, the Centre of National Socialistic Ideological and Educational Research. As the head of the Office of Foreign Affairs of the NSDAP (the APA), Rosenberg was largely responsible for Romania's joining the Axis. He also played an important role in the preparation and planning of the attack on Norway. Under the influence of Quisling, he persuaded Raeder that an attack on Norway was necessary owing to the threat of Great Britain's possible actions. The tribunal declared Rosenberg primarily responsible for the formulation and execution of occupation policies in the Occupied Eastern Territories. He was informed by Hitler of the coming attack against the Soviet Union. In preparing the plans for the occupation, he had numerous conferences with Keitel, Raeder,

Göring, Funk, Ribbentrop and other high Reich authorities, before being appointed Reich Minister for the Occupied Eastern Territories. The tribunal sentenced Rosenberg to death.[68] The sentence was carried out.

The defendant Keitel played a significant role in the aggression against Austria (he attended the Schuschnigg conference in February 1938 with two other generals, where their presence, he admitted, was a 'military demonstration', and he commenced 'Case Otto'), Czechoslovakia (Hitler and Keitel considered making use of a possible incident such as the assassination of the German minister in Prague to preface the attack on Czechoslovakia; Keitel signed many directives and memoranda on 'Fall Grün' and he attended the negotiations with Hácha), Poland (he was present on 23 May 1939, when Hitler announced his decision to attack Poland and he had signed directives on 'Fall Weiss'), Denmark and Norway (he participated in the meeting of 12 December 1939, with Hitler, Jodl and Raeder; the Norway plans were placed under his direct and personal guidance) and Belgium and the Netherlands (he signed the orders for these attacks as well as the orders postponing them on numerous occasions). He was well informed of Hitler's plans against Greece and Yugoslavia. Keitel testified that he opposed the invasion of the Soviet Union for military reasons, and also because it would constitute a violation of the non-aggression pact. Nevertheless, he initialled 'Case Barbarossa' and he directed all army units to carry out the economic directives issued by Göring for the exploitation of Russian territory, food and raw materials. The tribunal sentenced him to death. The penalty was carried out.

With regard to the defendant Raeder, the tribunal noted that within the 15 years that he was in command of the German navy, he built its power, and he bore full responsibility for its expansion.[69] He was well aware of the secret armament plans, and he carried them out, in particular with regard to submarines. He admitted that the German navy violated the Versailles Treaty, insisting it was 'a matter of honour for every man' to do so. Raeder insisted that he believed the questions of Austria and Czechoslovakia would be settled peacefully, despite his contribution to Germany's fast armament. The tribunal did not believe his claims, citing instead the directive of 24 June 1937 from von Blomberg requiring special preparations for war against Austria. Moreover, it was known that at the meeting on 12 May 1934 Raeder had already rallied in favour of commencing a war without any notice. He was present at the Hossbach Conference of 5 November 1937 and the Obersalzburg briefing of 22 August 1939. He received the plans for the 'Fall Grün' and 'Fall Weiss' operations. The tribunal noted that the conception of the invasion of Norway first arose in the mind of Raeder and not that of Hitler. He defended himself against the responsibility for the Greek invasion by claiming that the German navy had no interest in Greece. However, the tribunal pointed to meetings that Raeder had attended at which Hitler had announced his plans to attack Greece. He had also received Hitler's directive on Yugoslavia. The tribunal did not consider it an excuse that Raeder voiced objections against the invasion against the USSR, since his objections were based on strategy concerns (he had objections against the Russian campaign before the defeat of England; he urged on Hitler an aggressive Mediterranean policy as an alternative to the attack on Russia). Once the decision to attack Russia had been made, he gave permission six days before the invasion of the Soviet Union to attack Russian submarines in the Baltic Sea. The tribunal sentenced Raeder to life in prison.[70] However, he left prison in 1955 owing to health concerns. He died in 1960.

The next defendant was Jodl. Although his immediate superior was the defendant Keitel, he reported directly to Hitler on operational matters.[71] The tribunal was not persuaded when Jodl defended himself on the ground he was a soldier sworn to obedience, and not a politician; and that his staff and planning work left him no time for other matters. He said that when he signed or initialled orders, memoranda and letters, he did so for Hitler and often in the absence of Keitel. Although he claimed that as a soldier he had to obey Hitler, he said that he often tried to obstruct certain measures by delay. The tribunal concluded that, in the strict military sense, Jodl was the actual planner of the war and responsible in large measure for the strategy and conduct of operations. Entries in Jodl's diary were evidence against him; they revealed that Hitler instructed both him and Keitel to keep up military pressure against Austria, and that the 'Case Otto' directive was initialled by Jodl. In planning the attack on Czechoslovakia, Jodl was very active; he conferred with the propaganda experts on justifying the invasion and appropriately presenting the operation in light of international law. The tribunal demonstrated that he had participated in the debate on the Norway invasion, and signed many orders regarding the operations in the West. He was very active in planning the attacks against Greece and Yugoslavia, and he commenced the invasion against the USSR himself, claiming that Hitler feared an attack by Russia and so attacked first. The tribunal sentenced him to death.[72] The penalty was carried out.

In regard to the defendant von Neurath, the tribunal stressed his role in the armament of Germany.[73] It was von Neurath who advised Hitler in connection with the withdrawal from the Disarmament Conference and the League of Nations, and the institution of rearmament. He was a key figure in the negotiation of the Naval Accord entered into between Germany and England on 18 June 1935. Von Neurath also played an important part in Hitler's decision to reoccupy the Rhineland. He took part in the Hossbach Conference of 5 November 1937. He testified that he had been so shocked by Hitler's statements that he had a heart attack. Shortly thereafter, he offered to resign, and his resignation was accepted on 4 February 1938. Yet even with the knowledge of Hitler's aggressive plans he retained a formal relationship with the Nazi regime as minister without portfolio, president of the Secret Cabinet Council and a member of the Defence Council. Moreover, he took charge of the Foreign Office at the time of the occupation of Austria, and participated in the negotiations with Czechoslovakia preceding the Munich Pact; he contended that he entered these discussions only to urge Hitler to make every effort to settle the issues by peaceful means. His objections did not prevent him from being appointed Protector for Bohemia and Moravia on 18 March 1939. The tribunal sentenced him to 15 years in prison. However, von Neurath left the prison in 1954 owing to his poor health. He died in 1956.

The next group of defendants consisted of individuals who were charged with conspiracy and the crime against peace, but were acquitted of the former charge and only found liable for the latter.

Frick was among these defendants. The tribunal decided that Frick, as the Minister of the Interior, was largely responsible for bringing the German nation under the complete control of the NSDAP, since he introduced the legislation which suppressed the trade unions, the church and the Jews.[74] The evidence did not show that he participated in any of the conferences at which Hitler outlined his aggressive intentions. Consequently, the tribunal took the view that Frick was not a member of the common plan or conspiracy to wage aggressive war. However, under the provisions of the Reich Defence Law of 4 September 1938, Frick became General Plenipotentiary for the Administration of the Reich. He was made responsible for war administration, except the military and economic aspects, in the event of Hitler's proclaiming a state of defence. The Reich Ministries of Justice, Education, Religion and the Office of Spatial Planning were made subordinate to him. He was therefore responsible for laws incorporating into the Reich the Sudetenland, Memel, Danzig, the Eastern territories (West Prussia and Posen) and Eupen, Malmedy and Moresnot. He was placed in charge of the actual incorporation, and of the establishment of German administration over these territories. He was tasked with ensuring close cooperation between Germany and the occupied territories, which required him to supply German civil servants for the administrations in all occupied territories. He was sentenced to death.[75] The penalty was carried out.

The next defendant, Funk, became active in the economic field after the Nazi plans to wage aggressive war had been clearly defined.[76] His representatives attended conferences at which a gigantic increase in armaments was announced, the Ministry of Economics was instructed in this regard and financing of war was discussed. Funk's subordinates sent a memorandum to the military command on the use of prisoners of war to make up labour deficiencies. His letters and speeches demonstrate that he was involved in the Reich's economic preparations for war (he transferred into gold all foreign exchange resources available to Germany, implemented price controls and strengthened the Reichsbank). Funk participated in the economic planning which preceded the attack on the USSR, in particular with regard to raw materials. He started preparations for the implementation of a special occupational currency. The tribunal took notice of the fact that Funk was never a dominant figure in the planning of aggressive war, since his operations were controlled by Göring. Nonetheless, he participated in the economic preparations for certain aggressive wars (mainly against Poland and the USSR). Therefore, even though he was not guilty of conspiracy, he was guilty of the crime against peace. He was sentenced to life in prison.[77] However, he was released from prison in 1957 owing to health concerns. He died in 1960.

As for the defendant Dönitz, the tribunal noted that he was a line officer performing strictly tactical duties. He was not present at the important conferences when plans for aggressive wars were announced, and there was no evidence he was informed about the decisions reached there.[78] Dönitz could, however, be charged with waging aggressive war. He was no mere army or division commander. The U-boat arm was the principal part of the German fleet and Dönitz was its leader, in charge of the fleet of submarines that did the greatest damage to the allied naval forces. Owing to the significance of his position, Raeder suggested to Hitler to make Dönitz his successor, which took place on 30 January 1943. From January 1943, Dönitz was consulted almost continuously by Hitler. The tribunal pointed out that, as late as April 1945, when Dönitz knew the struggle was hopeless, he urged the German navy to continue its fight. On 1 May 1945, he became the head of state and, as such, ordered the Wehrmacht to continue its war in the East, until capitulation on 9 May 1945, ostensibly to ensure that the civilian population might be evacuated. The tribunal decided that, although he had not participated in conspiracy to wage aggressive war, he was guilty of crimes against humanity, and sentenced him to 10 years in prison.[79] He served the full term of his sentence and was released from prison on 1 October 1956. He died in 1980.

As for the next defendant, Seyss-Inquart, the tribunal pointed out his special involvement in the aggression against Austria (he met Hitler in Linz on 12 March 1938 and welcomed the German troops entering Austria), culminating in his appointment as Chancellor of Austria as a result of German threats of invasion.[80] Seyss-Inquart had also contributed to the acts of aggression against Czechoslovakia, for example by means of advocating for the declaration of independence in Slovakia on 11 March. He was in charge of management of territories (Polish and Dutch) that were under occupation as a result of aggressive war, and that were of great importance during further wars of aggression conducted by Germany. For these reasons, although he was not declared guilty of conspiracy, he was nonetheless declared guilty of the crime against peace, and he was sentenced to death.[81] The penalty was carried out.

The next group of defendants consisted of individuals who were charged with both conspiracy to wage aggressive war and with crimes against peace, but who were acquitted of these charges. The cases of Schacht and von Papen appear to be most interesting, since they were the only two individuals against whom the charges of war crimes and war against humanity were not brought, and therefore the prosecution had to focus on the sole issue of the crime against peace.

The defendant Schacht was an active supporter of the Nazi Party before its accession to power.[82] He played a significant role in the armament of

Germany, because he used the resources of the Reichsbank to obtain money to fund the armament. As Minister of Economics and as Plenipotentiary General for War Economy, he was active in organising the German economy for war. On 3 May 1935, he sent a memorandum to Hitler stating that the accomplishment of the armament programme with speed and in quantity was the most important objective of German policy. Schacht, by April 1936, began to lose his influence as the central figure in the German rearmament effort when Göring was appointed first Coordinator for Raw Materials and Foreign Exchange, and then in October 1936 Plenipotentiary for the Four-Year Plan, with the task of putting the entire economy in a state of readiness for war. Schacht disagreed with Göring on many matters, and he slowly began to withdraw from many of the methods of funding the armament effort. Eventually, on 2 January 1939, he attempted to persuade Hitler to reduce the armament spending, which led to his dismissal from the position of president of the Reichsbank and, in January 1943, also from the position of minister without portfolio. He was arrested by the Gestapo on 23 July 1944 and sent to a concentration camp – a fact that decidedly spoke in his favour before the tribunal – which eventually decided that despite Schacht's key position within the armament programme, and therefore his contribution to the rise of Nazi military power, arming a state was not a crime in itself. Schacht continued to claim that all he wanted was a strong and independent German state; as soon as he learnt of Hitler's aggressive plans, he took measures to prevent their completion. He also claimed that after von Fritsch and von Blomberg were dismissed, he was a supporter of eliminating Hitler, even if that meant his assassination. The tribunal confirmed Schacht's participation in the aggression against Austria and Czechoslovakia, considering that he had set the rate of exchange and orchestrated the incorporation of their national banks into the Reich. However, the tribunal was unable to find evidence of Schacht's involvement in planning even one aggressive war. The tribunal therefore ruled that he was clearly not one of the inner circle around Hitler most closely involved with this common plan, and he was regarded by this group with undisguised hostility. Since the prosecution was unable to demonstrate Schacht's guilt beyond reasonable doubt, the tribunal had no other option but to acquit him. The Soviet judge was strongly opposed to this decision. He filed a dissenting opinion[83] in which he noted that Schacht established contact with Göring in December 1930, and with Hitler at the beginning of 1931. He was responsible for the contacts with the industrialists. He demanded that von Papen resign his post as Reich Chancellor in favour of Hitler. In 1932, Schacht collected signatures of German industrialists, urging them to come out in favour of Hitler's appointment as chancellor. He was a proponent of Hitler and the Nazis. When, on 17 March 1933, Schacht was appointed president of the Reichsbank, he transformed it into a national socialist institution. Once Schacht was appointed Minister of Economy, he implemented a new funding programme and was in charge of the economic mobilisation. The Soviet judge pointed out that von Blomberg testified that

Schacht was fully cognisant of the plans for development and increase of the German armed forces, since he participated in military exercises, and in September 1934 in a conversation with the then American ambassador he said that Germany would seek new territories even through war if necessary. The defendant wished to enter into negotiations with the United States to ensure that the US refrained from offering assistance to Great Britain. It was therefore not true that Schacht disagreed with the aggressive German politics. Notably, his resignation from the position of president of the Reichsbank had nothing to do with the armament process, according to Göring's claims. Puhl's testimony suggested instead that Schacht was trying to avoid responsibility for certain financial operations.

It must be noted that the prosecution had expected Schacht's acquittal,[84] and the reasoning presented in the judgment of the International Military Tribunal suggests that in his case it was decided that he had left the Nazis too early on to be considered guilty of conspiracy or crime against peace.[85]

The defendant von Papen was often referred to as the 'devil in a top hat'. The tribunal noted that he had helped Hitler form the coalition cabinet and aided in his appointment as chancellor.[86] However, he was not uncritical towards the Nazi regime; he had warned against Nazi attempts to suppress the freedom of the press and the church. In June 1934, in the wave of violence which accompanied the so-called Röhm Purge, von Papen was taken into custody by the SS, and subsequently released. In analysing the role von Papen played in the context of the aggression against Austria, the tribunal decided that the only charge that could be made against him was supporting Austrian Nazis at the position of minister in Vienna, which ostensibly led to the *Anschluss* of Austria, as well as his involvement in a number of intrigues. Indeed, von Papen organised a conference between Schuschnigg and Hitler in Berchtesgaden on 12 February 1938, where he advised Schuschnigg to comply with Hitler's demands. However, on 10 March 1938, just before the *Anschluss*, he returned to Berlin. The tribunal held no evidence to demonstrate that von Papen supported Austria's occupation. He retired after the *Anschluss* and steered clear of politics, with the exception of serving as German ambassador to Turkey. The tribunal ruled that von Papen had violated the principles of political ethics, but that such conduct in itself did not constitute a crime. Since prosecution was unable to prove beyond reasonable doubt that von Papen's actions were intended to lead to aggressive actions, the only option was to acquit the defendant.

The Soviet judge disagreed. In his dissenting opinion, he presented von Papen's actions in the service of the Nazi regime, in particular his aid in the seizure of Austria.[87] Nikitchenko invoked also the testimony of the American ambassador, who claimed that the seizure of Austria was the first step towards war, and that the actions of von Papen were aimed at calming down global public opinion.

With regard to the remaining two defendants, Sauckel[88] and Speer,[89] the tribunal offered no elaboration on the grounds of the decision to acquit them of the charges of conspiracy and the crime against peace. The ruling is limited to noting that the defendants were neither associated with the common plan to wage aggressive war nor sufficiently involved in planning and waging aggressive war to be considered guilty of such charges. With regard to Sauckel, the tribunal pointed out that he held the function of leader of the armament industry only at a time when aggressive wars were already underway, and his actions contributed to the war effort to the same extent as all other enterprises. In the tribunal's opinion, therefore, just as Schacht had left the Nazis too early, Sauckel and Speer rose to positions of power too late.[90] Nonetheless, both of them were convicted of war crimes and crimes against humanity.[91] Sauckel was sentenced to death.[92] The penalty was carried out. Speer was sentenced to 20 years in prison.[93] He served the penalty in full, leaving prison on 1 October 1966. He died in 1981.

The last group of defendants consisted of individuals who were charged with conspiracy but not the crime against peace. All of these defendants were acquitted. In the great majority of cases, the tribunal offered no elaboration as to the grounds for this decision.

With regard to Kaltenbrunner, the tribunal was certain that he was active in the Nazi intrigue against the Schuschnigg government.[94] On the night of 11 March 1938, Kaltenbrunner was in command of the SS detachment that entered the Federal Chancellery, where Seyss-Inquart was negotiating with President Miklas. However, the Anschluss, although it was an aggressive act, was not charged as an aggressive war and thus a crime against peace, and there was no evidence connecting Kaltenbrunner with plans to wage aggressive war on any other front. Therefore, the tribunal cleared him of the conspiracy charge. In the case of Frank, the evidence did not satisfy the tribunal that he was sufficiently connected with the common plan to wage aggressive war to allow the tribunal to convict him on count 1.[95] The situation was similar in the case of Streicher, who was never present at any of the important conferences when Hitler presented his aggressive plans and there was no evidence that he was connected with the formulation of the policies that led to war.[96] Nonetheless, Kaltenbrunner, Frank and Streicher were all convicted on counts of war crimes and crimes against humanity[97] and sentenced to death.[98] The penalties were carried out.

With regard to the defendant von Schirach, the tribunal found evidence to prove beyond doubt that he had participated in the psychological and educational preparations for war.[99] He conducted intensive Nazi propaganda efforts through the organisations of which he was the leader. Moreover, in agreement with Himmler, he supplied candidates for the SS and established close collaboration between Hitler, Jugend and the Wehrmacht. However, what the tribunal found to be decisive was that von Schirach was not involved in the development of Hitler's plan for territorial expansion by means of aggressive war, or that he participated in the planning or preparation of any of the wars of aggression. It appears that the case of von Schirach is a good illustration of a mistake on the part of the prosecution, in terms of indicting him only on the count of conspiracy.[100] Von Schirach was convicted of crime against humanity[101] and sentenced to 20 years in prison.[102] He served the sentence in full and was released from prison on 1 October 1966. He died in 1974.

With regard to *Fritzsche*, it was found that he had been spreading the Nazi doctrine.[103] He was the head of the Home Press Division of the Ministry of Popular Enlightenment and Propaganda and thus supervised the German press of 2,300 daily newspapers and, in November 1942, he was made head of the Radio Division. In the tribunal's opinion, he was responsible for propaganda campaigns carried out before each major act of aggression, and he instructed the press how the actions or wars against specific states should be dealt with. Yet he was merely a conduit to the press of the instructions handed him by Otto Dietrich. Fritzsche, with other officials of the Propaganda Ministry, was present at Göbbels' daily staff conferences. After 1943 Fritzsche himself occasionally held these conferences, but only when Göbbels and his state secretaries were absent. Even then his only function was to transmit Göbbels' directives. In the opinion of the tribunal, Fritzsche never achieved sufficient stature to attend the planning conferences which led to aggressive war nor was there any evidence that he was informed of the decisions taken at these conferences. He never even had a conversation with Hitler.

Fritzsche's acquittal was opposed by the Soviet judge, who filed a dissenting opinion on the matter. He pointed out that, since 1942, Fritzsche was de facto the director of the Reich Press and later the Plenipotentiary for the Political Organisation of the Greater German Radio, that is, in charge of the German radio.[104] Nikitchenko emphasised the impact that propaganda had alongside military and economic actions. It is indeed difficult to understand why the tribunal acquitted Fritzsche, considering that it convicted Streicher for incitement to crimes against humanity.[105]

Finally, with regard to Bormann, the tribunal explained its decision to clear him of the conspiracy charge by stating that the evidence did not show that Bormann knew of Hitler's plans to prepare, initiate or wage aggressive wars and did not participate in their fulfilment.[106] He attended none of the important conferences when Hitler revealed his plans for aggression, nor could knowledge of them be conclusively inferred from the positions he held. It was only when he became head of the Party chancellery in 1941, and later in 1943 secretary to Hitler, when his positions gave him the necessary access to such knowledge. Nonetheless, Bormann was declared guilty of war crimes and crimes against humanity[107] and sentenced to death *in absentia*.[108] He most probably died in Berlin in May 1945.

4.3 The Tokyo trial

On 19 January 1946, General Douglas MacArthur issued a special proclamation ordering the establishment of an International Military Tribunal for the Far East with its seat in Tokyo. The tribunal was to try Japanese war criminals. The scale of the Tokyo trial was massive. It lasted for more than two years, consisted of 818 sessions and included the testimony of 419 witnesses and 779 affidavits.[109]

The adjudicating panel consisted of judges representing 11 nations: Sir William Flood Webb (Australia) as the president of the tribunal, Stuart E. McDougall (Canada), Ju-Ao Mei (China), Henri Bernard (France), Lord Patrick (Great Britain), Radhabinod Pal (India), Bernard Röling (the Netherlands), Erima H. Northcraft (New Zealand), Delfin Jaranilla (Philippines), I. M. Zarianov (USSR) and John P. Higgins (United States), who tendered his resignation on 21 June 1946 and was succeeded by Myron H. Cramer (United States).[110] The judges in Tokyo, in contrast to Nuremberg, had no alternates. The chief prosecutor was Joseph B. Keenan (United States).

The indictment was filed on 29 April 1946, the first formal session took place on 3 May 1946 and the judgment was entered on 12 November 1948.

The prosecution brought 55 charges divided into three groups, of which the first one pertained to the crime against peace and consisted of counts 1–36.[111] Counts 1–5 concerned a conspiracy to wage aggressive war or war in violation of international law, treaties, agreements and assurances. Under count 1, between 1928 and 1945 the defendants participated in a conspiracy, the object of which was that Japan should secure the military, naval, political and economic domination of East Asia and of the Pacific and Indian Oceans, and of all countries and islands therein and bordering thereon. For this purpose, Japan alone or in combination with other countries having similar objects, or who could be induced or coerced to join therein, was to wage declared or undeclared war or wars of aggression, and war or wars in violation of international law, treaties, agreements and assurances, against any country or countries which might oppose that purpose.

The prosecution's starting point was therefore to assume that there had been one gigantic conspiracy to wage aggressive wars between 1931 and 1945 but, in order to prevent the acquittal of any of the defendants (should the tribunal decide that a conspiracy of this scale and duration was implausible), it also delineated smaller conspiracies that together contributed to the main one. Consequently, count 2 pertained to a conspiracy with the objective of Japan's waging aggressive war against China, with the purpose of gaining control over Manchuria. Count 3 pertained to aggressive war against China, aimed at dominating China. Count 4 pertained to aggressive war against the United States, Great Britain, France, the Netherlands, China, Portugal, Thailand, the Philippines and the Soviet Union, in order to secure domination over East Asia and the Pacific and Indian Oceans. Count 5 pertained to a conspiracy between the defendants and Germany and Italy in order to wage war against the countries listed in count 4, with the purpose of securing worldwide domination, and special domination for each of these countries in their own sphere.

Counts 6–36 referred to crime against peace. Specifically, counts 6–17 covered planning and preparing wars of aggression against Australia, Canada,

China, France, India, the Netherlands, New Zealand, the Philippines, Thailand, the Soviet Union, Great Britain and the United States. Counts 18–26 covered initiating wars of aggression against the above-listed countries, with the exception of the Netherlands. Counts 27–36 covered waging wars of aggression against all the countries against which war had been planned.

The prosecution went to great lengths to offer evidence of how the defendants, having formed a conspiracy, took over power in Japan, by means that included *coup d'états*, assassinations and infiltrations. The indictment discussed the specific features of the Japanese political system in order to be able accurately to assign the responsibility for Japan's aggressive policies. The importance of the *Hakko Ichiu* principles was presented; these principles advocated the superiority of the Japanese race and the holy mission of subordinating Greater East Asia and the whole world. The indictment also pointed out that Great Britain and the United States were presented as the key enemies.[112] Further, the prosecution offered an analysis of the subsequent stages of the Japanese aggression against specific states.

In selecting the defendants to be tried by the tribunal, the prosecution relied on four guidelines.[113] First of all, individuals against whom no charges of the crime against peace could be made were to be avoided. Secondly, the defendants had to represent a variety of authorities and a variety of degrees of aggression. Thirdly, the defendants had to be individuals to whom key responsibility could be assigned. Fourthly, only individuals against whom strong evidence was available were to be indicted. Eventually, the following individuals were charged: Sadao Araki, Kenji Dohihara, Kingoro Hashimoto, Shunroko Hata, Kiichiro Hiranuma, Koki Hirota, Naoki Hoshino, Seishiro Itagaki, Okinori Kaya, Koichi Kido, Heitaro Kimura, Kuniaki Koiso, Iwane Matsui, Yosuke Matsuoka, Jiro Minami, Akira Muto, Osami Nagano, Takasumi Oka, Shumei Okawa, Hiroshi Oshima, Kenryo Sato, Mamoru Shigemitsu, Shigetaro Shimada, Toshio Shiratori, Teiichi Suzuki, Shigenori Togo, Hideki Tojo and Yoshiiro Umezu.

Okawa, whose writings and speeches continued to swell the numbers of supporters of war, was declared mentally unfit.[114] Two defendants, Matsuoka and Nagano, died before the trial was over, respectively on 26 June 1946 and 5 January 1947.

The tribunal ruled that there had indeed been a conspiracy to secure Japan's domination over East Asia, west and south-west Pacific and Indian Oceans, and certain islands therein. However, despite aspirations of some of the defendants to this effect, the tribunal believed that the prosecution had failed to prove that there had been a conspiracy to ensure domination over North and South America.[115] With this reservation, the tribunal believed count 1 to have been proved[116] and, consequently, there was no need to consider counts 2 and 3 (where the purpose of the conspiracy had been narrowed down) and count 4 (which pertained to the same conspiracy as count 1, but offered more detail on it). On the other hand, the tribunal ruled that there was no evidence of a conspiracy between Germany, Italy and Japan, with the purpose of worldwide domination and division of the world into specific spheres of domination (count 5), even though admittedly certain defendants had dreams of such worldwide domination.

In considering the nature and essence of the conspiracy, the Tokyo Tribunal established that the conspiracy resulted in the planning and preparation of war. Therefore, since all defendants were charged with participating in the conspiracy, it was not necessary to consider counts 6–17, which pertained to planning and preparation for specific wars of aggression.[117] This argumentation is not surprising: while the Charter of the International Military Tribunal listed a conspiracy to plan, prepare, initiate and wage aggressive war, the Charter of the International Military Tribunal for the Far East only specified punish ability of a conspiracy to wage aggressive war.[118] Interestingly, the conspiracy charge was problematic in the Tokyo trial in that Japan had no leader who could be considered equivalent to Hitler, and thus no meetings were held that could be attended by all defendants, and it was difficult to pinpoint one specific plan that had been consequently put into action.[119]

The tribunal ruled, in connection with the counts of initiating and waging aggressive war, that these two counts should not be considered separately, since in this specific case they coincide. The tribunal decided to investigate the guilt solely with regard to the waging of aggressive war, rather than initiating it, and without disregarding counts 18–26, proposed to abstain from their consideration.[120]

As for counts 27–36, pertaining to waging aggressive war or war in violation of international law, treaties, agreements and assurances against specific countries, the tribunal ruled that Japan had indeed waged aggressive war against China, the Commonwealth, France, the Netherlands, the Soviet Union and the United States. Since the tribunal considered the charge of count 27 (waging aggressive war) proven, it abstained from ruling with regard to count 28, which also pertained to waging war against China, but to a narrower extent.[121] The tribunal stated that it was beyond doubt that a war of aggression had been waged against the Philippines, but for the sake of technical accuracy it was considered part of the war of aggression waged against the United States, because during the period of the war the Philippines was not a completely sovereign state.[122] Consequently, the tribunal gave no specific ruling as to the charge of count 30 (war against the Philippines). The justices decided that the prosecution failed to prove that Japan had waged war against Thailand, and count 34 was consequently dismissed.[123]

For the sake of full information it should be added that Justice Pal, in his dissenting opinion, expressed his belief that all the defendants should be acquitted; Justice Bernard claimed that, given the procedural errors, the tribunal should not have ruled on the guilt of the defendants; and Justice Röling in a number of cases noted that the judgment should have been more severe, amounting to the death penalty rather than imprisonment (Oka, Sato and Shimada), while in other cases advocated the acquittal of the defendants who had been found guilty by the tribunal (Hata, Hirota, Kido, Shigemitsu and Togo).[124]

Table 4.2 Accused and convicted in the trial before the IMTFE

Name	*Convicted of:*										*Penalty*
	1. (conspiracy)	*27. (China)*	*29. (US)*	*31.(UK)*	*32. (Netherlands)*	*33. (France)*	*35. (USSR – Khassan)*	*36. (USSR – Nomonhan)*	*54. (war crimes)*	*55.(failure to prevent war crimes)*	
Araki	+	+	No	No	No	No	No	No	No	No	Life imprisonment
Dohihara	+	+	+	+	+	No	+	+	+	–	Death
Hashimoto	+	+	No	No	No	N/A	N/A	N/A	No	No	Life imprisonment
Hata	+	+	+	+	+	N/A	No	No	No	+	Life imprisonment
Hiranuma	+	+	+	+	+	No	No	+	No	No	Life imprisonment
Hirota	+	+	No	No	No	No	No	N/A	No	+	Death
Hoshino	+	+	+	+	+	No	No	N/A	No	No	Life imprisonment
Itagaki	+	+	+	+	+	No	+	+	+	–	Death
Kaya	+	+	+	+	+	N/A	N/A	N/A	No	No	Life imprisonment
Kido	+	+	+	+	+	No	No	No	No	No	Life imprisonment
Kimura	+	+	+	+	+	N/A	N/A	N/A	+	+	Death
Koiso	+	+	+	+	+	N/A	N/A	No	No	+	Life imprisonment
Matsui	No	No	No	No	No	N/A	No	No	No	+	Death
Minami	+	+	No	No	no	N/A	N/A	N/A	No	No	Life imprisonment
Muto	+	+	+	+	+	No	N/A	No	+	+	Death
Oka	+	+	+	+	+	N/A	N/A	N/A	No	No	Life imprisonment
Oshima	+	No	No	No	No	N/A	N/A	N/A	No	No	Life imprisonment
Sato	+	+	+	+	+	N/A	N/A	N/A	+	+	Life imprisonment
Shigemitsu	no	+	+	+	+	+	No	N/A	No	+	7 years imprisonment
Shimada	+	+	+	+	+	N/A	N/A	N/A	No	No	Life imprisonment
Shiratori	+	No	No	No	No	N/A	N/A	N/A	N/A	N/A	Life imprisonment
Suzuki	+	+	+	+	+	N/A	No	No	No	No	Life imprisonment
Togo	+	+	+	+	+	N/A	N/A	No	No	No	20 years imprisonment
Tojo	+	+	+	+	+	+	N/A	No	+	–	Death
Umezu	+	+	+	+	+	N/A	N/A	No	No	No	Life imprisonment

Source: Author.

The most logical division of the defendants appears to be along the lines of the military affiliation: the majority of them were military men, whereas a minority were affiliated with the diplomatic service.

The defendant Tojo was considered the leader of the conspiracy, a Göring-like figure.[125] Tojo was charged, inter alia, with participation in conspiracy and waging aggressive war against China, the United States, the Commonwealth, the Netherlands, France and the Soviet Union (Nomonhan). The tribunal noted that since he became Chief of Staff of the Kwantung Army in June 1937, he was associated with the conspirators as a principal in almost all of their activities. He planned and prepared for an attack on the USSR. Since May 1938, when he was recalled from the field to become Vice Minister of War, he played an important part in the mobilisation of the Japanese economy for war. He opposed suggestions for a peace or compromise with China. He became Minister of War in July 1940, and thereafter was largely responsible for the making of the plans and waging of the wars. As prime minister between October 1941 and July 1944, he supported the policy of totally conquering of China. In the negotiations before the attack on Pearl Harbor, he tried to secure Japan's domination in East and South Asia. In the tribunal's opinion, Tojo bore major responsibility for Japan's criminal attacks on her neighbours. Yet he should be cleared of the charge of the crime against peace with regard to the Soviet Union in 1939, since at the time he held no position of power. He was sentenced to death. The penalty was carried out.[126]

The defendant Araki was a Japanese military officer of high rank. He was accused of participation in conspiracy and waging aggressive war against China, the United States, the Commonwealth, the Netherlands, France and the Soviet Union.[127] The tribunal considered the defendant guilty of participation in conspiracy. It noted that Araki was an energetic proponent of the army policy of political domination at home and of military aggression abroad. As a member of different cabinets, he advanced the army policy to prepare for wars of aggression by stimulating the warlike spirit of the young men of Japan, for example by his speeches and by control of the press inciting and preparing the Japanese people for war. He both approved and actively supported the policies undertaken by the Japanese army in Manchuria and Jehol to separate that territory politically from China, to create a Japanese-controlled government and to place its economy under the domination of Japan. As for the charge of waging aggressive war against China, the tribunal pointed out that Araki, as the Minister for War in the period 1931–1934, continued the war with China and gave his full support to the occupation of Chinese territories. From May 1938 until August 1939, he was Minister of Education, in which capacity he approved and collaborated in military operations in other parts of China. Araki was cleared of other charges by reason of lack of evidence. He was sentenced to life in prison, but did not serve the term in full. He was released from prison in 1955 owing to health concerns. He died in 1966.

Dohihara was a general in the Japanese army. He was charged, inter alia, with participation in conspiracy and waging aggressive war against China, the United States, the Commonwealth, the Netherlands, France and the Soviet Union.[128] According to the tribunal, he was involved in the initiation and development of the war of aggression waged against China in Manchuria and in the subsequent establishment of the Japanese-dominated state of Manchukuo. He was also involved in aggressive actions in other parts of China. Dohihara also participated in political intrigues and closely cooperated with other military leaders in the development, preparation and execution of their plans to bring East and South East Asia under Japanese domination. For this reason, he was guilty of the conspiracy charge. As a general, he participated in wars of aggression against other countries; for example he was a military leader of the Lake Khassan fighting, and at Nomonhan, a part of the army he commanded took part in the fighting. However, the tribunal cleared Dohihara of the charge of war against France, since the decision had only been made in February 1945 and, moreover, the prosecution presented insufficient evidence of the defendant's participation in this war. He was sentenced to death. The penalty was carried out.

Hashimoto was charged with participation in conspiracy and waging aggressive war against China, the United States, the Commonwealth and the Netherlands.[129] The tribunal stressed that he joined the conspiracy early, and that none of the conspirators held more extreme views than he did. He advocated the expansion of Japan through the seizure of Manchuria by force of arms as well as the use of force against all Japan's neighbours for the accomplishment of the aims of the conspirators. He was an ardent admirer of government by military dictatorship. He was a principal in many of the activities whose purpose was to suppress the opposition, including plots designed to overthrow existing cabinets. His publications and the activities of the societies he founded or supported were largely devoted to the destruction of democracy and the establishment of a form of government more favourable to the use of war for achieving the expansion of Japan. In his publications, he advocated an alliance with Germany and Italy, which were bent on similar schemes of expansion and agitated for a great increase in the armaments of Japan. For these reasons, the tribunal ruled that Hashimoto was a principal in the formation of the conspiracy and contributed largely to its execution. He was also declared guilty of aggressive war against China, having played a part in the planning of the Mukden Incident, being a commander of the army that fought there and having done everything within his power to secure the war's success. The tribunal cleared him of all the other charges owing to lack of evidence and sentenced him to 20 years in prison, a term he did not serve in full. He was released from prison in 1954. He died in 1957.

Hata was charged with participation in a conspiracy and waging aggressive war against China, the United States, the Commonwealth, the Netherlands and the Soviet Union.[130] The tribunal ruled that he was guilty of the conspiracy charge as well as the charge of aggressive war with the above-listed countries, with the exception of the Soviet Union. As emphasised by the tribunal, as the Minister for War between August 1939 and July 1940, Hata contributed substantially to the formulation and execution of the aggressive plans and exerted considerable influence on government policy. Under his influence, the war in China was waged with renewed vigour; the Wang Ching Wei Government was established at Nanking; the plans for control of French Indochina were developed; the negotiations with the Netherlands in relation to matters concerning the Netherlands East Indies were conducted; and an agreement with Germany was negotiated. From March 1941 to November 1944, as Commander in Chief of the expeditionary forces in China, he continued to wage war in that country. Afterwards he continued to wage war against China and the Western powers as Inspector General of Military Education, one of the highest active military posts in the Japanese army. Hata was cleared of the charge of aggressive war against the Soviet Union, because when the Lake Khassan hostilities occurred, he was in Central China, and at the time of the Nomonhan Incident, he was Aide-de-Camp to the emperor. The tribunal noted that Hata became War Minister just a little more than a week before the conclusion of the incident. Hata was sentenced to life in prison, but he did not serve the sentence in full. He was released from prison in 1954. He died in 1962.

Itagaki was charged with participation in a conspiracy and waging aggressive war against China, the United States, the Commonwealth, the Netherlands, France and the Soviet Union.[131] The tribunal ruled that he was guilty of the conspiracy charge as well as the charge of aggressive war with the above-listed countries, with the exception of France. The tribunal noted that he had joined the conspiracy by the year 1931, with the immediate object that Japan should seize Manchuria by force of arms. He helped to engineer the Mukden Incident and played a principal part in the establishment of Manchukuo. In 1934, as Vice Chief of Staff of the Kwantung Army, he was active in setting up puppet regimes in Inner Mongolia and North China. Itagaki supported Japan's military occupation of Outer Mongolia as a threat to the territories of the USSR. He used the phrase 'Anti-Communism' to serve as a pretext for Japanese aggression in North China. He took part in the fighting at Marco Polo Bridge in July 1937 as a divisional commander. When he became Minister for War in May 1938, the attacks on China were intensified and extended. He was a party to the ministerial conferences, where he favoured the decision to set up a puppet regime in China to arrange for the exploitation of these areas. As Minister for War in the Hiranuma Cabinet, he was again responsible for the prosecution of the war against China, and for the expansion of Japan's armaments. He was an advocate of a military alliance among Japan, Germany and Italy. He obtained by a trick the consent of the emperor to the use of force against the USSR at Lake Khassan. He was still War Minister during the fighting at Nomonhan. He was a strong supporter of the declaration of Japan's so-called 'New Order' in East Asia and the South Seas, even though he recognised that the attempt to set up the

New Order must lead to war with the USSR, France and Great Britain. He participated in direct fighting, as a commander, in China, Korea and Singapore up to the time of Japan's surrender. His subordinate armies defended Java, Sumatra, Malaya, the Andaman and Nicobar Islands and Borneo. The tribunal offered no elaboration as to his acquittal of the charge of waging war against France. Itagaki was sentenced to death. The penalty was carried out.

Kimura was charged with participation in a conspiracy and waging aggressive war against China, the United States, the Commonwealth and the Netherlands.[132] The tribunal found him guilty as charged. In the statement of grounds, the tribunal noted that, initially, he was engaged in administrative work in the War Ministry. The situation changed when he became Vice Minister for War in April 1941. During his service in this position he was in daily contact with the War Minister and other ministers, vice ministers and bureau chiefs. He was also Councillor of the Planning Board and Councillor of the Total War Research Institute. He had therefore full knowledge of the plans and preparations for the Pacific War and the hostilities in China. Kimura was himself not a leader but he supported the aggressive plans and participated in the formulation and development of the aggressive policies. He was active in direct fighting. He commanded the army in Burma until Japan's surrender, even though he had full knowledge of the illegality of the Pacific War. The tribunal sentenced Kimura to death. The penalty was carried out.

Koiso was charged with participation in a conspiracy and waging aggressive war against China, the United States, the Commonwealth, the Netherlands and the Soviet Union (Nomonhan).[133] The tribunal ruled that he was guilty of the charges, with the exception of waging war against the Soviet Union. The tribunal noted that Koiso had joined the conspiracy in 1931 by participating as one of the leaders of the March Incident, the purpose of which was to overthrow the government. After 1932 he played a leading role in the development of the Japanese plans for expansion as the Chief of Staff of the Kwantung Army. He prepared or concurred in proposals and plans for the political and economic organisation of Manchukuo. He was aware – as the tribunal pointed out – of Japan's aggressive plans, and he went beyond the scope of the normal duties of a Chief of Staff in advising on political and economic matters to further them. While he was Chief of Staff, the military invasion of Jehol and renewed fighting in Manchuria took place. As Overseas Minister, Koiso supported and took part in the direction of the war in China, the beginning of the occupation of French Indochina, and the negotiations intended to obtain concessions from and eventual economic domination of the Netherlands East Indies. During the same period, he advocated the plan for Japan to advance 'in all directions'. When he became prime minister in July 1944, he urged and directed the waging of the war against the Western powers. He retired as prime minister only when it became clear that the war was lost for Japan. However, the tribunal found that there was no evidence that he played any part in the hostilities at Nomonhan. Koiso was sentenced to life in prison. He died in the Sugamo prison in 1950.

The only defendant acquitted both of the conspiracy charge and of the charge of the crime against peace was Matsui.[134] Matsui was charged with participation in a conspiracy and waging aggressive war against China, the United States, the Commonwealth, the Netherlands, France and the Soviet Union. In providing the reasoning for clearing Matsui of these charges, the tribunal noted that, although his close association with the conspirators might suggest that he must have been aware of their purposes and policies, the evidence did not justify a finding that he was a conspirator himself. Matsui was a senior officer of the Japanese army, ranking as a general. He was army commander in Central China. With his troops, he captured the city of Nanking on 13 December 1937. Despite this fact, the tribunal decided that his military service in China in 1937 and 1938 could not be regarded as the waging of an aggressive war; it was the duty of the prosecution to tender evidence which would justify an inference that he had knowledge of the criminal character of that war which, however, in the tribunal's opinion, had not been done. Nonetheless, Matsui was found guilty of war crimes and sentenced to death. The penalty was carried out.

Minami was charged with participation in a conspiracy and waging aggressive war against China, the United States, the Commonwealth and the Netherlands.[135] The tribunal found him guilty only of the charges of conspiracy and war with China. In the statement of reasons, the tribunal noted that, prior to the Mukden Incident, Minami had already associated himself with the conspirators in their advocacy of militarism, and of the expansion of Japan into Manchuria. Therefore, in his capacity of Minister for War and, despite an order to this effect, he took no adequate steps to prevent the incident, which led to the occupation of Manchuria by Japan's army. Minami was convinced that Japan should take over Manchuria and Mongolia for reasons of self-defence. From December 1934 to March 1936, as Commander in Chief of the Kwantung Army, he completed the conquest of Manchuria and aided in the exploitation of that part of China. As noted by the tribunal, Minami was responsible for setting up puppet governments in North China and Inner Mongolia. He was in part responsible for the development of Manchuria as a base for an attack on the USSR. He supported the destruction of the national government of China. The tribunal offered no elaboration as to the grounds of the decision to clear Minami of the remaining charges. He was sentenced to life in prison, but he did not serve the sentence in full. He was released from prison in 1954 owing to health concerns.

Muto was charged with participation in a conspiracy and waging aggressive war against China, the United States, the Commonwealth, the Netherlands, France and the Soviet Union (Nomonhan).[136] The tribunal ruled that he was guilty of the charges, with the exception of waging war against France and the Soviet Union. The tribunal noted that, prior to holding the post of Chief of the Military Affairs Bureau of the Ministry of War, Muto was not involved in the making of high policy, and there is no evidence that in this period he, alone or with others, tried to effect it. When he became Chief of the Military

Affairs Bureau, he joined the conspiracy and began to play an important part in planning, preparing and waging wars of aggression. The tribunal was forced to acquit Muto of the charge of waging war against the Soviet Union: when he became Chief of the Military Affairs Bureau, the fighting at Nomonhan was over, and he was Chief of Staff in the Philippines when Japan attacked France in French Indochina in March 1945 and thus had no part in the waging of this war. Nonetheless, the tribunal sentenced him to death. The penalty was carried out.

Oka, an officer in the Japanese navy, was charged with participation in a conspiracy and waging aggressive war against China, the United States, the Commonwealth and the Netherlands.[137] The tribunal found him guilty as charged, noting that Oka was an active member of the conspiracy during his tenure of office as Chief of the Naval Affairs Bureau and was an active and influential member of the conspiracy. He attended conferences where he participated in the formation and execution of the policy to wage aggressive war against China and the Western powers. The tribunal sentenced him to life in prison, but he did not serve the sentence in full. He was released from prison in 1954.

Sato was charged with participation in a conspiracy and waging aggressive war against China, the United States, the Commonwealth and the Netherlands.[138] The tribunal found him guilty as charged. In the judgment, the tribunal specified that, in 1937, Sato was a member of the Military Affairs Bureau and thereafter he held a number of other positions directly connected with the war. In 1938 he presented the General Mobilization Law to the parliament and made a speech in support of it. It was only in February 1941, when Sato was appointed Chief of the Military Affairs Section of the Military Affairs Bureau, and then when (in April 1942) he attained a position which enabled him to influence the making of policy. For the tribunal, the crucial question was whether Sato was aware that the conspirators' designs were criminal, for thereafter he furthered the development and execution of these designs. In responding to this question, the tribunal invoked Sato's speech of 1938 that, in the judges' opinion, proved that the defendant was fully aware of the army's plans toward China and that he predicted war would occur with the Soviet Union, when a sufficient level of armament and production was reached. The tribunal was thus able to consider him a participant of the conspiracy. The fact that he held positions of power in the government and in the army made it possible to find him guilty on the counts of waging war against the above-listed countries. Sato was sentenced to life in prison, but he did not serve the full term. He was released in 1956.

Shimada was charged with participation in a conspiracy and waging aggressive war against China, the United States, the Commonwealth and the Netherlands.[139] The tribunal found him guilty as charged. In explaining its reasoning, the tribunal stated that, until October 1941, Shimada was simply a naval officer and had no part in the conspiracy. The situation changed when he became first a senior naval officer and then Navy Minister (he held that office until August 1944) and Chief of the Navy General Staff (from February to August 1944). He held positions of significant power in the crucial period from the formation of the Tojo cabinet until the attack on the Western powers. He took part in all the decisions in planning and launching the attack on 7 December 1941, and thereafter played a principal role in waging the war against the United States. The tribunal rejected his defence, based on the claim that his actions were undertaken in self-defence owing to economic and military 'encirclement' of Japan. Shimada was sentenced to life in prison, but he did not serve the full term. He was released in 1955.

Suzuki was charged with participation in a conspiracy and waging aggressive war against China, the United States, the Commonwealth, the Netherlands and the Soviet Union.[140] The tribunal found him guilty, with the exception of the charge of war against the Soviet Union. The tribunal stated that as a lieutenant colonel and member of the Military Affairs Bureau in 1932, he was an active member of the conspiracy. He supported a government that would work towards the accomplishment of the goals of the conspiracy. After the assassination of Premier Inukai in May 1932, he threatened similar acts of violence. During his service with the bureau, he insisted that the USSR was the absolute enemy of Japan and assisted in the preparations then being made to wage aggressive war against it. However, the tribunal ruled that there was no evidence that Suzuki had participated in waging war against the USSR. Furthermore, Suzuki was one of the organisers and head of the political and administrative division of the Asia Development Board and, as such, he actively furthered the exploitation of the parts of China occupied by Japan. Suzuki also became president of the Planning Board (replacing Hoshino) and continued in that position until the fall of the Tojo cabinet on 19 July 1944; thanks to this position, he regularly attended the meetings of the Liaison Conference, the virtual policy-making body for Japan. What was crucial, in the tribunal's opinion, was that Suzuki was present at most of the important conferences leading to the initiation and waging of aggressive wars against the allied powers. Suzuki was sentenced to life in prison, but he did not serve the full term. He was released in 1955.

Umezu was included among the defendants at the last minute and at a very clear directive of the Soviet Union.[141] He was charged with participation in a conspiracy and waging aggressive war against China, the United States, the Commonwealth, the Netherlands and the Soviet Union (Nomonhan).[142] The tribunal found him guilty of the charges, with the exception of the charge of aggressive war against the Soviet Union. The tribunal noted that while in command of Japanese troops in North China from 1934 to 1936, Umezu continued the Japanese aggression in that country. He set up a pro-Japanese local government and, under threat of force, compelled the Chinese to enter in to the Ho-Umezu Agreement of June 1935.

He was Vice Minister for War form March 1936 to May 1938, while the National Policy Plans of 1936 and the Plan for Important Industries of 1937 were decided upon. These plans were one of the prime causes of the Pacific War.

Umezu played an important part in the refusal to endorse the Ugaki cabinet. When the fighting in China broke out anew in July 1937 at Marco Polo Bridge, he was aware of it and approved of the plans to carry on with the war. He was a member of the Cabinet Planning Board, as well as of many other boards and commissions which largely contributed to the formulation of the aggressive plans and to preparations necessary for the execution of these plans. In December 1937, Umezu received from the Chief of Staff of the Kwantung Army plans for preparation for the attack on the USSR, plans for the strengthening of the Kwantung Army, and plans for installations in Inner Mongolia, which were of vital importance both in the preparation for war with the USSR and in connection with the war with China. As the commander of the Kwantung Army between 1939 and 1944, he continued the direction of the economy of Manchukuo, made plans for the occupation of Soviet territories and made plans for the military administration of the Soviet areas to be occupied. Moreover, Umezu served as Chief of the Army General Staff from July 1944 until Japan's surrender, thereby playing a principal part in the waging of the war against China and the Western powers. With reference to his acquittal of the charge of aggressive war against the USSR, the tribunal stated that the fighting at Nomonhan had begun before he took command of the Kwantung Army, and it had ceased immediately thereafter. Umezu was sentenced to life in prison. He died in prison in 1949.

The remaining defendants were either professional politicians or diplomats.

Hiranuma was charged with participation in a conspiracy and waging aggressive war against China, the United States, the Commonwealth, the Netherlands, France and the Soviet Union.[143] The tribunal found him guilty of the charges, with the exception of the charge of aggressive war against France and the Soviet Union (Khassan). The tribunal noted that Hiranuma became a member of the conspiracy, if not at the very beginning, then shortly afterwards. From October 1941 until April 1945 he was one of the senior statesmen. He attended the meeting of senior statesmen on 29 November 1941 to advise the emperor on the question of peace or war with the Western powers, where the decision was made that war was inevitable. At the meeting of the senior statesmen held on 5 April 1945, he strongly opposed any overtures for peace and advocated that Japan should fight to the end. These facts demonstrate that he was one of the leaders of the conspiracy and an active participant in furthering its policy. However, the tribunal cleared him of the charges of waging war against France and the Soviet Union, owing to the lack of evidence of his direct involvement therein. Hiranuma was sentenced to life in prison, but he did not serve the sentence in full. He was released from prison in 1955.

Hirota was a politician believed to be the godfather of the Japanese conspiracy.[144] He was charged with participation in a conspiracy and waging aggressive war against China, the United States, the Commonwealth, the Netherlands, France and the Soviet Union (Khassan).[145] The tribunal noted that Hirota, in the period 1933–1938, initially as the foreign minister and later as the prime minister, was at times the originator and at other times a supporter of the aggressive plans. In the same period, Japan had taken over Manchuria and had taken steps aimed a separating it from China. It was Hirota's cabinet that formulated and adopted the national policy of expansion in East and South Asia. In 1936 he forced the execution of the Anti-Comintern Pact, which was an element of aggressive anti-Soviet policy. He fully supported the military operations in China, and once the real policy towards China was clarified, he made every effort to subjugate China. In the tribunal's opinion, Hirota was either responsible for the plans of continued war with China, as well as plans of other wars, or was a supporter of such plans. For these reasons, the tribunal decided that Hirota had been a member of the conspiracy since 1933, and as a foreign minister was involved in the war against China. He was cleared of the other charges, since there was evidence to prove that he had opposed the war with the Western powers and, from 1938 onwards, he held no public office and there was no evidence of his participation in the other wars. Hirota was sentenced to death. The penalty was carried out.

Hoshino was charged with participation in a conspiracy and waging aggressive war against China, the United States, the Commonwealth, the Netherlands, France and the Soviet Union (Khassan).[146] The tribunal found him guilty of the charges, with the exception of the charge of aggressive war against France and the Soviet Union. The tribunal noted in particular Hoshino's part in the aggression against China. From 1932 onwards, the defendant held a number of offices in Manchuria (Manchukuo), using the resources of this area to serve the military needs of Japan. Although he was nominally a servant of the Government of Manchukuo, and had been so for eight years, he was recalled to Japan in 1940 to become a minister without portfolio and president of the Planning Board. In this position he was the leader in the special steps being taken to equip Japan for the continuation of the aggressive war then being waged in China, and for wars of aggression contemplated against other countries. From April 1941, his official functions were reduced, but upon the accession of Tojo as prime minister in October 1941, Hoshino became the Chief Secretary of the Cabinet and soon after a Councillor of the Planning Board. Therefore, he was in close association with all the preparations for the aggressive war already determined. For these reasons, the tribunal decided that Hoshino was an active member of the conspiracy in the period 1932–1941 and was directly involved with the wars against China, the United States, the Commonwealth and the Netherlands, but that there was no evidence that he participated in waging aggressive war against the Soviet Union and France. Hoshino was sentenced to life in prison, but he did not serve the sentence in full. He was released from prison in 1955.

Kaya was a minister of finance, amongst his other functions. He was charged with participation in a conspiracy and waging aggressive war against China, the United States, the Commonwealth and the Netherlands.[147] The tribunal found him guilty as charged, noting that he had taken part in the formulation of the aggressive policies of Japan, and in the financial, economic and industrial preparation of Japan for the execution of those policies. Throughout this period, particularly as Finance Minister in the first Konoye and Tojo cabinets, and as president of the North China Development Company, he was actively engaged in the preparation for and the carrying out of aggressive wars in China and against the Western powers. He was an active member of the conspiracy alleged in count 1 and was adjudged guilty under that count. As a minister of finance and president of the North China Development Company, he was involved in the preparation and waging of aggressive war against China and the Western powers. The tribunal dismissed the claims that Kaya, as a civilian holding administrative positions, was not consulted with regard to the wars of aggression, and thus could not be responsible for the crime against peace.[148] It would be difficult to believe that, for example, the construction of the Burma-Siam railway line could have been completed without the knowledge thereof on the part of the minister of finance.[149] Kaya was sentenced to life in prison, but he did not serve the sentence in full. He was released from prison in 1955.

Kido was charged with participation in a conspiracy and waging aggressive war against China, the United States, the Commonwealth, the Netherlands, France and the Soviet Union.[150] The tribunal found him guilty of the charges, with the exception of the charge of aggressive war against France and the Soviet Union. As noted by the tribunal, in the period 1930–1936, even though the defendant was a member of the emperor's household and was therefore clearly aware of the political and military actions against Manchuria, he could not have participated in the conspiracy at the time. Only when in 1937 he became a cabinet member did he adopt the views of the conspirators and devote himself to their policy. He was zealous in the pursuit of the war with China, resisting the efforts of the general staff to shorten the war. He was intent on the complete military and political domination of China. As Education Minister, he applied himself to the development of a strong warlike spirit in Japan. When he became Lord Keeper of the Privy Seal, Kido was active in the development of a scheme to implement a totalitarian political system. He advised the emperor and used his influence, including by political intrigue, so as to further the aims of the conspiracy, that is, the domination of China and the whole of East Asia, as well as the areas to the south. As for the war against the Western powers, Kido hesitated, because doubts of complete success were entertained within the navy. In spite of these fears, he was determined to pursue the aggressive war against China, and lent himself, although with less confidence, to the projected war against Great Britain and the Netherlands and, in case of need, against the United States. Despite his doubts, he continued in pursuit of the purposes of the conspiracy. He was largely instrumental in securing the office of prime minister for Tojo with the emperor, and refrained from advising the emperor to take any stand against the war with the Western powers. The tribunal explained its decision to acquit Kido of the charges of waging war against France and the Soviet Union, citing lack of evidence. Kido was sentenced to life in prison, but he did not serve the sentence in full. He was released from prison in 1955.

Oshima, although an army officer, was a diplomat first and foremost. He was charged with participation in a conspiracy and waging aggressive war against China, the United States, the Commonwealth and the Netherlands.[151] The tribunal found him guilty solely of the conspiracy charge. In presenting the reasons for its decision, the tribunal noted that Oshima was responsible for the alliance with Germany. He was first military attaché of the Japanese embassy in Berlin, later being promoted to the post of ambassador there. While holding these positions, he dealt directly with Foreign Minister Ribbentrop, in an endeavour to involve Japan in a full military alliance with Germany. He supported the aggressive policy of the army faction, even in opposition to the Foreign Ministry. Although Oshima was one of the principal conspirators, he took no direct part in the war in China or the Pacific War. Oshima was sentenced to life in prison, but he did not serve the sentence in full. He was released from prison in 1955.

Shigemitsu was yet another diplomat among the defendants; he too was included in this group at the last minute at the insistence on the part of the Soviet Union.[152] He was charged with participation in a conspiracy and waging aggressive war against China, the United States, the Commonwealth, the Netherlands, France and the Soviet Union (Khassan).[153] He was acquitted of the conspiracy charge and of the charge of war with the Soviet Union, but found guilty of the remaining charges. The tribunal noted that there was no evidence that Shigemitsu played any part in the making of policy as councillor of the Board of Manchurian Affairs, and in his other capacities (he served as ambassador to the Soviet Union, Great Britain and China) he never exceeded the functions proper to these offices. The tribunal ruled that he could not be considered a conspirator also for the reason that he repeatedly gave advice to the Foreign Office, which was opposed to the policies of the conspirators. By 1943, when he became Foreign Minister, the policy of the conspirators to wage certain wars of aggression had been settled and was in course of execution. Thereafter, there was neither further formulation nor development of that policy. Yet, in 1943, when he was appointed to a ministerial position, despite being fully aware that so far as Japan was concerned, the Pacific war was a war of aggression and despite his previous advice against the politics of expansion, he began to play a principal part in waging that war until he resigned on 13 April 1945. The ruling of guilty, at least to an extent, was a surprise; most observers had been certain of his acquittal.[154] Shigemitsu was sentenced to seven years in prison, but he did not serve the sentence in full. He was released from prison in 1950.

Yet another diplomat, Shiratori, was charged with participation in a conspiracy and waging aggressive war against China, the United States, the Commonwealth and the Netherlands.[155] The tribunal found him guilty solely of the conspiracy charge. He came into prominence as chief of the Information Bureau of the Foreign Office; in that position he justified Japan's seizure of Manchuria to the press worldwide. He advocated early that Japan should withdraw from the League of Nations. He supported the setting up of a puppet government in Manchuria. He was a minister to Sweden from June 1933 to April 1937, and his letters from this period demonstrate his full support for aggressive war. For example, he claimed that Russian influence should be expelled from the Far East, by force if necessary. Upon his return to Japan, he published articles advocating a totalitarian form of government for Japan and an expansionist policy. As ambassador to Rome and then to Berlin, he participated in the negotiations of a pact with Germany and Italy. He went so far as to refuse to comply with the instructions of the Foreign Minister when the wishes of the conspirators were not met. He carried on propaganda designed to excuse Germany's pact with the Soviet Union. He argued that that Japan should attack China, Russia and the Western powers, and should establish the 'New Order'. He was a proponent of attacking Singapore. His role ended when he became ill in April 1941, and resigned the position of adviser to the Foreign Office in July of that year. The tribunal explained that Shiratori was acquitted of the charges of aggressive wars because he never occupied such a position as would justify a finding that he waged any war of aggression. He was sentenced to life in prison. He died in prison in 1949.

Togo was charged with participation in a conspiracy and waging aggressive war against China, the United States, the Commonwealth, the Netherlands and the Soviet Union (Nomonhan).[156] The tribunal found him guilty of the charges, with the exception of the charge of aggressive war against the Soviet Union. The tribunal pointed out that Togo as Foreign Minister in the Tojo cabinet from October 1941 until September 1942 participated in the planning and preparing for the war. He attended cabinet meetings and conferences and concurred in all decisions adopted. He played a leading role in the negotiations with the United States. He collaborated with other members of the cabinet in the conduct of the war in the Pacific, as well as in the waging of the war in China. Togo claimed in his defence that he had agreed to the cabinet appointment on the assurance that every effort would be made to bring the negotiations with the United States to a successful conclusion. The tribunal, however, observed that when the negotiations failed and war became inevitable, rather than resign in protest, he continued in office and supported the war (Togo returned to the position of Foreign Minister in 1945 in the Suzuki cabinet). As for the decision to clear Togo of the charge of war with the Soviet Union, the tribunal noted that the defendant's only part in relation to that charge was to sign the post-war agreement between the USSR and Japan settling the boundary between Manchuria and Outer

Mongolia. The partial ruling of guilty was a surprise; observers tended to be certain of his acquittal.[157] Togo was sentenced to 20 years in prison. He died in prison in 1948.

4.4 Trials before courts in the occupation zones in Germany

When Gustav Krupp von Bohlen und Halbach was removed from the list of the defendants before the International Military Tribunal (he was declared medically unfit to stand trial) and when the tribunal declined the prosecution's request to extend the list of defendants to include Gustav's son Alfried Krupp von Bohlen, the question arose of organising another trial for representatives of industry.[158] Jackson believed that those holding positions of power in the industrial spheres were as guilty of the crime against peace as politicians, diplomats and members of the military;[159] it was the industrialists who contributed to the rearmament of Germany at such a fast pace. It remained to be decided whether the representatives of the biggest industrial concerns should be tried under the London Agreement, that is, before another joint international military tribunal, or whether national or occupation zone courts would be more appropriate.

Consultations carried out on 5 April 1946 revealed that the Soviet Union was in favour of a series of trials under the London Agreement; France preferred at least one more such trial, provided that it should be shorter than the trial underway in Nuremberg; and Great Britain, initially in favour of proceedings before a national court, eventually endorsed the idea of another trial before an international military tribunal.[160] Americans officially avoided stating that they would not participate in another trial before an international military tribunal, but this position was motivated solely by anxiety over potential diplomatic repercussions resulting from a unilateral departure from the London Agreement.[161]

In the end, another trial before an international military tribunal was not held. The Americans ultimately decided to declare that they would not endorse this option. The decision was undoubtedly motivated by the massive expenses that the United States incurred in connection with the proceedings before the International Military Tribunal No 1. The costs were generated, first, by the need to conduct the proceedings in four languages and, secondly, by the perception that the United States hosted the trial and therefore was responsible for the room and board of the delegations of the remaining states.[162] The Americans were also concerned that the presidency of the second international tribunal might go to a Soviet representative, an option they found unacceptable.[163] There were also predictions that the trial of German industrialists may become a failure of the prosecution owing to the likely acquittal of Schacht in the Nuremberg trial (which did in fact occur), and that it may be perceived as targeting a specific category of individuals, owing to the participation of the French Left and of the Soviet representatives.[164] The American delegation believed that a trial before an occupation zone court would be less expensive, given that it would only need to proceed in two languages (English and German) and, moreover, the procedure would be more straightforward and clearer to the Americans.[165] On these grounds, on 22 January 1947 the American ambassadors notified the governments of Great Britain, France and the Soviet Union that they saw no need for another meeting of the prosecutors from the four states, as requested by the French.[166] In the opinion of the American government, an international military tribunal convened under the London Agreement was not appropriate for the trial of the remaining main German criminals; the trials should occur in the national and occupation zone courts. In this way, each of the occupying states – France, Great Britain, the United States and the Soviet Union – were solely responsible for bringing to justice the criminals in their occupation zones.

In the end, in each of the occupation zones of Germany, a series of trials of war criminals was held. However, all accessible data suggest that only in the trials before the American military courts (that is, the so-called subsequent Nuremberg trials) and the trials before the French military courts did the judges investigate charges of the crime against peace.

4.4.1 Subsequent Nuremberg trials before American military courts

The Americans established occupation zone courts on 18 October 1946, under a regulation of the occupation government. The legal basis for their functioning was the Control Council Law No 10. The courts were intended to try German criminals for the crime against peace, war crimes and crimes against humanity.[167] Twelve more Nuremberg trials were held before these courts, lasting in total from December 1946 to April 1949.

The chief prosecutor Telford Taylor was fully in charge of the selection of defendants. He admitted that the choices he made were contingent not only on the gravity of the violations but also on the likelihood of a fast and relatively inexpensive trial, which in turn depended on the accessibility of evidence and on whether or not the suspects were already in American hands.[168] Taylor realised that the trials would only extend to a very small number from among those who were guilty solely of the crimes listed in the Control Council Law No 10.[169] However, owing to the necessity to wrap up proceedings quickly and to avoid the impression that the prosecution was intent on charging all representatives of a given professional or economic group, he made certain presumptions as to the number of defendants.

The prosecution gave priority to the charge of crimes against peace[170] but, in the end, this charge was filed in only 4 out of the 12 Nuremberg trials (in the IG Farben trial, the Krupp trial, the Ministries trial and the High Command trial). The results were not impressive. From among 68 individuals charged with the crime against peace, only five were found guilty of it (two of these, von Weizsäcker and Wörmann, were cleared of charges after they filed motions to correct judgments).

The prosecution considered bringing charges of the crime against peace in two more cases: the Milch case (*United States v Erhard Milch (Case No 2)*) and the Hostages trial (*United States v Wilhelm List (Case No 7)*).[171] However, the decision was made not to file such charges, since the prosecution held very strong evidence with regard to war crimes and crimes against humanity, sufficient to convict the defendants. Certainly the decision not to file the charge of crimes against peace in the Milch case and in the Hostages trial contributed to the prompt conclusion of the trials, but it turned out to be a tactical error. Taylor had regrets about it: in the case of Milch, a general inspector and field marshal of the Luftwaffe, Göring's deputy in the Aviation Ministry and a member of the Central Planning Office, it would have been relatively easy to prove that he had committed crimes against peace, especially since Milch had attended the key conferences convened by Hitler. Taylor believed that having Milch convicted on the charge of crimes against peace would have encouraged other panels before which such charges were filed.[172] Owing to their complexity, the cases involving charges of crimes against peace were considered by the American military courts last, at the end of 1948 and the beginning of 1949.

Chronologically, the first trial among the subsequent Nuremberg trials at which the charges of aggressive war came up was the so-called IG Farben case, that is, *United States v Carl Krauch et al (Case No 6)*.

The indictment was filed on 3 May 1947, the trial began on 27 August 1947 and the judgment was entered on 29–30 July 1948. The judges in this case were: Curtis Grover Shake (presiding judge), former Chief Judge of the Supreme Court of Indiana; Paul M. Hebert, dean of the Law School of the Louisiana State University; James Morris, Supreme Court Justice from North Dakota; and Clarence F. Merrell, a lawyer from Indiana.

The defendants in the case had all been members of the managing bodies and other high officials of IG Farben Industrie AG (InteressenGemeinschaft Farbenindustrie Aktiengesellschaft): Otto Ambros, Max Brüggemann (removed from the trial on 9 September 1947 owing to health concerns), Ernst Bürgin, Heinrich Bütefisch, Walter Dürrfeld, Heinrich Gattineau, Fritz Gajewski, Paul Häfliger, Erich von der Heyde, Heinrich Hörlein, Max Ilgner, Friedrich Jähne, August von Knieriem, Carl Krauch, Hans Kühne, Hans Kugler, Carl Lautenschläger, Wilhelm Mann, Heinrich Oster, Hermann Schmitz, Georg von Schnitzler, Fritz ter Meer, Christian Schneider and Carl Wurster.

All of the defendants were charged as follows: acting through the instrumentality of Farben and otherwise, with other persons, during a period of years preceding 8 May 1945, they participated in the planning, preparation, initiation and waging of wars of aggression and invasions of other countries, which wars of aggression and invasions were also in violation of international laws and treaties (count 1).[173] The indictment read further that all of the defendants, acting through the instrumentality of Farben and otherwise, with other persons, during a period of years preceding 8 May 1945, participated in the formulation and execution of a common plan or conspiracy to commit war crimes as defined by Control Council Law No 10, or acts which constituted such war crimes (including war crimes and crimes against humanity that were committed as integral parts of crimes against peace). It was emphasised that the defendants were on trial for acts they committed individually as well as for acts of other individuals who acted in execution of the common plan or conspiracy. Moreover, it was stated that all charges, that is, also the charges of war crimes and crimes against humanity, were contemplated under the charge of conspiracy (count 5).[174]

The prosecution presented IG Farben as a chemical and synthetic conglomerate that had already been a major factor in the First World War.[175] Its significance increased as Germany began its rearmament before the Second World War, owing to the production of synthetic gasoline and rubber required by the mechanised and aviation units of the military. IG Farben had lent financial support to the Nazis, spread Nazi propaganda and collected intelligence data in foreign countries through its subsidiaries, closely cooperated with Wehrmacht in matters of armament and equipment, was aware of Hitler's plans of aggressive war at least since 1936, systematically plundered the occupied countries and enslaved the population of these countries.[176]

The prosecution believed that, compared with the other 'industrial' trials, in the IG Farben case the evidence it held was the strongest, especially with regard to the charges of aggressive war.[177] The prosecution was confident that it would be able to prove, first, that the management of IG even before Hitler's accession to power had desired a dictatorship that would be able to act without taking the whims of the masses into consideration and, secondly, that it had wanted to dominate the entire European chemical industry and, if possible, to do so also outside Europe. Thirdly, even before Hitler seized power, IG Farben had entered agreements with him for government support for the expansion of its synthetic gasoline facilities. Fourthly, IG Farben had supported Hitler's accession to power and the reinforcement of his authority by means of substantial financial contributions and systematic propaganda. Fifthly, IG Farben had collaborated closely with Hitler and the German military leaders and had willingly participated in the development of a gigantic German army and air force. Sixthly, in the conflict between Schacht, who believed that unlimited armament was a threat to the financial stability of Germany, and Göring, who held the opposite belief, IG Farben took the latter's side. Seventhly, Carl Krauch, the director of IG Farben, had been Göring's direct counsel and the leading figure of the entire chemical industry. Eighthly, IG Farben had accounted for 75 per cent of Göring's Four-Year Plan, which was the basis of Germany's armament. Ninthly, owing to their strategic position in the production of rubber, petrol, munitions and poison gas, the managers of IG Farben had been aware of the fact that the rearmament efforts by far exceeded any conceivable defence measures. Tenthly, IG Farben had prepared plans of seizure of the chemical industries in the countries over which Germany was to take control, and implemented them immediately after the countries had been subdued. Finally, IG Farben participated in the conferences with military and political leadership; the conferences consisted not in exchange of purely technical information, but were extremely aggressive and pro-war in nature. The prosecution pointed also, inter alia, to the Krauch report, in which the defendant argued that Germany and its allies had to become powerful enough to exceed the power of all other states of the world combined.[178]

However, the prosecution failed to convince the tribunal. All the defendants were acquitted of the charge of the crime against peace and of the charge of conspiracy to commit such a crime. In explaining the reasons for their decision, the judges stated that the International Military Tribunal had been very careful with regard to charges of the crime against peace and conspiracy charges, and only convicted defendants of these two charges when strong evidence had been provided that the defendants had awareness of the crimes and had actively participated in their commission.[179] The judges explained that only persons who remained as close to Hitler as Hess, or persons who participated in the conferences on 5 November 1937, 23 May 1939, 22 August 1939 and 23 November 1939 could have been aware of Hitler's aggressive plans. The judges disagreed with the claim that at some point in Germany there was general awareness of Hitler's intentions; they cited a number of Hitler's speeches in which he renounced violence[180] and the conspirators made efforts to keep their plans secret.[181] Invoking again the ruling of the International Military Tribunal, the judges noted that armament as such is not a crime, and none among the defendants was a military expert. It cannot therefore be assumed that they knew that the scale of military production exceeded the scope of self-defence.[182]

The judges pointed out that the International Military Tribunal had set a standard for determining participation in crimes against peace at the level of individuals who run a state; the defendants in the IG Farben trial were neither high government officials nor high-ranking military officers.[183] They were not leaders but followers, and therefore could not be punished for any participation in crimes against peace.[184] Had the judges adopted a different view, and assigned the defendants responsibility for crimes against peace, it would have resulted in a situation where the great majority of Germans would have to be considered guilty of crimes against peace, and the guilt would be not individual but collective 'to which the corollary of mass punishment is the logical result for which there is no precedent in international law and no justification in human relations'. Good citizens may not be placed in a position where no matter what they do, they are either criminals or traitors.

In considering the guilt of the individual defendants, the judges first focused on the four persons who had held the highest positions: Krauch, Schmitz, von Schnitzler and ter Meer. The judges declared that these persons had participated in the process of Germany's armament, but decided that it had not been proved beyond reasonable doubt that they were engaged in these actions with the awareness that they were preparing Germany for aggressive war.[185] In the case of Krauch, the court ruled that his report, invoked by the prosecution, proved only that Krauch had intended to strengthen Germany which, in his opinion, was surrounded by other strong foreign powers, which could lead to war.[186] The court noted that Krauch spoke to Hitler on only one occasion, in 1944; moreover, he was scolded by Göring on that day.[187] He was responsible for the establishment and functioning, within IG Farben, of War Economic Central Office of Farben for all matters of military economy and questions of military policy (Vermittlungsstelle W), which collected data on the armament process, but the agency had no impact on policy-making.[188] Moreover, the government positions held by Krauch gave him no decision-making authority, since his role was limited to providing expert opinions.[189]

The court decided in regard to the remaining 19 defendants that there was no need to investigate whether they were aware of Germany's preparations for aggressive war, given that the positions they held were lower than those of the other four defendants.[190]

Judge Hebert disagreed with the reasoning behind the judgment. In his dissenting opinion, he argued that the role that IG Farben played was immense, and the management was aware that it was not involved in normal business activity but rather in preparations for war, as evidenced, for example, by the fact that it destroyed documentation.[191] However, since the defendants' guilt had not been proved beyond reasonable doubt, it was necessary to acquit them.

The acquittal of all defendants of the charge of crimes against peace and of the charge of conspiracy is definitely controversial, especially in the light of the fact that during the consultations between the allied powers as to the possibility of bringing industry representatives to trial, three from among the six names that were listed on that occasion were connected with IG Farben (Schmitz, von Schnitzler, Ilgner).[192] The ruling in the IG Farben case undoubtedly influenced the decision to acquit Schacht and Speer of the charge of crimes against peace before the International Military Tribunal, and to acquit of the same charge Hermann Röchling (whose trial is discussed in more detail below) before the French occupation court, even though the judges were fully aware that the concern had played an inherent part in the construction of Germany's machinery of war.[193] Some of the defendants were convicted for war crimes and crimes against humanity, but none of the sentences exceeded eight years' imprisonment.

The next trial of German industrialists was the Krupp trial, that is, *United States v Alfried Krupp von Bohlen und Halbach (Case No 10).* In this trial too all the defendants were charged with the crime against peace and participation in a conspiracy to commit crimes against peace. The indictment was filed on 16 August 1947, the trial began on 8 December 1947 and the judgment was entered on 31 July 1948. The adjudicating panel's members were Hu C. Anderson of the Court of Appeals of the State of Tennessee, Edward

James Daly of the Supreme Court of Connecticut and William John Wilkins of the Supreme Court of Washington.

Gustav Krupp von Bohlen und Halbach should have been the principal defendant in the trial, since he was the leader of Krupp, but the condition of his health made it impossible. Instead, the prosecution charged his son, Alfried Krupp von Bohlen und Halbach. He held his first positions of power in the company starting in 1937, and from 1940 onwards he was practically in charge of the entire company, having taken over most of his father's duties. Beside him, the following persons were the defendants: Friedrich von Bülow, Karl Eberhardt, Eduard Houdremont, Max Ihn, Friedrich Janssen, Heinrich Korschan, Hans Kupke, Heinrich Lehmann, Ewald Löser, Erich Müller and Karl Pfirsch.

The charges brought against the representatives of Krupp mirrored those brought in the case of IG Farben. Count 1 pertained to crimes against peace, and count 4 – participation in a conspiracy.[194] After the trial had already begun, prosecution withdrew these charges with regard to Kupke, Lehmann and von Bülow.[195]

The prosecution argued that the Krupp enterprise had been a leader of secret and illegal armament, and the Krupp family had been engaged in the armament process for 133 years.[196] It noted that the Krupp enterprise was the principal manufacturer of large calibre artillery and armour plate, as well as the largest private builder of U-boats and warships, and the second largest producer of iron and coal in Germany, and thus had contributed substantially to the ability of the Third Reich to wage its invasions and wars of aggression.[197] The prosecution also alleged that, beginning as early as 1919, Krupp violated the Treaty of Versailles and misinformed supervisory authorities.[198] Krupp supported Hitler, subsidised the NSDAP,[199] synchronised its activities with the German government and used its foreign affiliates to carry out extensive espionage.[200] Immediately after the indictment was read and the opening speeches of the prosecution were delivered, the defence counsels filed a motion dated 11 March 1948 for an acquittal on the charges of crimes against peace and conspiracy to commit crimes against peace.[201] They argued that the defendants had not participated in Hitler's most important conference, at which plans for aggressive wars were discussed, they were familiar neither with the proceedings at these conferences nor the plans of aggressive wars discussed therein and thus did not have the relevant state of mind. None of the defendants played a significant political role, and therefore it was difficult to charge them with waging aggressive war.

The motion was granted. On 5 April 1948 the military tribunal acquitted all defendants of the charges of the crime against peace and conspiracy to commit such a crime. The reasons for this decision were explained in an opinion dated 11 June 1948. In the opinion, the military tribunal stated clearly that it was not claiming that industrialists could under no circumstances be tried for the crime against peace but that, in this specific case, their guilt had not been proved beyond reasonable doubt.[202] The conspiracy in which the Krupp leadership had allegedly participated did not pertain to any specific war.[203] The tribunal dismissed the line of reasoning that a person could be considered guilty of participation in a conspiracy before plans for specific wars were crystallised.[204] Furthermore, the tribunal asserted that it was wrong to distinguish between a Nazi conspiracy and a separate Krupp conspiracy.[205] It noted that the defendants had not participated in Hitler's most important conferences and were not informed of the decision made therein.[206] The tribunal also took into consideration the fact that Speer, who had held higher positions than the defendants, had been acquitted of the charges of conspiracy and the crime against peace.[207]

The tribunal's judgment was appended with two opinions that touched upon the issue of responsibility for the crime of aggression and further explained the reasons behind the decision to acquit the defendants of the charge of crimes against peace.

Judge Anderson in his opinion argued that the prosecution attempted to prove the existence of a separate and private conspiracy (independent from the Nazi conspiracy) to result in the commission of the crime against peace.[208] The prosecution must make out a prima facie case of guilt by competent and relevant evidence, and the proceedings against Gustav Krupp could not be used as an argument against the other defendants.[209] It is also difficult to argue in a believable manner that the defendants had been aware of the plans for aggression, given that all such plans were secret, and strict censorship prevailed.[210] In Anderson's opinion, the acquittal of Speer eliminated the possibility of convicting the defendants in the Krupp case.[211] He noted that no responsibility should be placed on private citizens who aid in the war effort if they had no vote and impact as to the waging of the war or the decision to continue it;[212] to do otherwise is to engage in mass punishment.[213]

Judge Wilkins stated that there could be no doubt that Gustav Krupp must have been aware of Hitler's aggressive plans, just like the other defendants who held top positions.[214] However, given the immense discretionary power that Gustav Krupp had in the enterprise, there may be some doubt as to whether the defendants had any impact on the course of events; an interpretation of this fact in favour of the defendants led the tribunal to make the decision to acquit them.[215]

The judgment may be considered a scandal, given that all the defendants had held top positions in a heavy industry enterprise and, therefore, based on the quantity of equipment ordered, delivery deadlines and production plans, they must have been aware of the plans for aggressive wars.[216] The allies had seemed in agreement as to the notion that Krupp representatives should be tried, inter alia, for crimes against peace in the subsequent trials of Nazi criminals. On the other hand, the military tribunal's judgment, disappointing as it was for the prosecution, was rather predictable, given the acquittal of Schacht and Speer of the charges of crimes against peace.[217] All it took to obtain an acquittal was proof that the defendants were not aware of Hitler's plans.[218] The atmosphere in 1948 was also very different from that in 1946, the time of the Nuremberg trial. Two years later, it was much more favourable towards the industrialists.[219] The defence counsels felt much more confident, which was clearly visible in some incidents in the courtroom.[220] Public opinion, not only in Germany but also in the West, demanded the acquittal of Krupp representatives of all charges, and return of the property they had forfeited under the judgment.[221] General Lucius Clay (military governor of the American occupation zone) withstood these demands, but his successor John J. McCloy did not; he returned the property to the Krupp family and released from imprisonment all defendants convicted for war crimes and crimes against humanity.[222]

The next trial at which the charge of the crime again peace was bought was the High Command trial (OKW trial, from the German name: Oberkommando der Wehrmacht), that is, *United States v Wilhelm von Leeb et al (Case No 12).*

The indictment was filed on 28 November 1947, the trial started on 5 February 1948 and the judgment was rendered on 28 October 1948. The judges in this case were John C. Young, former president of the Supreme Court of Colorado, Justin W. Harding, a former judge from Alaska and Winfield B. Hale, an appellate court judge from Tennessee.

The prosecution had wanted to put all the top leadership of the German army on the defence stand. It approached Great Britain with a request to hand over Gerd von Rundstedt, Walter von Brauchitsch and Erich von Mannstein. However, the British authorities refused to hand over the generals, assuring the prosecution that they would be put on trial in Great Britain.[223] Preparations for the trial proceeded with no urgency. Consequently, von Brauchitsch died free in 1949, von Runstedt's health was too fragile for him to be put on trial and the case of von Mannstein became politicised, even though he was eventually tried for war crimes in 1949 and sentenced to 18 years in prison. He did not serve the sentence in full; he was released in 1953 owing to his failing health.[224]

In Nuremberg, the highest-ranking German commander put before the American tribunal was Wilhelm von Leeb who was, after von Runstedt, the top ranking German marshal during the Second World War (formally, he ranked fifth). The following defendants were indicted along with him: Karl Hollidt, Hermann Hoth, Georg Karl Freidrich Wilhelm von Küchler, Rudolf Lehmann, Hermann Reinecke, Hans Reinhardt, Karl von Roques, Hans von Salmuth, Otto Schniewind, Hugo Sperrle, Walter Warlimont, Otto Wöhler and Johannes Blaskowitz, who committed suicide on 5 February 1948. All defendants were members of the High Command, that is, the authority in charge of the armed forces that was responsible for coordinating the three types of forces and all military affairs.

All defendants were charged with the crime against peace (count 1) and participation in a conspiracy (count 4).[225]

The prosecution stressed the special role and status of soldiers in Germany, citing the quip by the Marquis de Mirabeau: 'Prussia is not a state with an army, but an army with a state'.[226] It presented the relations between Wehrmacht and Hitler and the role he played in the specific acts of aggression.[227] It pointed out that the defendants had participated in Hitler's conferences where plans for aggressive wars were discussed. This last factor had apparently been decisive in the sentencing of Keitel, Jodl, Raeder and von Neurath by the International Military Tribunal for the crime against peace.[228]

Yet the American tribunal decided to acquit all defendants of the charge of the crime against peace. The charge of conspiracy to commit the crime against peace was dismissed, since the tribunal argued that it was fully included in the former charge.[229]

In explaining the grounds for its decision, the tribunal discussed the nature and characteristics of war and argued that war was the implementation of a specific policy by means of force; if the policy has a criminal aspect, either in terms of its intent or in terms of its purpose, it is only because the individuals behind this policy have this criminal intent and purpose.[230] If therefore the defendants had no impact on the shaping of the policy, they cannot be considered guilty of the crime against peace.[231] Actions undertaken by commanders and staff officers who were below policy-making level, consisting in planning campaigns or undertaking operations against other states in line with the orders they received, did not amount to the crime against peace.[232] The boundary between the criminal and the excusable participation in the waging of an aggressive war by an individual engaged in it was somewhere between the dictator, the supreme commander and the common soldier.[233] The tribunal argued that the defendants may have failed to live up to their moral obligations, but that could not be considered a crime.[234] The fact that there was evidence of the defendants' opposition to Hitler's plans was interpreted in their favour.[235] Most of the defendants were nonetheless convicted of other crimes (crimes against humanity and war crimes). The sentences ranged from three years' imprisonment to life in prison.

As illustrated by the argumentation cited above, the tribunal – somewhat surprisingly – considered the position of the defendants to be essentially the same as the position of ordinary soldiers. Why should Admiral Schniewind, who had been in charge of planning the invasion of Norway and Denmark, be less guilty than Keitel or Dönitz?[236] Clearly, in the few years that had passed after the war, the situation had radically changed in favour of the defendants.

The only conviction for the crime against peace in the subsequent Nuremberg trials occurred in the so-called Ministries trial (also known as the Wilhelmstrasse trial), that is, *United States v Ernst von Weizsäcker et al (Case No 11).*

The indictment was filed on 4 November 1947, proceedings began on 6 January 1948 and the judgment was presented on 11–13 April 1949. The judges were: William C. Christianson, former judge of the supreme court of the state of Minnesota; Leon W. Powers, former judge of the supreme court of the state of Iowa; and Robert F. Maguire, an attorney from the state of Oregon.

There were 21 defendants in the case. The charge of the crime against peace was brought against 17 of them (count 1), as was the charge of conspiracy to commit the crime against peace (count 2). Those accused of these crimes were: Ernst von Weizsäcker, Wilchelm Keppler, Ernst Bohle, Ernst Wörmann, Karl Ritter, Otto von Erdmannsdorff, Edmund Veesenmayer, Hans Heinrich Lammers, Wilhelm Stuckart, Richard Walther Darré, Otto Meissner, Otto Dietrich, Gottlob Berger, Walter Schellenberg, Lutz Schwerin von Krosigk, Paul Körner and Paul Pleiger. After the indictment was filed, the prosecution applied for the dismissal of these two charges with regard to Bohle, von Erdmannsdorff and Meissner.[237] The tribunal granted the application.

As for the count of conspiracy, the tribunal ruled that no defendant could be convicted of it, because no sufficiently convincing evidence to this effect had been presented.[238] What remained was the charge of the crime against peace brought against the defendants.

From among those convicted on the count of the crime against peace, von Weizsäcker generated the greatest interest, because he had many friends in those countries where he had served as the German ambassador.[239] The prosecution argued that von Weizsäcker had played a pivotal role in preparing the diplomatic plans, in general preparation, and in the diplomatic stage of aggressive wars.[240] The defence pointed to the fact that von Weizsäcker did not support the Nazi plans, was active in the opposition movement and even went so far as to want Hitler's removal from his position.[241] However, the tribunal decided that good intentions were not enough to be relieved of criminal responsibility.[242] It noted that von Weizsäcker, as a secretary of state at the Foreign Ministry, had oversight over all units of the ministry, and thus issued them with instructions and received information from them.[243] He did not participate in Hitler's conferences, but – in the opinion of the tribunal – was informed of the decisions that had been reached there, for example by von Ribbentrop. He was therefore aware of the plans for aggression.

Von Weizsäcker was found guilty of the count of the crime against peace, but only with regard to Czechoslovakia. The tribunal decided that he had knowledge of the plans for the invasion and had played an important part therein, by means of conducting the negotiations with Czechoslovakia and with the allied forces.[244] The steps he took with the purpose of warning of the invasion were described by the tribunal as 'anaemic'.[245]

He was acquitted of the charge of the crime against peace with regard to the other states listed in the indictment. The tribunal admitted that von Weizsäcker had knowledge of the plans for the aggression, but he himself participated neither in the planning or preparing nor in the waging of aggressive war. For instance, in the case of Austria, he supported certain political moves, but had no desire for the invasion;[246] he was in charge of implementing the plans rather than designing them.[247] Also in his favour was the fact that he tried to warn other states of the possibility of aggression (eg with regard to the aggression against Poland[248]), he often advised his superiors to abstain from specific aggressive plans (in the case of the Sudetenland,[249] Belgium, the Netherlands, Luxembourg[250] and Russia[251]), in a few cases he was unable to have any impact on Hitler's decisions (eg in the case of Russia) or there was not time for him to take the necessary preventive measures (Denmark and Norway[252]); he had also never advised in favour of attacking the United States.[253]

Judge Powers disagreed with the judgment that partially found the defendant guilty of the crime against peace. Powers believed that the actions taken with regard to Czechoslovakia could overall not be considered a crime against peace.[254] He doubted whether von Weizsäcker was aware of the plans of aggression and whether in fact von Ribbentrop had shared all the relevant information with him.[255] Even if the matter of lacking awareness of the aggressive nature of Germany's actions, Powers argued, the defendant hardly played a sufficiently important role in politics to be able to prevent the German aggression.[256]

Von Weizsäcker was sentenced to seven years in prison.[257] However, owing to the length and complexity of the proceedings, the tribunal allowed the defendants whose interests might have been injured to file memoranda for the correction of errors and alleged facts.[258] All defendants who had been convicted of the crime against peace took this opportunity, including von Weizsäcker. In the end, the tribunal cleared him of the charge of the crime against peace with regard to Czechoslovakia, as it concluded that during the negotiations with representatives of Czechoslovakia, he had not misled them as to Hitler's intentions;[259] von Weizsäcker did not participate in any stage of the commission of the crime against peace, since he neither planned nor prepared nor waged the attack, and therefore should be acquitted.[260] His punishment was reduced to five years in prison. Following a decision of John J. McCloy, von Weizsäcker was released in 1950.[261] He died in 1951.

The next diplomat convicted of the crime against peace was Keppler, who played a special part in the Austrian aggression: it was Keppler who communicated to Austria the German ultimatum, demanding that Schuschnigg be replaced by Seyss-Inquart or else the German army would invade.[262] The tribunal accepted that Keppler was Hitler's direct representative in Austria, and was involved in the execution of the plans of invasion that had been made before his arrival in Vienna. Keppler was also declared guilty of aggression against Czechoslovakia. The tribunal noted that he had participated in Göring's conferences where Slovaks were being encouraged to strive for independence from Czechs.[263] What worked primarily to Keppler's disadvantage was his presence in Hitler's headquarters during the negotiations with Hácha, and the fact that he conducted the negotiations with Slovakia with respect to the treaty of friendship and defence that was to lead to the division of Czechoslovakia. Again, Judge Powers dissented; he argued that the defendant had not initiated the invasion against

Czechoslovakia and Austria and had no desire for the army to enter their territories.[264] Nonetheless, the tribunal sentenced Keppler to 10 years in prison, and refused to change the ruling after Keppler's memorandum was filed.[265] Keppler was released under McCloy's January 1951 decision.[266] He died in 1960.

Wörmann, head of the political division in the Foreign Ministry in the key period 1938–1943, was also convicted of the crime against peace. The prosecution claimed that he had been assigned many tasks of major importance that required absolute discretion. On the other hand, the defence argued that the position he held was relatively low, and that he was in conflict with von Ribbentrop.[267] The tribunal initially decided that the defendant was responsible for the diplomatic preparations for the war with Poland and diplomatic actions when war was already underway.[268] The documents that the defendant had sent to German outposts abroad, including the White Book on the invasion of Poland, were indicated as evidence.[269] He was also responsible for the decisions of the High Command taken after the Polish invasion, such as the closing of borders and for the negotiations with Slovakia as to the use of its territory to facilitate the attack against Poland.[270] As for the aggression against Czechoslovakia, the tribunal ruled that Wörmann's part in it was insignificant.[271] As for the actions aimed against Denmark, the prosecution failed to present convincing evidence of Wörmann's participation in the aggression.[272] With regard to the charge of the crime against peace in other countries, the tribunal decided that the defendant neither waged aggressive war nor participated in the formulation or execution of a plan of such a war.[273] Wörmann was initially sentenced to seven years in prison, but when he filed the memorandum, the tribunal changed its position, clearing him of the charge of aggression against Poland under the *de minimis* clause.[274] The tribunal came to the conclusion that the documents Wörmann had received must have made him aware of the plans for the aggression, but nonetheless his part in the execution and implementation of these plans was minor. Since doubts remained as to his precise contribution to the aggression, they had to be interpreted in favour of the defendant and, consequently, he should be cleared of the charge.[275] Wörmann's sentence was reduced to five years in prison[276]. He did not, however, serve the sentence in full; he was released in January 1950. He died in 1979.

Another defendant convicted of the crime against peace was Lammers. The tribunal believed that, owing to the positions he held (head of the Reich Chancellery and minister), Lammers had policy-making influence.[277] The tribunal noted that Lammers had drafted the Four-Year Plan, and thus was in the position to make accommodation for the needs arising out of aggressive wars. He was a member of the Ministers' Committee established by Göring in 1936 and, as such, contributed to the work on the fundamental decisions. He was one of the select few individuals (next to Hitler and Göring) who had signed the Reich Defense Law of 4 September 1938. He was a member of the Council for the Defence of the Reich, the very authority in charge of preparations for war. He signed the decree establishing the Ministerial Council for Reich Defense, which drafted the plans of aggression against Poland.

Lammers was found guilty of aggression against Czechoslovakia (he participated in the conference with Hácha and signed the decree establishing the Reich Protectorate of Bohemia and Moravia),[278] Poland, Norway, Russia (on top of his involvement in the preparations for the aggression, there were many decrees which he had signed pertaining to the administration of these territories), Belgium, the Netherlands and Luxembourg (three months before the invasion, he transmitted to Nazi dignitaries plans of invasion against these states).[279] He was, on the other hand, acquitted of the charges of aggression against Austria and Denmark, since there was no evidence of his active role in the invasions against these states.[280] Judge Powers dissented again; he believed that the individuals involved in the drafting of the Four-Year Plan were not necessarily aware of the plans for the aggression.[281]

Lammers was sentenced to 20 years in prison;[282] the ruling was not amended after this memorandum was considered. However, under McCloy's decision of January 1951, his sentence was reduced to 10 years in prison.[283] He died in 1962.

The last defendant found guilty of the charge of the crime against peace was Körner, whose part in the execution of the Four-Year Plan was particularly emphasised by the tribunal.[284] Interestingly, Körner attempted to defend Göring (and thus himself) by claiming that he was a man of peace.[285] In light of the Nuremberg judgment there was no chance of this argumentation being accepted. The tribunal decided that Körner, who often acted as Göring's deputy at important meetings, must have been aware of the plans of aggression and, moreover, must have had an impact on the formulation of the plans for aggressive wars.[286] In view of these arguments, the tribunal sentenced Körner to 15 years in prison.[287] The ruling was not amended despite the memorandum, but McCloy's 1951 decision resulted in a reduction of Körner's sentence to 10 years.[288] Körner died in 1957.

As for the remaining defendants, the prosecution insisted that Ritter and Veesenmayer had played a key part, right beside von Weizsäcker and Keppler, in the diplomatic planning and preparations for the aggressive wars.[289] As for Stuckart, it was noted that together with Lammers he was responsible for the incorporation of the subdued territories, and was one of the main administrators thereof.[290] Darré was responsible for the mobilisation of agriculture for the purposes of the aggressions.[291] Schwerin von Krosigk was in charge of the economic preparation for the aggression, and hosted the first cabinet meeting after Hitler's electoral victory.[292] Pleiger was involved in the organisation and establishment of Herman Göring Works. Berger assisted Lammers in the establishment of the Fifth Column in other states.[293] Dietrich was heavily involved in propaganda, and Schellenberg was behind the Venlo incident which was used to justify the invasion against the Netherlands, and was also the creator of SS Einsatzgruppen.[294]

The tribunal decided that all the defendants apart from von Weizsäcker, Keppler, Wörmann, Lammers and Körner should be cleared of the charge of the crime against peace. It ruled that the defendants were not aware of the plans of aggression, either because the positions they held were too low or too far removed from waging aggressive wars (Berger, Veesenmayer), or because they did not participate in Hitler's conferences where the plans for aggression were revealed, or there was no evidence that they were informed of the decisions made at these conferences (Darré, Dietrich, Stuckart).[295] In spite of this, most of the defendants received prison sentences, since they were convicted on counts of war crimes or crimes against humanity.

4.4.2 Trials before French courts

In the French zone, the General Tribunal at Rastatt of the Military Government for the French Zone of Occupation in Germany was established. It heard one case that pertained to the crime against peace, namely the case of directors of the Röchling enterprise and specifically Hermann Röchling, Ernst Röchling, Hans Lothar von Gemmingen-Hornberg, Albert Maier and Wilhelm Rodenhauser.

The panel consisted of one Belgian judge, Elleboudt, one Dutch judge, Baron van Tuyll and five French judges: Marcel Pihier as the presiding judge, Hornbostel, Tschiember, Lévy and Roger Toillon.[296] Charles Gerthoffer prosecuted. The indictment was filed on 25 November 1945 and later modified on 15 April 1948 so as to withdraw the charge of the crime against peace against all defendants, with the exception of Hermann Röchling, who was on trial *in absentia*.[297] The judgment in the first instance was issued on 30 June 1948.

The prosecution pointed out that Röchling was in close touch with Hitler (commencing at the latest in 1933 when he helped raise large amounts of money to support Hitler) as well as other key officials in the Reich.[298] He was involved in military and economic espionage, and supported the so-called 'Independence for Alsace' movement. He was behind the boom in the steel industry accomplished as a part of the Four-Year Plan. He was responsible for the Nazi exploitation of the steel industry and the plunder of iron ore and steel in the occupied territories, most importantly France. The charges against him alleged that he advocated and contributed to the preparation for and waging of wars of aggression, and exploited the resources and population of occupied territories with a view to strengthening the military potential of the Reich.

The tribunal conceded that Röchling participated in the conferences with Göring in the period 1936–1937, where the issues of armament were discussed, but argued that did not constitute a sufficient reason to conclude that he was informed of the preparations for the wars of aggression, and the fact of armament itself is not necessarily a symptom leading up to aggressive war.[299] Therefore, the tribunal was forced to conclude that Röchling did not participate in the preparation for wars of aggression.[300] Yet the tribunal ruled that after the attack against Poland in 1939 no doubt could remain as to the fact that wars of aggression were being waged; despite this, the defendant accepted high administrative positions. He became the Reich Commissioner of the iron industry of the departments of Moselle and Meurthe-et-Moselle Sud and did everything in his power to increase steel production to benefit the Reich. When in 1942 he was appointed Reichsbeauftragter, he was put in charge of the exploitation of Norway, Alsace, Lorraine, Luxembourg, Styria, South Carinthia, Bohemia and Moravia, Poland, Ukraine and Serbia, with extensive powers to employ any measures necessary to increase the production of steel. In this way, he contributed for three years to the war effort.[301] Röchling was sentenced to seven years in prison[302] for a number of reasons. First, his actions and the personal initiative he took (especially in his position as plenipotentiary) contributed to the enslavement of the steel industry in the occupied territories with the aim of increasing the military potential of the Reich. Secondly, his actions and personal initiative as the president of the 'Reich Association Iron' led to an increase in iron and steel production for the purpose of conducting aggressive wars. Thirdly, he provided advice to the Reich government with regard to deportations of the populations of the occupied territories with a view to using them for slave labour and to fight against their own countries.[303]

Röchling's case did not end with the ruling of the General Tribunal of the Military Government for the French Zone of Occupation. The Supreme Court of the Military Government issued a judgment in his case on 25 January 1949. The adjudicating panel was composed of French judges (Fournier, Weninger, At, Tournier and Gous), as well as a Dutch judge (Meijer) and Belgian judge (Huens). Gerthoffer prosecuted.

The court of appeal cleared the defendant from the charge of the crime against peace. In its statement of grounds, the court explained that the key factor was whether Röchling's cooperation with Hitler and Göring in the preparation and waging of wars of aggression was sufficient and whether he had been sufficiently aware of his involvement, particularly considering that it was Göring that was in charge of all matters connected to resources.[304] The court also noted that under the Charter of the International Military Tribunal as well as under the Control Council Law No 10 only the principal authors of or participants in crimes against peace were to be prosecuted and punished.[305] The court decided that it had no other option but to acquit the defendant, because sufficient evidence had not been adduced to establish that his participation in the rearmament had for its purpose the facilitation of invasions of other countries or wars of aggression in violation of international law and treaties.[306] As the Nuremberg Tribunal had implied earlier, the rearmament of a country in itself did not necessarily imply the intention to wage aggressive war. The defendant had held no leadership position in the war effort, and he had become the head of the metallurgical industry only a considerable time after the wars of aggression had been launched.[307] He had doubtless supported the war effort with his actions, but that did not by itself amount to participation in the conduct of war. However, owing to the defendant's participation in war crimes, the court sentenced him to 10 years in prison, deprivation of civil rights and forfeiture of assets. Röchling was scheduled for release in October 1955, but he was pardoned and released in 1951. He died in 1955.

4.5 Trials before national courts

4.5.1 Trials before the Supreme National Tribunal in Poland

In Poland, the decree of 22 January 1946 established the Supreme National Tribunal, competent inter alia in the following cases:

> cases regarding crimes of persons who, under the Moscow Declaration of the three allied powers: the United States of North America, the Union of Soviet Socialist Republics and Great Britain, on the responsibility of Nazis for the atrocities they committed, will be surrendered to the prosecuting authorities of the Republic of Poland for the crimes committed on the territory of the Polish State under enemy occupation.[308]

The Supreme National Tribunal's jurisdiction was modelled after the Charter of the International Military Tribunal. It heard cases with charges of crimes against peace, war crimes, crimes against humanity and participation in criminal organisations. Where possible, provisions of the Polish criminal law were invoked.

An overview of the judgments issued by the Supreme National Tribunal suggests that the charge of the crime against peace was usually brought by the prosecution as a part of a larger set of charges, all connected with membership of the NSDAP. The Supreme National Tribunal discussed the issue of Germany's aggression at considerable length but refrained from addressing the matter of individual responsibility of the defendants for the crime against peace, focusing instead on their responsibility for war crimes and crimes against humanity.[309] Only in three cases, namely the cases of the defendants Arthur Greiser, Albert Forster and Ludwik Fischer, did the Supreme National Tribunal give separate consideration to the crime against peace, attempting to decide whether the defendants were responsible for it, separately from the issue of their responsibility for war crime and crimes against humanity.

The trial of *Arthur Greiser*[310] took place before the Supreme National Tribunal in Poznań in the period 21 June 1946–9 July 1946, that is, it was concluded before the judgment of the Nuremberg Tribunal was entered (sic). The adjudicating panel was composed of Kazimierz Bzowski (presiding judge), professional judges Emil Stanislaw Rappaport and Witold Kutzner and lay judges Zygmunt Piękniewski, Czeslaw Grajek, Jerzy Nowacki and Longin Szymański.

The relevant charges against Artur Greiser read as follows:

> That, between 1930 and May, 1945, within the territories of the Third Reich, of the Free City of Danzig, and of Poland, as one of the leaders of the German National Socialist Workers' Party (NSDAP) he took part in the activities of a criminal organisation, which that party was, its purpose being through violence, waging of aggressive wars and the commission of crimes, to establish in Europe and in particular in the states bordering on Germany, among them that of Poland, the national-socialist regime and to incorporate into Germany foreign territories, in particular' some of the territories of which the Polish State was composed by virtue of the Treaty of Versailles.[311]

He was also accused of the following:

> That, on behalf of the said Nazi Party (NSDAP), he was in charge of its branch acting· under the same name in the territory of the Free City of Danzig, and that in this capacity he, between 1933 and 1st September, 1939, conspired with the chief government organs of the German Reich with a view to: (1) Causing warlike activities whose purpose was to separate part of the territories of the Polish State, and subsequently to deprive the remaining territories of that State of their independence, which was accomplished by the aggression against Poland begun on 1st September, 1939, and subsequently by means of the military occupation of the whole country carried out in violation of the principles of the law of nations; (2) Arbitrarily depriving the Polish State of the rights to which it was entitled in the territory of the Free City of Danzig by virtue of Article 104 of the Treaty of Versailles and of the Polish-Danzig Agreement concluded in Paris on 9th November, 1920, as well as of the Convention subsequently concluded on the basis of the aforesaid treaty and agreement, and of the legally binding decisions of international bodies; [...] this object having been achieved by the appointment by the Danzig Senate on 23rd August, 1939, of Albert Forster, a subordinate to the Führer of the Third Reich and Gauleiter of the National-Socialist Party in Danzig, to the post of Stadtoberhaupt (Governor) of the Free City of Danzig, and who by a law of 1st September, 1939, set aside the constitution of the Free City of Danzig, and arbitrarily incorporated it to the German Reich.

The prosecution attempted to prove that Greiser, in his capacity of the president of the Senate of the Free City of Danzig as well as the deputy to

Gauleiter, prepared, led and then – together with Forster and other NSDAP members – waged in the area of the Free City of Danzig the aggression against Poland, as prescribed by the party line.[312] The prosecution argued that this made Greiser guilty not only of the preparation of an aggressive war against Poland, but also of launching its initial stage, that is, the violation of the statute of the Free City of Danzig and of the internationally granted rights that Poland held in that area. It pointed out that the Senate resolution of 23 August 1939, creating the position of the mayor of the Free City of Danzig and appointing Albert Forster as the mayor, was signed by none other than Greiser;[313] it was Forster who proclaimed, on 1 September 1939, the law repealing the Constitution of the Free City and integrating it into the Reich.

The defence claimed that the defendant had been opposed to war, that he had attempted to solve all conflicts peacefully and that the changes in the law had been implemented with full knowledge of Poles and the High Commissioner of the League of Nations.[314] It tried to minimise Greiser's role, pointing out that he had only implemented the Führer's decrees, that the laws which he had proposed were censored in Berlin and that forces such as the SS and the Gestapo received their orders directly from Himmler.[315] As Greiser himself argued, those responsible for the crimes with which he was charged, that is Hitler and Himmler, were already dead.[316]

The prosecutor countered that if an individual joins a certain team where unconditional discipline and obedience are required, and if this individual accepts the team's worldview and methods then, consequently, this individual also accepts the responsibility for following the orders.[317]

The tribunal took note of the arguments of the prosecution, found Greiser guilty as charged and sentenced him to death. He was described by the tribunal as having been one of Hitler's most active and most trusted collaborators 'in the implementation of the plan for German superpower in Central and Eastern Europe by means of military and biological aggression and cultural annihilation (genocide) of the neighbouring peoples, and in particular the Polish Nation, so hated by the Germans'.[318] The tribunal noted the special significance of Danzig, the city which – in the opinion of the expert witness Professor Ludwik Ehrlich – was to play the party of an 'entry gate' in the Nazi conspiracy. From this 'gate', the Nazi military force was to unfurl, with the objective of subduing Poland and making it into German *Lebensraum* once and for all.[319] The tribunal characterised Greiser as a man of no scruples, principles or morality, chosen by Hitler precisely for this reason to carry out Hitler's plan with respect to Danzig.

Both the indictment and the judgment indicate that it was Forster who was primarily responsible for the separation of Danzig from Poland and the conversion of Danzing into a German base for the aggression against Poland. Greiser's fault mostly consisted in remaining in close touch with Forster; this was essentially the reason why he was convicted of the crime against peace, without a further elaboration of the issue.

Greiser was sentenced to death and executed on 21 July 1946.

The trial of Albert Forster[320] took place before the Supreme National Tribunal in Gdańsk (formerly Danzig) in the period 5–27 April 1948. The adjudicating panel consisted of three professional judges (Stanislaw Rybczyński, Józef Zembaty and Henryk Cieśluk) and four lay judges (Stanisław Stasiak, Stanislaw Stefański, Henryk Wójcicki and Janusz Wierusz-Kowalski).

Forster's indictment read:

> Starting in September 1923 in the territory of the German Reich, and starting on 24 October 1930 in the territory of the Free City of Danzig, and until the fall of the Reich in 1945, he participated in the criminal organisation under the name of National Socialist German Workers' Party (NSDAP), with the party's objective (to be achieved by means of violence, aggressive war, war crimes and crimes against humanity) to incorporate into the Reich the neighbouring lands, and in particular the territory of the Republic of Poland and the territories separated from the Reich under the Treaty of Versailles and constituting the territory of the Free City of Danzig, and to introduce in these territories a Nazi state, as demonstrated by the fact that on 15 October 1930 he was appointed, at Hitler's discretion, Gauleiter, the commissary leader of the party in the Free City of Danzig, with special representation powers later confirmed on 12 July 1933 by Hitler as in his capacity as Chancellor; based on these powers, and in contravention of international agreements, he exercised actual control over the Senate of the Free City of Danzig, while continuing in his capacity of Gauleiter, when on 23 August 1939, in violation of international agreements and the constitution, he took over from the Senate the function of Staatsoberhaupt von Danzig, after which on 1 September 1939 he was in charge of NSDAP action which led to an unlawful incorporation of Danzig into the Reich; he subsequently became the leader of the civilian government in Danzig, with powers later extended to Western Prussia, and on 26 October 1939 he became governor of the Danzig-West Prussia province.[321]

Further charges read:

> In the period October 1933–1 September 1939, as Gauleiter in charge of the implementation of the NSDAP plan in Danzig, in cooperation with the top party authorities and top authorities of the Reich government, he carried out by increments action with the following objectives: to unlawfully deprive the Polish State of rights in the Free City of Danzig vested in this State by Article 104 of the Treaty of Versailles and the Polish-Danzig agreement, as well as the convention signed pursuant to this treaty and this agreement; to violate international agreements that guarantee the status of the Free City of Danzig; [...] to prepare and wage aggressive military action with a view to separating a part of the territory of the Polish State and subsequently to depriving this State of its

> sovereignty, where this action accomplished its goal on 1 September 1939: by the proclamation, effected by the defendant, of a law on the incorporation of the Free City of Danzig into the Reich, and by the waging of aggressive military action against the Polish state, such action in this territory involving the SS-Heimwehr and other party units organised under the supervision of the defendant.[322]

The tribunal found Forster guilty as charged. In the elaboration of the grounds for the decision, the tribunal additionally noted the importance of the Pomerania region and the city of Danzig as the 'geographic lungs of the country'.[323] It also pointed out the importance of Danzig for the Nazis, who had considered the possibility of delegalisation of NSDAP in Germany and planned to move the headquarters to Danzig in that case.[324]

The tribunal explained that, thanks to Forster, the city of Danzig became the focal point 'from which came the attack against the principle of collective security and against the League of Nations, and the gateway to the aggression against Poland'.[325] Forster's work was divided into three stages. The first stage included the time from his arrival in Danzig on 24 October 1930 to the Nazi surge to power in Germany in 1933. In this period, Forster prepared the Danzig branch of the NSDAP for a takeover of power; began the preparation for the violation of treaties and international agreements; tried to eliminate opposition; prepared the party for the expected tasks ahead; organised militias such as the SS; and dismantled the legal regulations in force.[326] The second stage lasted from 1933 to 1 September 1939. Forster's actions in that period were guided by the motto of *Zurück zum Reich*, that is, aimed at the incorporation of Danzig into the Reich.[327] He worked to undermine the Danzig Senate and pushed for a new election (which the NSDAP won using terror and forgery).[328] From that time on, international obligation began to be violated openly and the policy of *Gleichshaltung*, that is, forcible institutional coordination of the Free City with the Reich, was put into effect.[329] Danzig was being incrementally incorporated into the Reich. Forster was responsible for military exercises of the Nazi units stationed in Danzig, as evidenced by the exercises organised for the Nazi youth, the invitation of military instructors and officers from the Reich, weapon supply mobilisation, facilitation of military services in Germany and the visits of warships (the heavy cruiser *Admiral Scheer* in 1935, the light cruiser *Leipzig* in 1936 and, finally, the battleship *Schlezwig-Holstein*, which on 1 September 1939 at 4.45 am fired the first shot towards the shore, at targets in Westerplatte and Gdynia).[330] The decree of 23 August 1939 created a legal framework for the status quo. Danzig was incorporated into the Reich, and Forster's appointment as the mayor of the Free City of Danzig was, in the tribunal's opinion, a bold international provocation, aiming to push Poland into military action. Once this plan failed, a different incident was used to justify the attack against Poland.[331] In the third stage, that is, from the moment when Danzig was incorporated into the Reich in violation on the Treaty of Versailles and international agreements until the liberation of the city in April 1945,

Forster's part in the crime against peace consisted in his appointment as the head of the civil administration in the Reich's territory after decrees were issued proclaiming the return of Danzig into the Reich.[332]

The tribunal pointed out that Forster must have been aware of the status of Danzig and, consequently, that the work he carried out for the party violated the Treaty of Versailles, the Constitution of the Free City of Danzig and the agreements between Poland and the Free City of Danzig.[333] Forster himself admitted that he knew that the laws of 23 August and 1 September violated both the constitution and international law; in his defence, he noted that his actions met no opposition from the High Commissioner of the League of Nations in Danzig and the representatives of Poland.[334] The tribunal stated that Forster was one of the best students and followers of national socialism, and that he worked to implement Hitler's plans and even, to some extent, helped to create them.[335] He was highly valued in the NSDAP and knew such Nazi figures as Hitler, Göbbels, Streicher, Göring and Bormann.[336] The tribunal argued that he had worked in close cooperation with top NSDAP authorities and the government of the Reich, that he as Gauleiter personally received instructions from Hitler and the Danzig police at his command participated in military operations in Poland on 1 September.[337] Furthermore, he was a seasoned politician, he understood the inner workings of the Nazi imperialist policy and might even be considered one of the creators of this policy, as evidenced by his authorisation by Hitler to negotiate with British representatives.[338]

Forster was sentenced to death and most likely executed on 28 February 1952.[339]

The charge of the crime against peace was also made in the trial *of Ludwik Fischer, Ludwik Leist, Józef Meisinger* and *Maks Daume*, which took place before the Supreme National Tribunal in Warsaw in the period 17 December 1946–24 February 1947. The adjudicating panel included professional judges Mieczyslaw Güntner, Maurycy Grudziński, Stanislaw Rybczyński and Józef Zembaty, as well as lay judges Jan Nepomucen Miller, Jerzy Jodłowski and Eugeniusz Kembrowski. The indictment against all defendants read as follows:

> They participated in a criminal organisation under the name of National Socialist German Workers' Party (NSDAP), created and led by Führer and Chancellor of the German Reich Adolf Hitler; this party established as its objective: the submission to its power of other nations, and the implementation of the national socialism in other European countries, by means of planning, organising and committing: a) a crime against peace, that is, the waging of wars forbidden by the Briand-Kellogg Pact, and in relation to Poland forbidden specifically also by the non-aggression pact of 1934, such wars having as their objective the incorporation into the Reich of neighbouring lands, primarily the territories of the Republic of Poland, and the submission to its powers and implementation of national socialism in other countries in Europe.[340]

Fischer was the only defendant of this group to be found guilty of the crime against peace, solely on the basis of the fact that he was a member of a group of political leaders; members of this group must have had a particularly strong grasp of methods and objectives of the party, and had been expected to demonstrate initiative and leadership skills.[341] Consequently, the tribunal decided that at this level Fischer consciously and purposefully participated in the planning, organisation and commission of the crime against peace by the criminal organisation NSDAP. In Fischer's case, therefore, the responsibility for the crime against peace was closely tied to his membership in the NSDAP, considered a criminal organisation by the Nuremberg Tribunal, which also held it responsible for the crime against peace. The remaining defendants were acquitted, since they had not held positions of power.

The judgment in the case of Fischer et al is somewhat difficult to interpret. It is unclear to determine whether the tribunal's intention was to convict Fischer for the crime against peace or whether it was for the membership in the NSDAP, which was responsible for the crime against peace. The judgment offers very little elaboration in this respect.

4.5.2 Trials before the Chinese Military Tribunal in Nanking

Trials of war criminals before the Chinese tribunals were held on the basis of the law of 24 October 1946. The law stipulated that, in trials pertaining to war crimes, the main source of law would be the international law.[342] The law moreover provided that the definition of war criminals included (but was not limited to) the following categories of persons: 'alien combatants or non-combatants who, prior to or during the war, violate an International Treaty, International Convention or International Guarantee by planning, conspiring for, preparing to start or supporting, an aggression against the Republic of China, or doing the same in an unlawful war'.[343] Thus an autonomous definition of the crime against peace was created, to be used in trials of war criminals before national courts.

Available sources suggest that the charge of the crime against peace was brought in the trial of Takashi Sakai before the Chinese War Crimes Military Tribunal in Nanking. Takashi Sakai was a Japanese military commander in China in the period 1939–1945 and during the hostilities between China and Japan after the Mukden Incident of 1931.

The charges against the defendant were as follows: that he was one of the leaders who were instrumental in Japan's aggression against China; that soon after the Mukden incident he instigated Li Chi Chun and his followers to form a gang for the purpose of creating disturbances in Peking and Tientsin and to organise terrorist activities; that as a result the Secretary of the Kuomintang office in Tientsin, Li Min Yueh, and a correspondent of the Shanghai Daily Chu Shao-tien, were assassinated; that in February 1934, attempts were made on the lives of a Chinese general, Ma Chun-shan, and of the chairman of the Provincial Government of Hopei, Yu Hsueh-chung, in Tientsin; that in May 1934, he threatened to attack Peking and Tientsin by artillery and air force, and demanded the dismissal of the heads of the local Chinese authorities in the province of Hopei; and that as a commander of the Japanese 23rd Army in Kwantung, which was then operating in South China, he ordered his subordinates to assist in setting up a puppet administration and in organising a so-called Peace Army in an effort to overthrow the Chinese Government.[344]

Sakai's defence invoked the international protocol of 1901, pursuant to which Japan and 10 other states had the right to keep troops in certain areas of China, including Tientsin and other locations in the province of Hopei, to maintain free communication between Peking and the sea and to ensure safe passage of foreigners and observation of international agreements. It also argued that Sakai could not be convicted of the crime against peace, as all he did was follow orders from his government.[345]

The arguments of the defence proved insufficient. Sakai was found guilty of participation in a war of aggression (as well as war crimes) and sentenced to death by a judgment of August 1946. The tribunal invoked the Charter of the International Military Tribunal, Charter of the International Military Tribunal for the Far East, Control Council Law No 10, as well as the Nuremberg judgment, which points to the Briand-Kellogg Pact, to which Japan was a party, as the source of responsibility for crimes against peace.[346] The Nanking Tribunal noted that the Charter of the International Military Tribunal provides for the responsibility of each person (sic) involved in the commission of the crime against peace.[347]

It appears that Sakai's only responsibility was for the armed action undertaken as a part of a war of aggression. The judgment found Sakai guilty of participation in a war of aggression.[348] Clearly in his case, the scope of responsibility for the crime against peace was considerably expanded.[349]

It is unclear whether the Nanking Tribunal, in issuing the judgment which convicted Sakai for the crime against peace, considered only his conduct in the period 1939–1945, or whether it also took into account the hostilities that occurred before the war but after the Mukden incident. It is possible that his earlier conduct was considered criminal not under international law but under the national law of China.[350] What the tribunal stated explicitly was that, in the commission of the crime against peace, Sakai violated the Briand-Kellogg Pact and the Nine-Power Treaty of 6 February 1922 in which the parties undertook to respect the sovereignty, independence and the territorial and administrative integrity of China.[351] Sakai was sentenced to death. The penalty was carried out.

4.6 Conclusions

Despite the efforts to find precedents, it remains clear that the first trials at which examination occurred of the crime against peace, that is, the crime of aggression, were the trials in Nuremberg and in Tokyo (with the exception of the trial of Arthur Greiser). Subsequent proceedings where the charge of the crime against peace was brought also took place in the aftermath of the Second World War and made explicit reference to the Nuremberg trial and judgment. Not all individuals who could be considered responsible for the aggression underlying the Second World War were brought to justice. In Germany, after the subsequent Nuremberg trials the courts no longer heard cases with charges of the crime against peace.[352] The situation in Japan was much the same. Interestingly, no citizen of Italy was tried for the crime against peace, even though many war crime trials were held.[353] In the satellite states of Nazi Germany there were a few trials which examined issues related to the responsibility for waging aggressive war, but they tended to be conducted in the perspective of treason and collaboration with the enemy, that is, a national disaster rather than a crime against peace with consequences for the entire international community.[354] Finland was an exception. Under Soviet pressure, a report was drafted, analysing the policy of the Finnish government from 1938 to the 1944 armistice.[355] On the basis of this report, top Finnish officials from the period of the war were charged with leading Finland to take the side of Germany. The trial lasted from 15 November 1945 to 21 February 1946. As Ian Brownlie pointed out, the value of this trial from the legal standpoint is very low: the laws under which the defendants were tried actually stated that they were guilty, and the trial essentially consisted in the examination of facts concerning specific individuals.[356] The trial was perceived as political vengeance and the very opposite of justice, particularly in light of the fact that Väinö Tanner, widely known for his pacifist convictions, was among those tried and convicted.[357]

The issue of responsibility for the crime against peace arose again in the debates surrounding the American involvement in Vietnam. Bertrand Russell and Jean-Paul Sartre, with the assistance of several others, established a quasi-tribunal to investigate the war crimes committed by the Americans in Vietnam, as well as the legality of the American intervention.[358] The tribunal was constituted in November 1966, and was conducted in two sessions in 1967, in Stockholm and Copenhagen. This body, established by philosophers and consisting mostly of non-lawyers, ruled that the United States was guilty of aggression.[359] The United States ignored the proceedings before the tribunal, which it considered a typical show trial. Indeed, the Russell-Sartre tribunal was a tribunal in name only, and had nothing in common with a true trial where legal nuances of responsibility for the crime of aggression are considered.

In the decades following the Nuremberg trial and other trials triggered by the Second World War, there were no serious attempts to try individuals for the crime of aggression. It was only at the beginning of the 1990s, with Iraq's invasion of Kuwait on 2 August 1990, that a number of commentators declared that a crime against peace had been committed and that those responsible for it should be tried in court.[360] There were no doubts whatsoever that aggression had indeed occurred.[361] Importantly, political leaders such as George Bush and Margaret Thatcher spoke out with regard to the issue of responsibility for the crime against peace.[362] The Security Council, in its resolution of 29 November 1990, authorised the use of all necessary means to stop Iraq.[363] The coalition defeated Iraq, but after the victory failed to pursue those guilty of the aggression.[364]

It was only after the second war with Iraq in 2003 that the Iraqi Special Tribunal was established, offering a real opportunity to try those guilty of the crime against peace.[365] The statute of the Iraqi Special Tribunal provided for the punishability of 'the abuse of position and the pursuit of policies that were about to lead to the threat of war or the use of the armed forces of Iraq against an Arab country ...'.[366] This can be considered a type of the crime of aggression, albeit a narrowly defined one: under the statute, it was impossible to try Saddam Hussein and his proponents for the aggression against Iran and Israel, for example.[367] This selective approach may be somewhat jarring, but it is based on the definition of aggression that had previously existed under the Iraqi Criminal Code, and the statute of the Special Tribunal was largely based on that code. During the first interrogation of Saddam Hussein, on 1 July 2004, an unspecific charge of waging war against Kuwait was formulated.[368] However, a trial with respect to the crime against peace was never held. Hussein and several top officials of the Baath party had already been sentenced to death in the first trial, focused on the massacre in Dujail village in 1982. Hussein was executed on 30 December 2006.

To recapitulate: in the last 70 years, there has been no trial where an individual would be tried for the crime against peace. The crime against peace has been consistently ignored in the numerous proceedings concerning war crimes.[369]

5 Scope of individual responsibility for the crime of aggression

5.1 Perpetrator of the crime of aggression

Until the 20th century, international law operated on the principle that an individual was not subject thereto, and could not be held responsible in light of international law, not even for the gravest of crimes under the law of nations.[1] In the case of the crime of aggression, the doctrine of the act of state was of particular importance. Under this doctrine, a natural person acting on behalf of a state's body cannot be held responsible for his or her actions in the office.[2] The person represents the state, and it is the state that must bear full and exclusive responsibility for the actions of its bodies.[3] Therefore, the crime of aggression is a crime of the state and an individual cannot be held responsible for it.

The Treaty of Versailles, and then the subsequent documents which made it possible to bring individuals to justice for crimes such as war crimes and eventually the crime against peace, meant that this principle was no longer in force. The new approach was validated by the Nuremberg Tribunal when it declared that international law imposes duties and responsibilities directly on individuals.[4] The International Military Tribunal ruled that 'crimes against international law are committed by men, not by abstract entities, and only by punishing individuals who commit such crimes can the provisions of international law be enforced'.[5]

While debate as to whether individuals can be subject to international law was extraordinarily heated,[6] at present it is generally accepted that an individual can indeed be subject to international responsibility, and this approach is reflected in a multitude of international documents.[7] The principle of individual responsibility has become the cornerstone of international criminal law.[8]

In a debate on the scope of responsibility of aggression, it is necessary to consider exactly who can be charged with this crime. Does the responsibility extend to each individual engaged in armed operations on the side of the aggressor state, or does it only pertain to the top representatives of this state?

The wording of the Charter of the International Military Tribunal is unclear in this respect. On the one hand, the charter specifies that the tribunal's jurisdiction covers only the major war criminals of the European Axis countries. Furthermore, it stipulates that leaders, organisers, instigators and accomplices participating in the formulation or execution of a common plan or conspiracy to commit for example crimes against peace are responsible for all acts performed by any persons in execution of such plan.[9] Clearly, for those who established the tribunal, it was important that the prosecution's attention should be focused on those who had planned and waged the Second World War. The chief prosecutor Jackson also emphasised that he wished to bring to justice the persons who had planned and designed the crimes: the leaders and the instigators.[10]

On the other hand, the above-mentioned excerpt of the Charter of the International Military Tribunal limits the jurisdiction of this tribunal only. It does not therefore preclude bringing other, less prominent individuals responsible for aggression to justice before other tribunals. What must become the focal point is the provisions of the charter that establish the jurisdiction of the tribunals as pertaining to not only those engaged in planning, preparation and initiation of a war of aggression, but also those who engaged in waging such a war.[11] The notion of 'waging a war' is broad enough to cover not only the top representatives of a state, that is, those who make the decisions to engage in military operations, but also the lower-grade soldiers who participate in these operations. Theoretically, any person who in any manner contributed to the military operations on the side of the aggressor could be charged with the crime against peace.[12]

This interpretation has proved unacceptable to many critics; it has even been called a tool of 'systematic holocaust'.[13] It was argued that nobody, for example, made an effort to focus on the Japanese pilots who carried out the attack on Pearl Harbor, or their immediate superiors: all the attention went to those who had made the political decision to attack.[14] It is therefore unsurprising that the option of significantly extending the circle of those potentially responsible for the crime of aggression was generally rejected in documents and trials. Control Council Law No 10 had already specified that the charge of the crime against peace could be made only against persons who 'held a high political, civil or military (including General Staff) position in Germany or in one of its Allies, co-belligerents or satellites or held high position in the financial, industrial or economic life of any such country'.[15]

Both the Nuremberg and the Tokyo judgments support the suggestion, clearly present in the Control Council Law No 10, that from the judges' perspective it was crucial whether the defendants had held high positions. It is particularly clear in the statement of grounds of the Tokyo Tribunal in the sections pertaining to the defendants Muto and Sato, where the tribunal expressly makes the connection between their participation in a conspiracy to commit a crime against peace with their holding a specific office.[16]

However, automatically tying the high position held by an individual with his responsibility for the crime of aggression appears misled.[17] The determination of whether the individual actually had impact on the state's policy is more important than the formal fact of holding an office. This aspect was emphasised in the subsequent Nuremberg trials, where the distinction was made between leaders and followers.[18] It was accepted that responsibility for the crime against peace must be limited to those in political, military and industrial circles who were in charge of designing and implementing policy:[19] otherwise the entire population of the aggressor state could be charged with the crime against peace, leading to the absurd situation with low-ranking soldiers, farmers supplying the army with produce and even housewives manufacturing the most basic goods used by the military industry being placed on the defendants' bench.[20] In the same vein, the Charter of the International Military Tribunal makes reference to major criminals only.[21] In the case of the High Command, it was similarly argued that Hitler, even if his absolute power is presumed, could not possibly have formulated and implemented the policy of aggressive war on his own: he needed the support of many others at the stage of the preparing, planning and waging such a war.[22] However, only those who held positions giving them actual influence on the state's policy can bear criminal responsibility for the crime against peace.[23]

The reference to, and reliance upon, the notion of impact on policy as a condition for assigning responsibility for the crime of aggression is understandable, given that the Nuremberg Tribunal pointed to the Briand-Kellogg Pact as the source of criminalisation of aggressive war: the pact specifically forbids the use of war as a policy instrument.[24] Moreover, if the question is asked whose participation is necessary to accomplish a crime against peace, it becomes evident that a low-ranking soldier is easily replaceable, whereas a visionary politician is not.[25] Thus, somebody's potential influence on policy is not necessarily crucial in determining the circle of those potentially guilty, but it must be considered in determining the cause-and-effect relationship between the actions of a given person and the commission of the crime of aggression.[26]

Jurisprudence to date has not been consistent in terms of factoring a defendant's impact on policy into the sentencing. Consequently, it is difficult to draw a clear line distinguishing between those who can and those who cannot be considered responsible for the crime of aggression. On the one hand, for example in Schacht's case, despite the fact that he had held a high position (including the position of Minister of the Economy), it was decided that he remained outside the strict sphere of power. The interpretation of the tribunal's ruling appears to be that he had no impact on the shaping of specific political and military plans. On the other hand, Funk, that is, Schacht's successor, was found responsible. He had held the same positions as Schacht, and yet the tribunal clearly decided that he had sufficient policy impact.

The judgment of the Nuremberg Tribunal in the case of Frick, the judgment of the American military tribunal in the Ministries trial and the judgments of the Supreme National Tribunal in Poland demonstrate that responsibility for the crime against peace can also be assigned to individuals who had no impact on the shaping of German policy, but who played a significant role in the implementation of that policy.[27] Conversely, Fritzsche, who was aware of the aggressive nature of the war and who obeyed all orders, was acquitted of the crime against peace by the International Military Tribunal, precisely due to the finding that he had no impact on the shaping of the policy.[28]

The single greatest controversy pertains to the responsibility of the military commanders. In the High Command trial, all defendants were found to have had no impact on policy, and to have been ordinary military personnel simply doing their job – and yet the Nuremberg Tribunal convicted Raeder and Keitel, despite the finding that they were not leaders, had no policy impact, had no decision-making powers and had no special influence among the top-ranking officials.[29] The Nuremberg Tribunal decided that Jodl and Dönitz had influence on Hitler's decisions as to the scale of the military operations, and therefore found them guilty of the crime against peace; the American military tribunal decided that Reinhardt, Warlimont and von Salmuth, with whom Hitler consulted on his decisions and who advised him to escalate the military operations, were not responsible for the war of aggression.[30] Dönitz, it was noted, was a military man who eventually became a state leader.[31] Judge Röling argued that the army was only an instrument in the hands of politicians, and military personnel may only be responsible for the crime against peace if they make decisions of political significance.[32] This principle, however, is not consistently reflected in the judgments.

The inconsistency of the rulings could result from the fact that the judges in Nuremberg attempted to distinguish between the grounds for responsibility for the participation in a conspiracy (holding a relevant office and having impact on policy) and the grounds for responsibility for the crime against peace, where the Nuremberg Tribunal at least appeared to be of the opinion that proof of significant involvement was sufficient.[33] In the subsequent Nuremberg trials, attempts were made to apply the grounds for responsibility for the participation in the conspiracy to the issue of responsibility for the crime against peace. Even these attempts were, however, inconsistent, as illustrated by the judgments in the Ministries trial and the High Command trial.

Documents relating to individual responsibility for aggression produced at later dates searched for a way to increase the precision in determining the circle of those potentially responsible. The Draft Code of Crimes against the Peace and Security of Mankind of 1996 stipulates that only an individual who, as leader or organiser, actively participates in or orders the planning, preparation, initiation or waging of aggression committed by a state shall be responsible for a crime of aggression.[34] However, the comments to the draft propose that these concepts should be interpreted broadly, so as to encompass not only cabinet members but also individuals holding high positions in military, diplomatic and political circles or industry.[35] They also suggest that aggression may only be committed by agents of states, when those agents use the power at their disposal to issue orders to commit the crime of aggression, or make available the means necessary to commit it.[36]

The above appears to suggest that private persons cannot be charged with aggression. This interpretation is unacceptable: clearly it should be possible to charge a person who is not a cabinet member but who has relevant impact on public issues or on the economy with the crime of aggression.[37] Neither the charters of the International Military Tribunals nor the Control Council Law No 10 differentiate between state representatives and private persons. It is therefore possible to charge individuals from both of these categories with the crime against peace[38] (for instance, the Tokyo Tribunal convicted Hashimoto, who held no high positions, but whose publications and range of influence provided evidence that he was an instigator of the conspiracy).[39] On the other hand, both the Tokyo and the Nuremberg Tribunals decided not to convict the industrialists who had contributed to Japan's and Germany's potential for aggressive war. Possibly, therefore, the position of the International Law Commission was a result of the jurisprudence in cases involving the crime against peace where the defendants were industry representatives.

In the course of work on the approach to the crime of aggression in the Statute of the International Criminal Court (ICC), one of the elements consistently beyond disagreement was that the crime of aggression is a leadership crime, that is, a crime committed by those who have impact on policy.[40] For this reason, Article 8 *bis* in the wording adopted by the review conference stipulates that a crime of aggression can only be committed by a person in a position effectively to exercise control over or to direct the political or military action of a state.[41] The Special Working Group on the Crime of Aggression pointed out that the language of this provision was sufficiently broad to include persons such as industrialists.[42] Therefore, the crime of aggression is not necessarily limited to high-ranking government officials.[43] During the negotiations it was noted that the leadership criterion applied to all forms of participation in the crime listed in the statute,[44] and the provision on responsibility of commanders was inapplicable to the crime of aggression.[45]

5.2 *Actus reus*

The key difficulty in determining the principles of responsibility for aggression appears to consist in a precise specification of the criminal act, the *actus reus.*

The first problem arises immediately on the attempt to determine what exactly is to be defined: is it 'aggression', 'an act of aggression', 'a war of aggression' or 'a war in violation of international treaties'? The proceedings before the Nuremberg Tribunal offer no clear guidance in this respect. While the Charter of the International Military Tribunal pertained solely to the criminalisation of aggressive war, the prosecution used the notions of foreign aggression,[46] aggressive action,[47] assault, invasion, aggressive war[48] and general war of aggression.[49] Moreover, the prosecution applied the same scrutiny to the hostilities against Poland, which the tribunal classified as a war of aggression, as it did to the *Anschluss* of Austria, which the tribunal deemed to have constituted an act of aggression.[50]

In contemplating the wording of the indictment, it is nonetheless to a certain extent possible to find some method in the application of terminology. The same cannot be said for the judgment. In the text of the judgment, the tribunal switches freely between the terms: acts of aggression,[51] aggressive acts,[52] aggressive war,[53] war of aggression,[54] aggression,[55] aggressive step,[56] seizure,[57] acts of aggressive war[58] and plain aggression.[59] The inconsistency in classifying the various actions was particularly striking in the considerations regarding the hostilities against Poland.[60] The tribunal tended to approach different actions in the same manner, treating them on a par with one another and denoting all of them as 'acts of aggression'.[61] It might lend legitimacy to the claim that in the Nuremberg trial, the difference between a war of aggression and other acts of aggression hardly mattered, because all aggressive conduct was punished either under the heading of conspiracy or of a crime against peace.[62] However, the fact remains that the International Military Tribunal explained the acquittal of Kaltenbrunner of the conspiracy charge by pointing out that he had been engaged in the actions against Austria, and these actions amounted to an act of aggression rather than aggressive war; if so, Kaltenbrunner could not have been guilty of a conspiracy to commit a crime against peace.[63]

Even assuming that the Nuremberg Tribunal distinguished between non-criminal acts of aggression (actions in Austria and Czechoslovakia) and criminal wars of aggression (where the attack on Poland was chronologically the first), the differentiation does not hold in an analysis of the subsequent Nuremberg trials. In the Ministries trial, the American military tribunal classified the actions against Austria and Czechoslovakia as invasions forming a part of aggression[64] and thus decided they were crimes against peace.[65] Judge Powers disagreed: he argued that many measures short of war may be perceived as aggressive in nature. They may be condemned but, unless they constitute a breach of the peace, it is a misuse of language to label them crimes against peace.[66]

Proponents of punishability of solely wars of aggression could invoke General Assembly Resolution 3314, according to which only a war of aggression is a crime.[67] This argument, however, is not too strong, given that the resolution stresses the political, rather than the criminal, dimension of the problem.[68] In the course of the negotiations of the definition of aggression in the statute of the ICC it was suggested that only a war of aggression should be considered a crime.[69] Eventually, however, it was aggression that was penalised, and the definition of aggression relies on the term 'acts of aggression'. This appears to be a good solution, since relying on the notion of war had always been problematic.[70] Attempts to draw a boundary between the (still allowable) acts of aggression and the level of aggressive war are dangerous. For example, even today there are scholars who argue that the actions of the Soviet Union against Poland and Finland may have constituted acts of aggression, but they never escalated to the level of a crime against peace, and so could not be tried in court.[71]

The General Introduction to Elements of Crimes (paragraph 7) lists three objective elements of each crime: the conduct, the consequence and the circumstances.[72] The circumstances must pertain either directly to the crime or to the context of the crime.[73]

In the case of the crime of aggression, the jurisprudence indicates that it can occur both by commission and by omission.[74] The person who has the ability to influence policy is responsible not only for active engagement in the aggressive actions, but also for failure to prevent or at least deter the execution of an aggressive plan.[75]

Article 8 *bis* adopted by the review conference of the ICC stipulates that a crime of aggression only occurs if there is the use of armed force by a state against the sovereignty, territorial integrity or political independence of another state, or in any other manner inconsistent with the Charter of the United Nations. This approach provides two of the elements necessary to determine the *actus reus* – the conduct (use of armed force) and the specification of the legal obligation that is violated (the Charter of the United Nations).[76]

The wording of Article 8 *bis* does not contain a reference to the threat of use of armed force, despite the fact that, in the subsequent Nuremberg trials, defendants guilty of invading Austria and Czechoslovakia (two states against whom a threat of force had been used) were convicted.[77] The example of these two states may be considered insufficient, given that the Nuremberg Tribunal did not classify the actions against them as aggressive war and consequently a crime against peace. Yet, the same tribunal decided that the actions against Denmark did constitute aggressive war, even though they essentially corresponded in nature to the events in Austria and Czechoslovakia.[78] The definition adopted by the ICC is therefore inconsistent with the jurisprudence, which may be an attempt reasonably to limit the jurisdiction of the ICC so as to avoid complications in cases of trying mere threats of aggression.[79] It would certainly be difficult to conduct proceedings in a case where there was a threat of aggression but no actual aggression. Moreover, it would be difficult to determine where acceptable pressure ends and punishable threats of the use of force begin.[80]

Article 8 *bis* invokes the list of acts of aggression first included in General Assembly Resolution 3314. It is, however, not stated whether the list is open-ended. Arguments against this interpretation include the principle of legality, as well as the model already adopted in the statute of the ICC with regard to war crimes (generally, the catalogue of war crimes is closed; it is possible to extend it by amendment).[81] However, this approach only allows for the criminalisation of new types of crimes that become effective in the future.

Those responsible for committing the actions that might result in the necessity of the amendment would go unpunished.[82] It has, however, been pointed out that even if the list were open-ended the principle of legality would not be violated: the statute of the ICC contains certain safety valves such as the invocation of the principle of *nullum crimen sine lege* (Article 22), the option to invoke a mistake of law (Article 32) and the reservation that the ICC only has jurisdiction over the most serious crimes (Article 5).[83]

As for the consequence, it is rather difficult to determine what the consequences of the crime of aggression should consist of. The third proposal of the Preparatory Committee of the ICC suggested that a crime of aggression can only be considered to have occurred if it resulted in annexation or armed occupation. A review of jurisprudence on the crime of aggression suggests that in the cases of Germany and Japan the focus was on the states' desire to conquer and take over what was in possession of other nations, and to win dominance.[84] The International Military Tribunal for the Far East decided to classify the Lake Khassan incidents as a crime against peace solely because their objective was to gain control over strategically important territory.

Accepting that the crime of aggression must be tied to a desire for territorial or economic gains, or interfering with internal affairs of the victim state, means that not every violation of the Charter of the United Nations can be classified as the crime of aggression.[85] This in turn leads back to the question: if the objective is to prevent a state from committing a crime, or to prevent the installation of weapons of mass destruction, is armed action still considered to constitute the crime of aggression?[86]

Article 8 *bis*, in line with the majority of earlier drafts, points to the consequence or objective of aggression, that is, the violation of sovereignty, territorial integrity or political independence of another state.[87] No reference is made to consequences of aggression, such as depriving people of their right to self-determination, freedom and independence, or other inalienable rights, even though such items were included in numerous earlier drafts.[88] Occupation and annexation as necessary consequences of aggression are also not listed. The states insisted that it was impossible to list all objectives and consequences of aggression, and that the Security Council in its decisions paid little attention to the objective of the aggressor's armed action. Moreover, the use of terms such as occupation results in shifting the debate towards the sphere of *ius in bello*.[89]

As far as the circumstances of the criminal act are concerned, in the case of the crime of aggression it must be first and foremost pointed out that it is a crime of the state.[90] No individual can be found responsible without the state being found responsible first.[91] The act of the perpetrator must be committed as a part of the state's aggression.[92] The use of force against another state cannot be considered a crime if it fits within the scope of self-defence. It would be overly optimistic to assume that this element of *actus reus* is beyond debate. Scholars have pointed out that in certain cases aggression may be committed by extra-state entities,[93] and defining aggression as a crime that can only be committed by a state is a reflection of an antiquated approach to the issues of international peace and security.[94] It is true that with regard to war crimes, the jurisdiction of the ICC extends to violations of the law of war occurring in internal conflicts. In a similar fashion, the definition of aggression could be stretched to incorporate cases of illegal use of force inside a state.[95]

If it is accepted that an individual's responsibility for aggression must arise out of a state's responsibility for this aggression, then consequently, it is impossible to commit aggression without setting into motion the machinery of the state.[96] Waging a war of aggression is a collective endeavour, a combination of individual actions that is more than a sum thereof, since the actions must be interrelated, coordinated and organised.[97] The crime of aggression cannot be committed individually, because it is collective in its essence.[98] It also means that reciprocal attacks of hostile groups within one state (eg the government and partisan militias) may not be classified as the crime of aggression.[99]

A notion often repeated in the debates on responsibility for aggression is that of a threshold where a given action becomes aggression; it is sometimes considered an element of *actus reus* (circumstance).[100] It has been argued, for example, that aggression must involve large-scale operations resulting in serious consequences.[101] Criminal responsibility, in this line of argument, is only an option in clear-cut cases:[102] hard core.[103] If aggression is the mega-crime, it cannot be trivialised by the application of the label to the lesser cases of violations of territorial integrity.[104] The well known principle of *de minimis non curat lex* offers a way to avoid classifying border tensions as aggression[105] (although the Tokyo Tribunal did consider the 12-day fighting at Lake Khassan on 31 July–11 August 1938 a crime of aggression).

In the negotiations in the Special Working Group on the Crime of Aggression, the determination of this threshold was an important issue. The gravity of the crime of aggression was emphasised either by specifying that an evident violation of international law is necessary, or by providing that aggression must result in annexation or occupation, or by criminalising only wars of aggression.[106] The extent of debates on the threshold issue may be somewhat surprising, given that the statute of the ICC expressly states that the tribunal has jurisdiction only in cases of most serious crimes of international concern.[107] On the other hand, with regard to war crimes it is specified that the ICC's jurisdiction pertains to war crimes committed as part of a plan or policy or as part of a large-scale commission of such crimes.[108] It does not mean that killing a single prisoner of war is not a war crime; what it means is that this crime will fall under the jurisdiction of national courts and not of the ICC. On the strength of a similar reasoning, it could be argued that the ICC should have jurisdiction over the gravest acts of aggression – the less grave acts of aggression, while beyond the ICCs jurisdiction, would nonetheless remain criminal in nature.[109]

Article 8 *bis* stipulates that, in order to qualify as a crime of aggression, an act of aggression must constitute a manifest violation of the Charter of the United Nations. Not each act of aggression falls within the jurisdiction of the

ICC.[110] The term 'manifest' is used here objectively, which has been clearly articulated in the debates on the elements of the crime.[111] If the ICC rules that a given violation of the Charter of the United Nations is 'manifest', this ruling is final and precludes the need to examine whether the violating party believed it to be manifest.[112] The 'manifest' qualification must refer to both the character of the act and to its gravity and scale.[113] According to Understandings 'No one component can be significant enough to satisfy the manifest standard by itself.

On the one hand, a threshold clause in the ICC's definition can be viewed negatively, since invoking circumstances such as violation of sovereignty automatically positions an act of aggression as rather serious.[114] On the other hand, all acts of aggression listed in General Assembly Resolution 3314 are implemented in this definition, and it is sometimes argued that not all of them are serious enough to merit the attention of the ICC – therefore, a threshold clause is necessary.[115]

5.3 Stages of aggression

The Charters of the International Military Tribunal and of the International Military Tribunal for the Far East, Control Council Law No 10 and the Draft Code of Crimes against the Peace and Security of Mankind of 1996 all make provisions for punishability of planning, preparation, initiation and waging of a war of aggression. Article 8 *bis* too stipulates that responsibility for the crime of aggression arises out of the planning, preparation, initiation or execution of an act of aggression. However, since the crime of aggression is a crime of a state rather than of an individual, a distinction must be made between preparations for an act of aggression undertaken by the state, that is, a collective of individuals (discussed below) from an individual's preparation for the engagement in the crime of aggression at some of its stages.

It is very difficult to separate in time the subsequent stages of aggression. Planning generally consists in the design of a certain scheme of action for a specific war of aggression; preparation is the implementation of the plan before armed operations begin; initiation is the moment the war is launched; waging continues until the armed operations finally cease.[116]

The planning and preparation stage is crucial.[117] However, in order to convict a defendant for participation in the planning of an aggression, general policy declarations do not suffice. It is necessary to provide evidence of a specific plan for war, and the defendant's participation in the drafting of this plan.[118] The Nuremberg Tribunal ruled that planning is possible even under a dictatorship, because the implementation of the plan must rely on multiple actors, and these actors cannot deny responsibility simply by claiming that their efforts were directed by one man.[119] For the International Military Tribunal the planning of aggression was particularly reprehensible, because it revealed the full scope of the criminal intentions of the defendants.[120] For this reason, the tribunal repeatedly noted the participation of defendants (eg Göring, Raeder, von Neurath) in the conferences where the aggressive plans were presented. The International Military Tribunal for the Far East was similarly meticulous in listing the conferences in which the defendants had participated. Both tribunals also took specific note of each defendant's participation in planning the particular campaigns. Interestingly, however, no defendants were convicted solely for planning the aggression. Participation in this stage was punished only when specific steps were later taken actually to implement the plans.[121]

The tribunals tended to assign preparation lesser significance than planning,[122] as illustrated for example by the acquittals of Speer and Schacht.[123] However, it was noted that the defendants had participated in the preparations, be it economic (Funk, Kaya), administrative (Rosenberg), diplomatic (von Ribbentrop, Rosenberg, Oshima, Togo and Wörmann) or military (Göring, Keitel, Raeder, Jodl and Tojo).

The punishability of merely planning or preparing for an aggression is controversial. If the aggression fails to materialise, preparations must be considered a threat of aggression, rather than actual aggression. The Draft Code of Crimes against the Peace and Security of Mankind of 1996 and the definition adopted by the review conference of the ICC both disallow the punishability of the threat of aggression. Historically, to date, planning and preparation for aggression have only been punished when actual aggression followed. Typically, defendants were found guilty of participation in all stages of the aggression (Göring, Keitel and Jodl). It seems to be generally agreed that an individual can be convicted solely for participation in the planning or preparation stages (eg Funk) only if the aggression actually occurred.[124]

Theoretically, the International Military Tribunal should have considered separately the issue of responsibility for the sole act of initiation of a war of aggression (considered the gravest of crimes).[125] In practice, the matter was given very little attention. The tribunal decided that the initiation of the war was a result of a political decision taken by Hitler.[126] The International Military Tribunal for the Far East treated the initiation of the war of aggression as an element of armed operations, and it too gave no consideration to the issue of responsibility for the sole act of initiation of a war of aggression. Judge Jaranilla, however, pointed out that it was possible for an individual to be responsible for initiating the war, but not for waging it, and vice versa.[127]

In the trials on the crime against peace, no one has to date been found directly guilty of initiating a war of aggression. Göring came the closest, in being declared the driving force behind the German aggression ('moving force for aggressive war, second only to Hitler').[128] If the initiation of war were contemplated in purely military terms, then the responsibility would fall to the top commanding officers, Keitel and Jodl.[129] However, assigning individual responsibility for the sole act initiation of a war of aggression seems a purely theoretical concept, and it is probably included in the recent draft of the Code of Crimes against the Peace and Security of Mankind for historical reasons.

The key problem is the determination of what constitutes the waging of a war of aggression, or – using a more contemporary terminology – the execution of an act of aggression. In theory, any person who joined the perpetrators and shared with them their know-how could be prosecuted for waging the war.[130] However, the crucial question is how to distinguish between the actions that support the military effort and are criminal in nature, and those that are permissible.[131]

An answer might be revealed by reviewing the cases of dependents convicted solely for the waging of a war of aggression, such as Dönitz and Shigemitsu; these two cases, however, differ considerably. Dönitz was the tactical leader most of the time, but the International Military Tribunal found him guilty mostly on the strength of the fact that he was a commander of a submarine flotilla. Moreover, Judge Powers pointed out that his previous actions were also important.[132] Shigemitsu, on the other hand, was found guilty of waging war owing to his holding the position of Minister for War.

The majority of those found guilty of waging a war of aggression were responsible for military operations (eg Göring, Keitel, Raeder and Jodl). However, it is not only armies that are capable of waging wars.[133] The tribunal decided that other types of actions, even purely administrative ones (eg Rosenberg, Frick and Seyss-Inquart) may be classified as waging war. In the case of von Ribbentrop, the fact that he signed laws incorporating new areas into the Reich and establishing protectorates was classified as waging war. Von Weizsäcker and Keppler were found guilty of waging war (or invasion) because they had signed papers and participated in diplomatic conferences. In the Röchling trial, the court of first instance ruled that exploitation of conquered territories constitutes a form of waging war – yet in the case of Sauckel it was argued that a person cannot be found guilty of waging a war of aggression just because he was in charge of organising forced labour. In terms of involvement in the economy and industry, Schacht and Funk were acquitted of the charge of waging war, but the conviction of Göring, Lammers and Körner may be interpreted to see such actions as forms of aggression.

The documents that formed the legal basis for the trials on the crime against peace made provisions for the punishability of a conspiracy. The notion of conspiracy originated from the Anglo-Saxon legal systems, which generally punish the agreement to commit acts in violation of law or morality.[134] Each participant in the conspiracy, even if joined only at a later stage, is subject to punishment.[135] However, upholding this traditional interpretation of the conspiracy notion would result, under the circumstances, in prosecuting a great many suspects, something the International Military Tribunal was not ready to handle.[136] The conspiracy charge was convenient in that the network of conspirators could be extended if it suited the prosecution.[137] One problem was the risk of assigning the guilt collectively.[138] Another problem was that the notion of conspiracy was foreign to the continental legal systems,[139] a point already argued by Gros at the London conference.[140]

The tribunals attempted to narrow down the notion of conspiracy and to specify when participation in a conspiracy is a crime. The International Military Tribunal ruled that the conspiracy must be clearly criminal in nature, and its activities cannot be too far removed in time from the moment of decision or action.[141] In order to determine that a person participated in a conspiracy it is necessary to provide evidence that this person participated in a specific criminal common plan. It is not sufficient to prove that the person supported a given political agenda. In the Krupp case, the tribunal endeavoured to summarise the conditions under which a conspiracy is criminal, with the conclusion that there must be a concrete plan, at least two participants to it, the purpose of the conspiracy must be criminal and clearly stated, and there can be no prolonged time lapse between the plan and the decisions or actions.[142]

The separate listing of conspiracy in the Charter of the International Military Tribunal (as well as in the Charter of the International Military Tribunal for the Far East and the Control Council Law No 10) is superfluous.[143] The charge of conspiracy can be reduced to the charges of planning and preparation for the crime of aggression.[144] This is the logic that the International Military Tribunal for the Far East followed in ruling that the charge of planning and preparation for a war of aggression were included in the conspiracy charge.[145] The definition of the ICC sensibly and correctly omits the wording with regard to a conspiracy.

5.4 *Mens rea*

Most criminal law systems require, in order to establish that an individual is criminally responsible for a given act, a specific subjective disposition of the perpetrator towards the act (*mens rea*).

Jurisprudence on the crime against peace suggests that the tribunals (particularly the American ones) paid special attention to the *mens rea* aspect of the crime, focusing on the need to prove that the defendant was aware of committing aggression and had the intent, motivation or objective (although the terminology for the latter component was inconsistent).

In the High Command trial, the tribunal ruled that waging war was a crime when the persons at policy-making level had a criminal intent when designing the policy.[146] There must be 'actual knowledge that an aggressive war is intended and that if launched it will be an aggressive war'.[147] In the Farben case, it ruled that the knowledge, state of mind and motives of a given defendant at a given time and in a given situation must be taken into account.[148]

The absence of criminal intent, motivation or objective was invoked by the tribunal particularly when explaining the grounds for acquittal of the defendants. In the case of von Papen, the Nuremberg Tribunal stated that his purpose was not armed occupation of another state but the subversion of a legitimate government and strengthening a party in the opposition, both designed to lead to annexation. In the cases of Pleiger and Röchling, the tribunals pointed out that, despite their participation in the process of armament, such actions were not criminal, unless undertaken with the intent and objective of invading another state. The reasoning was similar in the case of Schacht.

The cases of military industrialists provide a clear illustration of the significance of proof of criminal intentions in terms of assigning responsibility for aggression.[149] Each state tries to be prepared in the event of war – even Switzerland. Unless there is evidence that the preparations are intended to lead to a war of aggression, no claims of a crime against peace may be made.[150] Many countries prepare simulations of military operations, draft various scenarios and carry out military exercises. As long as there is no aggressive intent, such operations are not criminal.[151] If a defendant acts with honourable motives, the will to engage in armed action is there – but if the objective is to protect one's own state or to protect the population of another state from human rights violations, that person cannot be punished for the crime of aggression.[152] The argument that the defendant internally disagreed with the plan of aggression (as in the case of von Weizsäcker) and attempted to sabotage it must, however, be approached with great caution. The general assumption is that a person predicts the natural consequences of his intentional acts.[153] Good intentions are not enough. It is not permissible to commit serious crimes with the hope that they will prevent other crimes. General kindness is no excuse for participating in a crime, and tacit disagreement is no defence to criminal responsibility,[154]

On the other hand, even if there is evidence that the intentions of the defendant were aggressive, but the war is declared to have been legal, the defendant must still be considered innocent.[155]

Yoram Dinstein notes that proving *animus aggressionis* is necessary only in relation to a small number of individuals; otherwise, proving awareness of participation in aggression is enough.[156] This is probably the reason why the issue of awareness of the criminality of certain acts has been discussed in jurisprudence and academia more than the criminal intent. In determining guilt, awareness is more important than intent, in that intent can be proved by offering evidence of the defendant's awareness that the plan or policy was aggressive.[157]

Nobody can be convicted of the crime against peace without proof that the person was aware of the criminal nature of his or her actions:[158] the focus is on the person's subjective awareness.[159] Suspicion is not sufficient to determine that a person was aware of participating in a crime against peace.[160] Judge Anderson additionally noted that awareness of preparations for war is not enough; the defendant must be proved to have been aware that the war was to be aggressive in nature.[161]

It has been justly argued that nobody can be condemned for taking part in a war in the belief of protecting one's country.[162] State representatives often base their decisions on patriotism and loyalty, which must be taken into consideration when determining *mens rea.*[163] The American tribunal pointed out, in the Ministries trial, that it is unreasonable to require that a person who takes part in armed operations should engage in an independent investigation to verify whether the government is guilty of aggression as fighting unfolds.[164] On the other hand, the Nuremberg Tribunal noted that the defendants who were aware of Hitler's goals, cooperated with him, and thus became a part of his plan, could not be acquitted by claiming that Hitler used them if they did in fact understand what they were doing.[165]

Both in Nuremberg and in Tokyo, the best proof of awareness of the crime against peace consisted in participation in the conferences where the aggressive plans were revealed. The Nuremberg Tribunal painstakingly listed the participation of Göring, von Ribbentrop, Keitel, Rosenberg, Raeder, Jodl, von Neurath and Funk in the most important conferences.[166] Conversely, absence at these conferences often led to acquittal, at least of the conspiracy charge (Frick, Fritzsche, Streicher, Dönitz, Bormann). In the Krupp Trial, the American military tribunal pointed out that those absent at the conferences might nonetheless have been aware of the plans; the example of Hess was cited – despite his absence at the conferences, his relations with Hitler were so close that he must have been aware of his plans.[167] The International Military Tribunal's judgment on Bormann implicitly suggests that holding a specific office can constitute evidence of awareness of the criminal nature of certain actions. In the Ministries trial, with regard to Wörmann, the tribunal ruled that the defendant should have realised Hitler's plans and intentions based on the documents he received in his official capacity.[168] Yet other rulings of American military tribunals suggest that industrialists were not similarly compelled to draw logical conclusions from the facts they knew,[169] and the generals in the High Command trial were not as aware of the criminality of their proceedings as were Jodl and Dönitz, despite having attended the same conferences.[170]

The inconsistency of standards was something of a trademark of the subsequent Nuremberg trials. An attempt to determine, on the basis of these rulings, which positions automatically led to awareness of the state's involvement in aggression, is doomed to fail. What explanation could there be for the acquittals of Bormann, Frick, Funk and Schacht, who held positions of power and must have been involved in the implementation of plans as much as von Neurath and Hess?[171]

The International Law Commission, in the comments accompanying the Draft Code of Crimes against the Peace and Security of Mankind of 1996, specifically noted the importance of *mens rea.* The commission pointed out that participation in aggression is not in itself sufficient to convict for the crime against peace. It is necessary to prove that this participation had been intentional and had taken place knowingly as part of a plan or policy of aggression.[172] The Special Working Group on the Crime of Aggression, in the debates on the definition of the crime of aggression and its elements, also noted that the crime of aggression must be committed with the intent and knowledge, but eventually decided to omit these aspects in the definition, since they are listed in Article 30 of the statute of the ICC.[173]

Article 30 of the ICC's statute is the first comprehensive attempt to determine the *mens rea*, or the mental element of the international crime. It stipulates that a person 'shall be criminally responsible and liable for punishment for a crime within the jurisdiction of the Court only if the material elements are committed with intent and knowledge'.[174] As for 'intent', the statute specifies that a person has intent where, in relation to conduct, that person means to engage in the conduct, and in relation to a consequence, that person means to cause that consequence or is aware that it will occur in the ordinary course of events.[175] As for 'knowledge', the statute further explains that it means awareness that a circumstance exists or a consequence will occur in the ordinary course of events.[176]

In the amendments to the elements of crime adopted by the review conference it is explicitly stated that 'the perpetrator was aware of the factual circumstances that established that such a use of armed force was inconsistent with the Charter of the United Nations' (element 4) and 'was aware of the factual circumstances that established such a manifest violation of the Charter of the United Nations' (element 6). In the introduction to the elements of crime, it is explained in line with the conclusions of the Special Working Group that this is not intended to mean that the prosecution must prove the defendant had carried out a review of the legal aspects of the legality of the use of force in light of the charter. The recommendation of the Special Working Group is that the defendants must be aware of the facts, not of the legal doctrines and principles that determine when the use of armed force violates the charter. A requirement of legal awareness might lead to adverse consequences: potential perpetrators might be encouraged purposefully to neglect understanding the legality of their actions, or to rely on legal expertise of doubtful quality but supportive of their position.

5.5 Grounds for excluding criminal responsibility owing to lack of guilt

A number of circumstances may exclude the guilt of the defendant and thus relieve the defendant of responsibility under international criminal law. Some of these circumstances are listed in the statute of the ICC. The statute, however, does not differentiate between the circumstances that exclude guilt and those that exclude unlawfulness. Furthermore, the statute gives the ICC the right to consider other grounds for excluding criminal responsibility.[177]

The circumstances of greatest significance in the case of aggression include mental incapacity (insanity), mistake of fact and mistake of law, order and duress.

It may seem unlikely for a defendant in an aggression case to invoke insanity in order to escape responsibility for the crime. Given that the crime against peace can only be committed collectively, the other participants would certainly notice that one of their number is insane. On the other hand, if a handful of individuals strive for world domination, as the Germans and the Japanese did during the Second World War, is it *Realpolitik*, or is it collective insanity? If the latter interpretation is allowed, then a group of perpetrators may include a person who 'suffers from a mental disease or defect that destroys that person's capacity to appreciate the unlawfulness or nature of his or her conduct, or capacity to control his or her conduct to conform to the requirements of law'.[178]

Insanity arising out of a mental disease was never directly invoked in a trial concerning the crime against peace. The Nuremberg Tribunal did, however, investigate whether Hess's mental state was conducive to his standing trial, and the Tokyo Tribunal found Okawa insane and placed him in psychiatric care.

Insanity may also arise out of intoxication, which – in the wording of the statute of the ICC – may:

> ... destroy that person's capacity to appreciate the unlawfulness or nature of his or her conduct, or capacity to control his or her conduct to conform to the requirements of law, unless the person has become voluntarily intoxicated under such circumstances that the person knew, or disregarded the risk, that, as a result of the intoxication, he or she was likely to engage in conduct constituting a crime within the jurisdiction of the Court.[179]

It is debatable whether this circumstance will be significant in terms of responsibility for the crime of aggression, which requires planning and preparation difficult to accomplish under involuntary intoxication.[180] It is unlikely that the courts investigating the crime of aggression will deal with drug and alcohol addicts (although, on a related note, historians have established that Göbbels, who escaped trial by committing suicide, was a morphine addict).

In contrast, the option to invoke a mistake of fact is incredibly important in the case of the crime of aggression.[181] This circumstance is frequently included in national legal systems, in line with the principle of *ignorantia facti excusat*.

It is easy to imagine that a person mistakenly believes that there are circumstances that make this person's actions legal.[182] If a head of a state makes the decision to attack on the basis of mistaken data that suggest that invasion by another state is imminent, there is the possibility to invoke a mistake of fact.[183] Under pressure, when preparing for war and waging war, the phenomenon that von Clausewitz labelled 'fog of war' can occur: events tend to be exaggerated in perception, and assigned disproportionate significance.[184] A state that falls victims to an attack, be it real or imaginary, and that experiences extreme emotional tension, may not be able objectively to determine whether its actions constitute self-defence or aggression.[185] Politicians never have full knowledge, yet they must try to stay a step ahead of their enemies.

They make the decision to use armed force blind. It is difficult to hold it against them if they use this force with the objective of protecting their state. Using the services available to them, they must assess the enemy's intent, capacity and power, and decide whether they can rely on their sources, especially when the information they provide is different from what is officially announced.

The option of invoking mistake at law is as important as mistake of fact. National legal systems tend to operate on the principle of *ignorantia iuris non excusat*, but international law does not: not everybody is expected to know and understand international regulations.[186] International agreements regarding the use of force are very imprecise. The Charter of the United Nations invites multiple interpretations, and the absence of a clear definition of aggression and self-defence produces a grey area where it is impossible to determine clearly whether the use of force was unlawful (eg humanitarian intervention or preventive self-defence). It is quite easy to imagine a person admitting a violation of the territorial integrity of another state, and having acted with full awareness, yet with the objective not to conquer, but to protect the population from crimes against humanity. What if a politician or military officer asks several lawyers to assess the legality of a course of action, and receives an opinion to the effect that this course of action is fully legal, whereas in fact it constitutes aggression?[187]

Generally, high-ranking representatives of a state can be expected to be familiar with international law. However, in the case of the ban on aggression, given all the nuances of the right to self-defence, even those individuals in top positions of power may claim mistake of law to be relieved of responsibility.[188] All doubts should be interpreted in favour of the defendant.[189] Thus, in the case of the crime of aggression, the principle of *ignorantia iuris excusat* should hold.[190] However, and it is a point raised in the debates on the elements of the crime of aggression, invoking mistake at law at the ICC will be most difficult, considering that the ICC will only handle cases of manifest violations of the Charter of the United Nations. Nonetheless, the option remains open, especially if, in the future, the jurisdiction of the ICC is gradually expanded, and an increased number of situations qualify as 'manifest violations of the Charter'.

One of the most typically used defences in cases of crimes under international law is following an order of a superior. If this defence were effective every time it is invoked, the Nuremberg Tribunal would have been unable to convict anyone except Hitler (who was already dead at the time).[191] The chief prosecutor in Nuremberg did not rule out the possibility that acting under orders would have an impact on the tribunal's decision,[192] but eventually the Charter of the International Military Tribunal regulated the issue quite clearly, leaving some room for manoeuvre in extraordinary circumstances.[193] Under the charter, the fact that a defendant acted pursuant to an order of his government or of a superior did not free him from responsibility, but could be considered in mitigation of punishment if the tribunal determined that justice so required.[194] Before the Nuremberg Tribunal, there was no option of completely relieving a defendant of responsibility on the strength of acting under orders; there was a strong desire to punish all top-ranking Nazi defendants, and their probable lines of defence were pre-emptively closed.[195] The International Military Tribunal argued in favour of this decision by explaining that Hitler could not have waged the war on his own – he needed collaborators, and these collaborators had no right to use the leader-follower relationship as a defence.[196] Nonetheless, since in the end the Charter of the International Military Tribunal included the option of invoking action pursuant to orders to mitigate punishment, the tribunal had to give consideration to this issue. The tribunal found it crucial to determine the extent to which the person following orders was able, despite being subordinated, actually to decide freely whether or not to obey the order.[197] The Nuremberg defendants failed to persuade the tribunal that they had been in no position to decide freely. On the contrary, many of them were proved to have been very eager to obey the orders they received.[198]

The Charter of the International Military Tribunal implements the concept of absolute liability: acting pursuant to orders does not, in any event, relieve a person from responsibility for crimes of international law, but may be considered in mitigation of punishment. In line with this reasoning, an order has no impact on the issue of guilt. The Charters of the International Military Tribunal for the Far East, the International Criminal Tribunal for the former Yugoslavia and the International Criminal Tribunal for Rwanda also rely on this principle. The Draft Code of Crimes against the Peace and Security of Mankind of 1996 also implements this principle, even though the 1954 draft proposed that an order should relieve a person from responsibility if the person was not in a position to disobey the order.[199] Clearly, the older concept of conditional liability is no longer prevalent. Conditional liability posits that an order may constitute a premise that excludes criminal responsibility, except in cases where the order was evidently unlawful.[200]

The statute of the ICC is built on yet another concept. Under the statute, an order can relieve a person from responsibility if three conditions are met jointly: the person was under a legal obligation to obey orders of the government or the superior in question; the person did not know that the order was unlawful; and the order was not manifestly unlawful.[201] This is an attempt at finding a middle ground between conditional and absolute liability. It suggests that acting under orders should not be perceived as a separate circumstance that excludes responsibility, but rather as one of the circumstances that must be taken into account when investigating *mens rea*.[202] When the statute of the ICC requires an examination of whether the perpetrator knew that the order was unlawful, it references the defendant's knowledge (awareness), which is necessary to convict. Acting under orders can also be contemplated in terms of mistake of law and mistake of fact: to escape responsibility it is necessary to prove that the defendant believed the order to be lawful; if the defendant was wrong, mistake of law can be invoked.[203]

It has been argued that in the case of the crime of aggression, that is, by definition a crime of leadership, provisions invoking responsibility of superiors and acting under orders should have no application.[204] The approach makes sense, given the general consensus that only persons who have policy impact (which usually is connected with holding a relevant position of power) may be held responsible for the crime of aggression – essentially, it is the very principle of *respondent superior*, under which superiors are responsible for the actions of their subordinates. The Charter of the International Military Tribunal clearly stipulated that leaders, organisers, instigators and accomplices participating in the formulation or execution of a common plan or conspiracy to commit the crime against peace are responsible for all acts performed by any persons in execution of such plan.[205] On the other hand, relieving a person of responsibility, despite his or her participation in hostilities, on the strength of the fact that this person had no impact on the decision to wage aggressive war, is in fact a modified version of the idea of acting under orders, or being bound by law.

In the course of the Special Working Group's discussions it was noted that, in addition to the controversies discussed above, one must also realise that in many cases the superiors in question are themselves subordinated to other persons.[206] The issue is particularly problematic in the case of military commanders. Under the definition adopted by the review conference, they are covered by the definition of the crime of aggression, because they exercise control over a state's armed forces. In the discussions it was, however, strongly pointed out that a situation must be avoided in which military commanders would question orders received from politicians.[207] High-ranking military commanders have the option of expressing their views with regard to a contemplated use of force, and therefore it should be up to the judges to determine their responsibility. The commanders may, in any case, invoke mistake of fact or of law. Since the statute of the ICC offers the option of invoking not only mistake of law and mistake of fact, but also the separate circumstance of acting under orders, it seems that the defendants in aggression trials should be able to invoke this circumstance.[208] It can of course be argued that a person who receives the order to commit the crime of aggression should refuse to obey it. Sociology, however, has demonstrated that most individuals, when issued an order, tend to want to obey it.[209] Moreover, soldiers usually have a limited understanding of circumstances, being told only as much as they need to know.[210] Only the persons at the highest level of command may have a better, broader understanding of the factors involved. A situation where each unit commander could challenge an order, dispute the decision on the positioning of troops and demand documents for review is unacceptable and impracticable.[211]

In aggression trials held to date, Jodl invoked acting under orders as a circumstance excluding liability. He argued that a soldier's duty is to obey and to carry out orders.[212] In his case, the tribunal decided that he had been one of the chief architects of the plan of aggressive war, so he could not escape responsibility. The case of Takashi Sakai included similar argumentation. However, in stating the grounds for the ruling in his case, and for the dismissal of these arguments, the tribunal only pointed to the relevant provisions of law, including the Charter of the International Military Tribunal.[213]

Another circumstance that excludes responsibility under the statute of the ICC is conduct caused by duress resulting from a threat of imminent death or of continuing or imminent serious bodily harm against the defendant or another person. The conditions for effectively invoking this defence are as follows: the defendant acted necessarily and reasonably to avoid this threat, provided that the defendant did not intend to cause a greater harm than the one sought to be avoided; the threat was either made by other persons, or constituted by other circumstances beyond the defendant's control.[214]

Duress was invoked in the Ministries trial, where it was argued that the defendants were forced to engage in the conduct they were charged with, and they were unable to refuse to obey the instructions they received, or to refuse to participate in the criminal agenda.[215] However, as the American military tribunal correctly noted, the defendants had many options open to them. If they were afraid that a refusal to cooperate would lead to losing their position, or that their resignation would not be accepted, they still had other opportunities to avoid participating in a crime. No supervisor would leave them in their high-powered positions if they continued to challenge instruction or oppose the implementation of the criminal plans and failed to collaborate.[216] If defendants invoke duress, it is again necessary to examine if they were in a position to make a moral choice. If the defendant's intent was fully in line with the general criminal plan, no exclusion of responsibility is possible.[217] It must also be noted that in the case of the crime against peace, it is difficult to argue that the decision to participate is made under duress.[218] The parties with decision-making powers consider the arguments in favour and against the aggression, and deliberate on the use of force: consequently, it is rare, if at all possible, to commit the crime against peace under duress.[219]

5.6 Conclusions

Individual responsibility for aggression arises out of a state's responsibility for this aggression. Consequently, the problems in defining state aggression lead to problems in determining the *actus reus* and *mens rea* of the crime of aggression.[220]

The problems persist even if it is accepted that the norms that penalise the conduct of individuals may not be identical with those determining the responsibility of states. Can an individual bear responsibility solely for military aggression, or is economic aggression relevant too? Can the crime be committed solely by a representative of a state, or do extra-state entities count as well? Should the crime be defined in a general, abstract manner, or is a list of specific acts of aggression necessary? Is it aggression, an act of aggression, or a war of aggression that needs a definition? There are good reasons for the feeling of *déjà vu* here.

The jurisprudence is so inconsistent that every argument can be countered. Additionally, the cases of the German and Japanese aggression during the Second World War are very clear-cut, and thus hardly provide a good starting point for far-reaching conclusions.[221]

On a more optimistic note, the fact that the review conference managed to adopt a definition of the crime of aggression proves that a certain consensus has been reached as to the principles of responsibility for aggression. First, the crime of aggression can be committed solely by a person with significant influence on a state's policy, which is usually connected with holding high office in that state. This principle applies throughout all forms of participation in the crime listed in the statute of the ICC.[222] Secondly, not only a war of aggression, but each and every act of aggression is punishable, as long as it is sufficiently serious. Only the use of armed force by a state against another state in violation of the Charter of the United Nations qualifies as an act of aggression. Planning and preparation for an act of aggression are only punishable if the aggression actually materialises. Thirdly, to convict a defendant for the crime of aggression it is necessary to determine that the defendant had the intent to commit aggression and was aware of the scope, significance and consequences of the conduct under investigation. Therefore, all potential circumstances excluding responsibility must be taken into consideration.

It is sometimes argued that the difficulty in precisely capturing the *actus reus* aspect of the crime of aggression should lead to courts placing greater emphasis on the *mens rea* aspect, that is, the guilt of the defendant.[223] This approach would make it extremely difficult to assign responsibility for the crime of aggression, since proving intent and awareness of criminality of conduct is always a challenge. Even with evidence of violation of the territorial integrity of a state by another state, the prosecution would risk failure in terms of proving the mental factor.[224] Moreover, a reliance on proving the pro-war attitude of the defendant does not eliminate the problem of lacking a definition of aggression. The subjective aspect of a crime is strictly connected with its objective aspect:[225] it is impossible to determine whether the perpetrator was aware that the conduct amounted to aggression without being able to specify what constitutes aggression as such.

Part III

Difficulties and risks

6 Procedural difficulties

Even though the legal basis for criminalising aggression is rather frail, it is possible to try individuals in court for this crime, as history has demonstrated. The task is, however, quite arduous. Many procedural difficulties arise, and – especially in national courts – they may prove insurmountable. Most of the problems are likely to stem from the fact that the crime of aggression is primarily a crime of a state, and pertains to the state's highest representatives.

If holding a trial actually proves possible, with no legal limitations standing in the way, it still is necessary to consider whether the benefits of proceeding (such as assigning the responsibility for aggression and punishing those guilty of the crime) outweigh the adverse outcomes. How will the aggression trial impact the maintenance – or the restoration – of peace and security? How does aggression relate to crimes recognised under international humanitarian law? What about the consequences of the trial for the integrity of the international criminal law system, and the trust it garners?

6.1 Lack of jurisdiction

The first problem a court encounters in a prospective aggression trial is the determination of the court's jurisdiction with regard to the crime of aggression.

Typically, jurisdiction of the courts in the aggressor state is territorial: the court of the state in whose territory the aggression was committed has jurisdiction over the perpetrator of the crime.[1] If in the territory of state A aggression against state B was planned and prepared, and subsequently an attack against state B originated in the territory of state A, the courts in state A will have jurisdiction over the perpetrators of the aggression against state B, since it was in state A that the acts that qualify as aggression occurred. Even if it is assumed that in the situation described above, aggression is in fact committed in the territory of state B, the courts in state A nonetheless have the jurisdiction over the perpetrators – the active personal principle (*compétence personnelle active*) stipulates the courts of the state whose citizen committed a crime outside of this state have jurisdiction in the case of this citizen.

However, it would be illusory to believe that the courts in the state that committed the aggression are truly going to bring the perpetrators of the crime of aggression to justice. Doing so would necessitate charging the state's top politicians and, generally, top politicians have ways of influencing the criminal policy of the state in which they operate. National courts tend to refrain from opposing government policy, especially in terms of foreign affairs.[2] They always have the option of invoking Montesquieu's notions of the separation of the executive, legislative and judicial powers: a decision to use armed force is easily classified as purely political and therefore outside the remit of the judiciary.[3] Conversely, it is difficult to imagine a trial of the instigators of a war of aggression that was won and that achieved the intended political effects.[4] Courts of the aggressor state can only bring the perpetrators of the crime of aggression to justice if the aggression fails to achieve its intended outcomes, and the regime responsible for the aggression collapses. It is not often that these conditions are met.

As for the courts in the state that is the victim of aggression, they might theoretically have jurisdiction under the principle of objective territorial jurisdiction. Under this principle, a state is authorised to punish the crimes that generated result in this state's territory, either partially or exclusively (even if the crimes themselves were committed beyond this territory).[5] In the case of the crime of aggression, the definition of which almost always requires a violation of territorial integrity, political independence or sovereignty, it is evident that the results will occur in the territory of the victim state. The authorities of the victim state might also invoke the passive personal principle (*compétence personnelle passive*). This principle authorises a state to exercise jurisdiction over a perpetrator of a crime if citizens of the said state fell victim to this crime. It is also possible to invoke the protective principle, which grants a state the power to try a perpetrator of a crime intended to bring damage to the primary interests or values of the state, regardless of the perpetrator's and the victim's citizenship. Clearly, sovereignty, territorial integrity and political independence are a state's primary interests and values. However, if the victim state loses as a result of the aggression, and peace is reinstated on the aggressor's terms, it is unlikely that the victim state's courts will have an opportunity to engage in a meaningful aggression trial.

The International Law Commission, in the comments to the 1996 draft of the Code of Crimes against the Peace and Security of Mankind, proposed that only international criminal courts should have jurisdiction over the crime of aggression, because in every case of an individual standing trial for aggression it is necessary to determine the aggression on the part of a state, which no national court can do (unless with regard to the state's own citizens). Otherwise, as observed by the Commission, the fundamental principle of international law, *par in parem imperium non habet*, would be violated.[6] This opinion, however, is not necessarily correct. The state that is a victim of aggression is authorised to bring to justice the perpetrators of aggression aimed directly at this state. The Special Working Group on the Crime of Aggression reached this conclusion too. The group agreed that in the case of aggression, concurrent jurisdiction arises where the perpetrator acts in one state and the consequences are felt in another.[7]

Theoretically, there is also the option of bringing the perpetrators of the crime of aggression to trial in a court of a third party state. It could be assumed that the crime of aggression belongs to a group of crimes that are generally condemned under international law, and the states are allowed to invoke the principle of universal jurisdiction towards the perpetrators of the crime.[8] This type of jurisdiction is contingent on the nature of the crime: for the exercise of the jurisdiction, the place where the crime was committed, the citizenship of the victim and the connection to the state that exercises jurisdiction are irrelevant.[9]

The proponents of the universal jurisdiction approach usually cite the judgment of the International Court of Justice (ICJ) in the Barcelona Traction case, which includes the following words:

> In particular, an essential distinction should be drawn between the obligations of a State towards the international community as a whole, and those arising vis-à-vis another State in the field of diplomatic protection. By their very nature the former are the concern of all States. In view of the importance of the rights involved, all States can be held to have a legal interest in their protection; they are obligations *erga omnes*.[10]

The ICJ named the ban on aggression as the first item on the list of imperative norms of *erga omnes* nature.[11] However, those sceptical towards the principle of universal jurisdiction point out that in the above-mentioned ruling, the ICJ referred to *erga omnes* obligations, but never to a right to *actio popularis*.[12]

Typically, aggression is listed among the crimes to which universal jurisdiction applies, but little regard is given to the consequences arising out of such classification.[13] The fact remains that not a single international agreement allows for the exercise of universal jurisdiction with regard to the crime of aggression. The 1996 draft of the Code of Crimes against the Peace and Security of Mankind acknowledges the principle of universal jurisdiction, but precludes its applicability to the crime of aggression.[14] Considering that the greatest anxiety in relation to the exercise of universal jurisdiction stems from its possible politicisation (and clearly this would be a factor in an aggression trial), it is doubtful whether a crime of this nature should actually fall under the principle of universal jurisdiction, especially given the absence of a legally binding definition of aggression.[15] There were good reasons why the resolution of the review conference stipulated that adopting the amendments to the statute of the International Criminal Court (ICC) should not be interpreted as creating the right or obligation to exercise domestic jurisdiction with respect to an act of aggression committed by another state.[16]

The key difficulty with aggression proceedings lies in providing the court (be it a court in the aggressor state, the victim state or a third party state) with a legal basis of jurisdiction. In order to do so, the crime of aggression would have to be included in the national criminal regulations of this state, which generally is not the case. Only international judicial authorities may have other options open. At the moment, solely the ICC appears to possibly have the chance of having its jurisdiction extended to cover the crime of aggression in near future.

The states agreed that the provisions adopted by the 2010 review conference and pertaining to the crime of aggression may not be retroactive.[17] Consequently, Articles 15 *bis* and *ter* stipulate that the ICC would have the power to try only such cases of aggression that occur at the earliest one year after the entry into force of the amendment to the statute defining the crime of aggression, which in turn will occur when it is ratified or adopted by 30 parties. Furthermore, the wording in Understandings (paras 1 and 3) emphasises that the ICC may exercise jurisdiction only with respect to crimes of aggression committed after a decision in accordance with Article 15 *bis* and *ter* is taken (after 1 January 2017) and one year after the ratification or acceptance of the amendments by 30 states parties, whichever is the later.

Moreover, each party to the statute of the ICC may, prior to ratifying or adopting the amendment, submit a declaration stating that it does not accept jurisdiction of the ICC over a crime of aggression arising from any act of aggression committed by that state.[18] However, the declaration only applies to jurisdiction exercised on grounds of state referral and prosecutor's *proprio motu* referral. The state may withdraw this declaration at any time; it is obliged to consider withdrawing it three years after submitting the declaration. States that will submit the definitions will naturally come under heavy public opinion criticism. However, even if the declaration is not submitted, representatives of a state may not necessarily be prosecuted for aggression committed on behalf of that state. The amendments pertaining to the crime of aggression were adopted under the Article 121(5) procedure, meaning that they continue to be binding only on those states that accept them.[19] The procedure outlined in Article 121(5) was designed as an exception from the principles specified in Article 12 of the statute of the ICC. Article 12 allows the option of bringing to trial citizens of states that are not parties to the statute, if they commit a crime under the jurisdiction of the ICC on the territory of a state that is a party to the statute.[20] The logic behind this mechanism is that the states would not wish, in a matter as serious as the definitions of specific crimes, a vote on certain amendments to be sufficient to make their citizens face responsibility for crimes this state had decided not to criminalise. Consequently, a 'negative interpretation' of Article 121(5) excludes the ICC's jurisdiction with regard to crimes introduced by means of an amendment, and committed by the citizens or on the territory of a state that did not ratify the amendment. This mechanism applies both to the already adopted amendments to Article 8 on war crimes, and to the crime of aggression.[21] During the negotiations, there were also efforts to develop a 'positive interpretation', in line with which it would after all be possible to exercise jurisdiction with regard to crimes committed by a state that did not ratify the amendments. Such an interpretation contradicts the wording of Article 121(5), but it provides an explanation as to why the opt-out mechanism was established.[22]

As a result, once the amendments to the statute of the ICC come into force, apart from states that are not parties to the ICC's statute, two more categories of states will be created: states that are parties to the statute of the ICC, but that have rejected the option of exercise of the ICC's jurisdiction in regard to themselves in terms of the crime of aggression (declaration under Article 15 *bis* 4) and states completely rejecting the provisions pertaining to aggression. Table 6.1 lists the potential situations in terms of jurisdiction.

In the course of proceedings in the Special Working Group on the Crime of Aggression it appeared clear that in cases where the aggressor state is not party to the ICC's statute, but the victim state is, and vice versa, the ICC should have jurisdiction.[23] This principle is currently in force with regard to war crimes, crimes against humanity and genocide: under Article 12(2), the ICC has jurisdiction if the crime was committed in a territory of a state that is party to the statute, or by the nationals of such a state. However, the review conference decided on a different approach with regard to the crime of aggression. In Article 15 *bis* 5 it stipulated that in respect of a state that is not a party to the statute, the ICC will not exercise its jurisdiction over the crime of aggression when committed by that state's nationals or on its territory. As a result, the ICC's jurisdiction is severely limited.

Most doubts arise with respect to situation 3 (as outlined in Table 6.1). In the past, commentators tended to agree that the ICC should have jurisdiction under such circumstances. However, these opinions were voiced when it still appeared that the ICC would have jurisdiction over aggression committed, for example, against a state that is not a party to the statute, if this aggression were committed by the nationals of a state that is a party. However, given how limited the jurisdiction is with regard to nationals of states that are not parties to the statute, it is no longer evident that the ICC should have jurisdiction in situation 3, particularly considering the wording of Article 121(5). The wording appears to eliminate such an option.

Interestingly, if the crime of aggression is committed by the nationals of a state that is not a party to the statute of the ICC or of a state that has rejected the amendments on aggression, or has submitted the declaration under Article 15 *ter* 4, or when the victim state is not a party to the statute, the ICC may nonetheless exercise its jurisdiction in a situation in which the crime appears to have been committed is referred to the prosecutor by the Security Council acting under Chapter VII of the Charter of the United Nations.[24]

The ICC may also exercise its jurisdiction when the state whose nationals have committed the crime accepts its jurisdiction, or – with certain restrictions – when the state in whose territory the aggression was committed does so.[25] While the former situation is purely theoretical, the latter is relatively

Table 6.1 ICC jurisdiction on crime of aggression in case of state referral or prosecutor *proprio motu* referral

Does ICC have jurisdiction on crime of aggression?	*Victim Party to the Rome Statute Amendments accepted*	*Victim Party to the Rome Statute Declaration upon Art. 15* bis *4*	*Victim Party to the Rome Statute Amendments not accepted*	*Victim Non-party to the Rome Statute*
Aggressor Party to the Rome Statute Amendments accepted	1. YES	2. YES	3. NO	4. NO
Aggressor Party to the Rome Statute Declaration upon Art 15 *bis* 4	5. NO	6. NO	7. NO	8. NO
Aggressor Party to the Rome Statute Amendments not accepted	9. NO	10. NO	11. NO	12. NO
Aggressor Non-party to the Rome Statute	13. NO	14. NO	15. NO	16. NO

Source: Author's own compilation.

likely. However, if the state that has committed the aggression is not a party to the statute of the ICC or has not adopted the amendments or submitted the declaration under Article 15 *bis* 4, the ICC will nonetheless not have jurisdiction. The ICC will also be unable to exercise its jurisdiction if the Security Council uses the powers granted to it under Article 16 of the statute of the ICC and decides that an investigation in a case should not be commenced, or – if commenced – suspended for 12 months (the suspension may be renewed for subsequent 12-month periods endlessly). It may be difficult for the Security Council to reach such a decision, given how many of its permanent members have veto power, but practice has demonstrated it is not impossible.[26] Interestingly, the Special Working Group on the Crime of Aggression also considered the possibility of granting the Security Council red light powers, which would prohibit the ICC from investigating and trying a given case forever.[27] In the end, this option was not included in the regulations.

One more problem is noteworthy in terms of the jurisdiction of the ICC. The ICC's statute includes the principle of complementarity, under which a case is considered admissible only if the state which has jurisdiction over it is unwilling or unable genuinely to prosecute the perpetrator.[28] This system stands no chance of functioning properly with regard to the crime of aggression. Most states lack criminal laws pertaining to this crime, and thus can be generally considered unable to prosecute its perpetrators.[29] However, if the states succeed in introducing the definition of aggression into the statute of the ICC and, in so doing, give the ICC jurisdiction over the crime of aggression, it may provide a push towards legislative changes at the national level, much as happened with regard to war crimes, crimes against humanity and genocide, although – as mentioned above – the wording of the Understandings on domestic jurisdiction over the crime of aggression discourages rather than encourages changes in national legal orders.

6.2 Surrender of person charged with a crime of aggression

Even if a national court decides that it has jurisdiction and is therefore capable of proceeding with an aggression trial, the problem is likely to arise that the perpetrator is out of the territory of the state whose court is willing to conduct the trial. If that is the case, it is necessary to apply for the extradition of the perpetrator.

Extradition is 'a transfer (based on an agreement between states) of a person located in the territory where one of the states has power, to another state who is competent to prosecute this person on grounds of the commission by this person of a given crime'.[30] There are two main reasons why states use extradition. First, under some circumstances a state has no jurisdiction towards a specific person, but justice demands that the perpetrator should not walk away unpunished. Secondly, another state might have more of an interest in bringing a criminal to justice, and at the same time have easier access to evidence and thus an opportunity to proceed with criminal prosecution more efficiently.[31]

Anglo-Saxon states tend to take the position that citizenship is not an obstacle to extradition. Most states, however, do not allow the extradition of their citizens.[32] It is in conflict with the principle of *aut iudicare aut dedere*, under which a state should either surrender a criminal or put him or her on trial. Setting aside the discussion of whether this duty arises under customary law or merely under agreements, it is reasonable to ask whether the principle should under any circumstances apply to the crime of aggression. The International Law Commission had its doubts; under the 1996 draft of the Code, the principle of *aut iudicare aut dedere* does not apply to the crime of aggression.[33] Moreover, reports of the Special Rapporteur of the International Law Commission feature very few remarks on the crime of aggression,[34] and from among the states that sent comments to these reports, only Poland and Russia listed the war of aggression/crime against peace, while South Africa only made a reference to it in connection with the Princeton Principles on universal jurisdiction.[35]

What could stand in the way of extradition of a person charged with aggression is the principle of not granting extradition if the alleged offence is a political offence.[36] Whether an act qualifies as a political offence is determined by the state that holds the individual to be potentially extradited. The very notion of 'political offences' is debatable. Offences that are purely (absolutely and objectively) political can probably be defined as 'punishable acts aimed directly against the state, its sovereignty and political organisation'.[37] Given that aggression is by definition directed against a state's sovereignty, it is very likely to be classified as a political offence. However, it must be noted that the principle of not granting extradition in cases of political offenders is closely tied to the institution of asylum, that is, the very opposite of extradition.[38] In this context it is important to point out that certain international documents note that the perpetrator of the crime against peace may not exercise the right to asylum[39] and may not be granted the status of refugee.[40]

Another obstacle is the requirement that a given offence must be punishable both under the laws of the state requesting extradition and of the state from which it is requested, that is, the principle of double criminality.[41] Since many criminal codes contain no provisions that criminalise aggression, this condition may be difficult to satisfy. By way of example, the General Assembly resolutions that reinforce the obligation to cooperate in matters of extradition and bringing criminals to justice refer exclusively to war crimes and crimes against humanity;[42] the issue of aggression is not mentioned.

In the case of the ICC, the term 'surrender' is used, rather than 'extradition'.[43] This is unlikely to make the ICC much more successful with accomplishing the transfer of the perpetrator than the specific states. The ICC will not only have to deal with a general lack of willingness to cooperate, but also with issues arising out of the agreements inspired by Article 98 of its statute.

Under these provisions, the ICC may not proceed with a request for surrender which would require the requested state to act inconsistently with its obligations under international agreements pursuant to which the consent of a sending state is required to surrender a person of that state to the ICC. In such cases, the ICC must first obtain the cooperation of the sending state for the giving of consent for the surrender.

It is precisely this regulation that provides the legal basis for two-party agreements between the United States and other countries, in which these countries undertake not to surrender or transfer in any manner and for any purpose American nationals remaining on their territory to the ICC without express consent on the part of the United States.[44] They also undertake not to transfer or expel American nationals to a third state for the purpose of their transfer to the ICC. These agreements are in contradiction to the obligations of the states parties to the statute of the ICC, since they render the ICC's objectives moot to a large extent.[45] The ban on surrender pertains not only to perpetrators of crimes, but also to witnesses and victims of these crimes. Nonetheless, such agreements are in place, and states will almost certainly invoke them.

6.3 Identification of aggressor

In the case of the crime of aggression, the procedure for determining the identity of the aggressor is even more of a challenge than defining the crime itself.[46] This is, however, the key issue in terms of criminal responsibility, if only because in a definition of aggression that is not very precise, the essence lies in the manner in which the aggressor is determined.

In the inter-war period, the establishment of an impartial body to determine the aggressor was suggested.[47] Most drafts of international agreements from that period stipulate that the aggressor would be determined by the Council of the League of Nations in a unanimous decision.[48] Treaty of Mutual Assistance provided additionally that the council should reach this decision within four days.[49] Owing to the fact that the council was a political body, it was proposed that the unanimity requirement should be replaced with a majority, to avoid an impasse if a contradiction of political interests occurred.[50] Representatives of the United States, on the other hand, in the negotiations of the treaty of mutual assistance, suggested that the Permanent Court of International Justice (PCIJ) should determine the aggressor.[51] In the end, the two most important agreements of the inter-war period, that is, the Covenant of the League of Nations and the Briand-Kellogg Pact left it up to the states to determine whether aggression had occurred and on whose part,[52] effectively leading to anarchy in international law.[53]

The problem of determination of the aggressor arose also in the course of the work on the definition of the crime of aggression and terms of exercising jurisdiction with regard to this crime in the statute of the ICC. The institutions listed by the Special Working Group on the Crime of Aggression as candidates for determining the aggressor state (and consequently paving the way towards prosecuting individuals before the ICC) included the Security Council, the General Assembly, the ICJ and the ICC itself.

For many states, only the Security Council seemed to be an acceptable option to determine the aggressor, given that the determination of a specific conduct on the part of a state is necessary to proceed with assigning individual responsibility.[54] It was argued that the logic and structure of the Charter of the United Nations clearly pointed to this solution.[55] The key argument was the wording of Article 39 of the Charter of the United Nations, under which the Security Council determines the existence of any act of aggression, in conjunction with the fact that Article 5(2) of the statute of the ICC stipulates that its provisions on the crime of aggression must be consistent with the relevant provisions of the Charter of the United Nations.

The opponents of the idea that the Security Council should determine the aggressor and consequently give the green light to the jurisdiction of the ICC pointed out that the Security Council is a political body, and therefore cannot play the part of a court.[56] The collective security system must be efficient in its operations; it is impossible to demand from the council – weighted down with the legal consequences of determination of the aggressor – to observe the rules of evidence and postpone a decision owing to the need to examine witnesses or hear the explanations of those potentially charged with crimes.[57] The council's decisions stem from political premises and are political and not judicial in nature.[58] Granting the Security Council sole power to determine aggression would undermine the efficiency and independence of the ICC.[59] Moreover, the decision-making system within the Security Council gives the veto right to China, France, Russia, the United States and Great Britain. These states will certainly use their veto power if there is a risk of their (or their allies') determination as aggressors.[60] The solution would officially place states and citizens at unequal positions in the eyes of the law, which is directly in contradiction of the fundamental principles of criminal law.[61] A situation where selected members of the United Nations have the power to block criminal proceedings against their nationals is unacceptable.[62] Furthermore, granting the Security Council the power to determine aggression contradicts yet another principle of criminal law, namely that nobody should be a judge in his or her own case.[63] The Security Council, in contrast to a court, by definition cannot be impartial; yet impartiality should be expected from a body that has a significant impact on court proceedings.[64]

It was also argued that, in the case of self-defence, in line with the Charter of the United Nations, the states determine themselves whether the situation requires the use of force or not.[65] On the other hand, in the case of self-defence, reference is made to an armed attack, and not to aggression, and the two notions do not necessarily overlap. The Security Council itself (as was noted) allowed the option of the use of force being examined by an independent body, since this solution was proposed during the Iraq-Iran conflict.[66]

Even if the Security Council is deemed to be the only body with the power to determine aggression, the regulations of the Charter of the United Nations pertain to aggression as a crime committed by a state and not to the liability of individuals, which is to be examined by the ICC.[67] For example, Article 39 of the Charter of the United Nations refers solely to the imposition of sanctions by the Security Council[68] and has no application in terms of individual responsibility.[69] Moreover, the Security Council's potential for action will not be limited, if only because it will still be the council that will be in charge of the ruling's enforcement, and possibly also have the formal right to reduce the punishment or even to grant full amnesty.[70] In addition, the Security Council has special powers under Articles 13, 16 and 103 of the statute of the ICC, and so a violation of the Charter of the United Nations[71] is out of the question.

In the end, the decision was made to grant the Security Council the power to determine the aggressor. A number of procedural problems result from this decision. It must be decided, for example, whether the resolution of the Security Council should be adopted on the basis of Chapter VII or as a procedural decision. Should the determination of aggression be included in the resolution's preamble or its body? Is it necessary to state explicitly that aggression occurred, or is an implicit reference sufficient?[72] However, the key consideration was what the ICC should do if the Security Council fails to determine the state that is responsible for the aggression. There is no procedure that would force the council to make the decision. The situation of no determination of whether aggression occurred and who committed it is quite likely to arise given that, to date, the Security Council has very rarely used the term 'aggression' in its resolutions.[73] In obvious cases, such as the Iraqi aggression against Kuwait, the council failed to determine aggression.[74] It did, however, refer to aggression in relatively borderline cases, such as the operations of South Rhodesia against other states, including Angola, Botswana, Mozambique and Zambia,[75] as well as South Africa against Angola, Botswana, Lesotho, the Seychelles and other southern African states,[76] attacks of mercenaries against Benin[77] and the attack of Israel against Tunisia.[78]

If the Security Council fails to make the determination of aggression, it was suggested that the ICC should either refrain from proceeding, or be allowed to proceed after the lapse of a certain period (such as six months); essentially, the ICC would then decide on its own whether or not an act of aggression had been committed. The General Assembly and the ICJ were also candidates for the determination of the aggressor.

Proponents of granting the decision power in this respect to the General Assembly noted that under the Charter of the United Nations, the Assembly is authorised to debate any matter or issue that falls within the scope of the charter[79] and may consider the general principles of cooperation in the maintenance of international peace and security.[80] Furthermore, the powers under the resolution *United for Peace* were cited in this context.[81]

The membership in the General Assembly is undoubtedly more democratic than in the Security Council, and it has demonstrated greater courage in classifying certain situations as aggression. It has, for example, made this determination with regard to China's intervention in Korea,[82] Namibia's occupation by South Africa[83] and other operations undertaken by South Africa against other African states,[84] by Portugal against Guinea-Bissau and Cape Verde,[85] Israel's attack against Iranian nuclear facilities[86] and against Lebanon[87] and also Israel's operations against the Palestinian population[88] and in the Golan Heights.[89] The General Assembly spoke of acts of aggression against Bosnia and Herzegovina.[90] Yet despite the courage (or lack of consideration) on the part of the General Assembly with respect to labelling certain actions as acts of aggression, it is important to remember that this body is also political in nature. If arguments were raised, with reference to the Security Council, to the effect that it is unacceptable that a political decision should determine legal responsibility, then these arguments remain just as valid with reference to the General Assembly. Just as the 15 members of the Security Council take into account, in their decision-making process, their own interests and *Realpolitik* considerations, so do the 193 members of the United Nations – the tangle of interests is just proportionately greater.

Numerous suggestions had been made proposing that the ICJ should determine both aggression and the aggressor. Under the Charter of the United Nations, it is the ICJ that is the principal judicial organ of the United Nations.[91] If the issue of aggression is considered to be legal in nature, then allowing the ICJ to determine it seems like the most obvious solution.[92] Another argument in favour of this option is the fact that the ICJ was never shy to mention aggression in its judicature in discussing the powers of the specific authorities,[93] imposing temporary measures to prevent acts of aggression[94] and in cases of legal disputes pertaining to illegal use of force.[95] However, in most cases the ICJ made no direct reference to aggression, focusing on the broad notion of the use of force instead.

The ICJ has stated on a number of occasions that when it made references to aggression it never questioned the solutions adopted by the Security Council, but referred solely to the legal aspects of the situation considered by the council.[96] Moreover, the restrictions that the charter imposes on the General Assembly do not pertain to the ICJ and, consequently, the ICC is free to examine a given situation at the same time as it is being examined by the council.[97]

However, under the charter, the ICJ may give advisory opinions solely when requested by the Security Council, the General Assembly or specialised agencies authorised to request such opinions on legal questions arising within the scope of their activities.[98] Consequently, one of these bodies would have to request a legal opinion, and thus the issue of potential inaction on the part of the Security Council or the General Assembly would remain unsolved: whether an issue is forwarded to the ICJ remains is a purely political decision.[99]

It was also pointed out that granting the ICJ the power to determine aggression would lead to unnecessarily overlapping efforts, and particularly since the standards of evidence are different before the ICJ and the ICC.[100] Also noted was the relatively lengthy period that is usually necessary for the ICJ to issue its ruling. It is also uncertain whether the ICJ could offer a ruling on aggression in an advisory opinion, if the question is under dispute between states.[101] The ICJ may examine issues as to which there is a debate between states, but only on the condition that those states have come to an agreement as to submitting the issue to be decided by the ICC, or have prior to the debate lodged a declaration giving the ICC mandatory jurisdiction *ipso facto* and without a specific agreement to this effect.[102] It is, however, difficult to expect states who are accusing one another of aggression to submit the case for a court to decide: the risk of one of them being determined the aggressor is too great. The issue could potentially be resolved by the implementation of a jurisdiction clause under which the ICJ would have the power to determine aggression in each case, in which the ICC could have jurisdiction. In this scenario, it would not be necessary to rely on other United Nations bodies or agencies, and neither would there be a need for the parties to the dispute to come to an agreement.

It was also suggested that the ICC should itself decide whether or not aggression had occurred.[103] It was pointed out that, in the proceedings before the Nuremberg and Tokyo Tribunals, there were also no other authorities to determine aggression (with the exception of China's attack on Manchuria).[104] Under the statute of the ICC, any dispute concerning the judicial functions of the ICC should be settled by the decision of the ICC.[105] Furthermore, Article 5 of the statute of the ICC grants it jurisdiction over the crime of aggression.[106]

On the other hand, it was argued that, as for the International Military Tribunal's independence of other bodies, it must be noted that the London Agreement was signed before the Charter of the United Nations came into force.[107] Moreover, a situation should not be encouraged in which a body outside of the United Nations system has powers exceeding those of the Security Council.[108] Also, if the ICC is free to decide whether or not aggression occurred, its position will be too politicised.[109] Ideally, a judge would not have to determine aggression, but rather would be able to focus solely on whether a given individual is responsible for acts the commission of which has already been confirmed.[110] Then, however, the question inevitably arises: if another body determines whether aggression occurred, can the ICC still be considered independent?

Eventually, the review conference decided in Article 15 *ter* 8 that a failure on the part of the Security Council to assess a given case within six months of notification means that the prosecutor may proceed, after the Pre-trial Division of the ICC has authorised the commencement of the investigation, and the Security Council did not exercise the right granted thereto under Article 16. The determination of aggression by a body other than the ICC should have no bearing on the ICCs decisions. A situation may therefore arise where the Security Council decides that aggression did occur, but the ICC in its proceedings rules that in fact it had not. Importantly, in the case of a Security Council referral, the council does not have to determine whether an act of aggression occurred; it only has to give the green light to the prosecutor to instigate proceeding in the given case.

With respect to the ICC, the problem of the authority to determine aggression was solved largely in favour of the Security Council (although in the opinion of the five permanent members of the council, the council is still not favoured enough in the balance).

It is interesting to consider whether national courts would be able to carry out aggression trials if the Security Council declared that no aggression had occurred. It seems very unlikely, as it would occur in violation of the above-mentioned principle of *par in parem non habet iudicium*.

6.4 *Immunity*

The crime of aggression may only be committed by persons who have impact on the policy of a given state. It is therefore the crime of heads of state, heads of governments and government members, as well as highest commanders.[111] These persons serve the highest functions in the state and, as such, have certain privileges and immunities.

The notion of immunity was endorsed under the Peace of Westphalia: since it was agreed that all states were equal, then representatives of sovereign units must have immunity from being subject to legal proceedings in other states, under the principle of *par in parem non habet iudicium*.[112] The impossibility of assigning responsibility to individuals holding certain positions stemmed also from the doctrine of the acts of the state (individuals cannot be held responsible for actions undertaken on behalf of the state), derived from the tradition of personalising power.[113]

At present, the issue of immunity is regulated by a number of international conventions.[114] Immunity, that is, the exclusion of certain units, persons or property from a state's jurisdiction,[115] may be divided into two types: immunity *ratione personae*, connected with holding a specific office (a person is protected by this immunity for as long as he or she holds this office) and immunity *ratione materiae*, granted to a person serving a specific official function.[116] The latter is applicable to all state officials, while the former is limited to a narrow group of persons, such as the head of the state, head of the cabinet, minister of foreign affairs, and diplomats. Immunity *ratione personae* has practically unlimited scope in terms of criminal responsibility, and pertains both to actions undertaken in an official capacity and privately.[117]

When the institutionalisation of international criminal law began, there was a debate as to whether holding a specific office should indeed prevent the trial of an individual. The report of the Commission on Responsibility of the Authors of the War and on Enforcement of Penalties noted that there was no reason whatsoever why a rank, even a top rank, should protect an individual under any circumstances.[118] The Commission also pointed out that this principle must extend to the former head of the state, if great outrages against the laws and customs of war and the laws of humanity had occurred, because inability to investigate and try such outrages 'would shock the conscience of civilized mankind':[119]

> Principles of the laws and customs of war and the laws of humanity which have been violated would be incomplete if he were not brought to trial and if other offenders less highly placed were punished; moreover, the trial of the offenders might be seriously prejudiced if they attempted and were able to plead the superior orders of a sovereign against whom no steps had been or were being taken.[120]

These notions were quite revolutionary; the reaction of American and Japanese representatives was very critical, claiming that, with regard to the head of state, only political responsibility (and not legal responsibility) applies.[121] Eventually, the Treaty of Versailles included provisions assigning responsibility to the German emperor, although he was never brought to trial.

The problem of top state representatives being protected from liability for international crimes returned in the run-up to the Nuremberg trial. Jackson in his report claimed that the doctrine under which a head of state is immune from legal liability is obsolete, and the idea of the immunity of a head of state is a relic of the doctrine of the divine right of kings.[122] He argued against accepting the paradox that legal responsibility should be the least where power is the greatest.[123] Both the London International Assembly and the United Nations War Crimes Commission had made similar recommendations earlier.[124]

The charter of the International Military Tribunal stipulated that the official position of defendants, whether as heads of state or responsible officials in government departments, should not be considered as freeing them from responsibility or mitigating punishment.[125] This solution is hardly surprising, considering that the Nuremberg trial had been specifically organised to reach those whose power had been the greatest.[126] The Nuremberg Tribunal stated, with regard to the issue of immunity, that a person who violates the laws of war cannot obtain immunity while acting in pursuance of the authority of the state, if the state in authorising that action moves outside its competence under international law.[127]

The principle under which criminal liability for international law crimes regardless of the position held by an individual was implemented in the statutes of all the international criminal tribunals.[128] It was also listed among the Nuremberg principles, in the draft Code of Crimes against the Peace and Security of Mankind, and in other international conventions.[129] The claim that it now comprises a part of customary law is no longer controversial.[130]

Furthermore, under the Rules of Procedure and Evidence of the ICC, 'abuse of power or official capacity' is an aggravating circumstance, which the ICC must take into account.[131] The proceedings before the International Criminal Tribunal for the former Yugoslavia against Slobadan Milošević,[132] judgment of the Special Court of Sierra Leone in the case of Charles Taylor[133] as well as the issue of a warrant of arrest by the ICC against Omar Hassan Ahmad Al-Bashir,[134] all confirm the above.

However, as demonstrated by the judgment of the ICJ in the case concerning the arrest warrant of 11 April 2000 (*Democratic Republic of the Congo v Belgium*), immunities may in some cases provide protection from criminal responsibility for international crimes.[135] The ICJ observed that in international law it is firmly established that, as is also the case for diplomatic and consular agents, certain holders of high-ranking office, such as heads of state, heads of government and ministers of foreign affairs, enjoy immunities from the jurisdiction of other states, both civil and criminal.[136] While they hold this office, such persons cannot be subject to the jurisdiction of third-party states, even with regard to acts performed by them in a private capacity, or before they held the office.[137] While in office, such persons only come under the jurisdiction of courts in their own countries, as well as institutions such as the International Criminal Tribunal for the former Yugoslavia, the International Criminal Tribunal for Rwanda, the ICC or foreign national courts, provided that their immunity is previously waived by the state they represent.[138] Third party states may only exercise their jurisdiction with regard to such persons if these persons cease holding public office, and even then only with regard to acts performed before or after holding the office, or performed while holding the office, but in a private capacity.

This judgment of the ICJ is controversial, because it constitutes a step backward in comparison with previous international law regulations.[139] However, in the context of responsibility for aggression it nonetheless appears to be just and well balanced. In the case of the crime of aggression, there is a real risk that states might make mutual accusations of illegal armed action, and then attempt to bring to justice top-ranking state representatives. Respecting functional immunity of top-ranking officials would be conducive to avoiding such mutual accusations, and the politically motivated criminal trials that might result.[140] On the other hand, the crime against peace most certainly falls beyond the scope of acceptable diplomatic and consular functions, considering that it is in direct contradiction, for example, to the objective of encouraging friendly relations.[141]

Interestingly, the statute of the ICC stipulates that the ICC may not proceed with a request for surrender or assistance which would require the requested state to act inconsistently with its obligations under international law with respect to the state or diplomatic immunity of a person or property of a third state, unless the ICC can first obtain the cooperation of that third state for the waiver of the immunity.[142] In consequence, a state may not protect its top representatives, but a third party state may do so.

Formal regulations pertaining to immunities do not reveal the full answer as to whether the criminal courts have actually heeded them in the course of their operation. An investigation of the actual court practice is necessary to find this answer.

Ministers and prime ministers were brought to trial both before the International Military Tribunal and the International Military Tribunal of the Far East. However, apart from Dönitz, no head of state was charged,[143] even though the allies could have charged the Italian king Victor Emanuel III[144] or the Japanese emperor Hirohito. The latter case is especially telling, given that it was often noted that the slightest signal from the emperor could have stopped Japan's participation in the war.[145] The decision to spare the emperor from facing the IMTFE was most likely predicated by hopes of better political cooperation with the Japanese elites after the war, and gaining support for the administration in the time of occupation.[146] It was also cited that, in contrast to Germany, Japan did not lose its sovereignty, and so the emperor's immunity held.[147] Nonetheless, the decision was debated even among the judges.[148]

The only person to invoke his immunity (in this case, diplomatic) was Oshima. The International Military Tribunal for the Far East ruled, however, that this type of immunity is only valid with regard to the jurisdiction of the country where its holder is accredited, and besides, is ineffective with regard to crimes under international law.[149]

6.5 Rights of a person charged with a crime of aggression

In an aggression trial, just like in any other court trial, it is necessary to guarantee that the defendant has certain rights and that these rights are respected. It is a *sine qua non* condition to consider the trial just and fair.[150] Of course, even the fairest of trials may end in unjust judgments that are misinformed as to the facts and consequently make wrong decisions as to the culpability of the defendant. However, it is usually the trials where the rights of defendants are violated that lead to unjust convictions.

In trials examining the cases of the gravest crimes of international law, there is often a tendency to dismiss the rights of the defendants. The implied suggestion is that, given the scale of violations committed by the defendants, they should consider themselves lucky to stand trial, instead of simply being put in front of a firing squad.[151]

The fundamental procedural guarantees are listed in the International Covenant on Civil and Political Rights of 1966.[152] It is in the light of these guarantees that potential violations of the rights of the defendants in aggression trials must be considered. Both the statute and the rules of procedure and evidence of the ICC implement the standards required under the International Covenant on Civil and Political Rights, as well as those elaborated by the Human Rights Committee. The rights guaranteed to defendants include, for example, the right to remain silent, protection against the burden of evidence being shifted onto the defendant and the guarantee of certain rights during the investigation, that is, before the trial actually begins.[153] Moreover, the statute of the ICC refers to 'fair hearing', which means that the rights guaranteed to defendants should be interpreted in line with the developments in human rights in this area.[154]

In terms of actual practice, it is necessary to investigate the proceedings in aggression trials, such as the proceedings before the International Military Tribunal or the International Military Tribunal for the Far East. Naturally, the International Covenant on Civil and Political Rights was not in force during the Nuremberg and Tokyo trials. Nonetheless, the charters of both these tribunals (as well as the Control Council Law No 10) stipulated that fair trial for the defendants would be ensured.[155] The procedural guarantees listed in the statutes of the International Military Tribunal and the International Military Tribunal for the Far East included the following: the indictment specifying in detail the charges against the defendants, and of all the documents lodged with the indictment, in a language the defendant understands, is to be furnished to the defendant at a reasonable time before the trial; the preliminary examination of the defendant and the trial are to be conducted in, or translated into, a language which the defendant understands; the defendant is to have the right to conduct his own defence before the tribunal or to have the assistance of a counsel (a professional attorney selected by the defendant or another person authorised to act in this capacity by the tribunal); during any preliminary examination or trial, the defendant is to have the right to give any explanation relevant to the charges made against him; the defendant is to have the right (himself or through his counsel) to present evidence in support of his defence, and to cross-examine any witness called by the prosecution.[156] Essentially, the guarantees listed in the charters of the tribunals corresponded to today's standards as specified in the International Covenant on Civil and Political Rights. Even if certain rules were not explicitly listed, they were implicit in the necessity to ensure a fair trial. Both the Nuremberg and Tokyo charters actually made guarantees to defendants that exceeded the standards under the law at the time,[157] and the course of proceedings at least formally ensured equal treatments of the parties.[158] It seems therefore legitimate to discuss the rights of defendants under the covenant on the one hand, and invoke examples from past court practice in aggression trials on the other.

One of the key procedural guarantees is the right to a just and public examination of the case by an independent and impartial court that has jurisdiction in the case. The impartiality of the judges is the easiest among these factors to challenge. The impartiality, that is, absence of bias on the part of the judge towards the defendant, is subject both to the subjective test (with respect to the judge's own beliefs and opinions) as well as the objective test (the guarantees on the part of the judge that rule out judicial bias).[159]

Unfortunately, considering the aggression trials held to date, it is impossible to uphold the notion of impartiality, since all the judges in these trials represented the states that had won the war.[160] No representatives of neutral states were allowed to sit on the panels. It has been argued that the defendants never have the right to choose the judges who try them, and they always have to rely on the fair trial guarantee – but it hardly sounds convincing under the circumstances.[161] If the judges fail to live up to the impartiality requirement, the principle of fair trial is effectively ruined. In the case of aggression, the problem of judges' impartiality is particularly pronounced, because any citizen of the victim state may feel a victim of the aggression, and therefore any judge originally from the state that was attacked may be challenged on grounds of partiality.

It would be difficult to argue that the International Military Tribunal for the Far East was impartial,[162] considering that Judge Jaranilla, who sat on the panel, had survived the Bataan death march and was a prisoner of the Japanese forces; Judge Cramer had prior to the trial drafted the legal opinion for Roosevelt with regard to the Pearl Harbor attack; Judge Webb had investigated the Japanese crimes committed in New Guinea as the Australian commissioner for war crimes[163] (and with his conduct in the courtroom clearly demonstrated his bias and dismissive attitude towards the defendants and witnesses they called[164]). Even before the trial began, it was evident that the Russian, Philippine and Chinese judges would favour very strict sentences.[165] The Indian judge, on the other hand, commented at the very outset of the trial that he believed all of the defendants in the Tokyo trial should be acquitted, because it was thanks to them that Asia was set free.[166]

As a side note to the topic of the jurisdiction of the court, it should also be noted that the judges should be qualified to carry out the proceedings. In cases relating to the crime of aggression, judges should be well versed not only in criminal law, but also in international law. From among the panel members of the International Military Tribunal for the Far East, only one judge (Pal) was a specialist in this area of law.[167] While it may seem self-explanatory that a judge should be fluent in the language of the proceedings, practice demonstrates that it is not always the case. The trial in Tokyo was carried out in only two official languages, English and Japanese. The French and Russian judges were unable to follow the proceedings properly, because their knowledge of these languages was minimal.[168]

In discussing whether the Tokyo trial meets the criteria of a fair trial, it is also necessary to consider the prolonged absences of the judges, as well as the substitutions in panel membership while the proceedings were underway.[169] At the first formal sitting of the court, on 3 May 1946, 9 out of 11 judges were present in the courtroom. Judge Pal arrived on 17 May, and the Philippine Judge Jaranilla – on 9 June, having missed six days of presentations of evidence. Judge Cramer, who replaced Judge Higgins, arrived as late as 22 July.[170] Judge Pal won the ranking for most absent, missing 80 out of 417 days of the tribunal's sessions.[171] Judge Webb missed the defence of 10 defendants.[172] Considering that the capital penalty sentences with regard to the Japanese criminals were passed with votes such as 6:5 (Hirota) and 7:4 (other defendants), each day missed during the presentations of the defence could actually be worth a life.[173] Moreover, not even one single meeting was held with all the judges present to discuss the final wording of the judgment (a fact that Judge Bernard made specific complaints about).[174]

They key principle in criminal proceedings is the assumption of innocence, from which it follows, inter alia, that members of the adjudicating panel should not commence proceedings with a firm belief that the defendants are actually guilty as charged.[175] The defendant may not be treated as if he was guilty, and all doubts should be interpreted in favour of the defendant.[176] Sadly, court practice has not been commendable in this aspect. The charter of the International Military Tribunal was drafted with specific defendants in mind.[177] In the course of the negotiations of the London Agreement, Jackson insisted that the tribunal should have jurisdiction over conspiracy to commit the crime against peace, with the specific objective of reaching individuals such as Ley and von Ribbentrop.[178] Nikitchenko openly claimed that the culpability of the potential defendants was beyond question, and the only issue was the punishment;[179] evidence suggests that Jackson held the same belief.[180] In this context it may appear shocking that the same persons who negotiated the Charter of the International Military Tribunal later sat on its panel (Nikitchenko, Falco) or acted as prosecutors or assistant prosecutors (Jackson, Trainin, Gros, Fyfe). How could the authors of the charter of the International Military Tribunal, who drafted it with specific defendants in mind, be expected truly to apply the principle of *in dubio pro reo*?[181] The claims that the sentences in the Nuremberg and Tokyo trials were predetermined seem therefore to be potentially well founded.[182]

'Equality of arms', that is, the notion that the rights of defendants should guarantee proper preparation of the defence and access to the same options that are available to the prosecution, has been a popular topic recently.[183] In order to satisfy these requirements, the defendant should most definitely receive a copy of the indictment with sufficient notice; the indictment should be drafted in a language that the defendant can understand; the defendant must have enough time to prepare his defence, and must have access to a translator if necessary. In both Nuremberg and Tokyo, the defendants received the indictment no later than 30 days before the trial, in their mother tongue.[184] However, in the case of Bormann the court decided to proceed *in absentia*, which is controversial in that practically it left the defendant unable to exercise the right to prepare his defence and be heard by the court.[185] The quality of the translation was criticised, but not beyond what is typical in proceedings where translation is necessary.

As for the right to have a defence counsel, it was respected in all trials; the attorneys who provided the defence in the Nuremberg trial were exceedingly competent.[186] There were, however, complaints that the defendants were only able to contact their defence counsels very shortly before the trial or even only during its initial days.[187] Nonetheless, as the trials progressed, efforts were made to facilitate the defence, for example by appointing an official to advise the defendants as to their rights and the selection of the defence counsel (Nuremberg trial)[188] or by assigning the defendants American defence counsel who were familiar with the Anglo-Saxon procedure applied in the proceedings (Tokyo trial).[189] The situation of the defendants was much bleaker in the Supreme National Tribunal in Poland, where the attorneys themselves declared that they were unwilling to defend their clients. Today many lawyers see participation in international law criminal cases as publicity, especially when it comes to defendants who held top offices, and consequently good defence counsel willing to do their best for their clients seem to be in ready supply.

The biggest problem that plagued the courts, and will probably continue to be a challenge in the ICC, is the lack of access to documentation and the impossibility of examining all core witnesses for the defence.[190] States cannot be expected to reveal their confidential and secret documents, and most documents relevant in the cases are bound to have this designation, given that they pertain to key issues in national defence, sovereignty and territorial integrity. With regard to witnesses, the defendants would probably wish to bring to the stand top politicians, who tend to hide behind their immunities in order to avoid being examined. Also, courts are likely to reject motions to examine for example a president or a prime minister, in order to prevent the trial from becoming too politicised. The problem naturally rests on the fact that aggression trials are inherently heavily political.

For example, the defence counsels in the Tokyo trial complained that many of their motions for evidence were rejected.[191] The Tokyo Tribunal (which, in comparison with the Nuremberg one, failed notoriously in terms of fair trial guarantees) disallowed examination of witnesses more than once. Moreover, it adopted an absurd rule under which a witness could not be called if this witness had previously offered a written statement and it could not be proved that this person had lied – which was extremely difficult to accomplish without examining the witness in court.[192] Owing to the unequal treatment of the prosecution and the defence, Judge Bernard concluded that the principle of equality of arms had been violated, and cited this fact as one of the reasons why it was impossible properly to assess the responsibility of the defendants.[193]

As for the ICC, it is of paramount importance which body determines aggression: if it is the Security Council or the General Assembly, no rules of evidence apply, and there is no requirement to examine witnesses and potential defendants, so the latter have no opportunity to present their points of view.[194] This is why the Special Working Group on the Crime of Aggression specifically noted that defendants are allowed to challenge, in the course of the proceedings, the determinations of the Security Council, and the ICC itself is not bound by these determinations either.[195]

The right of defendants to appeal to a higher instance court or tribunal to review their cases should also be universally guaranteed. Sadly, this right has not been respected in the aggression trials undertaken to date. For example, the charter of the International Military Tribunal stipulated that the judgment of the tribunal as to the guilt or the innocence of any defendant was final and not subject to review,[196] with the reservation that the Control Council for Germany could at any time reduce or otherwise alter the sentences.[197] The council reviewed the applications for sentence reductions within five days. As for the judgment of the International Military Tribunal for the Far East, the review period was even shorter and amounted to only three days. It is difficult to believe this period would be sufficient to consider all legal and factual aspects of the case.

To recapitulate: as shown above, the opinions that the Nuremberg trial was not subject to criticism,[198] or that it was completely fair,[199] appear to be exaggerated.

6.6 Statute of limitations and amnesty law

In many jurisdictions, after a given period elapses, a perpetrator may avoid responsibility, because a statute of limitations applies to the perpetrator's actions.[200] The idea that legal responsibility is limited in time derives from the understanding that after the lapse of a certain period, actions fade in human memory, and punishment is no longer necessary in terms of both justice and deterrence.[201] In relation to the crime of aggression, the application of a statute of limitations seems particularly important: initiation of proceedings in an aggression case many years after the events is definitely not conducive to improving relations between the aggressor and victim states, and is likely to rekindle political conflicts that may have already been extinguished. Arguments have been made to the effect that no statutes of limitations should apply to the prosecution of so-called core crimes of international criminal law, but this position actually appears debatable with respect to the crime of aggression.

The inapplicability of statutes of limitations to the crimes under the jurisdiction of the International Military Tribunal may be derived (and has been argued to derive) from the London Agreement, which was designated as unlimited in time.[202] Even so, the Charter of the International Military Tribunal pertained solely to crimes committed by citizens of the European Axis powers; legal acts of more universal nature should probably prevail in this context.

The Convention on the Non-Applicability of Statutory Limitations to War Crimes and Crimes Against Humanity, adopted by General Assembly Resolution 2391 of 26 November 1968, invokes General Assembly Resolution 95 of 11 December 1946, which in turn upholds the principles of the charter and judgment of the International Military Tribunal.[203] However, the convention explicitly specifies that no statutory limitations apply to war crimes and crimes against humanity.[204] What is more, it also provides that 'war crimes' should be understood in line with the definition in the Charter of the International Military Tribunal, that is, as particularly the 'grave breaches' enumerated in the Geneva Conventions of 12 August 1949 for the protection of war victims. It is therefore impossible legitimately to argue that the convention pertains to the crime of aggression; on the contrary, the convention explicitly narrows down the interpretations of the term 'war crimes' to exclude the crime of aggression.

Similarly, the European Convention on the Non-Applicability of Statutory Limitation to Crimes against Humanity and War Crimes, adopted in Strasburg on 25 January 1974, specifies that it only has application to crimes against humanity and war crimes, in particular those listed as grave violations in the Geneva Conventions of 1949.[205]

Only the statute of the ICC stipulates that the crimes within the jurisdiction of the ICC (ie including the crime of aggression) are not subject to any statute of limitations.[206] Yet the crime of aggression falls within the ICC's jurisdiction only theoretically at the moment.

The view that the gravest crimes of international law should not be subject to any statute of limitations is often believed to derive from customary law. If aggression is the gravest of crimes, and the 'less grave' war crimes are not subject to statutes of limitations, then naturally the crime of aggression should not be subject to them either. It is, however, difficult to uphold this reasoning. First, states have made the conscious decision not to include aggression in the conventions on the non-applicability of statutory limitation.[207] Secondly, both of these conventions have been ratified by a very limited number of states: only 54 in the case of the United Nations Convention,[208] and only seven in the case of the European one (including Belgium, the Netherlands and Romania).[209] Thus, there seems to be very little evidence that the non-applicability of statutory limitation to the gravest crimes of international law is actually rooted in customary law.[210]

The application of statutes of limitations is an expression of the state's criminal policy from a general, long-term perspective, In contrast, abolitions in conjunction with amnesty (further jointly referred to as amnesty)[211] reflect the state's decision not to prosecute specific types of crimes under specific types of circumstances, that is, they represent the state's short-term criminal policy with regard to specific objectives.

Amnesties tend to be declared in the final phases of a conflict or when a conflict has recently ceased, in order to encourage disarmament and help restore peace; often, it is the price that must be paid for the surrender of the representatives of the old regime.[212] Amnesty as an institution is controversial in that, while an individual pardon is specific to circumstances and typically occurs after a court has ruled on the guilt and the punishment, amnesty (with its universal applicability) does nothing to discourage crime and its attendant moral shortcomings.[213]

Clearly, a law firmly entrenched in a national legal order, such as an amnesty, may not take precedence over international law, and is not formally binding on third party states. But does international law actually prohibit amnesties pertaining to perpetrators of crimes against peace? Of the numerous international agreements, only the Control Council Law No 10 expressly stated that no amnesty granted under the Nazi regime could be admitted as a bar to trial or punishment.[214] The statutes of the International Criminal Tribunal for the former Yugoslavia and the International Criminal Tribunal for Rwanda include no references to amnesties. Both tribunals were established by the Security Council with the objective of restoring peace, and it appears that the Security Council believed that an amnesty would be in contravention of this objective.[215] The problem is that neither of the tribunals has jurisdiction over the crime of aggression. The ICC, on the other hand, is allowed to consider amnesty a factor that can preclude prosecution in a given case.[216]

Legal theory proposes a list of conditions that an amnesty must satisfy in order to be considered legal from the international law perspective. First, it must have a specific objective, such as for example commencement of the process of reconciliation. Secondly, it must be implemented together with other measures, such as truth commissions or a vetting and screening process, the objective of which is, in addition to the documentation of violations, also the prevention of such crimes being recommitted in the future. Thirdly, it must either be negotiated by the national forces in conflict or adopted under the guidance and approval of an international organisation such as the United Nations and, moreover, it must be accepted by a majority of the society to which it pertains. Fourthly, it may not extend to persons with the greatest responsibility for the crimes that were committed. Fifthly, it must go hand in hand with a promise of compensation to be paid to the victims. Finally, the state must be considered unable to prosecute the perpetrators.[217] These conditions are applicable to amnesties that pertain to war crimes, crimes against humanity and genocide. They might be also applicable to the crime of aggression, with the exception of the fourth condition, since only the persons with greatest responsibility for the aggressive policy are punishable for this crime. Consequently, insisting on this condition would make it effectively impossible to have an amnesty pertaining to the crime against peace.

6.7 The principle of *nullum crimen sine lege*

One of the most fundamental arguments raised against the legitimacy of all aggression trials was the violation of the principle of *nullum crimen sine lege*, one of the fundamental principles of criminal law. Unfortunately, even today problems remain in adhering to this principle in scenarios in which individuals are assigned criminal responsibility for the crime of aggression.

Nullum crimen sine lege originated in Roman law, but was further developed in the time of the French revolution, in the context of protection from arbitrary deprivation of freedom by a despot.[218] The principle works to the effect that an act is not punishable if it was not criminal and punishable at the time of commission of the act (*nullum crimen sine lege poenali anteriori*). It also results in a ban on retroactive criminal legislation (*nullum crimen sine lege praevia, lex retro non agit*) and the necessity to specify strictly the parameters of the act that is criminalised (*nullum crimen sine lege certa*), which is only achievable by means of laws codified in writing, as opposed to customary law or laws of minor significance (*nullum crimen sine lege scripta*). Finally, it also leads to a prohibition on relying on analogies in criminal law.[219]

At the core of these principles lies the notion that an act that is permitted by law cannot be punishable, since it would not be just to punish without due warning.[220] During the Nuremberg trial, Hermann Jahreiss, one of Jodl's defence counsels, argued in particular that prosecuting defendants for the crime against peace makes law retroactive, and as such anticipates the legal regime of a global state.[221] If aggression is a crime, how can the initial neutrality of the United States be explained, along with the absence of sanctions against the Soviet Union for the aggression against Poland and Finland?[222]

There had been attempts to challenge this position. The International Military Tribunal ruled that *nullum crimen sine lege* is not a limitation of sovereignty but rather a guarantee of justice,[223] that it is not unjust to punish those who violated treaties and assurances, and who attacked neighbouring states without warning. Under the circumstances, the attackers must have realised their wrongdoing; it would be unjust to leave this wrongdoing without legal consequences.[224] Jackson argued also that the absence of a precedent (ie a previous aggression trial) was immaterial, since the Nazis in power were fully aware that 'launching aggressive war or the institution of war by treachery was illegal'.[225] Another argument invoked the fact that piracy was and had been punishable, despite the fact that no specific code made it a crime, and individuals were in fact punished for engaging in piracy.[226] Similarly, the first person to stand trial for murder might argue that that the court had no jurisdiction in the case.[227] If it is accepted that aggression has been illegal since time immemorial, challenging the law on the grounds of it being retroactive is unfounded: what occurred was a period of temporary impunity that was a failure of politicians, but not a failure of the law.[228] Thus, even if the previous regime found certain types of conduct acceptable, a reasonable person must have been aware of the wrongdoing, and therefore should be punished by the new regime.[229]

Theorists of law also noted that not all national legal systems prohibit retroactivity.[230] Moreover, it typically pertains only to the types of conduct that have no impact on the international community. There is no point in requiring that all crimes should be accounted for in codified law; international law is a primitive legal order, and strict observance of this principle will effectively annihilate it.[231]

Even if it is assumed, for the sake of argument, in the period immediately following the Second World War that the principle of *nullum crimen sine lege* was not considered absolute,[232] in today's reality there is no denying its fundamental role in international criminal law. It features in the statute of the

ICC that stipulates that a person is criminally responsible under the statute unless the conduct in question constitutes, at the time it takes place, a crime within the jurisdiction of the ICC.[233] Moreover, the statute provides that the definition of a crime should be strictly construed and not be extended by analogy and, in case of ambiguity, the definition should be interpreted in favour of the person being investigated, prosecuted or convicted.[234]

That aggression is nowadays considered a crime is beyond doubt. The problem lies not in proving that aggression is a crime, but rather in specifying precisely what this crime consists of. The two aspects of *mens rea* and *actus reus* of the crime must be delineated with sufficient precision so that a potential perpetrator could anticipate the consequences of his or her actions.[235]

It has been argued that the interpretation of *nullum crimen sine lege* should take into account the particular nature of international law:[236] since no catalogue of international crimes exists, it is unreasonable to expect regulations to be very specific.[237] The objective of international law is to express certain general principles of law and justice, as they are accepted by the international community, rather than to observe strictly legal notions.[238] The principle of *nullum crimen sine lege* should therefore be considered in terms of its procedural applications, and understood as ideal rather than immediately achievable (although efforts should be made to observe it).[239]

These arguments are somewhat weak. Criminal law, be it national or international, applies to specific individuals, and practice has demonstrated that individuals may (and on occasion do) pay the highest price for disobeying its regulations. It must therefore be predictable. If law is based on perceptions, whether personal or more widely held, it is not predictable.[240] The principle of *nullum crimen sine lege* should not be discounted when the law punishes for something that it is not able to define.

On the other hand, the law requires only a general awareness of the provisions that criminalise certain conduct, rather than full consensus as to the meaning of all terms used to define the crime as applicable to every imaginable situation.[241] The International Covenant on Civil and Political Rights, which also incorporates the principle of *nullum crimen sine lege*, stipulates that its application may not prejudice the trial and punishment of any person for any act or omission which, at the time when it was committed, was criminal according to the general principles of law recognised by the community of nations.[242]

Most definitely in the case of the crime of aggression references to customary or natural law do not suffice;[243] such norms lack the precision necessary in criminal law. The problem of differentiating between aggression and self-defence persists despite the ruling of the International Military Tribunal that each state has the right to self-defence, but it is the court that determines whether it was properly exercised.[244] The definition adopted by the review conference also fails to solve the problem of potential violations of *nullum crimen sine lege.* It provides for the punishablity of acts of aggression, understood as the use of armed force by a state against the sovereignty, territorial integrity or political independence of another state, or in another manner in violation of the Charter of the United Nations. However, the regulations of the charter are notoriously imprecise and are often interpreted to contradictory effect. This is why it was decided that only an act of aggression that constitutes a manifest violation of the Charter of the United Nations potentially gives rise to responsibility. This then leads to another problem: how manifest must the violation of the charter be in order to trigger an individual's responsibility? It appears that, in line with the *in dubio pro reo* principle, only in the most truly blatant cases of aggression will the perpetrators be charged; the inexactitude of the definition of the crime will be less evident under such circumstances.[245] Moreover, the crime of aggression is a crime of leaders and not followers; consequently, it is not necessary to make the wording so precise as to be transparent to the average citizen.[246] In any event, in borderline situations defendants always have the option of invoking a mistake of law, which may exonerate them from responsibility.

As for the provisions adopted by the review conference, it is probably unnecessary to take fright and to declare that violations of *nullum crimen sine lege* are certain to occur.[247] It is, however, important to appreciate the risk inherent in a broad interpretation of the definition of the crime of aggression. The definition cannot be flexible and change like a chameleon depending on the circumstances.[248] Problematically, the statute of the ICC, while it forbids extending the definition of the crime of aggression by analogy, at the same time fails to prohibit new interpretations of the existing regulations.[249]

For the sake of completing the argument, it should be noted that, with regard to international courts, the principle of *nullum crimen sine poena* is not applicable: in the absence of an international criminal code, no law specifies the penalties for the specific violations of international law.[250] It is not the potential penalty but rather the gravity of the violation that is of paramount importance in international criminal law.[251] In order for a crime of international law to be punishable, it is sufficient to demonstrate the existence of a relevant prohibition.[252]

6.8 Conclusions

Bringing defendants to court on charges of aggression gives rise to a number of procedural difficulties, many of which are insurmountable. The first obstacle consists in finding the legal basis to give the courts of a given state jurisdiction over the perpetrators of the aggression. The problem is absent only in relation to two states, the aggressor and the victim. However, the same two states may either have no interest in undertaking the proceedings or be too weak to initiate them with success. Third party states may invoke the principle of universal jurisdiction, but a number of arguments suggest that the principle is actually not applicable to the crime of aggression. As for the international courts, only the ICC may, at some point in the future, have the relevant jurisdiction. Yet even then the ICC's jurisdiction will be severely limited.

The optimistic scenario assumes that the courts in the aggressor state will give a fair trial to the perpetrators of aggression. Failing that (ie realistically in most cases), the problem of surrendering the defendants will arise. Extradition is only possible if a given act is punishable both under the laws of the requesting and of the requested state. This condition is likely to be difficult to satisfy, considering that few criminal codes actually contain regulations that stipulate punishablity of the perpetrators of aggression against other states. Moreover, states may attempt to protect specific individuals from extradition by classifying the acts they are charged with as political in nature. With regard to the crime of aggression, it is very easy to argue in favour of such classification.

One of the pivotal issues was designating the body with the power to determine whether aggression has in fact occurred. The review conference decided to place this power in the hands of the Security Council. Should the council fail to take action, the ICC has the discretion to act. Furthermore, it remains unclear whether national courts are also obliged to wait for the Security Council to determine aggression before initiating proceedings.

Aggression is a crime of the leaders of states, and aggression trials are therefore vulnerable to the risk that the perpetrators will invoke their immunities to avoid responsibility. Doubtless this obstacle pertains to national courts: as confirmed by the judicature of the ICJ, national courts must respect immunities of top-ranking representatives of states. The obstacle is also likely to arise in proceedings before the ICC, because states are free to deny the surrender of a person on grounds of respecting the individual's privileges and immunities.

It is unclear whether it is possible to ensure that defendants in aggression trials are guaranteed all procedural rights envisaged in the fundamental documents in the area of human rights. ICC practice demonstrates that this tends to be problematic. If aggression trials are held mostly before the ICC, there are reasons to be optimistic, since the ICC's statute incorporates all fair trial guarantees. Unfortunately, the ICC is not able to ensure that defendants have access to all documents useful in constructing their defence. There is no mechanism forcing states to present documentation relevant to the decision to use armed force; regulations proposing such a mechanism would be unenforceable. If defendants charged with the crime of aggression are tried before national courts, there are no guarantees of judges' impartiality and the presumption of innocence.

It is only under the statute of the ICC that the statutes of limitations are not applicable to the crime of aggression. Even this singular regulation is problematic, given that the ICC does not actually have jurisdiction in cases of aggression. Certainly the non-applicability of statutes of limitations to the crime of aggression cannot be derived from customary law. It also does not appear that amnesty could be banned with regard to perpetrators of the crime of aggression, especially if the objective of the amnesty is to facilitate the process of reconciliation, as disputing the differences as to who initiated the war is unlikely to promote this objective.

Finally, violation of *nullum crimen sine lege* remains a problem with regard to the crime of aggression. At present, the legal basis for criminalising aggression is so shaky that it is debatable whether aggression is indeed a crime (although denying it may be perceived as exceedingly radical). Even if the criminality of aggression is conceded, along with the principle of individual responsibility for it, the absence of a precise definition remains an issue. A possible solution may consist in bringing charges only in the most manifest cases of aggression and, in all the other cases, interpreting all doubts in favour of the defendants.

7 Impact of aggression trials

7.1 Peace and security

When the world's most powerful states designed the global collective security system, they clearly pointed out the objective of this process: ensuring peace and security. These two elements have priority over all other values, such as justice, human rights, economic growth and social progress.

In the context of responsibility for war crimes, crimes against humanity and genocide, an oft-repeated phrase is that there can be no peace without justice, and no justice when impunity reigns.[1] Just as often cited are the words of Pope Paul VI, spoken on the World Day for Peace in 1972: 'If you want Peace, work for Justice'.[2] At the same time, it is stressed that the main reason why international crimes must be punished is in order to preserve the international order and to ensure the maintenance of peace and security.[3] Unfortunately, in the specific case of the crime of aggression, the two objectives – peace and justice – may come into conflict.[4] Should this problem arise, the approach based on the axiological roots of the United Nations system dictates that peace should prevail over justice.[5]

The United Nations has assigned to the Security Council the principal responsibility for maintaining peace and security. Thousands of pages could be written about the inertia that seems to pervade the Security Council, and about the conflicts that it failed to prevent. Nonetheless, the international community continues to vest in the United Nations its hopes for maintaining or restoring peace. It is therefore important to study the risks associated with potential aggression trials in terms of the operations of the Security Council, in particular in the context of trials before the International Criminal Court (ICC).

The Security Council, as noted above, is typically reluctant to classify a given situation as aggression and to determine the aggressor. Its resolutions tend to use more neutral terms, such as violation or breach of the peace, since in such cases it is not obliged to point to the party responsible for the illegal use of armed force, and is still free to employ all the measures stipulated in Chapter VII of the Charter of the United Nations.[6]

While this unwillingness to determine aggression may be jarring at times, it does make negotiations with all the parties to the conflict much easier. The aggressor state is not explicitly negatively branded, and thus is more willing to debate the options of conflict resolution.[7] If the Security Council announces its decision as to the guilty party while the conflict is still raging, armed action might continue longer than it otherwise would. Under such circumstances, the state considered the aggressor has nothing to lose, and its representatives will understand that they are about to face the criminal consequences of their actions; only victory may protect them from these consequences, since only as victors do they have a chance of escaping accountability. Consequently, once a state is declared to be the aggressor, it has motivation to fight until the end[8] and to refute the good offices of the Security Council.[9] After all, there is a lot of truth to the French saying: *le désespoir redouble le courage*. Stigmatising one of the parties could also lead to the (equally undesirable) attitude of 'they can only hang us once': if the persons leading the aggression feel that their fate is sealed, they may continue to engage in criminal conduct, with the understanding that the consequences of one violation and many violations will essentially be the same.[10] It is therefore not surprising that the Security Council may decide, under certain circumstances, that refraining from the determination of the aggressor may be a wiser course of action.[11]

The Security Council, it must be noted, is an institution that is not judicial, but rather political in nature, and its objective is not justice, but rather peace.[12] The superpowers rejected the notion that the actions commanded by the Security Council must not only be in compliance with the international law, but also with justice. They decided that the task of the Security Council is to prevent illegal use of force and, failing that, to punish it; achieving a just resolution of the conflict falls beyond this scope.[13] It has been argued that the Security Council should prevent aggression in a manner consistent with law and justice.[14] However, striving after justice must be contained within certain limitations, otherwise threatening to destabilise peaceful relations.[15]

After the establishment of the ICC, there is now another institution (somewhat in competition with the Security Council) in the field of peace and security.[16] In fulfilling its mission, the Security Council may either rely on the international criminal jurisdiction, or consider it redundant or even detrimental.[17] Consequently, the Security Council was granted the special power in relation to the ICC: it can suspend proceedings of the ICC in a given case for a period of 12 months[18] and, once the period lapses, it can renew the decision perpetually.

In the context of the crime of aggression it was also decided that the Security Council should have the final say as to whether aggression actually occurred. However, the Security Council's determination is important only in that it gives the green light for the proceedings before the ICC to commence; it has no impact on the further course of the proceedings. The defendants must have the option of proving that there had been no aggression. In terms of respecting defendants' rights, this is the only acceptable solution. In terms of the Security Council's position, the matter is not necessarily that clear. If the defendants present evidence that the ICC finds sufficient to decide, despite the determination of the Security Council, that aggression had not in fact occurred, it may undermine the credibility of the Security Council (none too strong at the best of times).[19] A safety valve is built into the system in that the ICC is only to investigate and prosecute manifest cases of aggression, so the situations of conflicts of opinions between the Security Council and the ICC are unlikely, although unfortunately not impossible.

One of the key arguments in favour of bringing perpetrators of aggression to trial is that it serves to prevent other cases of aggression. This argument is rooted in the notion of achieving peace by means of law.[20] Criminalising aggression is designed as a mechanism to prevent further conflicts[21] or conflict escalation.[22] Conversely, not criminalising it under international law encourages aggression.[23] It is also argued that it is impossible to tell how many wars would be prevented by the punishability of aggression,[24] just as it is impossible to tell how many more murders would occur if the crime were not punishable.[25] Moreover, the punishability of certain conduct reinforces the idea that this conduct is wrong,[26] while in all certainty impunity is not a deterrent.[27] If states are perceived as rational, then it should be possible to deter them from certain actions.[28] If leaders are aware that waging an illegal war places them at risk of criminal liability, they will hesitate to do so.[29]

The preventive function of international criminal law is a weak argument in that it relies not on a scientifically proven impact of penalisation on the rates of international crimes, but solely on the hope that, in the future, this preventive effect will occur.[30] It is nonetheless often invoked, since there is no good alternative justification of the usefulness and rationality of an international criminal justice system.[31] The deterrent effect fails to prevent crime even in national legal orders, despite the presence of the enforcement agencies. On an international scale, the deterrent effect is further reduced by factors such as hatred, fanatical patriotism, prospects of victory and martyrdom.[32]

Prevention can be contemplated in either general or specific terms. In the former case, the deterrent effect may only arise if there is clear understanding of which actions are to be avoided. The regulations pertaining to the use of force certainly lack such clarity. Of course, one might argue that the uncertainty as to the regulations of international law, coupled with the real possibility of criminal responsibility for certain actions, may result in a decrease in the number of doubtfully-legal interventions.[33] However, the consequences may be both positive and negative. While the number of cases where force is used may decrease, it is by no means synonymous with an increase in peace and security. States may well abstain from acting in support of human rights, and undertaking military interventions in support of these rights, in the absence of a relevant decision of the Security Council.[34] Often, keeping the peace requires the use of force. What is more, if (as it is often argued) the system of collective security is ineffective, the Security Council fails to live up to the expectations and states are forced to take matters into their own hands in terms of protecting their essential interests, it is not at all surprising that many states choose to ignore the law when the price is their very survival.[35] This is how the United States explains its reasons for opposing every institution that may limit its options as far as interest protection is concerned.[36] Benjamin Ferencz noted that those who are innocent are not afraid of the law,[37] which is definitely true. However, in this case, 'innocent' should be read as 'passive'.

The deterrent effect will only be achieved if aggression trials become a regular occurrence. If prosecution for aggression is the exception rather than the rule, most individuals in power will hesitate to believe that they might actually be held criminally responsible for illegal use of force.[38] Moreover, when debating the decision on possible aggression, usually the decisive factor is not the risk of criminal responsibility but rather the potential (or certainty) of victory.[39] What drives the invasions of new lands is the desire for power and for a place in history – a desire strong enough to overpower even the fear of death.[40]

In a more specific manner, the preventive effect of regulation was argued, for example, by claiming that, had Germany been punished for waging the First World War, it may not have waged the Second World War.[41] This cannot be determined, however, with any degree of certainty. The Treaty of Versailles did, for example, propose that Wilhelm II should be punished, and the emperor – despite the fact that punishment never materialised – remained outside national politics for the rest of his life. It was Hitler and his collaborators who waged the Second World War.

It has been argued that, in order for a punishment to be effective, the one who punishes must not be a criminal, the punishable act must be considered unacceptable by society and the other parties involved in the system must abstain from committing similar acts.[42] In the aggression trials conducted to date, none of these conditions has actually been met. The situation may change if the ICC is tasked with prosecuting aggression not only in theory, as it is now, but also in practice – yet even then it will not be fully different. For example, the permanent members of the Security Council may theoretically ensure their impunity by means of determining that no acts of aggression occurred in a given situation (they would, however, need to vote unanimously, with no permanent member exercising its power of veto). Considering the power of skilful propaganda, aggression may actually turn out to be socially acceptable, especially in authoritarian states and new or emerging democracies: wars of aggression are not officially waged nowadays, having been replaced by policing operations, humanitarian interventions, peaceful demonstrations and so on.

Aggression is also problematic in that it pertains to top-ranking state officials. It is therefore impossible for a state to give up, as sometimes happen in cases of war crimes, a number of lesser criminals in order to protect its image, and to protect those in power from responsibility. The problem is that the same persons who may potentially face criminal responsibility make the decisions on the deployment of armed force, and may use this force for their own protection. Moreover, it is usually the same persons that negotiate the peace conditions. It has been argued that the indictment brought by Richard Goldston, prosecutor of the International Criminal Tribunal for the Former Yugoslavia, against Radovan Karadžić and Ratko Mladić, or the indictment brought by David M. Crane, the prosecutor of the Special Court for Sierra Leone, against Charles Taylor, made the conflicts last longer that they would otherwise have done.[43] On a similar note, Togo (sentenced by the International Military Tribunal for the Far East) warned that an attempt to bring the emperor Hirohito to trial would cause Japan to continue fighting until her last breath.[44]

Furthermore, given that the potential defendants hold high state offices, they represent the state. A public trial of these defendants may thus be perceived as humiliating to the whole nation. The public opinion may understand why it is necessary to surrender a leader who allowed a massacre of innocents, but it will be much more difficult to convince society why a person who claimed to be fighting in self-defence, of for freedom, democracy etc is now to stand trial as an aggressor. The provisions assigning responsibility for the First World War to the emperor Wilhelm II were referred to as 'shame paragraphs', and nearly ended the ceasefire.[45]

The stigma of a charge of aggression marks not only the limited number of defendants, but also their whole nation. In consequence, it reinforces hatred and the sense of being wronged, and may lead to tension on national or ethnic grounds. The problem of aggression tends to culminate in heated debates engaging entire societies; the most minuscule details of shared history are analysed time and again; not only the use of force, but also all real and perceived mutual offences are invoked. The situation is not conducive to peace and reconciliation. An aggression trial thus seems unlikely to foster unity between nations or to contribute to the restoration of peace.[46]

What is more, in today's reality peace is seldom threatened by international conflicts, which have become increasingly rare.[47] It is not so much aggression, but rather national-level instability, tensions and conflicts between individuals and groups, and policy decisions that disrupt peace.[48] Such occurrences, however, are not punishable under international criminal law.

7.2 International humanitarian law

Ever since the Nuremberg Tribunal referred to it as the supreme crime, aggression has been almost universally accepted as the gravest violation of international law. In trying to understand precisely why it is aggression that is considered the worst possible wrongdoing in international relations, it is necessary to study the words of the main prosecutor in the Nuremberg trial and of the judgment that was entered there: it is the Nuremberg heritage that is generally invoked as the key argument supporting the gravity of the crime of aggression.

Jackson argued: 'Any resort to war – to any kind of a war – is a resort to means that are inherently criminal. War inevitably is a course of killings, assaults, deprivations of liberty, and destruction of property'.[49] In his opinion, an unjustifiable war is 'the crime which comprehends all lesser crimes'.[50] In the most famous passage of the Nuremberg judgment, the tribunal stated that 'to initiate a war of aggression is not only an international crime; it is the supreme international crime differing only from other war crimes in that it contains within itself the accumulated evil of the whole'.[51]

These passages suggest that aggression is condemned under international criminal law because it leads to death and destruction.[52] Owing to the scale of the violations, it was decided in Nuremberg that prosecuting the defendants for war crimes would not suffice.[53] Ecer noted this in his report to the United Nations War Crimes Commission, in which he wrote that the reason the Second World War should be considered a crime not on the grounds that every aggression is a crime, but rather because it was a total war plagued with war crimes and crimes against humanity.[54] Similar sentiments were expressed in theoretical legal writings, by the proponents of aggression trials[55] and in indictments in trials beyond Nuremberg.[56] Clearly, the reason why trials for the crime against peace have been held to date is because the Second World War was plagued with war crimes.[57]

If that is the case, should it not be sufficient, in terms of international justice, for courts to hold trials for war crimes and crimes against humanity only, giving up their attempts to decide on the responsibility of those guilty of aggression? Almost every case of aggression leads to other crimes. Could prosecuting these crimes be a good alternative to prosecuting aggression itself?[58] After all, even if it is theoretically possible to imagine a scenario in which aggression occurs without any of its attendant violations of international humanitarian law, it is difficult to argue why the aggression should be condemned under such circumstances.[59]

Yet the answer to the above question is far from simple. It is contingent, for example, on deciding whether for the international community the abuse of rights of persons protected under international humanitarian law is as undesirable as the risk to the life and health of the combatants (given that their killing by the combatants of the opposing army is, in light of the law of armed conflicts, perfectly legal).[60] After all, if aggression had not occurred, the deaths would not have had to occur either.[61] Two different situations must be considered here: when a person voluntarily chooses to become a soldier, thus declaring his or her willingness to risk life and limb in politically ordered military action, and conversely, when mandatory conscription results from the state's need to defend itself from aggression. In the former case, it is perhaps not necessary to empathise with a soldier's difficult fate. In the latter, no simple judgments can be made. It is also important to remember that, had the aggression not occurred, the finances necessary to fund the state's defence could have been otherwise put to good use.

A recurrent notion in the debate on the criminalisation of aggression is that it would prevent the use of armed force, and thus diminish the scale of other associated crimes.[62] What we eliminate, therefore, is the cause and not the effect, *fons et origo* of other crimes.[63] However, this positive impact of punishability of aggression will steadily decrease, given that the great majority of conflicts today play out at a national level, while the proposed definitions of the crime of aggression pertain solely to violent outbursts in international relations.

On a separate note, it appears that the decision to give the International Military Tribunal jurisdiction over the crime against peace stemmed largely from the awareness that otherwise it might prove impossible to bring to trial persons serving top state functions.[64] State leaders tend not to commit war crimes; they merely wage the war during which war crimes are committed.[65] Prosecution on charges of aggressive war was thus perceived as the 'magic bullet capable of ensuring the conviction of those at the very top'.[66] Today, however, when the scope of responsibility of leaders for the actions of their subordinates has been increased and the notion of a joint criminal enterprise has been developed,[67] the potential for impunity of top-ranking state officials problem has been strongly limited, if not altogether eliminated.[68]

Another important question to ask is as follows: if the tribunals had not had jurisdiction over the crime against peace, would the final sentences for the defendants who stood accused of the crime against peace be much different? The answer is not necessarily in the affirmative. From among all the Nuremberg defendants, only von Papen and Schacht were charged solely with the crime against peace, that is, they were not additionally charged with war crimes and crimes against humanity. Both were acquitted. Only the case of Hess could be used to argue in favour of vesting jurisdiction over the crime against peace in the tribunal: he was acquitted of the charges of war crime and crimes against humanity, but found guilty, convicted and sentenced to life imprisonment for participation in a conspiracy to wage a war of aggression. The outcome was different in Tokyo, where 14 defendants (Araki, Hashimoto, Hiranuma, Hoshino, Kaya, Kido, Minami, Oka, Oshima, Shimada, Shiratori, Suzuki, Togo and Umezu) were convicted solely for the crime against peace. The example appears striking, but is in fact less so, considering that none of these defendants was sentenced to death, and all of them left prison before 1955. In all the other cases discussed in this book, defendants charged with the crime against peace were also convicted for war crimes or crimes against humanity.

When the crime of aggression is on trial next to 'traditional' war crimes, there are almost always attempts to challenge the fundamental principle of international humanitarian law, that is, that the norms of *ius in bello* and *ius ad bellum* are completely separate and mutually independent.[69] This is well illustrated by another passage from Jackson's opening statement, in which he argued that: 'an honestly defensive war is, of course, legal and saves those lawfully conducting it from criminality. But inherently criminal acts cannot be defended by showing that those who committed them were engaged in a war, when war itself is illegal'.[70] The following conclusions can be drawn from these words: killing (presumably of those who are not participating in the armed action) is only a crime when committed by the forces of the aggressor; attacking the combatants is only legal when undertaken by those fighting on the side of the state that is defending itself.[71] It is a very tempting approach. At first, it may seem that justice requires a differentiation between the situations of the aggressor and that of the party forced to defend itself. The state acting in self-defence should be free from the necessity to respect any principles in relation to the state that violated the most important principle of international law, that is, the ban on the use of armed force.[72]

Such an approach is extremely dangerous. While not necessarily formulated in bad faith, it does demonstrate a thorough failure to understand the mechanisms of the law of armed conflict. The rights and the duties arising out of the norms of the law of armed conflict cannot be separated. If there is a principle to the effect that civilians (not participating in the immediate armed action) cannot be attacked it means, first, that the civilians are protected from the consequences of the military operations but also, secondly, that the combatants on the opposing side are protected too, because the civilians cannot attack them without losing the protection afforded to them, thus risking criminal liability.[73]

Importantly, during an armed conflict it is very difficult to determine which state is the aggressor and which is acting in self-defence. Each party typically claims self-defence, while accusing the other one of aggression. Consistent application of the principle that only the aggressor must observe international humanitarian law would merely serve to ensure inobservance of this law by either party, each claiming self-defence.

The Nuremberg Tribunal attempted to separate the concepts of *ius in bello* and *ius ad bellum*, but failed to do so consistently. As evidence of the ban of aggression being in force, it invoked the Hague Convention (IV), which pertains to the law of armed conflict, despite theoretically noting that these two areas of law are separate and distinct.[74] As a result, in many of the subsequent Nuremberg Trial, war crimes were considered in strict connection with the crime of aggression,[75] almost as if those fighting to defend themselves were incapable of committing atrocities.[76] Even in the cases where the courts affirmed the mutual independence of *ius in bello* and *ius ad bellum*, the considerations of whether aggression had occurred overshadowed the problem of crimes of humanitarian law.

A close reading of the judgments reveals that, in the course of the trials before the International Military Tribunal and the International Military Tribunal for the Far East, both the prosecutors and the judges focused their efforts on proving aggression, with war crimes and crimes against humanity moved to a position of secondary importance.[77] One could even note a certain American obsession with the crime against peace, which drew the attention away from, for example, crimes against the Jews in Europe.[78]

Unfortunately, investigating war crimes alongside the crime of aggression always centres the debate on the justification of the military operations, rather than on the real victims of the use of armed force.[79] What if aggression cannot be proved? The public opinion is most likely to be suspicious of all convictions of defendants charged with crimes of humanitarian law.[80] If there was no aggression, war crimes fade in significance, and their cruelty is diminished. What is more, the conviction of the so-called major criminals in Nuremberg and in Tokyo meant that, for many people, the issue of responsibility for the evils of the Second World War was finally put to rest. If the focus had not been on proving the conspiracy to commit aggression, what could have happened? Would Heinz Reinefarth, responsible for the slaughter of Warsaw's entire Wola district, have been considered by the allies a better witness than a defendant in the Nuremberg trial? Would the situation have been similar with Erich von dem Bach-Zelewski? Paradoxically, bringing aggression to trial did not actually help justice to be served on those guilty of war crimes, crimes against humanity and genocide.

7.3 The international criminal justice system

It is worthwhile to consider, in the context of the international justice system, the reasons for penalisation of certain types of conduct and whether these reasons apply to the crime of aggression. It is generally accepted that criminalisation arises out of the need to punish a wrongdoer or deter potential perpetrators from engaging in specific conduct.[81] The problem of punishability as deterrent has been discussed above. What should be added here is that prevention is only as useful insofar as it contributes to the general happiness of the population, in the words of Jeremy Bentham.[82] In the case of aggression, all side effects of prosecuting its perpetrators must be considered; should the procedure of prosecuting the crime of aggression prove to be too politically problematic, it would definitely not contribute to the overall well-being of the international community.[83]

As for the need to punish the wrongdoing, the question deserves an honest answer. What exactly is this wrongdoing that we wish to punish? Is it really the 'supreme international crime', that is, the violation of the norms regulating the use of force, or is it rather the specific war crimes and crimes against humanity perpetrated as an effect of this use of force?[84]

In terms of international crimes, it is often argued that one of the objectives of punishment is assigning the responsibility to specific individuals and, in doing so, absolving from that responsibility the remaining part of society. The process is intended to encourage reconciliation between the nations engaged in the conflict and determination of the historical truth.[85] In his opening statement, Jackson clearly stated that the responsibility should be assigned to individuals so as not to incriminate the entire German people.[86] It would in fact be perfect if, in case of aggression, it were possible to identify a group of individuals who were responsible for it, and thus release others from this responsibility. It is sometimes noted that the *raison d'être* of the aggression charge is that it should focus on the leaders.[87] However, the lines are blurred (eg in democracies) where the use of force is typically approved by a legislative body. Are all those who voted in favour to be held responsible?[88] And even on the assumption of the possibility of identifying a strict group of leaders, the effect would be: guilty leaders, an innocent nation.[89] Is that really so, and is that the way it should be?

In the trials to date, the decisions as to who to prosecute were made in rather a selective fashion.[90] Persons with strong ties to the armament industry were not put on trial, even though they often had the greatest vested interest in the continuation of military operations. The Japanese emperor escaped trial on purely political grounds.[91] It was almost as if a certain group had been selected to be sacrificed in order to protect others. Those whose fortunes had been made from war did not lose them after the Nuremberg and Tokyo trials. Quite the opposite: they gained additional legitimacy with the judgments of both tribunals, since the judgments clearly listed the main perpetrators. Consequently, attempts to bring others to trial seemed akin to abuse. Convicting only a small group of defendants for aggression meant in effect that responsibility was assigned to just a dozen or so individuals. Yet if waging a war of aggression can be likened to a concert played by the whole orchestra, is it really fair only to punish the conductor?[92] The politicians engaged in the crime of aggression on behalf of the larger group they represented. If they had emerged victorious, the entire nation would have reaped the benefits. Why should they stand alone when they are defeated?[93] It is therefore necessary to find a middle ground between collective responsibility (unacceptable in criminal law) and an excessively narrow interpretation of the leadership principle that tends to be applied in assigning responsibility for the crime of aggression.

One of the potential benefits of trials investigating international crimes is that it may help to reveal and determine the truth. The problem is that the truth tends to be the first victim of a war,[94] and each aggression trial soon turns into a battle for the historic truth.[95] The matter is relatively simple with war crimes: it is determined that somebody, for example, tortured a protected person during an armed conflict, and thus committed a war crime. The criminality of aggression, on the other hand, is contingent on a number of political circumstances, which often cannot be subject to full scrutiny owing to sensitive issues of state security.[96] In order to issue a just and truthful decision on who is responsible for aggression, it would be necessary to inspect state archives: an impossible feat. The likelihood that essential documents will only be revealed years after the relevant events is also much greater in aggression cases than, for example, in cases concerning war crimes.[97] For example, the International Military Tribunal ruled that Germany had no right to invoke self-defence to justify the aggression against Norway, but years after the trial, documents came to light that offered evidence of British preparations to move into Norwegian territories.[98] Another example, cited by Constantine Antonopoulos, is the Israeli attack on Iraqi nuclear facilities. The attack was universally condemned until Iraq used armed force against Kuwait and Iran and it was discovered that it had a nuclear weapons programme, at which point the perception changed radically.[99]

A review of the case is of course possible, but it is small consolation to a person who is executed following a death sentence, or who spends long years in prison (even though it must be noted that there is no option of the death penalty in the statute of the ICC, in contrast to some national legal orders). An acquittal issued years after the original sentence has the additional side effect of undermining the credibility of the court. Aggression trials therefore have the potential to do damage to the fragile framework of the hard-won respect for the international justice system and international criminal law.

Trials with charges of aggression are perceived as an expression of a certain policy. Of course there is a great deal of truth to the argument that each conflict has a political and economic background, but that hardly means that conflicts cannot be settled with the application of law.[100] A crime that is political in nature does not necessarily implicate political prosecution,[101] and the judges are not necessarily persuaded by purely political arguments.[102] However, the reputation of a political trial will persist with regard to trials for aggression as long as it is only those who lose that are tried for aggression, and the trials are tools wielded only by the victors.[103]

In each instance of attempts to bring to justice those guilty of aggression, accusations were made along the lines of 'victors' justice',[104] *vae victis*[105] or political revenge.[106] Until this day, the International Military Tribunal and the International Military Tribunal for the Far East are perceived as victors' courts.[107] Jackson tried to argue against these charges, explaining that the Nazis stood before the tribunal 'not because they lost the war, but because they started it'.[108] It was also stressed on multiple occasions that the allies chose to proceed in a manner that was the least convenient for them: a trial in which the defendants were allowed to present their defence in the presence of the public.[109] What is more, for each judgment, it is necessary to ensure that there is a power able to enforce it; at the time, it was the allies who had that power.[110] However, it would probably be a mistake to overestimate the altruistic motivations of the allies. Nuremberg was the perfect solution in that guilt was demonstrated before a court: the perfect façade of impartiality and fairness. Large-scale murders could not have been explained away in the era of public media. The Nuremberg solution satisfied both Churchill, who got the court he wanted, and Stalin, who got the mass executions he wanted.[111] 'Give them a fair trial, then hang them' is a quip, but one that came into being for a reason.[112]

Soviet representatives, that is, representatives of the state that was guilty of aggression against the Baltic states, Finland and Poland, sat on the adjudicating panel of the International Military Tribunal and the International Military Tribunal for the Far East. Importantly, the Soviet aggression against Poland was carried out pursuant to an agreement with the Nazis.[113] If, as was decided in the subsequent Nuremberg trials, the interventions in Austria and Czechoslovakia amounted to acts of aggression, all participants of the Munich conference were also guilty of the crime against peace.[114]

The defendants made attempts to use these circumstances in a *tu quoque* type of defence, best summarised as: 'If you have committed certain acts yourselves, how is it you are prosecuting us for the same acts?' (the so-called 'clean hands' principle).[115] This charge aims at eliminating legal discrimination.[116] As Judge Pal correctly noted, the same standards must be applied with consistency.[117] In the Ministries trial, the American military tribunal offered insight into the *tu quoque* approach. The tribunal's judges explained that it is not a defence to criminal responsibility to invoke that one of the parties who made the law either violates it or intends to violate it in the future.[118] It was also often stressed that the same standards applied to Germans as to the British, the Americans, the French and the Russians.[119] Furthermore, it was also argued from theoretical positions that a court has no bearing on the decision on who is charged and what they are charged with, and thus the accusations are pointless.[120] Finally, the clean hands principle has no application in criminal proceedings, and only the victors can try and convict the aggressors.[121]

Yet, for all the reasons and reasoning, the fact remains that the Nazis and the Japanese were brought to trial because they had lost the war, while the Soviets were not because they had won.[122] There are good grounds for the claim that the International Military Tribunal and the International Military Tribunal for the Far East were victors' courts.[123] Characteristically, there were no representatives of neutral states on the adjudicating panels, not to mention German or Japanese representatives.[124]

No radical change is likely to take place with the ICC gaining jurisdiction over the crime of aggression. Given that the Security Council has the prevailing vote as to whether prosecution proceeds, the permanent members of the Security Council as well as their allies will be in a position to ensure impunity. There is also the potential pressure on the prosecutor (not by any means unheard of) not to prosecute for crimes committed by specific states, under the threat of the withdrawal of these states' funding of the ICC.[125] Clearly, the crime of aggression is inherently burdened with double standards,[126] and the sense of unfairness resulting out of the unequal treatment of perpetrators of aggression definitely has the potential to undermine the efforts towards the construction of a consistent international justice system.[127]

Currently, international criminal law focuses on the rights of the victims, and adopts the perspective of the victims.[128] This approach, however, is difficult to implement with regard to aggression because of the difficulty in pinpointing the victim: is it the nation of the state that was attacked, or is it also the population of the aggressor state that was forced into participation in an armed conflict? Is everyone who was adversely affected by the aggression a victim? If so, all of them should have a claim for compensation from the defendants.[129] Yet the perpetrators, rich as they might be, will never be able to compensate the losses suffered by millions of individuals. In its essence, aggression is not targeted against specific individuals, just as is the case with other crimes of international law such as genocide and crimes against humanity: it is the state that is the target.[130]

The ICC strives for global jurisdiction. At present (3 June 2013) 122 states are parties to the ICC's statute. It is a good number, but so is the number of those states that chose not to ratify the statute. This list includes the United States, Russia, China and Israel. Among the many reasons why these states are not willing to sign the statute of the ICC, the latter's jurisdiction over the crime of aggression ranks quite high.[131] The implementation of the definition of aggression is guaranteed to serve as another argument for the opposition to the ICC. After all, the problem with defining aggression almost prevented the statute's adoption.[132] Even NGOs were sceptical of this crime.[133] This reluctance stems from states' awareness that, once the ICC has jurisdiction over the crime of aggression, it will begin to expand the scope of its jurisdiction to cover all forms of the use of force.[134] On the other hand, for many states it was precisely the ICC's jurisdiction over the crime of aggression that was of key importance, and the ICC's credibility is measured by the likelihood of its investigation of specific cases of aggression.[135] The problem is that the states for whom this is the key motivator may well turn their backs on the ICC if it undertakes an investigation into a case of aggression which, in the opinion of these states, constituted a legitimate use of force, or fails to investigate a case of alleged aggression that, in the opinion of these states, is a manifest violation of the Charter of the United Nations. Consequently, each instance of proceedings in matters related to aggression will inherently bear the risk of rescission on the part of states that are now parties to the statute of the ICC, or of scaring away those who are contemplating becoming a party thereto.

Finally, the likelihood of attacks against the ICC is even greater in light of the fact that the charges of aggression will be brought against top-ranking state officials. When Sudan's president Omar Al-Bashir was charged with numerous crimes against humanity and war crimes, it caused uproar among African states, with some of them threatening withdrawal of their support for the ICC.[136]

7.4 Conclusions

International criminal law is designed to protect the values that are of greatest importance to the international community, and that this community is able to protect.[137] Beyond doubt, peace is one of these essential values.[138] Legal theory explicitly names the right to peace as one of the key human rights.[139] It may appear that peace cannot be protected without the criminalisation of aggression.[140] It would be most ironic if the crime that gave the impulse for the establishment of the United Nations Organisation were left out of the statute of the ICC,[141] effectively rendering the ban on aggression an empty phrase.[142] The fundamental question is as follows: can the regulations of criminal law work to protect peace, or is the opposite true, that is, that these regulations are detrimental to the maintenance and restoration of peace?

There is no simple answer. The preventive effects of the criminalisation of aggression are debatable. Stigmatisation of a given state or its officials is certainly not conducive to a prompt resolution of the conflict. A trial for aggression may breed disagreements and become the cause of new conflicts. It may also be perceived as an attempt to humiliate a nation, and thus generate further adverse outcomes.

There is also a real risk that the charges of aggression may draw the attention away from crimes such as war crimes, crimes against humanity and genocide. Mass-scale human rights violations are perceived much less negatively when they are committed by a party officially declared by a court to have fought in self-defence. On the other hand, lesser criminals on the side of the aggressor may attempt to shift the responsibility onto the persons assigned the responsibility for aggression, and to play the part of victims of politics or circumstances. Hopefully, courts will consistently enforce the separation of *ius ad bellum* and *ius in bello*, and negative consequences such as those described above will be avoided.

The crime of aggression differs significantly from other crimes of international law, if only in that it relies to a much greater extent on the notion of the responsibility of the state. In the result, different rules of procedure and evidence apply in the case of aggression.[143] The Security Council is involved in the investigation of aggression, by necessity making the proceedings political.[144] Prosecution of aggression is also inescapably entrenched in double standards, since it is only the weak and the defeated that are brought to trial. Yet this issue is also present in any investigation of war crimes.

Aggression trials must be approached with great caution, because they are fraught with the risk of undermining the credibility of the courts, owing to the strongly political nature of the crime. The criticism directed against Nuremberg and Tokyo trials focused mainly on the proceedings with regard to the crime against peace.[145] The trials held to date have demonstrated that the courts are forced to analyse many years of history (or even centuries, as was the case with the proceedings before the Polish Supreme National Tribunal) to determine responsibility for aggression. With a context as broad as this, it is easy to forget that it is a specific individual who stands trial, and no individual can be held single-handedly responsible for decades of tense international relations.[146]

Arguably, a trial on charges of aggression satisfies the emotional needs of society at a given point in time.[147] The demand for court-administered judgment in all cases of violations of the peace stems from the common perception of law and politics, law and morality, and law and metaphysical ethics as fused together.[148] War and aggression being political in nature, it has also been argued that responsibility for them should accordingly be political and historical, and not criminal in nature.[149] However, with the implementation of the term 'aggression' into the acts of international law, aggression became a legal issue as well. War crimes too were for a long time perceived as purely political, yet today their interpretation in legal terms raises no objections.

What is the alternative to eliminating the crime of aggression from the jurisdiction of the ICC, as well as of national courts? Is it impunity?[150] To date, decades after Nuremberg, this crucial question of impunity has been only considered in the context of mass-scale violations of human rights.[151] Yet, possibly, this is precisely the issue deserving the focus. It would put an end to many pointless political diatribes and mutual international accusations. Courts would be able to concentrate on the real victims of military operations, most of whom suffer as a result of national, rather than international, conflicts. It is notable that most defendants convicted on charges of aggression were also found guilty of war crimes or crimes against humanity. It seems that, today, with the new broader interpretation of joint criminal enterprise and command responsibility, convicting leaders guilty of aggression on charges of the traditional crimes of international humanitarian law would present no significant problems.

Conclusion

From time immemorial, deploying armed force against other states was perceived as a legitimate method of either exercising existing rights or reaching for new ones. The law began to limit the options of waging war in earnest only when the carnage of the First World War demonstrated the extent of damage to civilisation and humanity inherent in military operations.

The Covenant of the League of Nations replaced the division into *bellum iustum* and *bellum iniustum* with the seemingly clearer notions of *bellum legale* and *bellum illegale*. Yet loopholes in the law meant that it was often still possible to use force legally. The situation changed with the adoption of the Briand-Kellogg Pact and later the Charter of the United Nations, both of which effectively eliminated the option of waging a war of aggression. Problematically, these two regulations (and many subsequent ones) used imprecise terms such as 'war as an instrument of national policy', 'self-defence' and 'aggression'. There is no binding and universally acceptable definition for any of these terms, leading to a multitude of interpretations.

The responsibility for maintaining peace and de facto limiting the use of force among states was vested in the United Nations in general, and the Security Council specifically. Unfortunately, the organisations failed to live up to the high expectations, and consequently many states still prefer to put their trust in the old principle of *si vis pacem para bellum*, tending to rely on a broad understanding of self-defence rather than on the efficiency of the system of collective security.

For decades, efforts have continued to define aggression – to very little avail. As yet, no universally legally binding document defines it. It might appear that a simple statement, to the effect that the use of force in violation of international law constitutes aggression, would solve this problem. It is, however, not the case: international law lacks precision. The states have intentionally worded all the regulations that limit the use of force in a most general manner, because their true intention was not at all to be deprived of the right to engage in war, should their interest come under risk. At present, while aggression has been delegalised, it still remains difficult to define *in abstracto*.

Yoram Dinstein argues that '[t]here is no way in which war can be waged as if it were a chess game. ... As a result, war simply must be a crime'.[1] Yet the states, even as they adopted the legal regulations that delegalised the aggressive use of armed force, were not particularly eager to penalise it. For the first time ever, individuals experienced sanctions for aggression after the Second World War. Even then the world's greatest powers preferred to make laws that applied only to the perpetrators of that specific aggression, that is, Germans and the Japanese, rather than to the general population.

Problems with phrasing the definition of the crime of aggression and formulating the conditions of exercising jurisdiction over this crime in the draft Code of Crimes against the Peace and Security of Mankind and the statute of the International Criminal Court (ICC) throw negative light on the suggestion that criminalisation of aggression arises out of customary law. It is also important to remember that the Code of Crimes against the Peace and Security of Mankind is not legally binding, while the relevant amendments to the statute of the ICC have yet to enter into force. The trials in Nuremberg and Tokyo evidently took place under unusual circumstances; it would be wise not to use these trials to jump to conclusions.

The responsibility of individuals for aggression derives from the state's responsibility for that aggression. Given that there is no universally binding definition of aggression committed by a state and that the regulations on the use of force are imprecise, the opposition to punishing individuals for the crime of aggression is hardly surprising. International law may not yet have advanced to the point where full criminalisation of aggression is viable (even if its evolution is headed that way).

The fact remains that, after Nuremberg, the crime against peace is listed among international crimes, along with war crimes, crimes against humanity and the crime of genocide. Aggression has also come under the jurisdiction of the ICC, and several states allow individuals to stand trial for aggression under their national laws. It has therefore become necessary to define the elements of aggression.

The crime of aggression may only be committed by individuals who have an impact on the political and/or military operations of a state. Consequently, it tends to be committed by those who hold top-ranking state positions. Aggression may also only be committed intentionally. It is, however, very difficult clearly to delineate the *actus reus* aspect of the crime. The assumption of an individual's responsibility must be preceded by aggression on the part of the state; since aggression on the part of the state is not well defined, it is difficult to provide a good definition of what the penalised conduct of the individual should comprise. Thus the court, in determining the culpability of the accused, should give particular consideration to the possibility of mistake of law and mistake of fact. There are also good reasons to respect the threshold clause that only calls for the prosecution of manifest cases of aggression. On the other hand, if the clause works to the effect that only violation on the scale that led to Nuremberg and Tokyo is prosecuted, the next aggression trial might not occur for decades. This is not to say that, at present, no attempts are made to subjugate other states or take over parts of their territories. However, it is usually carried out under the pretences of neutrally-sounding humanitarian intervention, peace operation, assistance of the state's own citizens, assistance in self-determination or anti-terrorist action. The invasions of today are executed with subtlety, so as not to come into blatant conflict with international law. Why move troops if placing the right people in the right posts will accomplish the same designs?

It has often been argued that, after the Nuremberg Trial, it would be impossible to go back and simply give up on criminalising aggression. Eventually, the relevant regulations were incorporated into the statute of the ICC. Whether or not the ICC will truly have jurisdiction over the crime remains to be seen. The term 'aggression' carries a massive load of negative emotions. Attaching it to a state, by naming this state the 'aggressor', stigmatises the state (which tends to be the victim state's intention). The inherent moral condemnation is what makes 'aggression' stand out.

Court trials of individuals charged with the crime of aggression are notoriously procedurally difficult, especially if they proceed before national courts. Two options arise with regard to these difficulties: overcome them, or ignore them. Either way, the focus truly should be on another issue, namely the potential adverse impact of such trials.

Aggression trials have the potential to undermine peace and security. Even assuming that there might indeed be a preventive effect of penalisation of aggression, in a situation where only manifest cases come to trial, it would be naïve to hope that penalisation can eliminate the twilight zone of imprecise regulations. Aggression occurs at the crossroads of law, politics and ethics, and consequently in every case its precise context must be investigated. Each aggression trial will thus trigger debates, engendering a rehash of problems old and new, as well as true and imaginary. The arguments are most likely to run on emotional rather than rational stances. Nations whose best interests lie with reconciliation may be drawn into disputes that directly hinder or possibly even prevent this outcome.

Criticising the concept of bringing the perpetrators of aggression to justice is not easy. It tends to give rise to accusations of ignorance of the terrifying fallout of aggression: the dead, the wounded, the horror of destruction. Yet at present, to say that, at this stage of advancement of international law, aggression should not be penalised is not at all the same as to say that perpetrators of war crimes and other crimes of international humanitarian law should go unpunished – quite the contrary. Giving up on determining those guilty of aggression may draw attention back to the crimes (and their perpetrators) that can be identified. Prosecuting the perpetrators of aggression diminishes the interest in prosecuting those guilty of abuse of – for example – civilians. Placing the blame for aggression on one of the parties to the conflict may make the atrocities committed by the victim appear less condemnable compared with those committed by the aggressor. The problem of aggression may overshadow all other crimes with which military operations are fraught, and that is not a worthy outcome.

As for the anxiety that top state officials are likely to escape responsibility when aggression is not criminalised, it appears to be somewhat misplaced. The principles of responsibility for war crimes are constructed in such a way that it is difficult for leaders to argue effectively that they personally committed no crimes, were aware of no violations of humanitarian law and, therefore, should not be punished. If such top officials are not tried today, it is not because no laws make it possible to assign to them responsibility for war crimes, but rather because the international criminal justice system is weak. It is a problem that the penalisation of aggression is very unlikely to fix. Cases of unlawful use of armed force which lead to no violations of the law of military conflicts are extremely rare, and often so insignificant that they would not in any event result in criminal responsibility.

Aggression trials also pose a serious risk to the international criminal justice system which is still only in its infancy. The hard-won respect for international judicial institutions may be lost, and international criminal law may forfeit its logically coherent structure. Aggression is very different from all the other crimes of international law for which individual perpetrators stand trial today. It is a crime committed collectively, yet the principles of assigning responsibility for it aim to eliminate collective responsibility. Furthermore, it is difficult to determine the victims of aggression, and consequently it is almost impossible to view aggression from the victim's perspective, as is the trend in international criminal law. Aggression can only be committed by top state officials, or individuals with significant power over such officials. Thus, in aggression trials the court faces the challenge of privileges and immunities on the part of the potential perpetrators, who – to make matters worse – may be perceived as having acted to protect their nation's honour or a policy the nation supported. Most importantly, however, the responsibility of individuals for aggression is inseparably linked to the state's responsibility for the same. With regard to aggression committed by a state, a special authority (along with a special responsibility) is vested in the Security Council. On the one hand, the Security Council's freedom may not be limited, yet on the other hand, the court before which the perpetrator is to stand trial must remain neutral and unbiased. The amendments made at the review conference seem to strike a good balance in this respect. Nonetheless, when aggression occurs, it is necessary not only to investigate the very issue of who used force first, but also all the relevant circumstances of this event. This in turn cannot be accomplished without resorting to top secret documents of the states in question. In practice, this is an impossible task. The use of force is closely tied to issues of security and sovereignty. No state is going freely to divulge such information to third parties.

Any body or authority that attempts to investigate a case of aggression must analyse the political background, with all its disputes and arguments. A public relations fallout is guaranteed. For this reason alone, the enthusiasm of some of the states that demand prompt jurisdiction of the ICC over the crime of aggression must be viewed with scepticism. If the ICC does indeed begin handling aggression cases, it stands to lose the credibility it has fought very hard to win in the decade since its establishment, and to disrupt the process of expansion of its jurisdiction. There is always going to be a case of aggression that, in the opinion of some states, should have been tried but was not, or conversely should not have been tried but went to trial. Each case of aggression tried by the ICC will swell the ranks of the court's opponents, or at the very least will generate distrust as to the its impartiality and independence.

Given the potential negative impact of aggression trials, one question is worthy of serious consideration: at this stage of advancement of international criminal law and its enforcement, is it really a good idea to prosecute and try aggression?

Notes

1 War as an institution of law

1 R. Numelin, *The Beginnings of Diplomacy. A Sociological Study of Intertribal and International Relations*, Philosophical Library, New York 1950, p. 104. See also Q. Wright, *A Study of War*, vol 1, The University of Chicago Press, Chicago 1944, pp. 53 ff. G. Bouthoul, *Traité de Sociologie. Les guerres. Éléments de polémologie. Méthodes. Doctrines et opinions sur la guerre, Morphologie. Éléments techniques, démographiques, économiques, psychologiques. Périodicité*, Payot, Paris 1951, pp. 18 ff.
2 C. Phillipson, *The International Law and Custom of Ancient Greece and Rome*, vol 2, MacMillan and Co. Limited, London 1911, p. 224.
3 Q. Wright, *A Study of War*, vol 1, p. 159.
4 On different causes of wars see S. Brown, *The Causes and Prevention of War*, St. Martin's Press, New York 1994, pp. 7 ff; R. J. Lieber, *No Common Power. Understanding International Relations*, 3rd edn, Georgetown University, Harper Collins College Publishers, New York 1995, pp. 240 ff.
5 Q. Wright, *A Study of War*, vol 1, pp. 34–35.
6 R. Numelin, *The Beginnings of Diplomacy*, p. 83 (see also the literature cited by the author).
7 J. S. Goldstein, *International Relations*, 2nd edn, Pearson-Longman, New York 2004, p. 123.
8 Y. Dinstein, *War, Aggression and Self-Defence*, 4th edn, Cambridge University Press, New York, Cambridge 2005, p. 73.
9 N. Solomon, 'Judaism and the ethics of war', *IRRC* 2005, no 858; G. Wilkes, 'Judaism and justice in war', in P. Robinson, *Just War in Comparative Perspective*, Ashgate, Hampshire 2003; L. Winowski, *Stosunek chrześcijaństwa pierwszych wieków do wojny*, Towarzystwo Naukowe KUL, Lublin 1947, pp. 2 ff.
10 P. Bandyopadhyay, *International Law and Custom in Ancient India*, Ramanand Vidya Bhawan, Goyal Offset Printers, Delhi 1982, pp. 86 ff; F. X. Clooney S.J., 'Pain but not harm: some classical resources Toward a Hindu' and G. Sinkh, 'Sikhism and just war', in P. Robinson, *Just War*, P. G. Lovett, *Justifying War: The Just War Tradition Until 1919*, The University of Oklahoma, Graduate College, Norman, Oklahoma 1982, pp. 27 ff.
11 S. Tchoan-Pao, *Le Droit des Gens et la Chine Antique. Tome I, Introduction. Partie I, Les Idées*, Jouve & Cie, Editeurs, Paris 1926, pp. 50 ff. See also T. M. Kane, 'Inauspicious tools: Chinese thought on the morality of warfare, in P. Robinson, *Just War*, P. G. Lovett, *Justifying War*, p. 28.
12 C. Phillipson, *The International Law and Custom*, vol 2, pp. 171 ff; F. Przetacznik, *The Philosophical and Legal Concept of War*, The Edwin Mellen Press, Lewiston 1994, pp. 49 ff.

13 W. Góralczyk, *Prawo międzynarodowe publiczne w zarysie*, 7th edn, Wydawnictwo Prawnicze PWN, Warszawa 2000, p. 414.

14 A. S. Hershey, *The Essentials of International Public Law*, The MacMillan Company, New York 1912, pp. 351–52, and further literature cited therein. See also Commission on the Responsibility of the Authors of the War and on Enforcement of Penalties, 'Report presented to the Preliminary Peace Conference', 29 March 1919, *AJIL* 1920, vol 14, p. 118, hereinafter *Report of the Commission on the Responsibility of the Authors of the War.*

15 Q. Wright, 'Changes in the conception of war', *AJIL* 1924, vol 18, pp. 755–56. See also H. Dembiński, *Wojna jako narzędzie prawa i przewrotu*, Towarzystwo Naukowe Katolickiego Uniwersytetu Lubelskiego, Lublin 1936, p. 11.

16 Y. Dinstein, *War, Aggression and Self-Defence*, p. 74.

17 A. S. Hershey, *The Essentials of International Public Law*, p. 349.

18 W. E. Hall, *A Treatise on International Law*, 3rd edn, Clarendon Press, Oxford 1890, pp. 64–65.

19 J. A. Cohan, 'Legal war: when does it exist, and when does it end?', *HastlntCompLRev* 2004, vol 27, pp. 254–55. Compare with C. Antonopoulos, *The Unilateral Use of Force by States in International Law*, A. N. Sakkoulas Publishers, Athens-Komotini 1997, pp. 8–9; M. S. McDougal, F. P. Feliciano, *The International Law of War*, New Haven Press, Dordrecht 1994, p. 98; C. B. E. McNair and A. D. Watts, *The Legal Effects of War*, Cambridge University Press, Cambridge 1966, pp. 2 ff.

20 I. Brownlie, *International Law and the Use of Force by States*, Oxford 1968, p. 34. C. A. Pompe refers also to another example, that of the naval Battle of Navarino of 1927, when the Ottoman armada was defeated by the allied force of British, French and Russian vessels. Despite the fact that thousands of people died, none of the parties claimed that war had taken place, and European ambassadors did not leave their diplomatic posts in Constantinople. C. A. Pompe, *Aggressive War. An International Crime*, Martinus Nijhoff, The Hague 1953, p. 7. For further similar examples see A. Cohan, 'Legal war', pp. 259 ff; I. Brownlie, *International Law and the Use of Force*, p. 28 ff; and A. M. Rifaat, *International Aggression. A Study of the Legal Concept: Its Development and Definition in International Law*, Almqvist & Wiksell International, Stockholm 1979, p. 19.

21 I. Brownlie, *International Law and the Use of Force*, p. 384.

22 Nowadays, the qualification of situation as a 'war' or another form of use of armed force can also have legal implications, eg in light of American civil law, see J. A. Cohan, 'Legal war', passim.

23 See I. Brownlie, *International Law and the Use of Force*, pp. 27 ff; C. Antonopoulos, *The Unilateral Use of Force*, p. 9.

24 'Recourse to "war" incurred a certain odium; "war" was a term which had acquired a deep psychological and emotional significance'. See I. Brownlie, *International Law and the Use of Force*, p. 27.

25 C. Antonopoulos, *The Unilateral Use of Force*, pp. 6–7.

26 L. Oppenheim, *International Law. A Treatise: vol II Disputes, War and Neutrality*, 7th edn, edited by H. Lauterpacht, Longmans, 1960, p.136.

27 The case pertains to arbitration between Portugal and Germany concerning the legality of forcible reprisals conducted by the German armed forces based in South West Africa (present-day Namibia) in October 1914 in the territory of Angola, then a Portuguese colony, in response to a frontier incident in which three German soldiers had been killed. This German military action in Angola resulted in an uprising of the native population and thus considerable loss of life and property. For commentary to the *Naulilaa* case see eg C. Antonopoulos, *The Unilateral Use of Force*, pp. 7–8; J. L. Brierly, *The Law of Nations. An Introduction*

to the International Law of Peace, 6th edn, edited by Sir Humphrey Waldock, Clarendon Press, Oxford 1963, pp. 400–401; C. H. M. Waldock, 'The regulation of the use of force by individual states in international law', *Recueil des cours* 1952-II, pp. 460 ff.

28 'Reprisals are acts of self-help by the injured State, acts in retaliation for acts contrary to international law on the part of the offending State, which have remained unrepressed after a demand for amends. In consequence of such measures, the observance of this or that rule of international law is temporarily suspended, in the relations between the two States. They are limited by considerations of humanity and the rules of good faith, applicable in the relations between States. They are illegal unless they are based upon a previous act contrary to international law. They seek to impose on the offending State reparation for the offence, the return to legality and the avoidance of new offences.' Excerpt from decision in *Naulilaa* case cited in G. Schwarzenberger, *International Law as Applied by International Courts and Tribunals*, Stevens & Sons, London 1957–1968, vol 2, pp. 48 ff.

29 I. Brownlie, *International Law and the Use of Force*, p. 40.

30 On the genesis of Hague Conferences see G. Bouthoul, *Traité de Sociologie*, p. 488.

31 '*Afin de rechercher les moyens les plus efficaces d'assurer à tous les peuples les bienfaits d'une paix réelle et durable et de mettre avant tout un terme au développement progressif des armements actuels.*' Excerpt from Russian note of 30 December 1898/11 January 1899, cited in R. Kolb, *Ius Contra Bellum. Le Droit International Relatif aux Maintien de la Paix*, Précis, Helbing & Lichtenhahn, Bruylant, Bruxelles 2003, p. 24.

32 The texts of both conventions (Hague I of 1899 and Hague I of 1907) are available at http://www.pca-cpa.org (last visited 3 June 2013). See A. S. Hershey, 'Convention for the peaceful adjustment of international differences', *AJIL* 1908, vol 2.

33 See G. W. Scott, 'Hague Convention restricting the use of force to recover on contract claims', *AJIL* 1908, vol 2.

34 J. Westlake, *International Law*, Part I, 2nd edn, Cambridge University Press, London 1913, p. 19.

35 R. Kolb, *Ius Contra Bellum*, p. 24.

36 See E. C. Stowell, 'Convention Relative to the Opening of Hostility', *AJIL* 1908, vol 2; Z. Cybichowski, *Rozpoczęcie i wypowiedzenie wojny w prawie państwowym i prawie narodów*, Wydawnictwo Seminarjum Prawa Publicznego Uniwersytetu Warszawskiego nr 6, Warszawa 1926, pp. 142 ff.

37 C. A. Pompe, *Aggressive War*, p. 4.

38 See 'The Bryan peace treaties', *AJIL* 1913, vol 7.

39 I. Brownlie, *International Law and the Use of Force*, p. 23.

40 ibid, pp. 23–24.

41 ibid, p. 47.

42 H. Wehberg, *The Outlawry of War*, Carnegie Endowment for International Peace, Washington 1931, p. 6.

43 ibid.

44 J. Westlake, *International Law*, p. 1.

45 J. L. Kunz, '*Bellum iustum* and *bellum legale*', *AJIL* 1951, vol 45, p. 528.

46 I. Brownlie, *International Law and the Use of Force*, p. 20.

47 Y. Dinstein, *War, Aggression and Self-Defence*, p. 74.

48 K. Baczkowski et al, *Historia*, Wydawnictwa Szkolne i Pedagogiczne, Warszawa 1997, p. 734. Compare with M. C. Bassiouni, 'World War I: "The war to end all wars" and the birth of a handicapped international criminal justice system', *DenJIntL&P* 2002, vol 30, p. 246.

49 D. D. N. Nsereko, 'Defining the crime of aggression: an important agenda item for the assembly of States Parties to the Rome Statute of the International Criminal Court', *Acta Iuridica* 2003, p. 261.

50 Compare with earlier propositions of Emeric Crucé (*Le nouveau Cynée*), William Penn (*Essay Toward the Present and Future Peace of Europe*), John Bellers (*Some Reasons for a European State*), Abbé de Saint-Pierre (*Project of Perpetual Peace*), Jean-Jacques Rousseau (*Jugement sur la Paix Perpetuelle*), Immanuel Kant (*Perpetual Peace*), William Ladd (*An Essay on a Congress of Nations*) and many others.

51 Excerpt from the President Wilson's Fourteen Points: 'XIV. A general association of nations must be formed under specific covenants for the purpose of affording mutual guarantees of political independence and territorial integrity to great and small states alike', available at http://wwi.lib.byu.edu/index.php/President_Wilson%27s_Fourteen_Points. (last visited 3 June 2013)

52 *LNOJ* 1920, p. 3.

53 F. P. Walters, *A History of the League of Nations*, vol 1, Oxford University Press, London 1952, p. 48.

54 C. Antonopoulos, *The Unilateral Use of Force*, p. 11.

55 W. Komarnicki, 'La définition de l'agresseur dans le droit international moderne', *Recueil des cours* 1949-II, p. 24; F. P. Walters, *A History of the League of Nations*, vol 1, p. 49.

56 F. P. Walters, *A History of the League of Nations*, vol 1, pp. 258 ff; J. B. Scott, 'Interpretation of Article X of the Covenant of the League of Nations', *AJIL* 1924, vol 18, p. 110; P. Wilson, *Aggression, Crime and International Security. Moral, Political and Legal Dimensions of International Relations*, Routledge, London 2012, p. 33.

57 The relevant resolution was not adopted, because unanimity could not be reached (Persia objected). I. Brownlie, *International Law and the Use of Force*, p. 64. See also J. B. Scott, 'Interpretation of Article X', pp. 108 ff.

58 W. Komarnicki, 'La définition de l'agresseur', p. 22.

59 I. Brownlie, *International Law and the Use of Force*, p. 62.

60 League of Nations 'Assembly report on the Sino-Japanese dispute', *AJIL* 1933, vol 27, Supplement, p. 131. See also M. O. Hudson, 'The report of the Assembly of the League of Nations on the Sino-Japanese dispute', *AJIL* 1933, vol 27.

61 Resolutions of Council of 12 December 1936, concerning intervention during civil war in Spain (*LNOJ* 1937, pp. 18. ff) and of 29 May 1937 (*LNOJ* 1937, pp. 333 ff). See I. Brownlie, *International Law and the Use of Force*, p. 64.

62 ibid, p. 56.

63 Article 12.

64 Article 15(9).

65 Article 12.

66 Article 13(4) and Article 15(7).

67 Article 13(4).

68 Article 15(6).

69 Article 12.

70 Article 15(7).

71 Article 15(8). Examples of internal affairs include: customs, immigration, citizenship, trade. R. Kolb, *Ius Contra Bellum*, p. 30.

72 Y. Dinstein, *War, Aggression and Self-Defence*, p. 81.

73 Article 12.

74 The Article 17 of the Covenant of LN stated: '1. In the event of a dispute between a Member of the League and a State which is not a Member of the League, or between States not Members of the League, the State or States not Members of the League shall be invited to accept the obligations of membership in the

League for the purposes of such dispute, upon such conditions as the Council may deem just. 2. If such invitation is accepted, the provisions of Articles 12 to 16 inclusive shall be applied with such modifications as may be deemed necessary by the Council. Upon such invitation being given the Council shall immediately institute an inquiry into the circumstances of the dispute and recommend such action as may seem best and most effectual in the circumstances. 3. If a State so invited shall refuse to accept the obligations of membership in the League for the purposes of such dispute, and shall resort to war against a Member of the League, the provisions of Article 16 shall be applicable as against the State taking such action. 4. If both parties to the dispute when so invited refuse to accept the obligations of membership in the League for the purposes of such dispute, the Council may take such measures and make such recommendations as will prevent hostilities and will result in the settlement of the dispute'.

75 H. Wehberg, *The Outlawry of War*, p. 8.

76 J. Zourek, 'La définition de l'agression et le droit international. Développements récents de la question', *Recueil des cours* 1957-II, p. 760.

77 Delegalisation of war was impossible owing to the objection of England. W. Czapliński, *Skutki prawne nielegalnego użycia siły w stosunkach międzynarodowych*, Polska Akademia Nauk, Agencja Scholar, Warszawa 1993, p. 16.

78 The dispute was a result of bombardment and occupation of the island of Corfu by Italy, which in turn had been the Italian response to the murder of Enrico Tellini (chairman of the commission to determine the boundary between Greece and Albania) by extremists within the Greek territory. F. P. Walters, *A History of the League of Nations*, vol 1, p. 244.

79 'Opinion of Commission of Jurists of the Janina-Corfu affair', *AJIL* 1924, vol 18, p. 541. See also C. H. M. Waldock, 'The regulation of the use of force', p. 475; I. Brownlie, *International Law and the Use of Force*, p. 221.

80 C. Antonopoulos, *The Unilateral Use of Force*, p. 14; C. H. M. Waldock, 'The regulation of the use of force', pp. 475–76.

81 See C. Antonopoulos, *The Unilateral Use of Force*, pp. 17 ff.

82 For more on sanctions applied by LN see H. Dembiński, *Wojna jako*, pp. 126 ff.

83 H. Wehberg, *The Outlawry of War*, p. 11.

84 I. Brownlie, *International Law and the Use of Force*, p. 58.

85 F. P. Walters, *A History of the League of Nations*, vol 1, pp. 61–63.

86 See Articles 8 and 9 of the LN Covenant.

87 See also F. Przetacznik, *The Philosophical and Legal Concept of War*, p. 333.

88 S. Brown, *The Causes and Prevention of War*, pp. 180–81.

89 W. Czapliński, *Skutki prawne nielegalnego*, p. 65–66.

90 For reasons behind the non-ratification of the LN Covenant by the United States see F. P. Walters, *A History of the League of Nations*, vol 1, pp. 258 ff.

91 See also F. Przetacznik, *The Philosophical and Legal Concept of War*, p. 349.

92 C. Antonopoulos, *The Unilateral Use of Force*, p. 12. Benjamin B. Ferencz describes Article 11 as a 'catch-all' provision. See B. B. Ferencz, *Defining International Aggression. The Search for World Peace. A Documentary History and Analysis*, vol 1, Oceana Publications Inc., New York 1975, p. 8.

93 H. Wehberg, *The Outlawry of War*, p. 9.

94 *LNOJ* 1920, pp. 33–38.

95 See *Arbitration and Security: Systematic Survey of the Arbitration Conventions and Treaties of Mutual Security Deposited with the League of Nations*, Legal Section of the Secretariat of the League of Nations, Geneva 1927; *Treaties for the Advancement of Peace between the United States and Other Powers Negotiated by the Honorable William J. Bryan, Secretary of the State of the United States*, Oxford University Press, New York 1920; F. Colt de Wolf, *General Synopsis of Treaties of Arbitration, Conciliation,*

Judicial Settlement, Security and Disarmament Actually in Force between Countries Invited to the Disarmament Conference, Carnegie Endowment for International Peace, Washington 1933; *Systematic Survey of Treaties for the Pacific Settlement of International Disputes, 1928–48*, vol 3, Secretariat of the United Nations, New York 1949.

96 Assembly's resolution no XIV(a) of 27 September 1922, *LNOJ* 1923, Special Supplement, no 16, pp. 114 ff, in B. B. Ferencz, *Defining International Aggression*, vol 1, p. 70.

97 *LNOJ* 1923, Special Supplement, no 16, pp. 203–206, in B. B. Ferencz, *Defining International Aggression*, vol 1, pp. 77 ff.

98 Article 1.

99 Article 2.

100 Article 4.

101 Article 5.

102 *LNOJ* 1923, Special Supplement, no 16, pp. 209–210.

103 *LNOJ* 1924, Special Supplement, no 26, pp. 129–68, in B. B. Ferencz, *Defining International Aggression*, vol 1, pp. 84 ff.

104 *LNOJ* 1924, Special Supplement, no 26, pp. 169–72, in B. B. Ferencz, *Defining International Aggression*, vol 1, pp. 124 ff, hereinafter *Draft Treaty of American Group*.

105 Article 1.

106 Article 8.

107 Article 6.

108 Article 4.

109 Article 5(1).

110 *LNOJ* 1924, Special Supplement, no 26, pp. 189–94, in B. B. Ferencz, *Defining International Aggression*, vol 1, pp. 132 ff.

111 B. B. Ferencz, *Defining International Aggression*, vol 1, p. 15; F. P. Walters, *A History of the League of Nations*, vol 1, p. 272.

112 Article 3.

113 Article 4. There were, however, certain exceptions from arbitration procedure, eg in a situation when the dispute arose out of a matter which in light of international law was solely within the domestic jurisdiction of a party (Article 5), but this did not preclude the option of review by the Council or Assembly based on the Article 11 of the LN Covenant. The other exceptions were cases in which the council adopted a recommendation unanimously, and one of the parties concerned accepted it before the protocol entered into force (Article 4 point 5), or disputes which were the result of the war conducted on the assent of the Council or Assembly (Article 4 point 6). On the exceptions see also H. Wehberg, *The Outlawry of War*, p. 28.

114 R. Kolb, *Ius Contra Bellum*, pp. 36–37.

115 See *General Report submitted to the Fifth Assembly on behalf of the First and Third Committees by M. Politis (Greece), Rapporteur for the First Committee, and M. Benes (Czechoslovakia), Rapporteur for the Third Committee, LNOJ* 1924, Special Supplement, no 26, p. 197, in B. B. Ferencz, *Defining International Aggression*, vol 1, p. 137.

116 Preamble (3).

117 Article 8.

118 Article 2.

119 Articles 11–15.

120 Article 11.

121 Article 10 underlined also that a state shall be presumed to be an aggressor (unless a unanimous decision of the council otherwise declare) if it has refused

to submit the dispute to the procedure of pacific settlement established in the LN Covenant and Protocol or if it has violated provisional measures enjoined by the council or if it has refused to accept the armistice or has violated its terms.

122 A draft of the Protocol was adopted unanimously by 48 LN members but it was signed by only 19 states and ratified by only one, Czechoslovakia. On the reasons for the rejection of the Protocol see F. P. Walters, *A History of the League of Nations*, vol 1, pp. 276 ff and also D. L. Lanza, *The Geneva Protocol of 1924: British Rejection of League of Nations Covenant Reform*, The University of Tennessee, Knoxville 1991.

123 LNTS, vol 106, pp. 260 ff.

124 LNTS, vol 107, pp. 444 ff.

125 LNTS, vol 157, pp. 353 ff. Concerning treaties signed by the USSR, an extremely useful tool is R. M. Slusser and J. F. Triska, *A Calendar of Soviet Treaties 1917–1957*, Stanford University Press, Stanford 1959.

126 LNTS, vol 60, pp. 152 ff.

127 LNTS, vol 70, pp. 401 ff.

128 LNTS, vol 54, pp. 289 ff.

129 Article 2(2).

130 Article 4(1).

131 Article 4(3).

132 Article 3.

133 Article 1.

134 S. E. Nahlik, *Wstęp do nauki prawa międzynarodowego*, Państwowe Wydawnictwo Naukowe, Warszawa 1967, p. 124.

135 H. Wehberg, *The Outlawry of War*, pp. 41–42.

136 I. Brownlie, *International Law and the Use of Force*, p. 71.

137 *LNOJ* 1927, p. 22.

138 I. Brownlie, *International Law and the Use of Force*, p. 72.

139 ibid.

140 ibid, p. 73; H. Dembiński, *Wojna jako*, p. 74.

141 On the genesis of the pact see H. Korczyk, *Traktat ogólny o wyrzeczeniu się wojny (Pakt Brianda-Kelloga). Geneza, zawarcie, recepcja, działanie*, Wydawnictwo Fundacji 'Historia pro Futuro', Warszawa 1993, pp. 5 ff.

142 Article 1.

143 G. von Glahn underlined that the pact 'represented nothing more than a moral preachment'. G. von Glahn, *Law Among Nations. An Introduction to Public International Law*, 4th edn, Macmillan Publishing Co., New York, 1981, p. 578. Compare with J. Zourek, 'La définition de l'agression', p. 768.

144 H. Korczyk, *Traktat ogólny o wyrzeczeniu*, pp. 29–30.

145 D. W. Bowett, *Self-defence in International Law*, Manchester University Press, Manchester 1958, pp. 135–36.

146 H. Wehberg, *The Outlawry of War*, p. 76; H. Dembiński, *Wojna jako*, pp. 111 ff.

147 C. H. M. Waldock, 'The regulation of the use of force', p. 474.

148 I. Brownlie, *International Law and the Use of Force*, p. 86.

149 C. Antonopoulos, *The Unilateral Use of Force*, p. 23.

150 A. M. Rifaat, *International Aggression*, p. 72.

151 See *Identic Notes of the Government of the United States to the Governments of Australia, Belgium, Canada, Czechoslovakia, France, Germany, Great Britain, India, The Irish Free State, Italy, Japan, New Zealand, Poland, South Africa Delivered at the Respective Foreign Offices, June 23, 1928*, *AJIL* 1928, vol 22, Supplement Official Documents, pp. 109 ff; 'Notes between the United States and other powers', *AJIL* 1929, vol 23, pp. 1 ff.

152 W. Morawiecki, *Walka o definicję agresji w prawie międzynarodowym*, Państwowe Wydawnictwo Naukowe, Warszawa 1956, pp. 118–119.

153 Great Britain formulated its own equivalent of the Monroe doctrine in the note of 19 May 1928, stating that 'there are certain regions of the world the welfare and integrity of which constitute a special and vital interest for our peace and safety'. See H. Wehberg, *The Outlawry of War*, p. 86; I. Brownlie, *International Law and the Use of Force*, pp. 235–36; J. T. Shotwell, *War as an Instrument of National Policy and Its Renunciation in the Pact of Paris*, Constable & Co Ltd, London 1929, pp. 194 ff.

154 H. Wehberg, *The Outlawry of War*, p. 75; I. Brownlie, *International Law and the Use of Force*, p. 90.

155 In the United States, there was a strong movement to outlaw war. Its founder, Salmon O. Levinson, had created the American Committee for the Outlawry of War in 1921. The efforts of the Carnegie Endowment for International Peace established by Andrew Carnegie in 1910 also had a certain impact in this respect. See H. Wehberg, *The Outlawry of War*, pp. 17 ff; H. Korczyk, *Traktat ogólny o wyrzeczeniu*, p. 6 ff; F. Przetacznik, *The Philosophical and Legal Concept of War*, pp. 250 ff; R. H. Ferrell, *Peace in Their Time. The Opinions of the Kellogg-Briand Pact*, New Haven, Yale University Press, London 1952, pp. 31 ff.

156 V. Maugham, *U.N.O. and War Crimes*, John Murray, Albemarle Street, London 1951, p. 68.

157 H. Korczyk, *Traktat ogólny o wyrzeczeniu*, p. 144.

158 International Law Association, *Report of the Thirty-Eighth Conference Held at Budapest in the Hungarian Academy of Science, September 6th to 10th, 1934*, London 1935, pp. 1–70.

159 See *AJIL*, Supplement, Research in International Law 1939, vol 33, p. 848.

160 Also San Marino, Yemen, Nepal, but there were doubts concerning their statehood.

161 M. N. Shaw, *International Law*, 5th edn, Cambridge 2003, p. 1017.

162 I. Brownlie, *International Law and the Use of Force*, p. 94.

163 This doctrine is derived from the principle of *ex iniuria ius non oritur, nemo ex propria turpitudine commodum capere potest.* Its origin is usually traced back to the declaration of Secretary Henry L. Stimson of 7 January 1932 to Japan and China with regard to the Manchurian incident. See also H. Korczyk, *Traktat ogólny o wyrzeczeniu*, pp. 197 ff; A. M. Rifaat, *International Aggression*, p. 81; W. Komarnicki, 'La definition de l'agresseur', pp. 62 ff; C. H. M. Waldock, 'The regulation of the use of force', p. 480. On its present meaning see R. Kolb, *Ius Contra Bellum*, pp. 44–45; A. Lagerwall, 'L'Administration du territoire irakien: Un exemple de reconnaissance et d'aide au maintien d'une occupation resultant d'un acte d'agression?', *RBDI* 2006, no 1, pp. 249 ff.

164 H. Wehberg, *The Outlawry of War*, p. 114.

165 H. Dembiński, *Wojna jako*, pp. 117–18.

166 LNTS, vol 93, p. 343.

167 See B. Broms, *Finland and the League of Nations*, Finnish Foreign Policy, Helsinki 1963, pp. 92–93.

168 *Polish Official Gazette* 1932, no 115, item 951. For more examples see I. Brownlie, *International Law and the Use of Force*, p. 103.

169 *Polish Official Gazette* 1934, no 16, item 124.

170 LNTS, vol 139, pp. 235–39.

171 LNTS, vol 153, pp. 155–59.

172 LNTS, vol 190, pp. 21 ff.

173 See the analysis of 30 drafts of the American Institute of International Justice in which there were propositions to outlaw war, in H. Wehberg, *The Outlawry of War*, pp. 68 ff.

174 Para 3 of the preamble of the Gondra Treaty, LNTS, vol 33, p. 36. See also V. B. Galeano, 'The Gondra Treaty', *Transactions of the Grotius Society* 1929, vol 15.
175 See J. B. Scott, 'The Sixth Pan-American Conference', *AJIL* 1928, vol 22, p. 357.
176 ibid, 'The Pan-American Conference on conciliation and arbitration', *AJIL* 1929, vol 23.
177 LNTS, vol 163, p. 393. See. P. C. Jessup, 'The Saavendra Lamas anti-war draft treaty', *AJIL* 1933, vol 27. This treaty was partially replaced by the American Treaty on Pacific Settlement (Pact of Bogotá) of 30 April 1948, UNTS, vol 30, pp. 55 ff.
178 R. Kolb, *Ius Contra Bellum*, p. 47.
179 See eg. the Montevideo Convention on the Rights and Duties of States of 26 December 1933, LNTS, vol 165, p. 19, Interamerican Treaty on Good Offices and Mediation adopted in Buenos Aires 23 December 1936, LNTS, vol 188, p. 80, Convention for the Maintenance, Preservation and Re-establishment of Peace and Additional Protocol relative to Non-Intervention, LNTS, vol 188, pp. 14 and 16, and also Declaration of American Principles adopted in Lima on 24 December 1938, *AJIL* 1940, vol 34, Supplement, pp. 200–201.
180 LNTS, vol 195, p. 229.
181 See H. Lauterpacht, '"Resort to war" and the interpretation of the covenant during the Manchurian dispute', *AJIL* 1934, vol 28.
182 L. H. Woolsey, 'The Leticia dispute between Columbia and Peru', *AJIL* 1933, vol 27.
183 See J. D. Singer and M. Small, *The Wages of War 1816–1965. A Statistical Handbook*, John Wiley & Sons, New York 1972, pp. 59 ff.
184 A. Wysocki, *Tajemnice dyplomatycznego sejfu*, Książka i Wiedza, Warszawa 1974, p. 64.
185 F. P. Walters, *A History of the League of Nations*, vol 2, pp. 801–802.
186 *LNOJ* 1939, pp. 505 ff, in: B. B. Ferencz, *Defining International Aggression*, vol 1, pp. 272 ff.
187 See H. Wehberg, *The Outlawry of War*, pp. 46 ff; F. Ryszka, *Norymberga. Prehistoria i ciąg dalszy*, Czytelnik, Warszawa 1982, pp. 76 ff. Wilson offers another example of a conflict, this time economic and political in scope: Ethiopia, Great Britain and Italy in 1926. P. Wilson, *Aggression, Crime and International Security*, p. 38.
188 I. Brownlie, *International Law and the Use of Force*, p. 66.
189 26 nations expressed their support for the principles formulated in the Atlantic Charter by signing on 1 January 1942 the joint Declaration by United Nations (United States of America, the United Kingdom of Great Britain and Northern Ireland, the Union of Soviet Socialist Republics, China, Australia, Belgium, Canada, Costa Rica, Cuba, Czechoslovakia, Dominican Republic, El Salvador, Greece, Guatemala, Haiti, Honduras, India, Luxembourg, the Netherlands, New Zealand, Nicaragua, Norway, Panama, Poland, South Africa, Yugoslavia), text available at http://www.ibiblio.org/pha/policy/1942/420101a.html (last visited 3 June 2013).
190 Text available at http://www.ibiblio.org/pha/policy/1943/431000a.html (last visited 3 June 2013).
191 Article 1(1).
192 Article 2(3). See also Chapter VI of the Charter of the United Nations.
193 Article 2(5).
194 Article 2(6).
195 Article 2(7).
196 Article 2(1).
197 Article 2(4).

198 T. Kearley, 'Regulation of preventive and preemptive force in the United Nations Charter: a search for original intent', *WyoLRev* 2003, no 3, p. 669.

199 Critics of the broad interpretation of the notion 'force' from the Article 2(4) of the Charter of the United Nations point out that during negotiations of the charter, the states had rejected Brazil's amendment according to which the term 'force' should embrace economic pressure. Moreover, in the subsequent documents of the UN, tools of economic coercion were qualified as a kind of intervention in the internal affairs of a state rather than use of force under Article 2(4) of the Charter of the United Nations. Compare with Declaration on Principles of International Law (GA resolution no 2625 of 24 October 1970) or Charter of Economic Rights and Duties of States (GA Resolution no 3281 of 12 December 1974) – Article 32. See also J. Zourek, 'La définition de l'agression', p. 834; ibid, *L'interdiction de l'Emploide la Force en Droit International*, A. W. Sijthoff-Leiden, Institute Henry Dunant, Genève 1974, p. 74; L. M. Goodrich, E. Hambro and A. P. Simons, *Charter of the United Nations. Commentary and Documents*, 3rd and revised edn, Columbia University Press, New York, London 1969, p. 49; D. W. Bowett, *Self-defence in International Law*, p. 188 and A. Jacewicz, *Pojęcie siły w Karcie Narodów Zjednoczonych*, Wydawnictwo Ministerstw Obrony Narodowej, Warszawa 1977, passim.

200 The term 'war' is used only in the preamble of the Charter of the United Nations and in articles referring to states which during the Second World War have been enemies – Articles 53, 77, 107. The notion of 'war' was replaced by 'armed conflict' or 'hostilities' etc in other international treaties; see eg Article 2 of the 1949 Geneva Conventions for the protection of war victims (UNTS, vol 1975, pp. 31 ff), Articles 44 and 45a of the 1961 Vienna Convention on diplomatic relations (UNTS, vol 500, p. 95.), Article 53 of the 1963 Vienna Convention on consular relations (UNTS, vol 596, p. 261), Articles 45 and 46 of the 1969 New York Convention on Special Missions (UNTS, vol 1400, p. 231) and Article 73 of the 1969 Vienna Convention on the Law of Treaties (UNTS, vol 1155, p. 331).

201 W. Czapliński, *Skutki prawne nielegalnego*, pp. 98–99.

202 In May 1946, Albania fired without warning at two British cruisers passing through Albanian territorial waters in the Corfu Strait. Albania claimed that foreign warships had no right to pass through without prior authorisation. Great Britain disagreed and responded to the effect that if, in the future, fire was opened on a British warship passing the channel, the fire would be returned. In October 1946 four British vessels entered the strait to see the reaction of Albania. Two of them struck mines. Great Britain did not want to approach the Security Council in this matter in fear of a Soviet veto. Instead, it decided to send into the strait vessels with the intention of sweeping the waters. Only afterwards did Great Britain present the matter to the council. After three months, the council ruled that the International Court of Justice (ICJ) should investigate the case. The ICJ decided that the British vessels did not violate the sovereignty of Albania when they passed the strait at full readiness to fire. Great Britain had the right to ensure the exercise of its right to innocent passage. However, the ICJ also decided that such a sweeping operation was in violation of the charter. ICJ, *Judgment on Corfu Channel (United Kingdom of Great Britain and Northern Ireland v Albania)*, 9 April 1949, pp. 29, 31–35. See also J. L. Brierly, *The Law of Nations*, pp. 421 ff and C. H. M. Waldock, 'The regulation of the use of force', pp. 499 ff.

203 GA Resolution no 2625 of 24 October 1970.

204 The Charter of the United Nations, apart from self-defence and action authorised by the Security Council, provided for the option of using armed force in relation to states that during the Second World War had been enemies of any of the

signatories of the charter, if the states responsible for such action had taken or authorised the action as a result of that war (Article 107 of the charter). Moreover, within a regional arrangement, it was possible to undertake armed action against an enemy state (defined in exactly the same manner as in Article 107), against the renewal of aggressive policy on the part of any such state (Article 53). It is, however, generally accepted that Article 107 lost its significance when the enemy states joined the United Nations Organisation, thereby becoming peace-loving states themselves (as defined by Article 4 of the charter). C. Berezowski, *Prawo międzynarodowe publiczne*, Wydawnictwa Uniwersytetu Warszawskiego, Warszawa 1970, p. 481.

205 Article 42.

206 Article 51.

207 Article 24(1).

208 Article 39.

209 F. L. Kirgis Jr, 'The Security Council's first fifty years', *AJIL* 1995, vol 89, p. 512. But see also T. Gazzini, *The Changing Rules on the Use of Force in International Law*, Manchester University Press, Manchester 2005, p. 8.

210 See as examples SC Resolution no 253 of 29 May 1968 or no 277 of 18 March 1970.

211 SC Resolutions: no 688 of 5 April 1991; no 794 of 3 December 1992; no 929 of 22 June 1994; no 1078 of 9 November 1996.

212 SC Resolutions: no 731 of 21 January 1992; no 748 of 31 March 1992 no 1054 of 26 April 1996; no 1070 of 16 August 1996; no 1267 of 15 October 1999; no 1333 of 19 December 2000; no 1368 of 12 September 2001; no 1373 of 28 September 2001; no 1377 of 12 November 2001; no 1438 of 14 October 2002; no 1440 of 24 October 2002; no 1450 of 13 December 2002; no 1465 of 13 February 2003.

213 SC Resolutions: no 1277 of 30 November 1999; no 1441 of 8 November 2002.

214 SC Resolutions: no 748 of 31 March 1992; no 1214 of 8 December 1998; no 1070 of 16 August 1996; no 1267 of 15 October 1999: no 1333 of 19 December 2000.

215 SC Resolutions: no 217 of 20 November 1965; no 418 of 4 November 1977.

216 SC Resolutions: no 841 of 16 June 1993; no 875 of 16 October 1993.

217 SC Resolution no 1408 of 6 May 2002.

218 SC Resolution no 1540 of 28 April 2004.

219 T. Gazzini, *The Changing Rules on the Use of Force*, pp. 31–32. On evolution of interpretation of the term 'threat to peace' see I. Österdahl, *Threat to the Peace. The Interpretation by the Security Council of Article 39 of the United Nations Charter*, Iustus Forlag, Uppsala 1998, passim.

220 Article 40.

221 W. Czapliński, *Skutki prawne nielegalnego*, p. 70.

222 Article 41.

223 Article 42.

224 C. Berezowski (ed.), *Prawo międzynarodowe publiczne*, p. 478.

225 Article 43.

226 The ICJ stated: 'It cannot be said that the Charter has left the Security Council impotent in the face of an emergency situation when agreements under article 43 have not be concluded'. ICJ, *Advisory opinion on certain expenses of the United Nations (Article 17, paragraph 2, of the Charter)*, 20 July 1962, p. 167.

227 The legal basis for these actions is unclear. See United Nations, *United Nations Peacekeeping Operations. Principles and Guidelines*, 2008, pp.13–14. See also T. Franck, *Recourse to Force. State Action Against Threats and Armed Attacks*, Cambridge University Press, Cambridge 2002, p. 39.

228 See United Nations, Department Peacekeeping Operations, Department of Field Support, *United Nations Peacekeeping Operations. Principles and Guidelines*, New York 2008, p. 31. See also L. Zapałowski, *Operacje pokojowe*, Krajowa Agencja Wydawnicza, Kraków 1989, p. 40; I. Popiuk-Rysińska, J. Zając, *Operacje pokojowe Narodów Zjednoczonych*, in J. Symonides (ed.), *Organizacja Narodów Zjednoczonych. Bilans i perspektywy*, Wydawnictwo Naukowe Scholar, Warszawa 2006, pp. 102 ff; S. R. Ratner, *The New UN Peacekeeping Building Peace in Lands of Conflict after the Cold War*, St Martin's Press, New York 1996, p. 10 ff.

229 Article 106.

230 See T. Gazzini, *The Changing Rules on the Use of Force*, pp. 35–36. See also resolutions mentioned by C. Gray, *International Law and the Use of Force*, 2nd edn, Oxford University Press, Oxford 2004, p. 187 ff. See also C. Gray, 'The use of force and the international legal order', in M. D. Evans (ed.), *International Law*, 2nd edn Oxford University Press, Oxford 2006, p. 590, where the author claims that 'Coalitions of the willing have replaced the plan for a standing army'.

231 Article 53. See also W. Czapliński, 'Organizacje regionalne a użycie siły. Kilka uwag na tle rozdziału VIII Karty NZ', *Krakowskie Studia Prawnicze* 2005, no 1.

232 See J. Kranz, *Wojna, pokój czy uspokajanie? Współczesne dylematy użycia siły zbrojnej*, Fundacja Centrum Stosunków Międzynarodowych, Warszawa 2006, p. 23. The best-known debate on the interpretation of a resolution authorising the use of force is SC Resolution no 1441 of 8 November 2002 (Iraq). The resolution was adopted pursuant to Chapter VII of the Charter of the United Nations. It stipulated that Iraq had not complied with the previous resolutions of the Security Council, which posed a threat to international peace and security, and that continued violations of Iraq's obligations would cause it to face serious consequences (paragraph 13). On the legality of the American operation in Iraq see the special issue of *American Journal of International Law* 2003, vol 97, and also W. Czapliński, 'Interwencja w Iraku z punktu widzenia prawa międzynarodowego', *Państwo i Prawo* 2004, no 1; J. Symonides, 'Wojna z Irakiem a prawo międzynarodowe', in R. Kuźniar (ed.), *Rocznik Strategiczny 2003/2004*, Wydawnictwo Naukowe Scholar, Warszawa 2004.

233 T. Gazzini, *The Changing Rules on the Use of Force*, p. 53.

234 Y. Dinstein, *War, Aggression and Self-Defence*, p. 288.

235 See eg SC Resolutions no 788 of 19 November 1992 or no 866 of 22 September 1993, commending ECOWAS for its efforts to restore peace, security and stability in Liberia.

236 See eg SC Resolution no 1244 of 10 June 1999 (situation in Kosovo after NATO intervention), or SC Resolution no 1483 of 22 May 2003 (situation in Iraq after American attack).

237 Y. Dinstein, *War, Aggression and Self-Defence* p. 291. See also R. B. Russell, *A History of the United Nations Charter. The Role of the United States 1940–45*, The Brookings Institution, Washington D.C. 1959, pp. 232–33; F. L. Kirgis Jr, 'The Security Council's first fifty years', p. 507.

238 D. Colard and J. F. Guilhaudis, *Le Droit de la Sécurité Internationale*, Masson, Paris 1986, p. 128.

239 SC Resolutions: no 82 of 25 June 1950; no 83 of 27 June 1950; no 84 of 7 July 1950. See L. Gelberg, 'Wojna w Korei w świetle prawa międzynarodowego', *Państwo i Prawo* 1950, no 10.

240 Like eg the establishment of the Peace-building Commission, with the following tasks: to bring together all relevant actors to marshal resources and to advise on and propose integrated strategies for post-conflict peace-building and recovery; to focus attention on the reconstruction and institution-building efforts necessary for recovery from conflict and to support the development of integrated strategies

in order to lay the foundation for sustainable development; to provide recommendations and information to improve the coordination of all relevant actors within and outside the United Nations, to develop best practices, to help to ensure predictable financing for early recovery activities and to extend the period of attention given by the international community to post-conflict recovery. SC Resolution 1645 and GA Resolution 60/180 of 20 December 2005.

241 R. Kuźniar, 'ONZ i porządek międzynarodowy', in J. Symonides (ed.), *Organizacja Narodów Zjednoczonych*, p. 770. See also G. Schwarzenberger, *International Law*, vol 3, p. 327.

242 R. Kuźniar, 'ONZ i porządek międzynarodowy', p. 780.

243 GA Resolution no 377 of 3 November 1950 was adopted with 52 votes in favour. Five states were against (the USSR, Poland, Ukraine, Belarus and Czechoslovakia), two abstained (India and Argentina) and Lebanon was absent. On the resolution *Uniting for Peace*, see T. Franck, *Recourse to Force*, pp. 33 ff.

244 Y. Dinstein, *War, Aggression and Self-Defence*, p. 317.

245 ICJ, *Advisory Opinion on Certain Expenses*, p. 163.

246 There are proposals to grant more powers to the General Assembly with regard to peace maintenance. See G. Clark and L. B. Sohn, *World Peace Through World Law*, Harvard University Press, Cambridge 1966, pp. 111 ff.

247 Until 2012 only 10 emergency special sessions took place: (i) 1–10 November 1956 *Middle East*, (ii) 4–10 November 1956 *Hungary*, (iii) 8–21 August 1958 *Middle East*, (iv) 17–19 September 1960 *Question of Congo*, (v) 17–18 June 1967 *Middle East*, (vi) 10–14 January 1980 *The situation in Afghanistan and its implications for international peace and security*, (vii) 22–29 July 1980, 20–28 April 1982, 25–26 June 1982, 16–19 August 1982 and 24 September 1982 *Question of Palestine*, (viii) 13–14 September 1981 *Question of Namibia*, (ix) 29 January–5 February 1982 *The situation in the occupied Arab territories*, (x) since 24 April 1997 *Illegal Israeli actions in Occupied East Jerusalem and the rest of the Occupied Palestinian Territory*. Full documentation is available at http://www.un.org/ga/sessions/emergency.shtml (last visited 3 June 2013).

248 A. Cassese, *Violence and Law in the Modern Age*, transl. S. J. K. Greenleaves, Polity Press, Cambridge 1988, p. 34.

249 J. Kranz, 'Nowe aspekty stosowania siły w stosunkach międzynarodowych', in J. Menkes (ed.), *Prawo międzynarodowe – Problemy i wyzwania. Księga pamiątkowa Prof. Renaty Sonnenfeld-Tomporek*, Wyższa Szkoła Handlu i Prawa im. Ryszarda Łazarskiego w Warszawie, Warszawa 2006, p. 334.

250 The wording of Article 51 suggests that the exercise of the right of self-defence is limited in time, that is, until the Security Council takes the necessary measures. However, practice has taken a different course. See R. Bierzanek, J. Symonides, *Prawo międzynarodowe*, pp. 385 and 390.

251 Note the contradiction: Article 51 stipulates that the Security Council should take measures 'to maintain international peace and security' once it is notified of the exercise of the right to self-defence. Yet once an armed attack has occurred, triggering the self-defence mechanism, international peace is shattered, and therefore can only be restored, but not maintained.

252 J. L. Brierly emphasised the differences between the English and French wording of the Charter of the United Nations (in the English version, 'if' is used); according to Brierly, it indicates a hypothesis rather than a necessary condition. See J. L. Brierly, *The Law of Nations*, p. 419.

253 ICJ, *Judgment on Oil Platforms (Islamic Republic of Iran v United States of America)*, 6 November 2003, eg para 6. See also I. Brownlie, *International Law and the Use of Force*, p. 214.

254 Y. Dinstein, *War, Aggression and Self-Defence*, p. 197.

255 ibid, pp. 188–89.
256 M. N. Shaw, *International Law*, p. 1030; C. Gray, 'The use of force', p. 601; Y. Dinstein, *War, Aggression and Self-Defence*, p. 187. See also J. Barcik, *Koncepcja samoobrony w prawie międzynarodowym w dobie 'wojny z terroryzmem'*, *Kwartalnik Prawa Publicznego* 2003, no 1, p. 108.
257 See M. Sapiro, 'Iraq: The shifting sands of pre-emptive self-defense', *AJIL* 2003, vol 97, p. 599.
258 This restrictive approach see eg in L. Dromi San Martino, *Legitima Defensa Internacional*, Ciudad Argentina, Editorial de Ciencia y Cultura, Buenos Aires 1998, pp. 30–31.
259 J. L. Brierly, *The Law of Nations*, p. 416–17.
260 L. M. Goodrich, E. Hambro and A. P. Simons, *Charter of the United Nations*, p. 334.
261 'It cannot therefore be held that article 51 is a provision which "subsumes and supervenes" customary international law. It rather demonstrates that in the field in question, the importance of which for the present dispute need hardly be stressed, customary international law continues to exist alongside treaty law. The areas governed by the two sources of law thus do not overlap exactly, and the rules do not have the same content.' ICJ, *Judgment on military and paramilitary activities in and against Nicaragua (Nicaragua v United States of America)*, 27 June 1986, para 176.
262 J. L. Brierly, *The Law of Nations*, pp. 404–405; C. H. M. Waldock, 'The regulation of the use of force', pp. 461 ff; S. Alexandrov, *Self-Defense Against the Use of Force in International Law*, Kluwer Law International, The Hague 1996, pp. 23 ff.
263 The steamer *Caroline* was used to support rebels during an uprising in Canada. The American Government did nothing to stop it, and Canadian soldiers crossed the American boundary and took part in fights that resulted in the deaths of a few Americans and the sinking of the *Caroline*. J. L. Brierly, *The Law of Nations*, p. 405; V. Epps, *International Law*, Caroline Academic Press, Durham 2005, pp. 364 ff.
264 '[...] necessity of self-defence, instant, overwhelming, and leaving no choice of means, and no moment for deliberation. It will be for it to show, also that the local authorities of Canada, even supposing the necessity of the moment authorised them to enter the territories of the United States at all, did nothing unreasonable or excessive; since the act justified by the necessity of self-defence, must be limited by that necessity, and kept clearly within it.' Excerpt printed in I. Brownlie, *Principles of Public International Law*, 6th edn, Oxford University Press, Oxford 2003, p. 701. For more on the *Caroline* incident and its impact on the development of international law, see M. A. Rogoff and E. Collins Jr, 'The *Caroline* incident and the development of international law', *BrookJIL* 1990, vol 16.
265 However, Dinstein claims that in the *Caroline* affair there was in fact an armed attack, in the form of support for the rebels. See Y. Dinstein, *War, Aggression and Self-Defence*, pp. 185 ff.
266 See eg C. H. M. Waldock, 'The regulation of the use of force', p. 498.
267 A. Sayed, *Quand le droit est face à son néant. Le droit à l'épreuve de l'emploi de l'arme nucléaire*, Bruylant, Bruxelles 1998, p. 138; T. L. H. McCormack, *Self-defense in International Law. The Israeli Raid on the Iraqi Nuclear Reactor*, St Martin's Press, New York 1996, p. 124. John Woo suggests that the most important is an interpretation of the notion 'imminent'. See J. Woo, 'Using force', *UnivChiLRev* 2004, vol 71, pp. 775 ff.
268 M. Skopets, 'Battered nation syndrome: relaxing the imminence requirement of self-defense in international law', *AmUnivLRev* 2006, vol 55, p. 756.
269 S. Alexandrov, *Self-Defense Against the Use of Force*, p. 149.
270 See SC Resolution no 487 of 19 June 1981. For more on the legal assessment of the Israeli attack see T. L. H. McCormack, *Self-defense in International Law*;

L. R. Beres, Y. Tsiddon-Chatto, 'Reconsidering Israel's destruction of Iraq's Osiraq nuclear reactor', *TempIntt&CompLJ* 1995, vol 9. Compare also with other publications of L. R. Beres in which the author claims that Israel has the right to preventive and pre-emptive actions.

271 SC Resolution no 573 of 4 October 1985.

272 See eg T. Christakis, 'Vers une reconnaissance de la notion de guerre préventive?', in K. Bannelier, O. Corten, T. Christakis and P. Klein (eds), *L'intervention en Iraq et le droit international*, Cedin Paris I, Centre de droit international ULB, Cahiers internationaux no 19, Editions Pedone, Paris 2004.

273 See A. Wasilkowski, 'Kilka uwag w kwestii użycia siły we współczesnym prawie międzynarodowym', in J. Menkes (ed.), *Prawo międzynarodowe*, p. 535. Compare with M. Sapiro, 'Iraq: The shifting sands', pp. 599 (especially footnotes) ff; E. Creegan, 'Justified uses of force and the crime of aggression', *JIntCrimJust* 2012, vol 10, pp. 72–73.

274 D. Colard and J. F. Guilhaudis, *Le Droit de la Sécurité Internationale*, p. 46 ff.

275 S. J. Barela, 'Preemptive or preventive war: a discussion of legal and moral standards', *DenvJIntL&Pol* 2004, vol 33, p. 36.

276 See eg Parliamentary Assembly, Council of Europe, *The concept of preventive war and its consequences for international relations*, 8 czerwca 2007, Doc 11293.

277 L. M. Goodrich, E. Hambro and A. P. Simons, *Charter of the United Nations*, p. 348.

278 Y. Dinstein, *War, Aggression and Self-Defence*, p. 270.

279 ibid, p. 255.

280 eg C. H. M. Waldock, 'The regulation of the use of force', p. 466; A. Cassese, *Violence and Law in the Modern Age*, p. 36; S. Murphy, *Principles of International Law*, Concise Hornbook Series, St Paul 2006, p. 442. For the opposite opinion see eg I. Brownlie, *International Law and the Use of Force*, p. 301; L. S. Sunga, *The Emerging System of International Criminal Law. Developments in Codification and Implementation*, Kluwer Law International, The Hague 1997, p. 77.

281 S. Alexandrov, *Self-Defense Against the Use of Force*, pp. 188–89.

282 W. Czapliński, *Skutki prawne nielegalnego*, pp. 37 ff.

283 T. Franck, *Recourse to Force*, pp. 76 ff.

284 W. Czapliński, *Skutki prawne nielegalnego*, p. 36.

285 See eg J. L. Brierly, *The Law of Nations*, p. 427; A. Wasilkowski, 'Kilka uwag w kwestii użycia siły we współczesnym prawie międzynarodowym', p. 537; Y. Dinstein, *War, Aggression and Self-Defence*, pp. 201 ff; D. W. Bowett, *Self-defence in International Law*, pp. 91–94. Compare with T. Schweisfurth, who treats such actions as lawful reprisals. T. Schweisfurth, 'Operations to rescue nationals in third states involving the use of force in relation to the protection of human rights', *GermYbkIntL* 1980, vol 23, p. 159.

286 ICJ, *Judgment on United States Diplomatic and Consular Staff in Tehran (United States of America v Iran)*, 24 May 1980, para 57. See also Y. Dinstein, *War, Aggression and Self-Defence*, p. 197.

287 W. Czaplin´ski, *Skutki prawne nielegalnego*, pp. 37 ff; C. H. M. Waldock, 'The Regulation of the use of force', p. 467.

288 W. Czapliński, *Skutki prawne nielegalnego*, p. 40.

289 Y. Dinstein, *War, Aggression and Self-Defence*, p. 233. This action was labelled as aggression by the USSR and states of the Third World. See P. M. Defarges, *Un monde d'ingérences*, Presses de Sciences Po, Mayenne 1997, p. 41.

290 See V. P. Nanda, 'The United States' action in the 1965 Dominican crisis: impact on world order – Part I', *DenvLJ* 1966, vol 43.

291 ibid, 'The United States' armed intervention in Grenada: impact on world order', *CalifWestIntLJ* 1984, vol 13.

292 ibid, 'The validity of the United States' intervention in Panama under international law', *AJIL* 1990, vol 84.
293 R. L. Griffiths, 'International law, the crime of aggression and the *ius ad bellum*', *IntCrimLRev* 2002, vol 2, p. 333.
294 M. N. Shaw, *International Law*, p. 1033; C. Gray, *International Law*, p. 7.
295 Y. Dinstein, *War, Aggression and Self-Defence*, p. 87.
296 R. Bierzanek, *Wojna a prawo międzynarodowe*, Wydawnictwo Ministerstwa Obrony Narodowej, Warszawa 1982, p. 11.
297 Y. Dinstein, *War, Aggression and Self-Defence*, p. 87; I. Brownlie, *Principles of Public International Law*, p. 700.
298 C. Vulcan, 'L'exécution des décisions de la Cour Internationale de Justice d'après la Charte des Nations Unies', *RGDIP* 1947, vol 51, pp. 187 and 195.
299 Article 94(2) of the Charter of the United Nations.
300 Y. Dinstein, *War, Aggression and Self-Defence*, p. 88; O. Schachter, 'The enforcement of international judicial and arbitral decisions', *AJIL* 1960, vol 54, pp. 15–16.
301 O. Schachter, 'The right of states to use armed force', *MichLRev* 1984, vol 82, pp. 1620, 1627.
302 See eg Article 7 of GA Resolution no 3314 of 14 December 1974, which states: 'Nothing in this Definition *[of aggression]* (...) could in any way prejudice the right to self-determination, freedom and independence, as derived from the Charter, of peoples forcibly deprived of that right and referred to in the Declaration on Principles of International Law concerning Friendly Relations and Co-operation among States in accordance with the Charter of the United Nations, particularly peoples under colonial and racist régimes or other forms of alien domination; not the right of these peoples to struggle to that end and to seek and receive support, in accordance with the principles of the Charter in conformity with the above-mentioned Declaration'. See also GA Resolutions no 1514 of 14 December 1960, para 2; no 2625 of 24 October 1970, para 6. Compare with R. L. Griffiths, *International Law*, pp. 356 ff; W. Czapliński, *Skutki prawne nielegalnego*, p. 33.
303 ICJ, *Judgment on military and paramilitary activities*, para 242. Compare with GA Resolutions no 2015 of 20 December 1965 and no 3070 of 30 November 1973.
304 A. M. Rifaat, *International Aggression*, pp. 274 and 317. See also GAOR, 29th session, *Report of the Special Committee on the Question of Defining Aggression*, A/9619 and Corr 1, 1974, pp. 15, 22, 26, 27, 32, 37, 38, 40.
305 See L. Doswald-Beck, 'The legal validity of military intervention by invitation of the government', *BritYbkIntL* 1985, vol 56; R. L. Griffiths, *International Law*, pp. 323 ff.
306 I. Brownlie, *Principles of Public International Law*, p. 708.
307 C. Gray, *International Law*, p. 7.
308 See eg C. Gray, 'The use of force', p. 595; M. N. Shaw, *International Law*, p. 1045; M. Byers, S. Chesterman, 'Changing the rules about rules? Unilateral humanitarian intervention and the future of international law', in J. L. Holzgrefe and R. O. Keohane (eds), *Humanitarian Intervention, Ethical, Legal and Political Dilemmas*, Cambridge University Press, Cambridge 2003, p. 177; S. Chesterman and *Just War or Just Peace?: Humanitarian Intervention and International Law*, Oxford University Press, Oxford 2003, p. 45; P. Malanczuk, *Humanitarian Intervention and the Legitimacy of the Use of Force*, Het Spinhuis, Amsterdam 1993, passim; and also A. Mężykowska, *Interwencja humanitarna w świetle prawa międzynarodowego*, Oficyna Wydawnicza Wyższej Szkoły Handlu i Prawa im. Ryszarda Łazarskiego, Warszawa 2008; D. Rudkowski, *Interwencja humanitarna w prawie międzynarodowym*, Wydawnictwo Sejmowe, Warszawa 2006; J. Zajadło, *Dylematy humanitarnej interwencji*, Arche, Gdańsk 2005.

309 J. Kranz, 'Nowe aspekty stosowania siły w stosunkach międzynarodowych', p. 350. Compare with a definition of A. Buchanan, 'Reforming the international law of humanitarian intervention', in J. L. Holzgrefe, R. O. Keohane (eds), *Humanitarian Intervention*, p. 130.
310 R. L. Griffiths, *International Law*, p. 351.
311 J. Kranz, 'Nowe aspekty stosowania siły w stosunkach międzynarodowych', p. 337.
312 ibid, p. 354.
313 International Commission on Intervention and State Security was established under the authority of Canadian government on 14 September 2000. Its members were Gareth Evans (Australia), Mohamed Sahnoun (Algeria), Gisèle Côté-Harper (Canada), Lee Hamilton (United States), Michael Ignatieff (Canada), Vladimir Lukin (Russia), Klaus Naumann (Germany), Cyril Ramaphosa (South Africa), Fidel V. Ramos (Philippines), Cornelio Sommaruga (Switzerland), Eduardo Stein Barillas (Guatemala), Ramesh Thakur (India). The report of the Commission *Responsibility to Protect* is available at http://responsibilitytoprotect.org/ICISS%20Report.pdf (last visited 3 June 2013).
314 In the report, the authors claim that states should have the responsibility to prevent (early warning, root cause prevention efforts, direct prevention efforts), to react (including military action) and to rebuild (reconstruction, reconciliation, elimination of causes of conflict).
315 ICISS, *Responsibility to Protect*, paras 4.10 ff.
316 ibid, paras 6.1 ff.
317 Report of the Secretary-General's High Panel on Threats, Challenges and Change, *A more secure world: Our shared responsibility, Report of the Secretary – General's High Level Panel on Threats, Challenges and Change*, United Nations, New York 2004, A/59/565.
318 Report of the Secretary-General, *In Larger Freedom: Towards Development, Security and Human Rights for All*, New York 2005, A/59/2005.
319 GA Resolution no 60/1 of 24 October 2005.
320 Y. Dinstein, *War, Aggression and Self-Defence*, p. 90.
321 GA Resolution no 375 of 6 December 1949.
322 GA Resolution no 2131 (XX) of 21 December 1965.
323 GA Resolution no 2734 (XXV) of 16 December 1970.
324 GA Resolution no 2625 of 24 October 1970.
325 GA Resolution no 42/22 of 8 November 1987.
326 Article 1, UNTS, vol 21, pp. 77 ff.
327 Article 5 point e, where war of aggression is condemned. UNTS, vol 119, pp. 3 ff.
328 Article 5, UNTS, vol 70, pp. 237 ff.
329 UNTS, vol 299, pp. 57 ff.
330 Article 4 points h and j, UNTS, vol 2158, pp. 3 ff.
331 A. M. Weisburd, *Use of Force. The Practice of States since World War II*, The Pennsylvania State University Press, Pennsylvania 1997, p. 308. Compare M. J. Glennon, *Limits of Law. Prerogatives of Power. Interventionism after Kosovo*, Palgrave, New York 2001, pp. 67 ff.
332 A. M. Weisburd, *Use of Force*, pp. 29 ff.
333 It has to be stressed that during the inter-war period no states justified their armed actions based on the right to resort to war under Article 15(7) of the LN Covenant. In all cases, states justified their armed actions eg by referring to self-defence.
334 W. Góralczyk, *Prawo międzynarodowe*, p. 414.
335 See A. M. Weisburd, *Use of Force*, pp. 1 ff.

336 O. Solera, *Defining the Crime of Aggression*, Cameron May, London 2007, p. 43; J. H. Westra, *International Law and the Use of Armed Force. The United Nations Charter and the Major Powers*, Contemporary Security Studies, Routledge, London 2007, p. 12.

337 T. M. Franck, 'Who killed Article 2(4)? Or: changing norms governing the use of force by states', *AJIL* 1970, vol 64, p. 809; T. M. Franck, 'What happens now? The United Nations after Iraq', *AJIL* 2003, vol 97, pp. 607, 610; T. M. Franck, 'Rethinking collective security', in M. N. Schmitt, J. Pejic (eds), *International Law and Armed Conflicts: Exploring the Faultlines. Essays in Honour of Yoram Dinstein*, Martinus Nijhoff Publishers, Leiden-Boston 2007, pp. 21 ff. See, however, L. Henkin, 'The reports of the death of Article 2(4) are greatly exaggerated', *AJIL* 1971, vol 65, p. 544.

338 On the impact of hegemonic position on implementation of international law see T. M. Franck, 'What happens now?'; D. F. Vats, 'Hegemonic international law', *AJIL* 2001, vol 95; J. E. Alvarez, 'Hegemonic international law revisited', *AJIL* 2003, vol 97; N. Kirsch, 'International law in times of hegemony: unequal power and the shaping of international legal order', *EJIL* 2005, vol 16.

339 C. Antonopoulos, *The Unilateral Use of Force*, pp. 30–31.

340 Y. Dinstein, *War, Aggression and Self-Defence*, p. 94.

341 B. Asrat, *Prohibition of Force under the UN Charter. A Study of Art. 2(4)*, Iustus Förlag, Juridiska Föreningenuppsala, Uppsala 1991, p. 51.

342 ICJ, *Judgment on military and paramilitary activities*, paras 188 ff.

2 The notion of aggression

1 I. Brownlie, *International Law and the Use of Force*, p. 351; N. Nyiri, *The United Nations' Search for a Definition of Aggression*, American University Studies, Series X, Political Science, vol 22, Peter Lang, New York 1989, pp. 21 ff.

2 I. Brownlie, *International Law and the Use of Force*, p. 351 and literature cited by the author; W. Morawiecki, 'Walka o definicję agresji', pp. 24–25. One of the most often cited agreements is the treaty of 3 January 1815 concluded in Vienna between Austria, England and France, where the wording is: '*Si les possessions d'aucune d'Elles (les Hautes Parties Contractantes) étaient attaquées, alors et dans ce cas, Elles s'engagent et s'obligent à se tenir pour attaquées toutes trois [...] pour repousser une telle aggression*'. See B. Broms, *The Definition of Aggression in the United Nations*, Turun Yliopisto, Turku 1968, p. 10.

3 J. Balicki, *Pojęcie agresji w prawie międzynarodowym*, Wydawnictwo Prawnicze, Warszawa 1952, p. 26; J. Stone, *Aggression and World Order. A Critique of United Nations Theories of Aggression*, Stevens & Sons Limited, London 1958, pp. 15 ff.

4 I. Brownlie, *International Law and the Use of Force*, p. 351; A. Van Wynen Thomas and A. J. Thomas Jr, *The Concept of Aggression in International Law*, Southern Methodist University Press, Dallas 1972, p. 15, W. Komarnicki, 'La définition de l'agresseur', p. 13.

5 I. Brownlie, *International Law and the Use of Force*, p. 351.

6 Article 10 of the LN Covenant ('external aggression').

7 Article 1(1), Article 39, Article 53(1) of the Charter of the United Nations; additionally, the notion of 'acts of aggression', '*acte d'agression*' is used in the title of Chapter VII, and in the French version of Article 51 the term '*agression armée*' is used.

8 See eg *Opinion of the Permanent Advisory Commission Regarding Assembly Resolutions XIV and XV*, *LNOJ* 1923, Special Supplement, no 16, p. 116, in B. B. Ferencz, *Defining International Aggression*, vol 1, p. 72, hereinafter *PAC opinion*; and Soviet, Italian and Spanish statements in B. B. Ferencz, *Defining International Aggression*, vol 1, pp. 92–93, 106–107, 117); *Second Report on a Draft Code of Offences Against*

the Peace and Security of Mankind by Mr J. Spiropoulos, Special Rapporteur, A/CN.4/44, *YbkIntLCom* 1951, vol 2, p. 69, hereinafter *Spiropoulos report*; League of Nations, Preparatory Commission for the Disarmament Conference, Committee on Arbitration and Security, *Memorandum on Articles 10, 11 and 16 of the Covenant, submitted by M. Rutgers, Rapporteur*, in B. B. Ferencz, *Defining International Aggression*, vol 1, pp. 173–74, hereinafter *Rutgers report*.

9 J. Maktos, 'La question de la définition de l'agression', *RDISDP* 1952, no 1, p. 6.

10 *Rutgers report*, p. 189.

11 E. Aroneanu, *La Définition de l'Agression. Exposé Objectif*, Les Editions Internationales, Paris 1958, p. 145.

12 M. S. McDougal and F. P. Feliciano, *The International Law of War*, p. 155.

13 The United Nations Conference on International Organization, Commission III Security Council, Committee 3 Enforcement Arrangements, Doc 881, III/3/46, 10 June 1945, *Report of Mr Paul-Boncour, Rapporteur, on Chapter VIII, Section B*, in B. B. Ferencz, *Defining International Aggression*, vol 1, p. 352, hereinafter *Boncour report*.

14 J. Stone, *Aggression and World Order*, p. 22.

15 *Rutgers report*, p. 189.

16 Argument used by Austen Chamberlain during his speech in the House of Commons on 24 November 1927. J. Diamandesco, *Le Problème de l'Agression dans le droit international public actuel. Deux aspects de l'organisation répressive: Définition de l'agression et détermination de l'agresseur*, Éditions A. Pedone, Paris 1935, pp. 46–47.

17 *Boncour report*, p. 352.

18 GAOR, 7th session, *Report of the Sixth Committee*, A/2322, 1952, p. 88.

19 *Spiropoulos report*, p. 69.

20 J. Maktos, 'La question de la définition de l'agression', p. 8.

21 A/2322, p. 87. See also L. B. Sohn, *Introduction*, in B. B. Ferencz, *Defining International Aggression*, vol 1, p. 1; C. A. Pompe, *Aggressive War*, p. 68.

22 A/2322, p. 87. GAOR, 23rd session, *Report of the Sixth Committee*, A/7402, 1968, p. 4. See also C. A. Pompe, *Aggressive War*, p. 88.

23 R. Bierzanek, 'Definicja agresji w świetle prac komitetu specjalnego ONZ', *Sprawy Międzynarodowe* 1970, p. 91.

24 A. Van Wynen Thomas and A. J. Thomas Jr, *The Concept of Aggression*, p. 10.

25 GAOR, 7th session, *Report by the Secretary-General*, Annexes, A/2211, 1952, pp. 53 ff. J. Balicki, 'O definicji agresji', *Państwo i Prawo* 1952, no 7, p. 49; W. Morawiecki, 'Walka o definicję agresji', pp. 20 ff.

26 League of Nations, Conference for the Reduction and Limitation of Armaments, General Commission, *Report of the Committee on Security Questions (Rapporteur: M. N. Politis)*, Conf. D. C.G./108, 24 May 1933, in B. B. Ferencz, *Defining International Aggression*, vol 1, p. 216), hereinafter *Politis report II*.

27 ibid, A/2322 p. 87. See also J. Balicki, 'O definicji agresji', p. 49; J. Žourek, 'La définition de l'agression', p. 811. M. Lachs, 'Walka o definicję agresji', *Wojskowy Przegląd Prawniczy* 1952, no 3, p. 449.

28 Preamble (9) of the GA Resolution no 3314 of 14 December 1974.

29 W. Czapliński, *Skutki prawne nielegalnego*, p. 28

30 L. B. Sohn, 'The definition of aggression', *VirLRev* 1959, vol 45, p. 698.

31 O. Solera, *Defining the Crime of Aggression*, p. 50 (see also statements of New Zealand's and Bolivia's delegates, ibid, pp. 51 ff). See also *Summary Report of Ninth Meeting of Committee III/3*, Doc 442, III/3/20, 19 May 1945, in B. B. Ferencz, *Defining International Aggression*, vol 1, pp. 345–48.

32 GAOR, 9th session, *Report of the Sixth Committee*, A/2806, 1954, p. 10.

33 A/2322, p. 87.

34 GAOR, 12th session, *Report of the 1956 Special Committee on the Question of Defining Aggression*, A/3574, 1956, p. 6.
35 A. Van Wynen Thomas and A. J. Thomas Jr, *The Concept of Aggression*, p. 11.
36 *PAC opinion*, p. 116.
37 ibid, p. 117. The signs revealing the impending aggression were supposed to be (in the following order): organisation on paper of industrial mobilisation, actual organisation of industrial mobilisation, collection of stocks of raw materials, setting-on-foot of war industries, preparation for military mobilisation, actual military mobilisation, hostilities.
38 *Commentary on the Definition of a Case of Aggression Drawn up by a Special Committee of the Temporary Mixed Commission*, *LNOJ* 1923, Special Supplement, no 16, Annex 4, pp. 184–85 in B. B. Ferencz, *Defining International Aggression*, vol 1, pp. 82–83, hereinafter *TMC comments*. These factors were: actual industrial and economic mobilisation, secret military mobilisation, air, chemical or naval attack, the presence of the armed forces of one party in the territory of another, refusal to withdraw armed forces behind a line or lines indicated by the council, a definitely aggressive policy and the consequent refusal of that party to submit the subject in dispute to the recommendation of the council or to the decision of the PCIJ and to accept the recommendation or decision when given.
39 *General Report submitted to the Fifth Assembly on behalf of the First and the Third Committees by M. Politis (Greece), Rapporteur for the First Committee, and M. Benes (Czechoslovakia), Rapporteur for the Third Committee*, *LNOJ* 1924, Special Supplement, no 26, p. 205 in B. B. Ferencz, *Defining International Aggression*, vol 1, p. 148, hereinafter *Politis I* or *Benes report*.
40 G. Ginsburgs, *Moscow's Road to Nuremberg. The Soviet Background to the Trial*, Martinus Nijhoff Publishers, The Hague 1996, p. 13.
41 *Polish Official Gazette* 1932, no 115, item 951.
42 *Politis report II*, p. 216.
43 *Rutgers report*, pp. 173 ff.
44 ibid, p. 174.
45 League of Nations, Conference for the Reduction and Limitation of Armaments, Minutes of the General Commission, 6 February 1933, in B. B. Ferencz, *Defining International Aggression*, vol 1, pp. 201 ff.
46 League of Nations, Conference for the Reduction and Limitation of Armaments, *Proposals of the French Delegation*, Geneva, 5 February 1932 in B. B. Ferencz, *Defining International Aggression*, vol 1, pp. 194 ff.
47 League of Nations, Conference for the Reduction and Limitation of Armaments, Minutes of the Political Commission, *General Discussion on Aggression*, 10 March 1933, in B. B. Ferencz, *Defining International Aggression*, vol 1, pp. 205 ff, hereinafter *General Discussion on Aggression*.
48 It was composed of representatives of Belgium, Cuba, Denmark, Estonia, Finland, France, Germany, Hungary, Italy, Poland, Spain, Switzerland, Turkey, the United Kingdom, the United States, the USSR and Yugoslavia.
49 There were the following differences: in the general part of Politis's definition there was reference to 'agreements in force between the parties'; among acts of aggression, an unauthorised presence of armed forces on foreign territory was excluded but 'provision of support to armed bands' was added; the notion of 'attack' was used instead of 'bombardment'; it was stressed that invasion 'with or without a declaration of war' is an act of aggression. Furthermore, grounds which could not justify aggression were indicated in the Annex but in contracts to the Soviet proposition they did not include such grounds as: possible danger to life or property of foreign residents, maintenance of political, economic or social order, infringement of international agreements, non-admission or

limitation of immigration, restriction of rights or privileges of foreign residents, infringement of the privileges of official representatives of other states, religious or anti-religious measures, refusal to allow armed forces transit to the territory of a third state. See more in J. Balicki, *Pojęcie agresji*, pp. 64–65.

50 The role of the Romanian representative, Nicolae Titulescu, cannot be underestimated. See W. Komarnicki, 'La definition de l'agresseur', p. 50.
51 *Polish Oficial Gazette* (Dziennik Ustaw) 1933, no 93, item 712.
52 LNTS, vol 148, pp. 79 ff.
53 ibid, pp. 211 ff.
54 J. Diamandesco, *Le Problème de l'Agression*, p. 173.
55 It is worth stressing that the London definition was included in Article 1 of the First Protocol of the Balkan Pact of 9 February 1934 signed by Greece, Romania, Turkey and Yugoslavia. LNTS, vol 153, pp. 156 ff.
56 See W. Czapliński, *Skutki prawne nielegalnego*, p. 26, A. Van Wynen Thomas and A. J. Thomas Jr, *The Concept of Aggression*, pp. 19–20.
57 Table 2.1.
58 *AJIL* 1937, vol 31, Supplement Official Documents, p. 53. According to Colombian reservation, 'That State shall be considered as an aggressor which becomes responsible for one or several of the following acts: (a) That its armed forces, to whatever branch they may belong, illegally cross the land, sea, or air frontiers of another State. When the violation of the territory of a State has been effected by irresponsible bands organized within or outside of its territory and which have received direct or indirect help from another State, such violation shall be considered equivalent, for the purpose of the present Article, to that effected by the regular forces of the State responsible for the aggression; (b) That it has intervened in a unilateral or illegal way in the internal or external affairs of another State; (that it has refused to fulfill a legally given arbitral decision or sentence of international justice.' Cited after A. M. Rifaat, *International Aggression*, p. 94.
59 A. M. Rifaat, *International Aggression*, p. 86.
60 All the signatory states considered this wording to be a list of typical acts of aggression, and not a definition. E. Aroneanu, *La Définition de l'Agression*, p. 173.
61 Article 9.
62 UNTS, vol 23, pp. 147 ff.
63 Article 5.
64 Article 1(c). See Table 2.1. Treaty available at http://www.africa-union.org/root/AU/Documents/Treaties/text/Non%20Aggression%20Common%20Defence%20Pacvol.pdf (last visited 3 June 2013).
65 R. B. Russell, *A History of the United Nations Charter*, p. 465.
66 ibid.
67 See *The Dumbarton Oaks Proposals for a General International Organization*, in B. B. Ferencz, *Defining International Aggression*, vol 1, p. 285.
68 O. Solera, *Defining the Crime of Aggression*, p. 50.
69 The United Nations Conference on International Organization, *Proposals of the Delegation of the Republic of Bolivia for the Organization of a System of Peace and* Security, Doc 2, G/14(r), 5 May 1945, in B. B. Ferencz, *Defining International Aggression*, vol 1, p. 313 ff..
70 The United Nations Conference on International Organization, *Observation of the Czechoslovak Government on the Dumbarton Oaks Proposals*, Doc 2, G/14(b), 1 May 1945, in B. B. Ferencz, *Defining International Aggression*, vol 1, pp. 307 ff.
71 The United Nations Conference on International Organization, *Proposed Amendments to the Dumbarton Oaks Proposals Submitted by the Philippine Delegation*, Doc 2, G/14(k), 5 May 1945 in B. B. Ferencz, *Defining International Aggression*, vol 1, pp. 322 ff.

72 N. Nyiri, *The United Nations' Search*, p. 37.
73 *Boncour report*, p. 352.
74 O. Solera, *Defining the Crime of Aggression*, p. 80; B. B. Ferencz, *Defining International Aggression*, p. 2.
75 GAOR 5th session, *USSR Draft Definition of Aggression*, Doc A/C.1/608, 1950, pp. 4–5.
76 N. Nyiri, *The United Nations' Search*, p. 85.
77 GA Resolution no 378 B of 17 November 1950.
78 GA Resolution no 380 (*Peace Through Deeds*) of 17 November 1950.
79 *Spiropoulos report*, p. 68.
80 GAOR, 6th session, *Report of the International Law Commission*, A/1858, 1951, p. 8.
81 Summary of the debate on the form of the definition; see O. Solera, *Defining the Crime of Aggression*, p. 85 ff.
82 A. Van Wynen Thomas and A. J. Thomas Jr, *The Concept of Aggression*, p. 7. According to Soviets, such a statement would be equal to saying that 'aggression' is 'aggression'. N. Nyiri, *The United Nations' Search*, p. 168.
83 A. Van Wynen Thomas and A. J. Thomas Jr, *The Concept of Aggression*, p. 10.
84 B. Broms, *The Definition of Aggression*, p. 61.
85 J. Žourek, 'La définition de l'agression', p. 800.
86 See *General Discussion on Aggression*, pp. 207 and 210. Compare with A. Van Wynen Thomas and A. J. Thomas Jr, *The Concept of Aggression*, p. 9.
87 B. Broms, *The Definition of Aggression*, p. 62.
88 O. Solera, *Defining the Crime of Aggression*, pp. 86, 88.
89 B. Broms, *The Definition of Aggression*, p. 62.
90 J. Stone, *Aggression and World Order*, p. 52.
91 GAOR, 6th session, *Report of the Sixth Committee*, A/2087, 1952, p. 16. B. Broms, *The Definition of Aggression*, p. 62.
92 GAOR, 9th session, *Report of the Special Committee on the Question of Defining Aggression*, A/2638, 1953, p. 5.
93 A/CN.4/L.7, A/CN.4/L.12, in A/1858, p. 9.
94 A/CN.4/L.11 and Corr.1, ibid.
95 ibid, pp. 9–10.
96 A/CN.4/L.8, ibid, 9. See also R. J. Alfaro, 'La question de la définition de l'agression', *RDISDP* 1951, no 4, p. 375.
97 'Aggression is the threat or use of force by a State or government against another State, in any manner, whatever the weapons employed and whether openly or otherwise, for any reason or for any purpose other than individual or collective self-defence or in pursuance of a decision or recommendation by a competent organ of the United Nations.' A/CN.4/48 and Corr 1 & 2, *YbkIntLCom* 1951, vol 2, p. 133.
98 Alfaro, Cordova and Francois voted in favour; Amado, Brierly, Hsu, el-Khouri, Sandström, Spiropoulos and Yepes were against; Hudson abstained; Scelle was absent.
99 Publications from that time provide further evidence; see biased articles such as J. Balicki, 'O definicji agresji' or A. Bramson, 'Definicja agresji a ustawy o obronie pokoju', *Sprawy Międzynarodowe* 1952.
100 A/2087, pp. 15 ff.
101 O. Solera, *Defining the Crime of Aggression*, p. 112.
102 ibid.
103 A/C.6/L.206, in A/1858 p. 12.
104 A/C.6/L.208, ibid, p. 13.
105 A/C.6/L.211, ibid, p. 14.
106 A/C.6/L.215, ibid, p. 15.
107 GA Resolution no 599 of 31 January 1952.

108 Responses were sent by: Belgium, Bolivia, Chile, Costa Rica, Denmark, Egypt, France, India, Indonesia, Iraq, the Netherlands, Nicaragua, the United Kingdom, the USSR and Yugoslavia. GAOR, 7th session, *Report of the Secretary General*, A/2162 and Add 1 and Add 2, 1952, pp. 2 ff.
109 A/2211, pp. 22 ff.
110 A/2087, pp. 12 ff.
111 GA Resolution no 688 of 20 December 1952. The following states became members of the Special Committee: Bolivia, Brazil, China, Dominican Republic, France, Iran, the Netherlands, Mexico, Norway, Pakistan, Poland, Syria, the United Kingdom, the United States and the USSR. The resolution establishing the committee points out the necessity of analysing the relationship between the definition of aggression and maintaining international peace and security as well as the development of international criminal law; the impact of the definition on the jurisdiction of the United Nations must also be considered.
112 A/2638, pp. 1–15.
113 A/AC.66/L.9, ibid, p. 15.
114 A/AC.66/L.4/Rev.3 and A/AC.66/L.7/Rev.2, ibid, p. 14.
115 A/AC.66/L.2/Rev.1, ibid, pp. 13–14.
116 A/AC.66/L.8, ibid, p. 14.
117 The comments were sent by: Argentina, Belarus, Denmark, France, India, Poland, Sweden, Ukraine, the United Kingdom, the USSR. See also B. Broms, *The Definition of Aggression*, pp. 65 ff.
118 A/2806, pp. 9–12.
119 ibid, p. 9.
120 GA Resolution no 895 of 4 December 1954. The following states were members of the second Special Committee: China, Czechoslovakia, Dominican Republic, France, Iraq, Israel, Mexico, the Netherlands, Norway, Panama, Paraguay, Peru, Philippines, Poland, Syria, the United Kingdom, the United States, the USSR, Yugoslavia.
121 A/AC.77/L.4, in A/3574, p. 17.
122 A/AC.77/L.7, ibid, p. 19.
123 A/AC.77/L.9, ibid, p. 20.
124 A/AC.6/L.336/Rev.2, ibid, p. 21.
125 A/AC.77/L.8/Rev.1, ibid, p. 22.
126 A/AC.77/L.10, ibid, s. 23.
127 A/AC.77/L.11, ibid.
128 ibid, p. 25.
129 ibid, pp. 1 ff.
130 GA Resolution no 1181 of 29 November 1957.
131 The following states were members of the committee in 1959: Australia, Ceylon, China, Czechoslovakia, Ecuador, El Salvador, France, Greece, Indonesia, Ireland, Japan, Lebanon, Mexico, Nepal, the Netherlands, Pakistan, Romania, the United Kingdom, Uruguay, the United States, the USSR.
132 The following states were members of the committee in 1962: Argentina, Bulgaria, China, Costa Rica, Cyprus, Czechoslovakia, Denmark, France, Ghana, Greece, Italy, Liberia, Mexico, the Netherlands, Nigeria, Panama, Philippines, Tunisia, the United Kingdom, the United States, the USSR.
133 The following states were members of the committee in 1965: Argentina, Bulgaria, Cameroon, Canada, Chile, China, Cyprus, El Salvador, France, Ghana, Guinea, Iceland, the Netherlands, Romania, Somalia, Syria, Turkey, the United Kingdom, the United States, the USSR.
134 The following states were members of the committee in 1967: Afghanistan, Austria, Bolivia, China, Congo, Costa Rica, Cyprus, Czechoslovakia, Ecuador, Finland, France, Gabon, Greece, Hungary, Iraq, Jordan, Morocco, Ruanda,

Senegal, Sudan, Trinidad and Tobago, Turkey, the United Kingdom, the United States, the USSR.

135 B. B. Ferencz, *Defining International Aggression*, vol 2, p. 8. It is worth noting here that 1962 was the year of the Cuban crisis; in 1963 there was a conflict between the Greek and Turkish communities in Cyprus; in 1964 the United States increased its involvement in Cambodia and Vietnam; in 1965 India clashed with Pakistan; and in 1967 war broke out in the Middle East. N. Nyiri, *The United Nations' Search*, p. 201.

136 B. Broms, *The Definition of Aggression*, p. 87.

137 GAOR, 22nd session, *Request of the USSR*, A/6833, 1967, pp. 1 ff.

138 GA Resolution no 2330. The following states became members of the Special Committee: Algeria, Australia, Bulgaria, Canada, Colombia, Congo, Cyprus, Czechoslovakia, Ecuador, Finland, France, Ghana, Guyana, Haiti, Indonesia, Iraq, Iran, Italy, Japan, Madagascar, Mexico, Norway, Romania, Sierra Leone, Spain, Sudan, Syria, Turkey, Uganda, the United Kingdom, United Arab Republic, Uruguay, the USSR, Yugoslavia.

139 N. Nyiri, *The United Nations' Search*, p. 218.

140 The Resolution establishing the Special Committee was invoked, with its wording: 'that there is a widespread conviction of the need to expedite the definition of aggression'. See GAOR, 23rd session, *Report of the Special Committee, Question of Defining Aggression*, A/7185/Rev.1, 1968, p. 12.

141 A/AC.134/L.3 and Corr 1 and 2, ibid, pp. 3 ff.

142 A/AC.134/L.4/Rev.1 and Corr 1, ibid, pp. 5 ff.

143 A/AC.134/L.6 and Add 1 and Add 2, ibid, pp. 7 ff.

144 O. Solera, *Defining the Crime of Aggression*, p. 152.

145 GA Resolution no 2420 of 18 December 1968.

146 GA Resolutions no 2549 of 12 December 1969, no 2644 of 25 November 1970, no 2781 of 3 December 1971, no 2967 of 14 December 1972, no 3105 of 12 December 1973.

147 A/AC.134/L.12 and Corr. 1, GAOR, 24th session, *Report of the Special Committee*, A/7620, 1969, p. 329.

148 A/AC 134 /L.16, ibid, p. 6.

149 A/AC 134/L.17 and Corr 1 and Add 1, ibid, p. 8.

150 N. Nyiri, *The United Nations' Search*, p. 247.

151 For example, the Arab states were most interested in ensuring that occupation and annexation were included in the list of acts of aggression, while African states (as well as the Arab states) put the emphasis on stating clearly that using force for self-determination was not aggression.

152 Article 1.

153 Article 2.

154 See Table 2.1.

155 Article 4.

156 N. Nyiri, *The United Nations' Search*, p. 328.

157 B. B. Ferencz, *Defining International Aggression*, vol 2, p. 2.

158 A. Van Wynen Thomas and A. J. Thomas Jr, *The Concept of Aggression*, p. 6.

159 See the discussion report on the legal character of Resolution 3314 in A. M. Rifaat, *International Aggression*, pp. 278 ff.

160 B. B. Ferencz points out the use of the term 'adopts' rather than 'declares', which would emphasise that the General Assembly was only confirming a customary norm. The issue, however, never even came up for debate. B. B. Ferencz, *Defining International Aggression*, vol 2, p. 26. For negative opinions on the customary character of the resolution, see S. D. Murphy, 'U.S. view of the crime of aggression', *AJIL* 2001, vol 95, pp. 400–401.

161 ICJ, *Judgment on military and paramilitary activities in and against Nicaragua*, para 195.
162 M. M. Gomaa, *The Definition of the Crime of Aggression and the ICC Jurisdiction over that Crime*, in M. Politi and G. Nesi, *The International Criminal Court and the Crime of Aggression*, Ashgate, Aldershot 2004, p. 74.
163 The Treaty has not entered into force thus it has not been published in UNTS. Its text is published in the Organization of American States Treaty Series, nos 46 and 61.
164 O. Solera, *Defining the Crime of Aggression*, s. 202, where also all the relevant GA resolutions are cited.
165 A/2638, p. 8.
166 ibid, p. 9; A/7620, p.16.
167 E. Aroneanu, *La Définition de l'Agression*, pp. 78 ff.
168 More in J. Žourek, 'La définition de l'agression', p. 831.
169 D. W. Bowett, *Self-defence in International Law*, p. 24, K. Skubiszewski, 'Use of force by states. Collective security. Law of war and neutrality', in M. Sørensen, *Manual of Public International Law*, St Martin's Press, New York 1968, p. 764.
170 A. Van Wynen Thomas and A. J. Thomas Jr, *The Concept of Aggression*, p. 84.
171 See A/2211, p. 69.
172 E. Aroneanu, *La Définition de l'Agression*, p. 74.
173 O. Solera, *Defining the Crime of Aggression*, p. 116.
174 A/2211, p. 74.
175 A/2638, p. 10. A. Van Wynen Thomas and A. J. Thomas Jr, *The Concept of Aggression*, p. 26.
176 A. Van Wynen Thomas and A. J. Thomas Jr, *The Concept of Aggression*, p. 27.
177 A/2638, p. 9.
178 O. Solera, *Defining the Crime of Aggression*, p. 136.
179 E. Aroneanu, *La Définition de l'Agression*, p. 240; S. Alexandrov, *Self-Defense against the Use of Force*, p. 113.
180 C. A. Pompe, *Aggressive War*, p. 48.
181 A/2638, p. 6.
182 J. Žourek, 'La définition de l'agression', p. 837.
183 O. Solera, *Defining the Crime of Aggression*, p. 77.
184 A/2211, p. 74.
185 C. A. Pompe, *Aggressive War*, p. 56.
186 E. Aroneanu, *La Définition de l'Agression*, p. 274.
187 A/3574, p. 10.
188 C. A. Pompe, *Aggressive War*, pp. 109 ff.
189 See Preamble (5) and Article 2 where it is stressed that 'aggression is the most serious and dangerous form of the illegal use of force'.
190 Y. Dinstein, *War, Aggression and Self-Defence*, p. 128.
191 Article 2(4) of the Charter of the United Nations. For a variety of historical examples of threats see N. Stürchler, *The Threat of Force in International Law*, Cambridge University Press, Cambridge 2007, pp. 127 ff.
192 See eg Córdova's proposition A/CN.4/L.10, A/1858, p. 9.
193 L. S. Sunga, *The Emerging System of International Criminal Law*, p. 60.
194 See P. H. Kooijmans, 'The enlargement of the concept "threat to peace', in R. J. Dupuy, *The Development of the Role of the Security Council, Peace-keeping and Peace-building*, M. Nijhoff, Dordrecht 1993, p. 120.
195 O. Solera, *Defining the Crime of Aggression*, p. 129.
196 Article 1 of GA Resolution no 3314 of 14 December 1974.
197 See Explanatory Note to the Article 1 of GA Resolution no 3314 of 14 December 1974.

198 Article 1.
199 W. Komarnicki, 'La définition de l'agresseur', p. 59.
200 GAOR, 25th session, *Report of the Special Committee*, A/8019, 1970, p. 8.
201 *YbkIntLCom* 1951, vol 2, p. 111, para 51.
202 ibid, p. 38, para 46.
203 W. Góralczyk, *Prawo międzynarodowe*, p. 417.
204 See Preamble (6) of GA Resolution 3314 of 14 December 1974 where the 'duty of states not to use armed force to deprive peoples of their right to self-determination, freedom and independence, or to disrupt territorial integrity' is stressed.
205 GAOR, 25th session, *Report of the Sixth Committee*, A/8171, 1970, p. 6. See also J. Stone, *Conflict Through Consensus. United Nations Approaches to Aggression*, The John Hopkins University Press, Baltimore 1977, pp. 66 ff.
206 R. Bierzanek, *Prawo międzynarodowe publiczne*, p. 88, J. Žourek, 'La définition de l'agression', p. 818.
207 See E. Aroneanu, *La Définition de l'Agression*, p. 226.
208 See Article 1, *Harvard Law School Draft Convention on the Rights and Duties of States in Case of Aggression*, according to which 'Aggression' is a resort to armed force by a state when such resort has been duly determined, by a means which the state is bound to accept, to constitute a violation of an obligation'. *AJIL* 1939, vol 33, Supplement: Research in International Law, p. 827.
209 Compare with *Draft Treaty of American Group*, pp. 169 ff, according to which aggressive war are measures of force not taken for the purpose of defence (Article 2) or for the protection of life (Article 5).
210 A/CN.4/L.6/Corr.1, in A/1858, p. 9. Compare with G. Amado, 'La question de la définition de l'agression', *RDISDP* 1952, no 2, p. 154.
211 A/CN.4/L.19, in A/1858, p. 10.
212 *Politis report I*, p. 204. For example, the Geneva Protocol of 1924 considered every instance of violation of the convention (Covenant of the League of Nations) and Protocol (Article 10) to be aggression.
213 ibid.
214 A. M. Rifaat, *International Aggression*, p. 75; M. S. McDougal and F. P. Feliciano, *The International Law of War*, p. 122; J. Diamandesco, *Le Problème de l'Agression*, p. 107. The interconnection between the terms is particularly clearly visible in the French version of Article 51 of the Charter of the United Nations, where self-defence is the response to armed aggression.
215 J. L. Brierly, *The Law of Nations*, p. 406. See also S. D. Bailey, *How Wars End, The United Nations and Termination of Armed Conflict, 1946–64*, vol 1, Clarendon Press, Oxford 1982, pp. 106 ff; P. Wilson, *Aggression, Crime and International Security*, p. 4.
216 I. Brownlie, *International Law and the Use of Force*, pp. 251–52.
217 '*Une nation qui veut la guerre est toujours en état de légitime défense*', cited after W. Czapliński, *Skutki prawne nielegalnego*, p. 28.
218 A. M. Weisburd, *Use of Force*, p. 304.
219 ibid, p. 307.
220 H. Wehberg, *The Outlawry of War*, p. 6.
221 ibid, p. 118.
222 J. Stone, *Aggression and World Order*, pp. 74–75.
223 A. Constantinou, *The Right of Self-defence under Customary International Law and Article 51 of the UN Charter*, Ant. Sakkoulas, Bruylant, Athènes, Bruxelles 2000, p. 58.
224 On the meaning of the Latin term *aggredior* from which the word 'aggression' is derived see A. Van Wynen Thomas and A. J. Thomas Jr, *The Concept of Aggression*, p. 14 and J. Stone, *Aggression and World Order*, p. 15.
225 *Politis report II*, p. 218. See also J. Žourek, 'La définition de l'agression', p. 819.

226 A/7620, p. 20; A/8019, p. 12; W. Morawiecki, 'Walka o definicję agresji', p. 235.
227 W. Góralczyk, *Prawo międzynarodowe*, p. 417.
228 O. Solera, *Defining the Crime of Aggression*, p. 63.
229 H. Wehberg, *The Outlawry of Law*, p. 105.
230 *PAC opinion*, p. 117; *TMC comments*, p. 185.
231 J. Maktos, 'La question de la définition de l'agression', p. 8.
232 League of Nations, Conference for the Reduction and Limitation of Armaments, *Discussion on Definition of Aggression*, Series B, Minutes of the General Commission, in B. B. Ferencz, *Defining International Aggression*, vol 1, p. 245.
233 B. B. Ferencz, *Defining International Aggression*, vol 2, p. 31.
234 See eg A/7620, pp. 20–21.
235 Article 2 of GA Resolution no 3314 of 14 December 1974.
236 B. B. Ferencz, *Defining International Aggression*, vol 1, p. 12.
237 On the difference between intent and motivation, see A. Van Wynen Thomas and A. J. Thomas Jr, *The Concept of Aggression*, p. 52.
238 O. Solera, *Defining the Crime of Aggression*, p. 106.
239 *PAC opinion*, p. 117.
240 See E. Aroneanu, *La Définition de l'Agression*, pp. 222–23.
241 See eg A/8019, p. 34.
242 See B. B. Ferencz, *Defining International Aggression*, vol 2, p. 8; N. Nyiri, *The United Nations' Search*, p. 22; J. Žourek, 'La définition de l'agression', p. 790.
243 Article 1(2).
244 N. Nyiri, *The United Nations' Search*, pp. 18 and 346.
245 W. Czapliński, *Skutki prawne nielegalnego*, p. 30.
246 R. Ranjeva and C. Cadoux, *Droit international public*, Edicef, Vanves 1992, p. 204.
247 A/8019, p. 13.
248 J. Žourek, 'La définition de l'agression', p. 843.
249 ibid, p. 844.
250 A. Van Wynen Thomas and A. J. Thomas Jr, *The Concept of Aggression*, p. 54.
251 O. Solera, *Defining the Crime of Aggression*, p. 178.
252 A/8019, pp.13–14.
253 Article 5(1) of GA Resolution no 3314 of 14 December 1974.
254 M. Flemming, 'Definicja agresji', *Wojskowy Przegląd Prawniczy* 1975, no 2, p. 211.
255 The inclusion of 'sovereignty' in Resolution 3314 caused a great deal of conflict, since the Soviet representatives believed the use of the term to be superfluous, as its sense was already covered by 'political independence' and 'territorial integrity', and moreover, it was not listed in Article 2(4) of the Charter of the United Nations. B. B. Ferencz, *Defining International Aggression*, vol 2, p. 27. Compare with N. Nyiri, *The United Nations' Search*, p. 366.
256 Y. Dinstein, *War, Aggression and Self-Defence*, p. 128.
257 O. Solera, *Defining the Crime of Aggression*, p. 199.
258 *PAC opinion*, p. 114.
259 ibid, p. 116.
260 ibid, p. 117.
261 These acts were labelled by Wacław Komarnicki as '*péchés capitaux*' of states. W. Komarnicki, 'La définition de l'agresseur', p. 45.
262 See eg London Conventions of 1933 and Saadabad Pact of 1937.
263 A/8019, p. 38; A/8171, p. 4.
264 J. Žourek, 'La définition de l'agression', p. 826.
265 During the First World War, almost all states declared war (apart from Turkey, which however was not a party to Hague III of 1907). In the period 1919–1939 the only declaration of war was made by Paraguay in 1934 during the Chaco conflict with Bolivia. See C. A. Pompe, *Aggressive War*, pp. 8–9.

266 A. Van Wynen Thomas and A. J. Thomas Jr, *The Concept of Aggression*, p. 6, R. J. Alfaro, 'La question de la définition de l'agression', p. 373.
267 The Netherlands declared war on Japan on 8 December 1941, before the attack on East India, and Japan declared war on the Netherlands on 11 January 1942, but on 5 December 1941 the Japanese command had already made the decision to attack. See M. S. McDougal and F. P. Feliciano, *The International Law of War*, p. 231.
268 A/2211, p. 60.
269 O. Solera, *Defining the Crime of Aggression*, p. 67.
270 A. Constantinou, *The Right of Self-defence*, p. 67.
271 See eg London Conventions of 1933 or GA Resolution no 3314 of 14 December 1974.
272 B. B. Ferencz, *Defining International Aggression*, vol 1, p. 11.
273 See eg London Conventions of 1933.
274 O. Solera, *Defining the Crime of Aggression*, pp. 71–72.
275 Y. Dinstein, *War, Aggression and Self-Defence*, p. 200. M. Flemming, 'Definicja agresji', p. 212.
276 *Politis report II*, p. 219.
277 See eg A/9619, p. 16. B. B. Ferencz, *Defining International Aggression*, vol 2, p. 36.
278 A/9619, p. 15. See also Indonesian comments, ibid, p. 19.
279 See propositions of 1969 and GA Resolution no 3314 of 14 December 1974.
280 O. Solera, *Defining the Crime of Aggression*, p. 68.
281 A/2211, p. 62.
282 See GA Resolution no 3314 of 14 December 1974 and 13 states proposition of 1969.
283 B. Broms, *The Definition of Aggression*, p. 150.
284 M. S. McDougal and F. P. Feliciano, *The International Law of War*, pp. 223–24.
285 A. M. Rifaat, *International Aggression*, pp. 127 and 270.
286 A/9619, p. 32.
287 A. M. Rifaat, *International Aggression*, p. 270.
288 ibid, p. 271. See also A. Constantinou, *The Right of Self-defence*, pp. 68 ff.
289 O. Solera, *Defining the Crime of Aggression*, p. 73.
290 J. Diamandesco, *Le Problème de l'Agression*, p. 153.
291 See League of Nations, Conference for the Reduction and Limitation of Armaments, *Report of the Committee on Security Questions: Statement by M. Politis, Chairman of the Committee, As to the Position of the Work*, Series B, Minutes of the General Commission in B. B. Ferencz, *Defining International Aggression*, vol 1, p. 240.
292 J. Diamandesco, *Le Problème de l'Agression*, p. 154.
293 A/2211, p. 63.
294 B. B. Ferencz, *Defining International Aggression*, vol 2, p. 35.
295 ibid, E. Aroneanu, *La Définition de l'Agression*, p. 88.
296 O. Solera, *Defining the Crime of Aggression*, p. 73.
297 A/2211, p. 63. J. Żourek, 'La définition de l'agression', p. 827, W. Morawiecki, 'Walka o definicję agresji', p. 230.
298 N. Nyiri, *The United Nations' Search*, p. 289.
299 GAOR, 29th session, *Report of Sixth Committee*, A/9890, 1974, p. 1. See also B. B. Ferencz, *Defining International Aggression*, vol 2, p. 67.
300 In the Philippines' proposition of 1945 this act was labelled as follows: 'to interfere with the internal affairs of another nation'.
301 B. Broms, *The Definition of Aggression*, p. 32.
302 C. A. Pompe, *Aggressive War*, p. 53.
303 J. Balicki, 'O definicji agresji', p. 51, A. M. Rifaat, *International Aggression*, pp. 218 ff.

304 E. Aroneanu, *La Définition de l'Agression*, p. 89.
305 M. S. McDougal and F. P. Feliciano, *The International Law of War*, p. 190.
306 O. Solera, *Defining the Crime of Aggression*, p. 78.
307 ICJ, *Judgment on military and paramilitary activities in and against Nicaragua*, para 115.
308 ibid, para 195.
309 ICJ, *Judgment on Armed Activities on the Territory of the Congo (Democratic Republic of Congo v Uganda)*, 19 December 2005, para 146 ff.
310 J. Kranz, 'Nowe aspekty stosowania siły w stosunkach międzynarodowych', p. 348.
311 ICTY, Appeals Chamber Judgment, *Prosecutor v Dusko Tadić* (IT-94-1-A), 15 July 1999, para 156.
312 See SC Resolutions no 1368 of 12 September 2001 and no 1373 of 28 September 2001.
313 Article 1(c)(viii).
314 Article 1(c)(xi).
315 See eg GA Resolution no 3314 of 14 December 1974.
316 See Bolivian proposition of 1945.
317 GAOR, 7th session, *Comments Received from Governments Regarding the Draft Code of Offences Against the Peace and Security of Mankind and the Question of Defining Aggression*, A/2162 and Add, 1953, p. 8.
318 See Yepes's proposition (A/CN.4/L.7). Compare with J. T. Shotwell, *War as an Instrument of National Policy*, p. 207.
319 *Rutgers report*, p. 174.
320 Article 5(2–4). See also. E. Aroneanu, *La Définition de l'Agression*, p. 287.
321 See GA Resolution no 378 of 17 November 1950, A/2211, p. 65.
322 *TMC comments*, pp. 183–84.
323 J. Stone, *Aggression and World Order*, pp. 108 ff.
324 B. B. Ferencz, *Defining International Aggression*, vol 2, p. 49.
325 I. Brownlie, *International Law and the Use of Force*, p. 351.
326 B. B. Ferencz, *Defining International Aggression*, vol 1, p. IX.
327 N. Nyiri, *The United Nations' Search*, p. 130.
328 ibid, p. 335.
329 W. Komarnicki, 'La definition de l'agresseur', p. 65.
330 O. Solera, *Defining the Crime of Aggression*, p. 197.
331 ibid, p. 15.
332 C. J. Chacko, 'International law and the concept of aggression', *IndJIntL* 1963, vol 3, p. 396.
333 B. Broms, *The Definition of Aggression*, p. 118.
334 A. Van Wynen Thomas and A. J. Thomas Jr, *The Concept of Aggression*, p. 12.
335 I. Brownlie, *International Law and the Use of Force*, p. 104.
336 A. Van Wynen Thomas and A. J. Thomas Jr, *The Concept of Aggression*, p. 12.
337 ibid, p. 13.
338 So-called 'zirkelquadratur'. C. A. Pompe, *Aggressive War*, p. 57.

3 The legal basis for criminalising aggression

1 I. Brownlie, *International Law and the Use of Force*, p. 157.
2 Y. Dinstein, *War, Aggression and Self-Defence*, p. 120.
3 W. A. Schabas, *An Introduction to the International Criminal Court*, 2nd edn, Cambridge University Press, Cambridge 2004, p. 3. M. C. Bassiouni, *World War I*, p. 250. Lippmann refers to the presidential address of Elihu Root to the American Society of International Law in which he proclaimed that the

international community shared an interest in the punishment of aggressive acts that interfered with the 'independence of nations', the 'inviolability of their territory' and the 'lives and property of citizens'. See M. Lippmann, 'The history, development, and decline of crimes against peace', *GeoWashIntLRev* 2004, vol 36, p. 958.

4 The commission was composed of 15 members, including: France, Italy, Japan, the United States and the United Kingdom had two representatives in the commission; other members (from Belgium, Greece, Poland, Romania and Serbia) were elected from states which had special interests. See *Report of the Commission on the Responsibility of the Authors of the War*, pp. 96–97.

5 ibid, p. 95.

6 ibid, p. 98.

7 ibid, p. 107.

8 ibid, p. 118.

9 ibid, pp. 118–119.

10 ibid, p. 119.

11 ibid, p. 120.

12 ibid, p. 133.

13 See *Memorandum of Reservations Presented by the Representatives of the United States to the Report of the Commission on Responsibilities*, 4 April 1919, *AJIL* 1920, vol 14, p. 128.

14 ibid, p. 137.

15 ibid, p. 136.

16 ibid, p. 139.

17 ibid, p. 140.

18 Article 231. Available at http://avalon.law.yale.edu. (Last visited 3 June 2013)

19 A. Klafkowski, *Prawo międzynarodowe publiczne*, p. 345.

20 Article 227.

21 M. C. Bassiouni, *World War I*, pp. 269–70.

22 Y. Dinstein, *War, Aggression and Self-Defence*, p. 117. Compare with K. Sellars, 'Delegitimizing aggression. First steps and false starts after the First World War', *JIntCrimJust* 2012, vol 10, pp. 13–14.

23 Article 227(3).

24 See J. F. Willis, *Prologue to Nuremberg: The Punishment of War Criminals of the First World War*, Duke University, Xerox University Microfilms, 1976, p. 199. Compare with D. Simons, 'L'Extradition de l'ex-Empereur d'Allemagne et la Hollande', *JDI* (Période de la guerre 1914–1919) 1919, vol 46, p. 957; M. C. Bassiouni, *World War I*, p. 280.

25 D. Simons, 'L'Extradition de l'ex-Empereur d'Allemagne et la Hollande', p. 960.

26 ibid.

27 F. Larnaude and A. de Lapradelle, 'Examen de la responsabilité pénale de l'empereur Guillaume II d'Allemagne', *JDI* (Période de la guerre 1914–1919) 1919, vol 46, p. 155.

28 ibid, p. 156.

29 *AJIL* Supplement 1920, vol 14, pp. 1 ff.

30 ibid, p. 185 ff.

31 *AJIL* Supplement 1921, vol 15, pp. 1 ff.

32 ibid, pp. 179 ff.

33 J. F. Willis, *Prologue to Nuremberg*, p. 329.

34 United Nations, General Assembly, International Law Commission, *Historical Survey of the Question of International Criminal Jurisdiction – Memorandum Submitted by the Secretary General, Topic: Question of International Criminal Jurisdiction*, New York 1949, A/CN.4/7/Rev.1, pp. 2–3 and 8 ff. Draft proposition, see B. B. Ferencz,

An International Criminal Court. A Step Toward World Peace – A Documentary History and Analysis, Volume I – Half a Century of Hope, Oceana Publications, Inc., London 1980, pp. 208–209.

35 See transcript of discussion at the committee meeting of 13 July 1920 in B. B. Ferencz, *An International Criminal Court*, vol 1, pp. 196 ff.

36 *Historical Survey of the Question of International Criminal Jurisdiction*, pp. 10–11. See the *voeu* in B. B. Ferencz, *An International Criminal Court*, vol 1, p. 237.

37 *Historical Survey of the Question of International Criminal Jurisdiction*, p. 11. See transcript of discussion in B. B. Ferencz, *An International Criminal Court*, vol 1, pp. 226 ff.

38 J. F. Willis, *Prologue to Nuremberg*, p. 344.

39 B. B. Ferencz, *An International Criminal Court*, vol 1, p. 255. For more on ILA initiatives see H. Wehberg, *The Outlawry of War*, p. 108 and T. Cyprian and J. Sawicki, *Prawo norymberskie, Bilans i perspektywy*, Wydawnictwo Eugeniusza Kuthana, Warszawa 1948, pp. 48 ff.

40 Text in *Historical Survey of the Question of International Criminal Jurisdiction*, p. 61 and B. B. Ferencz, *An International Criminal Court*, vol 1, p. 258.

41 See comments below draft articles.

42 Article 21(1)(a–c).

43 Article 21(2).

44 O. Solera, *Defining the Crime of Aggression*, p. 25, I. Brownlie, *International Law and the Use of Force*, p. 156.

45 Text of the *voeu* in *Historical Survey of the Question of International Criminal Jurisdiction*, p. 74.

46 Point 4.

47 Point 6.

48 Text of the proposition in V. V. Pella, *La guerre-crime et les criminels de guerre. Réflexions sur la justice pénale internationale. Ce qu'elle est et ce qu'elle devrait être*, Histoire et Société d'Aujourd'hui, Éditions de la Baconnière, Neuchatel 1964, pp. 129 ff. English translation in *Historical Survey of the Question of International Criminal Jurisdiction*, pp. 75 ff.

49 Article 35.

50 Article 36.

51 Text in B. B. Ferencz, *An International Criminal Court*, vol 1, pp. 247 ff. See also V. V. Pella, *La guerre-crime et les criminels de guerre*, p. 26.

52 Point 3.

53 Point 10.

54 Point 9B.

55 Point 8B.

56 *Historical Survey of the Question of International Criminal Jurisdiction*, p. 14 (resolution's text in ibid, pp. 70 ff).

57 The topic of a criminal code was raised again within the Union in 1929. See further V V. Pella, *La guerre-crime et les criminels de guerre*, pp. 26–27.

58 See V. V. Pella, 'Le code des crimes contre la paix et la securité de l'humanité (observations et réflexions)', *RDISDP* 1952, no 4, p. 341.

59 Title 2, Chapter 1, Point 1. Text of the proposition in V V. Pella, *La guerre-crime et les criminels de guerre*, p. 145.

60 Title 2, Chapter 2, Points 1–10.

61 Transcript of discussion on both conventions in B. B. Ferencz, *An International Criminal Court*, vol 1, pp. 269 ff.

62 Article 1. Text of the convention, in *Historical Survey of the Question of International Criminal Jurisdiction*, p. 88.

63 V V. Pella, *La guerre-crime et les criminels de guerre*, p. 28.

64 Convention for the Establishment of an International Criminal Court was signed by 13 states: Belgium, Bulgaria, Cuba, France, Greece, Monaco, the Netherlands, Romania, Spain, Czechoslovakia, Turkey, the USSR and Yugoslavia. None of them ratified the convention.
65 See B. B. Ferencz, *An International Criminal Court*, vol 1, pp. 40 ff.
66 G. A. Finch, 'The Nuremberg trial and international law', *AJIL* 1947, vol 41, p. 26.
67 A. M. Rifaat, *International Aggression*, p. 168.
68 G. Dean, 'Preface', in *The Case Against the Nazi War Criminals, Opening Statement for the United States of America by Robert H. Jackson and Other Documents, with Preface by Gordon Dean of Counsel for United States*, Alfred A. Knopf, New York 1946, p. v.
69 See first of all S. Glueck, *The Nuremberg Trial and Aggressive War*, Kraus Reprint Corporation, New York 1966, pp. 109 ff; United Nations War Crimes Commission, *History of the United Nations War Crimes Commission and the Development of the Laws of War*, His Majesty's Stationery Office, London 1948, p. 87.
70 T. Taylor, 'Nuremberg trials. War crimes and international law', *IntCon* April 1949, no 450, p. 127.
71 Representatives of Australia, Canada, China, India, New Zealand, the United Kingdom, Union of South Africa, the United States and the USSR participated in the conference as guests.
72 United Nations War Crimes Commission, *History of the United Nations War Crimes Commission*, pp. 93 ff.
73 In the United States the main proponents of an execution without a trial included Henry Morgenthau, Cordell Hull and Dwight Eisenhower. As it turned out, Roosevelt was under a stronger influence of Henry Stimson and John McCloy, who preferred that a court should be involved in the case of the Nazi criminals. See eg W. R. Harris, *Tyranny on Trial. The Evidence at Nuremberg*, Southern Methodist University Press, Dallas 1954, pp. 7 ff; B. F. Smith, *Reaching Judgment at Nuremberg*, Andre Deutsch, London 1977. pp. 22 Ff; J. R. Worth, 'Globalization and the myth of absolute national sovereignty: reconsidering the "UN-Signing" of the Rome Statute and the legacy of Senator Bricker', *IndLJ* 2004, vol 79, p. 249; B. B. Ferencz, 'Remarks made at Pace University School of Law on October 23, 1993', *PaceIntLRev* 1994, vol 6, p. 56; I. Brownlie, *International Law and the Use of Force*, p. 161; G. Dean, 'Preface', p. v; *Final Report to the Secretary of the Army on the Nuernberg War Crimes Trials Under Control Council Law No 10 by Telford Taylor, Brigadier General, U.S.A. Chief of Counsel for War Crimes*, Washington, D.C., 15 August 1949, p. 2 (*Taylor Report*); J. A. Bush, 'The "supreme crime" and its origins: the lost legislative history of the crime of aggressive war', *ColLRev* 2002, vol 102, p. 2350 (see also there the discussion on William Chamberlain Chanler, 1895–1981, whom the author believes to have been the first person to suggest a court trial). As for the position of the British government, on the one hand Winston Churchill is sometimes perceived as wanting a collective execution of the criminals, eg A. J. Kochavi, *Prelude to Nuremberg: Allied War Crimes Policy and the Question of Punishment*, University of North Carolina Press, Chapel Hill, 1998, pp. 63–91; C. A. Pompe, *Aggressive War*, p. 189 but, on the other hand, is remembered to have responded very strongly to Stalin's suggestion to this effect at the conference in Teheran. See J. J. Heydecker and J. Leeb, *Proces w Norymberdze*, Świat Książki, Warszawa 2006, p. 80 (original title: *Der Nürnberger Prozeß*, Verlag Kiepenheuer &Witsch, Köln 2003); W. J. Bosh, *Judgment on Nuremberg. American Attitudes toward the Major German War Crimes Trials*, North Caroline Press, Chapel Hill 1970, p. 23.
74 'Report to the President from Justice Robert H. Jackson, Chief of Counsel for the United States in the prosecution of Axis war criminals', 7 June 1945, *AJIL* 1945, vol 39, Supplement Official Documents, p. 182 (*Jackson Report*).

75 United Nations War Crimes Commission, *History of the United Nations War Crimes Commission*, p. 487.

76 'Italian Military Armistice of 3 and 29 September 1943', *AJIL* 1946, vol 40, Supplement, pp. 1 ff. 'Finland-Soviet Union Armistice of 19 September 1944', *AJIL* 1945, vol 39, Supplement, p. 85. 'United States-Great Britain-Soviet Union Armistice with Romania of 12 September 1944', ibid, p. 88. 'United States-Great Britain-Soviet Union with Bulgaria Armistice of 28 October 1944', ibid p. 93. 'United States-Great Britain-Soviet Union with Hungary Armistice of 20 January 1945', ibid p. 97. The claim of T. Cyprian and J. Sawicki to the effect that these documents listed war crimes and similar crimes, and therefore provided for a possibility of a trial for the crime against peace, must be considered an exaggeration. T. Cyprian and J. Sawicki, *Prawo norymberskie, Bilans i perspektywy*, pp. 556–57.

77 I. Brownlie, *International Law and the Use of Force*, p. 161.

78 The London International Assembly was an unofficial body established in 1941 on the initiative of Robert Cecil of Chelwood under the auspices of the League of Nations. Its members were appointed by the allied governments with their seat in London. The General Assembly drafted recommendations which it communicated to these governments via its members. United Nations War Crimes Commission, *History of the United Nations War Crimes Commission*, p. 99; *Historical Survey of the Question of International Criminal Jurisdiction*, p. 18.

79 Article 2 of the draft Convention on the Establishment of an International Criminal Court. Text of the convention in *Historical Survey of the Question of International Criminal Jurisdiction*, p. 98 and in B. B. Ferencz, *An International Criminal Court*, vol 1, p. 400. See also T. Cyprian and J. Sawicki, *Ludzie i sprawy Norymbergi*, Wydawnictwo Poznańskie, Poznań 1967, pp. 70 ff.

80 The United Nations Commission for the Investigation of War Crimes was established on 20 October 1943 (it was previously announced in the declaration of President Roosevelt and Lord Simon of 7 October 1942). Its membership included representatives of most allied states: Australia, Belgium, China, Czechoslovakia, France, Greece, the Netherlands, India, Luxembourg, Norway, Poland, Great Britain, the United States and Yugoslavia (but the membership differed from the list of representatives who negotiated the establishment of the commission). The USSR was not represented, because it had insisted that all 16 Soviet republics should be included. The argument offered was that the Ukrainian, Belarusian, Moldavian, Lithuania, Latvian, Estonian and Karel-Finnish Republic fell victim to aggression, just like the British protectorates. The remaining allies refused to accept this reasoning. The president of the commission was initially Sir Cecil Hurst, and then Lord Wright of Durley. See United Nations War Crimes Commission, *History of the United Nations War Crimes Commission*, pp. 109 ff; *Historical Survey of the Question of International Criminal Jurisdiction*, p. 20, F. Ryszka, *Norymberga. Prehistoria i ciąg dalszy*, Czytelnik, Warszawa 1982, p. 159, T. Taylor, 'Nuremberg trials', p. 128, T. Cyprian and J. Sawicki, *Ludzie i sprawy Norymbergi*, p. 63.

81 United Nations War Crimes Commission, *History of the United Nations War Crimes Commission*, p. 180.

82 ibid, p. 182.

83 Text of the resolution in B. B. Ferencz, *An International Criminal Court*, vol 1, pp. 425 ff.

84 United Nations War Crimes Commission, *History of the United Nations War Crimes Commission*, p. 181.

85 The majority report was adopted by representatives of Great Britain, the Netherlands and the United States. ibid, p. 182.

86 ibid. Text of the report in B. B. Ferencz, *An International Criminal Court*, vol 1, p. 414.
87 United Nations War Crimes Commission, *History of the United Nations War Crimes Commission*, p. 183.
88 ibid, p. 184.
89 ibid, p. 185.
90 Text of the memorandum in B. B. Ferencz, *An International Criminal Court*, vol 1, p. 438 and also available at http://avalon.law.yale.edu/imt/jack01.asp (last visited 3 June 2013).
91 *American Draft of Definitive Proposal, Presented to Foreign Ministers at San Francisco*, April 1945, in B. B. Ferencz, *Defining International Aggression*, vol 1, pp. 362–67.
92 ibid, p. 362.
93 ibid, p. 364.
94 *Jackson Report*, pp. 184–85.
95 ibid, p. 186.
96 ibid, p. 187. Compare with *Opening Statement for the United States of America by Robert H. Jackson*, in *The Case Against the Nazi War Criminals*, pp. 74–75, (*USA Opening Statement*).
97 *Jackson Report*, p. 187.
98 ibid, p. 187, *USA Opening Statement*, p. 77.
99 *Jackson Report*, p. 188, *USA Opening Statement*, pp. 74–75.
100 *Jackson Report*, p. 188, *USA Opening Statement*, p. 75.
101 *Jackson Report*, p. 189.
102 See *Formulation of the Nürnberg Principles – Report by J. Spiropoulos, Special Rapporteur*, A/CN.4/22, in *YbkIntLC* 1950, vol 2, United Nations, New York 1957, p. 182.
103 ibid.
104 ibid.
105 ibid, p. 183.
106 ibid. Also in B. B. Ferencz, *Defining International Aggression*, vol 1, p. 197.
107 O. Solera, *Defining the Crime of Aggression*, p. 211.
108 *Amendments Proposed by American Delegation*, 16 July 1945, in B. B. Ferencz, *Defining International Aggression*, vol 1, p. 377.
109 B. B. Ferencz, *Defining International Aggression*, vol 1, pp. 378–79, 387, 392. See also 'Definition of "aggression", suggested by American delegation as basis of discussion', 19 July 1945, ibid, p. 381 and 'Redraft of definition of 'crimes', submitted by American delegation', 25 July 1945, in O. Solera, *Defining the Crime of Aggression*, p. 225. The difference between the two definitions of aggression proposed by the American delegation consisted mainly in the omission from the list of the acts of aggression of naval blockade and support for armed bands. See also W. Morawiecki, *Walka o definicję agresji w prawie międzynarodowym*, Państwowe Wydawnictwo Naukowe, Warszawa 1956, pp. 247–48.
110 B. B. Ferencz, *Defining International Aggression*, vol 1, p. 390.
111 ibid, pp. 378–79.
112 O. Solera, *Defining the Crime of Aggression*, p. 212.
113 B. B. Ferencz, *Defining International Aggression*, vol 1, pp. 383, 387.
114 I. Brownlie, *International Law and the Use of Force*, p. 163.
115 A/CN.4/22, p. 184. Also B. B. Ferencz, *Defining International Aggression*, vol 1, pp. 380 ff.
116 O. Solera, *Defining the Crime of Aggression*, p. 213.
117 B. B. Ferencz, *Defining International Aggression*, vol 1, p. 382.
118 I. Brownlie, *International Law and the Use of Force*, p. 163.
119 B. B. Ferencz, *Defining International Aggression*, vol 1, p. 382.

120 ibid, p. 384.
121 ibid, pp. 382–83.
122 ibid, p. 383. The French referenced the resolution of the League of Nations of 1927 and the Briand-Kellogg Pact which, in their opinion, defined the crime of aggression.
123 ibid, p. 384.
124 ibid, p. 393.
125 ibid, p. 384.
126 ibid, p. 392.
127 A/CN.4/22, p. 184.
128 B. B. Ferencz, *Defining International Aggression*, vol 1, p. 385.
129 ibid, p. 395.
130 ibid, p. 385.
131 ibid, p. 391.
132 A/CN.4/22, p. 184.
133 O. Solera, *Defining the Crime of Aggression*, p. 222.
134 A/CN.4/22, p. 185.
135 O. Solera, *Defining the Crime of Aggression*, p. 227.
136 'Revised definition of "crimes", prepared by British delegation and accepted by French delegation', 28 July 1945, in B. B. Ferencz, *Defining International Aggression*, vol 1, pp. 397–98.
137 N. Nyiri, *The United Nations' Search*, p. 53.
138 'Revised definition of "crimes", prepared by British delegation to meet views of Soviet delegation', 28 July 1945, in B. B. Ferencz, *Defining International Aggression*, vol 1, p. 399. Also A/CN.4/22, pp. 185–86.
139 'Revised definition of "Crimes", submitted by American delegation', 30 July 1945, in B. B. Ferencz, *Defining International Aggression*, vol 1, p. 400. Also A/CN.4/22, p. 186.
140 'Notes on proposed definition of "Crimes", submitted by American delegation', 31 July 1945, in B. B. Ferencz, *Defining International Aggression*, vol 1, p. 401.
141 'Revision of definition of "Crimes", submitted by American delegation', 31 July 1945, in ibid, p. 402.
142 ibid, p. 404. A reference to a book by A. N. Trainin, which mentions a crime against peace was decisive. A. N. Trainin, *La responsabilité pénale des Hitlériens*, Presse Française étrangère, O. Zeluck, Éditeur Paris 1945, passim.
143 Article 6.
144 Among states which acceded to the London Agreement were: Australia, Belgium, Czechoslovakia, Denmark, Ethiopia, Greece, Haiti, Honduras, India, Luxembourg, the Netherlands, New Zealand, Norway, Panama, Paraguay, Poland, Uruguay, Venezuela and Yugoslavia.
145 W. A. Schabas, *An Introduction to the International Criminal Court*, p. 6.
146 *USA Opening Statement*, p. 71.
147 I. Brownlie, *International Law and the Use of Force*, p. 163.
148 N. Nyiri, *The United Nations' Search*, p. 40.
149 *USA Opening Statement*, p. 78.
150 ibid, p. 79.
151 O. Solera, *Defining the Crime of Aggression*, p. 212.
152 Symposium, The Fifth Annual Ernst C. Stiefel Symposium 1945–1995: Critical perspectives on the Nuremberg trials and state accountability, Panel I. Telford Taylor Panel: Critical perspectives on the Nuremberg trials, *NYSchJHR* 1995, vol 12, p. 498.
153 T. Cyprian, J. Sawicki, *Ludzie i sprawy Norymbergi*, p. 470.
154 N. Nyiri, *The United Nations' Search*, p. 45.

155 G. Dean, 'Preface', p. xii.
156 O. Solera, *Defining the Crime of Aggression*, p. 212.
157 *USA Opening Statement*, p. 3.
158 ibid, p. 11.
159 ibid, p. 48.
160 O. Solera, *Defining the Crime of Aggression*, pp. 241 ff.
161 'Indictment', in *The Case Against the Nazi War Criminals*, p. 115.
162 ibid, p. 136 and pp. 205–217.
163 International Military Tribunal (Nuremberg), 'Judgment and sentences', 1 October 1946, *AJIL* 1947, vol 41, Supplement, pp. 214–216 (*IMT Judgment*).
164 F. Ryszka, *Norymberga. Prehistoria i ciąg dalszy*, p. 268.
165 N. Nyiri, *The United Nations' Search*, p. 58.
166 *IMT Judgment*, p. 186.
167 ibid, p. 216.
168 ibid, pp. 217 ff.
169 ibid, p. 218.
170 Convention (IV) respecting the Laws and Customs of War on Land and its annex: Regulations concerning the Laws and Customs of War on Land. The Hague, 18 October 1907.
171 *IMT Judgment*, pp. 218–219.
172 ibid, p. 220.
173 Y. Dinstein, *War, Aggression and Self-Defence*, p. 120.
174 M. O'Donovan, 'Criminalizing war: toward a justifiable crime of aggression', *BostColIntl&CompLRev* 2007, vol 30, p. 513; L. Gardocki, *Zarys prawa karnego międzynarodowego*, Państwowe Wydawnictwo Naukowe, Warszawa 1985, p. 54.
175 G. A. Finch, 'The Nuremberg trial and international law', pp. 31–32.
176 V. Maugham, *U.N.O. and War Crimes*, John Murray, Albemarle Street, London 1951, p. 53.
177 Cited in G. A. Finch, 'The Nuremberg trial and international law', p. 32.
178 United Nations War Crimes Commission, *History of the United Nations War Crimes Commission*, p. 91.
179 ibid, p. 129.
180 eg Roosevelt statement of 12 March 1944. See S. Horwitz, 'The Tokyo trial', *IntCon* 1950, no 465, p. 478.
181 R. H. Minear, *Victors' Justice: The Tokyo War Crimes Trial*, Princeton University Press, Princeton 1971, p. 7; C. A. Pompe, *Aggressive War*, p. 180.
182 Available at http://avalon.law.yale.edu/wwii/cairo.asp (last visited 3 June 2013).
183 S. Horwitz, 'The Tokyo trial', p. 479; C. A. Pompe, *Aggressive War*, p. 179.
184 Available at http://www.ibiblio.org/pha/policy/1945/1945-08-02a.html (last visited 3 June 2013).
185 N. Boister and R. Cryer, *The Tokyo International Military Tribunal: A Reappraisal*, Oxford University Press, Oxford 2008, p. 119.
186 S. Horwitz, 'The Tokyo trial', pp. 479–80.
187 General Orders No 1, General Headquarters Supreme Commander for the Allied Powers, 19 January 1946, U.S. Department of State Publication 2675, pp. 5–10.
188 General Orders No 20, General Headquarters Supreme Commander for the Allied Powers, 26 April 1946, U.S. Department of State Publications 2675, pp. 11–16. Text of IMTFE statute, also in B. B. Ferencz, *Defining the Crime of Aggression*, vol 1, pp. 522 ff.
189 Article 5(2)(a).
190 K. Kittichaisaree, *International Criminal Law*, Oxford University Press, Oxford 2001, p. 207.
191 Article 5(1).

192 'Excerpts', in N. Boister and R. Cryer, *The Tokyo International Military Tribunal*, p. 122.
193 See 'IMTFE judgment', in B. V. A. Röling and C. F. Rüter, *The Tokyo Judgment, The International Military Tribunal for the Far East (I.M.T.F.E.) 29 April 1946–12 November 1948*, vol 1, APA – University Press Amsterdam BV, Amsterdam 1977, p. 15 (*IMTFE Judgment*).
194 ibid, passim (see first and foremost the tribunal's comments on Japanese attacks against Great Britain, the United States, the Netherlands).
195 ibid, pp. 26–27.
196 B. V. A. Röling and C. F. Rüter, *The Tokyo Judgment*, vol 2, pp. 527 ff.
197 ibid, p. 551.
198 ibid, p. 563.
199 ibid, p. 554.
200 ibid, pp. 1059 ff.
201 ibid, vol 1, p. 490.
202 ibid, pp. 485 ff.
203 Control Council Law No 10, Punishment of Persons Guilty of War Crimes, Crimes against Peace and Against Humanity, 20 December 1945, Official Gazette of the Control Council for Germany, No 3, 31 January 1946, pp. 50–55. Also in B. B. Ferencz, *Defining the Crime of Aggression*, pp. 491 ff.
204 Article II(1)(A).
205 B. B. Ferencz, *Defining International Aggression*, vol 1, p. 46.
206 T. Taylor, 'Nuremberg trials', p. 155. See also K. J. Heller, *The Nuremberg Military Tribunals and the Origins of International Criminal Law*, Oxford University Press, Oxford 2011, p. 180.
207 See ibid, p. 247.
208 *Trials of War Criminals before the Nuernberg Military Tribunals under Control Council Law No. 10, Nuernberg October 1946–April 1949*, United States Government Printing Office, Washington 1950, vol XI, p. 485.
209 *Taylor Report*, pp. 8–9.
210 *Taylor Report*, p. 31. See also Article X, Military Government of the United States Zone, Ordinance No 7, 18 October 1946, text in *Taylor Report*, p. 286.
211 ibid, p. 9.
212 United Nations War Crimes Commission, *Law Reports of Trials of War Criminals*, His Majesty's Stationery Office, London 1947, vol 1, pp. 122 ff.
213 ibid, vol 3, pp. 101–102.
214 ibid, vol 15, pp. 28 and 40. See also *Taylor Report*, pp. 7–8.
215 *Trials of War Criminals*, vol 14, p. 319.
216 ibid, p. 321.
217 See Article 45 of the Treaty of Peace with Italy, UNTS, vol 49, pp. 3 ff; Article 6 of the Peace Treaty with Hungary, UNTS, vol 41, pp. 167 ff; Article 5 of the Peace Treaty with Bulgaria, ibid, pp. 49 ff; Article 6 of the Peace Treaty with Romania, UNTS, vol 42, pp. 33 ff, Article 9 of the Peace Treaty with Finland, UNTS, vol 48, pp. 227 ff.
218 UNTS, vol 1696, pp. 124 ff.
219 Article 2.
220 I. Brownlie, *International Law and the Use of Force*, p. 176.
221 United Nations War Crimes Commission, *Law Reports*, vol 15, pp. 32–33.
222 ibid, p. 36
223 ibid, p. 29.
224 ibid, vol 3, pp. 105–107.
225 ibid, vol 7, pp. 82 ff.
226 ibid, vol 14, pp. 152 ff.

227 'It must be agreed that war aggression is a crime and all debates as to this issue are unnecessary', judgment in the case of L. Fischer et al, in T. Cyprian and J. Sawicki, *Siedem wyroków Najwyższego Trybunału Narodowego*, Instytut Zachodni, Poznań 1962, p. 57.

228 See an extensive analysis of contemporary national legislation on the crime of aggression by Astrid Reisinger Coracini: A. Reisinger Coracini, 'Evaluating domestic legislation on the customary crime of aggression under the Rome Statute's complementarity regime', in C. Stahn and G. Sluiter (eds), *The Emerging Practice of the International Criminal Court*, Brill 2009, pp. 725 ff. See also B. Van Schaack, '*Par in parem imperium non habet.* Complementarity and the crime of aggression', *JIntCrimJust* 2012, Special Issue vol 10, pp. 134 ff.

229 Article 113, *Polish Official Gazette* 1932, no 60, item 571. As emphasised by Marian Flemming, the provision was introduced to comply with obligations arising out of the Paris Pact. M. Flemming and J. Wojciechowska, *Zbrodnie wojenne. Przestępstwa przeciwko pokojowi, państwu i obronności. Rozdział XVI, XVII, XVIII Kodeksu Karnego. Komentarz*, Wydawnictwo C.H. Beck, Warszawa 1999, pp. 41–42. It is important to note that the notion of implementing into the national legal order provisions on punishability of inciting to war came up at the International Conference on Unification of Criminal Law held in Warsaw in 1927; in 1930 in Brussels a draft of a relevant law was presented. See J. B. Herzog, *Nuremberg: un échec fructueux?*, Librairie Générale de Droit et de Jurisprudence, Paris 1975, pp. 40 ff.

230 Article 96. *Polish Official Gazette* 1944, no 6, item 27.

231 L. Gardocki, *Zarys prawa karnego międzynarodowego*, p. 115.

232 Article 1. *Polish Official Gazette* 1950, no 58, item 521.

233 Article 2.

234 Article 117. *Polish Official Gazette* 1997, no 88, item 553 with subsequent changes.

235 M. Flemming and J. Wojciechowska, *Zbrodnie wojenne*, p. 38.

236 ibid, p. 43.

237 See ch 2. Renunciation of War, Article 9: 'Aspiring sincerely to an international peace based on justice and order, the Japanese people forever renounce war as a sovereign right of the nation and the threat or use of force as means of settling international disputes. In order to accomplish the aim of the preceding paragraph, land, sea, and air forces, as well as other war potential, will never be maintained. The right of belligerency of the state will not be recognized'. Text of the Constitution available at http://www.sangiin.go.jp/eng/law/index.htm (last visited 3 June 2013).

238 Chapter III. Crimes Related to Foreign Aggression: 'Article 81. (Instigation of Foreign Aggression) A person who agrees with a foreign state and thereby causes the state to exercise armed force against Japan shall be punished by the death penalty. Article 82. (Assistance to the Enemy) A person who, when a foreign state exercises armed force against Japan, sides with the state by engaging in the military service of such state, or otherwise affords military advantage to such state, shall be punished by the death penalty or imprisonment with work either for life or for a definite term of not less than 2 years. Articles 83, 84, 85 and 86 deleted. Article 87. (Attempts) An Attempt of any of the crimes proscribed under Articles 81 and 82 shall be punished. Article 88. (Preparations; Plots) A person who prepares for or plots any of the crimes proscribed under Articles 81 and 82 shall be punished by imprisonment with work for not less than 1 year but not more than 10 years. Article 89. Deleted'. Text of the code available at http://www.cas.go.jp/jp/seisaku/hourei/data/PC.pdf (last visited 3 June 2013).

239 Article 93 (Preparations or Plots for Private War) 'A person who prepares or plots to wage war privately upon a foreign state shall be punished by imprisonment

without work for not less than 3 months but not more than 5 years; provided, however, that the person who surrenders him/herself shall be exculpated'.

240 Article 94. (Violations of Neutrality Orders) 'A person who violates an order of neutrality in a war between foreign states shall be punished by imprisonment without work for not more than 3 years or a fine of not more than 500,000 yen'.

241 Grundgesetz für die Bundesrepublik Deutschland of 23 May 1949, available at http://www.bundestag.de/dokumente/rechtsgrundlagen/grundgesetz/index.html; English translation available at http://www.constitution.org/cons/germany.txt (last visited 3 June 2013).

242 Article 26. For more on German regulation, see M. Hummrich, *Der völkerrechtliche Straftatbestand der Aggression, Historische Entwicklung, Geltung und Definition im Hinblick auf das Statut des Internationalen Strafgerichtschofes*, Nomos Verlagsgesellschaft, Baden-Baden 2001, pp. 85 ff; C. Björn, *Die Strafbarkeit des Angriffskrieges und die Funktion seiner Strafbarkeit*, Duncker & Humblot, Berlin 2005.

243 Section 80 Preparation of a war of aggression: 'Whosoever prepares a war of aggression (Article 26(1) of the Basic Law) in which the Federal Republic of Germany is meant to participate and creates a danger of war for the Federal Republic of Germany, shall be liable to imprisonment for life or for not less than ten years'. Bundesgesetzblatt no 75, 19 November 1998, pp. 3322 ff. Available at http://www.bgbl.de (last visited 3 June 2013). English translation of German penal code, see http://legislationline.org/documents/section/criminal-codes (last visited 3 June 2013).

244 Section 80a Incitement to a war of aggression: 'Whosoever publicly incites to a war of aggression (section 80) in a meeting or through the dissemination of written materials (section 11(3)) within the Federal Republic of Germany shall be liable to imprisonment from three months to five years'.

245 C. Björn, *Die Strafbarkeit des Angriffskrieges und die Funktion seiner Strafbarkeit*, Duncker & Humblot, Berlin 2005, pp. 87–88. Interestingly, in the case of *R v Jones et al* [2006] UKHL 16 that was heard by the British House of Lords, the following observation was also made: 'the making of war and peace and the disposition of the armed forces has always been regarded as a discretionary power of the Crown into the exercise of which the courts will not enquire' (para 65). See also B. Van Schaack, '*Par in parem imperium non habet*', pp. 144–45.

246 Gesetz zur Einführung des Völkerstrafgesetzbuches, Bundesgesetzblatt no 42, 29 June 2002, pp. 2254 ff. Available at www.bgbl.de (last visited 3 June 2013).

247 United Nations War Crimes Commission, *History of the United Nations War Crimes Commission*, pp. 185–86.

248 ibid, p. 186.

249 A/CN.4/22, p. 188.

250 ibid.

251 A/C.6/69, 15 November 1946. See ibid.

252 GA Resolution no 95 of 11 December 1946.

253 See A/CN.4/22, p. 188.

254 United Nations, General Assembly, International Law Commission, *The Charter and Judgment of the Nürnberg Tribunal – History and Analysis: Memorandum submitted by the Secretary-General*, A/CN.4/5, pp. 15–16.

255 GA Resolution no 177 of 21 November 1947.

256 *YbkIntLC* 1949, pp. 183 ff.

257 ibid, pp. 196–97.

258 It is noteworthy that Jackson in his opening speech at the Nuremberg trial insisted that the objective of the law which serves as the basis of the prosecution of the Germans was to condemn aggression no matter who commits it. *USA*

Opening Statement, p. 88. See also M. Lippmann, 'The history, development, and decline of crimes against peace', p. 992.

259 GA Resolution no 488 of 12 December 1950.

260 See critical comments of states on ILC proposition of formulating Nuremberg principles, A/CN/4/45 and Add 1 and 2, in *YbkIntLC* 1951, vol 2, pp. 104 ff.

261 *Replies from Governments to Questionnaires of the International Law Commission*, A/CN.4/19, Add 1 and 2, in *YbkIntLC* 1950, vol 2, pp. 249 ff.

262 *Draft Code of Offences Against the Peace and Security of Mankind – Report by J. Spiropoulos, Special Rapporteur*, A/CN.4/25, in ibid, p. 261.

263 O. Solera, *Defining the Crime of Aggression*, p. 255.

264 A/CN.4/25, p. 261. Compare with Pella's proposition in *Mémorandum présenté par le Secrétariat*, A/CN.4/39, in *YbkIntLC* 1950, vol 2, pp. 278 ff.

265 O. Solera, *Defining the Crime of Aggression*, p. 260.

266 In the draft code, among international crimes, genocide, crimes against humanity and war crimes were also listed, points 10–12.

267 O. Solera, *Defining the Crime of Aggression*, pp. 262–63.

268 ibid, p. 262.

269 GA Resolutions no 897 of 4 December 1954 and no 1186 of 11 December 1957.

270 GA Resolutions no 33/97 of 16 December 1978 and no 35/49 of 4 December 1980.

271 GA Resolution nos 36/106 of 10 December 1981.

272 O. Solera, *Defining the Crime of Aggression*, pp. 283 ff.

273 Article 5.

274 A. L. Paulus, 'Peace through justice? The future of the crime of aggression in a time of crisis', *WayneLRev* 2004, vol 50, p. 17.

275 O. Solera, *Defining the Crime of Aggression*, p. 286.

276 *Draft Code of Crimes against the Peace and Security of Mankind. Titles and Texts of Articles Adopted by the Drafting Committee: Parts One and Two; Articles 1–26*, A/CN.4/L.459 and Corr 1 and Add 1, in *YbkIntLC* 1991, vol 1, pp. 187 ff.

277 Draft Article 17(2): 'Intervention in the internal or external affairs of a State consists of fomenting [armed] subversive or terrorist activities or by organizing, assisting or financing such activities, or supplying arms for the purpose of such activities, thereby [seriously] undermining the free exercise by that State of its sovereign rights'.

278 Draft Article 18 prohibited 'to establish or maintain by force, colonial domination or any other form of alien domination contrary to the right of peoples to self-determination as enshrined in the Charter of the United Nations'. Apart from the above mentioned crimes, in the 1991 draft the following crimes were also listed: genocide, apartheid, systematic or mass violations of human rights, serious war crimes, recruitment, use, financing and training of mercenaries, international terrorism, illicit traffic in narcotic drugs, wilful and severe damage to the environment.

279 Article 15.

280 Article 16. The greatest opponents to include threat of aggression in the code were Australia, the Netherlands, Paraguay, Switzerland, the United Kingdom and the United States. L. S. Sunga, *The Emerging System of International Criminal Law. Developments in Codification and Implementation*, Kluwer Law International, The Hague 1997, pp. 62–63.

281 B. B. Ferencz, 'An international criminal code and court: where they stand and where they're going', *ColJTransL* 1992, vol 30, p. 381. See *Comments and observations received from Governments*, A/CN.4/448 and Add 1, in *YbkIntLC* 1993, vol 2, pp. 62 ff.

282 *Draft Code of Crimes Against Peace and Security of Mankind*, in *YbkIntLC* 1996, vol 2, Part 2, pp. 17–56 (1996 Draft CCPSH).

283 Article 2(2).
284 Article 16.
285 GA Resolution no 51/160.
286 *YbkIntL* 1996, vol 2, p. 43.
287 ICTY, Trial Judgment, *Prosecutor v Furundzija* (IT-95-17/1-T), 10 December 1998, para 227.
288 A/CN.4/5, p. 24.
289 ibid, p. 28.
290 Article VI, UNTS, vol 78, pp. 277 ff.
291 GA Resolution no 260 of 9 December1948.
292 *Report on the Question of International Criminal Jurisdiction by Ricardo J. Alfaro, Special Rapporteur*, A/CN.4/15 and Corr 1, in *YbkIntLC* 1950, vol 2, p. 16.
293 ibid, p. 17.
294 *Report on the Question of International Criminal Jurisdiction by Emil Sandström, Special Rapporteur*, A/CN.4/20, in ibid, p. 22.
295 ibid.
296 GA Resolution no 489.
297 GAOR, 7th session, *Report of the Committee on International Criminal Jurisdiction*, 1–31 August 1951, A/2136, 1952, pp. 21–25.
298 GAOR, 9th session, *Report of the Committee on International Criminal Jurisdiction*, 27 July–20 August 1953, A/2645, 1954, p. 21.
299 GAOR, 7th session, *Comments Received from Governments Regarding the Report of the Committee on International Criminal Jurisdiction*, A/2186 and Add 1, 1952.
300 M. C. Bassiouni, 'From Versailles to Rwanda in seventy-five years: the need to establish a permanent international criminal court', *HarvHRJ* 1997, vol 10, p. 51.
301 GA Resolution no 898.
302 *YbkIntLC* 1983, vol 2, Part 2, p. 16.
303 GA Resolution no 44/39. See also GA Resolutions no 45/41 of 28 November 1990, no 46/54 of 9 December 1991, 47/33 of 25 November 1992, no 48/31 of 9 December 1993.
304 *YbkIntLC* 1992, vol 2, Part 2, pp. 58 ff.
305 *YbkIntLC* 1993, vol 2, Part 2, pp. 100 ff.
306 *YbkIntLC* 1994, vol 2, Part 2, pp. 20 ff.
307 ibid, p. 26.
308 GA Resolution no 49/53.
309 GAOR, 50th session, *Report of the Ad Hoc Committee on the Establishment of an International Criminal Court*, A/50/22, 1995. See O. Solera, *Defining the Crime of Aggression*, p. 337.
310 GA Resolution no 50/46.
311 O. Solera, *Defining the Crime of Aggression*, p. 341.
312 On the mentioned proposals, see R. Kherad, *La question de la définition du crime d'agression dans le statut de Rome. Entre pouvoir politique du Conseil de securité et compétence judiciaire de la Cour pénale internationale*, RGDIP 2005, no 2, pp. 349 ff.
313 *Decisions made by the Preparatory Committee at its Session held from 11 to 21 February 1997, Annex 1, Report of the Working Group at the Definition of Crimes*, A/AC.249/1997/L.5, 12 March 1997, pp. 13–14, available at http://www.iccnow.org/documents/DecisionsTaken11to21Feb97.pdf (last visited 3 June 2013). See also O. Solera, *Defining the Crime of Aggression*, pp. 350 ff.
314 O. Solera, *Defining the Crime of Aggression*, p. 353.
315 A/CONF.183/2/Add 1, in *Official Records of the United Nations Diplomatic Conference of Plenipotentiaries on the Establishment of an International Criminal Court (Summary Records of the Plenary Meetings and of the Meetings of the Committee of the Whole)*, vol 3, United Nations, New York 2002, pp. 14–15.

316 ibid, pp. 12–14.
317 M. C. Bassiouni, 'Observations concerning the 1997–1998 Preparatory Committee's Work', *DenvJIntL&Pol* 1997, vol 25, para 33.
318 GA Resolution no 51/207.
319 See O. Solera, *Defining the Crime of Aggression*, pp. 356 ff; K. Kittichaisaree, *International Criminal Law*, pp. 208–209.
320 O. Solera, *Defining the Crime of Aggression*, p. 357.
321 ibid, p. 358, M. H. Aransjani, 'The Rome Statute of the International Criminal Court', *AJIL* 1999, vol 93, p. 30.
322 O. Solera, *Defining the Crime of Aggression*, p. 363.
323 A/CONF.183/C.1/L.53, in *Official Records*, vol 3, p. 204.
324 O. Solera, *Defining the Crime of Aggression*, p. 369 (table).
325 ibid, p. 368.
326 A/CONF.183/C.1/L.59, in *Official Records*, vol 3, p. 212.
327 See Resolution F, A/CONF.183/C.1/L.75, in *Official Records*, vol 1, pp. 72–73.
328 Rome Statute of the International Criminal Court of 17 July 1998, UNTS, vol 2187, pp. 3 ff.
329 O. Triffterer (ed.), *Commentary on the Rome Statute of the International Criminal Court. Observers, Notes. Article by Article*, Nomos Verlaagesellschaft, Baden Baden 1999, pp. 105–106.
330 S. A. Fernández de Gurmendi, 'The Working Group on Aggression at the Preparatory Commission for the International Criminal Court', *FordhIntLJ* 2002, vol 25, p. 589. M. Schuster, 'The Rome Statute and the crime of aggression: a gordian knot in search of a sword', *CrimLF* 2003, vol 14, p. 1.
331 A. R. Lacanilao, 'The International Criminal Court in the balance: should the Security Council be given a role in the crime of aggression?', *Eyes on the ICC* 2004, vol 1, p. 106.
332 O. Triffterer (ed.), *Commentary on the Rome Statute*, p. 106. A. Cassese, *International Criminal Law*, Oxford University Press, Oxford 2003, p. 110.
333 M. Aziz Shukri, 'Will aggressors ever be tried before the ICC, in M. Politi and G. Nesi, *The International Criminal Court*, p. 37.
334 See propositions of Bahrain, Iraq, Lebanon, Lybia, Oman, Sudan, Syria and Yemen, PCNICC/1999/DP.11; Russian proposition, PCNICC/1999/DP.12; German proposition PCNICC/1999/DP.13, Colombian proposition, PCNICC/2000/WGCA/DP.1, Greece's and Portugal's proposition, PCNICC/1999/WGCA/DP.1. Available at http://untreaty.un.org/cod/icc/documents/aggression/aggressiondocs.htm (last visited 3 June 2013).
335 PCNICC/1999/WGCA/RT.1; see also PCNICC/1999/INF/2.
336 O. Solera, *Defining the Crime of Aggression*, p. 383.
337 See Italian oral suggestions of 13 March 2000, PCNICC/2000/WGCA/DP.3 and Colombia-Italy's proposition of the same day, PCNICC/2000/WGCA/DP.2.
338 PCNICC/2000/WGCA/RT.1. See also PCNICC/2001/WGCA/DP.2/Add 1.
339 See German proposition, PCNICC/2000/WGCA/DP.4; proposition of Greece and Portugal, PCNICC/2000/WGCA/DP.5; proposition of Bosnia and Herzegovina, New Zealand, Romania, PCNICC/2001/WGCA/DP.1 and PCNICC/2001/WGCA/DP.2; proposition of Guatemala, PCNICC/2001/WGCA/DP.3; Dutch proposition, PCNICC/2002/WGCA/DP.1; Colombian proposition, PCNICC/2002/WGCA/DP.3; proposition of Belgium, Cambodia, Sierra Leone and Thailand, PCNICC/2002/WGCA/DP.5.
340 PCNICC/2002/WGCA/RT.1 and Rev.1 and Rev.2.
341 PCNICC/2002/WGCA/L.1.
342 See Samoa's proposition, PCNICC/2002/WGCA/DP.2. See also PCNICC/2002/WGCA/RT.1.

343 ASP resolution, *Continuity of Work in Respect of the Crime of Aggression* ICC-ASP/1/Res 1, 9 September 2002.
344 ICC-ASP/4/Res 4, para 37.
345 See ICC-ASP/2/SWGCA/DP.1 and ICC-ASP/1/L.4.
346 O. Solera, *Defining the Crime of Aggression*, pp. 397–98.
347 See reports from informal meetings of SWGCA ICC-ASP/3/SWGCA/INF.1, ICC-ASP/4/32, Annex II, ICC-ASP/5/SWGCA/INF.1, ICC-ASP/6/SWGCA/INF.1, ICC-ASP/8/INF.2.
348 See reports from informal meetings of SWGCA, ICC-ASP/4/SWGCA/1, ICC-ASP/5/SWGCA/1, ICC-ASP/5/35, ICC-ASP/6/SWGCA/1, ICC-ASP/6/20/Add 1, Annex II , ICC-ASP/7/20, Annex III, ICC-ASP/7/20/Add 1, Annex II, and discussion papers ICC-ASP/4/32, Annex B, C, D, ICC-ASP/5/SWGCA/2, ICC-ASP/6/SWGCA/2, ICC-ASP/7/SWGCA/INF.1.
349 See documents ICC-ASP/6/SWGCA/INF.1, Annex III, IV.
350 ICC-ASP/7/20/Add 1, Appendix III, para 3.
351 ICC-ASP/7/20/Add 1, Appendix I, Annex Draft Amendments to the Rome Statute of the International Criminal Court on the Crime of Aggression.
352 See non-papers of 28 May 2009 (non-paper by the chairman on the elements of crimes, non-paper by the chairman on the conditions for the exercise of jurisdiction), ICC/ASP/8/INF.2, Annex I and II.
353 'The central topic in the review of the Statute, as mandated by the Rome Conference, is the crime of aggression. This crime is already contained in the Rome Statute, and we have therefore recognized it as one of the most serious crimes under international law. We have prepared as diligently as we could for the discussions here in Kampala on the possible inclusion of provisions in the Rome Statute that would define the crime and allow the Court to exercise its jurisdiction over this crime. The legal groundwork is in place, and the large task ahead of us consists of finding a solution, with the willingness to compromise from all of you, that assembles the largest possible political support. I appeal to you to approach these discussions with an open mind and with awareness of the historical task before you." Opening remarks by the president of the assembly, Ambassador Christian Wenaweser, 30 May 2012, available at http://www.icc-cpi.int (last visited 3 June 2013). Significantly, the speeches of Secretary General of the United Nations, Ban Ki-moon, President of the International Criminal Court, Sang-Hyun Song, Prosecutor of the ICC, Luis Moreno-Ocambo or former Secretary-General of the United Nations, Kofi Annan fail to mention the crime of aggression. Only the statement by President of the Republic of Uganda, Yoweri Kaguta Museveni uses similar words, pertaining however not to the crime of aggression, but rather a 'war of aggression' which is the opposite of a 'just war' (Speech of 31 May 2012). NGOs were also rather disinterested in the topic of the crime of aggression.
354 SWGCA held eight meetings during the review conference on 1, 4, and 7–9 June 2010.
355 RC/WGCA/3, 6 June 2010 and RC/11, Annex III, 10 June 2010, para 4. Roger S. Clark notes, however, that 'not everyone at the Working Group was entirely happy with everything'. See R. S. Clark, 'Negotiating provisions defining the crime of aggression, its elements and the conditions for ICC exercise of jurisdiction over it, *EJIL* 2010, vol 20, p. 1104.
356 In Article 9(1) (concerning Elements of Crimes) and in the *chapeau* of Article 20(3) the problem pertained solely to adding a reference to the crime of aggression. In Article 25(3) of the statute, it was suggested that the following wording should be added, in line with the Special Working Group's definition of the

crime of aggression: 'In respect of the crime of aggression, the provisions of this article shall apply only to persons in a position effectively to exercise control over or to direct the political or military action of a State'.

357 RC/11, para 16.

358 ibid, para 5.

359 See RC/11, Attachment 1 and Conference Room Paper on the crime of aggression, RC/WGCA/1/Rev.1, 6 June 2010 and RC/WGCA/1/Rev.2, 10 June 2010.

360 The option (included in the earlier version from the negotiations in the Special Working Group, RC/WGCA/1, 25 May 2010) to approach the General Assembly or the International Court of Justice, or simply for the prosecutor to proceed with the investigation without any need to approach any authorities for the determination of an act of aggression, was thus rejected.

361 RC/11, para 12 ff. See also the table in J. Trahan, 'The Rome Statute's amendments on the crime of aggression: negotiations at the Kampala Review Conference', *ICLR* 2011, vol 11, p. 63.

362 The United States is not a party to the statute. However, one of the goals of the conference was to secure general agreement, ie not only agreement among the states parties to the statute but also non-party states. Consequently, the non-party states had a significant impact on the wording of the amendments as they were finally adopted. See J. Van der Vyver, 'Prosecuting the crime of aggression in the International Criminal Court', *UMiamiNat'lSec&ArmedConflLawRev* 2010–2011, vol 1, p. 6; M. Politi, 'The ICC and the crime of aggression: a dream that came through and the reality ahead', *JIntCrimJust* 2012, Special Issue, vol 10, p. 269.

363 J. Trahan, 'The Rome Statute's amendments on the crime of aggression', pp. 67–68.

364 See RC/7 and RC/8, 10 June 2010.

365 The wording of the American proposal cited in J. Trahan, 'The Rome Statute's amendments on the crime of aggression', pp. 73–74.

366 ibid, pp. 77–78.

367 RC/Res 6 of 11 June 2010.

368 Review Conference of the Rome Statute of the International Criminal Court, Kampala 31 May–11 June 2010, Official Records, RC/9/11,p. 126.

369 K. J. Heller, 'The uncertain legal status of the aggression understandings, *JIntCrimJust* 2012, vol 10 pp. 229 ff.

370 C. Kress and L. von Holtzendorff, 'The Kampala compromise on the crime of aggression', *JIntCrimJust* 2010, vol 8, p. 1203.

371 Consequently, it is the entire group of judges assigned to the Pre-Trial Division of the ICC who will bear responsibility, and not only the three judges of any Pre-Trial Chamber. See M. Politi, 'The ICC and the crime of aggression', pp. 274–75.

372 RC/WGCA/1/Rev.2.

373 C. Wenaweser, 'Reaching the Kampala compromise on aggression: the chair's perspective', *LeidenJIntL* 2010, vol 23, p. 886.

374 See Kampala Diary of 8 June 2010 available at http://iccreviewconference.blogspot.com/ (last visited 3 June 2013).

375 C. Wenaweser, 'Reaching the Kampala compromise on aggression', p. 885.

376 ibid.

377 See the president' non-paper of 10 June 2010, reprinted in J. Trahan, 'The Rome Statute's amendments on the crime of aggression', p. 102. Compare RC/WGCA/2, 25 May 2010 with RC/10 and RC/DC/3, 11 June 2010.

378 The seven-year period is a reference to Article 123(1) and Article 124 of the statute of the International Criminal Court.

379 C. Wenaweser, 'Reaching the Kampala compromise on aggression', p. 887. J. Van der Vyver points out that the option to submit an opt-out declaration constitutes in its essence an exception to, or a deviation from, the rule contained in Article 120 of the ICC's statute. Article 120 specifies a prohibition on submitting reservations to the statute (in precise terms, Van der Vyver notes that the opt-out provisions are 'seemingly in conflict with the provision in the ICC statute that precludes States from ratifying the Statute subject to reservation'). J. Van der Vyver, 'Prosecuting the crime of aggression in the International Criminal Court', p. 44.

380 Niels Blokker and Claus Kress comment on the particularly high dramatic tension of the final hours: N. Blokker and C. Kress, A consensus agreement on the crime of aggression: impressions from Kampala', *LeidenJIntLaw* 2010, vol 23, p. 890; C. Kress and L. Von Holtzendorff, 'The Kampala compromise on the crime of aggression', *JICJ* 2010, vol 8, pp. 1179–80.

381 See Official Records RC/9/11, p. 121. See also C. Kress and L. von Holtzendorff, 'The Kampala compromise on the crime of aggression', p. 1180.

382 D. M. Ferencz compares the solution adopted in Kampala to a situation where a doctor puts a patient in a medically induced coma in order to save the patient's life. D. M. Ferencz, 'The crime of aggression: some personal reflections on Kampala', *LeidenJIntLaw* 2010, vol 23, p. 907.

383 J. Trahan, 'The Rome Statute's amendments on the crime of aggression', p. 87.

384 See Official Records RC/9/11, pp. 122 ff.

385 L. S. Sunga, *The Emerging System of International Criminal Law*, p. 44.

386 N. Nyiri, *The United Nations' Search*, p. 57.

387 R. H. Minear, *Victors' Justice*, p. 58.

388 J. N. Boeving, 'Aggression, international law, and the ICC: an argument for the withdrawal of aggression from the Rome Statute', *ColJTransL* 2005, vol 43, p. 559.

389 W. Czapliński, *Skutki prawne nielegalnego*, p. 199.

390 SC Resolutions no 808 of 22 February 1993 and no 827 of 25 May 1993.

391 SC Resolution no 955 of 8 November 1994.

392 C. Tomuschat, 'Crimes against peace and security of mankind and the recalcitrant third state', in Y. Dinstein and M. Tabory, *War Crimes in International Law*, Martinus Nijhoff Publishers, The Hague 1996, p. 53.

393 L. S. Sunga, *The Emerging System of International Criminal Law*, p. 49; H. S. Levie, 'The Statute of the International Tribunal for the Former Yugoslavia: a comparison with the past and a look at the future', *SyrJIntL&Com* 1995, vol 21, p. 7; M. Lippmann, 'The history, development, and decline of crimes against peace', pp. 1054–55.

394 A. Cassese, *International Criminal Law*, p. 110.

395 B. B. Ferencz, 'The crime of aggression', in B. B. Ferencz, *Substantive and Procedural Aspects of International Criminal Law. The Experience of International and National Courts, Commentary*, vol 1, Kluwer Law International, The Hague 2000, p. 54.

396 M. Schuster, 'The Rome Statute and the crime of aggression', p. 18.

397 L. Caflisch, 'Réflexions sur la création d'une cour criminelle internationale', in J. Makarczyk (ed.), *Theory of International Law at the Threshold of the 21st Century: Essays in Honour of Krzysztof Skubiszewski*, Kluwer Law International, The Hague 1996, p. 880.

398 T. Meron, 'Defining aggression for the International Criminal Court', *SuffTransLRev* 2001, vol 25, p. 7.

399 *USA Opening Statement*, pp. 77–78.

400 See *Jackson Report*, p. 187, and R. Jackson, 'Foreword', in S. Glueck, *The Nuremberg Trial and Aggressive War*, p. x.

401 F. B. Schick, 'The Nuremberg trial and the international law of the future', *AJIL* 1947, vol 41, p. 779.
402 A. L. Paulus, 'Peace through justice?', p. 6.
403 L. May, *Aggression and Crimes against Peace*, Cambridge University Press, Cambridge 2008, p. 22.
404 GAOR 51st session, *Report of the International Law Commission*, A/51/10, 1996.
405 J. F. Murphy, 'Crime against peace at the Nuremberg trial', in G. Ginsburgs and V. N. Kudriavtsev (eds), *The Nuremberg Trial and International Law*, Martinus Nijhoff, Dordrecht 1990, p. 153.
406 L. N. Sadat, *The International Criminal Court and the Transformation of International Law: Justice for New Millennium*, Transnational Publishers, Ardsley 2002, p. 138.

4 Trials of individuals charged with the crime of aggression

1 G. S. Maridakis, 'Un précedent du procès de Nuremberg tiré de l'histoire de la Grèce ancienne', *RHDI* Juillet–Décembre 1952, 5ème année.
2 C. A. Pompe, *Aggressive War*, pp. 118–119.
3 R. K. Woetzel and R. K. Woetzel, *The Nuremberg Trials in International Law*, Stevens & Sons Limited, London 1960, pp. 124–25.
4 M. Królikowski, P. Wiliński and J. Izydorczyk, *Podstawy prawa karnego międzynarodowego*, Oficyna Wolters Kluwer Business, Warszawa 2008, p. 52.
5 See further C. A. Pompe, *Aggressive War*, pp. 137 ff.
6 See eg G and Michałowska, 'Odpowiedzialność jednostki w prawie międzynarodowym', *Stosunki Międzynarodowe* 2000, no 3–4, p. 26; F. Przetacznik, *The Philosophical and Legal Concept of War*, The Edwin Mellen Press, Lewiston 1994, p. 365; J. M. Gulak, *Przypadek Napoleona jako precedens skazania za zbrodnię przeciwko pokojowi. Wkład Profesora Mariana Iwanejko w zakresie kształtowania się poglądu odpowiedzialności karnej jednostki za wywołanie wojny*, in *Aktualne problemy prawa międzynarodowego we współczesnym świecie. Księga pamiątkowa poświęcona pamięci Profesora Mariana Iwanejko. Materiały z ogólnopolskiej konferencji zorganizowanej przez Katedrę Prawa międzynarodowego i Porównawczego Akademii Ekonomicznej w Krakowie (Kraków, 27–28 września 1995)*, Akademia Ekonomiczna w Krakowie, Kraków 1995; S. Glueck, *The Nuernberg Trial and Aggressive War*, in G. Mettraux, *Perspectives on the Nuremberg Trial*, Oxford University Press, Oxford 2008, pp. 74–75.
7 See F. M. Anderson, *The Constitutions and Other Select Documents Illustrative of the History of France 1789–1901*, The H. W. Wilson Company, Minneapolis 1904, pp. 449 ff; see also M. Iwanejko, 'Przypadek Napoleona jako precedens skazania za zbrodnię przeciwko pokojowi', *Kultura i Społeczeństwo* 1972, no 3, pp. 64–65.
8 ibid, p. 468.
9 C. A. Pompe, *Aggressive War*, p. 150.
10 G. Michałowska, 'Odpowiedzialność jednostki w prawie międzynarodowym', p. 26.
11 M. Iwanejko, 'Przypadek Napoleona jako precedens skazania za zbrodnię przeciwko pokojowi', p. 60.
12 L. Gardocki, *Zarys prawa karnego międzynarodowego*, Państwowe Wydawnictwo Naukowe, Warszawa 1985, p. 28.
13 T. Cyprian and J. Sawicki, *Prawo norymberskie, Bilans i perspektywy*, Wydawnictwo Eugeniusza Kuthana, Warszawa 1948, p. 232.
14 M. N. Shaw, *International Law*, p. 159.
15 J. F. Willis, *Prologue to Nuremberg: The Punishment of War Criminals of the First World War*, Duke University, Xerox University Microfilms, 1976, p. 81.
16 M. C. Bassiouni, *World War I*, p. 268.

17 Article 227.
18 J. F. Willis, *Prologue to Nuremberg*, p. 152.
19 ibid, p. 151 and also *JDI* (Période de la guerre 1914–1919) 1919, vol 46, pp. 160–62.
20 J. F. Willis, *Prologue to Nuremberg*, p. 161.
21 ibid, p. 215.
22 F. Ryszka, *Norymberga. Prehistoria i ciąg dalszy*, Czytelnik, Warszawa 1982, p. 60, T. Cyprian and J. Sawicki, *Ludzie i sprawy Norymbergii*, Wydawnictwo Poznańskie, Poznań 1967, p. 23.
23 For a discussion of Dutch law, see W. Jellinek, 'L'ex-Empereur d'Allemagne Guillaume II en Hollande', *JDI* (Période de la guerre 1914–1919) 1919, vol 46, p. 167 and D. Simons, 'L'Extradition de l'ex-Empereur d'Allemagne et la Hollande', *JDI* (Période de la guerre 1914–1919) 1919, tome 46, pp. 954 ff.
24 See T. Cyprian and J. Sawicki, *Ludzie i sprawy Norymbergii*, pp. 23–24; T. Cyprian and J. Sawicki, *Prawo norymberskie, Bilans i perspektywy*, p. 18; L. Hankey, *Politics, Trials and Errors*, Pen in Hand, Oxford 1950, pp. 5 ff.
25 M. C. Bassiouni, *World War I*, p. 280, F. Ryszka, *Norymberga. Prehistoria i ciąg dalszy*, pp. 60–61, P. Wilson, *Aggression, Crime and International Security*, p. 30.
26 ibid.
27 E. Davidson, *The Trial of the Germans. An Account of the twenty-two defendants before the International Military Tribunal at Nuremberg*, The Macmillan Company, New York 1966, p. 4. See also K. Sellars, 'Delegitimising aggression', p. 16.
28 J. F. Willis, *Prologue to Nuremberg*, p. 221; M. C. Bassiouni, *World War I*, pp. 248 and 272.
29 T. Cyprian and J. Sawicki, *Ludzie i sprawy Norymbergii*, p. 26.
30 G. J. Bass, *Stay the Hand of the Vengeance - The Politics of War Crimes Tribunals*, Princeton University Press, Princeton 2002, p. 87.
31 J. F. Willis, *Prologue to Nuremberg*, p. 341.
32 ibid, p. 342.
33 ibid, p. 343.
34 ibid, p. 344.
35 *Trials of War Criminals*, vol 14, p. 321.
36 *IMT Judgment*, p. 173. For the minutes of the proceedings before the Tribunals, see International Military Tribunal, *Trial of the Major War Criminals before the International Military Tribunal, Nuremberg 14 November 1945–10 October 1946*, 42 vol, Nuremberg 1947–1949.
37 For biographical information on the judges, see eg P. M. Wald, 'Running the trial of the century: the Nuremberg legacy', in *Symposium, The Nuremberg Trials: A Reappraisal and Their Legacy*, *CardozoLRev* 2006, vol 27, pp. 1560 ff.
38 The British expectation was that the trial would last no longer than three weeks. W. R. Harris, *Tyranny on Trial*, p. 14.
39 *Jackson Report*, p. 183.
40 Charges were also brought against the Reich's cabinet (Die Reichsregierung), the leadership corps of the NSDAP (Das Korps der Politischen Leiter der Nationalsozialistischen Deutschen Arbeiterpartei), the secret state police, ie the Gestapo (Die Geheime Staatspolizei), SA (Die Sturmabteilungen der NSDAP), SD (Sicherheitsdienst), SS (Die Schutzstaffeln der Nationalsozialistischen Deutschen Arbeiterpartei), and the General Staff and High Command of the German armed forces. However, the responsibility of these organisations falls beyond the scope of this book.
41 *IMT Judgment*, p. 173.
42 'Indictment', in *The Case Against the Nazi War Criminals*, p. 115.
43 F. Biddle, 'Le procès de Nuremberg', *RIDP* 1948, no 1, p. 14.
44 'Indictment', pp. 117 ff.

45 Notably, neither the invasion against France in May 1940 nor the bombing of Great Britain were mentioned.
46 'Indictment', pp. 135 ff.
47 ibid, pp. 137 ff.
48 *IMT Judgment*, p. 173.
49 ibid, p. 175.
50 ibid, pp. 177 ff.
51 ibid, p. 184.
52 ibid, p. 185.
53 ibid, p. 187.
54 The International Military Tribunal assigned particular significance to the summit meetings on 5 November 1937, 23 May 1939, 22 August 1939 and of 23 November 1939. ibid, pp. 188 ff.
55 ibid, p. 222.
56 ibid, pp. 222–24.
57 ibid, p. 222.
58 T. Taylor, *Nuremberg Trials*, p. 151.
59 See *IMT Judgment*, pp. 272–73.
60 ibid, p. 331.
61 ibid, pp. 275–77.
62 ibid, p. 331.
63 *Nazi Conspiracy and Aggression*, Opinion and Judgment, Office of United States, Chief of Counsel for Prosecution of Axis Criminality, United States Government Printing Office, Washington 1947, p. 178.
64 *IMT Judgment*, pp. 278–79.
65 ibid, p. 332.
66 Where a defendant was sentenced to death by the International Military Tribunal, all of the executions were carried out on 16 October 1946.
67 *IMT Judgment*, pp. 286–87.
68 ibid, p. 332.
69 ibid, pp. 306–308.
70 ibid, p. 332.
71 ibid, pp. 314–315.
72 ibid, p. 332.
73 ibid, pp. 324–25.
74 Judgment of the International Military Tribunal against Frick with regard to the crime against peace, ibid, pp. 291–92.
75 ibid, p. 332.
76 ibid, pp. 296–97.
77 ibid, p. 332.
78 ibid, pp. 302–303.
79 ibid, p. 332.
80 ibid, pp. 319–20.
81 ibid, p. 332.
82 ibid, pp. 299–302.
83 *Nazi Conspiracy*, Opinion and Judgment, pp. 166 ff.
84 See Jackson's words at the meeting of main prosecutors on 5 April 1946, minutes of meeting, in *Taylor Report*, p. 270.
85 T. Taylor, *Nuremberg Trials*, p. 152.
86 *IMT Judgment*, pp. 316–318.
87 *Nazi Conspiracy*, Opinion and Judgment, pp. 172 ff.
88 *IMT Judgment*, p. 311.
89 ibid, p. 321.

90 T. Taylor, *Nuremberg Trials*, p. 152.
91 *IMT Judgment*, pp. 313 and 324 respectively.
92 ibid, p. 332.
93 ibid.
94 ibid, pp. 283–84.
95 ibid, p. 289.
96 ibid, p. 294.
97 ibid, pp. 286, 291, 296 respectively.
98 ibid, p. 323.
99 ibid, pp. 309–310.
100 T. Taylor, *Nuremberg Trials*, p. 153.
101 *IMT Judgment*, p. 311.
102 ibid, p. 323.
103 ibid, pp. 327–28.
104 *Nazi Conspiracy*, Opinion and Judgment, p. 175.
105 T. Taylor, *Nuremberg Trials*, p. 153.
106 *IMT Judgment*, ibid, p. 329.
107 ibid, p. 331.
108 ibid, p. 332.
109 *IMTFE Judgment*, p. 22.
110 Judge Higgins was convinced that the whole trial would last up to six months. When he realised that his assumptions were wrong, he resigned and returned to the United States to recommence his duties as justice of the Massachusetts Superior Court. For further information on the circumstances of nomination and resignation of Judge Higgins, see Y. Takatori, 'The forgotten judge at the Tokyo war crimes trial', *Massachusetts Historical Review* 2008, vol 10, pp. 115–41.
111 *IMTFE Judgment*, p. 20.
112 ibid, pp. 53 ff.
113 See S. Horwitz, 'The Tokyo trial', pp. 495–96.
114 Many authors have expressed their doubts as to whether Okawa truly was insane; he may have been simulating in order to escape responsibility. See A. C. Brackman, *The Other Nuremberg. The Untold Story of the Tokyo War Crimes Trial*, William Morrow and Company, Inc., New York 1987, pp. 101–5, B. V. A. Röling, A. Cassese, *The Tokyo Trial and Beyond. Reflections of a Peacemonger*, Polity Press, Cambridge 1993, p. 33.
115 *IMTFE Judgment*, p. 439.
116 ibid, p. 441.
117 ibid, p. 31.
118 S. Horwitz, 'The Tokyo trial', p. 55.
119 R. H. Minear, *Victors' Justice*, p. 131.
120 *IMTFE Judgment*, p. 32.
121 ibid, p. 441.
122 ibid.
123 It was noted in the judgment that in the period before 8 December 1941, ie the date of occupation of Thailand, the relationship between the two states was one of trust and cooperation. When Japanese troops entered Thailand, negotiations were underway on an alliance that in fact occurred two weeks later. Moreover, the Tokyo Tribunal noted that there were no demands from the Thai side to classify the Japanese actions as aggression.
124 For the judges' separate opinions, see B. V. A. Röling and C. F. Rüter, *The Tokyo Judgment*, vols 1–2.
125 *IMTFE Judgment*, pp. 61–62.
126 The executions were carried out on 23 December 1948.

127 See *IMTFE Judgment*, p. 443.
128 ibid, pp. 443–44.
129 ibid, pp. 444–45.
130 ibid, pp. 445–46.
131 ibid, pp. 448–49.
132 ibid, pp. 451–52.
133 ibid, pp. 452–53.
134 ibid, pp. 453–54.
135 ibid, pp. 454–55.
136 ibid, p. 455.
137 ibid, pp. 455–56.
138 ibid, pp. 456–57.
139 ibid, pp. 458–59.
140 ibid, p. 460.
141 S. Horwitz, 'The Tokyo trial', p. 496.
142 *IMTFE Judgment*, pp. 463–64.
143 ibid, p. 446.
144 A. C. Brackman, *The Other Nuremberg*, p. 274.
145 *IMTFE Judgment*, pp. 446–47.
146 ibid, p. 448.
147 ibid, p. 450.
148 A. C. Brackman, *The Other Nuremberg*, p. 331.
149 ibid, p. 274.
150 *IMTFE Judgment*, pp. 450–51.
151 ibid, p. 456.
152 S. Horwitz, 'The Tokyo trial', p. 496.
153 *IMTFE Judgment*, pp. 457–58.
154 A. C. Brackman, *The Other Nuremberg*, p. 277.
155 *IMTFE Judgment*, pp. 459–60.
156 ibid, p. 461.
157 A. C. Brackman, *The Other Nuremberg*, p. 277.
158 The British representative decided not to sign the prosecution's charges against Alfried Krupp von Bohlen; he supported the general idea of trying Alfried in the Nuremberg trial but was afraid that bringing charges against him would delay the beginning of the trial. *Taylor Report*, pp. 22–23. See also J. Sawicki, *Od Norymbergi do układu paryskiego. Za kulisami niemieckiego rewizjonizmu*, Wydawnictwo Ministerstwa Obrony Narodowej, 2nd edn, Warszawa 1956, pp. 35 ff.
159 *Taylor Report*, p. 23.
160 ibid, p. 271.
161 ibid, p. 272.
162 ibid, pp. 270 and 279.
163 ibid, p. 274.
164 ibid, p. 277.
165 ibid, pp. 26, 27, 282.
166 *Substance of Note Addressed by Embassies London, Moscow and Paris to British, French and Soviet Governments*, 22 January 1947, in ibid, p. 285.
167 See Military Government – Germany, Unites States Zone, *Ordinance No 7*, in ibid, pp. 286–91.
168 ibid, pp. 73 ff.
169 ibid, p. 74.
170 ibid, p. 64.
171 ibid, p. 67.
172 ibid, pp. 92–93.

173 The prosecution made the charges more specific by citing invasions and wars of aggression against Austria (1 March 1937), against Czechoslovakia (1 October 1938 and 15 March 1939), against Poland (1 September 1939), against the United Kingdom and France (3 September 1939), against Denmark and Norway (9 April 1940) against Belgium, the Netherlands and Luxembourg (10 May 1940), against Yugoslavia and Greece (6 April 1941), against the USSR (22 June 1941), against the United States (11 December 1941). See United Nations War Crimes Commission, *Law Reports*, vol 10, pp. 3–4.
174 ibid, p. 5.
175 *Trials of War Criminals*, vol 7, p. 16.
176 ibid, pp. 18 ff.
177 ibid, pp. 15 ff. See also T. Taylor, *Nuremberg Trials*, pp. 196–97.
178 *Trials of War Criminals*, vol 7, p. 175.
179 ibid, vol 8, p.1102.
180 ibid, pp. 1102, 1106–7, 1113.
181 ibid, p. 1107.
182 ibid, p. 1113.
183 ibid, pp. 1125–26.
184 ibid, p. 1126.
185 ibid, p. 1123.
186 ibid, p. 1116.
187 ibid, p. 1109.
188 United Nations War Crimes Commission, *Law Reports*, vol 10, p. 17.
189 *Trials of War Criminals*, vol 8, pp. 1114 ff.
190 ibid, p. 1124.
191 ibid, p. 1212.
192 *Taylor Report*, p. 273.
193 T. Taylor, *Nuremberg Trials*, p. 199.
194 United Nations War Crimes Commission, *Law Reports*, vol 10, pp. 71–75.
195 ibid, p. 71.
196 *Trials of War Criminals*, vol 9, pp. 10 ff.
197 ibid, p. 12.
198 ibid, p. 11.
199 ibid, p. 12.
200 ibid, pp. 15 ff.
201 *Defense Motion for Acquittal on the Charges of Crimes against Peace*, 11 March 1948, in ibid, pp. 356 ff.
202 ibid, p. 393.
203 ibid, p. 396.
204 United Nations War Crimes Commission, *Law Reports*, vol 10, p. 108.
205 *Trials of War Criminals*, vol 9, p. 400.
206 ibid, pp. 396 ff.
207 ibid, p. 397.
208 ibid, p. 407.
209 ibid, pp. 405 ff.
210 ibid, p. 437.
211 ibid, pp. 445 ff.
212 ibid, p. 449.
213 ibid, pp. 450–51.
214 ibid, p. 456.
215 ibid, pp. 457 ff.
216 T. Cyprian and J. Sawicki, *Nieznana Norymberga. Dwanaście procesów norymberskich*, Książka i Wiedza, Warszawa 1965, p. 277.

217 C. Goetz, 'Impressions of Telford Taylor at Nuremberg', *ColJTransL* 1999, vol 37, p. 671.
218 T. Taylor, *Nuremberg Trials*, p. 191.
219 J. A. Bush, 'Soldiers find wars: a life of Telford Taylor', *ColJTransL* 1999, vol 37, p. 682.
220 T. Cyprian and J. Sawicki, *Nieznana Norymberga. Dwanaście procesów norymberskich*, p. 276; J. A. Appleman, *Military Tribunals and International Crimes*, Greenwood Press Publishers, Westport 1954, reprint 1971, pp. 215–18.
221 J. A. Bush, 'The "supreme crime" and its origins', p. 2382.
222 C. Goetz, 'Impressions of Telford Taylor at Nuremberg', p. 672.
223 *Taylor Report*, p. 82.
224 ibid, p. 83, J. Sawicki, 'Od Norymbergi do układu paryskiego', pp. 311 ff.
225 United Nations War Crimes Commission, *Law Reports*, vol 12, pp. 2 ff.
226 *Trials of War Criminals*, vol 10, p. 62.
227 ibid, pp. 77 ff.
228 ibid, pp. 338 ff.
229 ibid, vol 11, pp. 482 ff.
230 ibid, pp. 485–86.
231 ibid, pp. 488–89.
232 ibid, pp. 490–91.
233 ibid, p. 486.
234 ibid, p. 489.
235 ibid, pp. 371 ff. See also United Nations War Crimes Commission, *Law Reports*, vol 12, pp. 12–13 and T. Cyprian and J. Sawicki, *Nieznana Norymberga. Dwanaście procesów norymberskich*, p. 309.
236 T. Taylor, *Nuremberg Trials*, p. 222.
237 *Trials of War Criminals*, vol 14, p. 323.
238 ibid, p. 436.
239 For more information on the Weizsäcker case see M. Lippmann, 'The good motive defense: Ernst von Weizsaecker and the Nazi Ministries case', *TouroIntLRev* 1997, vol 7.
240 *Trials of War Criminals*, vol 12, p. 24.
241 ibid, vol 14, pp. 340–41. See also M. Lippmann, 'The good motive defense', pp. 80 ff.
242 ibid, pp. 340–41.
243 ibid, p. 340.
244 ibid, pp. 348 ff.
245 ibid, p. 350.
246 ibid, p. 343.
247 ibid, p. 356.
248 ibid, pp. 357, 356, 369.
249 ibid, p. 343.
250 ibid, pp. 372, 375, 278.
251 ibid, pp. 381–83.
252 ibid, pp. 370, 372.
253 ibid, p. 385.
254 ibid, p. 880.
255 ibid, p. 891.
256 ibid, p. 892. Judge Powers used similar arguments in the case of Wörmann, ibid, p. 893.
257 ibid, p. 866.
258 ibid, pp. 943 ff.
259 ibid, p. 955.

260 ibid, pp. 950–56.
261 ibid, pp. 1002–4.
262 ibid, pp. 385–87.
263 ibid, p. 388.
264 ibid, p. 894.
265 ibid, p. 869.
266 ibid, p. 1004.
267 ibid, p. 391.
268 ibid, p. 393.
269 ibid, pp. 393–94.
270 ibid, pp. 393, 396.
271 ibid, p. 393.
272 ibid, p. 396.
273 ibid, p. 397.
274 ibid, p. 966.
275 ibid, pp. 965–66.
276 ibid, pp. 1002–4.
277 ibid, pp. 972–74.
278 ibid, pp. 407–8.
279 ibid, pp. 413–4.
280 ibid, pp. 406, 412.
281 ibid, p. 895.
282 ibid, p. 867.
283 ibid, pp. 1002–4.
284 ibid, p. 421.
285 ibid, p. 424.
286 ibid, p. 425.
287 ibid, p. 868.
288 ibid, pp. 1002–4.
289 ibid, vol 12, p. 24.
290 ibid, p. 24.
291 ibid.
292 ibid, pp. 24–25.
293 ibid, p. 30.
294 ibid.
295 ibid, vol 14, pp. 399, 416–417.
296 ibid, p. 1075.
297 ibid, p. 1076. For more information on the case of H. Röchling see W. W. Bishop, 'The case against Hermann Roechling and others', *AJIL* 1949, vol 43.
298 *Trials of War Criminals*, vol 14, p. 1065.
299 ibid, p. 1077.
300 ibid, p. 1078.
301 ibid, p. 1079.
302 ibid, p. 1089.
303 ibid, p. 1095.
304 ibid, p. 1107.
305 ibid, pp. 1107–8.
306 ibid, p. 1108.
307 ibid, p. 1109.
308 Article 13(1)(1) Decree of 22 January 1946 concerning the establishment of the Supreme National Tribunal, *Polish Official Gazette* 1946, no 5, item 46. By the decree of 17 October 1946, *Polish Official Gazette* 1946, no 59, item 325, Article 13 was derogated and the Article 51 was introduced, giving the tribunal jurisdiction

eg in cases of 'crimes committed by individuals who for these crimes will be surrendered under the Moscow Declaration of the three allied powers: the United States of North America, the Union of Soviet Socialist Republics, and Great Britain to the authorities of the Republic of Poland – with the exceptions of cases which the prosecutor of the Supreme National Tribunal submits to the prosecutor of the regional court, taking into account territorial jurisdiction as far as practicable'. For more information on the jurisdiction of the Supreme National Tribunal see T. Cyprian and J. Sawicki, *Siedem wyroków Najwyższego Trybunału Narodowego*, Instytut Zachodni, Poznań 1962, pp. XIII–XIV; and United Nations War Crimes Commission, *Law Reports*, vol 7, pp. 83 ff and also ibid, vol 13, pp. 106 ff.

309 See for instance the judgment of the Supreme National Tribunal of 10 July 1948 in the case of Joseph Buhler, which took place in Cracow from 17 June–10 July 1948, in T. Cyprian and J. Sawicki, *Siedem wyroków Najwyższego Trybunału Narodowego*, pp. 324 ff and also in United Nations War Crimes Commission, *Law Reports*, vol 14, pp. 23 ff. See also L. Kubicki, *Zbrodnie wojenne w świetle prawa polskiego*, Państwowe Wydawnictwo Naukowe, Warszawa 1963, pp. 36 ff.

310 See C. Łuczak, *Arthur Greiser*, PSO, Poznań 1997. See also the United Nations War Crimes Commission, *Law Reports*, vol 13, pp. 70 ff.

311 SNT Judgment of 9 July 1946, in T. Cyprian and J. Sawicki, *Siedem wyroków Najwyższego Trybunału Narodowego*, pp. 4–5, see also United Nations War Crimes Commission, *Law Reports*, vol 13, pp. 70.

312 J. Gumkowski and T. Kułakowski, *Zbrodniarze hitlerowscy przed Najwyższym Trybunałem Narodowym*, Wydawnictwo Prawnicze, Warszawa 1961, p. 10.

313 ibid, p. 6.

314 United Nations War Crimes Commission, *Law Reports*, vol 13, p. 103.

315 ibid, p. 102

316 J. Gumkowski and T. Kułakowski, *Zbrodniarze hitlerowscy przed Najwyższym Trybunałem Narodowym*, p. 54.

317 ibid, p. 62.

318 T. Cyprian and J. Sawicki, *Siedem wyroków Najwyższego Trybunału Narodowego*, pp. 10–11.

319 ibid, p. 11.

320 See M. Podgóreczny, *Albert Forster gauleiter i oskarżony*, Wydawnictwo Morskie, Gdańsk 1997.

321 SNT Judgment of 29 April 1948, in T. Cyprian and J. Sawicki, *Siedem wyroków Najwyższego Trybunału Narodowego*, pp. 263–64.

322 ibid, p. 264.

323 ibid, p. 270.

324 ibid, p. 276.

325 ibid. See also the opinion of Stanisław Kaszyński, *Polityka Forstera jako 'Gauleitera' na terenie Wolnego Miasta Gdańska oraz jako 'Reichsstatthaltera Gau Danzig-Westpreussen'*, in *Ekspertyzy i orzeczenia przed Najwyższym Trybunałem Narodowym*, vol 2, Ministerstwo Sprawiedliwości, Główna Komisja Badania Zbrodni Hitlerowskich w Polsce, Warszawa 1979, pp. 73 ff.

326 T. Cyprian and J. Sawicki, *Siedem wyroków Najwyż szego Trybunału Narodowego*, p. 281.

327 ibid, p. 282.

328 ibid, pp. 282–83.

329 ibid, p. 283.

330 ibid, p. 289.

331 ibid, p. 291.

332 ibid, p. 292.

333 ibid, pp. 276–77.
334 ibid, pp. 292–93.
335 ibid, p. 274.
336 ibid, p. 275.
337 ibid, p. 292.
338 ibid, p. 295.
339 It is not absolutely certain whether Forster was actually executed. See D. Mikłaszewicz, *Tajemnice procesu gdańskiego gauleitera*, available at http://miasta.gazeta.pl/trojmiasto/1,35635,2013658.html (last visited 15 December 2012).
340 SNT judgment of 3 March 1947, in T. Cyprian and J. Sawicki, *Siedem wyroków Najwyższego Trybunału Narodowego*, pp. 45–46.
341 ibid, p. 66.
342 Article I of the Law governing the Trial of War Criminals of 24 October 1946; see United Nations War Crimes Commission, *Law Reports*, vol 14, p. 152.
343 Article II, ibid, pp. 152–53.
344 ibid, p. 1.
345 ibid, p. 2.
346 ibid, pp. 3–4.
347 ibid, p. 4.
348 ibid, pp. 4–5.
349 I. Brownlie, *International Law and the Use of Force*, p. 182.
350 UNWCC, *Law Reports*, vol 14, pp. 5–6.
351 ibid, p. 6.
352 P. A. L. Weir, *The German War-Crimes Trials, 1949 to Present: Repercussions of American Involvement*, University Microfilms, A Xerox Company, Ann Arbor, Michigan 1973, p. 220. See also A. D. Rotfeld and F. Ryszka, 'Przedawnienie zbrodni hitlerowskich. Problem polityczny i prawny', in *Przedawnienie zbrodni hitlerowskich w NRF. Materiały sesji naukowej Komitetu Koordynacyjnego Badań Niemcoznawczych, Warszawa, 8 marca 1965*, Polski Instytut Spraw Międzynarodowych, Warszawa 1965, pp. 36 ff.
353 M. C. Bassiouni, *From Versailles to Rwanda in Seventy-Five Years*, pp. 30–31, L. Gardocki, *Zarys prawa karnego międzynarodowego*, p. 60.
354 I. Brownlie, *International Law and the Use of Force*, p. 184.
355 ibid, p. 183.
356 ibid, p. 184.
357 A. Sauvageot, *Histoire de Finlande*, vol 2, Imprimerie Nationale, Librairie Orientaliste Paul Geuthner, Paris 1968, pp. 470–71. Among the convicted defendants were also: Risto Ryti, former president of Finland (10 years of forced labour), Johan Wilhelm Rangell, former prime minister (6 years in strict prison), Edwin Linkomies, former prime minister (5.5 years in strict prison), Väinö Tanner, close friend of Juho Kusti Paasikivi (5.5 years in strict prison), Professor Toivo Mikael Kivimäki, former prime minister and Finland's plenipotentiary minister in Berlin in the period 1940–1944 (5 years in strict prison), Henrik Ramsay, former foreign minister (2.5 years in strict prison), as well as Antti Kukkonen and Tyko Reinikka, former ministers (2 years in prison). All those convicted ended up serving only half of their respective sentences, ibid.
358 W. J. Bosh, *Judgment on Nuremberg*, pp. 190–91, W. Czapliński, *Skutki prawne nielegalnego*, p. 203.
359 See the documents on this quasi-trial at http://www.vietnamese-american.org/contents.html (last visited 3 June 2013).
360 See eg L. R. Beres, 'Iraqi crimes and international law: the imperative to punish', *DenJIntL&Pol* 1993, vol 21, p. 338; T. R. Kleinberger, 'The Iraqi conflict: an assessment of possible war crimes and the call for adoption of an

International Criminal Code and Permanent International Criminal Tribunal', *NYLSchJInt&CompL* 1993, vol 14, pp. 77 ff; J. S. Robbins, 'War crimes: the case of Iraq', *FletFWorldAff* 1994, vol 18, p. 46; K. A. Williams, 'The Iraq-Kuwait crisis: an analysis of the unresolved issue of war crimes liability', *BrookJIntL* 1992, vol 18, pp. 393 ff; Y. Dinstein, *War, Aggression and Self-Defence*, p. 16, W. Czapliński, *Skutki prawne nielegalnego*, pp. 201–202.

361 A. Cassese, *International Criminal Law*, p. 113.

362 B. B. Ferencz, 'An international criminal code and court', p. 386. See also eg *New York Times*, 17 April 1991, *The Times* (London), 3 August 1990.

363 SC/Res/678.

364 B. B. Ferencz, *The Crime of Aggression*, p. 54.

365 The Iraqi Special Tribunal was established by the Iraqi Governing Council on 9 December 2003. On 10 December 2003 Paul Brehmer, authorised by the Coalition Provisional Authority, signed regulation no 48 with the tribunal's statute, which was subsequently promulgated in the *Official Gazette* and thus became incorporated into the legal order of Iraq. The statute of the tribunal is available at http://www.hrcr.org/hottopics/statute/ (last visited 3 June 2013). In October 2006 the government of Iraq amended the statute and changed the name of the tribunal to Iraqi Higher Criminal Court, with the new statute appearing in the *Official Gazette* In al-Waqaa'e No 4006 on 18 October 2006. The new statute is available at http://law.case.edu/saddamtrial/documents/IST_statute_official_english.pdf (last visited 15 December 2012). See P. Grzebyk, 'Le tribunal spécial iraquien: instrument de justice ou de vengeance', in S. Sur (ed.), *Annuaire Français de Relations Internationales* 2008, vol IX, La Documentation Française, Bruylant, Bruxelles 2008, pp. 131 ff.

366 Article 14 of the IST statute.

367 A. L. Paulus, 'Peace through justice?', pp. 30–31.

368 Judicial Chronicle, 'Saddam Hussein's first hearing', *JIntCrimJust 2004*, no 2, p. 927.

369 M. Lippmann, 'Prosecutions of Nazi war criminals before post-World War II domestic tribunals', *UnivMiamiInt&CompLRev* 1999–2000, vol 8, pp. 2 ff.

5 Scope of individual responsibility for the crime of aggression

1 A. Klafkowski, *Prawo międzynarodowe publiczne*, p. 147; G. Michałowska, 'Odpowiedzialność jednostki w prawie międzynarodowym', p. 25; S. Glueck, *The Nuremberg Trial and Aggressive War*, pp. 98 ff.

2 R. K. Woetzel, *The Nuremberg Trials in International Law*, pp. 68 ff.

3 W. Czapliński and A. Wyrozumska, *Prawo międzynarodowe publiczne*, pp. 251–53.

4 The International Military Tribunal referenced a ruling of the Supreme Court of the United States of America, *Ex parte Quirin* (1942 317 US 1), *IMT Judgment*, p. 220.

5 ibid, p. 221.

6 See F. Malakian, 'International criminal responsibility', in M. C. Bassiouni, *International Criminal Law, Volume I, Crimes*, 2nd edn, Transnational Publishers Inc., Ardsley, New York 1999, pp. 153 ff; A. Obote-Odora, *The Judging of War Criminals: Individual Criminal Responsibility Under International Law*, Akademitryck, Edsburg 1997, pp. 29 ff; R. K. Woetzel, *The Nuremberg Trials in International Law*, pp. 96 ff.

7 Article 6 IMT Charter, Article 49 I GC (the same wording as in Article 49 I GC is repeated in Article 50 II GC, Article 129 III GC, Article 146 IV GC, Article 7(1) ICTY statute, Article 6(1) ICTR statute, Article 25(1) ICC statute, Article 1 draft

CCPSH of 1954, Article 2 draft CCPSH of 1996 and so-called first Nuremberg principle.

8 Commentary to the draft CCPSH of 1996, p. 19.
9 Article VI(3).
10 *USA Opening Statement*, p. 13.
11 Article VI(2)(a).
12 Y. Dinstein, *War, Aggression and Self-Defence*, p. 133.
13 V. Maugham, *UNO and War Crimes*, p. 19.
14 G. P. Fletcher, *Romantics at War. Glory and Guilt in the Age of Terrorism*, Princeton University Press, Princeton, Oxford 2002, p. 5.
15 Article II(2)(f).
16 K. Kittichaisaree, *International Criminal Law*, p. 223. See also United Nations War Crimes Commission, *Law Reports*, vol 15, p. 147.
17 K. Kittichaisaree, *International Criminal Law*, p. 223.
18 *Trials of War Criminals*, vol 8, p. 1126.
19 ibid, p. 1124.
20 ibid, pp. 1124–25.
21 ibid, p. 1124.
22 ibid, vol 11, p. 486. Compare with *IMT Judgment*, p. 223.
23 *Trials of War Criminals*, vol 11, pp. 486–89.
24 R. D. Lumb, 'Individual responsibility for aggressive war: the crime against peace', *UnivQueensLJ* 1956–59, vol 3, p. 350.
25 L. May, *Aggression and Crimes against Peace*, p. 238.
26 ibid, 'Act and circumstance in the crime of aggression, symposium: war and responsibility', *JPolPhil* 2007, vol 15, p. 180.
27 C. A. Pompe, *Aggressive War*, p. 233.
28 See also the dissenting opinion of Judge Powers to the judgment in the Ministries case, *Trials of War Criminals*, vol 14, pp. 887 ff.
29 See PCNICC/2002/WGCA/L.1/Add 1, pp. 32 ff.
30 R. D. Lumb, 'Individual responsibility for aggressive war: the crime against peace', p. 350.
31 W. R. Harris, *Tyranny on Trial*, pp. 532–33.
32 B. V. A. Röling and C. F. Rüter, *The Tokyo Judgment*, vol 2, pp. 1061–62.
33 I. Brownlie, *International Law and the Use of Force*, p. 205.
34 Article 16.
35 Commentary to the draft CCPSH of 1996, p. 43.
36 ibid, pp. 19–20.
37 Y. Dinstein, *War, Aggression and Self-Defence*, p. 134.
38 A. Niang, 'Les individus en tant que personnes privées', in H. Ascensio, E. Decaux and A. Pellet, *Droit international pénal*, Cedin Paris X, Editions A. Pedone, Paris 2000, p. 228.
39 K. Kittichaisaree, *International Criminal Law*, p. 223.
40 M. Politi, 'The debate within the Preparatory Commission for the International Criminal Court', in M. Politi, G. Nesi, *The International Criminal Court*, p. 46. See ICC-ASP/5/SWGCA/INF.1, para 88.
41 ICC-ASP/7/SWGCA/INF.1.
42 ICC-ASP/7/20/Add/1, para 25; R. S. Clark, 'Negotiating provisions defining the crime of aggression', p. 1105.
43 Compare with R. Cryer, 'Aggression at the Court of Appeal', *JConf&SecL* 2005, vol 10, p. 214.
44 ICC-ASP/6/SWGCA/INF.1, para 11.
45 ICC-ASP/3/SWGCA/INF.1, para 54.
46 'Indictment', in *The Case Against the Nazi War Criminals*, pp. 125–26.

47 ibid, pp. 126–30.
48 ibid, pp. 130–31 and 133.
49 ibid, p. 132.
50 ibid, pp. 126 ff.
51 *IMT Judgment*, p. 197.
52 ibid, p. 186.
53 ibid, p. 192.
54 ibid, p. 186.
55 ibid, pp. 187–88.
56 ibid, p. 192.
57 ibid, p. 194.
58 ibid, p. 207.
59 ibid, p. 213.
60 ibid, pp. 197 ff.
61 ibid, p. 186.
62 W. Morawiecki, *Walka o definicję agresji w prawie międzynarodowym*, p. 252.
63 A/CN.4/5, p. 49.
64 *Trials of War Criminals*, vol 14, p. 323.
65 ibid, p. 331.
66 ibid, p. 882.
67 Article 5(2).
68 Y. Dinstein, *War, Aggression and Self-Defence*, p. 126. However, see also the comments of B. B. Ferencz, who claims the resolution had been drafted with responsibility in mind. B. B. Ferencz, 'Can aggression be deterred by law? "You have it in your power to make dreams of a more human world order under law come true"', Address to the Diplomatic Conference of Plenipotentiaries on the Establishment of an International Criminal Court, *PaceIntLRev* 1999, vol 11, p. 354.
69 See eg Russian proposition, PCNICC/1999/DP.12.
70 For example, during the trial in Tokyo a decision was made to reference internal Japanese decisions rather than specific attacks, because if a different approach had been adopted, The Netherlands would have been considered the aggressor and not the other way round. C. A. Pompe, *Aggressive War*, p. 32.
71 G. Ginsburgs, *Moscow's Road to Nuremberg*, pp. 127–29.
72 Elements of crimes were adopted by Assembly of States Parties and entered into force on 9 September 2002 (see ICC-ASP/1/3, 3–10 September 2002). Pursuant to art 9 of the ICC statute, 'Elements of Crimes shall assist the Court in the interpretation and application of articles 6, 7 and 8, consistent with the Statute'.
73 M. Królikowski, P. Wiliński, J. Izydorczyk, *Podstawy prawa karnego międzynarodowego*, p. 166.
74 See judgments concerning Weizsäcker, Wörmann, Kido or Minami.
75 *Trials of War Criminals*, vol 11, p. 488.
76 L. May, *Aggression and Crimes against Peace*, p. 230.
77 R. L. Griffiths, *International Law*, p. 367.
78 I. Brownlie, *International Law and the Use of Force*, p. 211.
79 Notably, in the course of work on the 1996 Draft Code of Crimes against the Peace and Security of Mankind it was also decided not to pursue criminalising a threat of aggression.
80 ICJ, *Advisory opinion on legality of the threat or use of nuclear powers*, 8 July 1996, paras 47 ff.
81 See Article 8(2)(b)(xx).
82 ICC-ASP/6/SWGCA/INF.1, para 50.
83 ibid, para 51.
84 I. Brownlie, *International Law and the Use of Force*, p. 208.

85 A. Cassese, *International Criminal Law*, p. 116.
86 ibid, p. 116.
87 See eg PCNICC/1999/DP.11 or PCNICC/1999/DP.13. See also H.-P. Kaul, 'The crime of aggression: definitional options for the way forward', in M. Politi, G. Nesi, *The International Criminal Court*, p. 102.
88 eg PCNICC/1999/DP.11.
89 ICC-ASP/5/SWGCA/INF.1, para 26
90 M. Politi, 'The debate within the Preparatory Commission for the International Criminal Court', p. 49.
91 J. Hogan-Doran and B. T. van Ginkel, 'Aggression as a crime under international law and the prosecution of individuals by the proposed International Criminal Court', *NIntLJ* 1996, vol 43, p. 324; K. Kittichaisaree, *International Criminal Law*, p. 207; draft CCPSH of 1996, p. 43.
92 L. May, 'Act and circumstance in the crime of aggression, symposium: war and responsibility', p. 174.
93 L. Condorelli, 'Conclusions générales', in M. Politi and G. Nesi, *The International Criminal Court*, p. 156.
94 R. Rayfuse, The Draft Code of Crimes Against the Peace and Security of Mankind: eating disorders at the International Law Commission', *CrimLF* 1997, vol 8, p. 60.
95 M. Schuster, 'The Rome Statute and the crime of aggression', p. 23.
96 F. Malakian, 'International criminal responsibility', p. 176.
97 L. May, *Aggression and Crimes against Peace*, pp. 174–76.
98 M. M. Gomaa, *The Definition*, in M. Politi and G. Nesi, *The International Criminal Court and the Crime of Aggression*, Ashgate, Aldershot 2004, p. 58. L. May, *Aggression and Crimes against Peace*, p. 235.
99 I. K. Müller-Schieke, 'Defining the crime of aggression under the statute of the International Criminal Court', *LeidenJIntL* 2001, vol 14, p. 420.
100 R. S. Clark, 'Rethinking aggression as a crime and formulating its elements: the final work-product of the Preparatory Commission for the International Criminal Court', *LeidenJIntL* 2002, vol 15, p. 876.
101 A. Cassese, *International Criminal Law*, p. 114, A. L. Paulus, 'Peace through justice?', p. 19.
102 L. May, *Aggression and Crimes against Peace*, pp. 91 ff.
103 C. Kress, 'Time for decision: some thoughts on the immediate future of the crime of aggression: a reply to Andreas Paulus', *EJIL* 2010 vol 20, p. 1139.
104 T. Meron, 'Defining Aggression', pp. 4 and 11.
105 S. A. Fernández de Gurmendi, 'The Working Group on Aggression at the Preparatory Commission for the International Criminal Court', *FordhIntLJ* 2002, vol 25, p. 597.
106 R. L. Griffiths, *International Law*, p. 319.
107 See Article 1, Article 5(1).
108 Article 8 (1).
109 David Scheffer points out that frivolous referrals are still possible based on Kampala amendments. D. Scheffer, 'The complex crime of aggression under the Rome Statute', *LeidenJIntL* 2010, vol 23, p. 899.
110 That does not mean that some acts of aggression will not result in individual responsibility. Kriangsak Kittichaisaree reminds us that the International Criminal Court is not the only court that can try individual for the crime of aggression; national courts have jurisdiction to do so too. K. Kittichaisaree, *International Criminal Law*, p. 217. On the other hand, Richard L. Griffiths argues that the function of the threshold clause is likely to be as an indicator of what types of illegal use of force constitute acts of aggression. R. L. Griffiths,

International Law, p. 366. With the above in mind, it appears worthwhile to invoke the words of Mary Ellen O'Connell and Mirakmal Niyazmatov, who claim that '[m]anifest adds nothing therefore but confusion'. M. E. O'Connell and M. Niyazmatov, 'What is aggression? Comparing the *ius ad bellum* and the ICC statute', *JIntCrimJust* 2012, vol 10, p. 204.

111 ICC/ASP/8/INF.2, Annex I, Article 8 *bis*, Introduction, point 3. See also A. Paulus, 'Second thoughts on the crime of aggression', *EJIL* 2010, vol 20, pp. 1121–22
112 ICC/ASP/8/INF.2, Explanatory Note, para 7.
113 Point 7 of Annex III, Understandings regarding the amendments to the Rome Statute of the International Criminal Court on the Crime of Aggression, Resolution RC/Res.6. However, there is no universal agreement as to whether the satisfaction of two requirements suffices (D. Scheffer, 'The Complex Crime of Aggression', p. 900) or whether all three requirements must irrevocably be met (C. Kress and L. Von Holtzendorff, 'The Kampala compromise', p. 1207).
114 ICC-ASP/5/SWGCA/INF.1, para 18.
115 ICC-ASP/6/SWGCA/1, para 25.
116 Y. Dinstein, *War, Aggression and Self-Defence*, p. 132.
117 *ICJ Judgment*, p. 221.
118 ibid, p. 222.
119 ibid, p. 223.
120 On the difference between a planning as a form of direct participation and a planning as a part of common plan, see K. J. Heller, *The Nuremberg Military Tribunals*, pp. 190–91.
121 United Nations War Crimes Commission, *Law Reports*, vol 15, pp. 148–49.
122 C. A. Pompe, *Aggressive War*, p. 219.
123 I. K. Müller-Schieke, 'Defining the crime of aggression', p. 417.
124 ICC-ASP/5/SWGCA/INF.1, para 39.
125 *IMT Judgment*, p. 186.
126 I. Brownlie, *International Law and the Use of Force*, p. 200.
127 B. V. A. Röling and C. F. Rüter, *The Tokyo Judgment*, vol 1, p. 503.
128 *IMT Judgment*, p. 273.
129 I. Brownlie, *International Law and the Use of Force*, p. 200.
130 R. S. Clark, 'Rethinking aggression as a crime and formulating its elements', p. 875.
131 R. K. Woetzel, *The Nuremberg Trials in International Law*, pp. 162–63.
132 *Trials of War Criminals*, vol 14, pp. 883–84.
133 G. P. Fletcher, *Romantics at War*, p. 76.
134 H. Donnedieu de Vabres, 'Le procès de Nuremberg devant les principes modernes du droit pénal international', *Recueil des Cours* 1947-I, p. 529. See also W. A. Schabas, *An Introduction to the International Criminal Court*, p. 103.
135 H. Donnedieu de Vabres, 'Le procès de Nuremberg', p. 531.
136 Y. Dinstein, *War, Aggression and Self-Defence*, p. 132.
137 R. H. Minear, *Victors' Justice*, p. 37.
138 W. A. Schabas, *An Introduction to the International Criminal Court*, p. 104.
139 L. Hugueney, 'Le procès de Nuremberg devant les principes modernes du droit pénal international', *RIDP* 1948, nos 3–4, p. 278.
140 B. B. Ferencz, *Defining International Aggression*, vol 1, p. 383.
141 *IMT Judgment*, p. 222.
142 *Trials of War Criminals*, vol 9, p. 411. See also K. J. Heller, *The Nuremberg Military Tribunals*, pp. 200–201.
143 I. Brownlie, *International Law and the Use of Force*, p. 201.

144 *Trials of War Criminals*, vol 9, p. 419.
145 Notably, two defendants (Oshima and Shiratori) were convicted solely on conspiracy charges, and were acquitted of charges of the crime against peace allegedly committed against the specific states.
146 ibid, vol 11, p. 488.
147 ibid.
148 ibid, vol 8, p. 1108.
149 Q. Wright, 'The law of the Nuremberg Trial', *AJIL* 1947, vol 41, p. 66.
150 *Trials of War Criminals*, vol 11, p. 488.
151 Y. Dinstein, *War, Aggression and Self-Defence*, p. 137.
152 L. May, *Aggression and Crimes against Peace*, p. 15.
153 *Trials of War Criminals*, vol 14, p. 341; see also pp. 349, 953.
154 ibid, p. 341.
155 Q. Wright, 'The law of the Nuremberg Trial', p. 67.
156 Y. Dinstein, 'The distinction between war crimes and crimes against peace', in Y. Dinstein and M. Tabory, *War Crimes in International Law*, p. 7.
157 B. B. Ferencz, 'The crime of aggression', p. 57.
158 J. Hogan-Doran and B. T. van Ginkel, 'Aggression as a crime under international law', p. 333, Y. Dinstein, *War, Aggression and Self-Defence*, p. 137.
159 L. May, *Aggression and Crimes against Peace*, p. 180.
160 *Trials of War Criminals*, vol 14, pp. 337, 417.
161 ibid, vol 9, p. 436.
162 ibid, vol 14, p. 337.
163 A. Obote-Odora, *The Judging of War Criminals*, p. 78.
164 *Trials of War Criminals*, vol 14, p. 337.
165 *IMT Judgment*, p. 223.
166 ibid, pp. 188 ff.
167 *Trials of War Criminals*, vol 9, p. 360.
168 ibid, vol 14, pp. 391, 966.
169 ibid, vol 8, p. 1287.
170 I. Brownlie, *International Law and the Use of Force*, p. 205.
171 ibid, p. 199.
172 Draft CCPSH of 1996, p. 43.
173 ICC-ASP/5/SWGCA/INF.1, Annex III, Item I, p. 21.
174 Article 30(1).
175 Article 30(2).
176 Article 30(3).
177 Article 31(3).
178 Article 31(1)(a).
179 Article 31(1)(b).
180 W. A. Schabas, *An Introduction to the International Criminal Court*, p. 112.
181 Article 32(1). Y. Dinstein, 'The distinction between war crimes and crimes against peace', p. 8.
182 See examples in R. S. Clark, 'The crime of aggression', in C. Stahn and G. Sluiter, *The Emerging Practice of the International Criminal Court*, p. 716.
183 R. S. Clark, 'Rethinking aggression as a crime and formulating its elements', p. 875, Y. Dinstein, *War, Aggression and Self-Defence*, p. 138.
184 L. May, *Aggression and Crimes against Peace*, p. 243; ibid, 'Act and circumstance in the crime of aggression', p. 181.
185 H. Wehberg, *The Outlawry of War*, p. 100.
186 Y. Dinstein, *War, Aggression and Self-Defence*, p. 138.
187 R. S. Clark, 'Rethinking aggression as a crime and formulating its elements', p. 876.

188 Y. Dinstein, *War, Aggression and Self-Defence*, p. 139, ibid, 'The distinction between war crimes and crimes against peace', p. 9.
189 G. M. Dawson, 'Defining substantive crimes within the subject matter jurisdiction of the International Criminal Court: what is the crime of aggression', *NYLSchJInt&CompL* 1999–2000, vol 19, p. 446.
190 J. Hogan-Doran, B. T. van Ginkel, 'Aggression as a crime under international law', p. 349.
191 G. A. Finch, 'The Nuremberg trial', p. 21.
192 *Jackson's Report*, p. 183.
193 L. Gardocki, *Zarys prawa karnego międzynarodowego*, p. 38.
194 Article VIII.
195 J. W. Grayson, 'The defence of superior orders in the International Criminal Court', *NJIL* 1995, vol 64, p. 248.
196 *IMT Judgment*, p. 223.
197 ibid, p. 221.
198 L. Gardocki, *Zarys prawa karnego międzynarodowego*, p. 56.
199 Article 4.
200 For more information on the notion of conditional liability see A. M. Maugeri, 'La responsabilité des supérieurs hiérarchiques et l'effet d'exonération de l'ordre du supérieur dans le statut de la Cour Pénale Internationale', in M. Chiavario (ed.), *La justice pénale internationale entre passé et avenir*, Dalloz, Paris, Milano, 2003, p. 323.
201 Article 33(1).
202 Y. Dinstein, *War, Aggression and Self-Defence*, p. 143.
203 J. W. Grayson, 'The defence of superior orders', p. 244. A. Obote-Odora, *The Judging of War Criminals*, p. 96, A. M. Maugeri, 'La responsabilité des supérieurs hiérarchiques', p. 324.
204 R. S. Clark, 'Rethinking aggression as a crime and formulating its elements', p. 885.
205 Article VI.
206 ICC-ASP/3/SWGCA/INF.1, para 58. However, see also ICC-ASP/4/32, para 44, where it is essentially agreed that the principle of leadership eliminates the option of invoking orders.
207 ICC-ASP/3/SWGCA/INF.1, para 59.
208 A. M. Maugeri, 'La responsabilité des supérieurs hiérarchiques', p. 322, L. May, 'Act and circumstance in the crime of aggression, symposium: war and responsibility', p. 185.
209 J. W. Grayson, 'The defence of superior orders', p. 251.
210 A. Obote-Odora, *The Judging of War Criminals*, p. 90.
211 J. A. Appleman, *Military Tribunals and International Crimes*, p. 55.
212 eg *Nazi Conspiracy and Aggression*, Supplement B, pp. 747 ff.
213 United Nations War Crimes Commission, *Law Reports*, vol 14, p. 5.
214 Article 31(1)(d).
215 *Trials of War Criminals*, vol 14, pp. 84 ff.
216 ibid, p. 339.
217 A. Obote-Odora, *The Judging of War Criminals*, p. 99.
218 Y. Dinstein, *War, Aggression and Self-Defence*, p. 140.
219 Y. Dinstein, 'The distinction between war crimes and crimes against peace', p. 11.
220 J. Stone, *Aggression and World Order*, p. 61.
221 F. Mitchell, *The Formulation of the Conception of Aggression*, International Association of Democratic Lawyers, Brussels 1952, p. 9; V. Maugham, *UNO and War Crimes*, p. 35; R. K. Woetzel, *The Nuremberg Trials in International Law*, p. 92.

222 See Article 25(3) of the ICC statute. It is perhaps important to note that the Special Working Groups eventually decided against implementing a provision that would make it impossible to assign responsibility for an attempt to commit aggression. The decision was made mostly on the strength of the argument that there are two safety valves in the statute that prevent excessive interpretation of punishability of aggression. First, the prosecutor should always consider whether to instigate proceedings in a given case, and strive to avoid rash decisions. Secondly, an external body (most likely the Security Council) will determine aggression: ICC-ASP/4/32, par 33 ff. It was also noted that most scenarios of attempted acts of aggression fit into the definition of the crime that has already been adopted: ICC-ASP/5/SWGCA/INF.1, para 42. Interestingly, the Special Working Group decided not to propose wording for a provision that would criminalise inciting to commit acts of aggression. It is surprising in that many instruments of human rights protection already include a ban on pro-war propaganda (eg Article 20 of the International Covenant on Civil and Political Rights), and GA Resolution no 110 on this issue was adopted on 3 November 1947. For more information see M. Kearney, *The Prohibition of Propaganda for War in International Law*, Oxford University Press, Oxford 2007.

223 C. A. Pompe, *Aggressive War*, p. 34, N. Nyiri, *The United Nations' Search*, p. 252.

224 A. Obote-Odora, *The Judging of War Criminals*, p. 78.

225 M. Schuster, 'The Rome Statute and the crime of aggression', p. 27, J. Stone, *Aggression and World Order*, p. 141.

6 Procedural difficulties

1 T. Ostropolski, *Zasada jurysdykcji uniwersalnej w prawie międzynarodowym*, Instytut Wydawniczy EuroPrawo, Warszawa 2008, pp. 24 ff.

2 A. L. Paulus, 'Peace through justice?', pp. 27–28.

3 For a discussion of relevant American rulings with comments, see C. Antonopoulos, 'Whatever happened to crimes against peace?', *JConf&SecL* 2001, vol 6, pp. 54 ff.

4 *USA Opening Statement*, p. 7.

5 See PCIJ, Judgment, *Lotus (France v Turkey)*, 7 September 1927, p. 23.

6 Draft CCPSH of 1996, p. 30.

7 ICC-ASP/7/SWGCA/2, para 38.

8 B. Stern, 'Better interpretation and enforcement of universal jurisdiction', in C. C. Joyner (sp. ed.), M. C. Bassiouni (gen. ed.), *Reining in impunity for international crimes and serious violations of fundamental human rights: proceedings of the Siracusa Conference 17–21 September 1998*, Siracusa, Association Internationale de Droit Pénal, Érès 1998, p. 179.

9 K. C. Randall, 'Universal jurisdiction under international law', *TexLRev* 1988, vol 66, p. 785.

10 ICJ, *Judgement an Barcelona Traction, Light and Power Co. Ltd.* (Belgium v. Spain), 5 February 1970, para. 33.

11 ibid, para 34.

12 W. Czapliński, A. Wyrozumska, *Prawo międzynarodowe publiczne*, pp. 20–28.

13 See eg M. C. Bassiouni, 'Universal jurisdiction for international crimes: historical Perspectives and contemporary Practice', *VirJIntL* 2001, vol 42, p. 107; Y. Dinstein, 'The distinction between war crimes and crimes against peace', p. 16. The crime against peace is also listed in *The Princeton Principles on Universal Jurisdiction* (principle no 2). See further on principles S. Macedo (ed.), *Universal Jurisdiction: National Courts and the Prosecution of Serious Crimes under International Law*, University of Pennsylvania Press, Philadelphia 2006, pp. 18 ff.

14 Article 8 of the draft CCPSH of 1996, p. 19.
15 O. Swaak-Goldman, 'Recent developments in international criminal law: trying to stay afloat between Scylla and Charybdis', *Int&CompLQ* 2005, vol 54, p. 700.
16 Understandings regarding the amendments to the Rome Statute of the International Criminal Court on the Crime of Aggression, para 5, Annex III, Resolution RC/Res.6.
17 ICC-ASP/3/SWGCA/INF.1, paras 8–9.
18 Article 15 *bis*, para 4. It is the so-called *opt-out* declaration, modelled after the instrument adopted in Article 124 of the statute of the International Criminal Court. The solution was proposed by the Special Working Group; see ICC-ASP/8/INF.2, paras 38–40.
19 It has been pointed out – accurately! – that Article 121(5) and Article 15 *bis*(4) contradict one another. See M. Milanovic, 'Aggression and legality. Custom in Kampala', *JIntCrimJust* 2012, vol 10, p. 180.
20 Mauro Politi claims that the second sentence of Article 121(5) was included upon the request of the permanent members of the Security Council in view of the future adoption amendments on crime of aggression. M. Politi, *The ICC and the Crime of Aggression*, p. 280.
21 A. Zimmermann, 'Amending the amendment Provisions of the Rome Statute. The Kampala compromise on the crime of aggression and the law of treaties', *JIntCrimJust* 2012, vol 10, p. 217.
22 See also C. Kress, L. von Holtzendorff, 'The Kampala compromise', p. 1213.
23 See ICC-ASP/7/20, paras 28 ff; ICC/ASP/7/20/Add 1, paras 34–39, ICC-ASP-8-INF.2, Annex II, para 5.
24 See Understandings, para 2, where a reference is made to Article 13 para b.
25 Article 12(2) of the ICC Statute.
26 See SC Resolution no 1422 of 12 July 2002. See further M. El Zeidy, 'The United States dropped the atomic bomb of Article 16 of the ICC Statute: Security Council power of deferrals and Resolution 1422', *VanderbiltJTransL* 2002, vol 35.
27 ICC-ASP/7/20/Add 1, paras 23–24.
28 Article 17(1)(a) and (b). In the course of the debates of the Special Working Group, the states agreed unanimously that Articles 17, 18 and 19 apply in their full extent to the crime of aggression, ICC-ASP/3/SWGCA/INF.1, para 27. For a more in-depth discussion of the principle of complementarity, see O. Solera, 'Complementary jurisdiction and international criminal justice', *IRRC* 2002, no 845.
29 W. Schabas, 'Origins of the criminalization of aggression: how crimes against peace became the supreme international crime', in M. Politi, G. Nesi, *The International Criminal Court*, p. 18; B. Van Schaack, *'Par in parem imperium non habet'*, p. 134.
30 B. Wierzbicki, *O azylach i ekstradycji przestępców*, Wydawnictwo Prawnicze, Warszawa 1982, p. 96.
31 I. A. Shearer, *Starke's International Law*, 11th edn, Butterworths, London, 1994, p. 317.
32 B. Wierzbicki, *O azylach i ekstradycji przestępców*, p. 110. See eg Article 6 of the European Convention on Extradition, Paris, 13 December 1957, UNTS, vol 359, pp. 273 ff; Article 7 of the Inter-American Convention on Extradition, Caracas, 25 February 1981, UNTS, vol 1752, pp. 177 ff.
33 See Article 9 of the draft CCPSH of 1996 and A/CN.4/571, para 51.
34 GA Resolution no 60/22 of 23 November 2005 authorised the inclusion of the topic of *Aut dedere aut iudicare* in the work of the International Law Commission. The commission appointed as its Special Rapporteur Zdzisław Galicki, who

prepared four reports: preliminary report of June 2006 (A/CN.4/571), second report of June 2007 (A/CN.4/585), third report of June 2008 (A/CN.4/603), and the fourth report of May 2011 (A/CN.4/648). In 2012, the commission decided to establish an open-ended Working Group under the chairmanship of Mr Kriangsak Kittichaisaree (the previous working groups were chaired by Alain Pellet and Enrique Candotti), A/67/10, para 206.

35 See states' comments in A/CN.4/579 and Add.1–4 of 2007; also A/CN.4/599 of 2008 and A/CN.4/612 of 2009.

36 See Article 3 of the European Convention on Extradition, Article 4 of the Inter-American Convention on Extradition.

37 B. Wierzbicki, *O azylach i ekstradycji przestępców*, p. 113.

38 L. Szpak, *Ekstradycja hitlerowskich zbrodniarzy wojennych ze szczególnym uwzględnieniem praktyki polskiej*, Ministerstwo Sprawiedliwości, Główna Komisja Badania Zbrodni Hitlerowskich w Polsce, Warszawa 1979.

39 See Article 1(2) of the Declaration on Territorial Asylum adopted by GA Resolution no 2312 of 14 December 1967.

40 See Article 1 para F of the Convention relating to the Status of Refugees, Geneva, 27 July 1951, UNTS, vol 189, pp. 137 ff.

41 Article 2(1) of the European Convention on Extradition, Article 3 of the Inter-American Convention on Extradition.

42 See eg GA Resolutions no 2840 of 18 December 1971 or no 3074 of 3 December 1973.

43 Arguments were offered to the effect that 'surrender' differs very significantly from 'extradition'. For example, the states themselves had the opportunity to participate in the design of the proceedings that their citizen will undergo if under such circumstances; such an option does not exist with regard to extraditing a citizen to another state. M. Płachta, *Międzynarodowy Trybunał Karny*, vol 1, p. 961.

44 D. Akande, 'The jurisdiction of the International Criminal Court over nationals of non-parties: legal basis and limits', *JIntCrimJust* 2003, vol 1, pp. 642 ff.

45 M. Płachta, *Międzynarodowy Trybunał Karny*, pp. 1193–95.

46 J. Diamandesco, *Le Problème de l'Agression*, p. 177.

47 The Dutch delegate Loder put forward a proposal to this effect within the League of Nations system in March 1919, ibid, p. 180, C. A. Pompe, *Aggressive War*, p. 72. Similar suggestions were made at the armament conference: J. Diamandesco, *Le Problème de l'Agression*, p. 24.

48 eg Article 4 of the Treaty of Mutual Assistance of 1923, Article 10 of the Geneva Protocol for the Pacific Settlement of International Disputes of 1924, Article 4 of the Rhineland Pact of 1925.

49 Article 4.

50 J. Diamandesco, *Le Problème de l'Agression*, pp. 202–204.

51 See Article 3 of the *Draft Treaty of American Group.*

52 C. A. Pompe, *Aggressive War*, p. 73.

53 J. Diamandesco, *Le Problème de l'Agression*, pp. 178 and 186.

54 J. N. Boeving, 'Aggression, international law, and the ICC', p. 576; F. Mitchell, 'The formulation of the conception of aggression', p. 22.

55 'Remarks by D. Stephen Mathias', in 'The definition of aggression and the ICC', *Proceedings of the Annual Meeting (American Society of International Law)*, vol 96 (13–16 March 2002), p. 181–82.

56 M. S. Stein, 'The Security Council, the International Criminal Court, and the crime of aggression: how exclusive is the Security Council's power to determine aggression?', *IndInt&CompLRev* 2005, vol 16, p. 5; D. D. N. Nsereko, 'Defining the crime of aggression', p. 285; Y. Dinstein, *War, Aggression and Self-Defence*,

p. 214, O. Solera, *Defining the Crime of Aggression*, p. 55. See also ICC-ASP/4/32, para 68.

57 M. S. Stein, 'The Security Council, the International Criminal Court, and the crime of aggression', p. 9.

58 C. A. Pompe, *Aggressive War*, p. 86; G. M. Dawson, 'Defining substantive crimes', p. 440; D. D. N. Nsereko, 'Defining the crime of aggression', p. 278

59 M. O'Donovan, 'Criminalizing war', p. 519; W. A. Schabas, *An Introduction to the International Criminal Court*, p. 32. See also ICC-ASP/4/32, para 74.

60 M. O'Donovan, 'Criminalizing war', p. 516.

61 C. Kress, 'Versailles-Nuremberg-The Hague Germany and international criminal law', *International Lawyer* 2006, vol 40, p. 38; J. Trahan, 'Defining "aggression"', p. 460.

62 M. S. Stein, 'The Security Council, the International Criminal Court, and the crime of aggression', p. 7.

63 ibid, p. 10.

64 A. R. Lacanilao, 'The International Criminal Court in the balance', p. 108.

65 M. S. Stein, 'The Security Council, the International Criminal Court, and the crime of aggression', pp. 14–15; P. Descaloupoulo-Livada, 'The crime of aggression: making operative the jurisdiction of the ICC – tendencies in the PrepCom', in *The Definition of Aggression and the ICC. Remarks by D. Stephen Mathias, Proceedings of the Annual Meeting (American Society of International Law)*, vol 96 (13–16 March 2002), p. 188.

66 See SC Resolution no 598 of 20 July 1987. See further S. M. Yengejeh, 'Reflections on the role of the Security Council in determining an act of aggression', in M. Politi, G. Nesi, *The International Criminal Court*, pp. 129–30.

67 B. B. Ferencz, 'The crime of aggression', p. 60; J. N. Boeving, 'Aggression, international law, and the ICC', p. 578; S. A. Fernández de Gurmendi, 'The Working Group on aggression', p. 602.

68 P. Escarameia, The ICC and the Security Council on aggression: overlapping competencies?, in M. Politi, G. Nesi, *The International Criminal Court*, p. 139.

69 A. R. Lacanilao, 'The International Criminal Court in the balance', p. 110.

70 S. Yee, 'A proposal to reformulate Article 23 of the ILC Draft Statute for an international criminal court', *HastingsInt&CompLRev* 1996, vol 19, p. 534.

71 ICC-ASP/5/SWGCA/INF.1, paras 53 ff.

72 See ICC-ASP/4/32, Annex II.C.

73 For a detailed discussion of all resolutions in which the Security Council classified a situation as an act of aggression or aggression, see PCNICC/2002/WGCA/L.1, pp. 115–21.

74 eg SC Resolution nos 660 and 661 of 6 August 1990, no 662 of 9 August 1990, no 678 of 29 November 1990. The Security Council used the phrase 'aggressive acts' solely with regard to the actions concerning diplomatic personnel in Kuwait (Iraq demanded that all foreign embassies should be closed); see SC Resolution no 667 of 16 September 1990.

75 See SC Resolutions no 326 of 2 February 1973, no 386 of 17 March 1976, no 411 of 30 June 1977, no 424 of 17 March 1978, no 445 of 8 March 1979, no 455 of 23 November 1979.

76 See SC Resolutions no 387 of 31 March 1976, no 418 of 4 November 1977, no 454 of 2 November 1979, no 496 of 15 December 1981, no 507 of 28 May 1982, no 527 of 15 December 1982, no 546 of 6 January 1984, no 568 of 21 June 1985, no 571 of 20 September 1985, no 572 of 30 September 1985, no 574 of 7 October 1985, no 577 of 6 December 1985, 580 of 30 December 1985, no 581 of 13 February 1986, no 602 of 25 November 1987.

77 SC Resolutions no 405 of 14 April 1977.
78 SC Resolutions no 573 of 4 October 1985, no 611 of 25 April 1988.
79 Article 10.
80 Article 11.
81 ICC-ASP/4/32, para 70.
82 See GA Resolutions no 498 and 500 of 18 May 1951, no 712 of 28 August 1953, no 2132 of 21 December 1965.
83 See GA Resolutions no 1899 of 13 November 1963, S-9/2 of 3 May 1978, no 36/121 A of 10 December 1981, no 37/233 A of 20 December 1982, no 38/36 A of 1 December 1983, no 39/50 A of 12 December 1984, no 40/97 A of 13 December 1985, no S-14/1 of 20 September 1986, no 41/39 A of 20 November 1986, no 42/14 A of 6 November 1987, no 43/26 A of 17 November 1988.
84 GA Resolutions 36/172 A and C of 17 December 1981, no 36/8 of 28 October 1981, no 38/39 A and C of 5 December 1983, no 39/72 A and G of 13 December 1984, no 1954 of 11 December 1963, no 1817 of 18 December 1962, no 2508 of 21 November 1969, no 38/14 of 22 November 1983.
85 GA Resolutions no 2795 of 10 December 1971, no 3061 of 2 November 1973, no 3113 of 12 December 1973.
86 See GA Resolutions no 36/27 of 13 November 1981, no 37/18 of 16 November 1982.
87 GA Resolution no 36/226 A of 17 December 1981.
88 GA Resolutions no 36/226 A of 17 December 1981, no 37/123 F of 20 December 1982, no 38/180 D of 19 December 1983, no 39/146 A of 14 December 1984, no 40/168 A of 16 December 1985, no 41/162 A of 4 December 1986, no 42/209 B of 11 December 1987, no 43/54 A of 6 December 1988, no 44/40 A of 4 December 1989, no 45/83 A of 13 December 1990, no 46/82 A of 16 December 1991.
89 GA Resolutions no ES-9/1 of 5 February 1982, no 37/123 A of 16 December 1982, no 38/180 A of 19 December 1983, no 39/146 B of 14 December 1984, no 40/168 B of 16 December 1985, no 41/162 B of 4 December 1986, no 42/209 C of 11 December 1987, no 43/54 B of 6 December 1988, no 44/40 B of 4 December 1989, no 45/83 B of 13 December 1990.
90 GA Resolutions no 46/242 of 25 August 1992, no 47/121 of 18 December 1992, no 48/88 of 20 December 1993, no 49/10 of 3 November 1994.
91 Article 92.
92 Matthias Schuster, however, emphasises that in the case of aggression, the determination pertains not to a right but to a fact. M. Schuster, 'The Rome Statute and the crime of aggression', p. 48.
93 ICJ, Advisory Opinion, *Certain expenses of the United Nations*; ICJ, Judgment, *United States Diplomatic and Consular Staff in Tehran*; ICJ, Judgment, *Military and paramilitary activities in and against Nicaragua*; ICJ, Order, *Application of the Convention on the Prevention and Punishment of the Crime of Genocide (Bosnia and Herzegovina v Yugoslavia)*, 8 April 1993.
94 See ICJ, Order, *Military and paramilitary activities in and against Nicaragua (Nicaragua v United States of America)*, 10 May 1984; ICJ, Order, *Frontier Dispute (Burkina Faso/Republic of Mali)*, 10 January 1986; ICJ, Order, *Land and Maritime Boundary between Cameroon and Nigeria (Cameroon v Nigeria)*, 15 March 1996; ICJ, Order, *Armed Activities on the Territory of the Congo (Democratic Republic of the Congo v Uganda)*, 1 July 2000.
95 ICJ, Judgment, *Military and paramilitary activities in and against Nicaragua*; ICJ, Judgment, *Armed Activities on the Territory of the Congo (Democratic Republic of Congo v Uganda)*, 19 December 2005.

96 ICJ, Judgment, *Military and paramilitary activities in and against Nicaragua*, paras 32 ff; see also a judgment of the International Court of Justice (ICJ) in the same case, dated 26 November 1984, paras 89 ff.
97 ICJ, Judgment, *United States Diplomatic and Consular Staff in Tehran*, para 40.
98 Article 96.
99 M. S. Stein, 'The Security Council, the International Criminal Court, and the crime of aggression', p. 33.
100 ICC-ASP/5/SWGCA/INF.1, para 60.
101 ICC-ASP/6/SWGCA/INF.1, para 31; M. Schuster, 'The Rome Statute and the crime of aggression', p. 48.
102 Article 36 of the ICJ statute.
103 ICC-ASP/7/SWGCA.INF.1.
104 C. A. Pompe, *Aggressive War*, p. 76.
105 Article 119.
106 ICC-ASP/4/32, para 74.
107 M. Schuster, 'The Rome Statute and the crime of aggression', pp. 36–37.
108 ibid, p. 38.
109 R. Peirce, 'Which of the Preparatory Commission's latest proposals for the definition of the crime of aggression and the exercise of jurisdiction should be adopted into the Rome Statute of the International Criminal Court?', *BYUJPubL* 2000–2001, vol 15, p. 298; T. Meron, 'Defining aggression', p. 13.
110 O. Solera, *Defining the Crime of Aggression*, p. 318.
111 T. Meron, 'Defining aggression', p. 3.
112 M. C. Bassiouni, *Introduction to International Criminal Law*, Transnational Publishers, Inc., Ardsley, New York 2003, p. 71.
113 E. Decaux, 'Les gouvernants', in H. Ascensio, E. Decaux, A. Pellet (eds), *Droit international pénal*, p. 183.
114 See International Law Commission, *Preliminary Report on Immunity of State Officials from Foreign Criminal Jurisdiction by Roman Anatolevich Kolodkin, Special Rapporteur*, A/CN.4/601, pp. 13 ff.
115 ibid, pp. 27 ff.
116 ibid, p. 37; D. Akande, 'The jurisdiction of the International Criminal Court', p. 641; W. Czapliński, *Skutki prawne nielegalnego*, p. 247.
117 D. Akande, 'The jurisdiction of the International Criminal Court', p. 641.
118 *Report of the Commission on the Responsibility of the Authors of the War*, p. 116.
119 ibid, p. 117.
120 ibid.
121 *Memorandum of Reservations Presented by the Representatives of the United States*, in ibid, p. 135; *Reservations by the Japanese Delegation*, 4 April 1919, in ibid, p. 152.
122 *Jackson report*, p. 182.
123 ibid. See also S. Glueck, *War Criminals. Their Prosecution and Punishment*, Alfred Knopf, New York 1944, pp. 123–24.
124 Interestingly, however, both the London International Assembly and the United Nations War Crimes Commission imposed certain restrictions on the responsibility of top state officials. United Nations War Crimes Commission, *History of the United Nations War Crimes Commission*, pp. 267 ff.
125 Article VII.
126 *USA Opening Statement*, p. 3.
127 *IMT Judgment*, p 221.
128 Article 7(2) of the ICTY statute, Article 6(2) of the ICTR statute, Article 27(1) of the ICC statute.
129 Third Nuremberg principle, Article 3 of the draft CCPSH of 1954; Article 7 of the draft CCPSH of 1996. For more information on international agreements that of the incorporate this principle see E. Decaux, 'Les gouvernants', pp. 191 ff.

130 MTKJ, Trial Judgment, *Prosecutor v Furundzija* (IT-95-17/1-T), 10 December 1998, para 140.
131 Article 145(2)(b).
132 Case IT-02-54. Pursuant to the trial order of 14 March 2006 proceedings were terminated due to the death of the defendant on 11 March 2006.
133 Special Court of Sierra Leone, Trial Chamber, Judgment, *Prosecutor v Charles Gankay Taylor*, SCSL 03-01-T, 18 May 2012. However, see primarily Appeal Chamber, Decision on Immunity from Jurisdiction, 31 May 2004, paras 43 ff.
134 ICC, First warrant of arrest issued by Pre-Trial Chamber I, 4 March 2009, ICC-02/05-01/09-1; Second warrant of arrest issued by Pre-Trial Chamber I, 12 July 2010, ICC-02/05-01/09-95.
135 ICJ, Judgment, *Arrest Warrant of 11 April 2000 (Democratic Republic of the Congo v Belgium)*, 14 February 2002.
136 ibid, para 51.
137 ibid, para 55.
138 ibid, para 61.
139 See S. Wirth, 'Immunity for core crimes? The ICJ's judgment in the *Congo v Belgium* case', *EJIL* 2002, vol 13, p. 881.
140 A. L. Paulus, 'Peace through justice?', p. 19.
141 Y. Dinstein, *War, Aggression and Self-Defence*, p. 147.
142 D. Akande, 'The jurisdiction of the International Criminal Court', p. 641, W. A. Schabas, *An Introduction to the International Criminal Court*, p. 81.
143 Notably, the wording of the Charter of the International Military Tribunal in Article VII included plural references to heads of state.
144 E. Decaux, 'Les gouvernants', p. 189.
145 M. C. Bassiouni, 'Searching for justice in the world of *Realpolitik*', *PaceIntLRev* 2000, vol 12, p. 225.
146 M. C. Bassiouni, 'From Versailles to Rwanda in seventy-five years', p. 35. See also P. Wilson, *Aggression, Crime and International Security*, p. 60–63.
147 L. Gardocki, *Zarys prawa karnego międzynarodowego*, p. 61.
148 B. V. A. Röling and C. F. Rüter, *The Tokyo Judgment*, vol 1, pp. 478, 494. See also L. Gardocki, *Zarys prawa karnego międzynarodowego*, p. 64; A. C. Brackman, *The Other Nuremberg*, pp. 387–88.
149 *IMTFE Judgment*, p. 456.
150 L. S. Sunga, *The Emerging System of International Criminal Law*, pp. 308 ff.
151 S. Glueck, *War Criminals*, p. 73.
152 Article 14. UNTS, vol 999, pp. 171 ff.
153 Articles 55, 66, 67 of the ICC Statute.
154 W. A. Schabas, *An Introduction to the International Criminal Court*, p. 98.
155 Article XVI.
156 ibid.
157 G. Schwarzenberger, *International Law*, vol 2, p. 472.
158 ibid, p. 474.
159 See ECHR judgment, *Piersack v Belgium*, 1 October 1982, Series A, no 53, p. 167 and *Hauschildt v Denmark*, 24 December 1989, Series A, no 154, p. 266.
160 L. Hankey, *Politics, Trials and Errors*, p. 2.
161 R. K. Woetzel, *The Nuremberg Trials in International Law* pp. 44–45.
162 See remarks made by B. V. A. Röling, 'The Nuremberg and the Tokyo trials in retrospect', in G. Mettraux, *Perspectives on the Nuremberg Trial*, p. 464.
163 R. H. Minear, *Victors' Justice*, pp. 82–83.
164 A. C. Brackman, *The Other Nuremberg*, p. 23, J. A. Appleman, *Military Tribunals and International Crimes*, pp. 243 ff.
165 B. V. A. Röling and A. Cassese, *The Tokyo Trial and Beyond*, p. 29.

166 ibid, A. C. Brackman, *The Other Nuremberg*, p. 344. There are good reasons why the monument to honour Judge Pal was raised near the temple of Yasukuni.
167 R. H. Minear, *Victors' Justice*, p. 86.
168 B. V. A. Röling and A. Cassese, *The Tokyo Trial and Beyond*, p. 30, G. Schwarzenberger, *International Law*, vol 2, p. 475.
169 The American judge John P. Higgins resigned from the bench of the International Military Tribunal for the Far East in July 1946, ie after a month of investigation evidence. He was replaced by Myron H. Cramer.
170 R. H. Minear, *Victors' Justice*, pp. 87–89.
171 ibid, p. 88.
172 A. C. Brackman, *The Other Nuremberg*, p. 338.
173 ibid, pp. 382–83, R. H. Minear, *Victors' Justice*, pp. 90–91, B. V. A. Röling and A. Cassese, *The Tokyo Trial and Beyond*, p. 64.
174 B. V. A. Röling and C. F. Rüter, *The Tokyo Judgment*, vol 1, p. 494. See also A. C. Brackman, *The Other Nuremberg*, p. 365; J. A. Appleman, *Military Tribunals and International Crimes*, p. 260; L. Hankey, *Politics, Trials and Errors*, p. 87; B. V. A. Röling and A. Cassese, *The Tokyo Trial and Beyond*, pp. 7, 62 ff.
175 See Article 66 of the ICC statute, ECHR, Judgment, *Barberà, Messegué and Jabardo v Spain*, 6 December 1988, Series A, no 146, p. 33.
176 W. A. Schabas, *An Introduction to the International Criminal Court*, pp. 95–97.
177 L. Hankey, *Politics, Trials and Errors*, p. 19.
178 B. B. Ferencz, *Defining International Aggression*, vol 1, p. 388.
179 ibid, pp. 385 and 390.
180 M. Lippman, 'Nuremberg: forty-five years later', *ConnecticutJIntL* 1991, vol 7, p. 37.
181 C. A. Pompe, *Aggressive War*, p. 193.
182 L. Hankey, *Politics, Trials and Errors*, p. 8
183 W. A. Schabas, *An Introduction to the International Criminal Court*, pp. 98 ff.
184 J. A. Appleman, *Military Tribunals and International Crimes*, p. 87.
185 L. S. Sunga, *The Emerging System of International Criminal Law*, p. 312.
186 J. A. Appleman, *Military Tribunals and International Crimes*, p. 89.
187 I. Bantekas and S. Nash, *International Criminal Law*, 3rd edn, Routledge Cavendish, London, New York 2007, p. 506.
188 Q. Wright, 'The law of the Nuremberg Trial', p. 52.
189 L. Gardocki, *Zarys prawa karnego międzynarodowego*, p. 61.
190 The states emphasised that in the case of the crime of aggression Article 57(3), Article 72, Article 93(4) and Article 99(5) all apply. Doubts were only expressed as to the applicability of Article 73 with regard to protection of document bearing the seal indicating state secrets of the aggressor state. ICC-ASP/4/32, paras 54–55.
191 See *Defense Appeal to General MacArthur*, 21 November 1948, reprinted in R. H. Minear, *Victors' Justice*, pp. 204 ff.
192 J. A. Appleman, *Military Tribunals and International Crimes*, p. 255, B. V. A. Röling, A. Cassese, *The Tokyo Trial and Beyond*, pp. 51 ff.
193 B. V. A. Röling and C. F. Rüter, *The Tokyo Judgment*, vol 1, p. 494.
194 R. L. Griffiths, *International Law*, p. 310; A. R. Lacanilao, 'The International Criminal Court in the balance', p. 113.
195 ICC-ASP/4/32, para 60.
196 Article XXVI.
197 Article XXIX.
198 R. K. Woetzel, *The Nuremberg Trials in International Law*, p. ix.
199 So B. B. Ferencz, *Remarks Made at Pace University School of Law*, p. 59.
200 If the statutes of limitation in the national legal order provide for no time limits after which prosecution is barred, the crimes never become barred. F. Weiss,

'Time limits for the prosecution of crimes against international law', *BYbkIntL* 1982, vol 53, p. 165.

201 L. Gardocki, *Zarys prawa karnego międzynarodowego*, p. 197.

202 A. Klafkowski, *Podstawowe problemy prawne likwidacji skutków wojny 1939–1945 a dwa państwa niemieckie*, Instytut Zachodni, Poznań 1966, p. 401.

203 UNTS, vol 754, pp. 73 ff.

204 Article I.

205 UNTS, vol 2245, pp. 307 ff.

206 Article 29.

207 Y. Dinstein, *War, Aggression and Self-Defence*, p. 135.

208 As of 15 December 2012.

209 ibid.

210 Y. Dinstein, *War, Aggression and Self-Defence*, p. 135.

211 Abolition consists in a statutory pardon for certain crimes. It is accomplished by specifying the type of crimes or by listing the sanction limits and dates before which the crimes must have been committed. As a consequence, proceedings may no longer be instigated, and those that had been instigated must be discontinued. In the case of an amnesty, on the other hand, it is not the crime but rather the punishment that is either cancelled or made more lenient. L. Gardocki, *Prawo karne*, 8th edn, Warszawa 2002, pp. 171 and 194.

212 M. P. Scharf, 'Justice versus peace', in S. B. Sewall, C. Kaysen, *The United States and the International Criminal Court. National Security and International Law*, Rowman & Littlefield Publishers, Inc., Lanham 2000.

213 M. Płachta, 'Jak pogodzić sprawiedliwość retrybutywną ze sprawiedliwością restytucyjną? Międzynarodowy Trybunał Karny a komisje pojednania i amnestie', *Ius et Lex* 2003, no 1, p. 106.

214 Article II(5).

215 Y. Naqvi, 'Amnesty for war crimes: defining the limits of international recognition', *IRRC* 2003, no 851, p. 615.

216 Articles 16, 17, 20, 53. M. Płachta, *Międzynarodowy Trybunał Karny*, pp. 1255 ff.

217 Y. Naqvi, 'Amnesty for war crimes', pp. 616–17; M. Płachta, *Międzynarodowy Trybunał Karny*, p. 11.

218 A. Cassese, *International Criminal Law*, pp. 141 ff; F. Weiss, 'Time limits for the prosecution of crimes', p. 174.

219 A. Cassese, *International Criminal Law*, pp. 141–42.

220 S. Glueck, *The Nuremberg Trial*, pp. 75–76.

221 The opinion of professor H. Jahreiss was published in *Nazi Conspiracy and Aggression*, Supplement B, pp. 3 ff. See also C. Kress, 'Versailles-Nuremberg-The Hague', pp. 21–22.

222 See opinion of Professor H. Jahreiss, pp. 9 ff. Compare with I. Brownlie, *International Law and the Use of Force*, p. 169.

223 *IMT Judgment*, p. 217.

224 See also S. Glueck, *The Nuernberg Trial*, pp. 89 ff.

225 *Jackson report*, p. 187.

226 S. Glueck, *The Nuremberg Trial*, p. 61; J. A. Appleman, *Military Tribunals and International Crimes*, p. 50; W. R. Harris, *Tyranny on Trial*, pp. 493 ff; B. V. A. Röling and A. Cassese, *The Tokyo Trial and Beyond*, p. 97.

227 *Nazi Conspiracy and Aggression*, Supplement A, p. 92.

228 ibid, pp. 88–89.

229 A. Obote-Odora, *The Judging of War Criminals*, pp. 76–77.

230 W. J. Bosh, *Judgment on Nuremberg*, p. 140.

231 ibid, pp. 138–39.

232 W. Schabas, 'Origins of the criminalization of aggression', p. 30.

233 Article 22(1).
234 Article 22(2).
235 A. Cassese, *International Criminal Law*, p. 145.
236 See Judge Jaranilla's opinion, in B. V. A. Röling and C. F. Rüter, *The Tokyo Judgment*, vol 1, p. 508; F. Weiss, 'Time limits for the prosecution of crimes', p. 183; V. V. Pella, *La guerre-crime et les criminels de guerre*, p. 83; S. Glueck, *The Nuremberg Trial*, p. 92.
237 J. A. Appleman, *Military Tribunals and International Crimes*, p. 48.
238 L. Leibman, 'From Nuremberg to Bosnia: consistent application of international law', *ClevStLRev* 1994, vol 42, p. 715.
239 R. K. Woetzel, *The Nuremberg Trials in International Law*, p. 112.
240 Judge Pal's opinion, in B. V. A. Röling and C. F. Rüter, *The Tokyo Judgment*, vol 2, pp. 11 ff.
241 R. L. Griffiths, *International Law*, p. 371.
242 Article 15(2) of the ICCPR and also Article 7(2) of the European Convention for the Protection of Human Rights and Fundamental Freedoms, 4 November 1950, UNTS, vol 213, pp. 212 ff. See C. Kress, '*Nulla poena nullum crimen sine lege*', in *Max Planck Encyclopedia of Public International Law,* available at http://www.mpepil.com (last visited 3 June 2013) and R. Cryer, 'Aggression at the Court of Appeal', p. 219.
243 R. K. Woetzel, *The Nuremberg Trials in International Law*, p. 169.
244 *IMT Judgment*, p. 207.
245 R. K. Woetzel, *The Nuremberg Trials in International Law*, p. 165.
246 R. L. Griffiths, *International Law*, p. 371.
247 However, Claus Kress and Leonie von Holtzendorff emphasise that Article 8 *bis* of the ICC Statute does not meet expectation of the 'highest standards of codification'. C. Kress and L. von Holtzendorff, 'The Kampala compromise', p. 1210.
248 R. Cryer, 'Aggression at the Court of Appeal', p. 223.
249 A. Cassese, *International Criminal Law*, p. 155.
250 ibid, p. 157.
251 C. A. Pompe, *Aggressive War*, pp. 258–59.
252 F. Weiss, 'Time limits for the prosecution of crimes', p. 175.

7 Impact of aggression trials

1 C. C. Joyner, 'Introduction', in C. C. Joyner (sp. ed.), M. C. Bassiouni (gen. ed.), *Reining in impunity for international crimes and serious violations of fundamental human rights*, p. 9.
2 Available at http://www.vatican.va/holy_father/paul_vi/messages/peace/documents/hf_p-vi_mes_19711208_v-world-day-for-peace_en.html (last visited 3 June 2013).
3 M. C. Bassiouni, *Introduction to International Criminal Law*, p. 680.
4 ibid, p. 702.
5 I. Tallgren, 'The sensibility and sense of international criminal law', *EJIL* 2002, vol 13, p. 593; L. Hankey, *Politics, Trials and Errors*, p. 26.
6 R. Kherad, 'La question de la définition du crime d'agression', pp. 340–41; J. N. Boeving, 'Aggression, international law, and the ICC', p. 580.
7 M. Schuster, 'The Rome Statute and the crime of aggression', p. 41.
8 L. Hankey, *Politics, Trials and Errors*, p. 55; B. D. Meltzer, '"War Crimes": the Nuremberg trial and the Tribunal for the Former Yugoslavia', *ValparaisoUnivLRev* 1996, vol 30, p. 904.
9 I. K. Müller-Schieke, 'Defining the crime of aggression', p. 421.
10 B. D. Meltzer, '"War Crimes": the Nuremberg trial and the Tribunal for the Former Yugoslavia', p. 904.

11 *Remarks by D. Stephen Mathias*, p. 184.
12 I. K. Müller-Schieke, 'Defining the crime of aggression', p. 421.
13 L. M. Goodrich, E. Hambro and A. P. Simons, *Charter of the United Nations*, pp. 27 ff. Interestingly, justice is only referred to in Article 2(3) of the Charter of the United Nations and in its preamble.
14 B. B. Ferencz, 'Can aggression be deterred by law?', pp. 355–56.
15 B. V. A. Röling and A. Cassese, *The Tokyo Trial and Beyond*, p. 96.
16 P. Malik, *Międzynarodowy Trybunał Karny a problematyka bezpieczeństwa światowego*, Wojskowy Przegląd Prawniczy 2003, no 3, p. 9.
17 M. Płachta, *Międzynarodowy Trybunał Karny*, p. 1223.
18 Article 16.
19 J. Trahan, 'Defining "Aggression": why the Preparatory Commission for the International Criminal Court has faced such a conundrum', *LoyolaLAInt&CompLRev* 2002, vol 24, p. 464; A. C. Carpenter, 'The International Criminal Court and the crime of aggression', *NJIntL* 1995, vol 64, p. 235.
20 T. Cyprian and J. Sawicki, *Przestępstwa międzynarodowe*, Wiedza Powszechna, Łódź 1948, p. 12.
21 D. Zolo, 'Peace through criminal law', *JIntCrimJust* 2004, vol 2, p. 727; M. O'Donovan, 'Criminalizing war', p. 509, N. Nyiri, *The United Nations' Search*, p. 39; T. Taylor, *Nuremberg and Vietnam*, Quadrangle Books, Chicago 1970, p. 75; J. F. Willis, *Prologue to Nuremberg*, p. 184.
22 G. M. Dawson, 'Defining substantive crimes', p. 431.
23 Y. Beigbeder, *Judging War Criminals. The Politics of International Justice*, Macmillan Press Ltd, New York 1999, p. 193.
24 B. B. Ferencz, 'Misguided fears about the International Criminal Court', *PaceIntLRev* 2003, vol 15, p. 242.
25 A/CN.4/15, p. 16.
26 I. Tallgren, 'The sensibility and sense of international criminal law', p. 570.
27 B. B. Ferencz, 'Can aggression be deterred by law?', p. 353.
28 L. May, *Aggression and Crimes against Peace*, p. 19.
29 Y. Dinstein, *War, Aggression and Self-Defence*, p. 117.
30 I. Tallgren, 'The sensibility and sense of international criminal law', p. 561.
31 ibid.
32 T. Meron, 'From Nuremberg to The Hague', *MilLRev* 1995, vol 149, p. 110.
33 M. O'Donovan, 'Criminalizing war', p. 527.
34 M. C. Van de Kieft, 'Uncertain risk: the United States military and the International Criminal Court', *CardozoLRev* 2002, vol 22, p. 2341.
35 A. R. Lacanilao, 'The International Criminal Court in the balance', p. 105.
36 ibid, p. 101.
37 B. B. Ferencz, 'Getting aggressive about preventing aggression', *BrownJWorldAff* 1999.
38 T. Meron, 'From Nuremberg to The Hague', p. 110.
39 So argued Robert Alphonso Taft, one of the biggest American opponents of the trial in Nuremberg and of aggression trials in general; see W. J. Bosh, *Judgment on Nuremberg*, pp. 75 ff.
40 J. A. Appleman, *Military Tribunals and International Crimes*, p. 10; G. A. Finch, 'The Nuremberg trial and international law', p. 35.
41 S. Glueck, *War Criminals*, p. 130.
42 W. J. Bosh, *Judgment on Nuremberg*, p. 227.
43 W. A. Schabas, 'United States hostility to the International Criminal Court: it's all about the Security Council', *EJIL* 2004, vol 15, p. 715.
44 A. C. Brackman, *The Other Nuremberg*, p. 35.
45 J. F. Willis, *Prologue to Nuremberg*, p. 210.

46 B. Van Schaack, *'Par in parem imperium non habet'*, p. 150.
47 See http://www.sipri.org/yearbook/2011/02/02A (last visited 3 June 2013).
48 M. C. Bassiouni, 'Nuremberg: forty years after', in *Forty Years After the Nuremberg and Tokyo Tribunals: The Impact of the War Crimes Trials on International and National Law, ASIL Proceedings* 1986, vol 80, p. 64. See also the statistics of the dead victims of wars and conflicts after the end of the Second World War (1945–2000); M. Leitenberg, 'Wojny i konflikty w latach 1945–2000: Ofiary śmiertelne', in R. Kuźniar and Z. Lachowski (eds), *Bezpieczeństwo międzynarodowe czasu przemian*, pp. 94 ff. The data clearly demonstrate that from among the 40 million dead, the majority lost their lives in civil wars and colonial wars.
49 *USA Opening Statement*, p. 76.
50 *Jackson report*, p. 186.
51 *IMT Judgment*, p. 186.
52 C. A. Pompe, *Aggressive War*, p. 177. E. Creegan, 'Justified uses of force', p. 68.
53 B. D. Meltzer, '"War Crimes": the Nuremberg trial and the Tribunal for the Former Yugoslavia', p. 897.
54 B. B. Ferencz, *An International Criminal Court*, vol 1, p. 421.
55 A. L. Paulus, 'Peace through justice?', pp. 2–3; Q. Wright, 'The law of the Nuremberg trial', p. 66; H. Kelsen, *Peace Through Law*, The University of North Carolina Press, Chapel Hill 1944, p. viii; B. V. A. Röling and A. Cassese, *The Tokyo Trial and Beyond*, p. 99; L. May, *Aggression and Crimes against Peace*, pp. 6; G. M. Dawson, 'Defining substantive crimes', p. 447; D. D. N. Nsereko, 'Defining the crime of aggression', p. 266; A. N. Trainin, *La responsabilité pénale*, p. 7; S. Glueck, *The Nuremberg Trial*, pp. 77, 79, 82, 83.
56 See eg *Trials of War Criminals*, vol 12, p. 13.
57 W. R. Harris, *Tyranny on Trial*, pp. 529 and 555.
58 J. Trahan, 'Defining "Aggression"', p. 465; I. K. Müller-Schieke, 'Defining the crime of aggression', p. 414.
59 L. May, *Aggression and Crimes against Peace*, p. 44.
60 See C. Kress, 'Time for decision', p. 1135 and also J. Trahan, 'The Rome Statute's amendments', p. 51.
61 A. L. Paulus, 'Peace through justice?', p. 8.
62 I. K. Müller-Schieke, 'Defining the crime of aggression', p. 414.
63 P. Calvocoressi, *Nuremberg. The Facts, the Law and the Consequences*, Chatto and Windus, London 1947, p. 42. See also *Closing Address for United Kingdom, Great Britain and Ireland by Sir Hartley Shawcross, Nazi Conspiracy and Aggression*, Supplement A, p. 76.
64 W. Schabas, 'Origins of the criminalization of aggression', p. 30.
65 B. D. Meltzer, '"War Crimes": the Nuremberg trial and the Tribunal for the Former Yugoslavia', p. 68.
66 W. Schabas, 'Origins of the criminalization of aggression', p. 31.
67 See A. M. Danner and J. S. Martinez, 'Guilty associations: joint criminal enterprise, command responsibility, and the development of international criminal law', *CalifLRev* 2005, vol 93.
68 W. Schabas, 'Origins of the criminalization of aggression', p. 30.
69 The principle was expressed in the preamble of the Protocol Additional to Geneva Conventions of 12 August 1949 (Protocol I) which read: 'Reaffirming further that the provisions of the Geneva Conventions of 12 August 1949 and of this Protocol must be fully applied in all circumstances to all persons who are protected by those instruments, without any adverse distinction based on the nature or origin of the armed conflict or on the causes espoused by or attributed to the Parties to the conflict'. UNTS, vol 1125, pp. 3 ff.
70 *USA Opening Statement*, p. 76.
71 A. L. Paulus, 'Peace through justice?', pp. 32–33.

72 F. Bugnion, 'Just wars, wars of aggression and international humanitarian law', *IRRC* 2002, no 847, p. 10.
73 See further ibid, pp. 16 ff.
74 *IMT Judgment*, p. 218.
75 It is, however, worth noting that eg the Netherlands Special Court of Cassation in the Trial of Willy Zuehlke pointed out the following: 'it is going too far to regard as war crimes all acts committed against the Netherlands or Netherlanders by the German forces and other organs during the war, solely on the grounds of the illegal nature of the war launched by the then German Reich'. United Nations War Crimes Commission, *Law Reports*, vol 15, p. 149.
76 See eg C. A. Pompe, *Aggressive War*, p. 559.
77 J. Trahan, 'Defining "Aggression"', p. 442.
78 M. R. Marrus, 'A Jewish lobby at Nuremberg: Jacob Robinson and the Institute of Jewish Affairs, 1945–946', *CardozoLRev* 2006, vol 27, p. 1652.
79 See RC/5, para 5.
80 See A. Paulus, 'Second thoughts on the crime of aggression', p. 1127.
81 M. O'Donovan, 'Criminalizing war', p. 524.
82 ibid, p. 525.
83 ibid, p. 526.
84 L. May, *Aggression and Crimes against Peace*, p. 225.
85 M. C. Bassiouni, *Introduction to International Criminal Law*, p. 724; M. Harroff-Travel, 'Do wars ever end? The work of the International Committee of the Red Cross when the guns fall silent', *IRRC* 2003, no 851, p. 484; M. Sassòli and A. A. Bouvier, *Un droit dans la guerre?*, Comité international de la Croix-Rouge, Genève 2003, p. 304; C. Antonopoulos, 'Whatever happened to crimes against peace?', p. 62.
86 *USA Opening Statement*, p. 9.
87 D. D. N. Nsereko, 'Defining the crime of aggression', p. 283.
88 J. N. Boeving, 'Aggression, international law, and the ICC', pp. 590–91.
89 C. A. Pompe, *Aggressive War*, p. 292.
90 See F. Ryszka, *Norymberga*, p. 245; N. Boister and R. Cryer, *The Tokyo International Military Tribunal*, p. 317; B. V. A. Röling and A. Cassese, *The Tokyo Trial and Beyond*, pp. 38 ff; R. H. Minear, *Victors' Justice*, pp. 105–107.
91 A. C. Brackman, *The Other Nuremberg*, p. 327; R. H. Minear, *Victors' Justice*, pp. 111, 113.
92 G. P. Fletcher, *Romantics at War*, p. 164.
93 ibid, p. 45. Rev. Andrzej Zwoliński notes that, particularly in democracies, the entire society is responsible for war, because it is the society that determines the prevailing ethics. K. A. Zwoliński, *Wojna. Wybrane zagadnienia*, Wydawnictwo WAM, Kraków 2003, p. 145.
94 G. Best, *War & Law Since 1945*, Clarendon Press, New York 1994, p. 382.
95 R. H. Minear, *Victors' Justice*, passim.
96 M. O'Donovan, 'Criminalizing war', p. 508.
97 R. S. Clark, 'Rethinking aggression as a crime', p. 886.
98 See *Trials of War Criminals*, vol 14, p. 336. Compare with L. Hankey, *Politics, Trials and Errors*, pp. 63 ff; W. Czapliński, *Skutki prawne nielegalnego*, p. 55.
99 C. Antonopoulos, 'Whatever happened to crimes against peace?', p. 42.
100 H. Kelsen, *Peace Through Law*, p. 24.
101 J. Hogan-Doran and B. T. van Ginkel, 'Aggression as a crime', p. 347.
102 B. B. Ferencz, 'The crime of aggression', p. 60.
103 C. A. Pompe, *Aggressive War*, p. 246.
104 Wilhelm II in his letter to Hindenburg dated 5 April 1921 wrote that he was unwilling to appear voluntarily before a court to be cleared of the charges, because the court designated to determine his responsibility was not so much an

organ of law as it was a victors' instrument, its purpose being to mask the political goals with the majesty of law. T. Cyprian and J. Sawicki, *Ludzie i sprawy Norymbergii*, p. 25. Similar arguments were used by Greiser; see J. Gumkowski and T. Kułakowski, *Zbrodniarze hitlerowscy przed Najwyższym Trybunałem Narodowym*, p. 60. See also B. V. A. Röling and A. Cassese, *The Tokyo Trial and Beyond*, p. 87.

105 L. Hankey, *Politics, Trials and Errors*, p. ix.

106 R. H. Minear, *Victors' Justice*, passim.

107 N. Boister and R. Cryer, *The Tokyo International Military Tribunal*, p. 310.

108 *USA Opening Statement*, p. 85.

109 *Symposium The Fifth Annual Ernst C. Stiefel Symposium*, p. 515.

110 ibid.

111 F. J. P. Veale, *Advance to Barbarism. How the Reversion to Barbarism in Warfare and War Trials Menaces Our Future*, C.C. Nelson Publishing Company, Appleton, Wisconsin 1953, p. 142.

112 B. V. A. Röling and A. Cassese, *The Tokyo Trial and Beyond*, p. 20.

113 For these reasons, Finch uses the term *participes criminis* to refer to the Russians. See G. A. Finch, 'The Nuremberg trial and international law', p. 28.

114 ibid, pp. 26 ff. Other examples cited in this context include Poland's military operations in Vilnius in 1920 and in the Zaolzie region in 1938; L. Hankey, *Politics, Trials and Errors*, p. 13; L. Gardocki, *Zarys prawa karnego międzynarodowego*, p. 58. As for the trial in Tokyo, it was noted that the adjudicating panel included one Dutch and one French judge, ie representatives of two states which were leading colonial wars at the time; A. C. Brackman, *The Other Nuremberg*, p. 213. Furthermore, it was also noted that it was the Soviet Union that declared war on Japan on 8 August 1945, and not the other way round; R. H. Minear, *Victors' Justice*, p. 95.

115 S. Yee, 'The "tu quoque" argument as a defence to international crimes, prosecution or punishment', *ChinJIntL* 2004, vol 3. pp. 92–93.

116 G. Schwarzenberger, *International Law*, vol 2, p. 509.

117 B. V. A. Röling and C. F. Rüter, *The Tokyo Judgment*, vol 2, p. 562.

118 *Trials of War Criminals*, vol 14, pp. 322–23.

119 T. Taylor, *Nuremberg Trials*, p. 216.

120 A. Obote-Odora, *The Judging of War Criminals*, p. 81.

121 F. Biddle, 'Le procès de Nuremberg', p. 6.

122 E. Davidson, *The Trial of the Germans*, p. 590; ibid, *The Nuremberg Fallacy. Wars and War Crimes Since World War II*, The Macmillan Company, New York 1973, p. 286; H. Kelsen, 'Will the judgment in the Nuremberg trial constitute a precedent in international law?', *IntLQ* 1947, vol 1, p. 171.

123 Q. Wright, 'The law of the Nuremberg Trial', p. 45.

124 R. H. Minear, *Victors' Justice*, p. 75.

125 See 'Open Panel Discussion: Should the United States join the International Criminal Court?', *UCDavisJIntL&Pol* 2002, vol 9, pp. 53, 59.

126 L. Hankey, *Politics, Trials and Errors*, p. 60.

127 A. R. Lacanilao, 'The International Criminal Court in the balance', p. 112.

128 J. N. Boeving, 'Aggression, international law, and the ICC', pp. 583 ff; T. van Boven, 'Accountability for international crimes: the victim's perspective', in C. C. Joyner (sp. ed.), M. C. Bassiouni (gen. ed.), *Reining in impunity for international crimes and serious violations of fundamental human rights*, pp. 350 ff.

129 Carsten Stahn notes that this in fact amounts to the constitution of 'a surrogate forum for interstate reparation through criminal proceeding before the ICC'. C. Stahn, 'The "end", the "beginning of the end" or the "end of the beginning"? Introducing debated and voices on the definition of "Aggression"', *LeidenJIntL* 2010, vol 23, p. 881. See also F. Rosenfeld, 'Individual civil responsibility for the crime of aggression', *JIntCrimJust* 2012, vol 10, pp. 249 ff.

130 J. N. Boeving, 'Aggression, international law, and the ICC', p. 587.
131 See eg M. C. Van de Kieft, 'Uncertain risk', pp. 2336–2337; K. Ailslieger, 'Why the United States should be wary of the International Criminal Court: concerns over sovereignty and constitutional guarantees', *WashburnLJ* 1999, vol 39, p. 84; L. J. Springrose, 'Aggression as a core crime in the Rome Statute Establishing and International Criminal Court', *StLouisWarsawTransLJ* 1999, vol 99, p. 152; W. A. Schabas, 'United States hostility', pp. 717–718; R. Peirce, 'Which of the Preparatory Commission's', p. 282; R. Kherad, 'La question de la définition du crime d'agression', p. 346; B. B. Ferencz, 'Getting aggressive about preventing aggression'; ibid, 'Misguided fears about the International Criminal Court', p. 235; S. D. Murphy, 'U.S. notification of intent not to become a party to the Rome Statute', *AJIL* 2002, vol 96, p. 724; M. A. Newton, 'Should the United States join the International Criminal Court?', *UCDavisJIntL&Pol* 2002, vol 9, p. 43; L. Jianping and W. Zhixiang, 'China's attitude towards the ICC', *JIntCrimJust* 2005, vol 3, pp. 608, 611.
132 I. K. Müller-Schieke, 'Defining the crime of aggression', p. 413.
133 L. N. Sadat, *The International Criminal Court*, p. 135. See also L. von Braun and A. Micus, 'Judicial independence at risk. Critical issues regarding the crime of aggression raised by selected human rights organizations', *JIntCrimJust* 2012, vol 10, pp.118 ff.
134 L. Condorelli, 'Conclusions générales', in M. Politi and G. Nesi, *The International Criminal Court*, pp. 158–59.
135 H. Abtahi, 'The Islamic Republic of Iran and the ICC', *JIntCrimJust* 2005, vol 3, p. 642 (see also Iran statement after the adoption of resolution RC/Res.6 on crime of aggression in Official Records, p. 125); L. J. Springrose, 'Aggression as a core crime', pp. 152–53; C. Kress, *Versailles-Nuremberg-The Hague*, p. 38.
136 See press conference of SGWCA of 13 February 2009, available at http://www.icc-cpi.int/NR/rdonlyres/9FCD3A51-6568-41DF-819F-5075C3857523/0/UNDOCPressConferenceonSWGCAENG.pdf (last visited 3 June 2013).
137 I. Tallgren, 'The sensibility and sense of international criminal law', p. 585.
138 D. D. N. Nsereko, 'Defining the crime of aggression', p. 265.
139 B. B. Ferencz, 'Can aggression be deterred by law?', p. 341; K. Drzewicki, *Trzecia generacja praw człowieka*, Sprawy Międzynarodowe 1983, no 10, pp. 89–91.
140 I. K. Müller-Schieke, 'Defining the crime of aggression', p. 414; C. Kress, *Versailles-Nuremberg-The Hague*, p. 38.
141 A. R. Lacanilao, 'The International Criminal Court in the balance', p. 100.
142 A. L. Paulus, 'Peace through justice?', p. 35.
143 T. Meron, 'Defining aggression', p. 3.
144 J. N. Boeving, 'Aggression, international law, and the ICC', pp. 582–83.
145 P. Wald, 'International criminal courts – a stormy adolescence', *VirJIntL* 2006, vol 46, p. 327.
146 It is enlightening to cite here a passage from the judgment of the Polish Supreme National Tribunal in the case of Forster to illustrate the scale of historical entanglement of an aggression trial: 'Suffice it to cite from our history events such as: murder by the armed forces of the Teutonic Order on 14 November 1308 of the population of Gdańsk and the area; the Order's bloody raids on the regions of Kujawy and Mazowsze in the 14th century; the support by the Duchy of Prussia of the Swedes when they invaded Poland in 1655–1657; the forcing of Poland, by means of the treaties of Bydgoszcz and Welawa, to give up the fiefdom from the Duchy of Prussia, which led to the subsequent development of the power of Prussia built by Frederic the Great at the expense of Poland'. T. Cyprian, J. Sawicki, *Siedem wyroków Najwyższego Trybunału Narodowego*, p. 269. Centuries of history were also investigated before the International Military Tribunal for the Far East. See J. A. Appleman, *Military Tribunals and International Crimes*, p. 256.

147 B. D. Meltzer, '"War Crimes": the Nuremberg trial and the Tribunal for the Former Yugoslavia', p. 900.
148 F. Ryszka, *Norymberga*, p. 193.
149 R. D. Lumb, 'Individual responsibility for aggressive war', p. 352.
150 I. Tallgren, 'The sensibility and sense of international criminal law', p. 587.
151 M. C. Bassiouni, 'The perennial conflict between international criminal justice and *Realpolitik*', *GeoStUnivLRev* 2006, vol 22, p. 559; see also C. C. Joyner (sp. ed.), M. C. Bassiouni (gen. ed.), *Reining in impunity for international crimes and serious violations of fundamental human rights*, p. 515.

Conclusion

1 Y. Dinstein, *War, Aggression and Self-Defence*, p. 120.

Bibliography

1 Documents

League of Nations

LNOJ 1920.
LNOJ 1923.
LNOJ 1924.
LNOJ 1927.
LNOJ 1937.
LNOJ 1939.

United Nations Organisation

A. Security Council Resolutions

82, 25 June 1950
83, 27 June 1950
84, 7 July 1950
217, 20 November 1965
253, 29 May 1968
277, 18 March 1970
326, 2 February 1973
386, 17 March 1976
387, 31 March 1976
405, 14 April 1977
411, 30 June 1977
418, 4 November 1977
424, 17 March 1978
445, 8 March 1979
454, 2 November 1979
455, 23 November 1979
487, 19 June 1981
496, 15 December 1981
507, 28 May 1982
527, 15 December 1982
546, 6 January 1984
568, 21 June 1985
571, 20 September 1985
572, 30 September 1985
573, 4 October 1985
574, 7 October 1985
577, 6 December 1985
580, 30 December 1985
581, 13 February 1986
598, 20 July 1987
602, 25 November 1987
611, 25 April 1988
660, 6 August 1990
661, 6 August 1990
662, 9 August 1990
667, 16 September 1990
678, 29 November 1990
688, 5 April 1991
731, 21 January 1992
748, 31 March 1992
788, 19 November 1992
794, 3 December 1992

808, 22 February 1993
827, 25 May 1993
841, 16 June 1993
866, 22 September 1993
875, 16 October 1993
929, 22 June 1994
955, 8 November 1994
1054, 26 April 1996
1070, 16 August 1996
1078, 9 November 1996
1214, 8 December 1998
1244, 10 June 1999
1267, 15 October 1999
1277, 30 November 1999
1333, 19 December 2000
1368, 12 September 2001
1373, 28 September 2001
1377, 12 November 2001
1408, 6 May 2002
1422, 12 July 2002
1438, 14 October 2002
1440, 24 October 2002
1441, 8 November 2002
1450, 13 December 2002
1465, 13 February 2003
1483, 22 May 2003
1540, 28 April 2004

B. General Assembly

RESOLUTIONS

95, 11 December 1946
110, 3 November 1947
177, 21 November 1947
260, 9 December 1948
375, 6 December 1949
377, 3 November 1950
378, 17 November 1950
380, 17 November 1950
488, 12 December 1950
489, 12 December 1950
498, 18 May 1951
500, 18 May 1951
599, 31 January 1952
688, 20 December 1952
712, 28 August 1953
895, 4 December 1954
897, 4 December 1954
898, 4 December 1954
1181, 29 November 1957
1186, 11 December 1957
1514, 14 December 1960
1817, 18 December 1962
1899, 13 November 1963
1954, 11 December 1963
2015, 20 December 1965
2131, 21 December 1965
2132, 21 December 1965
2312, 14 December 1967
2330, 18 December 1967
2391, 26 November 1968
2420, 18 December 1968
2508, 21 November 1969
2549, 12 December 1969
2625, 24 October 1970
2644, 25 November 1970
2737, 16 December 1970
2781, 3 December 1971
2795, 10 December 1971
2840, 18 December 1971
2967, 14 December 1972
3061, 2 November 1973
3070, 30 November 1973
3074, 3 December 1973
3105, 12 December 1973
3113, 12 December 1973
3281, 12 December 1974
3314, 14 December 1974
S-9/2, 3 May 1978
33/97, 16 December 1978
35/49, 4 December 1980
36/8, 28 October 1981
36/27, 13 November 1981
36/106, 10 December 1981
36/121, 10 December 1981
36/172, 17 December 1981
36/226, 17 December 1981
ES-9/1, 5 February 1982
37/18, 16 November 1982
37/123, 20 December 1982
37/233, 20 December 1982

38/14, 22 November 1983
38/36, 1 December 1983
38/39, 5 December 1983
38/180, 19 December 1983
39/50, 12 December 1984
39/72, 13 December 1984
39/146, 14 December 1984
40/97, 13 December 1985
40/168, 16 December 1985
S-14/1, 20 September 1986
41/39, 20 November 1986
41/162, 4 December 1986
42/14, 6 November 1987
42/22, 8 November 1987
42/209, 11 December 1987
43/26, 17 November 1988
44/39, 4 December 1989
44/40, 4 December 1989
43/54, 6 December 1988
45/41, 28 November 1990
45/83, 13 December 1990
46/54, 9 December 1991
46/82, 16 December 1991
46/242, 25 August 1992
47/33, 25 November 1992
47/121, 18 December 1992
48/31, 9 December 1993
48/88, 20 December 1993
49/10, 3 November 1994
49/53, 9 December 1994
50/46, 11 December 1995
51/160, 16 December 1996
51/207, 17 December 1996
1422, 12 July 2002
60/1, 24 October 2005
60/22, 23 November 2005

GENERAL ASSEMBLY OFFICIAL RECORDS

5th session, *USSR Draft Definition of Aggression*, A/C.1/608, 1950.
6th session, *Report of the International Law Commission*, A/1858, 1951.
6th session, *Report of the Sixth Committee*, A/2087, 1952.
7th session, *Report of the Committee on International Criminal Jurisdiction, 1 to 31 August 1951*, A/2136, 1952.
7th session, *Comments Received from Governments Regarding the Draft Code of Offences Against the Peace and Security of Mankind and the Question of Defining Aggression*, A/2162 and Add, 1952.
7th session, *Comments Received from Governments Regarding the Report of the Committee on International Criminal Jurisdiction*, A/2186 and Add 1, 1952.
7th session, *Report by the Secretary-General*, Annexes, A/2211, 1952.
7th session, *Report of the Sixth Committee*, A/2322, 1952.
9th session, *Report of the Special Committee on the Question of Defining Aggression*, A/2638, 1953.
9th session, *Report of the Committee on International Criminal Jurisdiction, 27 July–20 August 1953*, A/2645, 1954.
9th session, *Report of the Sixth Committee*, A/2806, 1954.
9th session, *Report of the Committee on International Criminal Jurisdiction*, A/2645, 27 July–20 August 1953.
12th session, *Report of the 1956 Special Committee on the Question of Defining Aggression*, A/3574, 1956.
22nd session, *Request of the USSR*, A/6833, 1967.
24th session, *Report of the Special Committee*, A/7620, 1969.
23rd session, *Report of the Special Committee, Question of Defining Aggression*, A/7185/Rev.1, 1968.
25th session, *Report of the Special* Committee, A/8019, 1970.
25th session, *Report of the Sixth Committee*, A/8171, 1970.

23rd session, *Report of the Sixth Committee*, A/7402, 1968.
29th Session, *Report of the Special Committee on the Question of Defining Aggression*, A/9619 and Corr 1, 1974.
29th session, *Report of Sixth Committee*, A/9890, 1974.
50th session, *Report of the Ad Hoc Committee on the Establishment of an International Criminal Court*, A/50/22, 1995.
51st session, *Report of the International Law Commission*, A/51/10, 1996.

C. International Law Commission

Historical Survey of the Question of International Criminal Jurisdiction – Memorandum Submitted by the Secretary General, Topic: Question of International Criminal Jurisdiction, New York 1949, A/CN.4/7/Rev.1, 1949.
The Charter and Judgment of the Nürnberg Tribunal – History and Analysis: Memorandum submitted by the Secretary-General, A/CN.4/5, 1949.
YbkIntLC 1949.
YbkIntLC 1950.
YbkIntLC 1951.
YbkIntLC 1983.
YbkIntLC 1991.
YbkIntLC 1992
YbkIntLC 1993.
YbkIntLC 1994.
YbkIntLC 1996.
Preliminary report on the obligation to extradite or prosecute (aut dedere aut judicare) by Mr Zdzislaw Galicki, Special Rapporteur, A/CN.4/571, 2006.
Second report on the obligation to extradite or prosecute (aut dedere aut judicare) by Mr Zdzislaw Galicki, Special Rapporteur, A/CN.4/585, 2007.
Preliminary Report on Immunity of State Officials from Foreign Criminal Jurisdiction by Roman Anatolevich Kolodkin, Special Rapporteur, A/CN.4/601, 2008.
Third report on the obligation to extradite or prosecute (aut dedere aut judicare) by Zdzislaw Galicki, Special Rapporteur, A/CN.4/603, 2008.
The obligation to extradite or prosecute (aut dedere aut judicare) Comments and information received from Governments, A/CN.4/579 and Add 1–4, 2007.
The obligation to extradite or prosecute (aut dedere aut judicare) Comments and information received from Governments, A/CN.4/599, 2008.
The obligation to extradite or prosecute (aut dedere aut judicare) Comments and information received from Governments, A/CN.4/612, 2009.
Fourth Report on the obligation to extradite or prosecute of the Special Rapporteur, Mr Zdzislaw Galicki, A/CN.4/648, 2011.
Report of the International Law Commission on the work of its sixty-fourth session, 7 May to 1 June and 2 July to 3 August 2012, A/67/10, 2012

D. International Court of Justice

JUDGMENTS

Corfu Channel (United Kingdom of Great Britain and Northern Ireland v Albania), 9 April 1949.

Barcelona Traction, Light and Power Company Limited (Belgium v Spain), 5 February 1970.
United States Diplomatic and Consular Staff in Tehran (United States of America v Iran), 24 May 1980.
Military and paramilitary activities in and against Nicaragua (Nicaragua v United States of America), 27 June 1986 and also 26 November 1984.
Arrest Warrant of 11 April 2000 (Democratic Republic of the Congo v Belgium), 14 February 2002.
Oil Platforms (Islamic Republic of Iran v United States of America), 6 November 2003.
Armed Activities on the Territory of the Congo (Democratic Republic of Congo v Uganda), 19 December 2005.

ADVISORY OPINIONS

Certain expenses of the United Nations (Article 17, paragraph 2, of the Charter), 20 July 1962.
Legality of the Threat or Use of Nuclear Weapons, 8 July 1996.

ORDERS

Military and paramilitary activities in and against Nicaragua (Nicaragua v United States of America), 10 May 1984.
Frontier Dispute (Burkina Faso/Republic of Mali), 10 January 1986.
Application of the Convention on the Prevention and Punishment of the Crime of Genocide (Bosnia and Herzegovina v Yugoslavia), 8 April 1993.
Land and Maritime Boundary between Cameroon and Nigeria (Cameroon v Nigeria), 15 March 1996.
Armed Activities on the Territory of the Congo (Democratic Republic of the Congo v Uganda), 1 July 2000.

International Criminal Court

PREPARATORY COMMITTEE ON THE ESTABLISHMENT OF AN INTERNATIONAL CRIMINAL COURT

A/AC.249/1997/L.5, 12 March 1997.

UNITED NATIONS DIPLOMATIC CONFERENCE OF PLENIPOTENTIARIES ON THE ESTABLISHMENT OF AN INTERNATIONAL CRIMINAL COURT

A/CONF.183/2/Add 1, 14 April 1998.
A/CONF.183/C.1/L.53, 6 July 1998.
A/CONF.183/C.1/L.59, 10 July 1998.
A/CONF.183/C.1/L.75, 17 July 1998.

PREPARATORY COMMISSION FOR THE ICC

PCNICC/1999/WGCA/DP.1, 7 December 1999.
PCNICC/1999/DP.11, 26 February 1999.

PCNICC/1999/DP.12, 29 July 1999.
PCNICC/1999/DP.13, 30 July 1999.
PCNICC/1999/INF/2, 2 August 1999.
PCNICC/1999/WGCA/RT.1, 9 December 1999.
PCNICC/2000/WGCA/DP.1, 1 March 2000.
PCNICC/2000/WGCA/DP.2, 17 March 2000.
PCNICC/2000/WGCA/DP.3, 24 March 2000.
PCNICC/2000/WGCA/DP.4, 13 November 2000.
PCNICC/2000/WGCA/DP.5, 28 November 2000.
PCNICC/2000/WGCA/RT.1, 29 March 2000.
PCNICC/2001/WGCA/DP.1, 23 February 2001.
PCNICC/2001/WGCA/DP.2, 20 September 2001.
PCNICC/2001/WGCA/DP.2/Add 1, 27 August 2001.
PCNICC/2001/WGCA/DP.3, 26 September 2001.
PCNICC/2002/WGCA/DP.1, 17 April 2002.
PCNICC/2002/WGCA/DP.2, 21 June 2002.
PCNICC/2002/WGCA/DP.3, 1 July 2002.
PCNICC/2002/WGCA/DP.5, 8 July 2002.
PCNICC/2002/WGCA/L.1, 24 January 2002.
PCNICC/2002/WGCA/RT.1, 1 April 2002.
PCNICC/2002/WGCA/RT.1/Rev.1, 10 July 2002.
PCNICC/2002/WGCA/RT.1/Rev.2, 11 July 2002.

ASSEMBLY OF STATES PARTIES TO THE ROME STATUTE

ICC-ASP/1/Res.1, 9 September 2002.
ICC-ASP/1/3, 3–10 September 2002.
ICC-ASP/1/L.4, 6 February 2003.
ICC-ASP/2/SWGCA/DP.1, 4 September 2003.
ICC-ASP/3/SWGCA/INF.1, 13 August 2004.
ICC-ASP/4/32, 15 June 2005.
ICC-ASP/4/SWGCA/1, 1 December 2005.
ICC-ASP/4/Res.4, 3 December 2005.
ICC-ASP/5/35, 1 February 2007.
ICC-ASP/5/SWGCA/INF.1, 5 September 2006.
ICC-ASP/5/SWGCA/1, 29 November 2006.
ICC-ASP/5/SWGCA/2, 16 January 2007.
ICC-ASP/6/20/Add 1, 6 June 2008.
ICC-ASP/6/SWGCA/1, 13 December 2007.
ICC-ASP/6/SWGCA/2, 14 May 2008.
ICC-ASP/6/SWGCA/INF.1, 25 July 2007.
ICC-ASP/7/20, 22 November 2008.
ICC-ASP/7/SWGCA/INF.1, 19 February 2009.
ICC-ASP/7/SWGCA/2, 20 February 2009.
ICC-ASP/8/INF.2, 10 July 2009.
RC/WGCA/1, 25 May 2010
RC/WGCA/2, 25 May 2010.
RC/WGCA/3, 6 June 2010.

RC/WGCA/1/Rev.1, 6 June 2010
RC/WGCA/1/Rev.2, 10 June 2010.
RC/5, 10 June 2010.
RC/7, 10 June 2010.
RC/8, 10 June 2010.
RC/10, 11 June 2010.
RC/DC/3, 11 June 2010.
RC/10.Add 1, 11 June 2010.
RC/Res.6, 11 June 2010.
RC/9/11, 11 June 2010.

WARRANTS

ICC-02/05-01/09-1, 4 March 2009.
ICC-02/05-01/09-95, 12 July 2010.

International Treaties

1907

Convention for the Pacific Settlement of International Disputes (Hague I), The Hague, 18 October 1907.
Convention on the Limitation of Employment of Force for Recovery of Contract Debts (Hague II), The Hague, 18 October 1907.
Convention Relative to the Opening of Hostilities (Hague III), The Hague, 18 October 1907.
Convention respecting the Laws and Customs of War on Land and its annex: Regulations concerning the Laws and Customs of War on Land (Hague IV), The Hague, 18 October 1907.

1919

Treaty of Peace between the Allied and Associated Powers and Germany, Versailles, 28 June 1919 (including Covenant of the League of Nations).
Treaty of Peace with Austria, Saint-Germain-en-Laye, 10 September 1919.
Treaty of Peace with Bulgaria, Neuilly, 27 November 1919.
Treaty of Peace with Hungary, Trianon, 4 June 1920.
Treaty of Peace with Turkey, Sèvres, 10 August 1920.

1923

Treaty to Avoid or Prevent Conflicts Between the American States ('Gondra Treaty'), Santiago de Chile, 3 May 1923.

1925

Treaty of Mutual Guarantee between Germany, Belgium, France, Great Britain and Italy (Rhineland Pact), Locarno, 16 October 1925.

Treaty of Arbitration between Poland and Germany, London, 1 December 1925.

Treaty of Mutual Guarantee between Poland and France, London, 1 December 1925.

Treaty of Friendship and Neutrality between USSR and Turkey, Paris, 17 December 1925.

1926

Treaty of Friendship and Security between Persia and Turkey, Teheran, 22 April 1926.

Treaty of Non-Aggression between USSR and Lithuania, Moscow, 28 September 1926.

1927

Treaty of Friendship and Security between Persia and Afghanistan, 27 November 1927.

Treaty of Neutrality and Non-Aggression between USSR and Persia, Moscow, 1 October 1927.

1928

General Act of Arbitration (Pacific Settlement of International Disputes), Geneva, 26 September 1928.

General Treaty for the Renunciation of War (Briand-Kellogg Pact), Paris, 27 August 1928.

1929

Protocol concerning entry into force of the General Treaty of August 27, 1928 for renunciation of war as an instrument of national policy (Litvinov Protocol) between Estonia, Latvia, Poland, Romania, USSR, Moscow, 9 February 1929.

1932

Pact of Non-Aggression between Poland and USSR, Moscow, 25 July 1932.

1933

Pact of Organization of Small Entente between Czechoslovakia, Romania and Yugoslavia, Geneva, 16 February 1933.

Convention for the Definition of Aggression between the Soviet Union, Afghanistan, Estonia, Latvia, Persia, Poland, Romania, Turkey, London, 3 July 1933.

Convention for the Definition of Aggression between the Soviet Union, Czechoslovakia, Romania, Turkey, Yugoslavia, London, 4 July 1933.

Convention for the Definition of Aggression between the Soviet Union and Lithuania, London, 5 July 1933.

Anti-War Treaty of Non-Aggression and Conciliation (Saavedra Lamas Treaty), Rio de Janeiro, 10 October 1933.
Convention on Rights and Duties of States, Montevideo, 26 December 1933.

1934

German-Polish Peace Declaration, Berlin, 26 January 1934.
Pact of Balkan Entente between Greece, Romania, Turkey, Yugoslavia with a Protocol, Athens, 9 February 1934.

1936

Convention to Coordinate, Extend, and Assure the Fulfillment of the Existing Treaties between the American States, Buenos Aires, 23 December 1936.
Convention for the Maintenance, Preservation and Re-establishment of Peace and Additional Protocol relative to Non-Intervention, Buenos Aires, 23 December 1936.
Inter-American Treaty on Good Offices and Mediation, Buenos Aires, 23 December 1936.

1937

Treaty of Non-Aggression between Afghanistan, Iraq, Iran, Turkey (Saadabad Pact), Teheran, 8 July 1937.

1945

Charter of the Arab League, Cairo, 22 March 1945.
Charter of the United Nations, San Francisco, 26 June 1945.
Agreement for the Prosecution and Punishment of Major War Criminals (London Agreement) and Charter of the International Military Tribunal (London Charter), London, 8 August 1945.

1947

Treaty of Peace with Bulgaria, Paris, 10 February 1947.
Treaty of Peace with Finland, Paris, 10 February 1947.
Treaty of Peace with Romania, Paris, 10 February 1947.
Treaty of Peace with Hungary, Paris, 10 February 1947.
Treaty of Peace with Italy, Paris, 10 February 1947.
Inter-American Treaty of Reciprocal Assistance (Rio Treaty), Rio de Janeiro, 2 September 1947.
Iraqi-Transjordanian Treaty of Brotherhood and Alliance, 14 April 1947.

1948

American Treaty on Pacific Settlement (Pact of Bogotá) Bogota, 30 April 1948.
Charter of the Organization of American States, Bogota, 30 April 1948.

Convention on the Prevention and Punishment of the Crime of Genocide, New York, 9 December 1948.

1949

Conventions for the protection of war victims, Geneva, 12 August 1949.

1950

Convention for the Protection of Human Rights and Fundamental Freedoms, Strasbourg, 4 November 1950.

1951

Convention relating to the Status of Refugees, Geneva, 27 July 1951.

1954

Agreement (with exchange of notes) on trade and intercourse between Tibet Region of China and India, Peking, 29 April 1954.

1957

European Convention on Extradition, Paris, 13 December 1957.

1961

Convention on diplomatic relations, Vienna, 18 April 1961.

1963

Convention on consular relations, Vienna, 24 April 1963.

1966

International Covenant on Civil and Political Rights, New York, 16 December 1966.

1968

Convention on the non-applicability of statutory limitations to war crimes and crimes against humanity, New York, 26 November 1968.

1969

Convention on Special Missions, New York, 16 December 1969.
Convention on the Law of Treaties, Vienna, 23 May 1969.

1974

European Convention on the Non-Applicability of Statutory Limitation to Crimes against Humanity and War Crimes, Strasbourg, 25 January 1974.

1975

Protocol of Amendment to the Inter-American Treaty of Reciprocal Assistance, San Jose, 26 July 1975.

1977

Additional Protocols to Geneva Conventions of 12 August 1949 for the protection of war victims, Geneva, 8 June 1977.

1981

Inter-American Convention on Extradition, Caracas, 25 February 1981.

1990

Treaty on the Final Settlement with Respect to Germany, Moscow, 12 September 1990.

1998

Statute of the International Criminal Court, Rome, 17 July 1998.

2003

Constitutive Act of the African Union, Lomé, 11 July 2000.

2005

African Union Non-Aggression and Common Defence Pact, Abuja, 31 January 2005.

Other official documents

1918

Congressional address of the United States President Woodrow Wilson, 8 January 1918.

1928

Identical Notes of the Government of the United States to the Governments of Australia, Belgium, Canada, Czechoslovakia, France, Germany, Great Britain, India, The Irish Free State, Italy, Japan, New Zealand, Poland, South Africa, Delivered at the Respective Foreign Offices, 23 June 1928.

1938

Declaration of American Principles, Lima, 24 December 1938.

1941

Atlantic Charter (UK, USA), 14 August 1941.

1942

Inter Allied Declaration on Punishment of the War Crimes (St James Declaration), London, 13 January 1942.

1943

Moscow Declaration (China, USA, UK, USSR), 30 October/1 December 1943.
Cairo Declaration (USA, UK, China), 1 December 1943.

1944

Military Armistice between UK, USA and Italy, 3 and 29 September 1943.
Military Armistice between USSR and Finland, 19 September 1944.
Military Armistice between UK, USA, USSR and Romania, 12 September 1944.
Military Armistice between UK, USA, USSR and Bulgaria, 28 October 1944.
Military Armistice between UK, USA, USSR and Hungary, 20 January 1945.

1945

Chapultepec Declaration, 3 March 1945.

1975

Final Act of the Conference on Security and Cooperation in Europe, Helsinki, 1 August 1975.

1990

Charter of Paris for a New Europe, Paris, 21 November 1990.

Reports (in chronological order)

Commission on the Responsibility of the Authors of the War and on Enforcement of Penalties, *Report Presented to the Preliminary Peace Conference*, 29 March 1919, *AJIL* 1920, vol 14.
Memorandum of Reservations Presented by the Representatives of the United States to the Report of the Commission on Responsibilities, 4 April 1919, *AJIL* 1920, vol 14.
Reservations by the Japanese Delegation, 4 April 1919, *AJIL* 1920, vol 14.
Opinion of Commission of Jurists of Janina-Corfu Affair, AJIL 1924, vol 18.
League of Nations Assembly Report on the Sino-Japanese Dispute, AJIL 1933, vol 27, Supplement.

International Law Association, *Report of the Thirty-Eighth Conference Held at Budapest in the Hungarian Academy of Science, September 6th to 10th, 1934*, London 1935.

Report to the President from Justice Robert H. Jackson, Chief of Counsel for the United States in the Prosecution of Axis War Criminals, 7 June 1945, *AJIL* 1945, vol 39, Supplement.

Final Report to the Secretary of the Army on the Nuernberg War Crimes Trials Under Control Council Law No 10 by Telford Taylor, Brigadier General, U.S.A. Chief of Counsel for War Crimes, Washington DC, 15 August 1949.

Report of the International Commission on Intervention and State Security, Responsibility to Protect, December 2001.

Report of the Secretary-General's High Panel on Threats, Challenges and Change, A more secure world: Our shared responsibility, Report of the Secretary-General's High Level Panel on Threats, Challenges and Change, United Nations, New York 2004, A/59/565.

Report of the Secretary-General, In Larger Freedom: Towards Development, Security and Human Rights for All, New York 2005, A/59/2005.

Parliamentary Assembly, Council of Europe, *The concept of preventive war and its consequences for international relations*, 8 June 2007, Doc 11293.

Judgments of international tribunals

ECHR, *Piersack v Belgium*, 1 October 1982.
ECHR, *Barberà, Messegué and Jabardo v Spain*, 6 December 1988.
ECHR, *Hauschildt v Denmark*, 24 December 1989.
IMT, *Hermann Göring et al*, 1 October 1946.
ICTY, *Prosecutor v Furundzija*, IT-95-17/1-T, 10 December 1998.
ICTY, *Prosecutor v Dusko Tadic*, IT-94-1-A, 15 July 1999.
ICTY, *Prosecutor v Slobodan Miloševi*, IT-02-54, 14 March 2006.
PICJ, *Lotus*, 7 September1927.
SCSL, *Prosecutor v Charles Gankay Taylor*, SCSL 03-01-T, 18 May 2012.
SCSL, Appeal Chamber, *Decision on Immunity from Jurisdiction*, 31 May 2004.

National and occupational regulations

Iraq

Statute of the Iraqi Special Tribunal, 10 December 2003.
Statute of the Iraqi High Criminal Tribunal, 18 October 2005.

Germany

Control Council Law no 10, 20 December 1945.
Basic Law for the Federal Republic of Germany, 23 May 1949.
Criminal Penal Code, 13 November 1998.
Act to Introduce the Code of Crimes against International Law, 26 June 2002.

Japan

General Order no 1 (IMTFE Charter) Supreme Commander for the Allied Powers, 19 January 1946.

General Order no 20, Supreme Commander for the Allied Powers, 26 April 1946.
Constitution of Japan, 3 November 1946.

Poland

Penal Code, 11 July 1932.
Penal Code of the Polish Army, 23 September 1944.
Decree on the Supreme National Tribunal, 22 January 1946.
Decree on the change of the decree of 22 January 1946 on the Supreme National Tribunal, 17 October 1946.
Law on the Protection of Peace, 29 December 1950.
Penal Code, 6 June1997.

2 Books

Alexandrov S., *Self-Defense against the Use of Force in International Law*, Kluwer Law International, The Hague 1996.
Anderson F. M., *The Constitutions and Other Select Documents Illustrative of the History of France 1789–1901*, The H. W. Wilson Company, Minneapolis 1904.
Antonopoulos C., *The Unilateral Use of Force by States in International Law*, Ant. N. Sakkoulas Publishers, Athens, Komotini 1997.
Appleman J. A., *Military Tribunals and International Crimes*, Greenwood Press Publishers, Westport 1954, reprinted 1971.
Arbitration and Security: Systematic Survey of the Arbitration Conventions and Treaties of Mutual Security Deposited with the League of Nations, Legal Section of the Secretariat of the League of Nations, Geneva 1927.
Aroneanu E., *La définition de l'agression. Exposé objectif*, Les Editions Internationales, Paris 1958.
Ascensio H., Decaux E. and Pellet A. (eds), *Droit international pénal*, Cedin Paris X, Editions A. Pedone, Paris 2000.
Asrat B., *Prohibition of Force under the UN Charter. A Study of Art. 2(4)*, Iustus Förlag, Juridiska Föreningenuppsala, Uppsala 1991.
Baczkowski K. et al, *Historia*, Wydawnictwa Szkolne i Pedagogiczne, Warszawa 1997.
Bailey S. D., *How Wars End, The United Nations and Termination of Armed Conflict, 1946–64*, vol 1, Clarendon Press, Oxford 1982.
Balicki J., *Pojęcie agresji w prawie międzynarodowym*, Wydawnictwo Prawnicze, Warszawa 1952.
Bandyopadhyay P., *International Law and Custom in Ancient India*, Ramanand Vidya Bhawan, Goyal Offset Printers, Delhi 1982.
Bannelier K., Corten O., Christakis T. and Klein P. (dir.), *L'intervention en Iraq et le droit international*, Cedin Paris I, Centre de droit international ULB, Cahiers internationaux no 19, Editions Pedone, Paris 2004.
Bantekas I. and Nash S., *International Criminal Law*, 3rd edn, Routledge Cavendish, London, New York 2007.
Barriga S. and Kress C., *The Travaux Préparatoires of the Crime of Aggression*, Cambridge University Press, Cambridge 2011.
Bass G. J., *Stay the Hand of the Vengeance – The Politics of War Crimes Tribunals*, Princeton University Press, Princeton 2002.

Bassiouni M. C., *Introduction to International Criminal Law*, Transnational Publishers, Inc., Ardsley, New York 2003.

Beigbeder Y., *Judging War Criminals. The Politics of International Justice*, Macmillan Press Ltd, New York 1999.

Best G., *War and Law Since 1945*, Clarendon Press, New York 1994.

Bierzanek R., *Wojna a prawo międzynarodowe*, Wydawnictwo Ministerstwa Obrony Narodowej, Warszawa 1982.

Bierzanek R. and Symonides J., *Prawo mie̜dzynarodowe publiczne*, Wydawnictwa Prawnicze PWN, wyd VI uaktualnione, Warszawa 2001.

Björn C., *Die Strafbarkeit des Angriffskrieges und die Funktion seiner Strafbarkeit*, Duncker & Humblot, Berlin 2005.

Boister N. and Cryer R., *The Tokyo International Military Tribunal: A Reappraisal*, Oxford University Press, Oxford 2008.

Bosh W. J., *Judgment on Nuremberg. American Attitudes Toward the Major German War Crimes Trials*, North Caroline Press, Chapel Hill 1970.

Bouthoul G., *Traité de sociologie. Les guerres. Éléments de polémologie. Méthodes. Doctrines et opinions sur la guerre. Morphologie. Éléments techniques, démographiques, économiques, psychologiques. Périodicité*, Payot, Paris 1951.

Bowett D. W., *Self-defence in International Law*, Manchester University Press, Manchester 1958.

Brackman A. C., *The Other Nuremberg. The Untold Story of the Tokyo War Crimes Trial*, William Morrow and Company, Inc., New York 1987.

Brierly J. L., *The Law of Nations. An Introduction to the International Law of Peace*, 6th edn, edited by Sir Humphrey Waldock, Clarendon Press, Oxford 1963.

Broms B., *Finland and the League of Nations*, Finnish Foreign Policy, Helsinki 1963.

Broms B., *The Definition of Aggression in the United Nations*, Turun Yliopisto, Turku 1968.

Brown S., *The Causes and Prevention of War*, St Martin's Press, New York 1994.

Brownlie I., *International Law and the Use of Force by States*, Oxford 1968.

Brownlie I., *Principles of Public International Law*, 6th edn, Oxford University Press, Oxford 2003.

Caflisch L., 'Réflexions sur la création d'une cour criminelle internationale', in J. Makarczyk (ed.), *Theory of International Law at the Threshold of the 21st Century. Essays in honour of Krzysztof Skubiszewski*, Kluwer Law International, The Hague 1996.

Calvocoressi P., *Nuremberg. The Facts, the Law and the Consequences*, Chatto and Windus, London 1947.

The Case Against the Nazi War Criminals, Opening Statement for the United States of America by Robert H. Jackson and Other Documents, with Preface by Gordon Dean of Counsel for United States, Alfred A. Knopf, New York 1946.

Cassese A., *International Criminal Law*, Oxford University Press, Oxford 2003.

Cassese A., *Violence and Law in the Modern Age*, transl S. J. K. Greenleaves, Polity Press, Cambridge 1988.

Chesterman S., *Just War or Just Peace? Humanitarian Intervention and International Law*, Oxford University Press, Oxford 2003.

Chiavario M. (ed.), *La justice pénale internationale entre passé et avenir*, Dalloz, Paris, Milano, 2003.

Clark G. and Sohn L. B., *World Peace Through World Law*, Harvard University Press, Cambridge 1966.

Clark R. S., 'The crime of aggression', in Stahn C., Sluiter G. (eds), *The Emerging Practice of the International Criminal Court*, Brill 2009.

Colard D. and Guilhaudis J. F., *Le droit de la sécurité internationale*, Masson, Paris 1986.

Colt de Wolf F., *General Synopsis of Treaties of Arbitration, Conciliation, Judicial Settlement, Security and Disarmament Actually in Force between Countries Invited to the Disarmament Conference*, Carnegie Endowment for International Peace, Washington 1933.

Constantinou A., *The Right of Self-defence Under Customary International Law and Article 51 of the UN Charter*, Ant. Sakkoulas, Bruylant, Athènes, Bruxelles 2000.

Cybichowski Z., *Rozpoczęcie i wypowiedzenie wojny w prawie państwowym i prawie narodów*, Wydawnictwo Seminarjum Prawa Publicznego Uniwersytetu Warszawskiego nr 6, Warszawa 1926.

Cyprian T. and Sawicki J., *Prawo norymberskie, Bilans i perspektywy*, Wydawnictwo Eugeniusza Kuthana, Warszawa 1948.

Cyprian T. and Sawicki J., *Przestępstwa międzynarodowe*, Wiedza Powszechna, Łódź 1948.

Cyprian T. and Sawicki J., *Siedem wyroków Najwyższego Trybunału Narodowego*, Instytut Zachodni, Poznań 1962.

Cyprian T. and Sawicki J., *Nieznana Norymberga. Dwanaś cie procesów norymberskich*, Książka i Wiedza, Warszawa 1965.

Cyprian T. and Sawicki J., *Ludzie i sprawy Norymbergii*, Wydawnictwo Poznańskie, Poznań 1967.

Czapliński W., *Skutki prawne nielegalnego użycia siły w stosunkach międzynarodowych*, Polska Akademia Nauk, Agencja Scholar, Warszawa 1993.

Czapliński W. and Wyrozumska A., *Prawo międzynarodowe publiczne. Zagadnienia systemowe*, 2 wyd, Warszawa 2004.

Davidson E., *The Trial of the Germans. An Account of the Twenty-two Defendants Before the International Military Tribunal at Nuremberg*, The Macmillan Company, New York 1966.

Davidson E., *The Nuremberg Fallacy. Wars and War Crimes Since World War II*, The Macmillan Company, New York 1973.

Defarges P. M., *Un monde d'ingérences*, Presses de Sciences Po, Mayenne 1997.

Dembin´ski H., *Wojna jako narze˛dzie prawa i przewrotu*, Towarzystwo Naukowe Katolickiego Uniwersytetu Lubelskiego, Lublin 1936.

Diamandesco J., *Le problème de l'agression dans le droit international public actuel. Deux aspects de l'organisation répressive: Définition de l'agression et détermination de l'agresseur*, Éditions A. Pedone, Paris 1935.

Dinstein Y., *War, Aggression and Self-Defence*, 4th edn, Cambridge University Press, New York, Cambridge 2005.

Dinstein Y. and Tabory M., *War Crimes in International Law*, Martinus Nijhoff Publishers, The Hague 1996.

Dromi San Martino L., *Legitima defensa internacional*, Ciudad Argentina, Editorial de Ciencia y Cultura, Buenos Aires 1998.

Dupuy R. J., *The Development of the Role of the Security Council, Peace-keeping and Peacebuilding*, Martinus Nijhoff, Dordrecht 1993.

Ekspertyzy i orzeczenia przed Najwyższym Trybunałem Narodowym, vol 1–9, prepared by C. Pilichowski, Ministerstwo Sprawiedliwości, Główna Komisja Badania Zbrodni Hitlerowskich w Polsce, Warszawa 1979–1982.

Epps V., *International Law*, Caroline Academic Press, Durham 2005.

Ferencz B. B., *Defining International Aggression. The Search for World Peace. A Documentary History of and Analysis.* vols 1–2, Oceana Publications, Inc., New York 1975.

Ferencz B. B., *An International Criminal Court. A Step Toward World Peace – A Documentary History and Analysis, Volume I – Half a Century of Hope, Volume II The Beginning of Wisdom*, Oceana Publications, Inc., London 1980.

Ferrell R. H., *Peace in Their Time. The Opinions of the Kellogg-Briand Pact*, New Haven, Yale University Press, London 1952.
Flemming M. and Wojciechowska J., *Zbrodnie wojenne. Przestępstwa przeciwko pokojowi, państwu i obronności. Rozdział XVI, XVII, XVIII Kodeksu Karnego. Komentarz*, Wydawnictwo C. H. Beck, Warszawa 1999.
Fletcher G. P., *Romantics at War. Glory and Guilt in the Age of Terrorism*, Princeton University Press, Princeton, Oxford 2002.
Franck T., *Recourse to Force. State Action Against Threats and Armed Attacks*, Cambridge University Press, Cambridge 2002.
Gardocki L., *Zarys prawa karnego międzynarodowego*, Państwowe Wydawnictwo Naukowe, Warszawa 1985.
Gardocki L., *Prawo karne*, 8 wyd zmienione, Wydawnictwo C. H. Beck, Warszawa 2002.
Gazzini T., *The Changing Rules on the Use of Force in International Law*, Manchester University Press, Manchester 2005.
Ginsburgs G., *Moscow's Road to Nuremberg. The Soviet Background to the Trial*, Martinus Nijhoff Publishers, The Hague 1996.
Ginsburgs G. and Kudriavtsev V. N. (ed.), *The Nuremberg Trial and International Law*, Martinus Nijhoff Publishers, Dordrecht 1990.
Glahn G. von, *Law Among Nations. An Introduction to Public International Law*, 4th edn, Macmillan Publishing C., New York 1981.
Glennon M. J., *Limits of Law. Prerogatives of Power. Interventionism after Kosovo*, Palgrave, New York 2001.
Glueck S., *War Criminals. Their Prosecution and Punishment*, Alfred Knopf, New York 1944.
Glueck S., *The Nuremberg Trial and Aggressive War*, Kraus Reprint Corporation, New York 1966.
Goldstein J. S., *International Relations*, 2nd edn, Pearson-Longman, New York 2004.
Goodrich L. M., Hambro E. and Simons A. P., *Charter of the United Nations. Commentary and Documents*, 3rd and revised edn, Columbia University Press, New York, London 1969.
Góralczyk W., *Prawo międzynarodowe publiczne w zarysie*, 7th edn, updated by S. Sawicki, Wydawnictwo Prawnicze PWN, Warszawa 2000.
Gray C., *International Law and the Use of Force*, 2nd edn, Oxford University Press, Oxford 2004.
Gumkowski J. and Kułakowski T., *Zbrodniarze hitlerowscy przed Najwyższym Trybunałem Narodowym*, Wydawnictwo Prawnicze, Warszawa 1961.
Hall W. E., *A Treatise on International Law*, 3rd edn, Clarendon Press, Oxford 1890.
Hankey L., *Politics, Trials and Errors*, Pen in Hand, Oxford 1950.
Harris W. R., *Tyranny on Trial. The Evidence at Nuremberg*, Southern Methodist University Press, Dallas 1954.
Heller K. J., *The Nuremberg Military Tribunals and the Origins of International Criminal Law*, Oxford University Press, Oxford 2011.
Hershey A. S., *The Essentials of International Public Law*, The MacMillan Company, New York 1912.
Herzog J. B., *Nuremberg: un échec fructueux?*, Librairie Générale de Droit et de Jurisprudence, Paris 1975.
Heydecker J. J. and Leeb J., *Proces w Norymberdze*, Świat Książki, Warszawa 2006.
Holzgrefe J. L., Keohane R. O. (eds), *Humanitarian Intervention, Ethical, Legal and Political Dilemmas*, Cambridge University Press, Cambridge 2003.

Hummrich M., *Der völkerrechtliche Straftatbestand der Aggression, Historische Entwicklung, Geltung und Definition im Hinblick auf das Statut des Internationalen Strafgerichtschofes, Nomos Verlagsgesellschaft*, Baden-Baden 2001.

International Military Tribunal, *Trial of the Major War Criminals before the International Military Tribunal, Nuremberg 14 November 1945–10 October 1946*, 42 vols, Nuremberg 1947–1949.

Jacewicz A., *Pojęcie siły w Karcie Narodów Zjednoczonych*, Wydawnictwo Ministerstwa Obrony Narodowej, Warszawa 1977.

Joyner C. C. (sp. ed.), Bassiouni M. C. (gen. ed.), *Reining in impunity for international crimes and serious violations of fundamental human rights: proceedings of the Siracusa Conference 17–21.09.1998*, Siracusa, Association Internationale de Droit Pénal, Érès 1998.

Kearney M., *The Prohibition of Propaganda for War in International Law*, Oxford University Press, Oxford 2007.

Kelsen H., *Peace Through Law*, The University of North Carolina Press, Chapel Hill 1944.

Kittichaisaree K., *International Criminal Law*, Oxford University Press, Oxford 2001.

Klafkowski A., *Prawo międzynarodowe publiczne*, 4th edn, Państwowe Wydawnictwo Naukowe, Warszawa 1964.

Klafkowski A., *Podstawowe problemy prawne likwidacji skutków wojny 1939–1945 a dwa państwa niemieckie*, Instytut Zachodni, Poznań 1966.

Kochavi A. J., *Prelude to Nuremberg: Allied War Crimes Policy and the Question of Punishment*, University of North Carolina Press, Chapel Hill, 1998.

Kolb R., *Ius contra bellum. Le droit international relatif aux maintien de la paix*, Précis, Helbing & Lichtenhahn, Bruylant, Bruxelles 2003.

Korczyk H., *Traktat ogólny o wyrzeczeniu się wojny (Pakt Brianda-Kelloga). Geneza, zawarcie, recepcja, działanie*, Wydawnictwo Fundacji 'Historia pro Futuro', Warszawa 1993.

Kranz J., *Wojna, pokój czy uspokajanie? Współczesne dylematy użycia siły zbrojnej*, Fundacja Centrum Stosunków Międzynarodowych, Warszawa 2006.

Królikowski M., Wiliński P. and Izydorczyk J., *Podstawy prawa karnego międzynarodowego*, Oficyna a Wolters Kluwer business, Warszawa 2008.

Kubicki L., *Zbrodnie wojenne w świetle prawa polskiego*, Państwowe Wydawnictwo Naukowe, Warszawa 1963.

Lanza D. L., *The Geneva Protocol of 1924: British Rejection of League of Nations Covenant Reform*, The University of Tennessee, Knoxville 1991.

Lieber R. J., *No Common Power. Understanding International Relations*, 3rd edn, Georgetown University, Harper Collins College Publishers, New York 1995.

Lovett P. G., *Justifying War: The Just War Tradition Until 1919*, The University of Oklahoma, Graduate College, Norman, Oklahoma 1982.

Łuczak C., *Arthur Greiser*, PSO, Poznań 1997.

Macedo S. (ed.), *Universal Jurisdiction: National Courts and the Prosecution of Serious Crimes under International Law*, University of Pennsylvania Press, Philadelphia 2006.

Malanczuk P., *Humanitarian Intervention and the Legitimacy of the Use of Force*, Het Spinhuis, Amsterdam 1993.

Maugham V., *U.N.O. and War Crimes*, John Murray, Albemarle Street, London 1951.

May L., *Aggression and Crimes against Peace*, Cambridge University Press, Cambridge 2008.

McCormack T. L. H. *Self-defense in International Law. The Israeli Raid on the Iraqi Nuclear Reactor*, St. Martin's Press, New York 1996.

McDougal M. S. and Feliciano F. P., *The International Law of War*, New Haven Press, Dordrecht 1994.

McNair C. B. E. and Watts A. D., *The Legal Effects of War*, Cambridge University Press, Cambridge 1966.

Mettraux G., *Perspectives on the Nuremberg Trial*, Oxford University Press, Oxford 2008.

Mężykowska A., *Interwencja humanitarna w świetle prawa międzynarodowego*, Oficyna Wydawnicza Wyższej Szkoły Handlu i Prawa im. Ryszarda Łazarskiego, Warszawa 2008.

Minear R. H., *Victors' Justice, The Tokyo War Crimes Trial*, Princeton University Press, Princeton 1971.

Morawiecki W., *Walka o definicję agresji w prawie międzynarodowym*, Państwowe Wydawnictwo Naukowe, Warszawa 1956.

Murphy S., *Principles of International Law*, Concise Hornbook Series, St Paul 2006.

Nahlik S. E., *Wstęp do nauki prawa międzynarodowego*, PWN, Warszawa 1967.

Nazi Conspiracy and Aggression, vols 1–8, Opinion and Judgment, Supplement A, Supplement B, Office of United States, Chief of Counsel for Prosecution of Axis Criminality, United States Government Printing Office, Washington 1947.

Numelin R., *The Beginnings of Diplomacy. A Sociological Study of Intertribal and International Relations*, Philosophical Library, New York 1950.

Nyiri N., *The United Nations' Search for a Definition of Aggression*, American University Studies, Series X, Political Science vol 22, Peter Lang, New York 1989.

Obote-Odora A., *The Judging of War Criminals: Individual Criminal Responsibility Under International Law*, Akademitryck, Edsburg 1997.

Oppenheim L., *International Law. A Treatise vol II Disputes, War and Neutrality*, 7th edn, edited by H. Lauterpacht, Longmans 1960.

Österdahl I., *Threat to the Peace. The Interpretation by the Security Council of Article 39 of the United Nations Charter*, Iustus Förlag, Uppsala 1998.

Pella V. V., *La guerre-crime et les criminels de guerre. Réflexions sur la justice pénale internationale. Ce qu'elle est et ce qu'elle devrait être*, Histoire et Société d'Aujourd'hui, Éditions de la Baconnière, Neuchatel 1964.

Phillipson C., *The International Law and Custom of Ancient Greece and Rome*, vols 1–2, MacMillan and Co Limited, London 1911.

Płachta M., *Międzynarodowy Trybunał Karny*, vols 1–2, Kantor Zakamycze, Zakamycze 2004.

Podgóreczny M., *Albert Forster gauleiter i oskarżony*, Wydawnictwo Morskie, Gdańsk 1997.

Politi M. and Nesi G., *The International Criminal Court and the Crime of Aggression*, Ashgate, Aldershot 2004.

Pompe C. A., *Aggressive War. An International Crime*, Martinus Nijhoff, The Hague 1953.

Przedawnienie zbrodni hitlerowskich w NRF. Materiały sesji naukowej Komitetu Koordynacyjnego Badań Niemcoznawczych, Warszawa, 8 marca 1965, Polski Instytut Spraw Międzynarodowych, Warszawa 1965.

Przetacznik F., *The Philosophical and Legal Concept of War*, The Edwin Mellen Press, Lewiston 1994.

Ranjeva R. and Cadoux C., *Droit international public*, Edicef, Vanves 1992.

Ratner S. R., *The New UN Peacekeeping Building Peace in Lands of Conflict After the Cold War*, St Martin's Press, New York 1996.

Rifaat A. M., *International Aggression. A Study of the Legal Concept: Its Development and Definition in International Law*, Almqvist & Wiksell International, Stockholm 1979.

Robinson P., *Just War in Comparative Perspective*, Ashgate, Hampshire 2003.

Röling B. V. A. and Rüter C. F., *The Tokyo Judgment, The International Military Tribunal for the Far East (IMTFE) 29 April 1946–12 November 1948*, vols 1–2, APA–University Press Amsterdam BV, Amsterdam 1977.
Röling B. V. A. and Cassese A., *The Tokyo Trial and Beyond. Reflections of a Peacemonger*, Polity Press, Cambridge 1993.
Rudkowski D., *Interwencja humanitarna w prawie międzynarodowym*, Wydawnictwo Sejmowe, Warszawa 2006.
Russell R. B., *A History of the United Nations Charter. The Role of the United States 1940–45*, The Brookings Institution, Washington DC 1959.
Ryszka F., *Norymberga. Prehistoria i ciąg dalszy*, Czytelnik, Warszawa 1982.
Sadat L. N., *The International Criminal Court and the Transformation of International Law: Justice for New Millennium*, Transnational Publishers, Ardsley 2002.
Sassòli M. and Bouvier A. A., *Un droit dans la guerre?*, Comité international de la Croix-Rouge, Genève 2003.
Sauvageot A., *Histoire de Finlande, Tome Seconde*, Imprimerie Nationale, Librairie Orientaliste Paul Geuthner, Paris 1968.
Sawicki J., *Od Norymbergi do układu paryskiego. Za kulisami niemieckiego rewizjonizmu*, Wydawnictwo Ministerstwa Obrony Narodowej, 2nd edn, Warszawa 1956.
Sayed A., *Quand le droit est face à son néant. Le droit à l'épreuve de l'emploi de l'arme nucléaire*, Bruylant, Bruxelles 1998.
Schwarzenberger G., *International Law as Applied by International Courts and Tribunals*, 3rd edn, Stevens & Sons, London 1957.
Schabas W. A., *An Introduction to the International Criminal Court*, 2nd edn, Cambridge University Press, Cambridge 2004.
Shaw M. N., *International Law*, 5th edn, Cambridge 2003.
Shearer I. A., *Starke's international law*, 11th edn, Butterworths, London, 1994.
Shotwell J. T., *War as an Instrument of National Policy and Its Renunciation in the Pact of Paris*, Constable & Co Ltd, London 1929.
Schwarzenberg G., *International Law As Applied by International Courts and Tribunals, Volumes II–III, The Law of Armed Conflict*, Stevens & Sons, London 1968.
Sewall S. B. and Kaysen C., *The United States and the International Criminal Court. National Security and International Law*, Rowman&Littlefield Publishers, Inc., Lanham 2000.
Singer J. D. and Small M., *The Wages of War 1816–1965. A statistical Handbook*, John Wiley & Sons, New York 1972.
Slusser R. M. and Triska J. F., *A Calendar of Soviet Treaties 1917–1957*, Stanford University Press, Stanford 1959.
Smith B. F., *Reaching Judgment at Nuremberg*, Andre Deutsch, London 1977.
Solera O., *Defining the Crime of Aggression*, Cameron May, London 2007.
Stone J., *Aggression and World Order. A Critique of United Nations Theories of Aggression*, Stevens & Sons Limited, London 1958.
Stone J., *Conflict Through Consensus. United Nations Approaches to Aggression*, The John Hopkins University Press, Baltimore 1977.
Stürchler N., *The Threat of Force in International Law*, Cambridge University Press, Cambridge 2007.
Szpak L., *Ekstradycja hitlerowskich zbrodniarzy wojennych ze szczególnym uwzględnieniem praktyki polskiej*, Ministerstwo Sprawiedliwości, Główna Komisja Badania Zbrodni Hitlerowskich w Polsce, Warszawa 1979.
Sunga L. S., *The Emerging System of International Criminal Law. Developments in Codification and Implementation*, Kluwer Law International, The Hague 1997.

Symonides J. (ed.), *Organizacja Narodów Zjednoczonych. Bilans i perspektywy*, Wydawnictwo Naukowe Scholar, Warszawa 2006.
Taylor T., *Nuremberg and Vietnam*, Quadrangle Books, Chicago 1970.
Tchoan-Pao S., *Le droit des Gens et la Chine Antique. Tome I. Introduction. Partie I. Les Idées*, Jouve & Cie, Editeurs, Paris 1926.
Trainin A. N., *La responsabilité pénale des Hitlériens*, Presse Française étrangère, O. Zeluck, Éditeur Paris 1945.
Treaties for the Advancement of Peace between the United States and Other Powers Negotiated by the Honourable William J. Bryan, Secretary of the State of the United States, Oxford University Press, New York 1920.
Trials of War Criminals Before the Nuernberg Military Tribunals under Control Council Law No 10, Nuernberg October 1946–April 1949, vols 1–15, United States Government Printing Office, Washington 1950.
Triffterer O. (ed.), *Commentary on the Rome Statute of the International Criminal Court. Observers, Notes. Article by Article*, Nomos Verlaagesellschaft, Baden-Baden 1999.
United Nations, Department Peacekeeping Operations, Department of Field Support, *United Nations Peacekeeping Operations. Principles and Guidelines*, New York 2008.
United Nations War Crimes Commission, *History of the United Nations War Crimes Commission and the Development of the Laws of War*, His Majesty's Stationery Office, London 1948.
United Nations War Crimes Commission, *Law Reports of Trials of War Criminals*, vols 1–15, His Majesty's Stationery Office, London 1947–1949.
Van Wynen Thomas A. and Thomas A. J. Jr, *The Concept of Aggression in International Law*, Southern Methodist University Press, Dallas 1972.
Veale F. J. P., *Advance to Barbarism. How the Reversion to Barbarism in Warfare and War Trials Menaces Our Future*, C.C. Nelson Publishing Company, Appleton, Wisconsin 1953.
Walters F. P., *A History of the League of Nations*, vols 1–2, Oxford University Press, London 1952.
Wehberg H., *The Outlawry of War*, Carnegie Endowment for International Peace, Washington 1931.
Weir P. A. L., *The German War-Crimes trials, 1949 to Present: Repercussions of American Involvement*, University Microfilms, A Xerox Company, Ann Arbor, Michigan 1973.
Weisburd A. M., *Use of Force. The Practice of States Since World War II*, The Pennsylvania State University Press, Pennsylvania 1997.
Westlake J., *International Law, Part I–II*, 2nd edn, Cambridge University Press, London 1913.
Westra J. H., *International Law and the Use of Armed Force. The United Nations Charter and the Major Powers*, Contemporary Security Studies, Routledge, London 2007.
Wierzbicki B., *O azylach i ekstradycji przestępców*, Wydawnictwo Prawnicze, Warszawa 1982.
Willis J. F., *Prologue to Nuremberg: The Punishment of War Criminals of the First World War*, Duke University, Xerox University Microfilms, 1976.
Wilson P., *Aggression, Crime and International Security. Moral, Political and Legal Dimensions of International Relations*, Routledge, London 2012.
Woetzel R. K., *The Nuremberg Trials in International Law*, Stevens & Sons Limited, London 1960.
Wright Q., *A Study of War*, vols 1–2, The University of Chicago Press, Chicago 1944.

Wysocki A., *Tajemnice dyplomatycznego sejfu*, Książka i Wiedza, Warszawa 1974.
Zajadło J., *Dylematy humanitarnej interwencji*, Arche, Gdańsk 2005.
Zapałowski L., *Operacje pokojowe*, Krajowa Agencja Wydawnicza, Kraków 1989.
Zwoliński A., *Wojna. Wybrane zagadnienia*, Wydawnictwo WAM, Kraków 2003.
Žourek J., *L'interdiction de l'Emploi de la Force en Droit International*, A. W. Sijthoff, Leiden, Instytu Henry Dunant, Genève 1974.

3 Articles

Abtahi H., 'The Islamic Republic of Iran and the ICC', *JIntCrimJust* 2005, vol 3.
Akande D., 'The jurisdiction of the International Criminal Court over nationals of non-parties: legal basis and limits', *JIntCrimJust* 2003, vol 1.
Ailslieger K., 'Why the United States should be wary of the International Criminal Court: concerns over sovereignty and constitutional guarantees', *WashburnLJ* 1999, vol 39.
Alfaro R. J., 'La question de la définition de l'agression', *RDISDP* 1951, no 4.
Alvarez J. E., 'Hegemonic international law revisited', *AJIL* 2003, vol 97.
Amado G., 'La question de la définition de l'agression', *RDISDP* 1952, no 2.
Antonopoulos C., 'Whatever happened to crimes against peace?', *JConf&SecL* 2001, vol 6.
Aransjani M. H., 'The Rome Statute of the International Criminal Court', *AJIL* 1999, vol 93.
Balicki J., 'O definicji agresji', *Państwo i Prawo* 1952, no 7.
Barcik J., 'Koncepcja samoobrony w prawie międzynarodowym w dobie "wojny z terroryzmem"', *Kwartalnik Prawa Publicznego* 2003, no 1.
Barela S. J., 'Pre-emptive or preventive war: a discussion of legal and moral standards', *DenvJIntL&Pol* 2004, vol 33.
Bassiouni M. C., 'From Versailles to Rwanda in seventy-five years: the need to establish a Permanent International Criminal Court', *HarvHRJ* 1997, vol 10.
Bassiouni M. C., 'Observations concerning the 1997–1998 Preparatory Committee's work', *DenJIntL&Pol* 1997, vol 25.
Bassiouni M. C., 'Searching for justice in the world of Realpolitik', *PaceIntLRev* 2000, vol 12.
Bassiouni M. C., 'Universal jurisdiction for international crimes: historical perspectives and contemporary practice', *VirJIntL* 2001, vol 42.
Bassiouni M. C., 'World War I: "the war to end all wars" and the birth of a handicapped international criminal justice system', *DenvJIntL&Pol* 2002, vol 30.
Bassiouni M. C., 'The perennial conflict between international criminal justice and Realpolitik', *GeoStUnivLRev* 2006, vol 22.
Beres L. R. and 'Iraqi crimes and international law: the imperative to punish', *DenJIntL&Pol* 1993, vol 21.
Beres L. R. and Tsiddon-Chatto Y., 'Reconsidering Israel's destruction of Iraq's Osiraq nuclear reactor', *TempInt&CompLJ* 1995, vol 9.
Biddle F., 'Le procès de Nuremberg', *RIDP* 1948, no 1.
Bierzanek R., 'Definicja agresji w świetle prac komitetu specjalnego ONZ', *Sprawy Międzynarodowe* 1970.
Bishop W. W., 'The case against Hermann Roechling and others', *AJIL* 1949, vol 43.
Blokker N. and Kress C., 'A consensus agreement on the crime of aggression: impressions from Kampala', *LeidenJIntLaw* 2010, vol 23.

Boeving J. N., 'Aggression, international law, and the ICC: an argument for the withdrawal of aggression from the Rome Statute', *ColJTransL* 2005, vol 43.

Bramson A., 'Definicja agresji a ustawy o obronie pokoju', *Sprawy Międzynarodowe* 1952.

von Braun L. and Micus A., 'Judicial independence at risk. Critical issues regarding the crime of aggression raised by selected human rights organizations', *JIntCrimJust* 2012, vol 10.

'The Bryan peace treaties', *AJIL* 1913, vol 7.

Bugnion F., 'Just wars, wars of aggression and international humanitarian law', *IRRC* 2002, no 847.

Bush J. A., 'Soldiers find wars: a life of Telford Taylor', *ColJTransL* 1999, vol 37.

Bush J. A., '"The supreme crime" and its origins: the lost legislative history of the crime of aggressive war', *ColLRev* 2002, vol 102.

Carpenter A. C., 'The International Criminal Court and the crime of aggression', *NJIntL* 1995, vol 64.

Chacko C. J., 'International law and the concept of aggression', *IndJIntL* 1963, vol 3.

Clark R. S., 'Rethinking aggression as a crime and formulating its elements: the final work-product of the Preparatory Commission for the International Criminal Court', *LeidenJIntL* 2002, vol 15.

Clark R. S., 'Negotiating provisions defining the crime of aggression, its elements and the conditions for ICC exercise of jurisdiction over it', *EJIL* 2010, vol 20.

Cohan J. A., 'Legal war: when does it exist, and when does it end?', *HastInt&CompLRev* 2004, vol 27.

Creegan E., 'Justified uses of force and the crime of aggression', *JIntCrimJust* 2012, Special Issue, vol 10.

Cryer R., 'Aggression at the Court of Appeal', *JConf&SecL* 2005, vol 10.

Czapliński W., 'Interwencja w Iraku z punktu widzenia prawa międzynarodowego', *Państwo i Prawo* 2004, no 1.

Czapliński W., 'Organizacje regionalne a użycie siły, Kilka uwag na tle rozdziału VIII Karty NZ', Krakowskie Studia Prawnicze 2005, no 1.

Danner A. M. and Martinez J. S., 'Guilty associations: joint criminal enterprise, command responsibility, and the development of international criminal law', *CalifLRev* 2005, vol 93.

Dawson G. M., 'Defining substantive crimes within the subject matter jurisdiction of the International Criminal court: what is the crime of aggression?', *NYLSchJInt&CompL* 1999–2000, vol 19.

Donnedieu de Vabres H., 'Le procès de Nuremberg devant les principes modernes du droit pénal international', *Recueil des cours* 1947-I.

Doswald-Beck L., 'The legal validity of military intervention by invitation of the government', *BritYbkIntL* 1985, vol 56.

Drzewicki K., 'Trzecia generacja praw człowieka', *Sprawy Międzynarodowe* 1983, no 10.

El Zeidy M., 'The United States dropped the atomic bomb of Article 16 of the ICC Statute: Security Council power of deferrals and Resolution 1422', *VanderbiltJTransL* 2002, vol 35.

Ferencz B. B., 'An international criminal code and court: where they stand and where they're going', *ColJTransL* 1992, vol 30.

Ferencz B. B., 'Remarks made at Pace University School of Law on October 23, 1993', *PaceIntLRev* 1994, vol 6.

Ferencz B. B., 'Getting aggressive about preventing aggression', *BrownJWorldAff* 1999.

Ferencz B. B., 'Can aggression be deterred by law? "You have it in your power to make dreams of a more human world order under law come true"', Address to the Diplomatic Conference of Plenipotentiaries on the Establishment of an International Criminal Court, *PaceIntLRev* 1999, vol 11.

Ferencz B. B., 'The crime of aggression', in *Substantive and Procedural Aspects of International Criminal Law. The Experience of International and National Courts, Commentary*, vol 1, Kluwer Law International, The Hague 2000.

Ferencz B. B., 'Misguided fears about the International Criminal Court', *PaceIntLRev* 2003, vol 15.

Ferencz D. M., 'The crime of aggression: some personal reflections on Kampala', *LeidenJIntLaw* 2010, vol 23.

Fernández de Gurmendi S. A., 'The Working Group on aggression at the Preparatory Commission for the International Criminal Court', *FordhIntLJ* 2002, vol 25.

Finch G. A., 'The Nuremberg trial and international law', *AJIL* 1947, vol 41.

Flemming M., 'Definicja agresji', *Wojskowy Przegląd Prawniczy* 1975, no 2.

'Forty years after the Nuremberg and Tokyo tribunals: the impact of the war crimes trials on international and national law', *ASIL Proceedings* 1986, vol 80.

Franck T. M., 'Who killed Article 2(4)? Or: changing norms governing the use of force by states', *AJIL* 1970, vol 64.

Franck T. M., 'What happens now? The United Nations after Iraq', *AJIL* 2003, vol 97.

Franck T., 'Rethinking collective security', in M. N. Schmitt, J. Pejic (eds), *International Law and Armed Conflicts: Exploring the Faultlines. Essays in Honour of Yoram Dinstein*, Martinus Nijhoff Publishers, Leiden-Boston 2007.

Galeano V. B., 'The Gondra Treaty', *Transactions of the Grotius Society* 1929, vol 15.

Gelberg L., 'Wojna w Korei w świetle prawa międzynarodowego', *Państwo i Prawo* 1950, no 10.

Goetz C., 'Impressions of Telford Taylor at Nuremberg', *ColJTransL* 1999, vol 37.

Gray C., 'The use of force and the international legal order', in M. D. Evans (ed.), *International Law*, 2nd edn Oxford University Press, Oxford 2006.

Grayson J. W., 'The defence of superior orders in the International Criminal Court', *NJIntL* 1995, vol 64.

Griffiths R. L., 'International law, the crime of aggression and the ius ad bellum', *IntCrimLRev* 2002, vol 2.

Gulak J. M., 'Przypadek Napoleona jako precedens skazania za zbrodnię przeciwko pokojowi. Wkład Profesora Mariana Iwanejko w zakresie kształtowania się poglądu odpowiedzialności karnej jednostki za wywołanie wojny', in *Aktualne problemy prawa międzynarodowego we współczesnym świecie. Księga pamiątkowa poświęcona pamięci Profesora Mariana Iwanejko. Materiały z ogólnopolskiej konferencji zorganizowanej przez Katedrę Prawa międzynarodowego i Porównawczego Akademii Ekonomicznej w Krakowie (Kraków, 27–28 września 1995)*, Akademia Ekonomiczna w Krakowie, Kraków 1995.

Grzebyk P., 'Le tribunal spécial iraquien: instrument de justice ou de vengeance', in S. Sur (ed.), *Annuaire Français de Relations Internationales* 2008, vol IX, La Documentation Française, Bruylant, Bruxelles 2008.

Harroff-Travel M., 'Do wars ever end? The work of the International Committee of the Red Cross: when the guns fall silent', *IRRC* 2003, no 851.

Heller K. J., 'The uncertain legal status of the aggression understandings', *JIntCrimJust* 2012, Special Issue, vol 10.

Henkin L., 'The reports of the death of Art. 2(4) are greatly exaggerated', *AJIL* 1971, vol 65.

Hershey A. S., 'Convention for the peaceful adjustment of international differences', *AJIL* 1908, vol 2.

Hogan-Doran J. and van Ginkel B. T., 'Aggression as a crime under international law and the prosecution of individuals by the proposed International Criminal Court', *NIntLJ* 1996, vol 43.

Horwitz S., 'The Tokyo trial', *IntCon* 1950, no 465.

Hudson M. O., 'The report of the assembly of the League of Nations on the Sino-Japanese dispute', *AJIL* 1933, vol 27.

Hugueney L., 'Le procès de Nuremberg devant les principes modernes du droit pénal international', *RIDP* 1948, nos 3–4.

Iwanejko M., 'Przypadek Napoleona jako precedens skazania za zbrodnię przeciwko pokojowi', *Kultura i Społeczeństwo* 1972, no 3.

Jellinek W., 'L'ex-Empereur d'Allemagne Guillaume II en Hollande', *JDI* (Période de la guerre 1914–1919) 1919, tome 46.

Jessup P. C., 'The Saavendra Lamas anti-war draft treaty', *AJIL* 1933, vol 27.

Jianping L. and Zhixiang W., 'China's attitude towards the ICC', *JIntCrimJust* 2005, vol 3.

'Judicial chronicle, Saddam Hussein's first hearing', *JIntCrimJust* 2004, no 2.

Kearley T., 'Regulation of preventive and preemptive force in the United Nations Charter; a search for original intent', *WyoLRev* 2003, no 3.

Kelsen H., 'Will the judgment in the Nuremberg trial constitute a precedent in international law?', *IntLQ* 1947, vol 1.

Kherad R., 'La question de la définition du crime d'agression dans le statut de Rome. Entre pouvoir politique du Conseil de securité et compétence judiciaire de la Cour pénale internationale', *RGDIP* 2005, no 2.

Kieft Van de C. M., 'Uncertain risk: the United States Military and the International Criminal Court', *CardozoLRev* 2002, vol 22.

Kirgis F. L. Jr, 'The Security Council's first fifty years', *AJIL* 1995, vol 89.

Kirsch N., 'International law in times of hegemony: unequal power and the shaping of international legal order', *EJIL* 2005, vol 16.

Kleinberger T. R., 'The Iraqi conflict: an assessment of possible war crimes and the call for adoption of an International Criminal Code and Permanent International Criminal Tribunal', *NYLSchJInt&CompL* 1993, vol 14.

Komarnicki W., 'La définition de l'agresseur dans le droit international moderne', *Recueil des cours* 1949-II.

Kranz J., 'Nowe aspekty stosowania siły w stosunkach międzynarodowych', in J. Menkes (ed.), *Prawo międzynarodowe – Problemy i wyzwania. Księga pamiątkowa Prof. Renaty Sonnenfeld-Tomporek*, Wyższa Szkoła Handlu i Prawa im. Ryszarda Łazarskiego w Warszawie, Warszawa 2006.

Kress C., 'Versailles-Nuremberg-The Hague Germany and international criminal law', *International Lawyer* 2006, vol 40.

Kress C., 'Time for decision: some thoughts on the immediate future of the crime of aggression: a reply to Andreas Paulus' *EJIL* 2010, vol 20.

Kress C. and von Holtzendorff L., 'The Kampala compromise on the crime of aggression', *JIntCrimJust* 2010, vol 8.

Kunz J. L., 'Bellum iustum and bellum legale', *AJIL* 1951, vol 45.

Kuźniar R., 'ONZ i porządek międzynarodowy', in J. Symonides (ed.), *Organizacja Narodów Zjednoczonych. Bilans i perspektywy*, Wyd Naukowe Scholar, Warszawa 2006.

Lacanilao A. R., 'The International Criminal Court in the balance: should the Security Council be given role in the crime of aggression?, *Eyes on the ICC* 2004, vol 1.

Lachs M., 'Walka o definicję agresji', *Wojskowy Przegląd Prawniczy* 1952, no 3.

Lagerwall A., 'L'Administration du territoire irakien: un exemple de reconnaissance et d'aide au maintien d'une occupation resultant d'un acte d'agression?', *RBDI* 2006, no 1.
Larnaude F. and de Lapradelle A., 'Examen de la responsabilité pénale de l'empereur Guillaume II d'Allemagne', *JDI* (Période de la guerre 1914–1919) 1919, tome 46.
Lauterpacht H., '"Resort to war" and the interpretation of the covenant during the Manchurian dispute', *AJIL* 1934, vol 28.
Leibman L., 'From Nuremberg to Bosnia: consistent application of international law', *ClevStLRev* 1994, vol 42.
Leitenberg M., 'Wojny i konflikty w latach 1945–2000: Ofiary śmiertelne', in R. Kuźniar, Z. Lachowski, *Bezpieczeństwo międzynarodowe czasu przemian. Zagrożenia-Koncepcje-Instytucje*, Polski Insytutu Spraw Międzynarodowych, Warszawa 2003.
Levie H. S., 'The Statute of the International Tribunal for the Former Yugoslavia: a comparison with the past and a look at the future', *SyrJIntL&Com* 1995, vol 21.
Lippman M., 'Nuremberg: forty-five years later', *ConnecticutJIntL* 1991, vol 7.
Lippmann M., 'The good motive defense: Ernst von Weizsaecker and the Nazi Ministries case', *TouroIntLRev* 1997, vol 7.
Lippmann M., 'Prosecutions of Nazi war criminals before post-World War II domestic tribunals', *UnivMiamiInt&CompLRev* 1999–2000, vol 8.
Lippman M., 'The history, development, and decline of crimes against peace', *Geo WashIntLRev* 2004, vol 36.
Lumb R. D., 'Individual responsibility for aggressive war: the crime against peace', *UnivQueensLJ* 1956–59, vol 3.
Maktos J., 'La question de la definition de l'agression', *RDISDP* 1952, no 1.
Malakian F., 'International criminal responsibility', in M. C. Bassiouni, *International Criminal Law*, vols 1–3, 2nd edn, Transnational Publishers Inc., Ardsley, New York 1999.
Malik P., 'Międzynarodowy Trybunał Karny a problematyka bezpieczeństwa światowego', *Wojskowy Przegląd Prawniczy* 2003, no 3.
Maridakis G. S., 'Un précedent du procès de Nuremberg tiré de l'histoire de la Grèce ancienne', *RHDI* Juillet–Decembre 1952, 5ème année.
Marrus M. R., 'A Jewish lobby at Nuremberg: Jacob Robinson and the Institute of Jewish Affairs, 1945–1946', *CardozoLRev* 2006, vol 27.
Mathias D. S., 'The Definition of aggression and the ICC. Remarks by D. Stephen Mathias', *Proceedings of the Annual meeting (American Society of International Law),* vol 96, (13–16 March 2002), p. 181–82.
May L., 'Act and circumstance in the crime of aggression, symposium: war and responsibility', *JPolPhil* 2007, vol 15.
Meltzer B. D., '"War crimes": the Nuremberg trial and the Tribunal for the Former Yugoslavia', *ValparaisoUnivLRev* 1996, vol 30.
Meron T., 'From Nuremberg to The Hague', *MilLRev* 1995, vol 149.
Meron T., 'Defining aggression for the International Criminal Court', *SuffTransLRev* 2001, vol 25.
Michałowska G., 'Odpowiedzialność jednostki w prawie międzynarodowym', *Stosunki Międzynarodowe* 2000, nos 3–4.
Milanovic M., 'Aggression and legality. Custom in Kampala', *JIntCrimJust* 2012, Special Issue, vol 10.
Mitchell F., 'The formulation of the conception of aggression', *International Association of Democratic Lawyers*, Brussels 1952.

Mitchell J. B., '"Pre-emptive war": is it constitutional?', *SantaClaraLRev* 2004, vol 44.

Murphy S. D., 'U.S. view of crime of aggression', *AJIL* 2001, vol 95.

Murphy S. D., 'U.S. notification of intent not to become a party to the Rome Statute', *AJIL* 2002, vol 96.

Müller-Schieke I. K., 'Defining the crime of aggression under the Statute of the International Criminal Court', *LeidenJIntL* 2001, vol 14.

Nanda V. P., 'The United States' action in the 1965 Dominican crisis: impact on world order – Part I', *DenvLJ* 1966, vol 43.

Nanda V. P., 'The United States armed intervention in Grenada: impact on world order', *CalifWestIntLJ* 1984, vol 13.

Nanda V. P., 'The validity of United States intervention in Panama under international law', *AJIL* 1990, vol 84.

Naqvi Y., 'Amnesty for war crimes: defining the limits of international recognition', *IRRC* 2003, no 851.

Newton M. A., 'Should the United States join the International Criminal Court?', *UCDavisJIntL&Pol* 2002, vol 9.

Niang A., 'Les individus en tant que personnes privées', in H. Ascensio, E. Decaux and A. Pellet (eds), *Droit international pénal*, Cedin Paris X, Editions A. Pedone, Paris 2000, p. 228.

Nsereko D. D. N., 'Defining the crime of aggression: an important agenda item for the assembly of States Parties to the Rome Statute of the International Criminal Court', *Acta Iuridica* 2003.

O'Connell M. E. and Niyazmatov M., 'What is aggression? Comparing the *ius ad bellum* and the ICC Statute', *JIntCrimJust* 2012, Special Issue, vol 10.

O'Donovan M., 'Criminalizing war: toward a justifiable crime of aggression', *BostCollnt&CompLRev* 2007, vol 30.

Official Records of the Review Conference of the Rome Statute of the International Criminal Court, Kampala 31 May–11 June 2010, International Criminal Court, The Hague 2010.

Official Records of the United Nations Diplomatic Conference of Plenipotentiaries on the Establishment of an International Criminal Court (Summary Records of the Plenary Meetings and of the Meetings of the Committee of the Whole), vols 1–3, United Nations, New York 2002.

'Open Panel discussion: should the United States join the International Criminal Court?', *UCDavisJIntL&Pol* 2002, vol 9.

Paulus A. L., 'Peace through justice? The future of the crime of aggression in a time of crisis', *WayneLRev* 2004, vol 50, no 1.

Paulus A., 'Second thoughts on the crime of aggression', *EJIL* 2010, vol 20.

Peirce R., 'Which of the Preparatory Commission's latest proposals for the definition of the crime of aggression and the exercise of jurisdiction should be adopted into the Rome Statute of the International Criminal Court?', *BYUJPubL* 2000–2001, vol 15.

Pella V. V., 'Le code des crimes contre la paix et la securité de l'humanité (observations et réflexions)', *RDISDP* 1952, no 4.

Płachta M., 'Jak pogodzic´ sprawiedliwos´c´ retrybutywna˛ ze sprawiedliwos´cia˛ restytucyjną? Międzynarodowy Trybunał Karny a komisje pojednania i amnestie', *Ius et Lex* 2003, no 1.

Politi M., 'The ICC and the crime of aggression. A dream that came through and the reality ahead', *JIntCrimJust* 2012, Special Issue, vol 10.

Popiuk-Rysińska I. and Zając J., 'Operacje pokojowe Narodów Zjednoczonych', in J. Symonides (ed.), *Organizacja Narodów Zjednoczonych. Bilans i perspektywy*', Wydawnictwo Naukowe Scholar, Warszawa 2006.

Pordea G. A., 'L'agression, ses critères déterminatifs et sa définition', *RDISDP* 1952, no 4.
Randall K. C., 'Universal jurisdiction under international law', *TexLRev* 1988, vol 66.
Rayfuse R., 'The Draft Code of Crimes against the Peace and Security of Mankind: eating disorders at the International Law Commission', *CrimLF* 1997, vol 8.
Reisinger Coracini A., 'Evaluating domestic legislation on the customary crime of aggression under the Rome Statute's complementarity regime', in Stahn C. and Sluiter G. (eds), *The Emerging Practice of the International Criminal Court*, Brill 2009.
Robbins J. S., 'War crimes: the case of Iraq', *FletcherFWorldAff* 1994, vol 18.
Rogoff M. A. and Collins E. Jr, 'The Caroline incident and the development of international law', *BrookJIL* 1990, vol 16.
Rosenfeld F., 'Individual civil responsibility for the crime of aggression', *JIntCrimJust* 2012, Special Issue, vol 10.
Sapiro M., 'Iraq: the shifting sands of preemptive self-defense', *AJIL* 2003, vol 97.
Schaack Van B., 'Par in parem imperium non habet. Complementarity and the crime of aggression', *JIntCrimJust* 2012, Special Issue, vol 10.
Schabas W. A., 'United States hostility to the International Criminal Court: it's all about the Security Council', *EJIL* 2004, vol 15.
Schachter O., 'The enforcement of international judicial and arbitral decisions', *AJIL* 1960, vol 54.
Schachter O., 'The right of states to use armed force', *MichLRev* 1984, vol 82.
Scheffer D., 'The complex crime of aggression under the Rome Statute', *LeidenJIntL* 2010, vol 23.
Schick F. B., 'The Nuremberg trial and the international law of the future', *AJIL* 1947, vol 41.
Schuster M., 'The Rome Statute and the crime of aggression: a gordian knot in search of a sword', *CrimLF* 2003, vol 14.
Schweisfurth T., 'Operations to rescue nationals in third states involving the use of force in relation to the protection of human rights', *GermYbkIntL* 1980, no 23.
Scott J. B., 'The Sixth Pan-American Conference', *AJIL* 1928, vol 22.
Scott J. B., 'The Pan-American Conference on conciliation and arbitration', *AJIL* 1929, vol 23.
Scott J. B., 'Interpretation of Article X of the Covenant of the League of Nations', *AJIL* 1924, vol 18.
Scott G. W., 'Hague Convention Restricting the Use of Force to Recover on Contract Claims', *AJIL* 1908, vol 2.
Sellars K., 'Delegitimising aggression. First steps and false starts after the First World War', *JIntCrimJust* 2012, Special Issue, vol 10.
Simons D., 'L'Extradition de l'ex-Empereur d'Allemagne et la Hollande', *JDI* (Période de la guerre 1914–1919) 1919, tome 46.
Skopets M., 'Battered nation syndrome: relaxing the imminence requirement of self-defense in international law', *AmUnivLRev* 2006, vol 55.
Skubiszewski K., 'Use of force by states. Collective security. Law of war and neutrality', in M. Sørensen, *Manual of Public International Law*, St Martin's Press, New York 1968.
Sohn L. B., 'The definition of aggression', *VirLRev* 1959, vol 45.
Solera O., 'Complementary jurisdiction and international criminal justice', *IRRC* 2002, no 845.
Solomon N., 'Judaism and the ethics of war', *IRRC* 2005, no 858.

Springrose L. J., 'Aggression as a core crime in the Rome Statute establishing and International Criminal Court', *StLouisWarsawTransLJ* 1999, vol 99.

Stahn C., 'The "end", the "beginning of the end" or the "end of the beginning"? Introducing debated and voices on the definition of aggression', *LeidenJIntL* 2010, vol 23.

Stein M. S., 'The Security Council, the International Criminal Court, and the crime of aggression: how exclusive is the Security Council's power to determine aggression?', *IndInt&CompLRev* 2005, vol 16.

Stowell E. C., 'Convention relative to the opening of hostility', *AJIL* 1908, vol 2.

Swaak-Goldman O., 'Recent developments in international criminal law: trying to stay afloat between Scylla and Charybdis', *Int&CompLQ* 2005, vol 54.

Symonides J., 'Wojna z Irakiem a prawo międzynarodowe', in R. Kuźniar (ed.), *Rocznik Strategiczny 2003/2004*, Wydawnictwo Naukowe Scholar, Warszawa 2004.

Symposium, the Fifth Annual Ernst C. Stiefel Symposium 1945–1995: Critical Perspectives on the Nuremberg Trials and State Accountability, Panel I. Telford Taylor Panel: Critical Perspectives on the Nuremberg Trial, NYSchJHR 1995, vol 12.

Takatori Y., 'The forgotten judge at the Tokyo war crimes trial', *Massachusetts Historical Review* 2008, vol 10.

Tallgren I., 'The sensibility and sense of international criminal law', *EJIL* 2002, vol 13.

Taylor T., 'Nuremberg trials. war crimes and international law', *IntCon* April 1949, no 450.

Tomuschat C., 'Crimes against Peace and Security of Mankind and the recalcitrant third state', in Y. Dinstein and M. Tabory, *War Crimes in International Law*, Martinus Nijhoff Publishers, The Hague 1996.

Trahan J., 'Defining "aggression": why the Preparatory Commission for the International Criminal Court has faced such a conundrum', *LoyolaLAInt&CompLRev* 2002, vol 24.

Trahan J., 'The Rome Statute's amendments on the crime of aggression: negotiations at the Kampala review conference', *ICLR* 2011, vol 11.

Vagts D. F., 'Hegemonic international law', *AJIL* 2001, vol 95.

Van der Vyver J., 'Prosecuting the crime of aggression in the International Criminal Court', *UMiamiNat'lSec&ArmedConflLawRev* 2010–2011, vol 1.

Vulcan C., 'L'Exécution des décisions de la Cour Internationale de Justice d'après la Charte des Nations Unies', *RGDIP* 1947, vol 51.

Wald P., 'International criminal courts – a stormy adolescence', *VirJIntL* 2006, vol 46.

Wald P. M., 'Running the trial of the century: the Nuremberg legacy', in *Symposium: The Nuremberg Trials: A Reappraisal and Their Legacy, CardozoLRev* 2006, vol 27.

Waldock C. H. M., 'The regulation of the use of force by individual states in international law', *Recueil des cours* 1952-II.

Wasilkowski A., 'Kilka uwag w kwestii użycia siły we współczesnym prawie międzynarodowym', in J. Menkes (ed.), *Prawo międzynarodowe – Problemy i wyzwania. Księga pamiątkowa Prof. Renaty Sonnenfeld-Tomporek*, Wyższa Szkoła Handlu i Prawa im. Ryszarda Łazarskiego w Warszawie, Warszawa 2006.

Weiss F., 'Time limits for the prosecution of crimes against international law', *BYbkIntL* 1982, vol 53.

Wenaweser C., 'Reaching the Kampala compromise on aggression: the chair's perspective', *LeidenJIntL* 2010, vol 23.

Williams K. A., 'The Iraq-Kuwait crisis: an analysis of the unresolved issue of war crimes liability', *BrookJIntL* 1992, vol 18.

Wirth S., 'Immunity for core crimes? The ICJ's judgment in the Congo v Belgium case', *EJIL* 2002, vol 13.

Woo J., 'Using force', *UnivChiLRev* 2004, vol 71.
Woolsey L. H., 'The Leticia dispute between Columbia and Peru', *AJIL* 1933, vol 27.
Worth J. R., 'Globalization and the myth of absolute national sovereignty: reconsidering the "UN-signing" of the Rome Statute and the legacy of Senator Bricker', *IndLJ* 2004, vol 79.
Wright Q., 'Changes in the conception of war', *AJIL* 1924, vol 18.
Wright Q., 'The law of the Nuremberg trial', *AJIL* 1947, vol 41.
Yee S., 'A proposal to reformulate Article 23 of the ILC Draft Statute for an International Criminal Court', *HastingsInt&CompLRev* 1996, vol 19.
Yee S., 'The Tu Quoque argument as a defence to international crimes, prosecution or punishment', *ChinJIntL* 2004, vol 3.
Zimmermann A., 'Amending the amendment provisions of the Rome Statute. The Kampala compromise on the crime of aggression and the law of treaties', *JIntCrimJust* 2012, Special Issue, vol 10.
Zolo D., 'Peace through criminal law', *JIntCrimJust* 2004, vol 2.
Žourek J., 'La définition de l'agression et le droit international. Développements récents de la question', *Recueil des cours* 1957-II.

4 Newspapers

The Times (London), 3 September 1990.
New York Times, 17 April 1991.

5 Websites

http://www.africa-union.org
http://www.bgbl.de
http://www.bundestag.de
http://www.cas.go.jp
http://www.hrcr.org
http://www.ibiblio.org
http://www.icc-cpi.int
http://www.iciss.ca
http://www.iccnow.org
http://iccreviewconference.blogspot.com
http://www.icj-cij.org
http://www.icty.org
http://law.case.edu
http://legislationline.org
http://wwi.lib.byu.edu
http://miasta.gazeta.pl/trojmiasto
http://www.mpepil.com
http://ota.ahds.ac.uk
http://www.sangiin.go.jp
http://www.sipri.org
http://www.un.org
http://www.vatican.va
http://www.vietnamese-american.org

Appendix

Biographies of the accused in the trial before the IMT

Bormann, Martin – Chief of Party Chancellery, Chief of Staff, Deputy of Führer in the NSDAP, secretary to Adolf Hitler, Reichsleiter, Reich Minister (1944–45), Member of Ministerial Council for the Defence of the Reich, Lieutenant General of SS.

Dönitz, Karl – On 1st May, 1945, he became the Head of State, succeeding Hitler, Commander-in-Chief of the German Navy (1945- 1943), Admiral (since 1942), Vice-Admiral (1940), commander of the submarine arm (1936), commander of the first U-boat flotilla (1935).

Frank, Hans – Reich Minister (1934–45), Governor General of Poland (1939–45), Bavarian Minister of Justice, Reich Commissioner and reformer of the Nazi state legal system, Reichsleiter, Lieutenant General of SS.

Frick, Wilhelm – Reich Protector of Bohemia-Moravia (1943–45), Plenipotentiary General for the Administration of the Reich (1939–43), Reich Minister of Interior (1933–43), Member of Reich Defence Council, Reichsleiter, Lieutenant General of SS.

Fritzsche, Hans – Chief of Radio Division in Reich Ministry for Public Enlightenment and Propaganda (1942–45), Chief of German Press Division in Reich Ministry for Public Enlightenment and Propaganda (1938–42), Chief of Wireless News Service (1932–37).

Funk, Walter – Member of Central Planning Board of Four-Year Plan (1943–45), Plenipotentiary General for the Economy (1939–45), President of Reichsbank (1939–45), Reich Minister of Economics (1938–45), Press Chief of the Reich Government and State Secretary in Reich Ministry for Public Enlightenment and Propaganda (1933–37), Member of Ministerial Council for the Defence of the Reich, Member of Small Ministerial Council of Four-Year Plan.

Göring, Hermann – Reich Marshal, Plenipotentiary for the Four-Year Plan (1936–45), Commander in Chief of German Air Force (1935–45), Reich Minister for Air (1933–45), Minister President of Prussia (1933–45), President of Reichstag (1932–45), Acting Reich Minister of Economics (1937–38), Chairman of Ministerial Council for the Defence of the Reich, Chairman of General Council of the Four-Year Plan, Member of Secret Cabinet Council, Lieutenant General of SS and SA.

Hess, Rudolf – Reich Minister without Portfolio (1933–41), Deputy of Hitler as Führer of NSDAP (1933–41), Member of Ministerial Council for the Defence of the Reich, Member of Secret Cabinet Council, Reichsleiter, Lieutenant General of SS and SA.

Jodl, Alfred – General, Chief of Armed Forces Operations Staff, High Command of the German Armed Forces (1939–45).

Kaltenbrunner, Ernst – Chief of Security Police and Security Service (1943–45), Chief of Reich Security Main Office (1943–45), State Secretary for Security in the Seyss-Inquart Cabinet of Austria, Chief of SS in Austria, Lieutenant General of SS and of Police.

Keitel, Wilhelm – Field Marshal, Chief of High Command of the German Armed Forces (1938–45), Chief of Armed Forces Office in Reich War Ministry (1935–38), Member of Ministerial Council for Defence of the Reich, Member of Secret Cabinet Council.

Krupp von Bohlen und Halbach, Gustav – company chairman of Friedrich Krupp AG heavy industry conglomerate (1909–41).

Ley, Robert – Reich Housing Commissioner (1942–45), Founder and Chief of the German Labor Front (1933–45), Chief of Party Organisation of NSDAP (1932–45), Reichsleiter, Lieutenant General of SA.

Neurath, Constantin Baron von – Reich Protector of Bohemia-Moravia (1939–43), Reich Minister of Foreign Affairs (1932–38), President of Secret Cabinet Council, Lieutenant General of SS, Member of Reich Defence Council.

Papen, Franz von – German Ambassador to Turkey (1939–44), German Minister Extraordinary and Plenipotentiary on Special Mission to Austria (1934–38).

Raeder, Erich – Admiral of the Fleet; Admiral Inspector of the Navy (1943–45), Chief of High Command of the German Navy (1935–43), Member of Secret Cabinet Council.

Ribbentrop, Joachim von – Reich Minister for Foreign Affairs (1938–45), Foreign Policy Adviser to Hitler (1933–45), German Ambassador in London (1936–38), Member of Secret Cabinet Council, Lieutenant General of SS.

Rosenberg, Alfred – Reich Minister for the Occupied Eastern Territories (1941–45), Chief of Foreign Policy Office of the NSDAP (1933–45), Plenipotentiary of the Führer for the Guidance of the Ideological and Philosophical Training and Education of the NSDAP, Reichsleiter, Lieutenant General of SS and SA.

Sauckel, Fritz – Plenipotentiary General for Labor Allocation in Four-Year Plan (1942–45), Reich Governor of Thuringia (1933–45), Gauleiter of NSDAP for Thuringia (1927–45), Lieutenant General of SS.

Schacht, Hjalmar – Reichminister without Portfolio (1937–43), President of Reichsbank (1923–30, 1933–39), Acting Reich Minister of Economics (1934–37), Plenipotentiary General for the War Economy (1935–37), Member of Small Ministerial Council of the Four-Year Plan.

Schirach, Baldur von – Gauleiter of Vienna (1940–45), Reich Youth Leader (1933–40), Reichsleiter.

Seyss-Inquart, Arthur – Reich Minister without Portfolio (1939–45), Reich Commissioner for the Occupied Netherlands (1940–45), Deputy Governor General in the Government General of Poland (1939–40), Reich Governor of Austria (1938–39), Federal Chancellor of Austria (1938), Minister of Interior and Security of Austria (1938), Lieutenant General of SS.

Speer, Albert – Co-chairman of Special staff organisation for fighter plane production, Member of Central Planning Board of the Four-Year Plan (1942–45), Plenipotentiary General for Armament Tasks of the Four-Year Plan (1942–45), Reich Minister for Armament and War Production (1942–45), Chief of Organisation Todt (1942–45).

Streicher, Julius – Publisher of 'Der Stürmer' and 'Fränkische Tageszeitung', Gauleiter of NSDAP for Franconia (1925–40), Lieutenant General of SA.

Biographies of the accused in the trial before IMTFE

Araki, Sadao – General, Minister of War (1931–34), Member of Supreme War Council (1934–36), Member of Cabinet Advisory Council on China (1937), Minister of Education (1938–39), Member of Cabinet Advisory Council (1940).

Dohihara, Kenji – General, Mayor of Mukden (1931), Chief Adviser to the North China autonomous Government, Commander in Chief of Japanese 5th Army Manchuria (1938–40), Supreme War Councilor (1940–43), Inspector General of Military Aviation (1941), Commander in Chief Eastern Army in Japan (1943), Commander of the 7th Area Army at Singapore (1944–45), Inspector General Military Training (1945).

Hashimoto, Kingoro – attached Army General Staff (1933), commanded an Artillery Regiment at the Rape of Nanking (1937), in command of Japanese forces which shelled the *Ladybird* and the *Panay* (1937), author of a large number of books, articles, public speeches advocating aggressive warfare, member of a number of societies instigating to aggressive warfare, elected to the Lower House of the Diet (1942).

Hata, Shunroku – Field Marshall, Divisional Commander in Manchuria (1933), Chief of Army Aviation Department (1935), Commander of the Taiwan Army (1936–37), Inspector General of Military Education and member of Supreme War Council (1937), Commander in Chief of the Expeditionary Force in Central China (1938, 1940–44), Member of Supreme War Council (1939), Minister of War (1939–40), Member of Board of Marshals and Admirals (1944), Inspector General of Military Education (1944).

Hiranuma, Kiichiro – Vice President and subsequently President of Privy Council (1930–39, 1945), Prime Minister (1939), Minister without Portfolio and for a time Home Minister and later Vice Premier (1940–41), Member of Thought Control Council (1941).

Hirota, Koki – Ambassador to the USSR (1930), Foreign Minister (1933–34, 1934–36, 1937–38), Prime Minister and for a time Foreign Minister concurrently (1936–37), Member of Cabinet Advisory Council (1940).

Hoshino, Naoki – Vice Minister Finance in the Manchukuo Government (1936), Chief of General Affairs in Manchukuo (1938), President of Planning Board and later Minister without Portfolio (1940–41), Chief Secretary and Minister of State (1941–44), Adviser to Finance Ministry (1944).

Itagaki, Seishiro – General, Vice Chief of Staff of Kwantung Army (1934), Commander 5th Division in China (1937), Chief of Staff of Kwantung Army (1936–37), Minister of War (1938–39) and concurrently President of the Manchurian Affairs Bureau of the Cabinet, Chief of Staff of Japanese Army in China (1939), Commander of Japanese Army in Korea (1941–45), Member of Supreme War Council (1943), Commander 7th Area Army in Singapore (1945).

Kaya, Okinori – Chief Secretary of Finance Ministry (1934), Minister of Finance (1937–38, 1941–44), on the Advisory Committee of China Affairs Board (1939), President of North China Development Company (1939–41).

Kido, Koichi – Chief Secretary to the Lord Keeper of the Privy Seal (1930), Minister of Education (1937), Minister of Welfare (1938), Home Minister (1939), Lord Keeper of the Privy Seal (1940–45), chief confidential adviser to the emperor.

Kimura, Heitaro – General, Chief of Staff of Kwantung Army (1940), Vice War Minister (1941–44), Member of Supreme War Council (1943), Commander in Chief Japanese Army, Burma (1944).

Koiso, Kuniaki – General, Vice War Minister (1932), Chief of Staff of Kwantung Army (1932–34), Commander Japanese Army in Korea (1935–36), Overseas Minister (1939, 1940), Governor General Korea (1942), Prime Minister (1944–45).

Matsui, Iwane – General, Member of Supreme War Council (1933), Commander in Chief of Japanese Forces in Central China (1937–38), Member of Cabinet Advisory Council (1938–40).

Matsuoka, Yosuke – President of South Manchurian Railway (1935–39), Member of Cabinet Advisory Council (1940), Foreign Minister (1940–41), author of publications and public speeches advocating aggressive warfare.

Minami, Jiro – War Minister (1931), Supreme War Councilor (1931–34), Commander in Chief of Kwantung Army (1934–36), Governor General of Korea (1936–42), Member of Privy Council (1942–45).

Muto, Akira – Chief of Military Affairs Bureau (1939–42), Commander 2nd Guards Division in Sumatra (1943), Chief of Staff of 14th Area Army in the Philippines (1944).

Nagano, Osumi – Admiral, Member of Supreme War Council, Navy Minister (1936–37), Commander in Chief of Combined Fleet (1937), Chief of Naval General Staff (1941–44), Supreme Naval Adviser to the emperor (1944).

Oka, Takasumi – Section Chief, General and Military Affairs Bureau of the Navy (1938), Chief of General and Military Affairs Bureaux of the Navy (1940–44), Vice Admiral (1942), Vice Navy Minister (1944), Commander in Chief Chinkai (Korea) Naval Station (1944–45).

Okawa, Shumei – organizer of the Mukden Incident (September 18th, 1931), author of publications and speeches advocating aggressive war for the expulsion by force of the white races from Asia.

Oshima, Hiroshi – Military Attaché in Berlin (1936), Ambassador to Germany (1938–39, 1941–45).

Sato, Kenryo – Lieutenant General, Member of Planning Board (1937–38), Chief of Military Affairs Section of Military Affairs Bureau of War Ministry (1941–42), Chief of Military Affairs Bureau of War Ministry (1942–44).

Shigemitsu, Mamoru – Minister to China (1931), Vice Foreign Minister (1933–36), Ambassador to the USSR, Great Britain, Nanking Puppet Government, Foreign Minister (1943–45) and concurrently Minister for Greater East Asia (1944–45).

Shimada, Shigetaro – Admiral, Chief of Staff of Combined Fleet (1930), Vice Chief of Naval General Staff (1935–37), Commander of Second Fleet (1937), Commander of China Fleet (1940), Navy Minister (1941), member of Supreme War Council (1944), Chief of Naval General Staff (1944).

Shiratori, Toshio – Chief of Information Bureau of Foreign Office (1930), Minister to Sweden, Norway, Denmark, Finland, Ambassador to Italy (1939).

Suzuki, Teiichi – Member of Military Affairs Section of War Ministry (1931), Official of Investigation Bureau of the Cabinet (1935), Regimental Commander of the 14th Regiment (1936), Chief of Political Affairs Division of China Affairs Board (1938–41), President of Cabinet Planning Board and Minister without Portfolio (1941–43), Cabinet Adviser (1943–44).

Togo, Shigenori – Ambassador to Germany and to USSR, Foreign Minister and Minister for Overseas Affairs (1941–42), Foreign Minister and Minister of Greater East Asia (1945).

Tojo, Hideki – General, Commander of the Military Police of the Kwantung Army (1935), Chief of Staff of Kwantung Army (1937), Vice War Minister (1938), Director

General of Military Aviation (1938–39), War Minister (1940–41), Prime Minister and War Minister concurrently (1941–44), during which period he was also, at times, Home Minister, Minister of Munitions, and Chief of General Staff.

Umezu, Yoshijiro – General, Chief of General Affairs Department of War Ministry (1931), Commander of the Japanese Forces in China (1934), Vice War Minister (1936–38), Commander of the Kwantung Army and Ambassador to Manchukuo (1939–44), Chief of General Staff (1944–45).

Biographies of the accused of crime of conspiracy or crime against peace in Farben case

Ambros, Otto – member of Vorstand (1938–45) and of several committees, manager of eight of the most important plants, member of control bodies in several Farben units, special consultant to chief of Research and Development Department, Four-Year Plan, chief of Special Committee (Chemical Warfare) of the Main Committee on Powder and Explosives in Armament Supply Office, chief of a number of units in the Economic Group Chemical Industry.

Bürgin, Ernst – member of Vorstand (1938–45), member of Technical Committee and Chemicals Committee, chief of Works Combine Central Germany and of the Bitterfeld and Wolfen plants, member of various Farben control groups in Germany, Norway, Switzerland, and Spain, collaborator of Krauch in the Four-Year Plan.

Bütefisch, Heinrich – deputy member of Vorstand (1934–38), full member of Vorstand (1938–45), member of several committees, deputy chief of Sparte I (1938–45), chief of the Leuna Works, chairman or member of control groups of many Farben concerns in the fields of chemicals, explosives, mining, synthetics etc in Germany, Poland, Austria, Czechoslovakia, Yugoslavia, Romania and Hungary, collaborator of Krauch in the Four-Year Plan, Production Commissioner for Oil, Ministry of Armaments, president of Technical Experts Committee, International Nitrogen Convention.

Dürrfeld, Walter – Prokurist of Farben (1941–44), chief of construction and installation at the Auschwitz plant, director of Auschwitz plant (1944–45).

Gajewski, Fritz – deputy member of Vorstand (1931–34), full member of Vorstand (1934–45), member of several committees, chief of Sparte III (1929–45) and of Works Combine Berlin (1931–45), manager of Agfa plants, member of board in numerous other subsidiaries and affiliates.

Gattineau, Heinrich – member of Vorstand Working Committee and of Farben's South-East Europe Committee, chief of Farben's Political Economy Department, officer or member of control groups in a dozen Farben units and subsidiaries in Germany and south-eastern Europe, colonel of SA, member of Council for Propaganda of German Economy.

Häfliger, Paul – deputy member of Vorstand (1926–38), full member of Vorstand (1938–45), member of several committees, vice chairman and deputy chief for metals of Sales Combine Chemicals, chairman or member of control groups in several Farben units, including concerns in Germany, Austria, Czechoslovakia, Norway and Italy.

Heyde, Erich von der – representative of Farben (1939–45), attached to Farben's Economic Policy Department, Berlin NW 7, counter-intelligence agent for Berlin

NW 7 and for a short period deputy to Schneider as chief of Farben's Counter-Intelligence Branch, High Command of the Armed Forces, member of the Reiter (mounted) SS, attached to the Military Economy and Armament Office of German High Command.

Hörlein, Heinrich – deputy member of Vorstand (1926–31), full member of Vorstand (1931–45), member of several committees, manager of Elberfeld plant.

Ilgner, Max – deputy member of Vorstand (1934–38), full member of Vorstand (1938–45), member of several committees, chief of Farben's Berlin NW7 office, manager of Schkopau Buna Works, deputy manager of Ammoniakwerk Merseburg, officer or member of central groups of 14 concerns in seven countries, including American IG Chemical Corporation, New York, chairman or member of several advisory committees to the government.

Jähne, Friedrich – deputy member of Vorstand (1934–38), full member of Vorstand (1938–45), member of Technical Committee, deputy chief of Works Combine Main Valley, chairman of the Farben Technical Commission, chief of engineering department of Hoechst plant, member of control boards of several Farben units, member of Greater Advisory Council, Reich Group Industry.

Knieriem, August von – deputy member of Vorstand (1926–31), full member of Vorstand (1931–45), member of several committees, principal attorney of Farben, member of board in several Farben units, member of several committees and subcommittees of Reich Group Industry.

Krauch, Carl – member of Vorstand and of its Control Committee, member and chairman of Supervisory Board (1940–45), chief of Sparte I, chief of Berlin Liaison Office, member of boards in a number of major Farben subsidiaries and affiliates, director of the Research and Development Department in the Office of German Raw Materials and Synthetics, under the Four-Year Plan, Plenipotentiary General for Special Questions of Chemical Production, Commissioner for Economic Development under Four-Year Plan, member of Directorate, Reich Research Council.

Kühne, Hans – member of Vorstand (1926–45) and of several committees, chief of Works Combine Lower Rhine, plant leader of Leverkusen plant, officer or member of supervisory boards in numerous Farben concerns within Germany and in other countries.

Kugler, Hans – member of several committees, chief of Sales Department Dyestuffs for Hungary, Romania, Yugoslavia, Czechoslovakia, Austria, Greece, Bulgaria, Turkey, the Near East and Africa.

Lautenschläger, Carl – deputy member of Vorstand (1931–38), full member of Vorstand (1938–45), member of Technical and Pharmaceuticals Committee, and chief of Works Combine Main Valley.

Mann, Wilhelm – deputy member of Vorstand (1931–34), full member of Vorstand (1934–45), member of several committees, chief of Sales Combine Pharmaceuticals, official or member of numerous control groups in Farben concerns, lieutenant of SA.

ter Meer, Fritz – deputy member of Vorstand (1931–34), full member of Vorstand (1934–45), member of several committees, chief of Sales Combine Pharmaceuticals, official or member of numerous control groups in Farben concerns.

Oster, Heinrich – deputy member of Vorstand (1928–31) and full member of Vorstand (1931–45), member of Working Committee and Commercial Committee, manager of Nitrogen Syndicate; chief of Farben's sales organisation for nitrogen and oil, member of several control groups in Germany, Austria, Norway and Yugoslavia.

Schmitz, Hermann – member of Vorstand (1925–45), member of Central Committee, chairman of Vorstand (1935–45), chairman or member of control groups in several Farben units or subsidiary and affiliated Farben concerns, chairman of the Currency Committee of the Reichsbank, member or chairman of control groups in several financial institutions.

Schneider, Christian – deputy member of Vorstand (1928–37), full member of Vorstand (1938–45), member of several committees, chief of Sparte I, chief of plant leaders and chief counter-intelligence agent of Vermittlungsstelle W, chief of Farben's Central Personnel Department, member of control bodies of several Farben units.

Schnitzler, Georg von – member of Vorstand (1926–45), member of several committees, chief of Dyestuffs Sales Combine, captain of SA, deputy chairman of Economic Group Chemical Industry, chairman of Council for Propaganda of German Economy, officer or member of supervisory boards of other Farben affiliates.

Wurster, Karl – member of Vorstand (1938–45). Member of Technical and Chemicals Committees, chief of Works Combine Upper Rhine (1940–45), member of supervisory boards in several Farben concerns, collaborator of Krauch in the Four-Year Plan, acting vice chairman of Presidium of Economic Group Chemical Industry.

Biographies of the accused of crime of conspiracy or crime against peace in Krupp case

Bülow, Friedrich von – official of Krupp, head of the Berlin office, military and political Chief of Counter-Intelligence at Krupp, Essen, direct representative of Krupp with Nazi officials, the Gestapo and SS, chief of the Works Police, Gusstahlfabrik, Essen.

Eberhardt, Karl – deputy member of Krupp Direktorium and Vorstand, successor to Karl Pfirsch as head of the War Material and Machine Sales Departments.

Houdremont, Eduard – member of the Krupp Direktorium and deputy member of the Vorstand, head of the Metallurgical, Steel and Machine Departments, plant leader, Gusstahlfabrik, Essen, Special Commissioner for Metal Substitutes in Reich Ministry for Armament and War Production and the Ministry of Economics.

Ihn, Max – deputy member of Krupp Direktorium and Vorstand, deputy to Ewald Loesser and Friedrich Janssen, deputy plant leader, Gusstahlfabrik, Essen.

Janssen, Friedrich – member of Krupp Direktorium and deputy member of the Vorstand, successor to Ewald Loeser as head of the Administrative and Finance Departments, head of the Berlin office.

Korschan, Heinrich – deputy member of Krupp Vorstand, head of the Department of Steel Plants and deputy head of the Metallurgical Department, trustee and administrator of Krupp wartime enterprises in Eastern and South-Eastern Europe, managing director of Krupp Bertha Werk, Breslau.

Krupp von Bohlen und Halbach, Alfried – sole owner, proprietor, active and directing head of Fried. Krupp, Essen, Leader of the Plants, directing head and owner respectively of Fried. Krupp AG, Deputy Chairman of Reich Association Iron and member of Presidium of Reich Association Coal, member of Armament Commission in the Office of Reich Minister for Armament and War Production, sponsoring member of SS.

Kupke, Hans – official of Krupp, head of experimental firing ranges at Essen, head of the foreign workers camps.

Lehmann, Heinrich – official of Fried. Krupp, deputy to Max Ihn and in charge of labour procurement.

Löser, Ewald – member of Vorstand and head of Administrative and Finance Departments of Fried. Krupp AG, Krupp representative in the Kleiner Kreis, Reich trustee for Phillips Radio, Eindhoven, Netherlands.

Müller, Erich – member of Krupp Vorstand and Direktorium, head of Artillery Designing and Machine Construction Departments and coordinator of artillery construction, armaments adviser to Hitler, adviser to the War Ministry, head of Armament Committee in the office of Reich Minister for Arms and Munitions, Chairman of Weapons Development Committee.

Pfirsch, Karl – deputy member of Krupp Direktorium and Vorstand, head of War Material and Machine Sales Departments, head of the Berlin office (1943–45).

Biographies of the accused of crime of conspiracy or crime against peace in the High Command case

Blaskowitz, Johannes – General, Commander in Chief Army Group Command 3 (1939), Commander in Chief 8th Army (1939), Commander in Chief 2nd Army (1939), Commander in Chief East (1939–40), Commander in Chief 9th Army (1940), Military Commander Northern France (1940), Commander in Chief 1st Army (1940–44), Acting Commander in Chief Army Group G (1944), Commander in Chief Army Group G (1944–45), Commander in Chief Army Group H (1945), Commander in Chief Netherlands and 25th Army (1945).

Hollidt, Karl – General, Commander of Infantry in District 9 (1938–39), Commander 52nd Infantry Division (1939), Chief of Staff 5th Army (1939), Chief of Staff to the Commander in Chief East (1939–40), Chief of Staff 9th Army (1940), Commander 50th Infantry Division (1940–42), Commanding General XVII Corps (1942), Commander Army Hollidt (1942–43), Commander in Chief 6th Army (1943–44).

Hoth, Hermann – General, Commanding General XV Corps (1938–40), Commander Panzer Group 3 (1940–41), Commander in Chief 17th Army (1941–42), Commander in Chief 4th Panzer Army (1942–43).

Küchler, Georg von – General of the Army, Commander in Chief 3rd Army (1939), Commander of East Prussian Defence Zone (1939), Commander in Chief 18th Army (1939–42), Commander in Chief Army Group North (1942–44).

Leeb, Wilhelm von – General of the Army, Commander in Chief 12th Army (1938), Commander in Chief Army Group C (1939–41), Commander in Chief Army Group North (1941–42).

Lehmann, Rudolf – Lieutenant-General, Judge Advocate, Ministerial Director of Army High Command and Chief of the Legal Division (1938–44), Judge Advocate-General of Army High Command (1944–45).

Reinecke, Hermann – Lieutenant-General, Infantry, Chief of the Department 'Armed Forces General Affairs' in the Army High Command (1939), Chief of General Office of Army High Command (1939–45), Chief of the National Socialist Guidance Staff of Army High Command (1943–45).

Reinhardt, Hans – General, Commander 4th Panzer Division (1938–40), Commanding General XLI Corps (1940–41), Commander of Panzer Group 3 (later 3rd Panzer Army) (1941–44), Acting Commander in Chief Army Group Centre (1944–45).

Roques, Karl von – Lieutenant-General, Infantry, Commander of a Division in the Zone of the Interior (1940–41), Commander Rear Area, Army Group South (1941–42), Commanding General of Group von Roques (1941), Commander Rear Area, Army Group A (1942).

Salmuth, Hans von – General, Chief of Staff Army Group Command 1 (1937–39), Chief of Staff Army Group North (1939), Chief of Staff Army Group B (1939–41), Commanding General XXX Corps (1941–42), Acting Commander in Chief 17th Army (1942), Acting Commander in Chief 4th Army (1942), Commander in Chief 2nd Army (1942–43), Commander in Chief 15th Army (1943–44).

Schniewind, Otto – Admiral, Chief of Navy Armament Office (1937–38), Chief of Navy Command Office and Chief of Staff of Naval War Staff (1938–41), Commander of the Fleet (1941–44), Commander of Naval Battle Forces in Norway (1942), Commander of Naval Group North (1943–44).

Sperrle, Hugo – General of the Army, Commander of the 'Condor Legion' in Spain (1936–37), Commanding General of Air Group 3 (1938–39), Commander in Chief Air Fleet 3 (1939–44).

Warlimont, Walter – Lieutenant-General, Artillery, Military Envoy to General Franco in Spain and Leader of the German Volunteer Corps (1936), Chief of Department National Defence in the Armed Forces Operation Staff (1938–44), Deputy Chief of Department National Defence in the Armed Forces Operation Staff (1942–44).

Wöhler, Otto – Lieutenant-General, Infantry, Operations Officer of the Army Group 5 (1938), Chief of Staff XVII Corps (1939–40), Chief of Staff 11th Army (1940–42), Chief of Staff Army Group Centre (1942–43), Commanding General I Corps (1943), Acting Commander XXVI Corps (1943), Commander in Chief 8th Army (1943–44), Commander in Chief Army Group South (1944–45).

Biographies of the accused of crime of conspiracy or crime against peace in the Ministries case

Berger, Gottlob – Lieutenant General of SS and of Waffen SS, Military Commander in Czechoslovakia (1944), Chief of Prisoner of War Affairs (1944–45), Chief of Political Directing Staff of Reich Ministry for the Occupied Eastern Territories (1943–45), Liaison Officer of Reichsfuehrer SS to Reich Minister for Occupied Eastern Territories (1942–45), Chief of SS Main Office (1940–45), Chief of Recruitment Office of Armed SS (1939).

Bohle, Ernst – Chief of Foreign Organization of NSDAP (1933–45), State Secretary of German Foreign Office (1937–41), Chief of Foreign Organisation in Foreign Office (1937–41), Gauleiter in NSDAP, Lieutenant General of SS.

Darre, Richard Walther – Reich Minister of Food and Agriculture (1933–45, inactive 1942–45), Chief of SS Race and Settlement Main Office (1931–38), Reichsleiter, Member of Small Ministerial Council of the Four-Year Plan, Lieutenant General of SS.

Dietrich, Otto – State Secretary in Reich Ministry for Public Enlightenment and Propaganda (1937–45), Press Chief of Reich Government (1937–45), Reich Press Chief of NSDAP (1932–45), Reichsleiter, Lieutenant General of SS.

Erdmannsdorff, Otto von – Deputy Chief of Political Division in German Foreign Office (1941–45), German Minister to Hungary (1937–41).

Keppler, Wilhelm – Reich Ministry of Economics (1939–45), State Secretary for Special Assignments, German Foreign Office (1938–45), Chairman of Supervisory Board of German Resettlement Trustee Company (1939–43), Reich Plenipotentiary for Austria (1938), Plenipotentiary for Economic Questions to the Führer and Reich Chancellor (1934–36), Plenipotentiary for Economic Questions to the Reich Chancellor (1933–34), Member of General Council of the Four-Year Plan, Lieutenant General of SS.

Körner, Paul – Member of Central Planning Board, Four-Year Plan (1942–45), State Secretary and Chief of Central Office of the Four-Year Plan (1936–45), State Secretary of Prussian State Ministry (1933–45), Deputy Chairman of General Council of the Four-Year Plan, Member of Small Ministerial Council of the Four-Year Plan, chairman of several organs of 'Hermann Göring' Inc., Lieutenant General of SS.

Lammers, Hans Heinrich – Reich Minister and Chief of Reich Chancellery (1937–45), State Secretary and Chief of Reich Chancellery (1933–37), Executive Secretary of Ministerial Council for the Defence of the Reich, Executive Secretary of Secret Cabinet Council, Lieutenant General of SS.

Meissner, Otto – Chief of Presidential Chancellery (1934–45), State Secretary with the Reich President (1923–34).

Pleiger, Paul – Director General, Chairman of Mining and Steel Works East (1943–45), General Manager of Mining and Steel Works East, (1941–43), Reich Plenipotentiary for Coal for the Occupied Territories (1942–45), Chairman of Reich Association Coal (1941–45), Reich Plenipotentiary for Coal (1941–45), Chief of Iron and Metals Section in the Office for German Raw Materials and Synthetic Materials, Four-Year Plan (1936–37), Member of Keppler Office (1933/34–36), Chairman of managing boards of several units of 'Hermann Göring' Inc.

Ritter, Karl – Ambassador for Special Assignments in German Foreign Office (1939–45), Liaison Officer of Reich Foreign Minister to High Command of the German Armed Forces, (1940–44).

Schellenberg, Walter – Brigadier General of SS, of Waffen SS, and of Police, Chief of Military Intelligence in Reich Security Main Office (1944–45), Chief of Foreign Intelligence in Reich Security Main Office (1941–45), Chief of Counter-intelligence Branch in Office of Secret State Police in Reich Security Main Office (1939/40–41).

Schwerin von Krosigk, Lutz – Foreign Minister in the so-called Dönitz Cabinet of Germany (1945), Reich Minister of Finance (1932–45), Member, Small Ministerial Council, Four-Year Plan.

Stuckart, Wilhelm – Acting Minister of Interior in so-called Dönitz Cabinet of Germany (1945), State Secretary of Reich Ministry of Interior (1943–45), Chief of Staff of the Plenipotentiary General for the Administration of the Reich (1939–45), State Secretary in Reich Ministry of Interior (1935–43), Lieutenant General of SS.

Veesenmayer, Edmund – German Minister to and Reich Plenipotentiary in Hungary (1944–45), Assistant to Wilhelm Keppler (1933–44), Brigadier General in SS.

Weizsäcker, Ernst von – German Ambassador to the Holy See (1943–45), State Secretary of Foreign Office (1938–43), Ministerial Director and Chief of Political Division in Foreign Office (1936–38), Brigadier General of SS.

Wörmann, Ernst – German Ambassador to China (1943–45), Under State Secretary and Chief of Political Division in German Foreign Office (1938–43), Embassy Counsellor, later Minister, in German Embassy in London (1936–38), Senior Colonel of SS.

Biographies of the accused of crime of conspiracy or crime against peace in the trial of Hermann Röchling and others

Gemmingen-Hornberg, Hans Lothar von – member of Supervisory Board of Trust Röchlingsche Eisen und Stahlwerke, member of Managerial Committee Southwest of the Reich Association Iron, economic representative for Saar.

Maier, Albert – financial director of Trust Röchlingsche Eisen und Stahlwerke, member of Managerial Committee Southwest of the Reich Association Iron.

Rodenhauser, Wilhelm – technical director of Trust Röchlingsche Eisen und Stahlwerke, member of Managerial Committee Southwest of the Reich Association Iron.

Röchling, Ernst – member of Supervisory Board of Trust Röchlingsche Eisen und Stahlwerke.

Röchling, Hermann – President of the Reich Association Iron (1942–44), director of Trust Röchlingsche Eisen und Stahlwerke, Reich Commissioner for the iron industry of the Departments Moselle and Meurthe-et-Moselle, Reich Minister of War Industries, member of War Industries Council of Reich Chamber of Commerce, Reich Plenipotentiary for the iron and steel industry on occupied territories.

Biographies of the accused of crime of conspiracy and crime against peace in the trial before the SNT

Daume, Maks – colonel of Police, section chief in the Headquarters of the Ordnungspolizei (1939–40).

Fischer, Ludwig – Lieutenant General of SA, dignitary of Warsaw district.

Forster, Albert – Reich Governor of Danzig-West Prussia (1939–45), Gauleiter of NSDAP for Danzig-West Prussia (1939–45), Gauleiter of NSDAP for Danzig (1930–39), Lieutenant General of SS.

Greiser, Arthur – Reich Governor and Gauleiter of NSDAP for Wartheland (1939–45), President of Senate, Free State of Danzig (1934–39), Lieutenant General in SS.

Leist, Ludwig – General major of SA, section chief in the Office of the Chief of Warsaw district (1939), plenipotentiary of the Governor for the city of Warsaw.

Meisinger, Josef – police attaché of Reich Embassy in Tokyo (1941–45), chief of security police and security service of Warsaw District (1939–41), Colonel of SS in Poland (1940).

Index